Perceptions of Infinity

PERCEPTIONS OF INFINITY

part of the *Under a Quicksilver Moon* series by
The International Library of Poetry

Noah Bevins, Editor

Perceptions of Infinity

Library of Congress
Cataloging in Publication Data

ISBN 0-7951-5053-9

Proudly manufactured in the United States of America by
Watermark Press
One Poetry Plaza
Owings Mills, MD 21117

poetry.COM
The International Library of Poetry

FOREWORD

Throughout life, we store information collected from experiences and try in some way to make sense of it. When we are not able to fully understand the things that occur in our lives, we often externalize the information. By doing this, we are afforded a different perspective, thus allowing us to think more clearly about difficult or perplexing events and emotions. Art is one of the ways in which people choose to externalize their thoughts.

Within the arts, modes of expression differ, but poetry is a very powerful tool by which people can share sometimes confusing, sometimes perfectly clear concepts and feelings with others. Intentions can run the gamut as well: The artists may simply want to share something that has touched their lives in some way, or they may want to get help to allay anxiety or uncertainty. The poetry within *Perceptions of Infinity* is from every point on the spectrum: every topic, every intention, every event or emotion imaginable. Some poems will speak to certain readers more than others, but it is always important to keep in mind that each verse is the voice of a poet, of a mind that needs to make sense of this world, of a heart that feels the effects of every moment in this life, and perhaps of a memory that is striving to surface. Nonetheless, recalling our yesterdays gives birth to our many forms of expression.

Melisa S. Mitchell
Senior Editor

Editor's Note

"So full of artless jealousy is guilt,
It spills itself in fear of being spilt."
—William Shakespeare, *Hamlet* (4.5.2764–65)

From Genesis to Shakespeare's tragedies, guilt has proven a popular literary theme for the intrigue, the controversy, and the emotions that accompany this profound concept. Shakespeare knew very well how to capture the audience's attention by exploiting the many roles guilt plays in our lives. Queen Gertrude, mother of the tragic prince of Denmark, spoke the words quoted above. With them, she describes guilt's tenacity and the power it often has over people's lives.

Besides its effects, however, Gertrude also alludes to the two definitions of guilt and how they play against each other. First, guilt is the responsibility for having done something wrong; second, it is the regret that accompanies such an offense. However, as modern psychologists have pointed out, many people can feel guilty for no apparent reason, and others are remorseless no matter their actions. Thus, guilt is as mysterious as it is powerful; its cause is hard to find, and its remedy is usually even more elusive. The causes for the mystique of this emotion arise out of a perception we build unconsciously throughout our lives, a system of beliefs that each of us applies to every decision we make. Thus, guilt can reveal itself in the simplest of situations, and it can have complicated repercussions on our psyches.

Brian Devine, author of "Confiteor" (1), understands guilt's consequences well. The very title of this poem implies guilt and the need to resolve it. Confiteor is a Latin word that means, "I confess." Beyond the translation, Confiteor is also a standard prayer in Catholicism. Used for a variety of purposes, it is primarily spoken before Mass as a confession of sins and a request for grace to rectify those sins. With such a weighty title, one would expect a reverential and dramatic situation to unfold, one describing grievous transgressions and a sincere need to plead for forgiveness. Yet, as the first lines demonstrate, the persona introduces the reader to a commonplace situation:

> *Too many nights you jigged around the strange trap's*
> *patient fare and scraped the cat's dish clean*
> *'til lured by cat food treadled on the pin's*
> *raw height, you climbed its scaffolding.*

The persona is trying to trap a mouse, a pest that has been eating his cat's food. However, the title and the detailed description in these lines alludes to more than just a passive interest in ridding his life of this annoyance. Not only has he waited patiently for the mouse to take the normal bait, the persona has now used as a lure the very thing that the persona does not want the mouse to eat: the cat food.

After planning and waiting and becoming preoccupied with the capture of this mouse, the persona finally gets his prize:

> *This ordinary morning I found you climbing still,*
> *your bright eyes as yet unglazed.*

Now that the mouse has taken the bait, the persona points out that the morning is "ordinary." The trapping of a mouse is rarely an event that would make a morning more than ordinary. Thus, the reader gets a clue here that the persona is already starting to feel guilty about hunting the mouse. By telling us what we already take for granted, the persona is simply reiterating the normalcy of the morning in an attempt to dispel the nervous guilt he is beginning to feel.

It is with the next line, however, that the reader becomes fully aware that the persona is starting to feel remorseful. The persona is struggling with the task of finishing off the mouse:

> *Don't call it murder, rephrase the term, as this*
> *wire harnessing from your soft flank is raised . . .*

The metaphorical relationship between the cyclic nature of sin, guilt, and forgiveness and the task of catching and killing a mouse is almost complete with these two lines. The persona seems to be asking the mouse for forgiveness, just as the confessor reciting the Confiteor before Mass asks for grace. After rationalizing the act, the persona seems to find redemption: He lifts the clamp of the trap from the mouse's body—as though to let it go. However, the true meaning of "rephrase the term" occurs to the reader when the persona nervously lets the clamp go for a "new release." He has transformed the act of killing the mouse from "murder" into "release." The use of the word "release" is very deliberate. In one sense, the persona is referring to the physical release of the camp on the mouse trap; in another, he alludes to the mouse's release from life, and in yet another, he is acknowledging the release his confession has on the emotional guilt from which he suffers.

Trapping and killing a mouse is hardly an activity that requires such an emotional and religious response. However, the poem acts as a metaphor for our universal need to seek redemption for our transgressions. Thus, while simply describing one person's attempt to kill a mouse, Brain Devine has covered two sides of a timeless and fundamental part of our humanity.

Similarly, Daniel Visconti contemplates the emotional impact guilt has on our lives in his poem "Futility" (1). This poem's persona is a child, and individuals learn to take responsibility for their actions during childhood. While such early encounters with guilt can cause destructive patterns of behavior, it also guides us to be responsible and ethical. However, learning that we are fallible can be terrifying or, as the persona in "Futility" observes, "deafening and sudden."

The first several lines of "Futility" contain vivid images describing the persona's environment:

> *I am speaking now of the July grass*
> *with steamy imprints where our shoes had fallen,*
> *the muggy sizzle of the early evening,*
> *the humidity drinkable with a straw . . .*

The persona is not alone; presumably, he is with siblings or friends, playing during a summer evening. Their environment is watching them, recording their every move by keeping "steamy imprints" of their footprints; it is a heavy, oppressive, almost tangible character. The rest of the persona's survey of his surroundings depicts a "path" of fireflies next to the "edge of the trees." The persona describes the fireflies as "lazy" and "meandering," and the persona and his companions are the predators hunting them:

> *and we, moving with clear purpose,*
> *captured them in pickle jars with lids*
> *stabbed with an ice pick.*

Again, another common activity, that of catching fireflies in a jar, becomes the source of guilt that far exceeds the severity of the act. The portrayal of the predator-like children and the murderous image of the ice pick act to hyperbolize this harmless childhood pastime into an epic hunt on the Serengeti. Up to this point, the persona has only the sensation of being watched; his guilt is not yet fully manifested. However, as the reader continues, the persona begins to interpret the natural phenomena around him as a judge convicting him of his crimes:

> *And in the depth of the night journey,*
> *when the storm outside rattled the screens,*
> *brought violent accusations against me . . .*

The persona has apparently retired indoors to enjoy his catch. Yet, his soul-searching, his "night journey," is now at its deepest. The outside world asserts itself again in the form of a violent storm. The persona is now fully aware of his offense; his conscience has turned into a storm, finding him guilty of encroaching on the natural world. Thus, the persona now focuses his attention on the source of his guilt, his jar of fireflies:

> *I lifted the jar off the shelf*
> *and stared at them, Japanese paper lanterns.*
> *What is their world like, so constrained, so futile,*
> *Yet so much like our own, always waiting . . .*

The image of the paper lanterns is well chosen. Not only does it describe the fireflies' delicate nature, but it also brings to mind the Japanese funerary custom of floating lanterns on water to honor the deceased. His childhood lack of responsibility has died, and his newfound culpability has now manifested itself in this innocent game. Therefore, like the fireflies bound in their jar, his own guilt and this new need to define the parameters of his moral accountability now trap him. Indeed, this realization is so profound that he releases the fireflies, unlike the persona in "Confiteor," who is bound by duty to keep his house pest-free. However, as the final two lines in "Futility" point out, the persona's act of compassion makes no difference to his guilty conscience:

And by the time the sun was above the dew-suckled fields
I unscrewed the lid, each turn more deafening and sudden.

This literal release, like the symbolic "new release" in "Confiteor," is a confession, a declaration of guilt to the judge that the persona has been facing all along: himself. Despite these confessions, however, neither persona has gained any lasting grace. By the last line in "Confiteor," the persona's mood is still "that of every man who's sinned." And in "Futility," the jar's lid, taking the place of the storm, continues to condemn the persona as a transgressor. Thus, the personas, representing all of humanity, must continually face the cycle of guilt and redemption in their lives.

With a genuine understanding of how ordinary events have extraordinary depth, these poets have explored a timeless and haunting facet of human existence. As a result of both poets' finesse and talented creativity, their poems provide a glimpse of the motivation behind some of the most intriguing and immortal epics in literature. Additionally, each poet in this anthology offers an insight into his or her views. I encourage you to read and contemplate each of the poets' thoughts and beliefs to help you better grasp your own feelings. Do not forget to read such memorable works as "Empty Jars" (3) by Sarah Devers, "The Envisionment" (3) by John Shepherd, "Vacant Queries of a Withering Rose" (3) by Erika Deoudes, "You Stick to Me Like Damp" (3) by Lisa Hall, and "Picasso's Women" (4) by Dawn Hopkins.

I would like to extend my sincere appreciation to all of the poets featured in this anthology. Congratulations on your ability to take difficult topics and transform them into powerful poetry. I wish you luck in all of your future creative enterprises.

The publication of this anthology has been a culmination of the efforts of many individuals, including judges, editors, assistant editors, customer service representatives, graphic artists, layout artists, office administrators, data entry staff, and mail-room personnel. I would like to thank all of these people for all their time and hard work that went into producing this anthology.

Noah Bevins
Editor

Cover Art: "Track of Dreams" by Bernard Edwards

Confiteor

Too many nights you jigged around the strange trap's
patient fare and scraped the cat's dish clean,
'til lured by cat food treadled on the pin's
raw height, you climbed its scaffolding.
This ordinary morning I found you climbing still,
your bright eyes as yet unglazed.
Don't call it murder, rephrase the term, as this
wire harnessing from your soft flank is raised,
and if your cocked-up ears still await the clamp
that spites my nervous hand, listen
to how I work this new release.
My mood is that of every man who's sinned.

Brian Devine

Futility

I am speaking now of the July grass
with steamy imprints where our shoes had fallen,
the muggy sizzle of the early evening,
the humidity drinkable with a straw,
the sky the color of dripping watermelons,

when the fireflies would come out,
meander along a lazy path along the edge of the trees,
and we, moving with clear purpose,
captured them in pickle jars with lids
stabbed with an ice pick.

And in the depth of the night journey,
when the storm outside rattled the screens,
brought violent accusations against me,
I lifted the jar off the shelf
and stared at them, Japanese paper lanterns.

What is their world like, so constrained, so futile,
yet so much like our own, always waiting,
lighting up our universe with sparks of violence and joy?
And by the time the sun was above the dew-suckled fields,
I unscrewed the lid, each turn more deafening and sudden.

Daniel Joseph Visconti

Your Marriage

Mend it like you mend those linen pants
you keep wearing because they go on so easily.
They do nothing for your shape,

always tearing at the middle
where thigh meets thigh, rubbing
until the pale brown threading gives

and bares the inner pink of your flesh—
you never notice the ripping until you feel
skin to skin with your own self

and realize how wonderful it feels
to have nothing between your legs.
But you mend again and again. With each new thread

the cloth becomes thicker, stronger,
and limbs acquire a careful pace and greater distance
from each other. One day the pants will not tear again,

and the feel of your skin, parted from itself
by scar tissue from the final mending,
will slowly begin to forget itself.

Denise Vargas Acosta

Empty Jars

Two blind tongues reaching to lick the other
raw—we kiss to distract our souls
from thirst and the need for thirst. Warm
and rusty, seasons-old water stood thin
in this shallow desert of leaving. And we
have used it all up
in wiping dirt from our hands: hands
fatigued by the silent dust of prayers
filtering through our bent fingers. While we
yet share an amnesia for dark and beautiful
things, a twinkling mirage of intensely
remembered love makes our hot throats
choke on our own words, as if we were filled
again. But with so many crying angels
we are flung down on the sand like empty
jars—waiting for a goodbye
that threatens only tears to flood our dry,
endless mouths.

Sarah Elizabeth Devers

The Envisionment

When the fire department burned our old barn,
I watched. The man with the mask went in for
A moment, then ran out towing fire; lucky
Thing he brought his own air to breathe.
The smoke twisted the sky into submission and
The mist hung for hours about my head,
And when it lifted there were only wet ashes,
Like the men in heavy coats had never been.
The foundation is still there; we store the
Winter hay on top of it so it doesn't mold
From the bottom.

In those days I used to sit on the hay bales
As Dad dragged them, two at a time, to the
Cows. He was giant, and could still
Recognize his son.

John Edward Shepherd

For the Slightest Sign

I roll out of bed, away from the thin linen
curtains which hang crookedly, barely trying
to hinder the early afternoon between the
heaviness of New England summer breezes. My
eyes adjust to the darkened shadow stepping
towards the mirror, something I wipe clean
from all the smudges every morning and every
night. Into it I lean so closely that my
uneven breath is plotted on the glass like
an echo-cardiogram. I quickly erase it with
my hands. Searching for the slightest sign,
something . . . anything, a map hidden among
my freckles, clues lining my crow's feet and
frown lines, a new line book marked in the
autobiography of my iris. I take a tissue
and wipe away my fingerprints from the pane
and return to my bed, cotton sheets clinging
to the moisture of the concentrated air,
faded almost to transparency.

Elizabeth Timpe

Rage

I've tasted rage the way a
middle-aged woman tastes rage,
a bag of potato chips, a container
of dip, and a few beers for dinner.

I've seen it, too—it's
the inside of an empty wine bottle,
lying on the floor at the end of the
bed, refracting light from the hallway
on Monday nights.

It leaves its scent, like the smoke
of 1,000 spent candles, clinging
to the damp stone walls
of a long forgotten chamber.

Unbidden guest,
I feel your presence even now,
engulfing fury, wandering ghost,
and I, its conquered, harboring host.

Linda R. Ritter

Vacant Queries of a Withering Rose

"How do I look?"
he asked womanishly, clad in a dress
adorned with black outlines of rich scarlet
polyester roses, stretched over his muscular form.
A curly black ponytail, standing upright,
mimicked his convincingly feminine gait,
shifting its weight with each barefoot stride.
I watched as an organized flood of crimson paint
dried on stretched charcoal cloth
upon two mahogany bamboo stalks.
"How does it look?" he asked,
holding up his creation:
a perfect image of a rose.
Over time, black veins of fabric
forced their way to the surface,
breaking up his once immaculate design.
As alizarin roses congregate upon the grim black
outline of my father's limestone name
and my mother's lifeless red dress
hangs beside a faded masterpiece, I long to answer.

Erika Deoudes

You Stick to Me Like Damp

You stick to me like damp
sand sticks to skin thickened
in California's fire
lying along the coast,
a godly child
its hills more yellow than is natural
swelling to sharp slopes—
like an abdomen, your
influence tiding against
me with unwashed
hair and newly brown shoulders.
My ocean manifests
itself on your shore.
Furious woman, we
sprung from something
that was so irrevocably
damaged, I fell asleep
sitting up, clutching.

Lisa Ashley Hall

Picasso's Women

He named you peasants
with a brush stroke,
coated the canvas
with anger and warm paint,

twisted your arms, heads, torsos
to fit his mad world.

But the Spaniard
could not hold your spirits captive.
Each curve screamed,
and the angles came alive.

Your eyes stared back
and witnessed the madness.
Beauty remained
in spite of his evil.

Your tormented creator
granted life and immortality, but

We are you
and the Minotaur
is dead.

Dawn Hopkins

Friends

You said once the blankets were the stairs
and I felt like a seductive poem
confined within the playground with red rubber floors
Bruises don't exist in playgrounds, you said, children do
I let you push my swing to and from the stars
I pretended to know the constellations
I took astronomy, but all I really remembered
was that Tyco Brahe had a gold nose
Everything was beautiful and nothing hurt
It was a quarter moon, not quite yet done
not old enough to play with us
I thought to kick you under its watchful eye
so we could fall to the floor like lovers in a romantic melodrama
We kissed and breathed and blamed confusion
We mixed and melted, and I cried
because when He threatens you with the rats in Room 101
you will ask them to do it to me, not Julia or yourself
Tomorrow you will find yourself singing
Nothing was beautiful and everything hurt

Idalmis Toro

Post-Abortion (The Final Dreamless Slumber)

When it was over and you were dead,
I fell into a dreamless slumber
for seventeen hours, and when I awoke,
my clothes were soiled,
the blanket saturated with blood.
Nearby, he gawked, as though it is
unnatural for the discarded to stain
the sheets, and I wondered, would he say
a prayer before he washed them?
I peeled off my clothes and climbed out of
bed to face the full-length mirror, nude.
Slender. My stomach was hollow.
I was 45, though 16 in years.
I went into the shower and stood under
the hot water, scrubbing and rinsing
until my flesh boiled
and the notion of a sympathetic God,
a prayer that I might forget you,
vanished like red water
through the drain.

Leah Penelope Polacco

Lost at the Dead Sea

I hate sea salt stinging my eyes and flesh.
Floating in this colorless limbo,
akimbo in the seam between Earth and sky,
I cannot sink,
but it burns to go under.
So I flap on the surface lightly,
like a snowless sprawling angel,
trying to cool the surface of my limbs.

In 110-degree heat, Bedouin men build fires
while darkly-draped women dance
in hot salty showers. An Israeli family
with a baby and a rifle prepares
a place to sleep. Motionless inside
our tent, I choke. He roams. We sweat.
We have lost our keys in the Dead Sea
and are waiting for a taxi from Jerusalem.
At sunrise, Hasidic men sing revival-style.
A Bedouin boy snaps the "Hollywood" slate
I have given him and cries, "Action!"

Stephanie Ann Lowe

1949

My father crawled out of the trenches
And met me yesterday
He looked different than the picture
Hanging on my vanity
Which must have been altered
By my mother
And her bridge club
That I always end up burning down
His skin was gray
Especially thick and gang green
Around his ankles
Eyes were too small apertures now
And he didn't have a gun
Or so I thought
Presumably he stopped working out
After the atomic bomb
He gave me a crew cut when I was asleep
Because I repulsed him with long hair
Always asking about my peach fuzz
When would I become a man?

Jackie Dacey

Love and Sadness

In loving memory of Melanie Kay Wilkerson, my loving aunt
Somehow the wind seems colder
without you by my side.
The tears of joy and happiness have faded
to darkness in my mind.
As I cry myself to sleep each night,
I replay the memories we shared
fighting to live our dreams.
And the sunshine always fell on me
as you smiled and wiped away my tears
and I know you will be with me everywhere I go.
Because without you I cannot go on.
Now all that exists are the treasures and memories
of our past together.
I will try harder to succeed in life
however, it will be difficult
since I no longer have your hand to guide me
lovingly through the hardships of life.
I will try to teach as you taught me,
to always forgive whether my fault or not.
And always listen with an open heart
as you did for me long before we were apart.
I will try to paint the world as I see it
without your hand over mine.
And I will try to be braver,
knowing you are very close by
and will always be with me in my heart, spirit, and mind.

Krystan Guimond

I Wish I Weren't So Stupid!

The most excellent thing to ever happen to me is you.
You came into my life and I became new.
Your heart is always there to give me your love.
Without asking anything in return, you are always there.
I WISH I WEREN'T SO STUPID!

You give me your everything from your very soul.
Yet I sometimes raise my voice and scowl.
I hurt you with my voice and the words I say.
But you are always there to tell me you love me.
I WISH I WEREN'T SO STUPID!

I want to always make you feel the same way you make me feel.
My love should always be total and strong.
Forevermore, I will love you.
Yet still I fall and with my face hurt you.
I WISH I WEREN'T SO STUPID!

Forgive me, my love, for I know not what I do.
My love for you is total and absolute.
My life belongs to you.
Mrs. Priny M. Boutcher, I love you.
I WISH I WEREN'T SO STUPID!

Though I am stupid so many times, I ask you to see
Past my flaws.
God knows how much I love you,
I will try to be better. But
I WISH I WEREN'T SO STUPID!

Your husband, in love with you forever,
Frederick

Frederick A. Boutcher

Pen and Paper

Thoughts come freely to my mind.
I find pen and paper—
Ink drifts across . . .
Like the surf beating against the shore—
To question this freedom—I shall not.
Thoughts come freely to my mind:
Pen and paper.

Jami Klimis

My Beloved

My beloved causes my passion to rise upward
toward its apex.
He begins with his sensitive touch, intense
affection, loving tenderness, and undying
devotion.

Kindling the emotion held so tightly inside
for so long.
He exhilarates my spirit, arousing it from
slumber.

Slowly leading me into a state of consciousness;
with it the blossoming of my emotions.
Becoming intoxicated by his passionate love.

The excitement magnifies and heightens the passion
to the point of becoming one with him.
With flowing synchronized movements,
the night ignites into an intense, passionate
frenzy.

Kathryn E. Westenberger

Oprah's Got Us Thinking Spiritually

We will have a change in our world
   and a change in the people
A change in the laws with humanitarian flaws
For Oprah has us thinking spiritually

The international games of supply and demand
   are beating the drums of the capitalist band
   and people are tired of the killing war zones
   weary of the bullies in the homes and on the thrones
For Oprah has us understanding spiritually

We will have a change in our attitudes
   and the way we treat each other
Lucy's African DNA gene is in every sister and brother
Black, brown, red, white, or yellow
   our human compassion makes us all mellow
For Oprah has us caring spiritually

And as night follows day
Spirit will lead the way
For Oprah has us loving and
Healing in many ways spiritually

Ida J. Dunson

Ballynahynch, Ireland

I remember, fondly
forests and beats,
especially Beat One

I remember white teeth . . . your teeth,
bad teeth, two teeth and Frank

I remember bad food, good drinks and Ernest
the bartender
pouring pints, half pints, whackers, gin
and vodka with two olives

AND I REMEMBER YOU

I recall fun stories, at all, at all, at alls,
laughs and many absolutelys
roaring fires, cold nights and warm hearts

AND I DO REMEMBER YOU

There were Martins and Michaels, Ernests,
Franks and Noels, afternoon siestas and
fresh air

I remember well my heart pounding and hooking
a hat whilst casting on the stream

BUT I REMEMBER THE MOST—YOU
happy meeting, sad goodbyes, and
many hopes of again
which never came

W. Elliott Hyland

Coffee

Shyness in the air
Alone in their despair
Saddened whispers seem to fly away.
Given madness
Inside souls of gladness
Somehow makes its way to me.
And when did you see
The hearts and minds
Of figures left in the past?
Will you stay to find out
What you're looking for
Or run, like with everything else?
Skipped on a pond in the mud, off a rock
What a headache we'll have in the morning,
And self-esteem fails to find some hope for valor
And the feeling sinks away with the cream.

Jessica Lynn Ritchards

As I

As I focused my eyes on you from across the way,
Your face so dark and full of mystery,
The look in your eyes captivated my soul.
With every glance, my body trembled.

As I let time surpass, closeness began.
In my mind something more was to be desired.
Only a truth was to be revealed,
Another stood in the way of my longing,
Kept quiet because of her love, which you shared.

As I allowed myself to let you in,
A feeling rendered my being.
Thoughts of your everything had taken over.
Into the depths of love I have fallen deeply.

As I played you out in my head,
She appeared never to let me in again.
Love is what she is to you;
Another is all I am for you.

As I lay here hopelessly dreaming of what would be.
As I lay here having fallen.
As I lay here hopelessly dreaming of what could have been.
As I lay here having fallen.

Deanna J. Gross

The Affair

For one there is a life tedious and mundane
Another whose life is filled with pain

At once it all passes with a look and a smile
An innuendo implying "won't you stay for a while?"

The days and the months fade into a blur
How quickly we've drifted from where we once were

The looks and the smiles are never dismissed
Implying a longing for that perfect kiss

The painful vacancy that cut like a knife
Is suddenly replaced with a love in your life

The tremendous emptiness you're so used to feeling
Is no longer the substance of your very being

A life of love cloaked by confusion
Which is reality and which is an illusion

Together we live in our separate fight
Never once questioning what's wrong or what's right

The lives which once were completely separate
Are joined together by the vacant not the desperate

Wrapped in each other we hold on tight
True love is a victory over the fight

April Norris

Reaching Out

The day is clear, the air vibrates
The children's laughter fills my ears
Young lovers go to seek their mates
My tired heart dissolves in tears

So fair my daughter as she gazes
With face raised upward toward the sky
As though she sings our Lord's sweet praises
To ruffled clouds where peace must lie

How can I bear to leave this home
The known, the promised, and the true
And journey far, unprepared, alone
To trade the old for something new. . . .

Oh, grant me strength to face this road
To tread with firm and measured stride
No looking back, no self-pitying ode
Dear God . . . don't turn thy face aside

Peggie Margaret Lyons

Having to Let Go

On this day, I say goodbye forever in our lives.
After death when we are at peace, I know I
will see you again. Of this, I am convinced.
The bits and pieces that I held of you in my
heart are now in someone else's hands.
I just hope that they are held with as
much love as I tried to give to you.
If they fall and they break,
I know you'll bounce right back.
Strong and smart you have always been;
hard and fragile I cannot help to be.
Time goes by and people change;
now it's time for me to go my way.
What you felt I never knew.
The scars I left, I never saw.
But now . . . now I feel you.
To GOD I pray that you forgive me.
If I had known what I feel today,
I would have NEVER left your side.
People make mistakes; I certainly did.
What goes around come around;
this was just my turn.
If you are happy, let it be.
Just know all I wanted was for you to love me!

Elizabeth S. Mendez

the value of a thirty-two cent stamp

a letter written with love and hope
folded and sealed in a white envelope
you would've sent it if you'd had a stamp
but you probably left it by the lamp
just a letter you wrote and held in your hand
so important to him but you wouldn't understand
what a few words could mean to a far-away heart
that's holding on to its love but tearing apart
from waiting and hoping
that a letter would arrive
a few days, two weeks
a month or more passed by
oh, i understand
even if you were mad
you would've sent a letter
if a stamp you'd had
too bad his poor heart
wasn't harder or stronger
for your man waited
but could wait no longer
he died never knowing
in a cold prison camp
that your love had the value
of a thirty-two cent stamp

Keith Kriner

Amazin' Tales

There are five kitties who all live with me.
Their antics are quite funny,
when they don't make me scream.

Bubba is the biggest,
three feet from nose to tail, and Sarge is the
roundest, as down the hall he rolls.

Cookie is the sweetest, except when she's
been hunting; then the way she spits and
hisses really amounts to something!

Mama Midnight is the shyest and the slyest,
as she goes her merry way; should you delay
her quest, you will surely rue the day!

But Smiley is the smallest and the meanest
one by far; she spits and hisses when no one's
near as she curls into her ball.

Petra Katrine Barajas

A Rock and My Life

I was back in nowhere again
No home to return to, no room at the inn

I don't need any help
I didn't need any help

Now I'm lost with only my thoughts
Not a friend to console in, not a friend in my heart

I don't need any help
I didn't need any help

More lies are coming my way
A lump in my throat and a sigh here to stay

I don't need any help
I didn't need any help

Once again her gray skies
Her broken down buildings and the tears in her eyes

I don't need any help
I didn't need any help

One day I'll get this town out of my heart
One day I'll get just one more start
That day I buy you screwed up
And forget it all away

David W. Ensor

After All We've Been Through

So you say I'm not the one for you?
How should I feel? What should I do?

How could you do this to me,
after all we've been through?

The good times, filled with laughter
and lust turned into love.
Are we made for each other
like a hand to a glove?

How could you do this to me,
after all we've been through?

If time apart is all that you need,
I'll give it to you and put aside my selfless greed.

How could you do this to me,
after all we've been through?

Don't turn my sunshine into dark and dreary rain,
nor my heartache into a sharp and piercing pain.

How could you do this to me,
after all we've been through?

As I sit and reflect what's on my heart,
It's okay that we part, NEVER MIND!

Sharon Denise Thompson

Hands of Time

Soft, warm, and supple,
Reaching out, needing, questioning.
Ready for patience and guidance
Through each new day.
These are the hands of a little child.

Seeking, searching, unwavering,
For life's mysteries to unravel.
Yearning for all the answers.
An unending quest for freedom,
And the chance to know and be known.
So are the hands of a growing young soul.

Hardened, yet knowing,
Gnarled and wrinkled with age.
Strong and wise from years of toil,
Yet still a need for kindness and love.
A beautiful story left to be told.
For these are the hands of one grown old.

Peggy R. Self

The Heart

With such a passionate feel for emotion,
The heart is a sacred place.
What a strong and loving devotion,
It helps us through struggles of life we must face.

The heart is where it all lies,
How we feel and how we act.
Your head sure does, but your heart has no denies.
Yet it's not always personal, but it all makes contact.

The heart shows us the way,
And guides us through life
As we live it day by day.
So strong yet fragile, it could be destroyed by a knife.

Without a good heart,
What would life be like?
Everything would just fall apart,
No flames burning, no matches to strike.

With a good heart, life can be better,
With this you can develop a good personality.
For all you do in life with a good heart, you'll get a good letter.
It can keep you in touch with reality.

Ashley Richey

Is Life Waiting for You?

happiness is not a fish that you can catch
some try, some cry, yet the fisherman is at end,
looks around the bend, finds nothing, nothing to spare,
wonders how, why compare?
this day is now and yesterday is gone
sometimes I wish life was easy,
not unexplainably cheesy
some people know and lie,
my mouth drops and wants to die
have you ever been in my play?
it's on every day, the cast, the crew, the lights,
sometimes I pray for the nights
my life on a plate sometimes seems to come in late
a package lost—how much does it cost?
the price unbearable, by far uncontrollable
is money really worth it?
I think not so, not one bit
how can one tell? once tried and fell
sometimes I can't help but think,
was I going to say pink?
is anybody there? does anyone care?
these are thoughts from my mind, some I wish people could find
please do, I welcome you to
life is waiting for you. . . .

Harper Holsinger

Insanity

The thickets are getting thicker,
And the stickers keep getting stickier;
The seeds of reason are beyond the reach of my neurons.
The thunder drowns my sense of ought,
And the fogbank blinds all rational thought.
I don't recall having a clear mental image in aeons.

The mythic banshee wails my soon demise.
I think, "only those in immortal sleep are wise."
I'm haunted by impossible dreams of forever and beyond.
Then I hear a whispering ocean breeze,
And some unseen presence gives my sad soul ease.
I find a fellowship that promises to secure a solid bond.

Suddenly, the thunderbolt becomes a lightning flash;
In its light, the ocean roar becomes a puddle splash.
And now, it seems that there is nothing I cannot explain.
How could I have been so dense?
Everything together all makes perfect sense,
So I know one thing for certain; Yes, I am insane.

Charles E. Mieir

My Baby, Belle

I can still recall the hour
When I was walking along the park
Biding my time before I could see a lark,

As I was carrying you in my tummy,
Telling everyone I meet
How happy I am and sometimes couldn't sleep,

Waiting for the time if it should come today
That if I'll have a boy, I would call him Ray.

Then suddenly I felt you move inside
Telling me, "I'm coming out, now set aside."
In turn I said, "I'll be happy to see you soon, my child."

So I packed my things, and off we went
To the hospital by the bend,
Told everyone there, I'll have a baby I can stare.

While counting the painful seconds
For my little creature to come out,
Patiently I waited for my baby to cry out.

Alas, by miracle of God's love,
Behold my baby so cute, so cuddly,
A baby girl I shall call . . . Belle.

Yvette Bautista Evangelista

I Dance Alone, Yet Not Alone

The wind's calling, the thunder's rolling;
Touching my heart, filling my soul
With Grandfather's love.

My heart beats with the drum,
My soul sings with the thunder,
My feet dance for Grandfather.

Though there's a crowd
When I enter the circle of life,
I enter alone; yet not alone,
for I dance with Grandfather by my side.

The wind's calling, the thunder's rolling;
Touching my heart, filling my soul
With Grandfather's love

I dance not for myself—
I dance for Grandfather,
I dance for The Old Ones,
I dance for the ones yet to be.

The wind's calling, the thunder's rolling;
Touching my heart, filling my soul
With Grandfather's Love.
I dance alone; yet not alone. . . .

Betty M. Gorby

Plucked from Memory

Cold, gray, still was the day.
Trees laced black against a patient sky,
Waiting to spew cradled flakes to soften the earth
        where the white goose walked
Stark
        across the arched footbridge
            to slip into the creek,
Soon to blend with the scene.

The house stood strong against the hill.
Veils of water beside a wheel
Bespoke it as mill.
Folk within by firelight warm,
        welcomed strangers as their own,
Shielding us off from harm.

Supped and tranquil for the long walk
        back,
Two little girls etched a day
Plucked from memory.

Genie Tarris

Sea of the Damned

Seizures
Darkness and pain come again
As demons from Hell to play.
The nightmare of the curse begins
And my soul is now covered with gray.

My body cries out to cease living.
I cannot endure another attack.
But the pain is never forgiving
And the darkness is always black.

My mind sees things from the past.
I always see lights and shapes so grand.
I am falling with nothing to grasp.
I am lost again in the Sea of the Damned.

I am weary of life with the curse.
Death by my own hand would stop the attacks
But I know something that would be worse,
Eternal damnation for a wrongful act.

My hands are tied and my fate is cast.
I must accept this curse and cruel strife.
Looking forward someday to peace at last
In God's kingdom and heavenly life.

Mark R. Fairall

confused love

sometimes you tell me you love me,
sometimes i think it's true,
sometimes you make me feel like you need me,
but i know i'll always need you.
sometimes you let me know you care.
sometimes i want to tell you things, but do i dare?
do i dare to tell you how i feel?
do i dare tell you that i think your love isn't real?
do i dare allow myself to love once more?
do i dare allow myself to feel the way i felt before?
should i tell you what i think in my head?
should i tell you what i think when i lie in bed?
i am so confused, i'm not for sure what to do.
i just keep thinking that all i need is you.
i'm afraid this is going to lead in the same path as before,
and i don't want to love someone that loves me no more.
you know what i went through before,
and when we talk about it, you say it's okay;
that makes me love you even more.
i've sat and thought about you today,
and i think i finally know what to say.
i know for sure now that i've loved you from the start,
and no matter what happens, you will have a place in my heart!

Samantha Horner

Life

Ashes to ashes
Dust to dust
And
God created me

I don't know what His plans are for me
But
He blew me into existence
Knowing I would make a difference

There is a future for me
You know
My life will unfold as days go by
Some days I'll be happy, some days I'll cry

And when the time comes
It's
Ashes to ashes
Dust to dust
I am going to
Return to where I came from

Karen Stowinsky

My Love for Nature

I am standing at the front of my boat
watching the twinkling stars and the
shimmering moon whisper in my ear, trying to
comfort me, for I sail alone.

I toss my finest herbs into my sister
sea, for I care for her lovingly.

Oh, how I love the Earth, for it supplies
life and happiness!

Oh, how I love adventure, for I see
things no one has seen before!

I explore the most beautiful places, for
I know where they are hidden.

I talk with animals, for they have many
secrets.

I swim with the life of the sea, for we
watch over each other.

I climb the highest mountain to talk
with God, for I am His.

I live alone, for I am a part of nature.

Marybeth Head

Forever Friend

There is a friend
Who comes in your life
Most times when you are walking
Through the hardest of times
She lovingly, tenderly
Begins caring for you
Wipes all your tears
And helps you start new
She sees not your weakness
Instead builds on your strength
Then watches with delight
As you spread your wings
She gives you a new song
To sing in the day
And looks on with delight
As you take time to pray
You know in this life
She will not steer you wrong
For her heart always hums a heavenly song
She will stand by your side
Through thick and or thin
Because deep in your heart
She is your "forever friend"

Tammie Stockley

Black Sunday

I had anticipated a day of glories,
the return of a long absent breed,
a young prodigy preparing for his mentor's mantle,
and a father giving up his own car to drive in his son's place.
Many here had won this race; a few had never won any.
Then there was him, "The Man in Black,"
a warrior so fierce, so determined, he was called "The Intimidator."
His competitive energy flowed through this day
from the command that brought 18,000 horsepower to life,
to the waving flag that sent 43 steeds chasing the carrot.
This day showed why he was truly "one tough customer."
Running flat-out in the last turn, on the last lap, his car hopped,
this warrior, my hero, sent careening head-on into a wall.
The crash didn't look so bad, but held our attention anyway
as "O'fer" celebrated a win at last, searching for his car owner.
Then the impossible happened,
the announcement we could never prepare for.
Everyone stood in stunned silence, blinking in disbelief,
the fiercest warrior in the land had left us for the next realm.

Steven C. Kroll

Be My Friend

To that lonely person who needs me
I tried to be your friend today,
Why I tried so ever hard.
But you wouldn't even acknowledge me,
Let alone be my friend.

I am not really sure what I did wrong,
But I know that I cannot give up.
I can see it in your eyes that you need a friend,
So I to try to figure out how to reach you.

You are new to me and I am new to you,
You know nothing of me and I of you.
So I come to you to know you,
So that I can call you my friend.

I know we must have something in common,
Whether it be sports, classes, or hobbies.
I know that we can connect on something,
And that will be our foundation to a great friendship.

So when I see you again tomorrow,
I will try again to be your friend.
For I know we share something together,
Something that will allow me to call you my friend.

Kevin A. Bost

Strong Wings

For Carl, Eagle Scout
Strong wings of the eagle
withstand storms and trials
soaring through God's blue sky
through miles and miles of flight

Never tiring, never giving up—
flying straight and true for days and nights
pausing only to gaze upon the world,
then reaching for greater heights.

An Eagle Scout spreads his wings
to embark on all the challenges of life
He travels over God's great land
and embraces learning through joy and strife

An Eagle Scout never stops trying
always reaching to meet his goal—
never forgetting his God and his purpose
continuing to pray and strengthen his soul.

Strong wings of the eagle
are developed with God's guiding hand
The wings of an Eagle Scout
are his faith in God and in this great land.

Carleta Rose Cates and David William Cates

Oracle of the Cosmos

As microcosms through space we fly
Unnoticed by the cosmic mist
Floating past fractured lives
And minds unscathed by rationale
Or cognizance of any burning desires.

Time exists only in the heart
And "too short, too short"
Echoes through the canyons of despair
Found within the murky depths
Behind its barren walls.

The oracle speaks and having spoken
Departs the cosmos leaving only
Bewilderment and desolation in its wake.
Ashes surround the sun,souls turn to dust
And fetuses weep in the womb.

Harken to the words written on the walls
"Repent—return to the ways of your fathers
Or perish within the noxious vapors
Which emanate from the swamp
You call civilization."

    Virginia Dawn Gardner

Magical October

The beautiful autumn,
Falling leaves of red and gold,
Brilliant colors in the Sun,
Announcing the season, bright and bold.

Shoppers hurry to Columbus Day sales.
The sound of wild geese, in formation V,
As every fall they never fail
To fly south for all to see.

Rising early to go to school,
Children run to catch the bus.
Daylight savings time, a changing rule,
Out of the darkness, they rush, rush, rush.

Halloween is a special day,
Dressing up in scary costume,
To go trick or treat in grand array,
Under the spell of magical moon.

The last rose of summer,
Competing with three or four.
Which one will Jack Frost miss
In Indian summer to bloom some more?

    Ann McCall

Set Free

You need no ropes to be tied down,
nor any other bonds, you see.
It only takes that prison called Earth
that makes you bound, not free.

To think these things, these books and dolls
could keep me from that gate.
The material things that I love best
could they somehow determine my fate?

Set me free, Lord! Set me free.
Take the scales off my eyes that I may see
what's truly important on this Earth,
not the things, but Christ's birth.

He's the one that you love so,
who took that lash and took the blow.
Thank you, Lord, for giving me, the one
who saves, the one who frees.

Thank you Lord and your Son, too,
for the things you're about to do.
Make me good and clean and right
that I may stand in thy holy sight.

    Krystal Smith

Happy Mother's Day

To the toughest eagle I know
when i think of mother, it's not just a word—
much more complicated than one has heard.
you must know everything, at once, today.
be serious, keep thing going, and play.
there are days that are confusing; you get by
and if you're lucky and pray—like an eagle fly.
motherhood is forever or while you're alive.
to be complete, it can't be a job from 9 to 5.
for your kids, through it all, you must be there—
it's a lifetime commitment, if you so dare.
you never get credit or even a thank you,
but with all the love, it's all right with you.
through my life you've given blood sweat and tears;
with the struggles, one never knows the fears.
you get by from day to day, and you'll cope;
as a mom, you'll never ever give up hope.
you seem to get help from your maker up above;
through the hard times, you remember the love.
even if you don't hear me, i want to say:
with my love, have a Happy Mother's Day.

    Judy A. Miller

Computerized

I got a new computer for Christmas.
It is supposed to be one of the best.
It's got a lot of attachments,
and you'd better believe I'm impressed.

It's got a mouse with a delicate clicker
and surfing the web is a thrill.
Interesting sites and plenty of chats
is the everyday run-of-the-mill.

I found friends that I didn't know I had
and they didn't know about me.
Touched base with the poor at heart
and rubbed elbows with the very elite.

I don't have to go to the park to have music,
it's right here at my door.
I've only to push a button
and I've got notes galore.

Between going to class and learning the rules,
only one fact seems to prevail—
the world is a better place
when a voice says, you've got mail.

    Joyce Elaine Campbell

I'm a Fool, but I'm Still in Love with You

When we first met, it was love at first sight,
We married one summer and we lived just right.
We made it through some bad times as well as some good.
Our marriage seemed to end, and I never understood!

Well, you left me one night and took my wedding ring,
You said I wasn't good enough to be your queen,
Well, I know you love me baby, and I love you too!
What is it going to take to get back with you!

It's been a great while since I've seen you,
I can't seem to smile because I feel so blue.
I Miss you so much that I cry myself to sleep.
I miss your sweet touch cause our love was so deep

Maybe you need to know, I need to let you go.
Oh, what a fool I've been, I'll never see you again.
You left me once, you'll leave me twice
Stop messing with my heart like a roll of the dice . . .

Well, the moral of the story is I'm still without you,
I have to move forward I got better things to do.
This chapter in my life must come to a close,
I will always love you and everybody knows.

    Darlene Hamm

The Glass Forest

Today I live in the Glass Forest.
I almost expect to see the little fairies
Flying about, from one iced branch to the next. . . .
But the terrible rain blizzard came last night.
It left each twig, stop sign, telephone wire,
And the whole length of barbed wire fence
Dipped in a sleeve of lacy glass.
Today they sparkle and shimmer in the sunshine.
Crystal branches explode when they touch each other.
Each blade of grass is encased in silver.
Every tip of the pine tree's needles has a
Diamond at the edge, ready to fall off
In the slightest gust of wind.
The skinny branches crowd together and twinkle
Like a giant silver spider web.
Rainbows sparkle on every glass shrouded limb.
Tubes of glass like drinking straws hang
From the trees and clink and tinkle.
Like tiny mirrors they reflect off of each other
In a shiny dance of light and sound.

Tawnya Mork

The Revelation of Women

The ravenous words in the tribal book give a meaning
with an amazing look
The luxurious letters fall into ancient place,
they are molded together without any indigenous trace

The loyalists structures are in depth in each bizarre size,
they are categorized items that will not hide
The imprisonment of passion is devoured into a mist,
for this is the time of mind and spirit elevation; there is no risk.

The women evolved from the essence of man,
we have the power of mankind in a cubicle plan
The exhilarating thoughts that float through our ominous heads
keep children awake in their beds.

We derived from a much stable source,
we were conjured up by the people's choice.
We, the women, are the ones to speak the word,
we share all grave images to be heard.

The revelation of women evolved from the rib cage of a man,
which contains the vibrance and life in the palm of everyone's hand.

Those who speak ill have no meaning,
for this is the revelation of women; it's just a beginning.

Jacqueline Denise Green

Faraway

Can you hear me whisper across the sea?
Have I lost you while I wait,
or is it love that echoes from a distance
as I watch the red rose turn gray?

Do I hear the piano play in silence,
or is it you moving in my thoughts?
So far away you stood; I could hardly see you
madly dancing into the rain.

Have I felt the warmth of your breath
standing here alone in the cold?
Is it the broken thorn that I found,
lay silently bleeding my soul.

Sailing away through the rough seas,
you find me—shelter in your shore—
gently washing across your sands.
I hear you whisper at my door.

The sun glares into my eyes;
I lay my heart in your hands;
you guide me through the stormy nights;
faraway you vanish into the unknown lands.

Syed M. Alam

Yesterday

I remember yesterday, the old days.
I like yesterday the joyous early breakfast
made by mam, the milk from cow, and yeah!
those beautiful stories given by grangma.

I like yesterday, the calm of the early field,
the duck asleep by river, all the quiet
hours of nature yield, before all the
chickens awake, and yeah! I like pigeons
when they all gathered together for grangpa's
corn every morning.

O, yeah! I remember those beautiful uniforms
we used to wear every day to school, it used
to be good. What happened to all the respect
we used to have for our elders, when will school start
teaching the old-fashioned way again?

Yesterday was perfect, I left my country with
pride, respect, love, but not by choice.
In my own I will find that old "la plus belle
des antilles." Haiti cherie, I will find my own sport,
and ride in my own field.

Exante Etienne

Passing

Well, it's been four days now,
Slowly sliding into five,
Since I said goodbye to E.T.
I guess by now he has arrived.

I know what people will think;
"Renée, it was only a cat.
He went no farther than the ground.
He died and that is that!"

But right now, I feel so strongly
He has just had cream, thick and sweet
He is happy and warm
Now he's sleeping at the Master's feet.

We were together for almost 20 years
And his age finally took hold
He couldn't get around much anymore
He would shake, like from the cold.

Surely he will be rewarded
For the friend he was to me
There will never be one to take his place
I love and miss you, E.T.

S. Renée Hunt

A "Yalie" Minuet

You ought to marry a "Yalie." This was bred in me.
"Oh, it would be awfully good for you." This was said to me.

"Yalies" are mostly sand-crowned, often have hazel eyes.
There are so presenting in their Brooks Brothers silk ties.
"Oh, he will look so good on you. Oh, me oh me oh my."

"Look for someone like your dad. Or Uncle Taylor, too.
Or someone like Cousin Carl. He was a 'Yalie,' too."

" 'Yalies' have a special flair. They have that savoir-fare.
Typically and often they are so debonair."

"You can expect carated rings, patrician friends, and yachts.
Oh, you will be in financial heaven. I truly kid you not."

So I did what they suggested. I listened to what they said.
I followed all their rules as "Yalie" and I were wed.

But guidelines were missing from their creed.
Big gaps were there in their breeding.
There were unexplored territories I needed to heed.
And one day I heard a "Yalie" pleading.

"I have basically met all your required needs.
Tell me what deeds did you bring to me."

Martha Deborah Hall

Capture the Laughter

For one selfish moment I would capture the laughter.
When bottled and sealed, I could remain inside forever
And bask in its sediment, to savor thereafter.
Like the clarity of a diamond, its presence always clear,
Never tiring of its contrast, seldom dull, perpetually clever,
Embraced for our pleasure, to guard and hold dear.

This champagne of life is destined to be shared.
The seal must be broken and uncorked with unbridled fervor,
As its bouquet and significance are boldly declared,
I know this verity and honor it with hesitant waiver.
Amidst the gossamer of the soul that floats on a calm autumn day
Is this prescription without cost, that invites us to play!

Engulfed by the inebriation that no other substance provides,
Like the fountain of youth, immersed to be kept,
I share with you my enticing divides
To quench your thirst; for I am keenly adept.
As the fragrance of that sound vaporizes the air,
Imprisonment is inevitable, when surrounded by its rapture.
You'll beseech for more potion and remain acutely aware,
When my pleasure fills all of your cups, as you capture the laughter!

Linda D. Boutin

The Surf

Time freezes when I sit by the water,
Watching the waves break on a warm summer night.
In the breeze I sit, while time freezes with fright:
Fear of going back the way I came,
Picking the same road I was on before.

Time freezes when I sit by the water,
Watching the waves break on a warm summer night.

"Go surf those waves," I say. It will help me
Stay on the new road I have found.
The waves glisten in the moonlight,
And they seem to listen to my every breath.
I never thought this road would lead to death.
"Stay off that old road," the waves say. "Stay
Here with us, and your troubles will go away."

Because time freezes when I sit by the water,
Watching the waves break on a warm summer night.

I see something among the waves. What
Is it? I cannot tell. It moves closer . . . closer.
It is a little boy with a face full of fear,
Telling me to stay on this road.

Michael John Avella

World and Opposites

To every beginning
There is an end
Just as roles in lives are playing
Until all acts are played and the curtain descends

To every win
There is a loss
A time to do the rhumba of Latin
And a time to join a procession of remorse

To every life
There is death
For it is just a while man must strife
Until it's demanded of his soul the living breathe

To every day
There is a night
As it is when the sun shines one can make hay
For at the moon's rise, one cannot challenge nature's fight

To every sowing
There is a reaping
A principle, not of man's scholastic reasoning
But of the almighty above's imposing

Olamide Abimbola Adams

Nanay

On my homecoming—after 25 years
Golden in years, platinum in grace . . .
The look of your face exhibits—not
The waning of love for me, in spite of
My many, many transgressions. . . . My coming
Home was like rain after a long, long drought
And—dearth . . . my mere presence was, to
One neighbor—an apparition of a prodigal son—
Long considered dead. Distraught and truly
Repentant, I poured my heart out to
Tatay (though way too late), the error
Of my ways, as Heaven released a torrent—
So heavy (as if saying),
"I am crying for you and with you," as
I shook feeling cold and weak. I promised
Tatay that, no more on my account shall I
Cause you pain. The harrowed lines . . . are
Hallow to me; they are telling of an era borne
To bridge my present . . . to yesterdays.
Under God's Heaven, there is no love greater
Than the love you have for me, my Nanay.

Eliseo Guerrero Cervantes

Breaking Free

Blackness.

All-consuming darkness.
A total feeling of being lost.
Searching but never finding.
Looking for light in this dark place.
Searching, searching,
Finding nothing but infinite darkness.
Finally, there is a small flicker of light.

Running, running headlong into the unknown.
Running towards the light,
Breaking free of the darkness.
Gone, without warning, the light is gone.

Alone again, alone in the darkness.
Alone to continue the search.
The search for light,
The search for life,
The search for happiness.
Searching but never finding,
Only all-consuming darkness.

Blackness.

Eric Kent Hammers

Only One

With a boy this special, can't believe his life is done,
your special little boy, only lived to be one.

No kindergarten, no prom, college isn't even a fact,
bet you cried your heart out to keep your love intact.

Never got to see him married, no grandchildren from this son,
because your precious little angel only lived to be one.

All the milestones of his life that you've had to miss,
wish you could blow away his pain with a loving, little kiss.

Got to see him giggle, maybe even talk,
got to see him crawl, maybe even walk.

Wish you could be with him now to tell him what to do,
wish you could have him back so he could be with you.

Know that he loves you, said a little dove.
Know that he looks out for you from way up above.

When it rains, he sees your tears,
and when you cry, he knows your fears.

He knows that you love him, just know that he's okay,
and if there wasn't a plan for him, he wouldn't have been led away.

Heather Caza

Oasis

The Ground, up-heaved and scorched, sprawls
limp like a corpse far as the eye can see.
The sparse vegetation stands indifferent.
It is silent.
The Sun, rising, casts shadows, but offers no
warmth. The purple-red glow stretches,
looming in the distance. Its reign is cold,
hollow, translucent.
It is silent.
The Air, cool, thick with the smell of
burning flesh, rolls in, covering everything
with a fine mist of immanent doom.
It is silent.
The Water, waiting quietly still is silent.
Sounds of distant screams and explosions
ripple under its surface, at odds with its
calm facade.
It is silent.
The Corpses, up-heaved and scorched, sprawls
limp like the ground far as the eye can see.
The Oasis, quiet separations mirage.

Christopher David Walrath

One True Love

To you I'm like a piece of string
That you have tied around your finger;
And in your mind is a thought
That my love for you won't linger.

When I had the chance to have you
I didn't take it as serious;
When I think of what I've done
The frustration makes me delirious.

At first my heart wasn't true . . .
Basically very unsure;
So I had to hold off
Until it was more mature.

After the things I have gone through in the past year
And entering into a new;
It makes me think and feel
That my life is meant to be with you.

Knowing what I want,
And having a heart that is now true,
Makes me believe now
That life with you won't make me blue.

Brandy Brown

Do We Really?

Do we really see?
Behind the playful grins, the hurt
That remains so well-concealed
Beneath the many layers of dirt.

Do we really know?
How they get from day to day,
Their dreams still waiting to be dreamt,
As on the cold, hard place they lay.

Do we really hear?
The chattering teeth, so cold
The night wind blowing through,
They long for something warm to hold.

Do we really feel?
Their need to be held and loved,
Never asking for the abuse
Which down their throats are daily shoved.

Do we really care?
Those who turn to look, so few
Will all God's people please stand and say
"YES, I REALLY, TRULY DO."

Stuart Ramnarine

Butterfly Honey

Butterfly honey
sounds real funny
when you're not in the mood for some.
But look real close
at that piece of toast
without a thing on top it looks dumb.
Butterfly honey
is better than money
'cause it won't fly away on the winds.
It doesn't take up much space
it won't make you lose face
but it might make you double your friends.
So run, get it today
without adieu or delay
'cause yesterday's stockpile won't last.
Knock yourself out
and shout out this tout:
Butterfly honey's a blast!
Make it known to the world
as this dish you unfurl
that this is one icon they can't clast.

William McCarty Ardrey

There's a Rainbow

There's a rainbow up in the sky.
Have you ever wondered what was on the other side?
So many colors running through and through.
Do you know that rainbows remind me so much of you?
I was down and out with a broken heart,
crying all the time, my life so torn apart.
Then I met the Master;
He wiped my tears away.
It was like that rainbow you see after the rain.
The rainbow's colors ring true through and through,
just like God's promises to me and you.
When I asked Jesus into my heart,
He gave me peace of mind,
I know we'll never part.
Like that promise of the rainbow you see after the rain,
I know He's going to stay with me,
and I will live with Him for all eternity.
Can you hear the Savior knocking?
Won't you please let Him in?
He will wipe your tears away, and
He will change your heart within.
Accept Him and don't delay, so you too can live with Him one day.

Aletha Pinder

In This Place

I am in a place where your world meets mine
Creating a kingdom of love, escaping time
The place where my ancestors lie
Because that's where their souls were claimed
As they looked into the clouds being lost
But becoming found, I hear the sound
Of two lovers placing footprints
In the sand, but the water demands
My full attention, sweeping the evidence
Of their love away, but what stays is the smell
Of salt, it lies around like the
Seaweed on the land
The sand sticks to my toes
The breeze goes and moves
With the water, I am the daughter of the Nile
So all the while being pulled in
The tide is getting higher, claiming my skin
As I place my feet within, I look above
And the clouds are creating a picture
Of their own, that's when I remember
I am all alone, just me and time
In this place where your world meets mine

Tiya Wiggins

The Pup

A puppy I am I am
I romp and play; you like me that way

A year old now, I'm a dog you say
There is no play
You forgot to feed me today
But that's okay; I love you anyway

I hear you say your going to take me away
Away what did I do
A place so cold I go
Can't play, can't get away
Shacking and scared in a cage I lay

Again I hear take him away
Away what did I do
What did I do

On a table it's hard and cold
She kissed me good night with a tear in her eye

I feel sleepy
Away I go
Why? I don't know
    Nikki M. Norrup

Happy Anniversary, My Darlin' Tim

Ten years ago we said, "I do,"
Knowing our love would always be true.
We said, "In good times and in bad,"
Never dreaming I could be so sad.
We said, "For better or for worse,"
Oh, the way your love made my heart burst.
We said, "In sickness and in health,"
Always standing side by side with whatever we were dealt.
We said, "Until death do us part,"
But even in death you remain in my heart.
Then you were told, "You may kiss the bride,"
And you did it with so much pride.
We were given three gifts from God.
As a father you had such a bond.
We've been married ten wonderful years,
Never knowing it would end with so many tears.
That sad day in July, I know God gave you wings to fly.
No one will ever know,
How I miss you so.
Ten years ago we said, "I do,"
Knowing our love would always remain true—
October 26,1990.
    Carrie White

I Am Justine

I am from sleeping in bed.
Slowly drifting away, not hearing what mom just said.
Dreaming forever on the clouds in the sky,
wanting but failing to open my eyes.

I am from the ocean, where my favorite foods are found.
The luscious smell of seafood drifting all around.
Lobsters and fishies, and Sharkies galore,
all are caught on the edge of the shore.

I am from a paradise called the Crystal Mall.
I could shop till I drop, but when I do I still crawl.
Always in search of nothing I need,
some call it shopping, but I call it greed.

I am from "Put that away!"
"Let's call it a day."
"They look up to you."
"Why not try something new?"

I am from my mother and my father,
of course everyone is, but don't bother.
Wherever I go, and whatever I say,
I am me in each and every way.
    Justine Rose Allard

A Wasted Life

Why would you stop now? Why would you let go?
Why would you just let your life pass by,
Like whirlwinds beneath your feet that blow?
I stop for nothing to get to the top,
I flip and trip over my own emotions, but still, I do not stop.
I take what I have and make the most of it,
I'm digging my foot into Hell to get to the top.
I'm like a lighter that hasn't been lit,
I'm an explosion just waiting for that click.
I frown upon you for doing so little,
For wasting the life that God has given.
Just to look at people like you gets me driven.
I wait for that one day
When all my work has come into play.
I will rise above others and conquer all odds,
For this I ask God to let me stay.
For every day I rise, you waste away;
Every time I drive, you are driven away.
This is my time to shine, because you did not.
You are a life that has been wasted away,
I am the decision maker, who will not let you stay.
    Alexander George Semba

Goodbye

I stood by this school through thick and thin
I have memories that make me laugh
When people dissed us it made me mad
I was defensive 'cause I knew the truth
That's the way it was—what could I do?
Now I sit here in a new school
I wanna come home, but I just can't
I miss the family we had
I miss you, my old school
I had some of the best times there
And I will be strong
It's time to recover,
So bye
There goes all the memories
It seems so dreary to say goodbye,
Yet I have to say goodbye,
Goodbye to the good times shared, it's time to part
Goodbye to the friends I've lost
Goodbye to the happiness they've cost
What's the point in being mad?
Goodbye, 'cause it's time for a new start,
Even though it breaks my heart
    Cindi Click

Searching

I have turned every dark dune
I have talked to the moon
Just to be with you
Just for the chance to be with you

Through the clouds I have looked
There I have found what I'm looking for
I have been looking for you
All this time I have been looking for you

The stars I have captured
And all the wonders of the world to you I have raptured
Only to give them to you
Because all I do I do it for you

Used all of my time to gather words
Wasted my days searching for words
Words beautiful enough to describe you
Words that could say how I feel about you

If I had to do it all again I would
If you gave me the chance I know I could
Because after everything is said and done I still love you
Until the end of time I won't stop loving you
    Joshua Gabriel Ortiz

Sleep

I will not go to sleep!
Not give in to the slumber!
I hug my teddy close to my chest
And look out the window,
Waiting for the morning sun.
It does not come; now I am confused.
Usually by now, I would be up and eating brekky.
Where is the golden circle?
When I go to sleep, I just wake up,
And the Sun is there.
I close my eyes.
The Sun is not coming,
And I am tired.
I give in to the slumber,
And go to sleep.
I open my eyes and it is morning,
And sunlight bathes my face.
I have slept but for a minute.
I could have waited a few more minutes
And seen it rise up like a bubble in the sea.
I will try again, tomorrow!

Ryan David Leith

Reflections

Look into mine eyes and tell me what you see.
Do you see all that I was?
All that I am?
All that I will be?

Do you see the very essence of my being?
The love in my heart?
The scars upon my soul?

No, of course you don't see.
You see what you choose to see.

I look into thine eyes and this is what I see:
You, who is the strongest tree in the forest.
You stand proud with your head held high.
You are surrounded by others,
Who hold their heads down and cry.

They weep for the memories they have forgotten,
For the loved ones they have lost,
For the blood that was shed,
Their souls pay the cost.

Look into mine eyes and tell me what you see.
For I am you and you are me.

Melissa Arlene Johnson

The Gift of Love

When I think of the greatest gift
I think of the gift of love,
And this great love is made complete
In the heavenly Father above.

He searched the world from east to west
Looking for a heart that was pure.
His eyes caught yours,
Looking up to Him so faithfully and sure.

Seeing your gentle, kind spirit and undeniable peace
Filled with patience and goodness too,
He leaned down to Earth, stretching out His arm
And bestowed this love on you.

But being the selfless, giving person you are
You knew it was a gift to give,
And so you lived out this love for me
By giving me a life to live.

So when I think of this gift of love
I think of the Lord and one other.
I think of the one who models this love;
I think of you, my mother.

Stacey Fields

Anger

Like a mob crazy for the blood of its victim
It has neither mind, nor soul
Like the thundering waves of an ocean gone mad in the winds
It envelops the mind and prevents rationality
Like a ravaging brush fire
It destroys all that is good in its path and leaves naught but chaos

Like the Nile's flood in full season
Nothing in its path has significance
Even the very life that breeds, it becomes minuscule
Its sole aim is to obliterate
And until it is vented, it remains like the mad mob
Whose satisfaction lies only in justice
Or what it deems to be justice

When the haze of the madness clears
The damage done comes clear
Oftentimes, the damage can be a righted
But most times, like spiritual death
It is irreparable

Is it worth it then we ask
Who knows, indeed, who cares

Chukwueloka Umeh

Life Is

Life is depending on God
For our daily existence on His Earth.

Life is perseverance,
Meaning not giving up.

Life is working diligently
To acquire what you need and want.

Life is learning new things,
Expanding on that knowledge,
And sharing what you have learned with others.

Life is making decisions,
Making the right decisions.

Life is making mistakes,
Learning from your errors,
Overcoming, refusing to stay stagnant!

Life is loving and receiving love,
Helping and receiving help,
Giving and being given to.

Life is,
Life is to live!

Latina Stroughter

Forever

Thank you for all the things we shared together,
For all the thoughts that were bound,
For all the moments we learned something new about ourselves.

But you must understand for a second,
It's me I need to find,
Me I need to remember,
Me I need to live for!

I don't mean to hurt you.
That's not my intention.
But if I do, I'm sorry,
But I must follow my heart!

So all I can say is that I love you,
Even though it may not seem like it now.
You'll always stay in my heart.
Through thick and thin,
Yours is the love I'll look back upon!

You'll always be part of me,
And when we meet again . . .
May it be the good times that we remember?
For this is what true hearts strive to keep!

Tamaryn Truter

Light of Day

The darkness is all around me,
I hold my tear-stained pillow tight,
Hoping for the light of day.

I live my life in the gray
And darkening days,
Hoping for the light of day.

Another lifeless day has ended
And still I pray for the
Light of day.

In the dark, I cry with no one to hold,
No one to console me,
No one to understand.

Slowly, my eyes are opening,
I see the Sun's rays through my window.
I watch the rainbow dancing across
My floor.

I can see the Light of Day,
As you come walking
Through my door.

Lori Diane Simons

My Harley

One day I bought a bike
It was a Harley, the kind I like
The color was azure blue
You can bet that I liked it, too.

I rode it fast, I rode it slow
I rode it everyplace I would go
It was so big and strong and good
I would get upon the seat and there I stood.

One day, I took it for a ride
A car hit me and I thought I had died
My clothes were torn, my watch was ruined
My biked looked like it had gone to the moon.

I rode to the Harley shop to get the parts
The dealer said the price of this will break your heart
I know the price I will need to pay
But fix her up—I want to play.

The next time out, I hit a dog, I hit a cat
I hit a truck right in the back
My teeth were loose, my back was strained
Everything I had was full of pain.

Thomas Anderson

Walking in the Autumn Woods

What a day for a stroll in the painted wood
and hearken nature's sound
through secret path and under bough,
forge stream that has yet to be found.

The wood elves have painted the forest
brilliant shades of fall.
Nature's magic appears to be
the most majestic power of all.

I come across a wall of stone
and marvel to myself.
Who has made this barrier of rock?
A native? A pilgrim? An elf?

Squirrels hurry to collect their food
along trunk and bough.
Their hustle and bustle remind me
that I really must go.

I head back east, toward suburb life,
to the crammed schedule of day.
But I am glad that I have stopped to see
nature's magical display.

A. J. Warren

My Love for You

Without you the stars burn out,
The sky turns black,
My world stays dark until you come back.
To hear your voice,
To see your face,
Brings my life purpose and a dream to chase.
I want to hold you close,
To kiss your lips,
And caress you softly with my fingertips.
You are my only passion,
My one desire.
When I'm with you, my heart's on fire.
Through the tunnel, you are my light.
My heart was blind,
But you gave it sight.
Angels sing when you are near.
I have no worry; I have no fear.
Every day without you is lifeless and dreary.
Struggling to breathe, I am tired and weary.
When you return, my strength is good as new;
My very soul I give to you.

Anonymous

Sorrows and Tragedies Overcome by Joy

Sorrows and tragedies,
Left unresolved,
Despise the human heart,
Cracking its emotional embers,
Which cannot be healed.

So dismal are our past woes,
We sink into the depths of soul.
Memories lie beneath its cover,
Concealed from the view of one's mind,
Leaving past recollections silenced from joy.

May the rippling tide of the clear water
Reflect your melancholy image,
And let the fire of your inner light
Burn infinite in jubilance.

May you recover from your past sorrows and tragedies
Left unresolved,
Despise the human heart,
Cracking its emotional embers,
Which cannot be healed.

Burn infinite in jubilance!

Ivy Casavant

Me

There are few who know me in this place
They just see a man
They never looked beyond my face
To see me for what I am

I am thought to be tough
And to have stone cold skin
But underneath this skin which is so rough
Is a caring man who lives deep within

I am a man who looks for love
Yet it has never been found
But I still pray to my God above
And he has never made a sound

Why I am here I know not
Just that I am here in this place
And soon I hope to be taught
To look beyond a mans face

To see the person inside
And not to judge by the skin
Because the cover always lied
Only truth can be found within

Robert LeChais Bomar

Eyeless Fear

Cover blinded, spinning 'round
Blackness, void, covered down
Spinning twirling, shooting slicing
Straight and curved
Wide and skinny, thin and sharp
Curving, narrowing to a point
Robed and cowled, deep inside
Eyes glow red, hands glow black
Poison, fear, death
Cover blinded, falling down
Spiraling in around the wrist
Sliding in between the ribs
Heart has burst wide, gaping wound
Forked tongue between the teeth
Slithering, flickering; scythe slashing down
Spiraling in past the wrist
Between the ribs
The grip of eyeless fear
Life gushing out the wound
Red, black, blind, fear, courage
Nothing

Tom Appleby

Surrender

Blackbirds cloud treetops, whispering
rumors of chill winds and winter plans.
Twittering tall tales of a summer
now lost beyond the sun's grasp.

Earth exhales her sodden breath
into swirling breezes of velvet twilight.
Slanted sunbeams run shimmering
toward autumn's magnetic embrace.

Elderly katydids stride slowly with
stiffness in their knees,
singing low, sad refrains
of coming frost and dying rose.

October has shredded summer's dress,
heavy-handed in her ruthless power.
Leaves tumble to their death in one last,
brief flash of flaming, passionate color.

Earth sighs.
The last surrender of her perfect love
contains a promise
born in dying autumn days.

Melissa Ellen Neill

Taking Chances

From the moment that our eyes met
I could feel it deep inside
Almost dared to think you were heaven sent
You're so beautiful I cried.

I've been here lonely for far too long
Thinking it would be this way forever
But then you appeared with a song
Bringing both hopes and dreams together.

So I sit by the phone
Hoping that you'll call
I don't want to be alone
And for you I'd risk the fall.

Can't you see I'm here waiting
For someone just like you
We're both giving and not taking
But together we can make it through.

I know its hard, you've been hurt before
My heart has had its share too
Slowly our trust builds more and more
Knowing I'll always be true.

D. L. Stone

New Soldier, Old Front, or More Slaughter in the Trenches

Leaning in the mud and muck
Cursing life, God, and luck
Awaiting the shrill call of death
In a silence too thick for breath
Gripping the iron and wood
Praying for their sanity or anything that would
Halt the call that will send me swift
Into oblivion's blinding dark rift
The blood pounding in my ears
The panic of just 18 years
Thrown unwilling into this strife
Wishing against the eclipse of my life
What about children and growing old
A long life is a wish too bold
Sacrifice for country, God, and kin
All that is wanted is to laugh again
Hear it, up and run, dodge and sway
Crying and praying to survive the day
Oh, God, oh, my
Now to die

Richard Bricker

Destined Together

If love as they say
was water,
we would be in the same glass;
You and I are destined from above.

If love as they say
was a tune,
we could make a symphony;
We create two souls into one.

And if love as they say
was the sun,
we could light the whole world;
Nothing can dim our light.

If love as they say
was a tree,
we'll share our growth on the same branch;
You and I will never be apart.

If love as they say
was food,
We'd be on the same recipe—
You and I are destined together.

Daniel Vardi

A Light in the Keyhole

When the doors close,
there is nothing I can do.

There is a light in the keyhole
where I can see through.
Where radiance is bliss
and settles like dew.

Where hope is an abundance
and dreams fly free.
There's a longing to get there,
but I need the key!

To go to the place
where worries are no more
is all I want,
please open the door.

Hope lies in green grass,
on the side I hold dear.
Never feeling it is my greatest fear.

I am perfectly happy now with all that I do
because there is a light in the keyhole
and I can see through.

Joey Lee Comstock

Insomnia

To slumber or not, I'm asking
Nothing equals its significance
Days are but respites between troubled nights
Your body weighs heavy, emotions rise
Things undone wear at the mind.

The clock ticks its hours
As our minds click in sequence
A voice is calling from beyond consciousness
Somewhere in the nights obscurity
You go to it like its victim.

Is it a compulsion to respond
To these nightly rituals of unrest
Old thoughts swirl, entangling to haunt you
While your subconscious succumbs
Leaving you no answers or a million.

Tranquilize the body you say
A grateful sigh one might heave
Until anxiety creeps its ugly head in silence
A habit is prelude to yet another
And alas, your mind has the last word.

Connie E. Rainbolt

Never

I never bothered you,
So I never knew.
I'm not sure who,
But someone laughed at you.

You were already on edge,
After that you fell off your ledge.
Those people shall never know
That they hurt you so.

You decided to take your life
With your own kitchen knife.
I never knew you would,
I didn't think you could.

Your own life was taken,
I thought you were happy, I was mistaken.
Never were you sad,
Until they made you mad.

I wish you would have stayed,
A friendship we could've made.
But as I see the moon,
I know I'll see you soon.

Jackie R. DeFrank

The Love Mildred Kuehl Has Shown

I look back on the years of my life
All the things I have been through
The good times, and the bad times
Would not have been the same without you

I often stumbled along the way
And made a mistake or two
You gave a few swats to correct me
But always followed them with "I love you"

The days of my life seemed to fly by
Because you and dad worked so very hard
You gave me a chance for an education
And allowed me to shoot for the stars

I have grown up into a man now
About to have a bride of my own
I only hope that I can show her
The same love that I have always been shown

A mother to me is more than words
She's everything I have done or still do
The way I was raised, the lessons I learned
She's love, she's life, she's home, she's you

Gregory Scott Kuehl

The Long Goodbye

The hardest thing, I think
Is when he looks at me with his soft, blue eyes and doesn't wink
He stares right through me, like there's nothing there to see
My image of a hero has not gone away
His greatness will never sway
He is a warrior in the battle of The Long Goodbye

Once in a while
I see a glimpse of what he was when I was a child
Good-hearted and kind he will always be, this anyone can see
Although I know he can never be the same
All because of life's cruel game
I try not to cry, as I ask God why
Why must he suffer The Long Goodbye

I will love him always, even when he's gone
In the end, he's in a better place
Even though his journey has been long
If this is one of life's difficult tests
I will try to take it for the best
But I still can't help but wonder why
Why The Long Goodbye

Alicia Pearson

Bitter

Feeling tormented and tortured inside
Trying to find a place for my pain to hide
Heart slowly turns to black
This is not what I've asked

Why is it that she tortures me
She shows no respect nor dignity
All I feel is hatred toward me
when all I need is love to set me free

All this hate I've tried to hide
makes me feel more denied
I can't keep letting this happen to me
I need to let my pain be set free

My voices start to speak to me
I love this pain which I feel
all these things within my brain
Oh, no I think I'm going insane

Maybe I should let it go . . .
Hate is all I feel from you
Maybe I should end it all
Just to prove my love to you

Steven Dewayne Mayes

Solitary Moment

One night I kept my eye on this precious woman dreaming
And the most amazing thing—I didn't believe what I was seeing.

From this moment on, time had lost control
For this thing that I was seeing was more precious than gold.

In all my twenty years, nothing quite compared
To the sparkle in her eye that told me she cared.

In a solitary moment, a lifetime would prevail;
That she would stand by me, even through gates of hell.

In all of my being I felt this to be true,
For in that solitary moment I learned, for her, that I would too.

Nothing will replace this solitary sparkle,
For knowledge beyond my years was really why I was marveled.

For I've learned not to cry if time can pull us away,
For something about "true" love has no option to wash away.

Can you let go and not be scared? It greatly reduces worry.
And how a speck of faith will correct those visions that are blurry!

In the blink of an eye, all these things must pass,
But the solitary moments will surely ever last.

David Lloyd

My Daddy

In memory of Eddie James Felder
Dear Daddy, I miss you so
More than anyone will ever know
I always imagined on my wedding day
That it would be you who gives me away
Well, Daddy that day is here
And I find it very hard to believe that you are not here
I'm finding it hard not to cry and not question why
But on this day . . . my wedding day
Is the day I need and miss you the most
Please look down on us from above
And be very confident of our commitment and love
Everyone has helped
To make my wedding day a dream come true
Even though I am without you
I know as grandpa lifts my veil
The soft breeze across my cheek
Is really the feel of you with the kiss that I seek
Just to let you know
No one could ever take
What should have been my daddy's place

Angelique Rochelle Felder

Alone, Completely Alone

I've lived a life of ugliness and blame.
I've known the extremes of heartaches and of pain.
There are scars from the dreams I've let go.
Wrinkles appear from the stress untold.

No one grieves with me over my tragedies,
Yet they all laugh over my catastrophes.
No one cares if I feel alive,
Yet they watch as I slowly die.

Betrayal has been my best friend.
Loneliness has been my guide.
Disappointment has been my major accomplishment.
Confusion has always been on my side.

Emptiness is my companion.
Solitude is my friend.
I am waltzing by myself
In this darkness I live in. . . .

Wandering silently, yet screaming for help;
No one comes to me and I seek no one out.
I go it alone because that's how I came.
Am I tired or am I completely insane?

April Lynn Wininger

My Fishing Spot

I wake up early and grab my pole and line.
I promise myself I'll catch a fish this time.
I walk down to the water, crystal clear.
I'm so glad I can finally come here.

I cast my line into the weeds and wait.
I made sure I brought lots of worms for bait.
Of course, scented lures work real well
Because I think that catching bass is swell.

I reel in twice and let my lure sink.
My line goes taut—I have a fish, I think.
I reel in, but this fish weighs a ton!
He takes my line and fast begins to run.

I give him slack, so as not to break my line.
I figure that this fight will take some time.
I wait until I feel him tire out
And reel him up on shore to end the bout.

I pick him up and give a moan as well—
It's not a bass, it is a pickerel.
I let him go, he swims off out of sight.
I cast again and hope a bass will bite.

Jason Skidgel

Dawning

For the ones who have proven there is love
What could she be fighting
in the beauty that surrounds her,
in this—our tempestuous night?
A hope dipped in shadow;
the night sky bowed to her there.
Attempts, oh how futile, to follow the sun.
It is this fate which we dread;
it is this ending, a closure through time;
somewhat unexpected—a single
light in the distant sky.
He who takes her hand and
wraps his love around her
terrestrial world, envelops her
in comfort.
The denying heart, a force to turn;
in times downtrodden, he brings
the moon;
in burrows deep, the stars do shine.
He lifts her up in thoughts so tender—
once barren mind reigns now fertile.

Suzanne Reed Mooney

Help Me, Lord

Lord, I'm slowly sinking
Your help is needed today
Here I sit without thinking
But your love is with me to stay.

My heart is heavily burdened
Saddened by this world's turmoil
To your path I have surrendered
Your wounds, my comforting oil.

Deep and sincere we're guided by prayer
You hear them ever so preciously
Offering your love for those who care
My thanks wasn't given so very graciously.

My life is now in remission
Shedding my tears wasn't from a hopeless plea
To be like you, my new commission
To others, this witness is confirmed in me.

The cross, my temptations do drown
This allows others to see Jesus in me
As I'm reviewing goals for your crown
Realizing now such pleasures aren't to be.

Elgina Bridgmon

Surround Me

Wash me in your heavenly light.
Let my heart with wings take flight.
Make me a candle, shining bright;
Surround me with your love.

Bring your heavenly light to me,
Open my heart so I can see,
Cause my doubts and fears to flee;
Surround me with your love.

Your heavenly light, your perfect gift,
On wings of angels my soul does lift.
With you here I no longer drift;
Surround me with your love.

Oh, how your heavenly light does shine;
I'm glad my life's no longer mine.
I place myself upon your vine;
Surround me with your love.

Your heavenly light, I'll always praise,
And unto you my hands I raise.
With awe I watch your glorious ways;
Surround me with your love.

Karon Leigh Towns

the lumberjack

timber, i shout, as i chop down weeds
seemingly trees that consume my space when
i need clarity most.
on occasion my alarm brings about
the evacuation of those who dwell
amongst my fickle furnishings.
you should see them run.
someday, i swear, those animals will
stampede over the last vine of support,
and then, where shall i exist?
such savagery in search of blood;
cannot help but find it, leaving a steady drip
as gentle as the morning rain tapping
on my window, when they do.
attempting to gaze out, my vision is again
screened by the metallic sheet
glazed over in rust.
its haggard appearance suggests stories
to tell of the forgotten artifact
that don't all have happy endings
with sunshine and ice cream.

Leo H. Anguiano

You, I'll Always Remember

I will still remember
The first time I talked to you
That would remain in my mind forever
These words are pure and true

I still remember the day,
When I looked deep inside your eyes
As I lie,
I keep seeing your brown eyes

Hey, boy,
It's you I'll always remember
You, I'll always try
To dream of in a land of wonder

Your smiles I will keep
Your love, they are so deep
Your words I will seek
You're the guy I wanted to pick

Even though it's impossible
Our friendship, I hope, will remain stable
'Cause it's you I'll always remember
That's a word for you to know forever.

Nur Ashikin

At Your Best . . . You Are Love

To Aaliyah Dana Haughton (1979–2001) miss ya, R.I.P.
You said, We are mirrors of what we see.
Positive motivating forces around us
Can make us believe? But how can we see?
If we couldn't foresee what happened to you.
The Angels will tell us that
love's true form is pure.
Life's a struggle, just get through it, just endure,
just be assured of a better tomorrow.
But instead of sorrow, just be secure,
But don't just follow, unless spirits make sure.

As heaven accepts you, A thought reveals
itself here, since not just your music, your
presence, the existence of the double A essence,
is now felt in silence, she left here.
Seems not enough to write on your love.
Almost impossible to sing or write this line.
This feeling choking ma heart's mind.
Seems we'll never find anyone like you,
from here below to up above.
Liyah hear, your heart to me
Sung that You are Love

Donald Soon Hyon

Black Speaks to White

I try to abide the courage to hide
what hurts me the most,
what kills me inside.

It kills outside too, it's true, you do!
If you only knew to be black,
and not blue.

Not to be blue for me, do you see that
you are the key to end all poverty?

For it's YOUR heart that's poor,
from outside to core!
(And the white man STILL asks what
my color's for!)

Black shows that we're whole,
we carry a soul that hasn't a liner
of hate or of coal.

We are not broken, I say at last.

It's YOU whose heart wanders
full of colored glass.

Michelle Kathryn Ferch

The Intimidator

You came into our home for every race
The man in black, you know the face
The world's most known driver
Who always came out a hero, a survivor

His ultimate goal—to win Daytona 500
He graced 1st place in Feb. 98
A smile, a trophy, a heart full of pride
His family, friends, and fans cheering by his side

A man who made others gain his respect
Especially on the track when they'd connect
Racing was his heart and soul
To give it all was his desired goal

How ironic for you to leave us this way
At that track, at the end of the day
All of us will remember the lessons you taught
Mostly the drivers and race tracks where you fought

We will all remember the legend, "The Intimidator"
A husband, a father, friend, and racer
Your memory will live on forever
Since you gave us a son to help us remember

Corinne F. Stickles

A Teen's Prayer

Who . . . would have ever known
That on that beautiful clear day
Many lives changed in an instant
As the world began to pray

As everywhere was in total chaos
And the sky turned its darkest gray
Everyone began to work together
And more began to pray

When things began to look their worst
And all some could do was pray
A rainbow appears out of Heaven
To ease our doubts and dismay

Through this time of great loss and devastation
And maybe even on another day
Remember God's rainbows speak to us
For its blessings you need only pray

So as you pray for guidance
To help you through the day
Keep searching for the rainbows
And He will show the way

Kimberly A. Wise

For My Love

I dedicate this poem to the woman I love.
There is this woman who has taken my heart.
I know that moment when she gave me her heart.
it was meant to be you and me.
As far as I know our love will grow.
All I do is to think about you.
Ever since I met you all I know is to love you.
You are beautiful and sweet.
Do you know you have swept me off my feet?
Keep it up please, never change not even for me.
I love you just the way you are.
You are my one and only star.
That lights up the sky.
That shows me there is no reason to be shy.
All I do is to let my heart go,
and let my words go with the flow.
You have given me love and you have given me life.
All I know is that I want you in my life.
I will love you until the day die.
All you are is my one true love.
That has come down from heaven above. . . .

Erney M. Ramirez

Strive

Stand strong, my son, my father said.
Be bold and brave when others flee.
See through the night that which is fear.
See through the pain, then all is clear.

I've seen the nights which never end
When all you want is a dearest friend
To chase from you that wicked sight;
To warm the chill from cold, cold night

While icy hands claw at your feet;
When terror's flag waves your defeat.
Please never from your foes retreat.
You must strive on to challenge meet.

And in your time I lend a hand
And bring to you my loyal band.
When the cries of anger cross the land,
You must strive on and make your stand.

You must survive and brave the night
Through vicious foe and fire fight
To show our foes the coming dawn
And prove to them we will strive on.

James Brandon Galliher

Two Sides

Take away my life and my troubles,
take away my torment; and my pain.
Wishing to be free, not to be here
wishing to be gone or to die.

My frustrating life, the tormenting pain,
my crying inner child that wants to go out and play.
No one to talk to, no one who understands.
I'm all alone in a corner, wondering where I stand.

My screaming heart, my crying mind
my eyes that see, my body that's blind.

The numbness that I feel, the cold seeping in,
the feeling of always being alone or never fitting in.

Wanting to be alone and wanting to cry,
wanting to let loose that scared child
that could be free, or try.

Wishing to be set free, wanting to see the world . . .
letting loose my mind and letting free my soul.

No one to talk to, no one that understands.
making all this trouble by myself, no one but me in my head.

Sarah Anne Ritchie

A Winter Rose

The icy winds blow
And life drags away
Beneath the thick wool of snow
A small rose chills
Its life-red bud smothered by frost

Our lives turn to hibernation
Crawling at the speed of tumbling flakes
Falling from Jack Frost's home in winter clouds
At mortal foot and bladed shoveling plow
Bringing aching back and frosted windshields

Inch by inch, abominable snow dunes climb
Foot by foot, steel cars roll endlessly
Until the piercing shard of renewal thrives
Onto the heaven-white banks of a dying season
Warming the crisp, waiting on newer days

Rivers soon flow from the last pale isles
Leaving way for regrown existence
And a once-gone rose breathes fresh
Razor thorns on crawling stems bloom crimson
And winter is forgotten, letting live spring forever

Robert W. Tokarz

So Sudden Gone

Life is so fragile
And death can be brutal,
Sudden, without warning,
Ugly, as if jealous of love.

Life is so fragile
A cry of suffocation,
A beat in rhythm stopped
In the midst of play.

And death can be brutal
Unreasoning,
Overwhelming goodness,
Undeterred by fear, or love.

Death can be sudden, without warning
A blockage, stifling a cry,
Blackening a tongue, dilating an eye,

And so the sudden cry it came: cradled in my arms
My beloved, lovely kitten died.
And I cried, even now.

So fragile, so sudden gone.
How, I ask, and why?

David Garrison Briggs

Sermon Herman and Amazing Grace

Sermon Herman and Amazing Grace
Were the names of a couple I knew
He'd preach from daylight until setting sun
And she would sing every song that she knew

Through fifty years they lived that way
And raised a family of seven
He would preach and she would sing
And each lived in their own little heaven

His sermons were not about the Bible
So his message never got through
Because Grace was smart and thought things out
And didn't want to be told what to do

His sermons were all about me, I, and mine
And with Grace this didn't seem right
So I guess the lessons we can learn here
Is to preach and sing instead of fight

The days are so short and life passes by
So try not to make it all sorrow
When he preaches just sing and let the bells ring
Because there may not be a tomorrow

Margaret Hardnack

Hope

This poem was written for my high school magazine.
Hope, you lead us and make us very hopeful;
You make nests among all the people.
Hope, you help us to dream a dream
And make people forget all their pains.
Hope, you are the rainbow of our mind;
You are always twinkling, radiating like a light.
Hope, you teach us how to go on
And yet train us not to hold on
When our rights are taken away.
Hope, you are precious but common;
You are radiant and yet sullen.
Hope, you are like a full moon;
You are the commitment of newly married couples.
Hope, you are the index of successful lives;
We cannot see you, but certainly you exist.
Hope, you are the rustle of a vast, green paddy field;
You are the means of living as a parentless child.
Hope, how can I portray you
When I see you emerging in millions of people
And they all want to see the world beautiful?

Russell Chowdhury

Slipping Away (Abbreviated)

I woke up in bed and I reached for your hair.
Discovered I was alone because you weren't there.

You were my love, and together, we shined.
But now I'm alone, and you're no longer mine.
What in the world did I think I was going to find?
I had you right beside me; I must have been blind.

Your eyes and your smile used to greet me each day.
I need your warmth and your kiss. Please show me the way.
Never could I go on without you here to stay.
That someday you'll return, I hope and I pray.

Desire one single thing, and that would be a brand new start.
If you'd give me just one chance, I promise we'll never part,
And the words that are spoken emanate straight from my heart.
I can't let you leave; I'm all torn apart.

I wish every night that my dreams will come true,
And I'll find myself sleeping again next to you.

But what can be done, for your love shines no more,
And without that love, I have a soul that's broken and poor,
And you'll never look back; you'll take your wings and you'll soar.
You'll find another who's better, another who loves you more. . . .

Ronald Joseph Colosi, Jr.

A Day I'll Remember

I sit on September 11 and watch TV,
I could not believe what I did see.
Terrorists in these planes did crash,
Hit the buildings with a bash.

I saw in awe and wanted to cry,
I watched and watched and my eyes weren't dry.
I watched with horror, I watched with fear
I could not stop from shedding a tear.

These crazy guys from another land,
they thought that they were making a stand.
No stand they made, but they will know,
how great our country is we will show.

You pick on us cause you've got nothing to do,
but now I think I'd hate to be you.
You see us come together, you see us unite,
now we see you hide in fright.

Our flags are waving, we are strong,
ever think now that you were wrong?
The planes blew up, our buildings fell,
now you terrorists will live in hell.

Charles Edward Hall

Daddy

Daddy, when I was young you duct-taped my bear's arm together.
Daddy, you put duct tape on my Band-aid to make it stick.
Daddy, when I broke my ankle you duct-taped a trash bag on my cast.
Daddy, as a teenager I need you the most.
Daddy, duct tape won't fix my broken heart.

Krystal A. Deans

Rainbow Rain

What is falling on my head
If feels like tiny beads of lead
I asked my mom what could this be
She looked up and then looked at me
Silly boy, those are just skittles, she said

Matt Keith Dills

Wind

As it brushes against my face,
As cold and warm as it is,
I must go through it.
If I really need to reach my destination,
I must walk through the wind.

Laura Lynne Peppenhorst

To Me

The caresses, the kisses, the laughter, the sun,
And still our love lingers when all that is done.
The hair is now white; the footsteps are slow,
But the love is much deeper before we must go.
We may not escape: old age has us in thrall.
But we've had the greatness and we've had it all:
We've had each other. We've had it all.

George DeMare

Farewell

I touch your eyes that are closed forever.
My fingers smooth out your hair that
Once was tied with ribbons.
I gently kiss your lips for the last time.
You were such a precious gift
Because for a brief moment
God let you be mine.

Patricia Conrad

gold

green shapes in different shades carry up
tall, vertical lines of grays stabbing blue
where curves all in white drift about the source
of shimmering gold, while here far below
this hard surface holds down a deeper place
of rugged stratum overlaying heat
which now and then seeps up to meet what is
so high, its will will not permit defeat

Peter Jameson Havens

Annual Date

Just why do I try to hide from the sad fate
That always comes on the same annual date
When doom and chronicles of despair loom cool,
Even if I have practiced the golden rule,

And I delay what I know must come today
When all freemen and kin must their tribute pay.
Into the box of blue, I must not be lax,
And so I lick the stamp and mail in my tax!

Larry Shine

My Grandpa Is Gone

My Grandpa is gone.
Those who see him in the sky are gone.
Those who saw him in the crash,
All bloody and bruised;
His great head lay down to rest.
Those who see him in the sky are gone.
My grandpa is gone.

Dustin Michael Edwards

L'amour

I met her 5 years ago.
She walked through those flipping doors,
And everybody went, whoa!
From then on changed were my mores.
Captivated by her eyes,
I behaved like a zombie the rest of the day.
It wasn't long until we traded cries.
That's the affectionate way.

Mozart Desrosiers

Ha! Or

You think you know how I feel about you.
You think you know what makes me happy.
You think you know what makes me tic.
You think you know . . . Ha!

I know that you are the only one I Love.
I know that you make me happy.
I know that you make the tic in me special.
I know you know . . . Ha!

Cheryl Ann Webber

Panther

A panther strolling in the night,
Watching its prey as it cowers in fright.
Eyes blazing with a fire held deep within,
Reflecting moonlight as cold as tin.
Running wildly, a crash in the night.
Panther, what makes you lust to fight?
With a squeal of pain, you win the fight
As you tear viciously into the night.

Jess Wyatt

The Very Special Angel That Was Sent from Above

There was a very special angel
That was sent to me from up above.
It was sent to me, so that I would
Have a very special lady in my life that I could love.
I almost thought that I was going to cry,
Until I had a chance to meet this very special angel the other day.
The day that I got to meet her,
All of the loneliness that was inside of me went away.

Brooke Jerome Williams

Victor's Poem

The once pretty sky has faded to black,
The smiling face, now a picture of sadness.
But behind the sadness always hides
The shining face of exuberance,
Waiting to be revealed.

When we are in our darkest moments,
We are like the nighttime sky,
Only temporarily losing sight
Of our shining soul.

Sheri Rosenthal

A Dream or a Nightmare?

I've seen the sunset,
I've seen the sunrise,
I've seen people's lives go by and by.
From the golden streets of Heaven
To the hot, murky Hell,
I've seen lives go by and by.
You can see a lot in a dream or a nightmare.
Me, I've had my share.

Dustin Livermore

Sweet Surrender

As the sun arises and the birds sing their songs,
I surrender to the dawning of a brand new day.
As I tune into the sights and sounds around me,
I surrender to the senses you have given me.
The touch of a child, the innocent laughter,
the warm glow of a smile encompass me.
I embrace life, love, joy, wisdom and peace
around me.
Yes, I surrender to the pulse of life flowing
through my veins.

Kelli Garden

Cry of the Wolf

A stark silhouette against the pale full moon.
A great lonely wolf cries its mournful tune.
Does he cry for his mate, is she gone, is she dead?
Listen to that cry, feel the pain, feel the dread,
And as your spine does tingle and your hair stands on end,
Listen with your heart the message he does send.
For times were not so long ago that wolf and man did share a common
Land of beauty, a place of love and care.
But now we speak with guns, with poison and the snare.
Could it be that mournful howl is but a plaintive prayer?

Mary Tripp

Silence

Silence!
Quiet! You . . .
with all that internal violence
think you not heard?
I hear the noise disguised as poise
it's a different language but the same word
thy countenance is peace
thy back is straight to say the least
so you think I am from out of the blue?
true silence is right within you

Charles Upton

A Horse's Epithet

Come walk with me along this lonely path.
I have but moments left to write my epithet.
My mind grows feeble, my limbs weak and sore.
My eyesight grows dimmer, my ears hear no more.

When once young and strong I used to play here.
I was bold and brave, without any fear.
I would chase the wind and not miss a stride,
Watch over the herd with wisdom and pride.

I was their leader, yes, I was their king.
They looked up to me, respected my being.
But those days are past; it's time to go home,
And the rest of this journey I must take alone.

Don't weep little one, give my neck one more pat;
Let me nuzzle your hand and drink from your hat.
Then let me lie down in the shade of the day
Where, in tranquil thought, I'll just slip away.

Joan "Ellis" Anderson

Poison

By the lumination from the firefly
I once walked a path on mountain high
I came upon a wickedly vivacious thought of a black rain
Falling upside down on a sideways plane
I hurriedly sipped from a glass of falling sunshine
Before long death would certainly be mine
Just how much and just how long
Poison in my blood is my reason to
Be gone

Mike Johnson

Attempt to Rekindle Love

A thunderbolt of hope
Through a sky of stained memories and destroyed dreams
Only to give life to what is now dried tears
No more room for pain, so grant another try
Walking along lonely, barren rivers
Once full of trust, now run dry
One vivid light of hope
Searching for a home, searching for life
Together we travel alone in pursuit of the lost city of dreams

Kobi Michelle Young

Crazy Angel

Heaven came down for a fallen city
Haunted roads shaking this cold gritty
Stopping in the middle of nowhere
That must be it over there
I feel blind behind this wall
It's too tall and I'm scared I might fall
I would, I could, and I never understood
Why angels could fly in and out of dreams

Hell is here looking for a fallen city
Where the streets are covered with the pity
Stopping just to gaze and stare
At how little we all care
I feel wrong along the outside and within
It's my sin wanting to get out again
Look down, look around, see two feet on the ground
Crazy angels fly in and out of my dreams

My vampire eyes are the daydreamers' lies
You can't see in 'cause they're hypnotized
Humpty Dumpty on the wall
Gets to see the Sun never fall

Jason Bryan Reese Jordan

Sadly, You Are Not My Love

When you hear me call your name,
Don't wonder why I'm calling.
When you see me cry in pain,
Don't wonder why I'm crying.
When you smell the scent of the rose
Petals I have pulled from the flower,
Don't wonder why I've pulled.
When you taste the beach air where I do hide,
Don't wonder why I've hidden.
When you feel the anger I do radiate
When I feel as though I'm dying,

Don't wonder why I'm dying.
Don't wonder why these things go on,
For sadly, you are not my love.

You are not my love who answers when I call your name.
You are not my love who's there to ease my crying pain.
You are not my love who has given me my rose flower.
You are not my love who'll sit and hide with me for hours.
You are not my love who understands my dying anger.
You are not my love who'll wonder of me ever longer.

Michaela Katzki

Shadow on the Wall

They pass by
They see you but they don't look
The laugh and cries pierce you
Thrills and chills you once had
Become thoughts you'd rather not have
They will push you away and pull you close
These games they play you don't comprehend
The reflection in the mirror is a person
Who doesn't understand
The image you see brings a tear
Facing reality shows the fear
The shadow on the wall is me passing by

Kristin A. Cisarik

Missing You

Days, months, and years gone by;
I find myself still missing you deeply inside.
The way you left was so unexpected—my heart destroyed.
Why, why, why, I employ?
This unfairness is so cruel,
It hurts so bad I'm still missing you.
I try to take it one day at a time.
Days, months, years—time isn't kind.
Memories of you bring back happiness of past years;
With those thoughts alone I can't hold back the tears.
I should be happy for the time we've spent together
But I'm hurting, I'm selfish; I thought we had forever.
I'm pretty sure the pain will eventually go away.
But I find myself still missing you anyway.

Vera Jackson

The Judas Betrayer Brand

There is little worse than a friendship gone bad.
Trust's betrayer grieves the spirit; renders the heart too sad!
The moment I realized it—suffered ten tears to cry.
How could you, my best friend, became my tormenter's best spy?

You wore a wire as we walked and in your car when we talked.
A word to them you needed not speak.
"Do you relate our conversations to others?" You said, "Oh, no!"
Yet our walks were set up to display an entrapment scenario.

In addition, betrayer, you gained my only other friend.
Your conscience came to pummel you, and toward the end,
You were impelled to call and implore, "please return."
How? Your Judas betrayer brand continues in my heart to burn!

Shelby Jean Peterson

September 11, 2001: A World Changed

I cannot comprehend what I just saw
The inside of Lucifer's gaping jaw?
I see destruction filtered through a lens
This should be from Hollywood's poisoned pens
The pain and fear are far too real to me
Their deaths, their sorrows more than tragedy
I cannot fix this problem in our world
Nor stop my tears as the flag is unfurled
I feel so guilty for getting to live
For all the pleasures that life has to give
Will time eventually dull the pain?
Will I ever feel like myself again?
I want to turn back time, to change our fate
I want our children to know love, not hate
Not fear, not suffering, how can it be?
I hope that God will hear my meager plea
For it cannot be God's one last great hope
That His children will learn how not to cope
How will I live in this world that is new
Yearning for peace and for evil's just due?

Lisa K. Fugit

His Shadow

A doorway stands far too open
In a grand light, empty field,
And if Death should number ten,
Then thy life to thee thou shall yield.
But if that doorway should stand closed,
Then know that your soul is forfeit.
And if your will would be imposed,
Let there be light lest it not be lit,
For deep in your heart there resides a shadow
Though of His presence so few of us know.

Saad Al-Ghawas

Love

Someday you will see
Everything that you mean to me
You will love me as I've loved you
Forever and always we'll always be true
You're the one I want always
So I hope someday you'll realize and stay
We could be so happy we are together
Don't you know it could be like this forever
All you have to do is stay
Until then all I can do is pray

Pamela Nicole Clemens

Like a Flower

Lady cries over the years she hasn't lived
The love she cherished didn't last
Whatever she gave, too little she received
Time passed her by too fast
Her face began to fade away
Her hair became finer and gray
Her tears froze in her salty eyes
Her lips stopped singing lullabies
She had many dreams
Although the years stole her time
She pretended her whole life had been
All she had ever wanted to find
Lady stared at the mirror
Time took her young years away
Weeping to remove her fears
Her salty tears of today
Tomorrow she won't be here
Like a flower, one day her beauty shone
The other day, just disappeared
From the world she had once known

Sandra Berlinski

To All My Beloved Children

I feel your sorrow and your pain.
I, through my son, have shed these tears.
In this time of fear and evil,
Know that I am here to help.
I dispatched my angels to join your forces
With blessed love that conquers hate.
Oh, how I hurt to see the choices my children make,
But I give you all the same chance to choose.
When a choice is made for wrong,
A thousand more are made for right.
Through the days ahead, please call on me.
I can carry you through to the end.
My dear, beloved children, do not fear;
I am here and have your loved ones.
Please, dear children, rest assured,
You are not alone in this fight against evil.
I will guide you on the path to home,
Where I will greet you with loving arms.
My dear, beloved children, come to me for comfort.
I love you. Stay strong.

Eleanor A. Mell

Life and Peace

Though life and peace are regarded together,
Still, far, far away from each other.

The end of life leads to another,
So beautiful and so fantastic.

The end of peace leads to war,
Whose progeny are so drastic.

Life spent by man can make stories;
Well, I would say,
Peace created by man can make histories.

Sanjay P. Kothari

My Love, My Life without You

My life, my love without you
    is nothing.
I go on living,
    only because I have to.
If I had to choose to
    live or Die?
But to live with out your love,
    I would rather die.
I would rather die than to live without you
    or your love for me.

Elizabeth Jane Miller

Eden, Our Eden

For Carol
In a valley, near the top of the mountain,
near the foot of a waterfall—
you, in the sunlight of a sunset by the falls.
Orange light glinting from your hazel eyes.
On a shady bank by the falls in heaven.
Leaning back against the weeping willow trunk
as the dappled sunlight filters down through the leaves,
caressing our upturned faces with its warmth.
We sit in comfortable silence,
listening to the sounds of our Eden.
The soft rumble of the water,
as it falls from the cliffs above.
As we gaze into the flowing current,
our souls would meet in waking dreams.
We would know that life is good.
That there is enough love,
at least for our Eden, and from our Eden,
our love would reach out to the world and embrace it.
In Eden, our Eden.

Jesse Gallagher

Words

Aren't my words enough?
My thoughts, my emotions exposed for everyone to feel
My heart, my dreams soaked through each letter
To write, I close my eyes and capture passion
I meditate, time expands, seconds last
I taste each word for flavor
I remember, I smile just right
I breathe slow, not wanting to miss anything
Allow me to jump into your soul
Will you feel me?
Words are power—close your eyes
Words allow you to see the wind
To feel the warmth of loving someone
To smell the seasons—breathe in autumn
To taste color—leaves like tangerine orange saffron
My words tell my story
Share in my sorrow, rejoice in my triumph
I laugh, I mourn, I am afraid
Hear me, feel me
I write words

Dawn Steward

My Guardian Angel

You made me smile when I was sad
And gave me strength when I was weak
You gave me love when I needed to be loved
And helped me through my private hell
When I was lost you brought me home
When I was alone you stood by my side
And you were there when I cried
Good and bad no matter what
You held my hand tight
To keep me safe through this my journey in life

Luisa Iasanzaniro

Country Life

As I sit here on the computer pondering a poem,
I can't think of anything because I'm stuck at home.
My mind attempts to travel, but it doesn't go too far
because my body can't travel without a working car.
I gaze at the endless acres and all of the trees
blocking the wind from the farms; the very sight bores me.
I wish I lived in town where I could travel on my feet,
but in the country without a car, the purpose is defeat.
So I leave you with this: Be thankful for your car,
because when you live in the middle of nowhere, gravel replaces tar.

Kari Ruth Aanesteed

Rebecca—a Little Girl

A little girl so sweet and true
Came to us out of the blue.
We didn't know she'd be here
A lovable baby ever so dear.
She coos and ahs and waves bye
And never forgets to say hi.
A smile so big she gives to me
A happier person I could not be.
She cuddles and babbles and kisses, too.
Everything to her is ever so new.
She talks with her hands and her loving eyes
Very rarely do we hear her cries.
I'm her Grandma don't you know
And Pap and I really love her so.
She loves her bath, her ducks, her Pap,
Swinging in her Little Tikes and just sitting on his lap.
We're glad God sent her here to stay
To love us and really brighten our day.
Rebecca Marie is her name
And her family is really glad she came.

Barbara Ann Smihal

Cherished Moments

You have been blessed
With a gift from God.
You have been given the honor
To be a parent.
Cherish the moment;
It all goes by too quickly.
Cherish the smiles and the hundreds of kisses.
Relish in the millions of hugs.
Smile when you wipe away those hand prints,
For soon they will be gone.
Savor the times you wrap your arms around them,
And protect them from harm.
You are considered their heroes,
In the future, their friends.
God has given you the gift of being parents.
Take the honor and cherish it.
Be an example.
Be a mentor.
Be his parents.
Love him.

Angela Dee Ellis

Since You Left

Since you left, I miss you so.
I know it's silly; it wasn't long ago.
Time takes forever. God, If you only knew.
Seconds seem like hours, when I'm missing you.
But the days will pass; our hearts will return.
Until this time, our passion inside will burn.
Do not worry; please don't despair.
Our love will remain strong, forever true to you, I swear.

Misty Lane Graham

If We Couldn't Stand the Rain

What beauty is there in a rose without the stubborn thorns?
How can we walk the extra mile without the painful corns?
What would come with the spring without the stinging bee?
How could we love the land without the raging sea?
What would be the honor of truth if for not the lies?
How could our soul be overjoyed without the quiet sighs?
How could we love the daylight hours without the darkest night?
How can we enjoy the laugh, if we never break down and cry?
How can we catch a breeze without the chill of the wind?
How can we experience salvation without the voice of sin?
How could we celebrate the winning if it wasn't for the trying?
How could we appreciate the living if it wasn't for the dying?
How could we ever fall in love without getting a broken heart?
How do we get to the finish line, if we can't get past the start?
What would be the point of joy if there was never any pain?
What good could come from sunshine, if we couldn't stand the rain?

Shelley Wilkins

Ocean Waves

As I stand high on this wall of rocks
I watch the waves come crashing down;
I am reminded of my loneliness
And realize that I could leave without a sound.
My body starts to feel heavy.
I'm being pulled lower and lower;
I can almost taste the salt
As my heart beats slower and slower.
All I can see is darkness.
I try for one final gasp of air.
But my chest collapses, and I am gone;
All this is a result of having no one to care.
But once again I'm standing here,
For alas! It was all a dream!
I realized I can't go through with it
Because, for myself, I need a chance to redeem.

Shawna Geier

How Is It Possible?

I never knew it was possible
to feel so alone in your company,
and yet, I wish for you to be with me.

I never knew it was possible
for a small bed to feel so big and empty
as the two of us lie here together,
and yet, I long to share closeness with you.

I never knew it was possible
to feel so rejected by a man who has pledged
his love to me,
and yet, I yearn to reach out to you.

I never knew it was possible
to feel such humiliation from asking you to
make love to me,
and yet, I desire your touch.

I never knew it was possible
to feel so dead inside,
and yet, I am still alive.

Lin LaRusse

How I Remember Mom

I do not remember her best for pies,
Nor her doughnuts, but for a sauce—not cooked,
A sauce of life that sparkled childish eyes
And frosted any picture while I looked.
She knew the recipe for a youthful dream,
Because her own was ever close at hand.
A cup of dew warmed by the sun's bright gleam
Could carry her into enchanted land.

She saw a bluebird waiting in a tree,
A hopeful chipmunk begging by a rock.
So she made a lyric to the bluebird's glee
And fed the chipmunk poems from her stock.
I do not remember her best for pies,
But for a sauce that sparkled childish eyes.

Donovan Marshall

Challenges

Life is filled with challenges.
I wake up to certain tasks that
I'll follow every day.

I must love; I must hate.
I must learn; I must obey.

I must believe; I must try.
I'll never give up; I must succeed.

It'll be in my way; I have to pass it.
I'll be mocked but should not respond.

For every challenge, an answer will appear.
But for love will you come near?

Trevor Murray

Dead of Winter

You dropped your winter in my splintered heart;
A leafless thought reaches out to my soul,
This loving, awful torment, sickly art,
No greens, or golds, all gray, no longer whole.
There were reasons explaining your charm;
A blinded lover running away, scared,
You turned my warmth into a colder harm,
And left me pictured times of places shared.
Our meeting the other we thought was fate;
The door I fastened you walked in through.
The lasting memories can desecrate,
Most treasured thoughts I lost before I knew.
If in these trying times you always find
Ways to keep on, we will create a bind.

Arielle Dawn Clary

Tomorrow's Rain

Night has fallen, dark green trees,
Into the meadow, whispering breeze.
Walk to the sound of the rain in the air;
It will lead you to nothing, just silent despair. . . .

Bristle upon bristle,
Pine upon pine,
Crackling of footsteps,
Crunch of a vine.

This is the forest that gathers the rain,
Not just of the people, but all of the pain.

We run, we jump,
We laugh, we fall.
This dark forest playground watches it all.
It collects and it gathers
All of yesterday's pain,
And transforms that sadness
To tomorrow's rain.

Bryon C. Myers

Love Is Fragile

Love can be fragile if not handled with care
A cruel word or gesture, a heart might tear
Sometimes without thinking we cause so much pain
The hurt we caused with nothing to gain
To say I am sorry are words merely spoken
To prove that you are, you need more than a token
I have tried to show that my love is real
But now only rejection is what I feel
If I could only take back the wrong I have done
And we could start anew, gazing at the setting sun
For it is one of the things that we most liked to do
Together in love, forever and true
People make mistakes and they say to forgive is divine
Forgive me my darling and please be mine

Bobbi MacMillan-Walker

Indelible

As you got behind the wheel that night;
You knew better—that it just wasn't right.
You told yourself you'll drive with care;
What happened next, it just wasn't fair.
You knew you'd get home safe, you had a feeling;
And because of your ignorance, I am now dealing.
You managed to escape with only a scratch;
But I guess you never really were attached.
To a stranger, a driver, who you never really knew;
If only you had gotten a hint or a clue.
I want you to know you can't bring her back;
I wish you could but it's the truth of a fact.
What you're about to go through has only begun;
Your actions of drinking and driving, can never be undone.

Melissa Adele Ramsay

Waterfall

Running water, as your color gleams so pure, so clear,
Has washed away all my thoughts, distilled all my fears!

Running water with your strength so powerful, your touch so gentle,
Welcomes and refreshes all to no one ever to be judgmental!

Running water with your sound so effortless, so relaxing,
Flows through me like my love for her, so true, so everlasting!

Running water with your path already chosen, never to stray,
Makes this epic of life to understand, never to tempt this Fate!

Running water with your taste so clean, so thought uplifting,
Quenches my thirst with me to whom no one else ever to be tempting!

Running water, as I fall into your depth never to be done,
As I jump into you, you into me, then we forever become ONE!

Arthur V. Casias

My Cats

Slinking silkily over my floors
On silent, smooth and slippery paws
Sitting patiently by my bed
With neat paws so prettily placed
Gently patting my sleeping face

Lazily stretching and scratching your nose
Stealthily tracking my unaware toes
Madly racing on scattering feet
Sleepily snoozing within the sun's heat

Stalking and scolding at bold, cheeky birds
Smiling and chirruping, my love's full of purrs
Tell me of love and devotion as arts
My soul kept alive with your loving hearts

When others around break my heart with their hate
When all other comforts have left my estate
Then I well know your love will be mine
Never to part 'til the end of time

Maureen E. Yates

Love

I am loved by God; I feel love when he's by my side.
Love makes me happy; I'm glad someone loves me.
Love is good feeling, like the song of my heart.
Love is so caring; I love and am loved, especially
from God above.

     Ethel Morris

Be Thankful

Be thankful for the things you have
Whether they are small or few
For somewhere there is someone else
Less fortunate than you.

If you have eyes to see your way,
If you have hands to work and play,

If you have ears that you may hear,
If you have a mind that is sound and clear,

If you have feet that you may walk,
If you have a voice so you can talk,

If you have a bed in which to lay,
If you have food to eat each day,

Then be thankful every day
For things you have and do.
Always remember there is someone else
Who has much less than you.

     Mary Alice Seiter

Dreams

They remain a part of your soul forever.
Shattered into a million pieces.
I remember how foolish I must have been
To think that they would come true.
They hold nothing for me now
Except to remind me of my blind faith
In life and all its wonders.
Sometimes I wonder if, perhaps,
It would have been different.
If it could have worked out the way I wanted it to.
But—no!
I am who I am.
It wouldn't have mattered anyhow.
They would have still been out of my reach.
It wouldn't have made a difference.
'Twas Fate that stepped in and added
A couple more to the pile of broken dreams.

     Marisa Sonali Wikramanayake

Our Special Place

In memory of Andrew O'Neal Powell, God's newest little angel
Sometimes, when I'm feeling so blue
I can catch a glimpse of you
It brings a smile to my face
To know you're in our special place
There I can hold you
And tell you everything
There I can rock you
And together we can sing
There, together we can talk
And through green fields, we can walk
There, I can watch you as you grow
In our special place where no one else can go
So when it gets quiet
And I need to see your face
I just slip off to our special place
There, I'm never ever alone
There in my mind, I can bring you home

     Bobbie Powell

So Mote It Be

'Tis a far cry from where
One once was
As of late, my quickening about a calling
Ill adhered
Beckons me towards a destiny
shadowed no longer

     Francis Sanz

The Vaccine

There is a treatment which cures all.
This treatment is available at all times if used properly.
It has been around from the beginning of our existence.
At times it has been forgotten.
But it is still more powerful than any medication.
This treatment is the most comforting of all.
It needs no needles.
It is not in a capsule or liquid form.
It is completely natural in its make.
It spawns from our hearts and soars from our souls.
I speak of the most cherished gift of humanity.
I speak of the gift of love.
It heals all who accept it.
Raising spirits and warming the souls of all its recipients.
I have been blessed to have received this precious gift.
I believe one should pass the cure on to all acquaintances.
I ask of you don't let the vaccine be forgotten again.
Keep humanity immune to hatred.

     David Michael Sprouse

Saved by Grace

There was a time I boldly spoke my peace.
But now I barely could show my face
Were it not for God's unfailing grace.
Ashamed am I of my sin-filled life
Full of struggles and filled with strife.
Wasted years full of pride
Many were the tears my loved ones cried.
Caring not the shame I caused
God heard their petitions and felt their pain
Dried their tears once believed were shed in vein.
He filled them with His abundant grace
And peace to calm the fears
That plagued them those many years.
It was at the cross of Jesus where first we met
And it was there He washed away my scarlet past
Releasing me from bondage long at last.
His forgiveness cleansed me whiter than snow
And by His pardon—I am now a sinner saved by His grace!

     Valeria M. Heikes

You

Since you are the one I can always talk to,
Can you tell me why I can get so blue?
You know my boy just don't treat me right,
and when he makes me cry,
you're the one who holds me tight.

I'm going to tell you, it's really going to
be hard for me,
but I have to tell him I don't love him,
like I used to be.

You're the first to realize I'm not all that bad.
Now I have something I never had.
The littlest things adore me,
even holding hands.
I hope you are the one
who truly understands.

So I hope your love will be happy and true.
It kinda hurts, 'cause I love you.

     Chrissy Warmbrodt

Sunrise-Set

The Sunrise falls over the dips and weavings of nature's past.
It coats our world with its undying love.
It works its magic day and night.
It is the calling card of every single bird of Heaven and Earth.
To thee, the Sunrise . . . one day, you will set, but you, you,
Will always go on forever.

Jenna M. Coakley

Angel

While I'm sitting, waiting here
Trying not to cry a tear
Hoping, watching, praying long
Trying to dream that nothing's wrong
Wishing high and staying low
Wondering when we're gonna know
Looking up into the sky
Wanting an angel to by us fly
And pour her luck upon us now
To keep her safe, only she'll know how
If only we could feel her pain
And how she's hurting and going insane
We'd know how to help and keep her cool
And not just throw this pity pool
All we can do is sit and pray
And patiently await the day
When she will return and be herself
'Cause that is truly the best kind of wealth

Lindsay Kaye Freeburnn

Lightning

It forks devastatingly through the storm,
Some if it causing mass destruction,
some barely reaching the ground.
The unharnessed power untouchable,
uncontrollable, unpredictable.
We watch, unabashed, awe over-taking us,
knowing not whether to seek cover,
thus losing its unimaginable hypnotic power,
or brave it, knowing it's some cataclysm
of life. . . .
As we are born, that power is inherent,
sleeping in us all.
And so we decide, decide wether to take
the path, leading to fireworks others dream
of . . . or fork off . . . to a quieter place,
still a part of the cosmic thunder,
yet coming up lame, quieter, more content
with what we are and what we know we could be.

Dean Thomas Andrews

if your love could only be mine

all worldly dreams i would resign;
she ever longs for hidden lore;
if your love could only be mine.

if but two eyes of green divine
could meet my glance forevermore,
all worldly dreams i would resign.

our gems would be the dew drop's shine;
our music floats on larks that soar.
if your love could only be mine.

the clouds would show a silver line
and a rainbow's tint would show them over;
if your could only be mine.

where is she now? she gives no sign.
that loyal heart, true to the core;
all worldly dreams i could resign
if your love could only be mine.

Aaron Anthony Gulbrnason

remembering

the dead man's whisper rests on my cold lips
the dead man's arms reach for my naked back
the dead man's shape falls 'cross my icy bed
the dead man's laughter mocks my empty house
the dead man's finger lured the steel trigger
the dead man's vision murdered my life's dream

Bonnie Jean Kurle

A Mother's Love

The feelings I have are so very new,
and that's because I now have you.
The first time I looked into that little face
I knew I entered such a magical place,
a place that only mothers can go,
a special love that only a mother could know.
The first time I looked into your eyes,
I softly and gently began to cry.
The first time I held your hand,
I knew my love could only grow and expand.
I watch you grow more every day,
and I realize you're so special in so many ways.
I never knew I could love this way,
and it just keeps growing every day.
I know you were sent from Heaven above
for me to protect and always love.
I never knew something so hard could feel so good,
and I would do it all again, I just know I would.

Carron Lynn Berger

East African Politics

Could say the difference is an illusion.
All the presidents will do anything to stay in power.
It is said the people have the power,
but it is also a fact that it is the money with the power.
Voters cast their votes with the influence of their stomachs,
thus the eminent leader after elections
views his victories as a right.
Hence dictatorship is legal,
for the people then pay back in kind.
And funny enough the bellies suffer, too,
evident by the usual hunger,
not that it surprises anyone else
apart from the international community,
which does not follow the events unfolding.
Thus lack of development in the region,
for one cannot treat an illness unknown to him or her.
And in the end, "the power has the people,"
not the people with the power.

Musubire Syrus

You Go So Far Away from Me

You did go so far away
and I could not say
that I did want you to stay.
But years later,
I for sure did know
that I forever was going
to be missing you!
So in my dreams I did see
that we one day
would be together again.
And then, my dear,
I would tell you to stay!

And today that dream is the truth
and we are together again!
So, forever stay!
I told you this time
that I did want you to stay!
So that dream belongs forever to you and me!

Liliane Murtsell Nilsson

If I Lost You

If I lost you I would die
A thousand times I would cry
I would feel so very sad
Because I would have lost what I once had
Because you are such a friend
I hope our friendship will never end

Jessica Lee Woodruff

If the World Was Blind

If the world was blind,
maybe then we'd see
the true side of beauty
deep within you and me.
No one could judge us
by our outer looks,
like the fancy covers
on expensive books.
We'd see with our hearts,
and not just our eyes,
and what we discover might be a surprise.
There would be no need to try to impress,
with the way we look,
or the way that we dress.
The only thing that would matter
is the way we would feel,
not phony or cheap,
but truthful and real.

Jesse M. Gantt

More than Friends

To Josh, for whom this poem was written
We have been best friends for five years,
Shared through the laughter and the tears,
Comforted each others deepest fears,
And held on to secrets no one ever hears.
Then one day you went away,
I begged and begged for you to stay,
I counted down each and every day,
Wishing you were here in the worst way.

I felt something I hadn't felt before.
We were just friends, but could there be more?
What had I hidden these feelings for?
I don't want to be just friends anymore.

And that's when I knew,
It had to be you.
This love is true,
Though secretly it grew.

Paula Anne White

Birth

Struggle, pressure, trying to break free,
energy burned, too blind to see.
Muscles contracting, forcing the day,
in such a hurry this thing to delay.
Warm and dark, submerged you have been,
used to the comforts offered within.
You know not what forces are shoving you away,
darkness becomes light, you enter the day.
Hands pull and grab and bruise your soft skin,
chill takes over, are you going to win?
Turned gently over, cloth wipes your brow,
a slap, a pain, you begin to howl.
Exhausted, tired, confused at this fray,
instruments suck and scrape your old world away.
You're wrapped in soft remnants and laid down to rest.
You hear a heart beating, you're at your Mother's breast.
People are smiling, laughing with mirth;
this is the thing that the world calls birth!

Ted Gerald Finchum

This Bird

A wisp of wind goes unseen beneath the bird's down wings.
It carries far across the land the song this small bird sings.
It sometimes sings of sorrow, but he never does complain.
It always sings of the joy in his heart that nothing can contain.
I cannot tell of what he says when he is atop the tree,
But this I know of what he sings: it's for my Father's glory.

Abigail Louise Bolay

special place

as i sail out to sea
i feel no pain, no grief, no misery
i feel not a thing as the wind blows through my hair
my mind is clear, i have not a single care
towards the horizon i long and gaze
to be part of the mystery, i wonder and praise
as the sun sets into the quiet sea
not the smallest thing shall disturb me
as i am lost in the slumber of purity
the place where there is no boundary
i am washed up by a gentle wave
and i have found that place that i have craved
that one place that lights up my soul
that one place that makes me feel so whole
that one place that makes me shimmer and glow
this is the place where i will learn and grow
this is the place where white clouds are a sign of purity
this is the place where God shall judge me

Eligia Angelina Guizar

Love

What is love I ask you, what makes it so?
The word is often tossed about
Can it really apply to what we know?

Does it mean with two that sex is shared
This is common and widespread
Or do these people bonded so, ever really care?

Time spent together, does that apply?
All manner of things to do
Sharing all and doing all, as day and night slip by

The exploration of each soul, the person lay exposed
Seeking, learning, sharing life
Is this what poets and romantics propose?

I suggest that these and more
Fulfills the needed bill
And I suggest that sacrifice
Is what love is want to fill

Randolph Joe Wolf

My First Love

My first love had said goodbye
And all I could do was sit and cry
Think of the memories and feelings we shared
It would have worked if only you had cared
People got between us and that is true
The lies we told, they were there, too
We don't trust and I see why
Could've been built with you and I
We could have been happy over time
To forgive and forget is no crime
Now it's too late, our time is through
I will still be here, no matter what you do
All I write is true in my heart
The day you left tore me apart
What it is I want you to know
You'll be in my heart, I will never let go
I will love you till the day I die
I will always think of you and I

Melissa A. Buel

Thinking of You

I think of you each morning,
I think of you each night.
Just thinking of you makes every dull day seem bright.
I think of you when we are together,
I think of you when we are apart.
You're always in my thoughts and forever in my heart

Diane Harbottle

They Said, He Said . . .

They said:
We didn't understand why he always acted that way.
We didn't understand why he'd always look away.
We didn't understand why he did the things he did.
We didn't understand why he never bothered with his kid.
We didn't understand why he seemed to hate his life.
We didn't understand why he always beat his wife.
We didn't understand why he chose the road he chose.
We didn't understand why he'd always overdose.
He said:
They didn't understand that I had a rough life.
They didn't understand that I really loved my wife.
They didn't understand that I felt like I was caged.
They didn't understand that I wished my life would change.
They didn't understand that I cried every night.
They didn't understand that I never wanted to fight.
They didn't understand that I never meant to hurt you.
They didn't understand and now he's gone and says, "I love you!"

Eilene Padilla

Untitled

Hurry and slowly worry
pen in my hand and a fist of fury
rare like black judges
hung juries
out of my jurisdiction
flurry and scurry with a pencil and paper
no stencil and tracer
no utensil is greater
full of it like a piñata
possess my spirit in them and a catastrophic case of stigmata
stigma enigma
insignia
anastrophe catastrophe
as bad as gossip
birds flock to me so I need a stick to bat you off with
mad and gothic
you are guile
our style shines like argyle

Winston Lawrence Greene

Forever My Angel

Such a short life gone in an hour.
It all spilled over like a leaning tower.
A life taken to go above,
Oh, how much we all miss and love.
To bring you back now is impossible.
You left us in that cold hospital.
It wasn't anyones fault.
God needed someone and took your spot.
You're not here physically but mentally you are.
Because our love and thoughts keep you close, not far.
You will stay in the sky of heaven to look down,
On all of us in this little town.
Angel this life, I do need help through.
I know you'll be here, because my angel is true.
Now my dear angel, watch over me.
Make sure I'm safe as you rest peacefully.
Forever my angel you will stay,
I shall pray for you day by day.

Amber Lee Mylet

Eyewash II

Oh, but the letter I,
The Devil's notion we must die,
Dreadful tears envelope a cry,
And I wonder at a fatal goodbye,
While racial tears form under the sky,
Colorless drops drip from under the eye.

William Royals

Grandmother's Smiles

The inner voice of a grandmother
Sitting so quiet and still, Smiles
Memories of childhood not forgotten
Though, years have passed
She struggles on.
Her family and friends are gone
Yet, she smiles,
Grandchildren, oh, what a joy
To watch and listen, their laughter she enjoys.
With open ears,
Your problems never too big, never too small.
She gives warm, loving and comforting advice.
Wrapped in hugs and kisses.
Her age, her hair so white
Her skin so soft, like petals of orchids
Her favorite floral dress and apron so worn.
Her eye sight almost gone.
Yet, she smiles

Sue Moore

DayStar

I look expectantly for this day to arise.
I look upon the dawn.
Colors are streaking towards a rainbow,
As distant thunder rolls.
Soft gentle rains fall.
Arise, oh, DayStar, in my heart.
Spread your awesome love around me.
Come unto me; impregnate me with your
Pure golden love.
Spread it through me, oh, my DayStar!
Here I am!
Oh, DayStar, arise in me your child.
Love through me; love through me!
I look upon your face, oh, DayStar!
You are so pure, so lovely, so manly, so strong!
Oh, DayStar, I love you!
Come dance with me upon the spreading dawn.
Celebrate our love, oh, DayStar!

Linda Marciele Throckmorton

How Do You Leave It All Behind?

How do you say goodbye
How do you leave it all behind
When love was so precious and new
When you lived for me and I lived for you
How do you sleep at night
How do you keep your pillow dry
When love burns to your soul
When pain and hurt attempts to control
How do you keep from crying
How do you keep your soul from dying
When love was all we had
When what was good turned bad
How do you stay stern and cold
How do you just grow old
When I sit and suffocate
When my longing doesn't wait
Why do you make me cry
And how can you leave it all behind

Ebony Vashti McClain-Owens

Inspired Vision

I have come to your tunnel in the earth
to find the universal secrets in my heart;
to decipher myself and branch out into a redwood tree.
I follow the blue bird. . . .
and find that gravity does not exist in the reality of naked truth.
I float away and find I am not alone.

Julie Soderberg

#22

Devastatingly boring seconds tick the time away
All the while I sit in my room
and with words I play
Without question, my mind is drifting
to another place
Someplace where all my world comes together
and I see your face
Looking at me, with resentment and pityless glory
Now I can see right through all the lies
I now know your true story
All the times I looked at you
and saw the pain inside
It was nothing but your wicked plan
and when I found out I could have died
from foolishness and stupidity
I just cannot believe
The balance of love and hate is tipped
so I can just barely grieve

Lisa Formoe

A Wonder to Us All

As I look at the night sky
What do I see?
God's great creation
Put there for me.

I see those millions and billions of stars
And look at Jupiter, Venus, and Mars.

Oh, why did God put
Those vast orbs in their place?
He did it so we could see
His beautiful face.

For God is a spirit and not a mere man,
But we can see Him in the works of His hands.

The vastness of the universe
Makes me feel small,
But He put it there to be
A wonder to us all.

Gene A. McCumber

The Rocks

The water rolls gently in waves
Traveling far in several days.
Just like two lovers, hand in hand,
The saltwater acts like woman and man.
Wave after wave rolls over each other;
But as the waves near the land,
As the water slides across the sand,
Upon the cruel, rough surface it doth break.
Love is what the land wants to take.
Huge, coarse rocks pierce the two apart,
The mind, the soul, yes, even the heart.
The waves, they curse, they scream with rage,
Hatred flowing across this page.
The sounds can be heard from far away,
And I must listen every day
To understand my lover's bliss.
The rocks are hurdles we must miss.
The rocks are hurdles we must miss.

Jennifer Rawls

Untitled

She was a radiant sight to see
her dark hair complimenting lightly tanned skin
The way she looked at me with those lovely eyes and pouting lips
And the shadows formed around us
as we walked together in the cool air
on that wonderful summer night

Robert Duffing

The Fallen Soldier

It drove him mad, like a splinter in his brain.
What was his duty? He couldn't think.
The pain was too great; fear clouded his thoughts.
He had fallen behind enemy lines, left to die.
The bullet pierced through his chest.
The shame was working its way through his body.
He had not fallen a hero. He was shot in the confusion of battle.
His duty was simple. Not to destroy the enemy,
Or rescue prisoners, but simply to return home.
Uncertain of what he was fighting for,
he broke his promise to his wife and son,
His brother and his mother and father.
Now he would die for nothing.
The faces of people he loved were fading.
There was no light like he'd expected. Instead, pitch black.
War was not hell to him. War was the creator of heroes.
But war left him unsatisfied. Now, it was too late.
He did not want to be a hero. He just wanted to be home.

Josh Akira Benner

Find Hope

I search for hope high and low
in the valleys and the mountaintops,
in the rivers and the air.
Where can I find hope when life is fill with despair?
As the dark lurks behind me and fear is at the door,
who holds the key to hope, and where do I go?
Do I seek hope from friends and family
or a stranger who smiled and said hello,
or find hope in the one
who rules the heavens and the Earth below?
When I get down on my knees and pray
and remember his promises,
I know that I am not alone.
He is love; he gave himself so freely,
without keeping an account for debt I may owe,
and only asks one simple thing—
believe that he love me, too.
That He, himself, holds the key to hope.

Janet E. Elizee

Me?

I am a hopeless dreamer who wants only to succeed.
I wonder what happens when you die.
I hear people calling from every side.
I see a way out, if I have the courage.
I want to get away from here.
I am a hopeless dreamer who wants only to succeed.
I pretend to be predictable.
I feel the pressure to be "normal."
I touch the stars as they flash by.
I worry that people see what I am.
I cry when I think of all the things I can't control.
I am a hopeless dreamer who wants only to succeed.
I understand that everyplace is the same.
I say that you can achieve anything, if you want.
I dream that I will be very successful.
I try to be what people want me to be.
I hope that I don't stretch too far.
I am a hopeless dreamer who wants only to succeed.

Jenifer Parsons

My Father

Time is passing,
But love is everlasting.
As we move on with our lives,
It was your strength and love we realize,
That kept us together in this confusing world.
And for that, we thank you, Lord!

Pamela A. Carter

Reflections

Ripples distort a reflection.
I struggle to see the lines, to see the form.
A strange familiarity brings a smile to my face
yet, the curving lips betray a sadness.
A sadness moving below the surface where the water kisses the air.
A sadness born of fear.
And fear, with her insecurity,
has sheltered the sadness near the muddy depths
away from the kiss, away from the light.
But time, with his ever-present persistence,
has urged the sun to dip its fingers into the depths
and touch the face of sadness.
Drawn to the light, attracted by the kiss,
the melancholy child struggles to the surface,
leaving fear behind,
making waves with courage
until a peace calms the waters.
And then I see me staring back at me.

Shari F. Bitsis

The Ups, the Downs

Sometimes I feel like I am on top of the world
Just so beautiful, content, and, oh, so thrilled
Other times I feel like the scum of the Earth
Wondering why my parents ever gave birth
To such a complicated and confused soul
I always had dreams, but never set any goals
One day I am just so happy and singing
The next day I am as mad and evil as a demon
On the good days, there's no stopping my greatest desires
On the bad days, I wouldn't care if the world were on fire
My state of mind is like a bomb waiting to explode
More like a volcano in its eruption mode
I have talked to family, friends, and teachers
I have even consulted with therapist and preachers
What shall I pray for? . . . A new brain
To correct the chemical imbalances that cause so much pain
In my life as well as the people I care about
I am manic-depressive without a doubt

Michele Thomas-Carter

Reflection

Who is the figure within the glass, face so familiar, yet unknown?
Two different worlds, set apart by dimension,
share every aspect the other has to offer.
How is it my tears of mourning can be seen but not felt?
Unwanted feelings try to free themselves, growing all the weary
in their bonds of imprisonment.
What becomes of this image as time removes it from sight?
The thoughts of such ordeals prove clarity can be found
in the most oblique of all situations.
Where does one turn to escape the burdens from which he runs?
Only in times of bravery will a tragedy disappear into the midst.
When will the sensations that shatter souls heal its wound?
This person, as close as it appears, can never be reached or helped.
Who determines how long the misery should last?
The time given for pain outweighs the cries which disagree.
With all in mind, I believe I know the answer to my present status.
It is I who am peering from behind the glass with hope to live
in the land that would be my salvation.

Adrian Rodriguez

Time Is . . .

Time is somewhat patient and then again not?
Because time goes forth and not back!
Time smiles when I succeed and laughs when I fail.
But time is still there pushing and watching me
As I fall and rise with all his grace,
By the second, minute, and hour of each day.

Emily Rosa

An Outing with Daddy

It seems as if the blackness grows with every day;
by and by I wish for a light.
I roam through this tunnel, blind as the bats.
I trip and fall, but manage to get up to proceed;
but only then do I realize:
This tunnel is my life, and it is black as night.
My fear begins to grow; something is amiss.
I run, and again I fall; I run, I fall.
I realize now that I am not alone.
I reach out to touch the person who walks with me
only to find that my hand is slapped away.
I know now that my companion is my father.
I turn to run, and again I fall;
I try to stand, and again I fall.
I am being pushed down by my "father."
"What have I done? Why do you push me down?"
He does not answer.
My father holds me down; I cannot get up—ever.

Nicholas Ravotti

States of America

America, America, you have many states.
How many are there?
There are so many.
Can you count?
America is growing, people are knowing.
We have people from Africa.
We have people from China.
Really, it does not matter.
We are all one family!
Our presidents were proud of this land
Because it is the land of the free!
We have no slaves. I am happy about that.
We are the land of the free.
No one person can take that away.
Indiana has corn.
Texas has cattle.
Each state has their own special thing.
America.

Pamela Megan Williams

The Black Sand Beach

Welcome to a place so real in my mind
I wish to make it ours—yours and mine
Welcome, my love, to my black sand beach
Where the waters are clear and skies are blue
Where the dolphins play and dance for you
Where the wind blows air that is so sweet
And the sunrise itself is considered a treat
Enjoy the warmth of the sun, as it rises above
Hear the beauty in the voice of never before seen
For my innermost heart wishes to talk
A rose petal path lies at your feet
A smile on your face, as our eyes meet
Hot spring baths of water so clean
Submerge yourself in the hot spring bath
Before you continue on the rose petal path
Hear the waves, as they kiss the black sands
A beautiful day has come to a close
Now, we must journey down the rose petal road. . . .

Rickey W. Potter

Lovesick Fool

I think I like you . . .
Wait, no, I know I do.
I can't bring myself to tell you,
But I wanna know if you feel the same way I do.
I wish I wasn't such a coward, and such a shy fool, too . . .
But I wanted to say it and tell you how much . . . I Love You!

Miranda Elizabeth Ruehlmann

The Bride

Here she comes floating down the isle,
So nervous she's afraid to smile.
Dad's legs are shaking,
Mom's knees are knocking.
Each seeing her life pass before them,
Wondering where and when time passed them.
Hoping all her dreams come true,
Praying he won't make her blue.
Family and friends come from far and wide,
To get a look at the lovely bride.
He waits in front for everyone to see,
Seems like hours, here comes his bride to be.
Saying their vows, voices cracking,
What was said when practicing.
Kissing the bride,
Hearts swell with pride.
To have and to hold,
From very young to very old.

Edna May Coyle

A Visit with My Thoughts

Sitting at the dining table as
I glanced out the window;
There I saw birds of
many kinds, a grey squirrel,
and blowing in the wind, a red bow.
This January day is very beautiful with snow.
All my little friends on the
ground are aglow.
My bird friends flying here and there,
are so beautiful in color;
I can do nothing, but stare.
What or whom could have made such beauty?
Each, has his own thoughts;
but, I think it was someone whom thought
it was his duty.
No one knows for sure,
but we all have our own thoughts
Not of man, nor animal, but of spirit.

Kasena Lee Sutherland

Will You

Come to me
when it's cold outside
and stars are devoid of their bright,
'cause I need your warm comfy hug
to hold me—
just to keep me living.
Shout to me
when I hide beneath silence and despair
and can't bear this icy loneliness,
'cause I need your strength
to aim my dreams—
just to keep me living.
Believe in me
when I sound insane;
eloping from this raging world,
'cause you give me the air that I breathe;
your heart is mine, yours is my blood—
that's what keeps us living.

Patricia Matthioli Luis

The Fish Hook's Final Catch

A selfish person reminds me so much of a fish hook
Always trying to hook you for what they can hook
You for and get out of you
But being like a fish hook
They finally get hooked themselves
Their final catch

Theresa Kathleen Meagher

The Child

I am a child who once had said,
"There is no one that loves me now."
I am sad and also lonely,
And still, I am left alone.
Oh, Lord, where are you now,
You have left me since I was small.
Still, now my life is incomplete.

Then on a great day, age seventeen,
My life suddenly changed.
I was standing inside a church
Accepting God in my life.
Now, listen here, son, I was always there.
It was you who wouldn't call me.
I was standing outside your door,
Please, let me inside.

Do come in, Lord, you know my needs,
Ask and you shall receive.

Jorge Candido Garcia

A Tribute to Our Veterans

As we approach this Memorial Day,
We need to pause and to reflect on the day.
To remember those brave men who left all
To answer their country's call.
To serve their country, many giving all.
To fight for freedom for one and all.
To keep their country and loved ones safe,
And to keep Old Glory flying high with pride.
He was someone's sweetheart, some mother's son,
some child's father, someone's brother,
and everyone's friend.
If it wasn't for his patriotism and sacrifice,
We would not be living in a land where freedom rings.
We owe our Veterans so much,
A debt we can never repay.
So if you see a Veteran on this very day,
Just say, thank you and God bless you,
As you hurry on your way.

Lavon P. Nunamaker

Missing You

You gave me light
You gave me life
You gave me love
You are my insight
Through all the bad and all the good
You loved me, you understood
I want to thank you for all the love
For you are an angel, an angel from above
Now all alone and feeling blue
Reflecting on memories and missing you
I can't pay you back for what you have done
But I want you to know of the life I've begun
I want you to know how bad I have felt
And the advice you have spoken and how much it has helped
My apologies for what I have put you through
I thank you and love you
But for now, I am just
Missing you

Justin Wade Heaton

Love

You bring me joy whenever I am sad
My heart goes wild when you touch my hands
I'll love you forever and ever more
Just as long as you show me the door
The door to your heart to let love in
So I can love you till the very end
Corinne Marie Hale

Rocks with Writings

Rocks with writings as far as I could see,
Nothing but rocks with writings.
Tripped over something the other day,
But what it was I can't really say.
Was in this place; so dark and deep.
Full of people; taking their final sleep.
Rocks with writings, as far as I could see.
Nothing but rocks with writings, Haunting me.
I remember the flowers, yes the beautiful flowers.
To count them all, would take hours and hours.
For the flowers were alive, seemed strange to me.
For the flowers were alive, seemed deranged to me.
For the flowers can still grow and bask in the sun.
But for the forever sleepers, the growing is done.
Rocks with writings as far as I could see,
Nothing but rocks with writings, Taunting me.
Tripped over something the other day,
But what it was I can't really say.

John D. Friest

To Wonder

Ever notice a man walking down the street
And wonder where he's going?
Gone or went?
Maybe to the grocery store
To get some honey for his wife.
Or to the bank
To get some money because he ran out.
Or maybe he's walking just to walk,
To clear the everyday headaches that come with being human.
And as the man turns the corner out of sight,
You wonder why the woman across the street
is going into a building.
Does she live there?
Or is she just here for a rendezvous?
To think that makes you wonder.
And as the sun goes down, the man and the woman are gone.
You go inside to lie down to much thinking.
To think that makes you wonder.

Christine Weremy

Clam Dip

You were a blast, a nice person to be around,
Always so happy and caring—
You held us together and kept us in touch.
At Christmas and Thanksgiving, they were so much fun—
with all the presents, the candy and soup,
but my favorite was the clam dip.
I remember that day in May when the phone rang—
Why would Grandpa be calling so late?
"Grandma is in the hospital, in intensive care!"
Mom and Dad go to see you, to hope everything was okay.
Waking up the next morning, hoping Mom and Dad would be home;
Wondering and worrying what was wrong.
"Come to the office, immediately!" There was Mom.
You were a lot of fun, a kind and gentle person to be around.
Christmas and Thanksgiving just aren't the same—
the house seems so empty because you aren't here.
I miss you a lot and wish you were here,
the best grandma to have and keep you in my mind forever!

Michelle Ragland

You Are

You are my Prince Charming
that takes me away from all my troubles and fears.

You are the light of my life
who lights the paths of my destiny.

You are the dream that was wished for and never came true.
Krystal Torres

Kristiana, the Chosen

God sent me a messenger
Who brought new life to my world.
She almost went to heaven,
But God allowed her life.

Her life has meaning, a message, a truth;
Her soul has depth, sweetness, inspiration.
She knelt one day in the field
And God gave . . . tore open the heavens and
Poured out blessings and power and strength
And might!

God sent this little one a protector—
Wherever she goes there is one to watch out!
An angelic presence surrounds her
So that no harm will befall. But instead,
The richest, best, the most glorious
Happenings occur so that the talent,
The promise will be known worldwide!

Cindy Bowen Simpson

She Was Only Seventeen

They called me on a Thursday to tell me you would soon go away
And sure enough you left this place later on that day.
I didn't understand it and oh, I got so mad,
Because you were one of the best friends I have ever had.
"Why?" was the question, "I don't know" was the reply,
at only seventeen, I lost another to the skies.
I miss you day and night, but I will not weep.
I'll smile and think of the memories I keep.
I know you are looking down, probably brushing your hair.
At seventeen, how's life up there?
Graduation won't be the same without you,
But I'll go on knowing you're with me at every day anew.
I love you and you'll never know how much,
and in the hospital I hope you felt my touch.
At only seventeen, I thought you had a long life to live
But you were taken, although, you were never our's to give
I hope I see you one day, but until then,
I'll be missing you until we meet again

Trena Jones

Dark Days

Somewhere between right and wrong
is a place we all know.
Where what's right seems wrong and
what's wrong can be right.
Tormented souls laughing or crying,
they're not sure which.
Pleasure and pain become as one; it
really doesn't matter, can't feel either.
Living nightmares to keep us awake,
for our dreams have died.
Blinded by darkness, that's okay—
there is no truth to see.
Maimed and bewildered—barely able to
recognize it was once whole;
Harsh voices cry out, hoarse from screaming
their prayers—a whisper, a murmur, a sigh.
Outward manifestation of what's deep
within. A truly frightening reflection!

Lisa Starr Hickson

The Wings of Love

Each person bears but one wing
When two people meet and fall in love,
They embrace and give each other the opportunity
To elevate and fly.
It takes two hearts to truly experience the gift of love,
And the joining of two wings to fly.

Diaja Akinloye

Love

What is love?
Is it an emotion,
A thought that someone is needed;
Or maybe it's a fear of dying alone
Which causes you to look for a companion?
None of these are true.
Love is but a word;
The experience is much more than words can describe.
You go mad for a person.
You get an obsession to keep that someone in your life.
Love—
What an experience.
Those who say it is better to have loved and lost
Haven't experienced it.
Those who have it:
Hold on tight and don't let go.
Cherish it, for when it's gone,
You'll regret losing it.

Nathaniel Ray Bibee

Closure

winter, spring, summer, fall
the things we shared I recall
four changing periods of time
that stand still to me
dreaming of what our love used to be
you still mean the world to me
feelings like this you should know
lips are shut words never flow
reminiscing about our kiss from the past
realizing it will be the last
soft and delicate our lips met
this feeling I will never forget
as I glanced at your ring, reality hit me
we were not meant to be
two souls intertwined for a time
their crossroads will never meet again
I believe two souls like ours should never part
in another life I will have your heart

Christian William Rhodes

The Curse

I can feel you dancing through my veins
like some strange curse
that I could never fade away
from the depths of my blind soul;
bleeding my pain into a loud cry,
drowning my life in a relentless sea of tears;
I face my demons, I face the lies, I face life.

I know I can be so strange;
my world seems lost in a day.
I know that things won't change;
my heart has become a dream so far away,
so sad and lifeless,
so eternal and endless.

So many worlds held in a hand,
so many words that can never be said;
the dark silence between us—
forever is a promise that has been lost.

Javier Osvaldo Henriquez

Undetermined Boundaries

What is it that keeps these hands writing?
The music of my inner core,
The freedom to express my mind,
For it is so unspoken here,
Such a struggle to define what is not
Intended for words.

Shabnam Modjarrad

Lover's Roulette

You'll keep on going until you'll be found
Just remember whatever goes around comes around
You have different girls, different times every night
You're still gone when the darkness turns to light
Just remember when the tables turn around
I won't be there for you, to help you out
I see you asking her for a quick dance
I'm not bothered, go on and take your chance
Is it your last, the question is, who knows?
But as fast as she came, she will go
One thing I know, you're time will come
And when it does, that's when I'll have my fun
Spin the wheel of fate, 'round and 'round she goes
Where she stops, Heaven or Hell, nobody knows
Me or her, this is the game where you win or lose
The way you're going now, you won't have to choose
The wheel is spinning now, I hope you placed your bet
You'd better watch out now, because you're playing lover's roulette

Sonia Bharaj

For My Son

Sometimes, things happen.
Sometimes, they are meant to be.
My love for you has never changed.
Just, someone else took your love from me.
I sit at home and wait,
Knowing and hoping it's not too late.
A card, a message, even a call.
Sometimes missing you so much
I crumble and fall.
No matter what, no matter when
I know in my heart I'll see you again.
To hold you and show you my love has not gone.
I want you now and I wanted you then.
My heart's getting too old to lose you again.
If next time I see you and hold you too tight.
Have patience with me, don't put up a fight.
Deal with my love, open your heart.
We both deserve a brand new start.

Teresa DeVivo

Icy Stillness

In the icy stillness we see not the beauty
Not the joy of the cleansing crystals
Nor the freshness of the frost
We see not the gift the Mother gives us
Not the beauty of the storm
Nor feel joy in our comforts
Look beyond the creature comforts
See what the Earth has given
This picture of gleaming white
In this glorious picture you will see
The sparkling of the cleansing
The beginning of the renewal
In this joy of our claiming
The whiteness of the day
Brings a joy to the Mother
The laughter of the children
The crackling of the wood
Are all we can ask of the day

Cheri M. Hodek

Seed

It is a place where beauty is born.
All of creation needs a seed for new birth,
And a place to feel peace when tattered and torn.
The seed for beauty is found in one place.
But I'm the only one who can go there,
For the place which holds this seed is in your wonderful face.
Mike Emert

A Bond That Cannot Be Broken

This poem is dedicated to the love of my life—he knows who he is.
Sitting here longing to be in your arms;
Knowing that you will protect me from all harm.
You are the only one I believe I can ever love;
You fit me perfectly as if you were sent from above.
Our relationship was perfect and free;
I belonged to you and you belonged to me.
Our bond is so strong, I know it will never break,
No matter how much confusion or mistakes that we make.
The love that we share is true
And because of this my heart will always belong to you.
I know in your heart you must feel the same,
Even though now it seems you are just causing me pain.
The pain is because right now we are not together,
Although in my heart I know that we are meant to be forever.
So my prayer is that one day you will see
And you will not hesitate to come back to me.
Jamila Wideman

In a Field

There he was
Twenty feet from the country road where I stood
No cares in the world or presidency to withstand any longer
Could it really be? Was I imagining?
I held one penny to my face; I squinted, I blinked
His profile matched exactly
Abraham Lincoln frolicking in a field
He once emancipated slaves
But now ran unruly like he, himself, had been freed
I saw his top hat on the side of the road
It was left behind and tattered
His hair matched his lackadaisical limbs
Free, floating, flying
Abraham Lincoln frolicking in a field
He danced a crazy dance
He ran a circuitous line
And as he skedaddled into the horizon
I think I saw him click his heels
Jessica Jenkins

I Belong Here

I belong here
Where the sky is blue,
And the wind blows freely.
Where the birds sing their carefree tunes,
And the Sun shines bright in my heart,
Especially on the cloudy days.
I belong here
Where my thoughts are clear,
And my creativity soars.
Where each and every day is brand new,
And the world keeps me in constant amazement,
Especially on the bad days.
I belong here
Where everything is right,
And heaven is so near.
Where my soul is filled with the joy of life
And I know I belong here
Especially with YOU!
Ruby Ann Cable

One Early Morning When the Sky Was Red

I sat by the river bed
One early morning when the sky was red.
I saw a deer stumble and then fled.
Then came a man smuggled with treasures,
Kicked his boots, and then struck with pleasure.
One early morning when the sky was red.
Brian Dennis Schubert

Like I Don't Know

What do you want from me?
I've given you my heart,
My soul, my love, my all.
And what do I get in return?
You go and cheat on me
Like I wouldn't find out.
Like I couldn't tell
Like I wouldn't know.
You started kissing me different,
Holding me different,
Loving me different.
But you couldn't come and tell me to my face
Because you're not that type of man
You're less than a man,
You're a dog.
And to think that I loved you.
I made that mistake once
And it's not going to happen to me again.
Ashley Jackson

The Rising Sun

In a small meadow a baby deer is born—
life is precious.

In a valley a little field mouse dies—
life is fragile.

There cannot be life without death.

Happiness without sorrow—good without evil.

We would not have Heaven without Hell.

No light if there was no darkness.

This is how it has been from the dawn of time.

Not all is good yet not all is evil.

Do not be quick to judge what you don't understand.

Nor judge by what you see for it is not just
to judge by one or the other.
Tabitha Cunningham

Truth

As I walk through the halls of eternity,
I am blinded by the darkness
Which allows me to see the truth.
My blood pours out of my open wounded heart
Like salty tears from my eyes when in utter pain.
My immortal soul is filled with fear
Which strikes me when I see the truth.
I wave my arms frantically,
As if trying to fly when I'm falling;
Instead I only touch the nothingness that thickly surrounds me.
Alas! I have found the end of infinity,
But instead I found the truth.
Which in the midst of the shadows
I could not bear.
The truth is:
It is a difficult task to find what you're looking for;
When you're lying cold
As the world bids you their last farewells.
Vanessa Ramirez

Hallelujah Chorus

Cottonwoods are the most elegant of trees
Their leaves hang gracefully
Not rustling, crackling, or crunching
But swaying in the breeze
Whispering
Hallelujah, Hallelujah, Hallelujah

Hannah Grant Pommersheim

Freedom

Capsized
and as you throw me overboard
I watch the water cover me
I breathe my last breath
I am dying
wondrous circular forms escape my mouth
I ponder quickly what you must be thinking
as you let me go
but darkness has flooded your face
and my world around me is loneliness and death
or in this death will I be alone?
can I give to you now
what you so desperately wanted then?
warmth infiltrates my thoughts
as I am to know it is cold
but I am past that
and the understanding sets in
you and your freedom

April Yvonne Jennison

One More

I've wished for one more Sunday, but what
would that be? My conscience reminds me of
my last Sunday. She cooked for me. I can't
have regrets because I did right, but one
more night of her saying, "Do you have plenty
of blankets?" One more Saturday at the
grocery store with, "What do you think we
should have for Sunday lunch?" One more
fish sandwich and small Sprite. Can we go to
Wal-Mart one more time? Can you fish with my
son as you walked with me? Will he remember
you or will I remind? One more Turkey Hash.
One more, "You drive careful now!" Just one
more, "I Love You." You've never missed anything; no matter how hard it was for you to
be there. One more tear on your shoulder;
but that would be for me and I have to let
you go for you—one more.

Christy Shealy Hauerwas

Heart Feelings

Here I am staring at the stars
Wiping the tear drops that keep on falling
Bring memories back to my mind.
Hoping and praying that you're doing fine
Because behind bars is not a good place to be
We've been through some hard times.
Thanks to God we've gotten through them
Now it's only you and I
That is left in the world.
All I ask from you
Is to love me forever!
To always make me proud
Just like you are doing now.
Even though you're far away
Every second you're on my mind
And just remember I'll always be waiting.
The day you get out I'll trap you in my arms
And never let you out!

Shelley Peoples

I Dream

I dream that tomorrow will be good day,
Not a nightmare for you or me.
I dream that I will see you again,
That you will be all right.
I dream that everything will work out for you and me.
I dream that you will be glad to see me.

Amber Froehlke

R.I.P., Matt

Inside my mind couldn't find a place to rest.
I can't take it any more, I'm feeling really stressed.
We used to run around the neighborhood, used to play in the streets;
Now you're in heaven—may your soul rest in peace.
Why'd you have to die such an early death?
Without you I feel there's nothing left.
You were always there to keep my head up;
Now it seems the rain will never let up.
Take me away from all this pressure, all this pain;
Show me the meaning of happiness again.
Broken-hearted as I glance at the casket—
It should never have been you, you should have lasted.
While the tears are rolling down my cheeks,
I look at our picture and steadily weep.
Hands clasped together, knees on the floor,
I'm begging the Lord: Bring me with you through heaven's door.
I'm lost and I'm weary and it's just not the same.
I wish it were I and not you burning in that sparkling flame.

Disha Parvatam

Who Am I?

As I sit and stare,
listening to the sound of the rain,
I look for him
I look for him everywhere
in my dreams, in my thoughts, in the sky
Mama said that he would come home one day,
but that was 14 years ago
"One day" comes and goes
She says he's my father, and that I look like him,
but when I look at myself, I see someone unwanted
I see someone that needs love
I see me
I look, and I look,
but it occurs to me that I don't know who I'm looking for
I know I have his nose, but I don't know his face
I don't know my father,
his name
I don't know

Cineca Anthony

New Horizons

Beyond the hills lies a fate
Of a life to remain unchanged
Yet to try and fight for life
This is an undeniable right
Feed the soul, cherish the body, nurture the mind
Let the mind run, the body reflect, and the soul cry
The top of the hill lies years ahead
And still we have many fears to dread
Though the light shines, there is fear in the soul
An action which only the spirit could control
Wish for tranquility and peace
Focus on your goal, lift the seas
Life shows promise yet many decline
A free gift given is life
If we can just push ahead, we surely can win
Climb the untaken path so that we might live
And to see what has yet to come
All we have to do is look beyond the horizon

Dustin McDonald

What Is Love?

Love is seeing him how no one else does.
Love is when you know he's not perfect, but you see him perfectly.
Love is thinking about him day and night.
Love is when he means the world to you.
Love is when no one else knows how you feel.
Love is the best feeling you can feel.

Sunie Ann White

The Little Angel

There she lay
In a crib
My infant sister
Her life not sustained
She wrapped her fragile hand
Around my finger
A small china dish
That would break so easily
Katie, Katie, I whispered her name
She gazed up into my eyes
Full of wires, IV's, and tubes
A half-sewn teddy bear
She couldn't breathe
Her hopes for life had perished
The doctors turned off the switch
The respirator brought her sustenance no more
My weeping mother slowly rocked her
Into eternal sleep

Kevin Myers

Still

You don't believe, you don't care, you're cold
Yet somehow you draw me in, luring me with your mysterious ways
You do everything I hate, say everything so vainly, but still
No matter what you do, I still—I can't stop—I don't know—maybe
I won't stop
You're always hurting me
You're the enemy of my dreams, still
I hope for you to be a part of them
I don't know what to do—if I told you, what would you do
Throw me aside after knowing you've captured me
Step on my heart after knowing you've stolen it
Leaving it black and tangled
Wipe your dirty feet all over my hope, smearing away its shine
Forsaken, disarrayed and dull, still it strives to keep a flicker
I can't help it—I can't help wondering
Do I
Am I in
It can't be?

Faryal Siddiqui

Alone

Have you ever stood outside your body,
Searching to find what lies beneath?
Why is it I can't please anybody?
Am I doomed to live a life without love
For I cannot afford to be alone
Nor afford to be happy
Everybody leaves me empty
Just give me a little fuel
I ask not for love, for love is nothing but heartbreak
I only ask for an answer
I am heard, but always a unanswered prayer
I have been forsaken by many and all
My heart breaks for emotion
My mind jumps in and says, never again
By the gods I am doomed
Or by God I am damned
Of which I do not know
I do know I cannot afford to be alone

Amy Lynn Boggs

What Will Bandage a Bleeding Heart

A heart is bleeding from anger and pain
Accusing everyone else when it's the only blame.
Things in the past you can not re do all you can
do is realize they are not because of you.
Watching as life slowly passes you by
Not taking time to create memories enjoy it and you don't know why.

Karla Mitchell

Recovery

Yes, we stand stunned and shed our tears.
We will soon recover and deal with our fears.
United we stand, divided we fall.
We did get knocked off our big wall.

We will find and bury our own,
And we will soon let it be known
That we will recover and face our fears.
Your day of reckoning will soon be near.

As you see, we have the freedom of choice
And you see our government hears our voice.
We will be knocking soon on your door,
And it won't be enough to even the score.

But you can see we are working on recovery.
We stand united and bond as thee,
And we look at the statue of liberty.
You couldn't extinguish the flame.
Our recovery will be the same.

Angela L. Pierce

New York City

Did you think
We didn't understand
Suffering,
That we'd never battled
Brother against brother
Or learned through pain and sacrifice
How to conquer tyranny?

These are not the first fires
That have burned here.
Every day, they burn and every day,
We forge from them a gift.

Our gift to the world is bigger
Than ourselves.
There is no way that anyone can take it back
Or make it disappear.

No towers are needed to reach this height.
No darkness can extinguish our light.

Raphael Badagliacca

A Shield of Tears—October 6, 1990

And so he leaves, this once "babe in my arms,"
this child-man of mine, to go to a far country, a vague somewhere.
I weep, fearing that he might end up learning
far more than anyone needs to learn or should have to learn;
for although the terror of war is just a whispered threat now,
in a moment war may be shouting its obscenities at him.
I weep because I will miss hearing his voice,
and shaking my head at the odd still-youth ideas
he has or things he has done.
I weep because he is afraid and he puts on a brave front,
and I am afraid and I cannot act so brave,
and I want to shield him from this shield
of sand and war he must be a part of;
I weep because of my own fear of losing him,
my first-born, the one who endured all my
bumbling mistakes as a young, teenage mother.
I weep . . . because I love him.
O God, please protect my son, my son.

Sandra Anderson

Living of the Swift

Living of the swift, always on the go.
Living of the swift, but nowhere to go.
Living of the swift, busy as can be.
Stop! Wait! Take a moment, if you please.
May I give a small advice if I could?
Take a walk in the park or in the wood.

Connie Riggleman

A New Beginning

When it was over I thought the pain would never end
And my heart would never mend
As all my warm days turned colder
I truly thought my life was over
But you came in a twinkling of an eye
And caught me completely by surprise
With your sweet smile and soft kiss
This was something I just couldn't resist
Visions of us together in time
An enchanted love, as your heart becomes one with mine
A fairy tale love, we live happily ever after
A never ending love, yes that's what I'm after
Step by step kiss by kiss
Slowly and surely you've granted my only wish
So no need to rush this is only the start
Soon you will have the key to my heart
This constant pain of my broken heart is now ending
I need you now you're my new beginning

Steven Graham

Not with You

Words could never express how I feel
Now, I know it's all too real
I still miss you every now and then
But I don't want you ever again
I hope I see you after this
I hope it's me that you miss
I still can't believe it turned out this way
And I think about it every day
But now I know you're truly gone
Now, I know you're not the one
Now, I know all your lies
Now, I know it's not her I despise
Years from now when I'm happy and free
You'll be sad you're not with me
And all the lies you've ever said
Will forever be gone from my head
And when you're sad and lonely, too
Just know I'm happy that I'm not with you

Nina Angela Biondo

One

Alone—but not weep, for what?
Sadness, darkness all around, simple world turned upside down.
Tell me how I need to cope, let me know there is some hope. . . .
I want to run, I want to scream;
some they say that is just too extreme.
Help me find my way; oh, please
pick me up off bent knees.
Pray, pray every day for everyone to be okay;
I see you, friend, upon tomorrow,
or will once again there be deep sorrow?
Uncertain world, please let me go—
love, life, what do they know?
I am one; what do I know?
I know when it's time to go.
So, here's farewell, not goodbye.
Please don't think I did not try.
I tried so hard; the pain was deep.
Now I lay me down to sleep. . . .

Michele A. June

Believe

There is a magical place
Where sometimes your enemy, you have to face.
Where most of our water comes from,
It has fish; yes, there are some.
Wherever you are, wherever you may be,
Sometimes you have to see
What's on the inside, not the outside of a human being.
Look around.
Don't make a sound,
And believe in yourself.

Kate Kinghorn

Lord up Above

Please, watch the one I love
For she's the world to me
It's hard for life to be
Even though she's an angel in disguise
I know with you her soul will lie
Even though it's hard for me to say
I know you had your reasons for taking her away
So, please, take care of her, better than any other
Because she is my Nanny
Nobody in this world is better than she
So, Lord, please, listen to my prayer

Danielle Skelly

Ode to Samurai

Velvety soft feet pitter-patter,
Following me wherever
Winding and wending like the finest silk.
Eyes like yellow sapphire,
Keen and aware,
Peer into my soul.
Melted chocolate in the Sun,
Wearing his stripes like a battle cry.
Fearless Samurai pounces
Hapless insects while I garden.
A day in the life of a feline warrior.

Laurel Rigoulot Osmun

My Wife

You don't know how often I wanted to look into your eyes
To touch your face
And to tell you how much I love you
But then God said
You may look at her, as you would a rose
Enjoy the beauty
Watch it grow
Do not pluck
And as in all roses
It is not for you only
But for others to enjoy

C. J. "Sweep" Ardeneaux

Forgotten Sounds

Meaningless chatter
forced into sobriety.
Never sealed by thoughts of others.
Childless dreams and pathetic murmurs
of a nation constricted by ignorance.
To fight against the eerie icy grip
of consciousness.
Stare down evil eyes with wicked intent,
for you see the scale tilting and shattering.
And the mind flows together on jagged
crystals of faith.

Krystal Lee Loewen

Twin Towers

The Twin Towers that used to stand tall and strong
Fell to the ground, but they're not there for long!
They were taken down by an evil force.
They fell to the ground because they had no choice.
So many lives lost, so much destruction.
It's a damn shame.
They say America is under attack
But that doesn't matter—
The Towers will be back,
And all the lives lost aren't gone for long,
They're just waiting for us in God's loving arms.

Marlene Batchelor

So Alone . . .

I feel so alone,
Part of the ground.
No one there or ever around.
You don't understand; don't tell me you do.
Don't say it unless you know that it's true.
Until you know the feelings inside,
Anticipating the hurt I tend to hide.
You don't know me at all, you see;
you don't know anything at all about me.
A stranger to you and everyone else,
I feel so alone.

Corey Ann Sharp

I Am Who I Am; Who I Am, I Will Be

I am who I am who I am I will be,
No wind can change me,
No gentle breeze may move me,
I am who I am who I am I will be,
I am who I am who I am I will be,
No wave can wash me of my sins only my Lord can in the end,
I am who I am who I am I will be,
I am who I am who I am I will be,
No creature can create me,
No peer can change my mind,
I am who I am who I am I will be.

Robin Goodman

Love

Love is like a ship,
Sailing through the sea.
You don't always know where it's heading,
So just let it be.

You may hit some trouble,
Such as thunder and rain,
Or your ship may get flooded,
And you hope for no pain.

Love is like a ship sailing through the sea.
You don't know where it's heading, so just let yourself free.

Nicole Ashley Aikin

Forgetfulness

I forgot to pray that all things are equal.
I forgot to be thankful for forgiveness.
I forgot to polish my soul with anointing.

How could you forget that the sun rises?
How could you forget all you promised?
How could you forget that love is a foundation?

I forgot that the world will not agree.
I forgot that I have no need to please you.
I forgot that there was only one thing that I must always do . . .

Acknowledge your love for me.

Angela Marie Bell

To the Man I Love

When the Sun no longer warms . . .
And the grass no longer grows

When the stars no longer shine . . .
And the moon no longer glows

When all the flowers have lost their scent . . .
And the ocean waves are completely spent

When the final day turns into night . . .
And the morn no longer comes

I will still love you.

Cheryl L. Altrich

Love

Love is like a never-ending ocean
You never know where it begins or where it ends
It flows like a tide
In and out, in and out
And when it comes crashing down
You have to be careful
Or you may cough up in it and drown
But just like an ocean
Love can be peaceful and calm
It can be dangerous or tranquil
But love is like a never-ending ocean

Emily Fayth Brass

Macho Man

Here I am and here I stand
A mighty man, a fighting man
A young man, an old man
And still always a man
Fearless
Relentless
Stubborn and true
There's nothing in the world I fear
I am steady and calm and my head is clear
Yet I realize now that that's not quite true
I'm afraid of your soft voice and of talking to you

Jason Daniel Bohnet

Winds of Growth

As we struggle against contrary winds,
We must remember a new life is about to begin.
When we go with the wind no effort is applied,
But, God gives us contrary winds to make us try.

So in our greatest hours each day,
Let's not push our winds away.
Welcome the struggles that are put in our paths,
And remember, our Lord will not make them last!

Thank Thee Lord for the winds that are blown.
For without these storms we could not have grown!

Barbara K. Nord

Sailor's Prayer

For the sailor in my life

Lord guide me on these seas. Return me
Safely to shore to the ones who wait for me.
Let not this jealous mistress of the deep
Steal me from the one who awaits my return.
Let me not see the dark watery grave.
Let me have yet more time ashore. Let this
Vessel quickly and safely return me home.
Home where my love awaits her sailor's
Return.
Amen.

Kathie Long Pahner

Birthday Reflections

A warm winter wind blew gently through the tree.
I walk by; it whispers your name softly to me,
Reminding me of today, and I fill with delight,
Celebrating and being with just you tonight.
Birthdays hint of aging, but not so with you.
To me, your grace and beauty each day is new.
They reflect the years of sunshine and giving.
Your deep love and affection make life truly worth living.
My heart fills with delight as it whispers your name
On this special celebration of the day you came.

Happy birthday, my love!

Patrick Austin

Save the Ozone

Save the ozone, the lifesaver of this day.
Stop the use of CFC that reacts with the UV rays.
The catastrophic birth of chlorine hitting the
ozone molecules . . .
Or you will find earth in a disfigure that
cannot be mended by any tool.
So stop the use of CFC, stop this ridiculous game,
or you will find no one but your own self to blame.

Dipti Surendra Pradhan

Turning Point

The waves of change are rushing over me as the river wild.
I devour this ascent like a child given his
first drop of milk from his mother's bosom.
In certainty, I shake off the embryonic
newness with awe—a change is in effect.
The flame of desire, at full combustion
signifies splendorific challenges awaiting me.
The peak perfection is emerging.
Even the pinnacle of Heaven cannot
surpass my changing delight—
only change itself could reshape this destiny.

Keshia LaAnnya Walker

My Pledge to You

You lay with me;
I hold you tight,
Never letting go till morning light.
The perfect day, the perfect night
Is to keep you long in my sight.
Don't ever fear, I'll hold you near
And keep you close till death draws near.
I'll keep you warm, I'll keep you safe;
I'll risk my life, I'll take your place.
I'll raise a toast when all is done
And give a cheer, for it's you I love.

Randy C. Habfast

Past

The pain I feel is so real.
My heart breaks every time
I think of that horrible place.

The images of him in my mind
are not so very kind.

This feeling is a ghost from my past
that seems to come into my mind
no matter where I am standing.

The final days of sorrow have come to an end
as a girl says goodbye to the memory of a not-so-kind man.

Stacy Nacole Shepard

Johnfred Daring

You gave me life, you made me strong,
but now you have journeyed on.
Time has passed as memories flood me,
tears flow so easily within my heart.
They say time eases your pain;
it's been a year, when will it start?
I miss your voice, so strong and full of life.
I miss your knowledge that gave me insight.
I miss your stubbornness that came about
when you were right.
I miss you each and every day of my life.

Tracy Hayes

Invitation to a Party

Last night I had a dream that I had too much to drink
It was only a dream, but when I awoke my slippers were gone
Now I think I will stay up from night till dawn
I do not want to lose any more slippers!

Sleepless nights, and racing minds . . .
My friends, please let us go and kill the fatted calf
Then, let us eat it off the same trencher
with our hands while we chant absurdities amongst ourselves
We'll drink our poison and make a toast to
endless nights, lost slippers, and lonely crowds
Salut!

Mauro Tambasco

Somewhere in Time

Somewhere in time, here I am.
Every corner I turn, I see myself
staring off into what I call time,
Not knowing where I am or where I will be,
Just knowing that somehow, I will be there
in that special place called time.
There, within myself, staring back in time,
and then only understanding that the
precious time I have viewed within will
give me the peace, love, beauty, solitude
and wisdom I have so desired.

Paula Marie Twitty

Why?

To all humankind

Why is it we run from church to church?
Why is it we all say we've been hurt?
Why do we run when God call our name?
Why can't we give God His fame?
Why can't we seek God face today?
Why is it you don't want to pray?
Why do birds fly in the sky?
Why do love ones have to die?
Why can't we let God's will be done?
Why not just believe, He is the mighty one?

Kim Kathleen Johnson

Hope

The dangers of my eyes will never cease.
The insecurities of my heart will go on forever.
Always be afraid; always be altered in thought.
I will not succumb to the evils of this society;
Will not give into death.
Be strong, be strong.
Do not die.
Live on in the minds of the warmhearted.
The cold will fall.
They cannot last forever.
There is hope yet!

Niki Leigh Barnes

Do We Dare to Dream?

Do we dare to dream of what love may hold?
Do we dare to share the events the day unfolds?
Do we dare to hope that these things may come true?
Is it possible for two hearts to connect through a touch?
When does one know when they care too much?
But should we choose not to dare, then what have we lost?
Perhaps happiness that could be shared.
For every broken heart that has to heal,
There is a lesson to be learned.
So dare to share and dare to care,
For life is far too short to live it all alone.

Sherry Lynn Davis

She Calls Herself the Ocean

Her torrent of waves crashing all about
She feels pain, she feels anger
She cannot contain
The power she holds deep inside the hollowness
All within her screams
Take me to a shore! Let me taste the sand!
She cannot hold back
What she is
For I yearn solace, comfort,
A shore of my own to walk upon
For it is all too confusing, wanting

Carissa Warman

Anywhere

I see you here, and I see you there.
Wherever you are, I'll be missing you anywhere.
Don't go away, don't go there,
'cause I'll be missing you anywhere.
But if you leave me and I hope you won't
there's still hope to be as one in love.
This is the poem that I wrote for you,
even knowing you left me without a clue,
but I'll still love you if you are there
because you remain in my heart
which keeps me warm here and there.

Kamil Horvath

I'm Crazy

I'm Crazy because of you,
Because you left me all alone.
Forever you said,
Never you always meant!

I'm Crazy because I can't see you anymore.
You left . . . never to return.
A love we once had,
So precious so true.

A love that made me so crazy,
All I do is think about you!

Chelsea Ann Elliott

Nothing Ever Makes a Bit of Sense

Claustrophobic
paranoia, microorganisms is all you
are. Feeding on plankton which is all the
low lives, like me. We are the puppets, the
moon our stage. We dance around happy. You,
like me, us. The screams echo through the
passages in the halls, the corridors of my
brain. The choice is ignorance. The chemical
imbalance of the sciences, the metric
conversion. Convert the cubic inch, what
will it become?

MiChelle Catherine Hansen

To Get Away

Wondering, oh, so far away
My mind slips into another dimension
Out there, somewhere away from here
So badly, I want to get away
From the shame, the blame, the loneliness
This new vacancy in my soul tugs so hard on my heart
This terror has brought my life to a new reality
One of fear, lament, and torture
Escaping the time, my mind lands in a world all its own
There I can do anything, be anything
But I am me and the sun will rise again.

Courtney Jo Vaughn

a lonely soul

when darkness comes with the night,
my lonely soul lets out a sigh,
my heart is scared
with life that teaches us in vain.
separate worlds are our domain,
but secret thoughts in my mind remain.
and feeling that to no one i can explain.
so with an empty heart, my lonely soul remains,
until another life i can obtain.
maybe in another life and time,
my heart's true pain will be erased.

Margie Deleon

Terror in the U.S.

Two Twin Towers, once standing tall
When terrorists crash planes and cause them to fall.
As these towers fall to the ground,
There are still so many people to be found.
So much tragedy, pain and horror;
It feels like there will be no tomorrow.
Our freedom will not be jeopardized
Because these people choose to terrorize.
America will stand strong and tall,
For these terrorists attacks
Will not stop us at all!

Lolita Kay McDaniel

Darkest Day

We were attacked by surprise
and we were afraid.
The sky grew dark and smoky
and we were afraid.
The world was no longer a peaceful place
and we were afraid.
But heroes arose from the ashes that day
and we were no longer afraid.
Our fear replaced with patriotism and courage,
For we have something they cannot destroy:
A spirit that will not be afraid.

Kasey Gray

America—Red, White, and Blue

America a land of opportunity, freedom and love.
America a place to be proud of.
With a flag flown high. Where it stands proud.
America—where people are free to shout out loud.

America—a flag of red, white, and blue.
America—what do those colors mean to you?
Red is for the bloodshed when each disaster strikes.
Blue is how we feel when we realize it is real.
White is when we start to wipe a clean slate.
Fifty stars for fifty states. United we stand.
America—red, white, and blue—oh what a land. We are proud of you.

Calev Beck

Nature's Wondrous Beauty

Climbing to the top.
Dare to look, or dare to walk.
Oh, wondrous beauty of natures wild.
Smell the sweet and dare to treat, thyself.
Only look, but do not touch.
Colors, colors, oh, so many.
Busting beauty, takes thy breath away, nature's wondrous beauty.

Reta Kaye Clayton

Left to Wonder

Terrorists would crash hijacked planes
on a beautiful day
into the New York World Trade Center
and leave the United States in dismay.

To see these famous buildings
crash to the ground below—
victims, sacrificed by terrorists exhibiting hatred,
for whatever reasons to be known.

What makes terrorists feel so supreme
when destruction, death and chaos is their goal?
They are not in the majority,
yet we, the majority, are put on "hold."

Pray for those who have died;
no longer are they in danger.
They are now safe with God;
we are left to wonder.

Elvira Traini Bowe

Hope

Through darkness
Through the shadows of despair
There is a light
A light that never ceases to exist
But we are oblivious to it
When we have lost it
It is not a buried treasure
It is not a needle in a haystack
When we open our eyes
We can see it
When we open our hearts
We can feel it
It is deep within our soul
That it cannot be deprived from us
If there is a tomorrow, there is hope
If there is love, there is hope
If there is faith, there is hope
The light will find us when we find the light

Justina Torre

Freckles

Freckles my cat
A calico breed
Slams her cabinet door when it's time to feed
No bags for her she prefers cans
Fancy feast is her favorite brand
She drinks water from the fish tank
Watch out fish, don't walk that plank
But the fish do not fear
Surprisingly enough, they want her near
They swim to the top to kiss her tongue
You'd think they would run!
She loves to play, and her toy chest is full
I know she is spoiled, but there is no rule
She has toys that squeak and some that roll
Even ones operated by remote control
But she is the sweetest at night lying in bed
With her blanket tucked around her
And her shark pillow under her head

Debra McClanahan

Myself

When I look at myself, I ask myself a question—
Who am I?
What happened to the person I saw before?
The answer to the question is simple.
You are just the same as before, but even better.
No one really changes on the inside,
But then, you can put on clothes,
And make-up can make you look different,
But it's just a cover.

Alisha Madonna

For My Daughter, Myranda

She came to me like Venus on the sea,
a ray of moonlight on the waves,
a fully formed new goddess washed in
by the surf on the beaches of my life.

I asked her name; she gazed at me
with brown eyes filled with the mystery
of planets and stars and faraway lands.
She repeated the question, who am I?

In need of an answer, I drew nearer and
saw in her hand a silver mirror.
Over her shoulder, I saw us two together
as her dark hair curled in the wind.

Deep within the glass, there passed a
recognition as her eyes met mine.
So different we looked, yet so much the same,
needing the other to reveal our own divinity.

Cynthia Ransom

Deeper (Bree)

You steal a glance, then look away.
You do not like what you see.
But what you saw was the outside;
You'll never know the real Bree.

You like to judge, but there is one flaw:
You only look at appearance.
But you've never heard how well she sings
Or seen her beautiful dance.

You do not know how much she's read
And will never read her poetry
Or help her as she paints the sky.
You'll never break past the sentry.

Open your heart and your mind.
Then you might be able to see
The diamond in the rough,
All she possesses, the real Bree.

Rosalyn Marie Grieder

A Weekend to Treasure

'Twas a weekend I'll long remember
your company was a great pleasure
Four days with treasured friends
which sadly came to an end

The warmth of your smiles that greeted each day
can only be matched by the sun's brightest rays
The walks on the beach in the cool sea breeze
with you alongside, miles were covered with ease

Sitting on the beach and enjoying the waves
we even had the pleasure of seeing some whales
The midnight stroll on the warm beach sand
staring at the stars in the sky beyond

I'm sure you'll agree, we had a great time
with memories we'll cherish for a long, long while
Life is certainly richer for having known you
and I hope we'll be friends forever and true

Govind Dhanraj

If I Could Give the World a Gift

If I could give the world a gift,
It would be one that would last forever,
It would be something that anyone could use.
It would make us all come together and make us feel better,
No matter black or white, it would tell us not to fight.
It would show us love and happiness,
And finally after all these years of waiting,
what we have wanted to see.
Peace on Earth for you and me!

Jeff Hudson

A New Friend

Little did I know so many months ago
That I would find a Friend who has
Touched me so.

I do not know why, or understand when
Or how you first became my Friend.

Maybe it is the way you smile
Or the way you say hello.

It may even be the way you make me feel
When you listen to the many tales I tell.

It could even be the manner in which you speak
That makes me feel at ease.

You have touched a part of me that will never end.

For this, my friend, I thank you for a Friendship
That I hope will have no end.

Lisa Marie Almeida

Soaring

Look upon a star;
Tell me what you see.
I see my destiny
Watching over me,

Reaching so high
Into the soaring sky,
Dreaming as you fly;
I can almost cry.

Going out into the world,
Seeing new things,
Watching over people,
And hearing the flap of birds' wings . . .

What a wonderful day;
I can't ask for any more,
But I just have to say
. . . SOAR. . . .

Daniel Marcel Godlin

Today and Tomorrow

As you live through the moments of TODAY
May you know each moment to be . . .
So much more than what you had hoped for
When this TODAY was still your TOMORROW!

As you look back from the end of TODAY,
May you know that you've been well-blessed
Far, far more than what you had hoped for
When this TODAY was just your TOMORROW!

In time you'll face each challenge of TODAY
Knowing you'll be given the strength to address them.
For you'll have th' assurance of mem'ries
Of each TODAY that was once TOMORROW!

And soon you will start each brand new TODAY—
With joy, not fear, for you'll know by then
Each trial will make you stronger . . . better—
Than when TODAY was just your TOMORROW!

Bradshaw E. Taylor

Complex Simplicity

Ashes to ashes and dust to dust, they say;
But what do they imply?
That death is just a simple stage that comes by and by?
Well, by and by come joy, sorrow and pain,
But ashes no longer flicker with fire and dust can never be a flame.
Ashes to ashes and dust to dust, they say;
But what is it they mean?
If death were such simplicity,
Life would only be a dream.

Kathryn Lott

Sunday Early Spring

The sky, a paperish, grayish wedge wood blue,
Framing house and tree alike.
The soft, shadowless misty sunlight
Color washing all.
The riverside willows,
Stealing ahead of their peers,
Standing aloofly
Draping their green finery,
The chill-wafting air, goosefleshing away
The spring sun's warm promise.
The voice of Gigli in the '38 recording
Of *La Boheme* in spirit
Equaling nature's vistas
The inner warmth
Of a large Scotch—or two
Sunday! Oh, Sunday!
Some Sunday!

Paul A. Haggerty

A Light

For I have come across a glow,
A brightness that I know not of.
It radiates a warmth that I cannot explain,
A light like no others before.

It is an energy that I have dreamed,
One not of this plane, but instead
A gift from He who rules all.
A reminder of the power of Love.

Though these words may be defined in ways
Other than what their true meaning is,
I shall endure in how they make me feel.
For to really feel is the freedom of Life.

My enormous thanks to the universe
For allowing me this moment of Glow,
This opportunity to touch an Energy
I did not think could ever be real.

Bill Bobbitt

The Angel I Never Saw

I awoke one morning and I saw her face
A heavenly angel so full of grace.

I quietly sat not uttering a word
Her beautiful voice was all that I heard.

Quietly watching, my eyes filled with tears
This angel from God has been with me for years.

Looking back I now know, she's been there each day
Blessing my life every step of the way.

I never saw her, nor did I know
That I have an angel who loves me so.

You see, God has blessed me with an angel so rare
No wings, no halo, nor gown does she wear.

He's given me an angel more special than any other
God's given me an angel disguised as my mother.

Veronica Faye Walskey

Just Can't Win

Trying to be romantic, but he's pulling my hair.
I ask for a glass of lemonade and he brings me a soda.
He's looking an hour for the car keys
when they're lying right in front of him.
Bumps his leg, instead of turning on the light.
Throws his jeans on the floor
when the basket is a foot away.
There is no one else like him and for that I am glad.
Boy, I can't wait to marry this man!

Melinda Lee Marvin

Let Me Go So I Can Come Back

I can go back hundreds of days with you
and see all that we have and need.
Sometimes I wondered what was there
and what we really would share.

Different times have come, and different paths in my life are here.
So I must pick and go on my road. . . . Please understand and hear.
It's nothing you've done or said or what you have lacked,
but it's about time I get my real life on track.

I'll keep you in my dreams at night.
The other things that try to separate us, I will fight.
I'm not saying this is my best choice.
But it's the one with most of God's voice.

When I'm not at home as much
and I really can't stay in touch,
as I get my emotional things and start to pack,
just please . . . let me go so I can come back.

Ryan K. Isaak

Thoughts

Whispers of love, I can still hear
Voice so sweet next to my ear.
Thoughts of you running through my brain.
You are the one, who keeps me sane.

Carefully listening to every word,
Not a thing, that goes unheard!
Vibes of thoughts from you,
Can be felt all the way through!

Love so dear, and so true,
To you each day through.
Joy from rings, of the telephone,
Wishing you and I were somewhere alone.

Prayers will be answered in time,
Hoping one day you'll be mine.
These are my thoughts I shall hold,
Deep down in my heart, my body, my soul.

Mary Ellen Mondt

Mosquito

Mosquito, oh, mosquito! Descendant of the ant
Sharp anger like that of the wasp
Flowing saliva as dynamic as a curse
Legs in the thorax like that of a monkey
Larva is your husband indeed

You sold malaria to the householder
You wait not for your financial returns
You sold malaria to the visitor
Without hesitating
You sold malaria to the nursing mother
Leaving her shivering intensely

Ah! You tiny mosquito
Making the elderly run insane
Worthy is the battle against you
To conquer the small diseases caused
To enjoy life in good health.

Adeyemi Idowu Badero

Being Young Again

I look at those days as if they were my last days
I didn't have much to worry about then
Though I was a loser I felt like a winner
I had a different mind set then
Now I'm in my twenties
But I look and feel in my teens
The real world don't capture me
I try to look at it as if I can't see
That not being young again is killing me

Elvis L. McCarter

The Last of His Kind

One man sitting in a forest;
One man all alone.
Wishing he had a son or daughter;
Wishing he wasn't on his own.

He's the last of his kind in the forest;
He's the last of his kind in the world.
When he dies it will all be over;
When he dies the leaves will be curled.

The trees are being cut down
And causing all this havoc.
He lies down with great sadness
While trying to sleep in his hammock.

It was a cold dark night that night
And the tree cutters had gone to bed.
The lonely man died that night
Before the dreams had reached his head.

Kate Kenward

Curse of the Immortal

Why does my life go on?
The misery is still going strong.
I've got no reason to smile.
My trust was misplaced all the while.
All I see is black.
All I feel is pain.
I just want to sever these vital veins.
Nothing in this world is right,
But my life just mustn't end,
So all these feelings I've got to fight.
Forever alone in this endless plight.
I see no end of pain in sight.
Life is my chronic disease,
And death, the only cure.
I want to treat myself and be forever pure,
But there is no way of release
For me, damned forevermore with this accursed disease.

Jonathan Roy Baker

The Ocean

Its gigantic waves seem to want to wash
away a certain memory,
The intricate shells and dazzling rocks seem
to want to say something,
Perhaps the story of their lives, all that they've been through.
The great seawall, father of all, towering over the
beach like a tremendous fortress,
Yet gentle enough to allow small children to run across it,
The seaweed waving in the glistening water as if to greet you,
The fresh salt smell makes your nose tingle,
The sandy floors are a perfect place to sit and
pour out your thoughts to the sea gulls,
Yet all they do is squawk for a reply.
The glorious ocean is a place to enjoy for
many years to come,
Anytime you want, it will be there,
Waiting for you.

Rachel-Leigh Phillips

Dreams

Dreams, what are they and why do we have them,
They are deepest and most delicate feelings and fears
we dream because we sometimes fear
that the circumstances that we're in will never change
and we've lost tracks of our real dreams, hopes, and fantasies.
What even your dreams are, always follow through with the good ones.
Never be afraid of a challenge,
because if you're a good person and follow your dreams
and ambitious you'll never go wrong.

Crystal Buchman

Denture Disasters

Have you ever had the roof of your mouth itch,
But you kept crocheting and didn't miss a stitch,
Though you felt you'd surely come un-glued,
While others observed, as you squirmed and stewed?

Or have you enjoyed a banquet, until
The strawberry shortcake completed your fill,
And suddenly a torturous strawberry seed
Embedded itself and cut short your feed?

Have you ever sneezed and become aware
That your teeth had departed into thin air.
And you had to retrieve them, while others stare,
But your toothless smile said you didn't care?

Did you ever lay your teeth upon a chair
And bite yourself when you sat down there?
Dentures may bring you problems galore,
But they're better than toothless like you were before!

Zula Richards Jones

Romantic

Romance is . . . dare I say romantic?
My thoughts thrive on it
My soul craves it
My heart worships it
Start a fire, it's time to get romantic
Is it that difficult?
Does it have to inhabit part of your brain?
Must you sell your soul to the devil?
One rose . . .
One kiss . . .
One term of endearment . . .
I'm not asking for your hand
I'm not asking for your heart
I'm not asking you to sweep me off my feet
and us ride off into the sunset
I just want some time, some love and some tenderness.
Is that too much to ask?

Pamela Dyer

Unbridled Passion

It's in our hearts, it's built in our soul.
No, it's not smarts, but it makes us bold.
Some come by it naturally, others have to change.
Go at it cheerfully and you'll see great range
in the spectrum of abilities that you possess.
As you strive with a conviction of the heart,
you know God plays such a large part.
A passion is created on your face
that neither man, nor time can erase.
It breaks us down, it builds us up,
it can't be measured in a cup.
With some goals it's big, with others small;
we feel it inside us, come one, come all
to this place of thought, of strife, of joy
in the mind of a little girl or boy,
where the "how thinker" decides with simple examination
this character trait that's called DETERMINATION.

Eric Schuller

Beauty of Earth

The sky is never-ending and beautiful in every way.
The ocean is like eternity with its great big waves.
A drop of water is like holding love within your palm.
The ocean is so beautiful, it makes me relaxed and calm.
A cloud is soft like a pillow on your bed,
The sky is so peaceful, you feel like an angel
Is watching over your head.
The ocean reminds me of everlasting love,
But nothing can replace the shape of clouds above!

Laura Panczuk

It Cannot Last

Time can play tricks on the mind.
It can make you believe in things that cannot be.
It can take from you the dreams that were.
And it can continue on and leave you behind.

Time can play games with the heart.
It can banish the memory of a love so strong.
It can defeat the drive that keeps love going.
And it can build a wall so high that with the world you must part.

Time cannot be bought and time cannot be rationed.
It cannot be made to last forever,
And it cannot be delayed.
It can only be met with courage and passion.

Time must be enjoyed before it is passed.
The time we have is limited,
And the limits cannot be bargained.
And above all, it cannot last.

Jeannie Foggia

Half a Soul

One soul was sent from God above
To a house down here on Earth.
But it really was just half a soul,
Until her sister's birth.

From that day on, though they knew it not,
Their lives were tied forever
With a special love that grew over the years,
Always bringing them closer together.

As life went on, they made their own way,
Staying in touch when they could,
Sharing things as sisters do,
Eventually motherhood.

Now, our daughters are like sisters together,
How else could it possibly be?
They have us as examples of sisterly love . . .
Thank God he gave you to me!

Rosalie Ruiz

Stained

My hands are stained crimson
From the blood that you shed
You feel no more pain
Because now you are dead

The world has held you down
And I have driven in the nails
I can almost see you that day
As I hear the beating and yells

The crimson stained on my hands
Is full of fear and guilt
I can almost see you that day
Atop the cross they built

But now you are alive
And you have gone back to your home
You have washed the crimson off our hands
And now we are free nevermore to roam

Benjamin Carder

On My Mind

Today I can't get you off my mind,
I miss you so much I can't stand it,
I miss you begging me to take you fishing
I miss your temper tantrums
I miss your smile
I miss your laugher
I miss everything about you,
and most of all I miss you,
my son.

Jana Taylor

Bless This House

Bless this house, Lord, for what it's worth,
and keep it in Your glory.
That all and everything we do,
we do it all, "no worry."

Bless this house, Lord, for it will hold
the new and all the old,
For every time we feel
the heat and even all the cold.

Bless this house, Lord, and our pockets,
for all is what we share.
Even when, at times, we fail
and cabinets are bare.

Bless this house, Lord, and our relationship,
for that will keep us whole.
Only You can bless this house
and my living soul.

Lily Yvonne De La Cerda

Waters Flow

I have seen the waters flow
Falling down,
Splashing the watery surface
Then flowing with no cease to an end.

Flowing like the mist falling on your face.
It runs freely
Just as a person would run a race.
Running wildly, getting to its destination point,
It reaches the falling line
And falls downward to its new beginning.

Splashing, splashing against the water's side
It flows like a bird flying smoothly in the sky.
Creatures moving,
Ripples or what looks like the skin of an older person,
Begin to form on the shiny surface.
The sun shining down giving it more shine than ever before.

Kristina Schaeffer

Inside

It's the thought that counts
to be so kind;
love is dead,
so am I.
You broke my heart,
once again.
You broke my mind, but still I'm fine.
Jaded I may be, because of you,
well that's me, affected by nothing, no harm to me.
Keep my walls up, stay away from me.
Trapped in my own hell, how much worse could it get?
I forgave you again, that's my only regret.
I let you back in, you tore it all down,
that's what makes the world go 'round.
Life sucks, then you die,
this is where I say
goodbye.

Daniel Fraser Adams

Interracial Harmony

I see my three sons faces—my three flavors of caramel,
chocolate, and the youngest, blackberry.
In retrospect, I never thought their destiny would lend;
could ever include the melody of love between these three.
Their brides' ivory faces denote the keys of harmony
and bring to life a song delighting of precious life, you see.
I now proclaim that black and white, the twine that they shall
meet, will blend to little notes and be my grandchildren—
the perfect tones and sounds of melody.

Martha Taylor

Untitled

So here I sit, but it doesn't matter
Because I might as well not be here
I can lie in that bed, but it doesn't matter
Because I'm not wanted there
You talk in riddles, tell me to go
But not what you really want
You scream and shout
Even call names
But it doesn't matter
Because I'm still here
Physically, but not emotionally
Not anymore
I can only hear so many times
That you don't care
So it doesn't matter anymore what you say
Or what I do
I'm finished with you

Orly Lilach Kirshenbaum

True Love

What is true love?
I don't know yet,
But I am close
Close to finding you
Where you are, I don't know
I'll find you and when I do
I will read this to you
And you will know how I feel
Your my love, my one true light
You give me strength to see, know, and love
When I look into your eyes, I am blind
Because all I see is you
It will never matter where we are
Because I will be there with you
I could never leave you,
All I can do is be with you
Because I love you

Michael DeMark

Coming of Age

Little girl hugging Mamma's knee
Knowing what she wants to be
Like Mamma
Young girl resting on the ground
Watching clouds move by
New place in her imagination found . . . flying free
Teenager with short cropped hair
Silver dangling from one ear
Feeling feelings
No one knows her, no one cares, sometimes not even herself
Coming of age, what does that mean?
Every few years she becomes another age
Who will she be . . . tomorrow? Like Mamma?
No! It's a different world
It's her world now to help shape and bend
And to be bent and shaped by it
So she will age to who she truly is

Jamie Cholaki

Wiggly, Wiggly

Wiggly, Wiggly was a pig
Wiggly, Wiggly loved to dig
He'd escape every time that's all I'll say
Put him anywhere, He'd dig away
The older he got, the more rude
'Til the farmers thought they'd have some
Food
Tasted so great, you could skip the fig
No more dig for Mr. Pig
Dallas Romine

Unreturned

My heart beats for her
But hers for another.
She's afraid of change, not ready to move on
I think she'll regret my love when it is gone.

The mind flows with passion and care
For where I wanna be, she is not there
Our paths are separate with different routes
With the screams of love, the silence mutes.

The body hides the heartbreak and pain
My tears fall like quiet drops of rain
Not a day goes by when I wish she were near
In my heart, my mind, and my body, I wish she were here.

My eyes close, for I do not wish to see
The fact that she doesn't feel the same for me
With each moment, you step farther away
The love is over, nothing left to say.
Jason Paul Larsen

Untitled

Is what I want
Only grazing my fingertips
And is what I need
Even more out of my reach
What I want is what I somewhat have
Yet I miss when not at my touch
It's the little things that are lacking
And it's the little things I need
But what I need is soon forgotten
When what I want is near
Then all things are forgotten
When you are with me
Everything is okay and nothing else matters
As the door closes, physical pain arrives
The only thoughts floating through my head
When will I see you next
I miss you already
Sarah Ann Noldy

Just One of Those Days!

Have you ever woke up thinking all is well,
Then all of sudden, it rings like a bell:
The kids all fuss, fight like mad;
Pretty soon, you feel mighty bad.

You work trying to keep the peace,
Clean the house—oh, what a mess.
You try to please your mate,
But your nerves cause you to hate.

You wonder now: Why did I get out of bed? . . .
Am I going to make it, when I feel so dead? . . .
But out of all of this gloom and despair,
A new burst of energy—yes, somebody cares.

I'm glad you're up there Lord to hear
All the earthly problems when I shed a tear.
You lift me up, giving me new light to see
All your love and blessings here for me.
Lorene May Ward

I've Loved; I've Lost

I've loved and lost, but do not despair,
For love comes again when hearts still care.
Time goes by, healing begins;
Fear not, I say, for hope springs anew—it's
Part of the plan—I tell this to you:
When you hear music, again it begins.
Enjoy the dance and have a ball.
We're here for the spring, maybe not for
The fall. . . .
Kathie T. LoMonaco

You Promised

You promised me I would see the light;
But I sit here, and it's dark as night.

You said that I would never see the rain;
But if this isn't rain, then why do I feel pain.

You promised me long ago that I would always feel secure;
But the way I feel right now, I'm not all that sure.

You promised that you would take care of me;
But now you're running away, you see.

You promised me a life of fame;
But my life hasn't changed; it's still the same.

You promised me I would see the light;
But I sit here, and it's dark as night.

You can forget me, 'cause from my thoughts you're dismissed;
But always remember that you promised.
Jessica Lynn Mitchell

Dream

A Dream:
The magic of the soul
The hopes of the heart
Deep down where emotions start.
A dream:
In so many ways
Is the only things that get us
Through our days
A hope that lies hidden something unknown
Except for when you're all alone
A Dream:
Is really to the mind
And is something that will happen in time.
A Dream:
Never lose it
Never let it get away
Tomorrow will be the dream of today.
Heather Frey

Anastasia

As I stare into your eyes
I dream of life without lies
With me and you together at last
Asking God to forget the past
My life meant so little before you
I'm just hoping that you someday feel this too
However, merely the chance that you may
Brings to me a wonderful day
Dreams are happiness in disguise
Dreams are life's little surprise
To think of something that will never be true
I just can't help loving you
I just can't help loving you
I am living a perfect life it seems
Then I wake up and see that these are just dreams
Why can't this dream be true?
I just can't help loving you
Chris Michael Hoffman

The Dress

I didn't want it, was even a little too big
but mom said it was the one.
It was violet, the most expensive of the rest,
found only at the best boutique.
The front was too low, the shoulders were too bulky,
patterned with flowers and . . . oh, what a mess.
I knew I was going to have to take it back.
But come the night of the dance, when I walked in, I knew . . .
It had to be the dress.

Jana Fay Rettig

I Still Wonder

Born in a shack, girdled with poverty—
You learn to live without a cry or a smile.
With the floor bruising your skin, ants crawling up your toes,
You took your first step. Without pride,

You were my prince without a throne or crown
Or even a king to guide you through.
For a silver spoon, I gave you love.
Somewhere along the line, I failed you in lessons of trust.

In a grownup world, you stand before me—
Your eyes still carry the shadow of sadness.
Years of struggle have brought us to this day.
I am proud of what you have become.

I hear praises everywhere you go.
A great young man you have become.
Once in a million years, I see you smile,
But still I wonder what makes you laugh.

I. Beatrice Fernando

Silly Me

Silly me,
Why didn't I see?
Why didn't I realize it was all coming to me?
I was blind in the situation,
It caused me pain through this demonstration.
If fate made it happen this way,
Then it should have happened that day.
I should have stopped myself from distortion,
Instead I created an unstoppable magic potion.
I nearly collapsed in the act,
But my mother had my back.
I put her in my disposition,
And created the worst head to head collision.
Me by myself,
And her with a frown.
Me looking shamefully,
And her on the ground.

Anna Belenky

Legacy

I dedicate this poem to my wonderful parents, Sara and Leroy Grindle.
My physical body is a mortal shell,
A temporary home where my soul dwells.

As I seek for goodness to prevail,
I must shun evil and all it entails.

If my earthly deeds reflect kindly love,
Someday I'll rejoice in the kingdom above.

But, if instead, I live with selfish intent,
My soul's misery I'll surely invent.

My time will come in the twinkling of an eye,
And my soul will depart to embrace the sky.

Let my legacy be, when this physical life ends,
That I lived by Grace, left nothing to mend.

Janice Trammell Cannon

Janel, God's Gracious Gift

Her life was given by God above
No choice of hers but for us to love
Our hearts were broken when we had learned
Her life would be different than the one we had preferred
The life she had to give was one of everlasting concern
As we think of all the pain she has endured
Her smile, her laughter made us assured
What God had given from above
Was our miracle for us to love

Gay Lenore Sanchez

True Love

You say you want to be more than friends
But you don't know where true love ends
This lustful way you show your feelings
In the end, it leaves me reeling

You think it's true love that you show
But I can tell you just don't know
True love waits until you're married
And there's no burden to be carried

If you can't keep your hands off someone
It probably means you're only in it for fun
You have no genuine feelings for them
You think that it's the sweetest of sins

But sin is sin, and so I say
And always, until comes the day
When I finally reach Heaven's gates
I will always say . . . that true love waits

Clinton James Wilcox

I Love Writing Poetry Each Day!

I love writing poetry each day.
It's a way of taking your worries away.
You relax as you write, and you cry a bit, too,
Because you review your own life and all you did do.
It's a way of expressing your feelings each day,
And it's a way of taking your tensions away.
It's a way of remembrances and your real feelings, too
Of all you've done in your life and still want to do!
I'm getting older, but it doesn't bother me
Because I know I'll keep aging each day, you see,
As you will, too, each day to day,
And you, too, someday will pass away.
I look forward to seeing my Lord someday,
And thanking Him sincerely for all He did do
For me, for my family and for you too!
Boo-hoo, Boo-hoo, Boo-hoo, Boo-hoo,
I want so much, my Lord, to be with you!

Margaret N. Mosanko

Ode to the Singing Spirits

In this world of matter, the world of sin
Where the voice of evil and the power of whim
Engage full effort to takeover and win,
. . . still, the sun of good would rise and shine

The bells of goodness would always ring
In the hearts of those who faithfully think,
"Never say 'never that a broken wing
Would heal,' and thus, the dove is fine"

Sooner or later, lust shall bring
Its own infraction: no blood but ink
But voices of those who always sing
Shall throw a party with cheese and wine

May all enjoy this life and cheer it
Playing a melody on the chords of the spirit
Singing with the voice of good whose merit:
Breakfasting on whims before they, on it, dine

Ghaleb M. Karouni

Learning to Wait

I turned my head to see if you were there.
But when I turned the space was bare.
So I walked on in faith that you would come
along.
Not noticing that I didn't wait for you to
lead me on.
As I walked I felt your presence escape.
It was then I realized that I should
learn to wait.

Tamara Nicole Guyton

My Prayer

Cleanse me, dear Lord, of my selfishness and greed.
Give me not what I want, but things that I need.
Make me hungry for your word, on that I will feed.
Make me thankful, dear Lord, for your mercies so free.

I am blessed by so much that you've given to me.
I've a roof o'er my head and a bed where I sleep.
I have food on my table, clothes to cover my back.
You've provided so much, there is little I lack.

Nothing, no nothing, but your kindness and grace,
To help me e'erywhere I go and with each day I face.
Just be my guide, comfort, strength, and my stay.
Help me always to love you and never too far to stray.

Thanks for all you have given, thanks for all you have done.
But most of all, precious Lord, thanks for giving your son
That we all can have new life and someday with you reign.
To live with you up in Heaven, as a child of the king.

Shari A. Angle

Mother Earth

Why is the world against me?
Why can't I get peace in this world?
The world that gave birth to every
living thing that I've learned to love hates me.
Everything I do in this world doesn't work.
Everything the world does doesn't work for me.
Why is the world against me?
The world that I've learned to love
the world that I've learned to call home.
My life is a mess because everything isn't working.
Am I doing something wrong to deserve this?
Am I the one to blame for all of this trouble?
Am I in this world to suffer?
I don't know the answers to all these questions.

I want the Earth to be my mother
and give me love, just like a mother
does to her kids.

Fumu Twala

Three Little Words

So easy to say when you don't mean it,
yet so difficult to say when you do.
Strange how three little words can mean and do so much.
When it's what you want to hear,
it can bring such joy and happiness,
or pain and confusion when you don't.
Three little words, which can so easily be felt,
yet so difficult to explain.
And different levels are so hard to describe to
one who doesn't or can't feel the same.
Three little words that wouldn't be said
if one didn't feel so.
Maybe "I love you" is so difficult for me to say
because I haven't said it in a long time to
somebody true,
or maybe because it means so much when I say it
to you.

Andrew Gehron

Love Began to Grow

Love began to grow from a cold heart
Like cupid had shot me with his love dart

I had thought it was better not to love again at all
But I guess after a while, I began to fall

Everything about him was great
He made me miss the love that I once had hate

Now, I love him with all my heart
I just wish we could be together and not so far apart

Andrea Ann Greway

Incomplete

Darkness everywhere I look, it surrounds, com-
pounds everything I breathe, touch. I fall
forgetting all every step of the way. I must
see, can't be blind to all, there's nowhere
else to fall. In my life with no escape it all
closes in to suffocate. Growing despair it's
everywhere trapped within me. Time predicates
the pain which escalates the shame, which
eliminates nothing. Growing up to swallow all
in today and tomorrow. Will it ever finish me off?
Dark mind, immune to light, everything backwards, not left to right. Looking within, back
at me, it all seems wrong. I see my shadow now
but then it's gone. Oh, god help me to see the
light buried inside of me. Now, yeah now's the
time to help me escape me.

Jason Hudgens

Life

As the years roll by and my hair turns gray,
As I sit and watch my grandchildren at play,
Life seems to have passed by in just a day.

Wasn't it yesterday that I was a little girl,
Putting wood shavings in my hair for curls;
In my fanciest skirt, I would whirl and whirl.

Then I was a teenager with a neat boyfriend,
I was in love with love that would never end;
I did not know my heart would break, not bend.

As a bride, my groom stood at my side.
It was a very fast roller coaster ride.
In my heart, true love would always abide.

Now here I am, an old, tired grandmother.
It's a job I would trade for no other.
Still, I wish to go back to being a mother.

Mary Jo Griese

Just Believe . . .

Jesus reached out His nail-pierced hand to me.
He said, I've come to set you free.
The pain and scars that are in your past,
Most assuredly will not last.

The father you've longed for, you'll find in me.
I alone am the missing key.
Take my hand and walk this way.
The price for you, I've already paid.

Trust in me with all of your heart.
Then from you, I will never depart.
Give me your life to mold into my plans.
You will be safe in my hands.

My love will fill the emptiness that you feel inside.
No longer will you need to run and hide.
For once you will feel whole and complete.
Through me there isn't anything that you can't beat.

Rachelle Faye Drabek

Storm Cloud

You're like a little storm cloud
High above the trees

You're like a little storm cloud
Making a pleasant breeze

I know you like it raining . . .
And when it's raining, you like it to stay

But I don't think you'll like it . . .
It's not raining today
Stephanie Patricia Kilgore

Skate Buds

I'm skating all alone,
Can barely land a trick;
Hear a ring on the phone,
Hey, maybe it's a chick.

It's my best friend, Chuck,
And he says he wants to skate.
Finally, to my way, some luck,
for skating alone, I do hate.

He arrives, my spirits rise,
And my skills come of the mud.
Then, in the corner of my eye,
I see Eric, my other best bud.

My skills increase even more.
Together, there is no trick we can't throw.
We work ourselves right to the core,
With each other's help, we've all gone pro.
Jon Levi Robinson

My Sunshine

In the morning when I awake,
Before I can wipe the sleep from my eyes,
I think of you.
As the morning turns to afternoon,
You are still in my thoughts:
I think of your warm smile—
It makes the edges of my mouth creep upward.
Afternoon ages into evening;
I think of your eyes,
Eyes that can melt diamonds.
The anticipation of getting to talk to you
Swells inside me;
The possibility of seeing you makes my heart race.
As I lay in bed waiting for sleep to come,
I hold my pillow and think of you.
I slip off to sleep smiling.
You are with me always.
John B. Sheppard

Thoughts

Thoughts of her running through my mind
Though my heart knows she is safe and sound
I'll think of her whenever I need to unwind
Only to her my heart is legally bound

My thoughts of her are only happy ones
For sad actions I'd rather not recall
She lighted my darkness and shone
Like a beam of light down a narrow hall

She is the meaning of my life
And when I see her unhappy or sad
It cuts like the blade of a knife
And I just feel horribly bad

However this could all be a dream
When I finally wake up in reality
Things could not be what they seem
Who knows she may have thoughts of me
Nick Jonathon Gilpin

Ripples

A flaming ball is drowning in the ocean.
It reaches out, but there is no one to help it.
It brings a quiet peace over the world.
A fish smoothly glides through the water,
Blissfully unaware of the drama it has witnessed.
Underwater fireflies come out and dance in the ripples
As an ivory orb sets itself in the sky.
A quiet washing lullaby sings the fish to sleep.
Beauty reigns supreme.
Elizabeth Barnes

Being Me

I'm a woman, a dreamer, a lover
and a little girl; I'm me . . .
I'm a writer, a poet, and a wisher
Don't you see that I'm me . . .
I'm just not everything I wish I could be
I'm a tender heart, a taker, a giver,
and sometimes a keeper,
I'm me . . . trying to please everyone,
to be everything they want me to be
I'm the ugly duckling turning into a swan;
my features change all the time
I'm me . . . always the mysterious one
I'm the quiet one and the sensitive one too
The watcher and the seeker of what's true
I'm all these things and maybe more, learning to live
And to adore the me who doesn't ask or tell,
But lets me just be me.
Laura Tilford

The Perfect Tan

Here I am
Feeling superior to those I left behind
On top of the city looking at the mountains
With nothing particular in mind

Lying here in my bed of grass
This beautiful sunny day
So quiet, so peaceful
With no clouds to get in the way

Soaking up the sun
Feeling like the trees around me
Collecting all of its warmth
Feeling its serenity

Feeling no urgency
Feeling no demand
This is complete pleasure
This is the perfect tan
Jason L. Burns

West Falmouth Harbor

A place of beauty nature made,
A place most worth an accolade
For all the pleasure it provides
As gently, shoreline feels the tides.

Some small, white sails adorn the sky
When young and old set out to try
To win the race, or just have fun
Relaxing 'neath the summer Sun.

A charming boathouse on the shore
Lends extra interest for the more
Artistic souls who sit, restraint,
Behind each canvas, daubing paint.

Depending on the time of year,
Some swimming scallops may appear.
Not all those shucked will reach the stove,
For eaten raw they're gourmet trove.
Garfield Manning Arthur

Untitled

The particles of sand, which comprise a beach,
are like moments of time.
Each is unique and special
and fulfills the destiny of each human being.
Then the waves of the ocean alter the order
and provide each person
with their unique destiny while on the Earth.
And only God can know
what that destiny may be.

David C. Mathews

Untitled (Nisha's Poem)

Live on for me and do all things the same
It's too hard to keep my sanity through all this rain
My eyes are welling, outburst of regret
I left words unspoken, love unexpressed

Memories in frames are failed attempts
To keep your smile replete
The graphic picture of your sleeping body
I find hard to defeat

If only someone could explain to me
All they say is it was destiny
I don't understand why you were ripped from me
They say God took you gently

I didn't even hear you leave
You escaped so quietly
I was too caught up in me to see
One day you could become a memory

Barrett Frances Jessica

I Cry

I cry for the people who never find love.
I cry for those who never have enough.
I cry for children lost and yet to be found.
I cry for babies whose fathers aren't around.

I cry for victims of domestic violence.
I cry for those afraid to break the silence.
I cry for people who are alone.
I cry for feelings that can't be shown.

I cry for those who cannot see.
I cry for human beings still not free.
I cry for those who cannot hear.
I cry for those who live in fear.

I cry for love that only goes one way.
I cry for anyone who hates every day.
I cry for all we've gone through.
I cry for me and I cry for you.

Krissy Beth Raab

Somebody Else?

Why do I run from the reality of me?
Scared perhaps that the person I am to be
is a person worth nothing—I run

far away from me and pretend to have
everything under control
yet my strength is nonexistent
and I am weak
I am scared and confused—I run

A race worth nothing; no prize in the end
only a life lived in pain
and all kept within
still—I run

I remind myself of someone else,
the person I want to be
Who it is exactly? I couldn't tell
All I know is it isn't me—I run

Amanda Marie Ferguson

Vacant

Your emptiness is ripping at my seams
And my nothingness is hard to face.
My tears are hollow
And your words are bare.
I stole that twinkle from your eye.
But now I've lost it.
I gave you the hope I had inside and you threw it away.
Now what is left is a shell.
Vacant and broken.

Jacqueline Callaway

Safe Place to Fall

I'm so tired
all I want is to sleep
all I want is to dream.
I want someone to believe in my goals,
and to tell me a story when my eyes won't close.
Someone to tell me it's okay when all my open doors have closed.
I'm so tired
all I want is to cry
all I want is to leave.
I want someone to be there to wipe my tears,
and see that all my walls aren't as thick as they appear.
Someone to comfort me through my deepest fears.
I'm so tired
all I want is to love
all I want is to let go.
I want someone to be there during the storm,
and take me to this soft place to fall.

Danielle Gantt

What Is Weakness?

Can it be pinpointed, thumb-tacked
on the maps of our characters?
Does it pervade the pathos
of our personalities?
Permeating our actions, like a lamprey
sucking on our host of intentions.
Is it meted out evenly or more to the bold,
less to the meek?
Is it prominent in the boastful,
elusive in the humble?
Does its existence make us
prone to judgement,
pliable to influence?
Does it warrant the first stone's throw,
Or does its ubiquity quarantine us all
from unobtainable divinity?
Liberating us to revel in our humanity.

Kathleen Jeanne O'Leary

The Last Soldier

What is going to happen when
The last soldier dies?
Who will be the pall bearers?
Who will say the last goodbye?
Who will be there to cry?
Will they have a lonely stone?
All alone, no one home, all had gone on.
Will they have a flag for the coffin?
Will they know; did we thank them often?

We need to think of what they did for our homes, lives, and land.
So many left to fight and protect.
Many died, kill or be killed, they said.
The rest came home not the same,
Never speaking of the bloody rain.
To their graves the stories go; history to never know.
What will we do when the last one dies?
Who will be there to say goodbye; to cry?

Barbara Cheryl Tepper

Sunset

Along the distant horizon there lies a sunset.
How far away it is and how close it looks, I really don't get.

Various colors of clouds above are constantly in motion,
The majestic reflection beaming across the ocean.

Sounds of waves crashing brings music to my ears.
Just watching a sunset clears my mind and all my fears.

Sadly I see the sunset disappear right before my eyes
As day goes to night and the sunset dies.

Joseph Alfiler De Los Reyes

Dream Come True

Summer vacation was over
And I arrived back to my rental cover.
As I prepared to return to the classroom,
A friend pulled me from my gloom.

It seems a house was up for sale
In a price range that was ideal.
The location was great,
But the house wasn't top rate.

I did some research into the buy,
And decided it could be suitable by and by.
As I made my purchasing plans,
Excitement grew as we shook hands.

After years of paying rent,
My money will finally be properly spent.
A home owner at last.
This is going to be a blast!

Sheila May Baker

Crazy Holidays—a Children's Poem

There once was a girl named Sarah Hayes,
who thought she knew all about holidays.
She said that on Easter bunnies hatched from eggs,
and the Easter baskets delivered themselves on chocolate legs!
She said that on Thanksgiving the turkey first had to shave
before presenting himself on that thankful day.
The potatoes and cranberries go off and get married—
the turkey jumped over the moon—
while the gravy ran away with the spoon!
She said that on Christmas our own Christmas tree
stays up all night watching TV.
She claims that all stockings go caroling that night,
and Santa's cookies had an enormous fight.
She is just plain crazy, you just have to see!
But . . . come to think about it, the little girl is me.
Because I too make up stories and tell people they're true,
I think we all have done that before—haven't you?

Marissa Rohanna Maharaj

Sunset over the Sycamores

The wind blows softly
Over the tall sycamores.
The water stands still
As a heron plucks a water snake from the pool.

Over the tall sycamores,
The sun winds slowly down.
As a heron plucks a water snake from the pool,
All creatures flee.

The sun winds slowly down
As the shadow rises.
All creatures flee
From the sound of a gunshot.

As the shadow rises,
The wind blows softly.
From the sound of a gunshot,
The water stands still.

Alyssa Claire Johnson

In His Arms

In his arms a dream comes and goes.
After a while it fades into gray,
Thus beginning a new kind of day.
Full of hope, love, and joyous inspiration,
His arms wrap around you in loving desperation.
Never to want another living soul,
He kisses you just to let you know,
That no matter what the day may bring
You will be in his arms for eternity.

Ashlie Keeling

Picture of Dreams

Breezes fresh as births of youthful young,
They blow tunes of songs that were never sung.
A beautiful land away from the slum,
Where things are the whole and not a crumb.
Mountains with wide whirlwinds within wonderful wonders,
Which waste and wash away harsh thoughts of thumping thunders.
Shining streams, streaming sounds of a spectacular superb story,
While wide and wet green grass graze give gapes of glorified glory.
Big bold bushes delivering black slithery shadowy spots,
But only courageous, colorful colors of habitation that never rot.
Clouds caught cleverly in creative creation,
For righteous reasons of resting relaxation.
That dream was created from my hands,
The mountains, ocean, sky, and sands.
My idea of a perfect world
Where things are straight,
But too bad they are swirled.

John P. Dessereau

In Memory

I wake up each morning and think of her;
Wondering if I will ever accomplish what she has done.
Can I be so loving and forgiving?
Can I be so vivacious and full of life?

Throughout the day as I grow weary, I think of her.
She had such strength and empathy.
Can I be so selfless and generous?
Can I show strength and yet remain soft?

When I have dinner with my family, I think of her.
She cherished every day and spoke with tenderness to everyone.
Can I have that thankfulness for life?
Can I find the patience to be gentle?

At night in the dark, I think of her.
She was our angel in life, and now, she's our angel in death.
I think of her every day.
I cry for her every night.

Heather Marie Blake

My Song

Can you hear my song?
Can you hear my song?
The song serves as a melody of a sad rhythm,
A sad rhythm that imitates the sounds
Of the starving and dying children,
The sounds of lonely land,
Naked without the people who were stolen
And put on ships that are now sunken.
Can you hear my song?
Can you hear my song?
The sad beat has now turned into a happy beat.
The beat plays the sounds of my people overcoming.
It plays the sounds of my ancestor's shackles being removed
And them being set free.
It plays the sound of Martin's dreams becoming a reality.
Can you hear my song?
It sings of you and me!

Clarine Thomas

Remember

Remember.
Remember me before you sleep,
Love forever you will keep.
Reality and dreams clash with life,
Exactly the way we want every night.
So many times I cried thinking of you,
Dreading a thought I already knew.
Even though you have better things to do,
Remember that I will always forever love you.

Tiffany Lynn Kuhn

Life

Look around at all the things that make us smile;
That make us cry.
What is going on? Why so many changes?
Not knowing one day to the next what challenges we may face.
We are on a journey, a never-ending journey.
Maybe I should think about it a little more clearly.
I have to take a stand and be strong.
I have to stay focused and be determined.
I have to face the good and the bad.
I have to move forward and keep my head up,
For this journey is too long.
A journey that will determine who I am.
I can't stand for what isn't right;
I have to pray that God guide me,
For this life will have many obstacles—
Ups and downs, also twists and turns.
God please keep me safe, for this journey is much too long. . . .

Retha Louis

The Nightmare

I sit on frozen waters; stars being eaten by the darkness.
Around me, nameless faces waiting to consume me.
I cry out to the heavens—breathy, ghostly, soundless.
I run towards the shelter in my desperate need to flee.
But they are all around me, wanting to include me.
And Lady Darkness leads them, a staff upon her hip.
They are eager soldiers, not a coward in their ranks.
And I am but a stranger in this land of no escape.
My legs are now both leaden.
Deadness underneath me.
My arms are rendered powerless in my attempt to fight.
And now I flail out madly with feathered arms beside me;
Their impact landing softly upon my enemy.
Now suddenly the darkness gives way to Lady Morning.
She wakens me and settles me into her lovely arms.
Lightness all around me bathes me in its softness.
And the frightening lair of darkness is a million miles away.

Dori Formby Weidmer

An Angel's Journey with the Flower Fairy

When you walk into a garden, what do you see?
Do you see the flower fairies looking down on me?
Have you joined them yet?
The angels I've asked say
They need more flower angels like you
To listen and guide, to teach and be taught,
To forever care and never cease to be amazed.
The angels I've heard
Have told me life does change.
One day, we will meet face to face.
Until that time, we shall remain in our place,
Still learning to trust, as the angels fly on by,
Painting their petals, what a detailed little job,
Every flower so perfect and created with love.
May your love never end,
May your heart grow with more friends.
May your life change its pace, only to see an angel's face.

Angela M. Grout

Eight Years

To me only death and pain linger near
I stand alone to master other's fear
with the power to cure the sun of its shame
upon my heart shadows have laid claim.
Oh, mother . . . it has been eight years since I cried
there is only emptiness inside.
I . . . I am.
Only I have the courage of a light I do not know
and the HOPE for a future longed for so.

Jennifer C. Lee

Love's Eye

Have you felt love within your heart
And did you know right from the start
That love within a person's eyes
They tell the truth, there are no lies

So look into my eyes and see
A love forever meant to be
Down deep within my soul are you
Your heart so sweet, your love so true

Reach for my hand and hold it tight
Together we shall conquer night
Death has no toll on love this strong
A road that's straight, this road so long

So hold me now, I sweetly kiss
My dreams with you I'll never miss
A feeling strong from up above
When in my heart that feeling's love. . . .

Steven J. Therrien

December's Candle

Darkness had set in,
Surrounding everything, both body and soul.
Who could have guessed that
Everything would eventually see the light once more?
There was no way to know when,
But somehow, they knew it would eventually occur.
The darkness, now only a memory.
Remembered, but rarely thought of.
Something that seemed to be so simple
Changed everything forever.
Though all the darkness was gone in minutes.
Nothing could explain it.
Though everyone knew what did it.
It was not a person alone,
It was people who gave a little more,
Those people who were there to listen,
Even if it seemed they had heard the story before.

Jessica W.

A Nation Still Lives

Yesterday, a tragedy, but tomorrow still lives on.
Terrorists attacked our freedom. Now many are dead and gone.
Some Americans tried to help and
Their lives were taken, too.
Others are living heroes,
But the devastation is still new.
A nation that stands so powerful
Now watches with fear and fright
As the media replays the actions
Of the four hijacked flights.
Though the casualty numbers are high
And the injured are many as well,
There lives still a nation
Through this tremendously deep hell.
Now it's time to pull together;
Put all our differences aside,
And fight as one great country with liberty and national pride.

Carey Dawn Stanton

My Love

My love is as a burning fire inside
I look toward you for help
You guide me, my love, with a light so bright
I cannot seem to go any other way
But to follow the path you have put before me
My love burning inside is never ending
I will follow you with all my heart and with nothing to turn back to
I thank you, my love, and my God, for putting me on this Earth
And I thank you for everything you have given me

Rebecca Lippold

Never Forgotten!

Gloom darkness fear, figments of our nations's imagination?
Unfortunately not!
The pain, torture, and despair are all too very real.
You left them for dead, their families and friends forever stripped.
All the victims of this tragic event shall always be remembered,
Their loss forever engraved in our hearts and on our minds.
Our pain is your own personal gain, you sick person.
Know this; for all the pain you cause, all the blood you spill—
You will never have our souls!
The damage you have done is to our physical being.
You brought chaos and devastation to our lives.
Unfortunately for the victims' families, friends, and neighbors—
Your disgusting acts of terrorism will forever remain.
Together, as a nation united, we shall pray that time will heal all.
One day you and your horrendous acts shall be a faded memory.
We now take a stand once and for all.
This is America and forever united, we stand!

Robbin Bernice Gullett

Remember

Remember the days when we were tight,
so tight I could still feel your embrace at night.
How could I have let you go
without thinking twice of my loss.
I only wish I hadn't done so.
'Cause now I know it wasn't lust.
Remember the secret meeting we had
which ended with me feeling bad?
How wrong of me to still care
when obviously you're over me,
leaving my broken heart bare—
no matter what, that's how it's going to be.
I'll always remember those days.
I try to leave them in the past where they belong,
but they come back to me in many ways.
Now those days are glued to my heart strong.
Remember.

Christelle Leora Seide

Bandit

We doze before the glowing embers,
Dreaming of days we've never seen.
You romp in dreams within your slumbers,
Your paws are twitching as you dream.

Oh, if we'd just been young together,
Oh, what walks we would have had.
You'd chase the rabbits through the heather,
And I'd run after, proud and glad.

The summer wind would cool our faces,
And rumple up your shining fur.
And oh, we'd see such wond'rous places
That we had never known were there.

But I was old when you were little,
And couldn't match your learning joy,
And now we both are old and brittle,
And only dream of pup and boy.

Roger Tempelton Stevens

Wish

I wish I were a flower blooming in the spring.
I wish I were a goldfish swimming in a cool spring.
I wish I were a rabbit hopping from tree to tree.
I wish I were a deer running gracefully.
I wish I were a dolphin playing happily in the sea.
I wish I were all these things living happily,
As God would want us to be.
Without all the peer pressure,
In peace and in harmony.

Kristy Holkenbrink

An American Tribute

From the sky came Satan's allies
To take the lives of those who had no clue;
Not once, but four.
Taking life with no regrets,
Satan's proud of his allies—
Their job was done with great success.
For the thousands who died so fast,
God will keep them close at hand.
For when Satan's allies meet with him,
They will soon understand murder is not
An act of heroism, but an act of coward.
Satan will show them the way to their new home he made for them.
For the many who died so quick,
God's home now is yours.
So God bless those who died and also those who have to carry on,
For God will keep them close to him.
God bless and God bless America.

John R. Turner

Trap Addict

Relationship is a drug . . .
You get high, excited, and happy first.
You get drawn in it,
and desire it more and more second.
When you decide to stay away from it,
you cannot stop thinking of it any longer.
Although you try to forget it,
you cannot help remembering it.
Then you get troubled, tortured,
and suffer, so you hurt yourself.
You feel like running away from reality,
and giving up everything in your life.
You lose yourself in the end. . . .

Love is a poison. . . .
It hurts me, torments me, suffers me, and then kills me. . . .

But we keep repeating it, right?

Misato Mimi Mukasa

Adoration

Style, charm, insatiable flair,
Wonderful smile, wavy hair,
Staring at me with eyes that care:
I am in awe with my situation.
Soft sweet pecks on my cheek,
Rubs me down head to feet,
Shouts from rooftops, yet covertly discreet;
Such a beautiful secret.
Glowing aura that everyone sees,
Smiles catch on like rampant disease,
Richly filled with nectar from honey bees;
You're my cavity-causing candy.
Patiently loving and eager to please . . .
Heart of gold, compassion extreme,
Capable of a love supreme,
My picture of an outstanding human being:
Your essence is incredible.

Monica Griffin

Drowning

Of tears, when does a stream become a river,
When an emotion, a tear?
The transparent line eludes me and I'm
In a state of exhaustion.
I am drowning in the tears I have not shed.
My love loves me not—or does he?
Who can tell without a straight word?
The juvenile approach persists and the water
Floods my lungs.

Shirley McLaughlin

Bright Lights

The sky is so bright I wish I
Were as bright as the bright
Light I see in the sky inside
I'm very dark and no one wants
To be my friend when I am in
Need but when everyone else is
In need of a good friend then
Is the only time I get friends
And I turned my back and explained why I was not going
To be there for them and then
They come back by saying
Something smart. People
Don't even ask how I feel
At all it makes me sick but
I know I am better than that so every time I look into the
Sky then I realize I have to
Go on with my business.

Ashley Erin Tobako

Angel

I look into my soul—and realize I've lost all sense of control
I've fallen for you—please let this be true.
Let our love always feel new.
Wrapping myself underneath your arm,
I am free from harm.
I never thought I could feel like this.
Emotions of happiness, no sorrow, no fear of tomorrow.
Happy and content
Erasing the memories of all the lonely nights I have spent.
Warmth and love
As if you've been sent down
From somewhere up above.
Friends before anything
Comforting and caring
Warm embrace
Putting a permanent smile
Upon my face.

Elin Jordan

Dante's Path: A Testament to a Child's Fear

The sky fell down today.
Gasps surrounded me . . .
shouts of fear,
astonishment—
as we watched the world crumble.
Pain envelopes me.
I trespass in the company of tortured faces,
bleeding eyes.
My apathy lays in shards, shattered by fanatical visions.
They died to show me.
I am forsaken—I tread fearfully through the valley.
Hatred flashes. Doom screams.
A booming testament of terror.
I open the door.
I step through the old, familiar smell.
I am in hell.

Courtney Hancock

Heartbeat

Would it continue . . .
If you weren't around?
Could it go on . . .
If your existence would cease?

Falling, stumbling toward forever
floating, swimming in love's river.
Hauntingly enchanting . . .
A beam of sunlight bursting through a dark cloud.

Hypnotizing moments of heat and lust,
Mesmerizing lifetimes of passion and love.

Tammy Mollohan

Thy Mountains, Part II

Let thy mountains sculpt you
Such chiseled faces o' time
Eternal seas wash so deeply blue
Within thy artist's living rhyme

Lose thyself within thy fold . . .

Their healing spirit flows into you
Trickling endless to thy distant sea
Scribe o' eagle wing in review
Shaping thy forms in enchanted mystery
Yea, lest their story ne'er be told . . .

Come, free thy tired mind
Explore riches o' thy inner soul
In nature what treasures find
What lasting pleasures enroll
Secret harmonies o' life embold . . .

Dennis Wangerin

September 11, 2001

Whisper of work,
Hum of the computers,
Laughter at the water cooler,
An explosion of noise.
Then it was quiet.

Among smoke and gloom
Rises a sound growing stronger
Confusion . . . unbelieving . . . desperation;
Screams . . . sirens . . . horns . . . crying—
Then it was quiet.

A part of us all
Among the ashes and papers;
Buried with the heroes—our brothers and sisters—
Voices never heard again.
It is too quiet.

Monica M. Michael

Let the Love Flow

When your heart is hurting and you feel tied
up in knots, let go of the angry feelings.
Once again, you'll feel topnotch.

An angry and resentful heart
can find no peace or joy.
Always hurting, always burning;
the fruits of love continuously destroyed.

Forgive those who do you wrong;
don't harbor thoughts of getting even.
Let love overcome the hurt;
the hurt and pain will soon be leaving.

Don't let your anger be in control.
You must learn how to forgive.
Stay in charge, let love flow forth.
Only then, can you truly live.

Sharon Abigail Anderson

I Remember

I remember when I was walking.
I heard a lot of people talking.
I looked up in the air; I breathed good air.
My eyes were getting blurry;
I thought my sneakers were flurry.
I put on my Nike Air and scream everywhere.
People glance at me; I was dressing fancy.
I was talking to Nancy, and she said,
"Boy, nasty—you look like a ghastly."
I went home crying.
I knew my brother was lying about ten dollars.
I just put on my shirt and tucked in my collar.

Alvin Brown

Surrender

To quit with sweet surrender
To no longer know the struggle
To only float through all that's before me
Oh! Yes! I too am tired
Tired of empty arms
And meaningless conversations
Tired of struggling in a world
Where no one knows, nor cares
Then I think of you
And in the name of love, I stand
Chained to the struggling forces within me
A human bondage I cannot ignore
For though this floating is so tempting
I know that it is the fantasy
Our bondage is my reality
I simply cannot surrender

Patricia A. Stock

I Am Somebody

I am somebody
I wonder exactly who though
I hear people say I am a child of God
I am a child of God

I pretend to be someone special
I feel other's care and love
I touch my own heart with questions
I worry who I really am
I am somebody

I understand now that I am a child of God
I say I know who I am
I dream about Heaven
I try to endure to the end
I hope I will be back in my heavenly Father's care

I am a child of God

Holly Louisa Casper

A Mother's Reflection

A mother's reflection in the kitchen window
staring into the summer air,
wondering where children are,
deep in thoughtful prayer.
A mother teaches the truth about all things,
showing she has the answer to life's trials.
She points to the Word of God,
which has taken her over many a mile.
She teaches the truth that only Jesus gives
to her children and their friends,
living her life as an example of His Word,
always going to the Lord when daylight ends.
A mother's reflection, a child can't do without,
for she teaches what true love really is.
I thank God for special mothers,
for they show me that Jesus lives. . . .

Karen Hopkins

Waves of Life

As I ride the waves of life,
I wonder where they might carry me;
I wonder what oceans lie ahead;
I wonder what dark storms and winds I will encounter.
Will the waves carry me towards my dreams,
Or will they lead me astray?
Will I find what I search for in earth's careless breath,
Or will it be yet another day without so much as a breeze?
For now, I sail on through life's perilous journey,
Not knowing what the future may hold,
Continuously wondering, continuously hoping,
To find all that these waves of life may hold.

Griffin William Bonacci

Let's Face It

I gave you life; I gave you breathe;
I gave you everything to pass the test

Of life's greatest challenges that you face;
You can go it at your own pace.

Whether you win or lose is up to you;
There is nothing more that I can do.
You have to start at the bottom to get over the hill,
And all in between is done by will.

Look at your challenges one by one
To see how many you have won.

The sacrifices you make as you journey through
Will make the test easier to do.
If you have held on and done your best,
I truly believe you will pass the test.

Jewel Virginia Norris

The Bridge to the Country above the One That Is, Part II

I will dress and rise,
wearing the clothes of the morning country.
Stand in the light of the morning country,
defending it
using this light and shelter it.
In it I find my dearest love
dressed in eternal, holy love
I will find eternal victory.
The certainty of the morning country
also hides your hopes.
In the light of the morning country,
but hidden to your eyes,
are holy rooms
filled with dreams and secrets
owned by my love.

Margareth Giskegarrd

The Farm

A building made of stone and wood
Barns and land around it stood
Held a family for many years
Watched each event, happiness and tears
A man and a woman with love in their hearts
Pledged their love, never to part
Had eleven children and many concerns
A lot of work, while the sun still burns
The house and the buildings could have told their tales
Of children growing and babies' wails
These people made this house a home
The house and the buildings couldn't do it alone
For many years, these buildings stood
Many a meal was cooked with wood
Carrying water from the well
Oh, what stories this farm could tell

Sona Lou Hollingshead

What If?

I wonder what it would be like, if I weren't,
Who I am, if something else were different.
Would I be able to do what I can? If I
Wasn't able to run right, would I have any
Friends, or if I looked unusual, would they
Be there till the end? I'm not sure that I
Would like to be different in any way; I'm
Just happy that I'm myself and that I am
Here today. I'll take this into
Consideration, a vow onto myself, to treat
Everyone with respect, and be thankful for
My health.

Danial S. Border

What Really Hurts

If I had only known
The way my life would be,
I really would have shown
A whole other side of me.
I wouldn't have been so easy to read,
I wouldn't be hurting like I do.
I wouldn't have worn my heart on my sleeve,
And I wouldn't be missing you.
I've been attracted to heartache forever,
And I believe I always will.
I thought that we'd always be together,
Now I'm too hurt to feel.
The cold that exists now in my eyes
Was put there by your words.
Yes, I do mean your lies.
And that's what really hurts.

Kasey Griggs

Masks

Lying down, under the dirt,
behind the pain and in front of hurt;
I can see the eyes I used to see,
that were drilled in the mask that was made for me.
Ah, that precious mask that I'd always wear,
to hide myself from vanity fair.
It would allow me to smile, laugh, and pretend,
and I could mix with others and fit right in.
But now it's over, and I see the truth.
Everyone wears a mask, in everything they do
Slipping it on again, just one more time to pretend.
We dance like puppets until the show finally ends.
My strings are cut, and my dance is done.
My soul and appearance have now become one.
There will be no more lies, and even fewer friends.
But life will be real, and worth living again.

Tim T. King

From Darkness to Dawn

Night as cold as death man's cheek
Inside the rusty iron bars
One artist painting 'n one dreaming afar
While the others fast asleep.
Poet, artist, and captive—me
Though lying in bed 'n reading
Yes my poor young heart is sinking
'cause in great turmoil is my country.
Picasso's white dove in my heart
Writhing, skinny, and losing feathers
so our polluted world politics weather
And chance of survival for one, so hard.
The moon out, night black as ghostly beast,
"It is always darkest before the day dawn."
Soon—my people, my country will be out of morn
The sun is rising in the east.

Andrew Saw

Confused Emotions

Emotions unmistakably
trampled over by words.
Accidental fragments spoken
causing distress to feelings and sensibility.
Thoughts not being contradicted,
but not exactly proven.
Love, passion, feelings, and emotions
can't be insured,
but security between the two
can be labor.
Enigmatic remarks often leave
the receiver guessing.

Dominique LeShanda Bobo

Days of My Life

As my life passes by one day at a time,
I'll try to describe it and put it in rhyme.
Some days are good, they make life worthwhile;
Everybody's happy, my day's filled with a smile.
Some days are bad, nothing seems to go right;
Nobody smiles, it's all bicker and fight.
Some days are depressing, the weather is rotten;
Everybody mopes, the good days are forgotten.
Some days are joyful, nothing goes wrong;
My steps filled with a skip and my heart with a song.
Some days are stressful—the world is a weight
Pushing down on my shoulders—too much on my plate.
Some days are fantastic, it's all laughing and fun;
Everywhere there's a rainbow, the sky's bright with the sun.
These days all pass one at a time.
It makes up my life so I've put it in rhyme.

Warren Liptrot

Retirement

Retirement . . . it'll fit you.
Don't worry about what you'll do.
Soon it will fit just like an old shoe.
And, Mondays, they'll never be blue.
Now, we're here to tell you it's true.
There'll be lots of things, not a few. . . .
Roads not yet traveled places to view
And lots of old friendships you can renew.
Days will slip by and you won't have a clue. . . .
What's the date? Oh, no! Bills are due!
You'll look back and say, "How time flew!"
So, we hope this little pre-view
Will convince you there's sooo much to do.
Next year we'll check in with you.
Not busy? We'll give you a few
Of the things we don't have time to do!

Betty Hoffman

My Last Tear

Watching the moonrise on the warm still night,
As a fog rolls atop the ground giving the sky an eerie light.
My heart pounds in rhythm with the quiet,
Hoping to hold you just one more night.
Together in each other's arms again we will be,
Softly embracing the past, which only my memory can see.
For the dancing we will do and kisses that we will share
Can only be from memory, for now you are not there.
In the still of the night as I sit beside your grave,
I wonder why you left and how you were so brave.
Many nights I stay by your side protecting you from harm,
Waiting to be with you again, holding you in my arms
My love grows stronger and this you will see;
One day again together we will be.
My eyes grow weary and the time draws near,
To taste your soft lips, and shed my last tear. . . .

Larry Christopher Gross

Waiting

Held-in tears, distant laughter.
Dreams of happiness, forgotten promises.
Hopes of forgiveness, searching for words.
Shattered emotions, withheld fury.
Helpless cries, endless pain.
Yearning fingertips, endured agony.
Hateful nights, precious hours.
Dazedly dancing, pitifully crawling.
Reaching frantically, walking aimlessly.
Faithfully drowning, senselessly diving.
Raging tantrums, remorseful encounters.
Yelling sessions, quietly waiting.

Kaitlyn Elisabeth Etter

When I Was Young

When I was young I trusted you.
To hold me when the wind blows,
to cover me when it rained,
and to catch me before I jumped into the sun's burning rays.
As the years went by, we grew apart.
You stayed here and I went there.
I could walk on my own
but I knew you were always here.
Now I'm older, all grown up.
My mind and body have changed
but the clear image of you still stands tall.
I'll hold on forever, but you'll have to let go. . . .
let me drift in the wind,
let me dance in the rain,
and allow me to be swallowed in sunshine.
I trusted you. Now you . . . trust yourself.

Megan Rhodes

Strategic Alignment

The dust swirled in ever-rising clouds,
The sounds becoming muffled and obscured.
I crouched deep within the space,
The space between the motes.

The wind whipped to a frenzied pitch,
The sounds, gasping to be heard.
The world around me being smothered,
Spaces filling with obscurity.

The sound moved sinuously between the gaps, oozing to release me.
I pressed against the shifting weight, stretching . . . stretching.

My fingertips touched the edge.
The contact charged the enveloping blanket,
Shattering the alignment . . . I was free.

There are sounds within sounds . . . spaces within spaces.

Duncan Ray

Rage

What is the beauty of hate?
Why do we let it incase us?
What have we accomplished by it?
Death? Immorality? Pain?
None of these things we want
Yet we keep letting them into our lives
What is the difference between you and I?
A simple pigmentation? Train of thought?
Are these reasons to kill each other?
To trade someone's life for revenge?
To feel a need to see the blood red fluid on our hands?
I ask you today is it worth it?
Is it worth it to slay our brothers?
Is it worth it to hear their cry?
Is it worth it to watch others suffer?
Is it worth it for them to die?

Andréa Danielle Hawkins

Faith in Heart

During the darkest hours in time
I felt these thoughts prick my mind
Hardly able to breathe to take away the pain
Staying in sleep not to face the day
Sweat beads on your upper brow and eyelash tips
Making salty water touch your lips
How you cry and yearn to scream in the night
To run for the very thing that brings you pain
Then out of the darkness is a comforting light
Jesus whispers in your ears that it will be all right
So don't forget in the shadow and the darkest part of your mind
That faith in heart is for yours and mine

Mika Baba

An Angel Is Coming Home

This is for my loving aunt Elsie Carr. Thank you for showing me love.

Answer my prayer I asked the Lord
Understand the memories I hold inside
Never forsake me and leave me alone
Trust in God for he has all the Love in His hands

Every day let the angels hold our hand
Listen to the words that are said
Show the tender loving kindness in your heart
In the morning let the day be bright
Every night let Jesus and Mary be at our sides

Carry us unto the midst of the skies
Another angel has earned their wings
Remember the kindness that she gave us
Reach and take our hands Lord for she is coming home

Sharon Rose Qualls

Darkened Regret

To my Jewl

The piece of my heart that makes me happy has long since eluded me
I can't even remember three days ago when you took it from me
I fell lower than before
The ceiling is like heaven with you smile shinning brightly through
The floor that I sank below
The well has run dry
Tears turn cold and disappear from where I used to cry
Is it worth writing this love?
With my cycle of bad to worse
Your much needed wonder
What you wanted was always better
Faded thoughts of a tender kiss from your lips put in a brighten age
But just before I take this one last step
And close the book
I'll turn this one last page to realize that you left

John Brandon Wills

Backstreet Boys

Backstreet Boys are mine
I will not forget them anytime
Backstreet Boys are my love, my life, and everything between
They are the hottest guys I have ever seen
A. J. is my favorite one
And for my heart, he has it won
Nick is the heartthrob
He has girls after him like a big huge mob
Howie's nickname is Sweet D
And of course he is very sweet to me
Brian has a voice of gold
In my heart, his voice I will always hold
Kevin is the big brother
And is loved by all of the girls' mothers
Backstreet Boys are mine
I will not forget them anytime

Tasha Nicole Eldred

My Pete

This blessed child born on Thanksgiving Day,
A day dark and cold, with snow on the way.
Born two weeks early and had a slow start,
But made up for it quickly and soon won my heart.
Now my sweet child has become a man,
A piece of the puzzle in God's grand plan.
Brave, smart, kind, and gentle is he,
God's gift of love to my family.
So it has been all of these years.
Through good times and bad, through laughter and tears,
We weathered together times of strife,
Me and my son, the light of my life.

Irene Livia Imbrogno

Within

There is a world full of hate and fears,
Where men without dreams cry endless tears.
This timorous place is dark and cold,
Where the devil rules your body and soul.
You never see this evil essence,
But deep inside you feel his presence.
In the distance are moans and screams,
Like raging waters and wild streams.
The grotesque sights are like no other,
Torture, pain, fear, and horror.
Many hope for a new tomorrow,
But what they find is sadness and sorrow.
To this place everyone attends,
For some the agony never ends.
But what you will find is inevitably true,
Is this evil place, lies within you.

Steven Wheeler

As God Is My Witness

Once in a lifetime the right love comes by
for a reason no one knows why.
You'll wake up one morning and nothing's the same.
As God is my witness, you're there the same.
Your kisses taste sweeter, your touch feels right,
you rush through the morning to get through the night.
Then you realize you're together for the rest of your lives,
so hold on to your love and hold on to your hearts,
but always remember you'll never be apart.
Because, as God is my witness, He sees the new.
I know in my heart this is what I want to do,
(I want to spend the rest of my life with you.)
If I had a dream for the two of us, it would be
("Whatever you do, don't change a thing, I love you just the same".)
As God is my witness, He is here
to be us together through the years.

Sharon K. Williams

On Earth and After

What will become of these words I speak
when I am gone from this rugged terrain?
What will become of my comforting beauty
when I disappear from this living in vain?
What will become of my lifelong faults
when I leave this hidden blunder?
What will become of my secret spirit
when I vanish from this common thunder?

Your words will be forgotten in time
when you are gone from this deep slumber.
Your beauty will be buried deep
when you disappear from these eyes of wonder.
Your faults will be shunned swiftly
when you leave this ocean of circles.
Your spirit will remain home indeed
when you vanish from this life of mortals.

Anjali Soi

The Eagle Takes Its Flight

The dampened air rests on the scarlet ground
as a river of red flows free.
They died for a cause of the freedom they found,
vowing never to flee.
Oh, mournful heart, the mother's song
cries out in agony.
Death at her door, her children gone,
lost to eternity.
From sorrow and pain a nation grew;
the red land now fertile and ripe.
From mother's cries to the brave and true,
the eagle now takes its flight.

Holly Jean Raiten

Promises You Turned to Lies

Promises you told,
Promises you didn't keep.
You told me you loved me,
You told me you cared.
Every day, more and more promises are made.
Every day, more and more are broken.
Promises that turned into lies.
Lies to keep me, lies to hurt me.
Lies that make me want to leave.
Every word or feeling expressed was a lie.
Every word hurt me inside,
Every word that you say I reply with a good bye.
Goodbye lies, goodbye you.
No more promises, no more lies.
No more pain to hurt me.
No more YOU!

Heather Anne Vickrey

Society

Revolutions from your abuses.
I can't explain all of my pain.
Restitution is the solution.
Please make up your mind and respect my kind.
Seems so inviting the feeling of dying.
I still live on. I still carry on.
I hear your conniving. I feel your spirit trying.
So deep inside a fear of genocide.
My attempts are in vain to let go of this pain.
Peace is fabricated. War is contemplated.
My ways seem so strange—well, your mind is deranged.
I ask for some respect, but am labeled a reject.
I don't think you understand or feel what I have manned.
To get back on track. The love that I lack.
I have to demand, I have to make up a stand.
No more from society. Please just let me be.

Josh Alan Flowers

Special Someone

God has blessed me with a special someone whom I will always love.
I wake up in the morning just to see your face.
I thank God for sending you my way.
I never knew what love was until I found you.
You were there for me like no one's ever been.
You will always be a part of me I will never let go.
You've been the only true love I ever had in my life.
Now that I found you, my life is complete.
I waited for the day when I would find someone like you.
My whole life, I've searched and searched;
I still hadn't found the right person until one day,
Heaven heard my prayer and brought you down into my life.
My life is much happier; it has more meaning to it.
My heart only belongs to you,
And you'll always have my love
From this day on and forevermore.

Monica Patlan

She

When you first opened your eyes, "She" was there.
When you first got mad, "She" calmed your stare.
On your first day of school, "She" got you through.
When your things got old, "She" bought you new.
When you spilled your drink, "She" filled your cup.
When you mentally fell, "She" picked you up.
"She" is always strong when you are weak.
"She" always found for you what you tried to seek.
"She" is always there, needed or not.
"She" always has love to fill that empty spot.
"She" is always in your heart, even after "She" is gone.
Never wanting her to depart, because, "She" is Mom.

Mitchell Thomas Phillips

Daddy

My guiding light, my solid rock, my best friend all the time.
My inspiration, my helping hand, my hero always kind.
My shoulder to cry on, my main man, he was always my number one fan.
My daddy was my everything, perfect in every way.
He always knew just what to say to take my fears away.
My daddy taught me everything that a girl should know
And left the rest to be discovered somewhere down the road.
My daddy loved to play the game or put on his cowboy boots.
He loved to sing, to laugh, or give his wife a smooch.
My daddy was a gracious man but stern when needed be.
He gave his heart, his love, his all to this community.
He loved to serve, to help, to teach, he gave all that he could.
He will always be remembered a man of his word.
Now I have to say goodbye with thousands of tears in my eyes.
But Daddy I love you with all of my heart,
And with my hero's spirit I will never part.

Lacy Lehman

Life Less Ordinary

"I think you'd be bored with my life," he says.
As if the thought of meeting the dawn with
him should fill my heart with despair.
As if it should matter to me whether he moves
like lightning or sunset.
All that is beautiful in the world sits in
silence while being looked upon. The ages
have not yet moved the majestic mountains,
and though the sea turns its tide, the moon
always knows where to find it, for it is
always close to shore.
So why then should I care if he greets me
with the force of the tempest or moth's
wings when all I want is his greeting?
Whether he arrives like legions or one
knight, it matters not. He is here.

Carla J. Andrejco

Real Life

What's real life?
My mother always told me,
Get a college degree.
Then get a good job,
It shouldn't be too hard.
Marry a nice man and buy a big house,
Don't just sit around laying on the couch.
Have a few kids,
Raise them right.
Send them off to college,
And hope they'll do alright.
Pray for grand-kids, then when they come,
You can retire now, for your work is done.
Is this real life though? How is it defined?
You'd have to live it out first,
And then make up your mind.

Felicia Lawrence

The Ocean and You

The waves race toward the shore
the black night wraps its arms around me
the salty air smells of life, of you.

The grains of sand blow away in the wind
time marches on as I sit and dream
darkness falls to light as the sun rises through the sea.

To you my mind wanders endlessly
my heart swells with love like the waves of the deep
a single tear rolls down my cheek.

For I know we will not meet again
until the sun sinks into the ocean. . . .

Samantha Elaine Phillips

Friends

Friends are like strangers: one minute
you know them, then you don't.
They're like the person you thought you could trust.
But in an instant it turns to rust, and you're
left standing there with a friendship in the dust.
I found my friend that I know will be
there until the end.
He never turns his back on me.
He shows me how a friendship is supposed to be.
I can talk to him about anything that's on my mind.
With ears wide open and focused on me,
that's the way a friendship should be.
But, my true best friend you can guarantee
will be with me eternally.
I love my best friend for showing me
what a real friendship means to me.

Brian Lee Westfall

Betrayal

u say that I hurt u
u say that I betrayed u
but did u ever stop to think. . . .
did u ever wonder. . . .
maybe I was the one that hurt her
maybe I was the one that betrayed her

u just go on with your life, blaming it all on me
look what she did to me, u say
look how she treated me
u look for pity to make u feel better

u need to face the truth. . . .
realize that u weren't the only one betrayed. . . .
see the other side of your story
then look into its eyes and u will find the truth. . . .
betrayal!

Andrea Jean Przybytek

Thoughts

The thought of your thoughts running over me . . .
What do I feel; what do I see?

I want to pour my thoughts on you;
Make your every wish come true;
Hold you in my arms and squeeze;
Float away on a warm summer breeze.
Let my kisses drip down your spine,
Followed by a trail of wine.
Yes I catch—not one bit a waste—
Against your body so good it tastes.
I could roll around on a cloud of you—
Soft and cozy; a pillow for two.
Whirl away on a thought of us
Spinning like a tornado, lost in lust.
If I could just touch you . . . yes, touch you. Outside my mind,
Lustful thoughts defined . . . intimacy frozen in time.

Bruno M. Naulls

We Are the Future

To every person there is a light,
that holds within them a course of delight.
We stand our ground we stand our fight,
for everything that is our right.
In the sky there is a kite,
in that dark blue night.
Open your eyes and see the sight,
because everything is not black and white.
We have our pride—we have our might.
We will not take your cruel hard bite.
We will succeed and not look back.
We are the future and that's the fact.

Stephanie Yuki Cali

A Moment Today

A moment today your future will make
As I witnessed on the streets one day
A young student wrapped in white linen
Lay there dying these words struggling to say
Hear me and please heed this warning
Pray that you listen to the words I say
The choices you make can haunt you forever
They may even get you carried away
Please tell my mamma that I really love her
Dear brothers and sisters don't go this way
I ask my father to please forgive me
For bringing pain to the family today
Play the music lowly, carry me slowly
The voice grew weak but he managed to say
I've made some choices not stopping to think
My actions will cost me my future today

Judy A. Hartz

A Dad

A dad can be old, and a dad can be strong.
A dad can be wise, and a dad can be young.

Some people just wouldn't know
That in my mind, dads are the heroes.

Sometimes we think, they push us too hard.
But we try and try, and sometimes we fall.
But dads pick us up and encourage us all.

They've taught us things they've learned in the past
To make us like them, for we could be their last.

They love us and cherish us,
For we could be their last,
But the one and only
Dads are, and always will be,
Our present, future, and past. . . .

Daniel David Gray

Heartache

A cold wind raps on the door,
silence creeps up on me.
Loneliness sweeps across the floor,
and tears roll down with every plea.
With so much I've done and so much I've not,
I'm feeling very low and empty.
But I hope you'll find within your heart,
to forgive me and make a brand new start.
I realize I've done you wrong,
and I want to make it right.
I want to feel one more time,
your arms holding me tight.
That's all I ask,
just one more chance.
Please, for me,
save the last dance.

Kyle Andrew Powers

Extraordinary

Thoughts of you make me smile through and through
My imagination shifts into maximum overdrive
Of what dreams may come or what reality can bring
You are a resurgence of energy, a pursuit of happiness
That makes the world a wonderful place to be
There aren't enough superlatives on earth to
Describe the extraordinary way you make me feel
Your presence exudes in every conversation we share
I can visualize your passionate smile and sweet continence
Your physical being is of no consequence
You have captivated my soul with your irresistible personality
I will never be the same

Anita Bonds-Kinchelow

Alone

Unspoken
Left to rot
Festering in your soul
Aching emptiness
Lost and alone
For a moment you reach out
To find nothing there
Nothing but tears
And loneliness
What happened to the arms that once held you
What happened to the love that once caressed you
Too long it was left un-taken and unused
Those arms got cold and withered
The love dried up from the heat of your glances
Alone, rotten, festering
To the end of your days

Jessica A. Sanchez

Four Seasons

You ended our affair mid-Vivaldi,
somewhere between *Autumn* and *Winter*,
diminishing the music of parting to a solo violin.
Fretful with tension, you shook your head
when I begged you to stay,
orchestrating your goodbye without words.
The minims spoke volumes,
missing the beat in syncopated pain,
unable to stave off the inevitable.
Pages rippled sorrow on the music stands
as I quavered through another season,
first to quit the concert hall farce.

Willing myself not to look, helpless,
I glanced back anyway.
Your chair already empty, as if we'd existed
only in a footnote.

Lindsay Hodges

Young Love

What's going on in the world when I want you but can't have you?
Though these feelings are new, I fully understand.
To do this I must place myself in your shoe
And realize you are still my man.
I realize what you want you do not know.
I realize you feel confused,
And even though I don't want it to show
I still feel used.
I know you still like me, want me,
And I still like you, want you,
But you just don't see
All the pain you put me through.
It's all good, all gravy.
I'll always forgive.
I'll still call you, and you'll call me baby.
And through eternity, my love for you will live.

Tiffany Deloach

Life's Too Short

Life's too short to waste away,
so live for tomorrow and today,
live your life the best you can,
and live to the fullest to every demand,
tell your family you love them forever,
tell your love you always be together,
be true to every promise that you make,
for a good friends sake,
always tell people that you care,
and that you will always be there,
remember live every day like there is no tomorrow,
with no sadness or sorrow.

   Christopher Dean Kniffin

Lawrence of Arabia

Study History from Afghanistan to Zimbabwe
You will find, with much abhorrence
The likes of T. E. Lawrence.

I'm thinking of *Lawrence of Arabia*.
What about you?

Staring eastward off a movie set
To the rising morn star that shudders beyond night-cold dunes
He on camel back, prefers dromedary to bactrian,
then looks into the distant future

Now, stop. The future's here
Lawrence incarnate lives again—the Arab and his rebirth
So, in what man today does T. E.'s spirit traipse the land?

I'm thinking of Edward Said.
What about you?

   Waciuma Billy Kimara

One Point of View

In a room of color I live
A life of sunshine and breezes.
My soul is nourished with fresh squeezed
lemonade and ideology.
As I wander under purple skies
and through blue clouds
I listen so hard to the world that
life
becomes
music
that becomes
life
that is the
music
that is
life.

   Krystal L. Cox

Cheri

Down into auburn eyes, I melt away.
Her soft, light hair gently sways;
Smile . . . sexy, soft,
I'm drawn deep within and find myself lost.

Who is this she that makes my heart explode?
A complex lady, a little girl;
She burns her mark forever in my soul.

I hear the rain that whispers her name;
I ache with the pain that says she'll go away
Forever.
Lost.

If meant to fly through some of this life together?
A cosmic event.
Star and Star,
Simultaneous Supernovas.

   Keith W. Snyder

A Passage to Heal

An empty vessel can be refilled;
Many things have many uses,
And you shouldn't give up.
When something you had seems empty, just remember,
An empty vessel can be refilled!

Time it will take,
But soon it will come,
That day when your vessel will be filled once again!

Today, your vessel has been refilled,
And soon enough, it will heal
To be refilled time and time again!

   Zaniesha Alexis Woods

My Dad's the Apple of My Eye

My dad is the apple of my eye.
My dad he will not see me cry.
I am sad because he might lie
in the Earth under the sky.
It is not so bad to rest an eye
because soon the paradise is neigh.
I'm so glad he'll awake anew,
pain and suffering no more too.
Glad to submit to kingdom grand,
where no one wicked will ever stand.
If God wills his end is not yet,
he will serve Jehovah his best.
And forever together all can rejoice,
praising Jehovah with a unified voice.
I love both dads you see with such force;
either way I can cope with whatever choice.

   Teresa Preve

Selected Few

There are only a selected few
That I give my heart to.
You are one that I have chosen
To lead me to my pot of gold.
You lead me and don't ask much,
Just to love you a whole bunch.
You are the one I will always love.
You are like a special dove.
You say I am your beautiful angel.
You see me from a different angle.
You help me with the good times
And encourage me through the bad times.
No matter what has happened, you are mine now,
And I really hope you know
I love you with all my heart,
Even though we are so far apart.

   Christina RaLynne Terrel

Lake of Glass

In the valley of mist lies a lake of glass.
The shimmering water splashes on the golden shore.
The smell of summer in the air, very few thoughts have no care.
The smooth glass-like surface does not move,
sounds of people dancing to music and getting in the groove.
It will not last forever; the summer season
will surely die.
But for now the power of music, song, and dance overpower.
Fire's glow on the lake's now dark shore.
Now that night has fallen everything is still.
How long will it last no one person knows; they soon will.
Morning comes, and the sun shoots across the
lake reflecting off the water.
All too soon it ends, and back to work we all go.
But we will return to this wonderful place;
next year we return to the lake of glass.

   Caleb Joel Nugent

Welcome

never shall I bear a tear
or feel the wind in my face
never shall a gray cloud dull the moon
or darken the stars
never shall a heavy foot tread on gentle blades
or the fringes of time
for my life has found love and life
and space is endless once more
for the reaching of hearts
and hands and joys
and the hands of time
bid thy welcome

Hugh J. Algeo, III

Time and Silence

How is it that I still love you
after all these years and all this silence?
You were not mine and never will be.
But it was that kiss so long ago
that lingers in my memory.
Yes, I see it now,
tenderness and sorrow
for the loss we suffered as our lips met.
It was a moment of hidden understanding but
a great divide for truth was revealed,
yet concealed in sorrow's past.
Our tears that night spoke for the union that will continuously
cry out from the depths of our souls.
It is far too much longing for one earthly life.
So perhaps we will meet in our next life
to walk together and dream again.

Christine Power

Through One

I've been blessed with precious souls;
These friends of mine, worth more than gold.
From God's own hand have come these gifts;
Bestowed on me to safely hold.
There've been times I've longed to cry
For bitter feelings of pain and strife,
For loneliness I'm cursed to feel,
And times I've wished to leave this life.
But it's too easy to run this way,
And selfish to hide from any fear.
You need me as I need you,
So I can stand to bear one tear.
Through only One can love exist;
From God alone comes help that mends.
So now I place you in His hands,
That we might be forever friends.

Abigail C. Shanks

Mending Hearts

As we grow in our tragic loss,
The tree mends itself back together.
Our hearts are broken with a hole inside,
But as time flows we heal and get better.
"Time heals all" we hear them say,
But there will always be a hole
As we go on with our lives
And we each have a piece of their soul.
The water flows through the broken tree
As the purest blood runs down
And they will all live forever in our hearts
As they are all heavenly bound.
Stored up in us is a piece of them,
And none of us will ever forget
The times we shared with these loving four
And how they kept their candles lit.

William Michael Costner

The Night

The night is nothing but paradise in my eyes.
The wind in my hair, the stars in the sky,
The smell of the grass. The night owl sings,
and the grass snake hisses, a sign meaning
the sun is coming and I must be hiding.
I run through the night with wind in
my hair hoping the sun would not be there. I run
over hills, valleys, and houses. I find my
home, and as I crawl inside I watch the
night fade and the sun shine bright.
Tears roll up in my eyes, and then I hide.
What am I?

Bethany Dickson

Prison RN

medical department work shared by one
education gained day by day
diligent by the pay check
intelligent enough, maybe
caring enough to stay
Attitude enough for a junkyard dog
Loyal up to a point

Personality depending on the mood
energy depending on the number of call outs
Resourceful when pushed
Sincere even with fingers crossed
Orn'ary all of the time
Nerves of steel
Nutty as a pecan log
entirely focused
lying like a dog

Jimmie S. Odom

Here Comes Number Three

Back there on the eighteenth row that black car sits in wait
Five hundred hungry miles till Victory Lane opens its gate
Nicknamed "Intimidator" as the legend came to be
Knock, knock on your backdoor, here comes number three
That country boy was born to race with winning in his blood
He moved up to the big time from that small track dirt and mud
A legend and a hero that the people came to see
Knock, knock on your backdoor, here comes number three
They went down to Daytona for the last lap of that race
And watched him help his son and brother take first and second place
When he pulled into Victory Lane it must have been a sight to see
The angels' trumpets sounded, here comes number three
I know for one I'll miss him, somehow it won't seem real
But he'd say, "let's go racing, hey how's that new car feel"
And in the paint's reflection a glimpse of him we'll see
Knock, knock on your backdoor, here comes number three

Richard E. Harris

The Chains of the Past

I shall not be held by the chains of the past.
I will not be held in bondage to the past.
The Past has come and gone,
becoming exactly what it has become—The Past.
I am not what I was,
For what I was then and what I am now
are at two totally different ends of life's spectrum.
I am not who I was,
For who I was then and who I am now
are two totally and completely different beings.
I am new,
I am evolved,
and as I reach forward,
I reach towards a better life,
for I will not be held by the chains of
The Past.

Warrene Renee Robinson

Sitting There

That tired look, those dreamy eyes,
That sound of wind, and how it cries.
That night so precious and dark,
Makes me want to just sit there.
Sitting there in the bright moonlight,
Makes me dream with not one fright.
How it makes me sit and wonder,
What if the sky should fall?
And as I lie there not a minute too soon,
I think of the days, and how the sun looks
Like a bright orange balloon
Just sitting there!

Carly Anne Sober

This Can't Be Heaven

This can't be heaven because you're not here with me,
Holding me, kissing me, loving me unconditionally.
This can't be hell because you're not here with me,
Yelling at me, hurting me, haunting me
With your all-knowing grin and your uncaring, hurtful gaze.
You reel me in with your game face;
You play me for the fool, thinking only of yourself,
Thinking that you broke my will;
Broke my heart is what you did.
You keep me hooked, thinking i have your heart,
But you kept it close by your side,
Got away with your crime.
You played your game well—how could you not win?
I had no defense against you—
how could I have a defense?
When I didn't think i needed one . . .

Dena Marie Sanford

Thoughts of Him

We gaze at the stars, imaginary ones will do
whatever it takes, just to be with you
wrapped in your arms, our heartbeats combine
so close together, our souls intertwine
together all night . . . as one
the night may be over, but the next day has begun
my love for you grows with each passing day
I never dreamed that I would love on this way
the intensity of my fear grows because we may say goodbye
but I dreamed our love will last . . . it is obvious why
our love is so strong, it will stay through the years
it will shine in the laughter, and brave through the tears
it will outlive all . . . the good and the bad
reminding us each day of the blessings we've had
we are so close now, you will remain in my soul
waking . . . with thoughts of you . . . my heart is now gold

Britnee Greenlee

Self Relic

Finding oneself is a journey . . . and the self is a treasure.
Paralyzed . . . frozen . . .
Still in my sarcophagus, waiting to be discovered.
The dust covers old ideas and concepts, yet they do not delay;
Metamorphosis on hold, harnessed by unseen forces unsaid
Knowledge of my existence—but am I real?
I know I am flesh, but I am unsure about the reality of my soul
For other powers keep the door shut,
Suffocating my potential, stifling my bloom.
Tradition over change like a gun to my head.
Stagnant is my growth yet I still succeed—
What is the answer?
Perhaps it is locked in here with me.
The darkness keeps me from finding it;
Maybe I'll just stay in here forever.

Arlene Parungao Laxamana

Life Comparison

In life, there is nothing to compare,
Not things, nor human.
If comparison were strong, life would be full of unfair judgement.
Look and understand beyond situations.
Not all beings are created the same.
Comparison only leads to shame,
A shame that cannot be hid forever.
Comparison makes us feel insecure.
Comparison makes us have unfulfilled expectations.
To be able to see and feel truly, so as to lead your unrestful mind,
No hate, but just dislike.
Think positive and live positive!

Tia Siew Kin

Beginning to End

As a seed of joy forms a fruit of a bearing tree
Beginning your stages in life so sweet as far as any can see
No lumps or rotten patches forms among your lovely surface
Just the tenderness of your touch I wonder do I deserve this
Cherishing the glow and the sparkle in your eye
I absorbed every teardrop as you begin to cry
I began to love what I have this wonderful fruit of mine
Something that's willing to grow with me only with a matter of time
I will not disown it or will I leave it astray
I will always love my wonderful fruit until my dying day
My fruit has grown with wonderful curves that I now adore
Into something solid and with love I give it much more
Ripe is what I'm seeing do I know whether it is alright
So I knelt down an prayed that I keep my fruit through the night
But now my fruit has withered into something I can't comprehend
Joyfulness fill my heart when I stayed with my fruit to the end

Andre Lamont Cuthbertson

College Life

As I sit here wondering
Who am I? and Why am I here?
The thought keeps coming back
It is certainly not to drink beer.
The pressures are great
And the time is well spent
But things are changing now
And I ponder, Will I make a dent?
Will someone look back and say,
"He made a difference in my life,"
Will someone say "I want to be like him,"
Or "He helped me through a time of strife."
All these thoughts run through my mind.
Am I running out of time?
Will the world remember me
Or will I just be another sad memory.

Kyle Wellmaker

My Addiction

I crave it when I cannot have it.
I feel like something is missing when it's not there.
I don't want to feel this way,
But my mind thinks that I need it.
The effects are unbearable,
And yet I keep going back.
It makes me feel good for a while,
But it never seems to last.
My friends try to make me stop,
Because they know what it's doing to me.
Every time I think that I'm over it, I'm not.
Whenever I see it, I just can't help myself.
I try to turn away,
And I know what I should do.
I really need help,
Because my addiction is you.

Jessica Sharpe

Confirmation

To my Bryan James
I know how you feel . . . But now I want to
here it! Every last bit of it!

Am I beautiful? Tell me so.
Do you love me? Say it.
Do you need me? Admit it.
Am I sexy? Show me.

I am a girl, a lady; sweet, sexy, beautiful,
intelligent, and in love with you.

Confirm what I know, I want to hear it,
Every last bit of it.

Amber Mowery

Mother Owl

I sat one night sodden and solitaire
beneath a darkened sky
when from the corner of my eye
I caught a glimpse of a sharp light.
To my surprise a lovely, sure breasted
mother owl was perched.
I too am a mother of two.
Mother owl and I shared a bond
in the midst of that shadowy sky.
She is as curious and wise as I.
Wide-eyed she hoots to me
her tales of flying high,
soul purpose for her young to survive.
Hushfully I tell her of my woe and glory.
Mother owl already knows,
and we realize there is no real hurry.

Andrea Leigh Scott

A Christmas Wish

It's Christmas again with that familiar jingle;
But will he forget once more? I mean that Kris Kringle.
I wished last year for only one thing,
But to me, I'm afraid, he never did bring.
Not the world or all riches could bring me delight;
It's something much smaller and still not in sight.
My Soldier had fallen and no longer marched on;
And still to this day, disbelief that he's gone.
So proudly he stood with beauty and grace;
And the actions of honor will never erase.
He stands now before me in memory and thought,
But in anger and fury is where I am caught.
The end of the madness that's guarded by night
Still can't be seen with bellowing light.
Maybe next Christmas I'll get what I desire
And that Soldier will help to put out the fire.

Keith John Furbacher

All Are Good

I don't know why all the fuss,
And I don't know which is better, a dog or a puss.
Both seem equally good to me.
While birds do nothing but sing twiddle-dee
And fish swim in the tank for all to see.
Iguanas are good for those people who are lazy,
And what's wrong with rats?
Why do we treat them worse than floor mats?
Is it because they're not as cute as mice,
Or is it because they're not as nice?
I don't know, but they're cool to me,
As long as I keep them clean, fed, and healthy.
So as far as I'm concerned all animals are good,
Even though some are quite misunderstood.
We have to remember that God made them too,
And that all you do to them shows the truth about you.

Kary Bledsoe, Jr.

Burnt Silence

Burnt leaves lie upon the ground in silence,
As I drown myself in tears of sorrow.
Gray skies fill the emptiness within my heart,
Completing me 'til 'morrow.
Daylight arrives with a cool autumn breeze;
Spring is here, yet the chill's borrowed.
Loneliness hinders my smile
With cold, blank stares that follow.
Quiet clamor, happy sadness;
Friendships lost in a world of madness.
I hear the laughter and compliance, yet
Burnt leaves lie upon the ground in silence.

Ellen Hurd

Thank You, Mother

I reminisce to a place in time
Where the memories are as sweet as honey
The love, joy and happiness were freely given
I didn't need any money
When the days got rough
And I fell apart
You stretched forth your hands
And held my heart
A single thank you is not enough
To show my respect for you
Sometimes I think you're the reason
The sky was painted pretty blue
So whenever you're down
And don't feel whole
Just remember that seed of joy
You planted in my soul

Todd Matthew Wynn

Control Life

I don't know what to do,
where is my other shoe
and who are you?
That's how I feel sometimes,
when I look in the mirror,
my thoughts are all boggled.
STOP!
Listen to the crickets, watch the ants,
oh, no, I have mud on my pants.
STOP!
Let go,
go with the flow.
You can't control the rain
you can't control people places or things.
You only live once
so why not do it with a punch?

Rhonda J. Ratliff

Skydiving

The gush of the wind
Trying its hardest to push you in the
Other direction,
But failing.
The feeling that you're not falling,
But actually being in the exact place that
You had started,
As if you were standing in one place on earth.
The sense that the world is growing rapidly,
Trying to catch you, just as a baseball player
Would a baseball.
The gravity only giving you a short period
In time—so small—lasting only seconds,
To let your mind wander as you
Gulp in all of the excitement
Before it ends.

Karlena Renae Johnson

Hourglass

Standing with the song of the wind,
He stood in bliss. Shadowed by a mist, his mind drifted.
He bent down, comfortable now as the tide charged towards him,
Ever so slowly.
He wandered around where you can't see.
Black now, his vision was halted from his tough eyelids,
The same covers that succeeded in opening the gates to Utopia.
Was this real? Am I really here?
As he reached to his west he knew
This was nothing close to a dream,
For she was right there,
Exactly like a thousand times before.

    Jeffrey Charles Beaudoin

The Universal Hurt

Every day I see racial discrimination
And every day I hear the names
They are taunted and booed across the nation
And excluded from childish games
Little children at elementary schools
Get made fun of every day
By those who disobey the rules
To put them down in every way
And the government will say
That everything is fair
Brainwashing us day by day
But do they really care?
I hope and pray that all of you
Don't hurt the feelings of others
Be careful what you say or do
And treat them like your brothers

    Linda Hood

this is it . . .

this is my paper, heavy with lead
these are my words, telling many stories
and i know you'd judge me
if you could read what i am writing
this is my paper, heavy with feelings
these are my thoughts, releasing much love
and I know you'd laugh at me
if you could read what i am thinking
this is my paper, heavy with burdens
these are my prayers, asking many things
and i know you'd ridicule me
if you could read what i am wishing
this is me, heavy with time
these are my being, showing my bare soul
and i still know you'd judge me
if you knew what i was writing

    Tyler Markey

The Greatest Happiness

Thoughts of you submerge deep within my mind
You're the warming of my intellect—the rhythms of my rhymes
Sunshine that overtakes cloudy skies
You're the center of an angels eyes and apple pies
Sent from above—you're the sound of love
With the pureness of an snow-white dove
You're the soothing wind of an oceans view
Sort of like heaven and too good to be true
On the hottest day, you're like summer rain
An undescribable feeling that can't be explained
You're the night's bright star in the mist of dawn
Your priceless treasure, finally won
You're an angel in disguise—three wishes in one
On the most boring days, thoughts of you is the greatest fun
My greatest happiness surpasses "sublime"
Yes, this angel I dream of is finally mine

    Maury Demetrius Golden

Mamma Cat

The birds are not as gay today, for
Mamma Cat has gone away.
A little stray who came in May.
Though very sick she made her way.
She had her kittens and watched them play,
And then their lives just went away.
So birds are not as gay today
For Mamma Cat has gone away.
A furry friend like her they say,
They hope to meet again someday,
Maybe in the month of May
When Mamma Cat went away.

    Joseph Bellucci

Angel with Broken Wings

Angels soar high up in the heavens
I felt that way once
Until it was all torn away
Now I have broken wings
And I'm falling back to Earth
I'm still an Angel but I will never fly
Now I am falling
No one to pick me up
But I'm still an Angel
Yet I will never fly
I'm hoping that everything will be alright
As long as I stay High
Angel with broken wings
Is there anyone who can fix these things?
I'm just a poor Angel with broken wings
Will I ever fly again?

    Jason Robert Van Nest

The Hourglass

Far into the future, where will I be?
From the year 2050, I look back to see
my determined and focused self had a spirit so free.
I built my future in the great uncertainty.
How I remember that day I learned to fly,
or when finally I met the stars in the sky.
How I strived for dreams with hardly a sound,
taking on life's hurdles with a single bound.
How I remember that day when Mom and Dad passed away.
They gave back to the Earth; it returned my first birth.
How new worries pushed college memories out of touch,
I see my priorities and prayers have changed so much.
As for a greatest accomplishment, my own family wins out
Now I realize it's loved ones that life's all about.
With life's journey closing in, full circle,
a grandma I sit, holding my daughter's own miracle.

    Leslie A. Novak

Nights of Hopelessness, Days of Desperation

Nights of hopelessness occur so often
While my heart continues to soften
All my memories swirl about it my head
'Til my happiness of the days is dead
I lie in bed and cry and whine
About how life can seem a swine
The hours pass on the clock by my head
Till it seems my misery has been justly fed
I feign until I fall asleep
My eyes no longer continue to seep
Daylight washes away my dreams like soap
My heart begins to fill with hope
To day night seems an apparition
These are the days of desperation
Each day brings my hope anew
Each night renders it askew

    Kimber Marie Faith

Life

Life is a highway.
You can choose any way to go, and I choose my way.
There are different paths to take.
You never know which choice to make.
Sometimes it's right; sometimes it's wrong,
but any which way you've got to be strong.

You can travel fast or slow;
it's your choice where you will go.
You can travel by car or train,
or even go by plane.
Any which way you've got to feel good.
Be happy and enjoy life just like you should.

Kimberly Dubin

Blessings

Blessings come in many forms
A friend, true love, good health, even storms
Some, we easily recognize, others we refuse—
They wouldn't be our lot if we could choose
But very often, what causes pain
Is certainly sunshine, which comes after rain
And unless we endure the storm clouds' drear
How will the brilliant Sun ever appear?
So when we take time to reflect
We realize we've been blessed—I do suspect
Thankful then, we all should be
For blessings abound, far as our eyes can see
Our jobs, homes—the air we breathe
The hard times that come before we succeed!
Together they all help us to be
A more complete humanity!

Denise Ursula Knight

You

When we first met it was like a dream come true.
And at that instant I knew it had to be you.
You were like someone that was sent from the heavens above.
And what I had for you was a heart full of love.
You treated me well like no one else did before.
Then all of a sudden my heart you chose to tore.
I didn't understand why you ended things this way.
You chose not to listen to the words I had to say.
Everyone told me that I had to forget about you.
But I wonder if you're trying to forget about me too.
Each and every day I sat there and cried.
Wondering why I even tried.
Months have passed and still you're in my mind.
Wondering if there is any hope to find.
But today I realized that I have to let you go.
And never again will I mention the name Yong Ho.

Lori Pham

Life

I have yet to begin my journey of life
Here, I sit, on my bed all curled up
Dreaming of my twelve wishes for each year of my life gone by
Laying with my first Brittany pup
I have just begun my journey
I have met my one true love
My thirty-six dreams flying like the doves up above
While I'm playing with my third Brittany pup
I have reached the middle of my journey
My babes are in their beds all curled up
My forty-eight dreams are resting with them
While I'm playing with my fourth Brittany pup
I have reached the end of my life journey
My babes with their sixth pup all grown and gone
My seventy-two dreams for them soaring over this lawn
While I'm laying with my first Brittany pup

Sara Persons

Forever Friends

You brighten my day when I am down
and stick by me when I frown;
you give me faith, courage and strength to follow my dreams,
no matter how impossible they may seem.

When life gets at me and I want to hide,
your support helps me abide
and though you aren't near all the time,
your spirit climbs all the mountains I climb.
I don't mean to get so mushy, it's not my style,
but I just want to say dear friend of mine:
through thick and thicker we shall stand
for forever you'll be my friend.

Diana Ida Kaaya

We

Seems like in the world today,
Everyone expects us to act a certain way.
You teach us empty morals and contradictions,
Then punish for us these afflictions.
Politicians lead the debate.
The only result I can see is hate.
We imitate the pushes you've shoved,
But we're all the same—we just need to be loved.
If we can't learn to see past labels and color,
How can we learn to live with one another?
Skinheads, punks, preps, and geeks,
I say it's the older generation who are mild-mannered freaks.
Stereotypes and class fill our innocence with pollution
When will someone stand and offer a solution?
We want to be happy, we want to be free,
Parents, this is your children—listen to We.

Maggie L. Day

Destructive Juices

To imagine ourselves a different race
A different breed, a different kind, a different species
Is unimaginable to many
To understand that souls exist
That other people respond as much as you
That they feel just like you
Is a difficult task for many
And so the world is corrupt
People have no imagination, no concept of humanity
Destruction without second thought
Thoughtlessness without guilt
Dreams are shattered by carelessness
Hopes are erased by overanalyzation
The world is a hopeless case
Nothing to accomplish or achieve
Only to wallow in our own destructive juices

Helen Hoffsommer

Who Can?

It hurts
The pain I feel inside
Is it for real,
Or all in my mind?

Who can I turn to
To make the pain go away?
Who can I turn to
To make all my fears go away?

Who can make the Sun shine in my day?
Who can make those lonely depressing days the ones
I will cherish forever long?
Hopefully the ones who will love me forever long!

Make all of my fears go away!
Make all of my pain go away!
Promise me you will love me all through the way!

Ryann Marie Gregoire

A Forbidden Passion

Unexpectedly escaping all moral excellence;
finding an inner peace of comfort and pleasure . . .
The few moments shared
are consumed with intense passion and harmony. . . .
I look deep into your eyes, and I am veiled in a world of
desire. . . .
Your gentle touch and soft sweet kiss compose passion
burning deep within my soul. . . .
Time stops; my body is numb. I am lost in your warm
embrace. . . .
Uncertainties that have circled in my mind are slowly
fading. . . .

    Nicole Majeski

Without You

So slow goes the time without you
I'm reaching just to grab your hand.
You drift so slowly out of sight
that I'm blinded by the light in your eyes.
I stand up and swim towards you
but I drown before I reach your mouth
and the arms drag me down
to the depths and darks of my lonely heart.

Hold my mouth open so I may scream.
Wake me from this nightmare,
this terrible dream.
I guess I knew you'd leave
like you always did before
leave me in the dark, leave me all alone.
Leave me just to sit
sit and think of you.

    Niki N. Price

Lost Love

Your love is painfully pierced into my heart.
Your face forever etched upon my eyes.
Your touch still felt on my lips.
If only for a lightning second as I wake from a dream.
Tears that fall from a memory that
lingers from the past.
I still carry with me wondering
how long this feeling will last.
A piece of my broken heart still falling for a time that is lost.
Some broken pieces I still keep with me—
but at what cost?
If I let go and the last piece falls—
will it be then
that your love will forever
be lost to my heart?

    Tamara L. Goins

My Sailor

Matthew Robert Amundson, US Navy
I miss you so and long for you . . .
To be home with us instead of there, so new . . .
'Tis so hard to send my child into the world of arms.
To be the little boy who fills my dreams . . .
The way you winked at every passerby,
Your smile, your laugh, your twinkling eyes.
You were so charming and full of life. . . .
No worries ever crossed your mind.
They are talking war, you say. . . .
I know it's true;
I just know how much I love you.
You're all grown up, I know that's true. . . .
But for me, your mom, worries subdue.
Take care, my sailor, be proud and true. . . .
For God and I are always with you.

    Sandra Ilene Amundson

Seasons of Love

Look outside at the spring sunshine.
My love for you is as bright.
Think of spring water on a hot summer day.
My love for you is as fresh and renewing.
Think of the first frost in the fall.
Your loving touch makes me shutter the same.
Think of the first snowfall in winter.
My love for you is as pure.
Let my love for you shine in your heart every minute.
Let my love for you refresh you daily.
May my love for you always be crisp.
Be forever my pure love.

    Robert Kent Mace

Always with Me

This poem is dedicated to my grandma, Ruth.
No matter what happens,
Or whatever changes life may bring,
In my heart you shall always be.
I will love you always
And cherish our memories forever
Because they can never be taken from me.
Right now, I'm feeling hurt and scared
Because a person I love won't always be here.
I'm trying to be as strong as you are for me,
But the thought of losing you
Is taking the life out of me.
I don't know what cards fate is going to deal,
But all I can do is tell you how I feel.
The angels may come and take you away,
But in my heart, you will always stay

    Lindsey Neal Wilhite

All Eyes on You

When it's your voice that rejoices
It's like magic that's strewn
Fulfilling the tenderness under a crescent moon
All eyes are on you
As you speak of romances, tales and tunes
Your funny faces and sexy moves
Turns heads and blasts laughs too
All eyes are on you
When your fingers touch ebony and ivory
There's nothing else that will do
Because those keys belong to you
All eyes are on you
When there's no one in sight
In pure dim light
I didn't believe what was seen
As your eyes were on me

    Aileen Liwanag Cayanan

September 11, 2001

Today is a day unlike any other;
because of evil, the world has forever changed.
It could have been my very own mother,
whose life was taken by the radically insane.
I feel sorrow, compassion, and love
for those many thousand innocent victims of war.
I have no doubt that we'll rise above,
but right now, my heart, like many, is still sore.
For the animals responsible, I have eternal hate,
for they have a created a darkness in our world.
A world without peace, a world that's irate.
Make no mistake, once the dust has settled,
everyone will see, that these haters of life
will pay for their deeds.
This war that was declared on September eleventh
will hopefully not be the end of civilization.

    Santiago Bernardez

Jesus Christ

Doesn't it make you cry
That for you and me He was crucified
That to cleanse us of our sins He would die
To the cross He was tied
He bled for us
So we could live
He died and still we sin and cuss
For us His life He would give
And then He arose
Because He is God's Son
And we should trust in Him wherever He goes
His name is Jesus Christ

Ashley Marie Maggard

Are You a Christian?

Are you a Christian?
What do those words mean to you?
Do you live the life
Or do you just get through?
Do you read your Bible
And pray every day
Or do you live in sin
And say what Man would say?
Have you really asked Jesus in your heart
Or do you just go to church and pretend that he's a part?
Do you show the light of Jesus at your school
Or do you say words like one of Satan's fools?
Do you have a relationship with Jesus Christ
Or do you live an unholy Devil's life
And if you were to die today, where would you go?
Heaven or Hell, or do you even know?

William Carney

Winter Pending

You are gone and I am free,
free to dream; to consider possibilities that never will be.
Wanting to take the next step with you.
Continuing the slow, sensuous dance of seduction, of love.

I am sad, restless,
wanting to speak your name; hear your answer.
Knowing I can't; knowing you won't.
Shaking my head at stupidity.
Railing against recklessness.
Feeling the hopelessness, the waste.
Seeing tomorrows slide away into the night.

I stare sightlessly into the darkness—
alone again, always,
as the first flakes begin to fall.
Winter has arrived.

Kate Stewart

Bubble

Response to the attack on America
Eighteen years on this earth in this country
And have never truly experienced pure evil.
My life seemingly lived inside a bubble of safety.
Eighteen years; now I struggle to keep the air in—
A hole punctured by the fall of two towers and people's lives lost.
I cover the hole, not wanting to believe; the air still escapes.
My world, my bubble, slowly starts to wither around me.
In reality, I struggle against what I have seen and denial sets in.
Eighteen years of thinking nothing bad could ever happen
And yet the world I thought I knew now seems foreign.
I watch the world carry on as it should,
But still I am standing alone and silently holding my bubble.
The air leaks; I cannot stop it.
I hold my breath, not wanting to lose the air,
And I fall as everything around me withers.

Carrie Nichole Chapman

I Already Have Her

One day, an angel came to Earth
It startled me at first
I gained my composure and the angel began to speak
"God has granted you a wish for all your years of sadness
You may choose any women in the world to have"
Without hesitation, I spoke your name
The angel looked at me with a puzzled look
And said, "You don't understand
You can have any woman on the face of the Earth
That will love you forever"
I looked at the angel and said to him
"I already have her"

Robert Donner

Terrorists

The planes came in the towers went down
many were lost many were found
people were scurrying searching everywhere
hoping and praying loved ones were there
the firemen searched leaving their wives
giving all they could to save many lives
the president came with a word to say
the people responsible will surely pay
the market was quiet sportsmen didn't play
showing love and reverence in a special way
freedom will flourish and rise to the top
because a nation like ours cannot be stopped
we all look to God for guidance and hope
with him leading the way everyone will cope
what seemed like the end of freedom we know
just started the seed for our country to grow

John W. Evans

Circus

Circus of people, clowns in funny faces
A bus and train in their last race
All getting nowhere, much slower than they knew
There was sanctuary among them but only to a few
The light is so bright, yet it's as dark as the night
They seem so far away, so far yet I can touch them
And I am part of it all
And they are deafened to my call
I climb a stairway to reach my perch
Hoping at last I can end my search
The wings of the devil, I'd love to grow
Straight up to Heaven I would go
But I do not possess those fantastic wings
If I would jump, only death it would bring
And my leap would be fatal
But I never, I never did like the Circus

Robin J. Labanoski

Hope for a Glorious Day

I stood alone at school one day
Shedding nothing but a tear
I had seen the likes of something sweet
The first day of the year
What else could have done this to me
But a girl I had not known
I was not the tough kid in the class now
But my softer side had shown
I kept the feelings inside of me as I grew up
Did not put them in view
If I could have expressed my emotions
If only she had knew
I start with a sparkle of hope
That's all I can say
With hope that tomorrow
Could be that glorious day

Andrew Craven J.

Memories Forever

The day was coming to an end,
I still hadn't said my last goodbye.
I rushed to see you,
Yet you got farther and farther away,
Rushing through the nasty crowd,
Pushing through impatient people,
Just to find out you were no longer there.

I sat down at the table where we were supposed to meet.
I cried in my hands, hoping it would wash away all the pain.
The pain hit me like a dart,
But I have realized you were never gone,
But always in my heart.

Kristin Elizabeth Uttenhove

Moon Tides

Ground swells . . . rising as moon tides.
The sun falls from the sky and the
world is silent in awe.
A perfect moment out of
time . . . as stillness surrounds
and silence overwhelms.
The world fills with tears
and echoes . . . rain falls
softly all around.
The air is charged with
something familiar and
unknown . . . each breath is
sharper than the last.
The colors of the rainbow
deepen . . . become new . . .
brighter.

Justin E. Boone

Dream

Everyone has their day
Even a losing team
It seems there's someone for everyone
But when it's my turn to dream.
They say it's better to have loved and lost
Than never to have loved at all
I'd like to see them try it
They'll see it's a much bigger fall.
How can you love someone so much
That it's always in your head
But when you finally tell them
They want to be friends instead.
Everyone has their day
But days always come to an end
How can it feel so bad
To be thought of as a friend.

Jason Christopher Vogel

Bonds

The bonds of friendship,
The bonds of truth,
The bonds of happiness,
The bonds of youth,
Throughout the many years that we have known
What makes us happy,
What's in our souls,
What's on each other's minds,
And what nobody else knows:
Each passing moment that I can recall
Of getting your letters
Or that first phone call.
The only thing I can think of
That I truly do fear
Is that I break any of the bonds
That draw us both near.

Jerrald P. Murphy

The Wish

In my quiet way, I wish for you angels
And hope like the Sun surrounds you, warm, so warm
Promises that keep and gentle compassion,
Someone to wipe your tears,
And chase away the pain—Truth to guide you,
And a song to fill your heart, and a rainbow that never ends
In my quiet way, I wish for your spirit,
Celestial beings dance and keep you safe, I pray
In my quiet way, I wish for your journey
His love will comfort you throughout your days,
Thoughts to inspire you,
And a song to fill your heart, and a rainbow that never ends

Denise Ambruson

A Lesson Well-Learned

I remember when we first met
Little did I know it was just a bet
I never could tell if you really cared
I assumed you did 'cause you were always there
When I found out that you had lied
It hurt me so much, all I could do was cry
I never thought this could happen to me
There's nothing I can do but let it be
Now when I look back at the past
The lesson you've taught me still lasts and lasts
For I have learned not to give my heart away
Until I know for sure that he is here to stay
Forgive and forget, people always say
They obviously have never felt this way
For if they had they would know
It's hard to forgive and just let go

Soua Yang

The Dance

Under a blanket of midnight
Lit by the fires of the ancestors
I wait for him
The fragrance of night fills my head
Blood courses through my temples, signaling his approach
He taunts me, eluding my grasp
His laughter is cruel; he enjoys my agony
He inches closer only to step back again
We dance like this for hours; the world falls away
In each salty droplet shed
At last he reaches for me, pulling me in with terrible strength
He clutches me to him; for a moment, I cannot breathe
I am everything and nothing;
I am disconnected atoms spinning madly out of control
Then, like the thief that he is, he is gone
Leaving no tangible evidence of our dance

Traci Fuller

Eight

Struggle to stay on that line,
so straight and true.
This task I partake only with you.
Keeping rhythm and time,
a fallacy of reason.
Controlling life and destiny
mimics the seasons.
As pleasing as it sounds,
as wounding as you are,
as ashamed as I get,
straight and narrow is the path we seek,
thought-soaked banter clouds, my sleep.
More and more our reason change,
as promises turn to shame.
That line that seemed so true and straight
reveals itself as a figure eight.

Michael C. Compo

My Mom

She's wonderful in every way.
She does every thing right every day.
Sometimes she can be very forgetful,
But that's okay, because she's so beautiful.
Every time something's troubling my mind,
She's very attentive, and yet she's kind.
She's fun, exciting. I love her. . . . She's mine!
But her energy wears off in time.
She works hard night and day,
Yet she's perfect in every way.
She and I could talk until dawn,
Just because she's my mom.

Alyssa DeWitt

Right Here Next to Me

East rises the sun,
and west, there it sets.
If only you could be
right here next to me.
Hearts and cards reading, "Will you be mine?"
Handing out gifts of affection on Valentine's.
Longing every second that you could be,
sharing this moment right here next to me.
Beautiful displays of light in the sky
of fireworks on the Fourth of July.
Oh, how I wish you could be
watching right here next to me.
Moments together, moments apart,
nothing will stand in the way of my heart.
Now that you're here, my mind open—heart wide.
I feel secured and safe, with you, right here by my side.

Theresa Do

Dirty Deeds

Twin Towers stood, now they burn.
To see them fall, my heart does yearn
To foresee justice, nothing rash,
Not to see peace turned to ash.
My soul goes out to mend those folks,
Whose wheel of life's now missing spokes.
Finding men on a hit list,
Guilty, but to a pacifist,
Other countries should not be blamed;
For these acts, they're inhumane.
Find those responsible, oh, yes.
Now to this world—an eternal test.
Nostradamus said it's near.
End of days—time to fear?
Other nations they all will heed,
Try not to spawn more dirty deeds.

Gareth McKenzie

I'll Give You My Heart

I'll give you my heart. I'll give you my
soul. I'll give you my life and let you
take control. Everything I have.
Everything I own. I'll give it to you, the
one who sits on the throne. I'll give
it to you. I'll give it all for you.
To show just how much I love you.
I'll give it to you. Every penny of
mine is yours. Everything I can't
live without is yours. Everything
that's anything to me I give it to you.
My thoughts make them pure. My fears
take away. My eyes make them bright.
Show everyone your light, and may
everything I do always glorify you.
You gave it all for me too.

Ellen Crill

A Smile

A tender embrace, a gentle smile,
A caring hand to hold awhile.

A dream we carry into the night
To silently face fears awful fright.

A heart to touch that love not knows;
With darkest rain, love's ill fate blows.

A soft hand to take and walk along,
Hopeful in that sweet, sweet song.

Now with this heart taking time to dance,
Hold tightly grace this precious chance.

Virginia Lee Alexander

Our Black Rose

Sister—rest in peace
Though she was a black rose, she was our rose.
When she became a bud, she reached for the sky.
When she bloomed, she spread her petals wide.
As buds appeared from her stem, they gave her life.
Then the buds bloomed, falling from her stem, and began their own strife.

Though she lived the life as a black rose, she was still a rose.
To look at her only a certain few could love.
Her life path was the wrong path but it was her path.
It was a path we all knew was not from above.

Though she bloomed as a black rose, she was still a rose.
And as her petals fell to the ground, one by one, year by year,
she knew she was forever lost and knew we would shed a tear.
Though she was a black rose, she was forever our rose.

Marie Ellen Fiola

Artist at the Park

I see your soul through your eyes
Whose beauty is seen in
The frolics of the fowls,
Smile of the flowers.

I read the works of your mind
Exquisitely carved in prose
So clear as the fountain,
So grand as the palace nearby.

I hear the music of your heart,
So soft, so sweet,
Like the chirping birds and
The whistling wind—so in love,
So enthralled by your beauty and tranquility.

I will come back again
To know where you've been.

Jose Rene Tamayo Tanoy

The Magic of Opposites

The magic of Your eyes shine brightly,
reflecting, reminding me of Your undying love.

The sweet smell of Your body
fills my nostrils, taunting, teasing.
Completeness . . .

Your soft, warm lips upon my own
stir unknown sensations within me;
the tingling remains even after You pull away.
Incompleteness . . .

Wanting, needing more of the touch,
of Your loving caresses,
You leave me; a sense of loss ensues.
I search for thee,
My love, My soul mate,
come to Me.

Naseem Kapdi

Pick Me

I'm all around each day, each year;
Looking for you to be my dear.
I'm growing each and every year;
Every day, yet I'm so very near,
Near to you and all my kind.
Walk slowly and see my cheer.

My colors, soft colors, some colors unseen;
Living in a world where I share your dreams.
Come take me home and show me off;
Make someone smile—I've seen the Nile!
Take me home and look at me;
Remember words and what I did see.
Please remember: Just pick me.

Mary Nolan

a dreamer's sequence

i swore when i saw silver shooting stars,
with glitter tails across the horizon,
planets were marbles to collect in jars
and rockets and airplanes raced toward the sun

i was staring into the midnight blue
when i caught a glimpse of the paper moon
captivated by its cellophane hue;
echoes of moonbeams; summer's eve in june

i strapped on my wings in the midst of the night
and fluttered across the fairy dust foam
the lil' paper moon was sleeping so tight
so i unstitched its thread and took it home

when i stapled it to my bedroom wall,
the moon was mine . . . i had stolen it all

Scarlett Carol Morris

Hey There

Hey there, child, I can hear you cry,
You are so confused and have no idea why,
Why did so many people have to die?
Begin to realize how precious this thing is called life.
Hey there, sir, thanks for the work you've done,
Your service was hard and way far from fun.
The suffering's not over, it's only begun.
Everyone's lost in this, nobody's won.
Hey there, angry man, you need to watch what you do,
They are also victims just like me and you.
The ones that you assault are Americans, too.
We all salute that waving red, white, and blue.
Hey there, world, you hear us cry out loud,
Thanks for your support, it is strongly needed now.
We know the men responsible must be very proud;
We need to stop their terror, it needs to end now.

John Michael Bousum

The Light

On the darkest night, the blackest space,
The loneliest place to be,
There's still a light, though barely in sight
That we all are able to see.
When fear suffocates us,
And the grief nearly blinds us,
And prayers seem lost in the wind
When times seem the worst
Like our lives have been cursed,
One day you'll feel you've been heard.
So close your eyes, weary friend
Here's my hand, to the end
Let's wait here with hope in our hearts.
We'll see that light, and it'll all be alright,
Because each day of our lives
Is the start.

Michele Maynard

Bridges

Bridges, their purpose ever so clear
They span rivers or valleys of air
But also they connect places of time
That exist but in the human mind
Such bridges of time, mainly the past
For our own well being were not meant to last
Although the past has memories in store
It also holds pain which can no longer endure
It is these bridges of which I speak
These bridges must burn before this night's sleep
So our joys and pleasures we can forever keep
Burn, bridges, burn set me free from my past
That which does not serve me let it not last
If it is not here now it was not meant to be
May I have the strength to set it free

Louis G. Gonot

Western in Summer

In summer when the campus wears a skirt of brilliant green,
The trees stretch out their leafy arms in welcome to her scene.
Each building opens wide its doors, the windows swing clear wide;
The lingering echo of the chimes stirs us to seek inside.

A soft perfume envelops us; we stop nostalgically
To capture once again the thrill of things that used to be.
Time marches on, the founder's gone, his dream is with us still—
"The spirit is the thing" alive and vibrant on the hill.

So, Western, in your glory, shine your beacon near and far.
Inspire us, drive us toward our goal, ere we must "cross the bar."
Ere summer's gone and life has flown; help us our dreams fulfill
And may we make a better world with spirit from the hill.

O, Western, you're a symphony . . .
Dressed in summer majesty!

Bess Martin

Fire Snuffed Out

Time has passed since you and I said goodbye,
but still in my heart lies a flame for you.
I know it shouldn't be allowed to burn,
I know I should snuff it out.
But I am afraid that if I let the fire die,
then I will die as well.
I gave you so much of my heart,
that if I let you go,
I don't know if my heart will be able to go on beating.
This may be against all logic,
but I fear it to be true.
And I just don't know if I have the courage
to step away from the fire,
into another form of heat;
I don't want to die.

Sarah Marie Sexton

Jacob

For Jacob

I look upon his little face, peaceful in slumber
His golden curls in wild array
Wide awake, big blue eyes, full of childish wonder
He looks to me and all I see—pure love
Making my heart thunder
The joy I feel when I take his hand
The warmth
I gaze down at the little face, looking up at me
Hand in hand, we walk in quiet harmony
This child and me
Gramma, he cries
Excited to see
A monarch butterfly, flying free
God has truly blessed me

Colleen Loraas

Forgiveness

I wrote a letter to forgive myself
for enduring seven years
of physical and emotional abuse.
I forgive myself for not leaving
the first time he punched me in the face.
I forgive myself for staying
after he locked me out of the house.
I forgive myself for staying awake many nights,
wondering which women he was with.
I forgive myself for pretending to be asleep
at night so he would not start an argument.
I forgive myself for leaving the house
early in the morning just to avoid him.
I am congratulating myself
for being strong enough to leave.

Tabitha Renee Edwards-Valere

Fill Me

Out of the depths of a broken spirit,
I call upon your holy name, oh, Lord,
that you might flood my parched soul
with your loving kindness.

Be enthroned in my heart and consume me.
Fill to overflowing the space
that you have reserved for your love,
which no earthly thing can ever replace.

For you alone have I been fashioned,
a vessel of honor chosen
for your good pleasure.

By your Spirit pour into my cup
your boundless love
that knows no measure.

James Clarence Revoir

I Long for You

I remember that first day
When I met you.
All the angels were singing
The song I will always remember . . .
It was a song about you,
A song of grace.
You saw me, and I turned away.
I tried to talk to you, but I didn't know what to say. . . .
I went up to you and pretended to be doing something else,
But I was just listening to your voice.
I didn't know what to do or what to say,
But I knew I should say hi.
I said hi, and then ran;
For I knew you heard and didn't know what to else to do.
Not a day goes by that I don't think of you.

Jeffrey A. Noll

Mama, Please Don't Worry . . .

Mama, here I am again.
So sit with me and talk for a little while.

You have been wondering where I've been.
The trouble I must be in.

Mama, don't you cry.
Let me wipe them tears from your eyes
Everything is all right.

Mama, it's time for me to hit the road again.
Ramble on to another place.
There are too many places I have to see.
I want to see them all.

Mama, before I go there's just one thing you need to know—
Just remember I love you, no matter where your boy rambles on. . . .

Christopher Mock

No Escape

"Hey Mac, can you spare me a dime?"
"Here you go, son."
"That's not what I had in mind."
"Hand over your wallet," the young man said.
"Gimmie your money, or you might be dead."
"Why do you beat me and make me cry?"
"Fork over the dough, if you don't want to die."
"Gimmie the cash, if you know what's best."
The old man says no. Gets shot in the chest.
The young man runs. You can hear him say.
"They ain't gonna catch me, no how, no way."
Goes into an alley to buy some drugs.
Gets in a scuffle with some local thugs.
They beat him with bats as he slowly dies,
Isn't it ironic; now, he cries.

Bill G. Gaul

Wounds Unbound

I die, I die; each time I lie, I die.
For I must die because of my lie.

Each time I lie, I get high.
For I get who I call.

Oh, that God will forgive my folly
And receive me higher than liar.

I now know that drugs don't heal, they kill.
Yet all my life I've lied,
Lied to get high and heal.
I have hurt many hearts.

But now, I die a liar!
Teach me, oh God, how to kneel and heal
The wounds I've left unbound.

Atieno Florence Mhonie

A Fantasy of Life

In a world of magical spells, where people
can change from one form to another,
nothing is what it appears to be, and nothing
is what it seems.
A world where there's a life of love and
nothing held back,
where you risk it all only to have one
chance of love and happiness without fear,
a world where people get along helping each
other through thick and thin,
to put aside the hatred of the past and
doing what we know in our hearts to be right
by turning the tides of history to a perfect
paradise for everyone to live together in a
fantasy of life.

Elaine Cooper

Steel Geranium

Sometimes, I feel like a steel geranium
in an iron garden with the
cloudy coppers nailed above me.

Sometimes, I feel like a wooden rose
among mahogany butterflies
with the sloping stump-strewn hills.

Sometimes, I feel like dripping gold,
slithering in the sun and
running down into expensive pools.

Sometimes, I feel like a shattered tree
in fragments, slicing through the earth;
real and painful,
beautiful and deadly,
like my birth.

Bryan Arthur Smith

The Rain

Silence is upon me,
Darkness surrounds all.
The thunder is rolling,
While raindrops fall.
Silence invites loneliness,
As darkness holds fear.
Thunder has its own powerful voice,
As raindrops form tears.
Tapping on my window, frantic with a rhythmic beat,
Running off the rooftop,
Its destiny it meets.
Puddles forming,
As rivers of tears.
Depression overcomes me,
As the storm grows near.

      Judith A. Bolton

The Face of a Friend

Gentle dewdrops caress my toes and splash softly—

I hasten to our secret spot.

The ebbing haze tinges delicately with
powder pink.

My breaths augment the wind's rhythm as it
disperses its warm, moist fragrance.

The birds herald my arrival and anticipate
the appearance of my friend.

Eyes now closed, warmth washes my face like
an ever-rising tide.

Heaven's curtains radiantly unveil—

and God smiles on the Earth.

      John Frank Grauch, V

Another Day Has Passed!

Another day has passed not to see your smiling faces.
To hold you in my arms, to smell your sweet scent.
Touch your soft face and run my fingers through your hair.
The sound of your voices are still planted fresh in my mind.
Laughter you girls gave me when we played.
When you girls would say, I love you Mommy, is never forgotten.
No one can ever replace the way you made me feel inside.
I never knew I could have so much love for someone.
I look back to the day when you were in my arms,
And I never felt so much love.
Remembering how much you wanted to walk and talk like me.
Your love is never forgotten,
And I carry my love within every breath I take.
One thing is true is my love for you will never stop growing.
Another day has passed till I will see you angels again. . . .

      RaJeana Price

Come Walk with Me

Come walk with me to an altar of prayer,
It won't take us long before we get there.
We'll kneel at the cross where Jesus died
To save the lost from the sinful cost.
Don't you know He loves you?
Don't you know He cares?
And His love with you He wants to share.
Come walk with me to an altar of prayer,
It won't take us long before we get there.
We'll talk to Jesus and confess every sin,
Jesus will hear us, if we bid Him in.
Then His blood will flow all o'er your soul
To cleanse your sin that has stained within.
Come walk with me to an altar of prayer,
It won't take us long before we get there.

      Vivian M. Fuller

Satisfaction

I have material possessions;
I am popular and good-looking.
I have a 4.0 GPA.
I am the best at sports, music, and the arts;
I'm not satisfied!
My family loves me for who I am;
My friends are loyal;
My coworkers respect me.
My job is not that stressful;
I am becoming satisfied. . . .
I have been given unspeakable joy,
Peace that surpasses all understanding,
Love for others that despise me;
God has given me eternal life.
I am satisfied.

      Jaclyn Schaer

A Touch of Madness

I sleep with you, you make love to me.
I am feeling so good, how can this be?
I am not deserving of this pleasure for free.
There must be a price for this pleasure to be had,
C'mon, it can't be all that bad.
There must be a price, but what can it be?
What type of torture is suited for me?
Perhaps a knife or a razor blade
To offset the good in our lusty charade.
Or maybe some nails hammered into my head
To drown out the wails I utter in bed.
Perhaps a bullet fired in the right place
Will wipe the smile off of my face.
Pleasure and goodness I surely don't deserve,
So hurt me now before I lose my nerve.

      Stephanie Marie Kuhn

Dreaming

I dream of dragons swift and sure
With shimmering scales and eyes so pure
With glittery wings that sparkle so bright
They soar over mountains and shade the moon's light
They glide to the clouds that blanket the sky
Their shadows pursue them wherever they fly

I dream of wizards with powers so great
Their magic they use to heal and create
And when you have neither your wisdom nor right
They come to the rescue and restore thy life

I dream an adventure to a far away place
With dragons and wizards and flying through space
There's beauty and wonder from bottom to top
And then . . . I wake up

      Darcey C. Schulwitz

A Look in Jesus's Soul through My Eyes

As I sit in this garden I see a valley of tears,
this world's destruction will make alive fears.
I am to suffer the pain and the sin,
upon my back I shall carry it like a thousand pins.
But out of love I do this for you,
I think not more than once about falling to the ground for you.
My knees are skinned from the thousands of falls
and my eyes are hazy from the thorns in my skull.
The whipping was gruesome, I even bled sweat.
I carried the cross, with splinters and rough wood,
tearing away at my whipped flesh.
To Heaven is where I would like you to go,
that is why I have made this sacrifice for you.
I love you, my children, and now I must go.
But I ask you this question, "Was my suffering for nothing?"

      Barbara Torres

Overcast

When I look to the moon at night
I see God's glory, love, and might.
I think about things out of this world,
but who cares? I am just another girl.
When I see the moon and its glorious light,
it tells me I'm alive and everything is alright.
But where is the moon when you need it the most,
under the clouds or shining over a different coast?
It's the thing I see first
and the light I see last,
except for when there is an overcast.
The moon and the stars are something God created,
so look up at night, for they may help you make it.

Ashley Brooke Hunt

What Is White?

What is white?
White is snow. White is a cloud.
White is the music when you sing aloud.
White is the color of breath in the night
and warmth in the stars that shine so bright.
White is a diamond ring that's pretty and sweet;
White is a wedding dress that's sewn very neat.
White makes me feel special and warm when I eat white rice
while sitting on the cold, cold ice.
When I feel white cotton, the bad things are forgotten and good
things come about.
White is the color of a bunny's fur and the sound of a cat when
it's about to purr.

White is beautiful in every kind of way.
White will comfort me every day.

Jenna Simon

Traveling to Australia

Even though it is very far away,
Australia is an interesting place.
You should think about it, just if you may.
Simply get on a plane with your suitcase.

The Great Barrier Reef is amazing.
The fish come swimming right up to you.
You always can see the different fish grazing.
You can also snorkel and scuba dive, too.

Sydney is also a great place to see.
The opera house looks like three sailing ships.
You can cruise the harbor, just off the sea.
Just make sure you don't fall and take a dip.

A whole new adventure is the outback.
There isn't much Australia seems to lack.

Chandra Clemens

Unity

Recycle my soul.
Make me a bird with wings;
let me feed off of a flower,
shine like a rainbow,
dance as a dolphin.
Reincarnate my heart.
Have me bound to the Earth as a river;
let me breathe as an anemone for eternity.
Let innocence be as natural as the sunset,
secure as the moonrise.
Bless my mind with metamorphosis,
so a butterfly I can be.
Transform this unclarity,
so I can be—
soul mates with me.

Melissa Marie Brechisci

Faraway Love

In a land far away, a love waits for me,
a love I've never met, one I'll never see.
Eyes as dark as mine, hearts that beat as one.
I never meant to fall; oh, what have I done?
This shouldn't have happened; it's not the right time.
But love has no rules, reason, or rhyme.
Seems I've known him forever; he's even in my dreams.
Then I awake all alone, how I want to scream.
I send to him this day, on the wings of a dove
all my thoughts and passion, and of course all my love.

Regina Nida

Sailing

For Dad

As the boat glides over the crystal blue,
Waves splash and splurge against the hull.
As the spray shoots into my face
In a foamy splash,
The salty ocean smells tickle my nose.
I can feel, with the gathering of wind,
The ropes between my fingers, begging to go.
The canvas sails are slapping the wind.
They threaten the sky.
They're in a race, but I can no longer
Hold them in place.
Off we go . . . just my boat and me,
Flying past the clouds
And over the glistening sea.

Elizabeth Lordan

Feelings Compel with Love

Love could be what you want it to be
but could hurt like thorns of a rose
could sting like a honeybee
it could be easy to get trapped in it
it could be easy to get out and turn to hatred
just be thankful if it happens to you
it makes life complete itself
it brings betrayal and seduction
which destroy the human race
but it is also makes each generation to continue
it turns the strong man to be weak
it makes the weak to go extra miles to get favor
it compelled every victim to do foolish things at times
but it's good to go through it all the same
thou should be grateful it happens all the same

Adenike Omolara Fashawe

Lefty's Song

Pity the romantic . . .
for all is seen in shades
of love . . . rather than the real.

Mired in total fantasy
and clinging to a dream.
Denying things are never such . . .
as we would have them seem.

Love borders on insanity.
What's real is not, what's not is real . . .
a thin line from depravity.

But in the end, would we admit
that love is all in vain?
The answer lies with those who share . . .
the knowledge of sweet pain.

Billy Alexander Dayers

Don't Knock the Hustle!

Some days you ball, some days you don't
when your body is pouring of a nerve,
wreaking of sweat.

Back and forth you run, repeating the pattern.
Your goal . . . to get the ball, and to you . . .
nothing else matters.

To get the ball in the basket,
to get the ball period, to rack up on personal points,
while your fans sit and cheer. . . .

A never-ending hustle, like the court is the streets,
to knock the other person . . . watching your feet.

To put on the uniform, the number you answer by,
that's the only drug that gets me high!

Victoria Gallardo

I Am There for You

I know times are rough
And I'm always there when stuff gets tough
There's no need to hesitate
You're my king and I'm your queen
Together we can get through anything
You don't have to wait
I've got ample time for you
My affections and concerns are real; if you only knew
Your sweet, gentle smile has faded with the times
All I'm trying to do is get back the spirit I wish were mine
People come and go, and storm clouds come with the passing Sun
Realize that you've got people that are here for you, Dun
No one can replace the man you've grown with and love
And no one is trying to
What I want you to know is that I love, care, and am here for you

Ayana M. Perez

Joy and Pain

First you receive joy then pain.
They always go hand in hand.
Life itself is joy and pain.
Never ending always around.

We go through life with joy and pain.
We try to live with them at our side.
Some days are good ones and some are bad.
Always joy and pain.

Love gives us both joy and pain.
Some days are happy and some days sad.
The one thing we can always count on
in this life are three little words
that carry so much weight:

Joy and pain.

David Allen Smith

The Darkness Inside of Me

There is a darkness inside of me—
a feeling I cannot escape.
This feeling is eating away at me.
I am as foolish as a jackanape.
Do you see the darkness in me?
I see the darkness in me—lingering
clinging to my soul like a shroud—
veiling the light that is there, too.
What am I supposed to do?
What on Earth am I supposed to do—
sit here and cry like a fool?
No-I will do something about it—change my life
change the direction I am going.
Runaway to the light—escape the maddening crush
of the darkness inside of me.

Rachel Embach

Sweet Escape

She lies awake, hoping God will take her
There's nothing left for her
Just shattered dreams and a broken home
Her time has come, she can feel it
Her heart is anxiously awaiting her sweet escape
There are no tears wept to dry
She just lies there
Then, it sets in
Her throat tightens, as she gasps for a breath that's not there
She knows it is time
She looks back on her life before her mind blackens
She smiles just a little
One last breath and she's gone
That's what it's like when you're waiting
Waiting for your sweet escape

Heather Mae Gomez

The Epitome of My Emotions

The epitome of my emotions
Lies beyond the reflection of the mirror
Image does not define my disposition
Thoughts and feelings are those that one must hear

My voice illustrates the scars and splendor
Of the eternal soul that rests within
The essence of its every endeavor
Lies in words that are too short to begin

Too many often judge by looks alone
And determine one's character by sight
Who should be disregarding what is shown
In an effort to do what they deem right

Speech is the key to being understood
For images are often misconstrued

Cara Iorianni

Reality

Never!
Turn your back on reality.
It won't go away.

Face it!
Although you don't see it every day.

Don't!
Argue with reality.
It drives its point home right away.

Seek it!
Although its presence makes you—prey.

A coward could never face it; the faint-hearted don't seek it.

But!
Reality—like death—will come someday.

Gerrold Johnson

The Window

Through my window, I see a world
A world of horror and hate
Through my window, I see all that is wrong
Yet I still peer out
In hopes of a new, fresh world

Through my window, I see the dirt of the world
I stare hard, in deep concentration
I take my rag in hand and sweep the glass
I peer out again

Through my window, I see a world
A world of dreams and love
Through my window, I see all that is right
Once again, I peer out
In hopes for my new, fresh world to remain this way forever

Jennifer Eve Homen

Your Love

Your love is like a leaf, fallen from a tree.
Away from me, please stay with me.
Your love is like a bell, ringing the last time.
Oh, what I would give to hear that sweet chime.
You swept me off my feet,
Sending my heart into retreat.
When I am around you I need to let you know
That I still love you so.
Your love is like a river, twisting and turning all about.
No one knows where it will turn out.
My stream is dying out, and running out of water.
Please come back one more time; you'll always have a place here.
Your love has given me something to live for,
But now it's gone, along with my poor soul.
Your love.

Joel Mellinger

As If I Am Prey

The birds hover over my head
circling as if I am prey

They switch positions
weaving an imaginary scarf
across the Sun-squinted
blue sky
Only a few decide not to play
and glide alone

It is not that enjoyment is not withdrawn
but a hand or claw inside pulls back,
preventing them
from joining the flying herd

They prefer the warmth of
a single string

Nathan Andre Gamache

new life

from the moment we are given life we begin to die
foolishly we yearn to grow older as a child
on the other hand, nearer to death we wish we
were young once again
searching for a purpose and never finding one
the questions of life are always unanswered
why do some flowers only bloom at night
why does the sun burn so violently
the sky is blue for what reason
why do we inflict pain upon loved ones
hurting the people closest to our hearts is unjustified
yes, life is cruel in certain ways
but it's whether you look up and smile or submit to fate
we all ask for a new life at some point but
we work with what we have

Roger Derrick Flores

the virtue of one

there she stands, all alone,
missing what was once there.
the fear sets in; she puts her head down;
she looks at the grave of what once was,
and she knows it will never be again.
she lives with discontent and anguish
upon her face.
i stand there proud and true, showing her the way.
she lifts her head and sees me.
a smile from her face lights up the sky,
and she says to me,
"i thought the world had come to end,
i don't believe it's true,
you showed me what i need to see,
and all i needed was you."

Felix Casio

Night Sky

I am a loving Grandma
I watch over my daughter
Who is now a mother

I hug her surrounding her with my cloak
My cloak is a fathomless black
That has winking diamonds in a celestial pattern
My daughter's children look at me after my husband has gone to bed
They look at the ornate patterns in my cloak and name them

Every so often one of my winking diamonds falls off
Then one of my grandchildren wish upon it
I lovingly watch my daughter with my iridescent face

My hood falls over my face sometimes, sometimes hiding parts of it
Sometimes hiding it all
I am a loving Grandma who loves her child and her grandchildren

Elizabeth Mae Stogner

Mountain Metaphor

Sometimes, on the way to the top of the mountain,
I pause.
The climb has left me weary
And I must regroup.
The stillness in the air forces personal thought.
Only, I am here to listen.
I look off to the side in the valley and
I begin to see myself there.
I cannot decide if I should collapse or cry.
I take in the air.
After a moment, I proceed.
I know that I am capable of conquering this
Mountain, and all others which may have once been difficult.
Now, it's easy to recognize the courage within myself.
And that is a great climb.

Sabrina Laughter Benedict

Not Like Peter Pan

Come dreams whisp'ring over me
lark hymns to cricket carols
come dreams dance butterfly-winged
mistymind to giddy glance
Spinning dizzily in a
carrousel . . . closed eyes . . . tickled
by the moons-and-stars-and-suns
O, smile First Quivered and Bit
O, hands First Clutched a dampened pillow . . .
Eyes sniffed, Battled Sleet
then tears
But now surrender
yield
melt
The young girl flutters . . . bye-bye.

Aimee Hui

Tomorrow

You ask me what 'tis like when time is gone
Does darkness fall or Sun still cast a light?
Do children play and birds still sing a song
Or do they fade away into the night?

Would God create a gift but for a while
A life of love begun, only to end?
A verdict passed in such a short-lived trial
It seems he must intend a greater plan.

Beyond the wall of life, there will be found
A path to walk which leads us to be free
From morbid chains of death, by which we're bound
The darkness conquered, once again we'll see

Barriers, first broken, then surpassed
Are trails far down the road to ever last.

Terrance Nicholas Toner

Interstate of Desolation

Traveling down this twisted road,
My brights are almost dim.
Detours, a bridge out, my speed has slowed,
The route ahead looks grim.

Highways, main streets . . . I don't go there,
I like the route less taken.
But exploration leads to nowhere,
And I often am left shaken.

No passersby, no headlights glare,
No pedestrians to cause strife.
It's lonely out here, I'm well aware;
This is the road of my life.

Holly Ann Meyer

Lost

Lately I've been so lost inside,
I feel like running away!
Away from all this pain and confusion!
Pain of family, confusion of friends!
Friends and family being such an embarrassment!
Embarrassment to the world that makes you want to scream!
Scream out to the world that you want to leave!
Leave this pain
Leave this confusion
Leave my friends
Leave my family
Leave the embarrassment
Lost . . . I've been lost!

Morgan P. Cagle

I Am From . . .

I am not from diamond rings or fancy cars,
nor from Einstein or a movie star.
The only claims to fame I own are a guy
who helped Custard and some king from France,
but they aren't who I am.
I am from the little things that surround me every day.
I am from my rabbit and the China cabinet.
I am from my memory box and my diary.
I am from the creek where I used to play.
I am from my barn which is filled with sweet smelling hay.
I am from my horse which I ride every day.
I am from the little puppies that romp around in the hay.
I am from all of these things and from these things are me.

Angela Distad

America

These last few days are in our minds
of the tragic events which took place
The unity in the air rides the winds
and reach every man, woman and face.

What is this word terrorism we know
that hurt and kill our innocent people
Brought to us by some unknown foe
and bring us together walking to the steeple

The nation became one to light candles at the hour
we salute the heroes with thought and flower
one can only hope and pray
there will never be a time like this day.

Chris John Marsicano

Don't Speak

Don't speak . . . some things don't need sayin'
Just watch . . . the games people are playin'
Listen . . . everyone is speakin'
In silence . . . my spirit does not weaken

Don't speak . . . look at my eyes, they're talkin'
Mouthless . . . my commitment I am hawkin'
Lips closed . . . I hear angels singin'
Wordless . . . my eyes and smile are screamin'

Don't speak . . . and while our lips are restin'
Listen . . . and learn better the lesson
Of silence . . . where there's no chance for lyin'
Without lies . . . there's no need for cryin'

Heart J. Fox

Bubble

Consider a bubble for a moment, if you will.
Quite an object of beauty, indeed?
Perfectly round, floating on air
Shiny with the iridescence of many colors.
Cheerful and content is the life of a bubble
As short and bitter as it ends.
Like the wings of a feathery butterfly
Frail is the luminous sphere of a bubble.
Falling softly as if not to break
Only to be shattered upon a world
So unlike its own makeup.
A flit of color and beauty, floating with grace
Splattering into a sticky liquid on the ground.

Marlene Behne

Mourning Blossoms

Holocaustic exodus,
A Daemon's design attained,
With Fins of Malice and Misery,
Doubt the mind, Deny the truth.

Coral Blossoms outside my domain,
Viewed with desolate senses parted,
Blind skies over rank and file,
Wastelands of grey, an Arctic Desert.

Creation has no conception, no sagacity,
The Wind blows still, here, my life Eternal,
Yet sitting in silence, I grasp to fail,
And all I see are the Coral Blossoms.

Chris Hebein

Our Mom

Our mom could kiss our tears away,
but as we got older
that job got harder
as we needed more than a kiss.
Our mom puts up with more than what anyone
else does in a lifetime.
Our mom has an unconditional love,
and that love is like a circle—never ending.
Our mom has the best job in the world—
just being Mom!
Being a mom is a reward!
Being a mom allows you to share the love you
have with the people you love the most!

Kim Beran

Unsung

Blessed be those who stay true to themselves.
Those who stand tall and those who do not, or
cower from fear, or wither from hatred, or
give up from despair, learned at an early
age. Hold your head up high and never, never
say goodbye. Have pity for those who loath
you and passion for those who embrace your
presence. Give a little bit of your time, or
share a little bit of your wealth, or teach
a little bit of your trade, learning from
others as they learn from you. But the last
thing you should ever want to be is just
like somebody else.

George B. Lyons

A Poem of Hope

Why can't things be my way for a change
Instead of always being against me
Why can't I have the good life for a change
Since happiness is to be free

I find beauty all around me
But with me it never stays
With time it comes to me
And with my heart it always plays

One day I will find my love
And she will always be in my heart
Everyone deserves to know love
Before this world they depart

Brandon Wayne Klein

A Hole in the Skyline

There is a hole in the skyline;
It saddens me.
It is something that should not be.

There is a hole in the skyline, so big and so dark;
It saddens me.
It is something that should not be.

There is a hole in the skyline where people once were;
It saddens me.
It is something that should not be.

There is a hole in the skyline and one in my heart;
It saddens me.
It is something that should not be.

Fran Trombetta

Blondie

Hey, hey, Blondie, I'm falling after you
Hey, hey, Blondie, what was I supposed to do
Hey, hey, Blondie, there are no words need to be said
Hey, hey, Blondie, you're messing with my head

Hey, hey, Blondie, I have given you it all
Hey, hey, Blondie, will you pick me up if I fall?
Hey, hey, Blondie, do you see the tears that drown my eyes?
Hey, hey, Blondie, I'm wasting my time

Hey, hey, Blondie, you're much too beautiful for me
Hey, hey, Blondie, your siren song makes a mess of me
What did you say before you left me all alone?
You said, I'm sorry if I was just leading you on

Douglas Michael Jay

Please

Every morning she puts on her black clothes,
Hating her dark life.
She sits alone on the way to school,
Uselessly trying to forget the silence
That engulfed the bus when she stepped on.
Walking through a mass of people in the hall,
She tries to ignore the rude comments.
She stares at the floor, memorizing all the cracks,
And pushes through the wall of bodies.
All she wants is a friend to save her from this darkness,
From the confusion deep inside of her.
The loud tormenting and the quiet whispering echo in her mind,
And she realizes that they will never understand.

Abbie V. Morgan

Can I?

Can I write you a poem,
tell you a secret,
or just sit close and inhale you?
Can I whisper sweet nothings
'til your ear starts to tickle
from the sweetness of the nothings
and our scents start to mingle into the one that once was two?
Can I tell you about attractions,
not the ones that detail the physical
or the ones that explain the mental
but the ones that evoke the emotional
as only attractions do?
Can I . . . with you?

Felepe Hassen Hall

Why?

Why was our country attacked with such force
Leaving Americans with such remorse?
Why were lives ended, some babes on the vine,
Never a chance to enjoy the sublime?
Why can't all love, today and tomorrow
Ending the times of hate and sorrow?
Why did this happen in the land of stripes and stars?
To us this can only be, in lands from afar.
Why can't we change this, starting today?
I think we can, if we all mend our ways.
Why not as a tribute to family and friends gone
Start all anew from this day on?
God bless America!

Catherine M. Sheffler

The Rest Is History

I seem to have lost my way; where is my home?
I've seen things I don't wanna see; my mind is lost.
These memories fade every day, can't find my soul.
My mind is lost today,
Can't seem to find my way.
There's gonna be hell to pay
when I find my way home.
A parent being lectured by their child,
a teacher without words to say, will the students be lost?
A school yard fight breaks out, who will break it up?
A black eye, a bloody nose, no hand to heal,
My mind is now made up; I'm gonna change
into something better, Lord only knows.

Christopher Holcomb

School—Are You Going?

School is starting, how are you going?
I was asked.
In just a day or two, it will be.
Classes will commence, and I will not want to be missed.
But will I go? This I do not know.
School is starting, HOW AM I GOING?
Be it by foot or bus by car or bike,
I will be there.

Rachel Arndt

As True Americans

Once we were a nation
secure in our thoughts.
Now, we are just scrutinizing
the things that we were taught.
However, as true Americans,
we will see that justice prevails.
And once again, above all,
we shall lead the world along a righteous trail.

Madeline M. Valentini

Where Pain Kneels

The steel and bodies fell in a heap.
For each one lost, a thousand weep.
But just as night to morning yields
So ends the rapture of the deep.

The oft-told tale of the phoenix reveals
True spirit rises from where pain kneels.
Their seeds of destruction will only reap
New life for those that Heaven shields.

MaryVance Duggan

Crushed Heart

I'm hurting so with a weight on my heart
That I couldn't break free if I tried.
This hurt that I feel, this weight on my heart,
Is truly tearing me up inside.
People tell me this hurt, this weight on my heart,
Is much less than I'm making it be.
But this hurt that I feel, this weight on my heart,
Is indeed very real to me.

Anita M. Grenier

Broken Hearts

I see the rain falling down,
but it doesn't seem to make a sound,
the world shuts out what can't get in
I'm wondering where it all began,
In this world with all its pain,
why can't we find love in the rain,
but when the rain stops falling, wouldn't you know.
Watch out because here comes the snow,
And then when you think the sun is out bright,
that's when it comes the darkest of night,
so that's what I mean when the snow's falling down
and the sun melt's it without any sound,
so if you believe me then here what I say
Stay away from the darkest of day

Theresa A. Goodwin

Let's Start Over

Three weeks ago, many lives were shattered.
To those few men, our pain did not matter.
For a cause that we will never understand,
They came into our peaceful, free land and
They tore apart our plans and our dreams
With horrific plots and deadly schemes.
But maybe we needed a wake-up call
To help us see what's important after all.
It's families and friends, freedom, and peace:
The color of skin, in importance, the least.
The cursing and fighting with our fellowman;
We can all stop now, start over again.
Let's do this for peace, let's do this for love,
The kind that comes from our Father above.

Susie Hill

The Pain That Does Not Rhyme, the Rhyme That Has No Pain

I was overcome by anger.
I was overwhelmed with hurt.
Hurt for all the things I missed,
Angry for all the wrong reasons.
In my head, a picture perfect family
That everyone shared but me.
In my heart, an emptiness
That everyone lacked and loved.
For my sake, she acted as both parents.
She wanted me to forget him and the past.
But how does one forget the future?
It only makes things worse when I lie to myself.
But at this moment I am content,
Content to think of all that lies
Within my heart and soul, I vent
The love that shines in my daughter's eyes.
So here I sit and look at her,
My reason to exist and be,
And when I'm overwhelmed with hurt, I'll know
'Twas he who missed out more than me.

April Bradley

A Silent Plea

My feet refuse to work,
as if it is some duty I may not shirk.
And my mouth refuses to give voice to tears,
and so I stand beside you, beset with fears.

It is true that despite my colored learning,
my heart knows only of yearning,
fair maiden, would you lend me your ear?
Spare me a thought, or smile, or pitiful tear.

Long have I watched and stood by,
as you walked suitors before me with a gleaming eye.
My rage grows daily, this is true, for to every dawn
there is a new one, another over which you fawn.

Oh, it is so unfair, that my admiration must be from afar,
must be as glances in a viewing hall,
and that my deep, cold fears won't allow me to stand tall.

Alas, I give but one pitiful statement more,
so that you may know that which I grieve for.
You spare me to time to bask in the light of your eyes,
but you have me, mind, heart, and soul.

Jeffrey Denton Bowers

A Penny for You

If I had a penny I would spend it all on you, in hopes that it would
take you on through. For a penny isn't much, but for you, it keeps us
in touch. For our friendship is more special than a penny or two.

Karen Nitsche

Why Remember?

I remember when we never talked, well, maybe just a nod
I remember the tone of your voice when your words struck me like a rod
I remember the hurt of my heart when you never returned my calls
I remember the days when we'd argue and our love would rise and fall
But ever since you lost your feelings for me
And locked your love away from me
I've been searching for the key
So why should I remember what wasn't meant to be?

Ralph Brown

Utopia Forever

I wake in the morning to the sweet smile on your face
That warms my very being like the Sun on my face
Invigorating voice of the sweetest siren
That leaves me utterly uxorious.
Your vivaciousness, alluring me to the nostalgia of us.
The enticement to have your sweet breath upon my skin,
To hold you once again, like a dewdrop in the petal of a rose,
To cradle you in this ultra utopia that I have found only in you, forever.

Michael Lynn Adams

What Is It All Worth?

From after death to before birth, we wonder, "What is it all worth?"
All the struggles, all the pain, all the hardships with no gain.
You must win, or you must cede. "One more try," you beg, you plead.
You strive. You give it all you can. "Why can't they just understand?"
All the work through every day, just like labor with no pay.
You make an effort, aim to please, but end up begging on your knees.
One more try, that's all I ask. I know I can complete this task.
But then I say, just to myself, "What is it all worth?"

I guess I'll never know until the end.

Nick Joseph McCollum

Grandma's Advice

Written by a wife, mother, grandmother, and a terminal cancer survivor
Oh, my, troubled little one, come sit here quietly by my side.
You must learn to relax a while for all anxious thoughts to subside.

Here love, come lay your little head against my shoulder, warm and firm.
Tell this old lady what causes such tears and anger to burn?

Heart of my heart, listen quietly, and understand what I am going to say.
Grandma will help you learn so in life you may easily find the right way.

So much hurt and pain should not be within such a tender young breast.
Lift that chin high and wipe the tears away; Grandma knows what is best.

Your life is like a rose bud, opening slowly within each moment you breathe.
Sweetheart, scatter those petals gently only upon the springtime breeze.

Dance through life's experiences, sprinkling star dust as you duck and sway.
Learn to walk unafraid amongst the people lost along the way.

Touch lightly the dangerous games of chance where you could fail.
Be heedful dipping in the oceans of knowledge where you unfurl your sail.

Hold strong within your heart the love of those you will leave behind.
Open wide those ears to hear within and the inner eyes that are blind.

Find the pattern in life child with joy, thus making all things right.
Look for God within and the ancient wisdom hidden there, inside the light.

Love from a joyous heart, my sweet, makes everyone's world go round.
Follow experienced advice from one who has lived it, for it is truly sound.

B. J. Marcou

Are You Watching

Do you look outside each morning
Just to see what God has built
And notice how the colors
Make Twilight stand so still

Do you watch as night light
Fades into dawn's early life
When dew drops might be there
And everything's all right

Walk into your day
Let your spirit show you how
The quiet turns to music
For all creatures, here and now

Donna Neal Stepp

Where I'm From

I am from a seed
Sewn inside the womb
I am from the pictures
Looked at inside my room
I am from God
Placed here for his reason
I am from the outside
Where we celebrate the season.

I'm from the nurse with four kids
From memories in jars
Placed perfectly with no lids
I'm from a man, short and tough
I am from a life that is rough.

I am from a home that is broken
I am from words that were unspoken
I am from here from the world
I am from water
With no shore
I am from the past
With a future and more.

I am from a dream
Pulled from a mind
I am from the ups and downs
I am from this time.

Heather Gresham

Thinking of You

To Megan
I stay up at night,
Thinking of you,
Of how things could be different,
Of how things could be true.

I think of us,
On how they used to be,
I think of how,
You used to look at me.

I think of the future,
On what could have been now,
I think of you back in my life,
But I don't know how.

I think of the memories,
That you've given me,
Things that I won't forget,
For eternity.

Now I'm thinking,
Of your thoughts too,
On how they have left me,
Feeling so blue.

So now I'm thinking,
Beyond and above,
That I just might,
Have fallen in love.

Ryan Hoffmeyer

My Inner Child

When I was just a little girl, I walked and jumped
I went up and down the seesaw and ended up bruised and lumped
Life was fun, no homework or work and every day was like a fairy tale
But as I have grown no more childish things for me
Homework, guys, the whole nine yards
Although I have grown and life is more complicated now
I still have an inner child inside

Gabby Labastida

Your Mother

Who would have ever thought your mother
could be the colorful dressed lady on the
side of the street.
Who could imagine their care giver to be the
evil weird lady down the street.
Who would admit their legal guardian to be the crazy woman locked up.

Nobody ever does know who anyone is.

Ana Veronica Arrambide

Troubles

when you have troubles don't worry
'cause you've always got a friend whose love will never end
he's always waiting to meet your needs and even listen to your pleads
he's the greatest friend anyone could have
so come on friend and put your trust in him
he'll never leave you out on a limb
he died for you, so don't think twice
just call on him, he's Jesus Christ

Drewey Andrew Watkins

Lights

The lights always seem so bright if you look at them long enough,
Or is it that they become dim?
I suppose that you can over analyze things and look at them too much,
And it all looks dim, just like the lights.
But this is life.
Lights, you can turn off, and then back on again,
Once life is off, there is no switch labeled "on."
I am okay with looking at the lights,
They tend to be prettier anyway.

Brandi Suder

Babies

You never know what a baby will turn out to be.
You don't know if the baby will be a boy or girl.
And if the baby is a boy the husband wonders what the baby will be like.
And if the baby is a girl the wife wonders what the the baby will be like.
So the baby sees this and wonders what the dad or mom will be like.
If the baby is a girl the baby wonders what mom will be like.
If the baby is a boy the baby wonders what dad will be like.
If the baby turns out to be a smart girl the dad wonders why.
If the baby turns to be a dumb boy the mom wonders why.
And if the baby turns to be a dumb girl the mom wonders why.
And if the baby turns out to be a smart boy the dad wonders why.
So the baby sees this and really wonders why mom and dad are like this.
Baby grows up and remembers how they were treated.
Baby gets older; parents see the baby growing.
Baby starts to make noises; parents wonder what they mean.
Parents take baby to ask a doctor what these sounds mean.
Doctor gives the parents a book on what sounds mean.
Parents look at book and remember when they were nasty to baby.
If the baby was a boy or girl and was dumb they wonder what mom is like.
If the baby was a boy or girl and was smart they wonder what dad is like.
Babies are sensitive be careful how you treat them.

John Craig

You Think You Know, but You Have No Idea

Tired, callused feet
Blistered, bleeding toes
Aching, strained muscles
All they see is a performance
Graceful, articulate movements
Strong, straight spine
Powerful, pointed feet
They take it for granted
Long, strenuous rehearsals
Tiresome, difficult classes
Constant, relentless exercise
You look so undaunted
Flawless, effortless steps
Perfect, smiling faces
Angelic, agile actions
Its hidden well
Sore, fatigued bodies
Exhausted, throbbing minds
Undamaged, boisterous souls
How do you do it?

Lydia Fein

Hearts Broken in Trusting Hands

The mornings grow darker
As the days go by
No one would wonder
No one knows why
I stand here alone
Just a girl in the rain
Not that they would care
The force or the strain
A single thing done
That cannot be undone
No hand can remake
Repaired by no one
Just a simple heartache
Nothing to compare
To the torments of the world
The lack of air
I'm just a stupid girl
Hurt though no one cares
I live in a strong world
There is no place for tears

Leona Mae Porter

Christy

To CG—love you always
In a world so far from heaven,
Full of heartbreak and fear,
It's hard to find someone you love,
A friend you hold so dear.

Some say it's just by chance or luck,
But me, I know what's true.
God placed us in each other's lives.
Each day I thank Him, too.

You're more than just a friend to me,
You're my baby sister, too.
If anything ever happened to you
I don't know what I'd do.

Eyes as green as emeralds,
Your hair, a lovely brown.
Your smile could brighten any day
And I hate to see you frown.

Christy, I wanted you to know
That I wrote this just for you.
And no matter what, no matter why,
I will always believe in you.

Amanda Isbell Morris

They Don't Stop and Say ...

As the cars pass by, so do the days;
so afraid, alone, scared, and unhappy.
As I cry myself to sleep each night and each day,
I never knew why they didn't stop and say "goodbye is not forever,
but someday somewhere, you shall see."
But what some people didn't say "if you have a heart,
you shall see that I am in you and you are in me forever, you'll see.
You will go on thinking about me, but I see you and feel you
in my heart forever and together, you shall see.
If it is not forever, then what should it be, for a second, minute,
hour, day, week, month, year, or forever until we die together,
we shall see whether it is or isn't."
And what other people didn't say "when you die,
you shall see if you go to Heaven where it is beautiful
or you go to Hell where you shall burn.
But if you go to Heaven and I go to Hell,
we shall be in each others' hearts forever.
Who will tell you and who will tell me, I am not sure,
but what I know is that forever is a long time for me.

Michael Lee Marceau

Sometimes There Are Cracks in the Sidewalk

Sometimes there are cracks in the sidewalks as you walk along through life

Sometimes there are holes, covered by leaves where your life used to
be . . . but you have moved on.

Sometimes the sidewalks ends abruptly in a street. This is where your
childhood ends and the adventures of adulthood begin.

You look with fondness at the sidewalks where your childhood was spent.
You look back at the sidewalk and grieve innocence lost. . . . you look back at
the sidewalk but only for a second; you have moved on.

Sometimes there are cracks in the sidewalk, but you try not to take them
to the street. As your walking the street of adulthood, you remember the
lessons you learned on the sidewalks, to walk with as much grace
and dignity as you can on the street of adulthood.

Sometimes there are cracks in the sidewalk, but you have moved on.
Remember that you should walk tall and proud on the street of adulthood;
someday that road will end eternity begins.

Sometimes there are cracks in the sidewalks. . . . but you have moved on!

Lorien D. Bourne

Dear . . .

Dear, I love the way you look at me and how you tell me what you see.
I love the way you say goodbye, even though I want to cry.
I love how you never mean forever,
And how you make things always better.

There's nothing in this world to find
that can be greater than love, this kind.
There's always way too much to see in a lifetime near to thee.
There's still that part of me that said, you want to leave, so go ahead.

I never meant it to be this way; I really always thought I'd stay.
I never meant to hurt you at all, I didn't want to see you fall.
I never thought you'd feel like this,
and think that to be with me was bliss.

I know it's torture to you, like hell
and you wish for me to break this spell.
I have been trying all along, to fall in love, just like our song.
I wish that something I could do to make you see it's nothing new.

I'll always be afraid, unsure I am no longer completely pure.
I'll always love you 'til the end, and I really want to be your friend.
I'll always know the pain I've caused and all that was counted, then lost.

I'm sorry things could not be better,
I'm sorry that you found this letter.
I wanted to go on with you, I wanted to be good and true.
I tried my very best, please know, but now I think that you should go.

April Highsmith

Other People's Lives

Other people's daughters fall apart,
waste away, wait away their lives
while other people's sons
work hard, live right.

And you sit, lumpish, lifeless,
alone.

Carol R. Strand

Depression

I wish you were in
My mind and heart
Able to understand this confusion
That nags at me endlessly
Bringing me down
I don't wanna go there again. . . .

Osila Grace Gomba

When It's Him I'm Thinking Of

I would have done so much for him
But he didn't care
He meant the world to me
But he wasn't there

I gave so much to make it work
But he didn't even try
Now my world is falling apart
Since he said goodbye

He has his eyes on someone new
He treats her very good
I can't help but wonder why
He didn't treat me like he should

Now I have a broken heart
That maybe time will heal
I wish that I had another chance
To tell him how I feel

Now I sit here lonely
With no one to love
Not just anyone will do
When it's him I'm thinking of

Philomena Dana DiFiore

Self-Esteem

The way for me to live
is to have no way.
My only habit should be
to have none.
I will be what I will be.
I will do what I will do.
All I want to do, or need to do,
is to stay in rhythm with myself.
Today I will work in rhythm with myself,
not with what I should be.
To work in rhythm with myself,
I must keep tuned into myself.
What I am, I am, when I am myself.
All I want is love.
Wanting myself loved,
to be lovable.
How do I get love?
I love.
Don't need love, be love.
Because I do love, I have love.
Love is love.
I am me; myself is who I'll be.
What I do is me;
that is who I am.

Marie Juanita Smith

One of Two

Once there were two women who never knew each other.
One you do not remember. The other you call Mother.
Two different lives shaped to make yours one;
One became your guiding star, the other became your sun.
The first gave you life, and the second taught you to live in it.
The first gave you a need for love, and the second was there to give it.
One gave you a nationality, the other gave you a name.
One gave you the seed of talent, the other gave you aim.
One gave you emotions, the other calmed your fears.
One saw your first sweet smile, the other dried your tears.
One gave you up—it was all that she could do.
The other prayed for a child, and God led her straight to you.
And now you ask me through your tears
The age old questions through the years;
Heredity or Environment—which are you the product of?
Neither, my darling—neither,
Just two different kinds of Love.

Joan Lafond

Verbal Murderer

I am a murderer. No one is dead, but I have killed them.
I didn't use a knife, nor did I use a gun. I didn't need it.
You see, I have the perfect weapon.
You can't pat me down for it, and it won't sound off the metal detectors.

Most people believe it not to be a weapon,
but a tool to help you go through life.
I warn you, though it seems harmless,
it is the greatest weapon unknown to most men.
So what is this great weapon of destruction?
It is no secret, it is the words that come from my lips.
So many people have died from the careless use of this weapon.

Many teenagers have killed themselves because of teasing.
Or they kill themselves, not wittingly,
but by listening to their friends when they are told drugs are cool.

You and I both have committed murder with our words.
Although it may seem like words really don't affect people,
just think about the last time words hurt you.
We may not be able to ban these weapons,
but we can control them.
It may seem like I'm an idealist,
but with your help I can become a realist.
People follow example.
The only question is, what example are you going to set?

Milton Ayala

My Untold Story

I looked out at the water gleaming as the sun hit it;
it seemed to call my name.
I walked toward it. It was a mysterious shade of green tempting, inviting.

My instincts raged like sirens.
Stay away, they told me, but, I didn't listen. I couldn't.
The waves gently lapping at the sand called to me. . . .
I stepped nearer to the water.
Cool water kissed my toes and caressed my bare feet.

I stepped in; water rose past my ankles, my knees,
my waist, my shoulders.
Soon, I was treading water effortlessly . . . freely.
Then the calm water turned; strong, angry rip tides pulled at my legs,
my arms splashed helplessly and my head struggled for the surface.

I tried to breathe, but took in only saltwater that burned my nose
and tore at my eyes.
I cried out. . . . I cried . . . but I never gave up—the tide was just too strong.

My chest gave a final heave. . . . and was flooded with burning water.
Then my breathing stopped. Everything was black.
The waves carried me back to the shore, gently rocking me.

Too late. My face was frozen . . .
frozen into a scream it would hold forever.
I am a child of the sea, and this is my untold story.

Laramie Wingfield

A Simple Prayer for Peace

I pray for peace in the Middle East.
I pray for peace in my hometown.
I pray for peace for our schools.
I pray for peace in the United States.
And most of all I pray for peace for all
those who have none!

Sheryl R. Dillon

Seeds of Evil

She looked in the mirror.
The only thing she saw staring back
Was a little body with a big stomach.
They tell her Jesus died for her sins,
But every night she dies
From her inability to bleed.

Jenna Stehney

Woes of a Third Shift Technician

The nights go by so slowly.
Day never seems to come.
I sit and wait forever but
I never see the sun.

The only light around me
is fluorescent and too bright.
I guess that is a hazard
of working late at night.

The moon is peeking out again
Trying to say Hello.
If only it could understand
How much I want to go.

I really want to leave here.
I want this night to end.
This life I lead is dull and
I don't even have a friend.

So I write this lonely poem
In the hopes that some sweet day
I get to see the sun again
To shine my grief away.

Tressie Norma Conway

A Tribute to a Fallen Comrade

Our hearts are deeply saddened
We lost someone so dear
Someone who brought much joy
Each time that he was near

He always had a smile
Wherever he might go
He always had a pleasant word
As he scurried to and fro

Although we lost a precious one
A part of him remains
The pleasant memories we possess
Will help to ease the pains

So why the sadness, why the tears
Let's dwell upon the happy years
The good he did that meant so much
To each and every life he touched

So if we must be sad today
Let's let the sadness we portray
Be for those poor unfortunate souls
Who happened never to have passed his way

Patricia West Cheney

Cry of the Wild

The world today is so unkind,
which brings to me these thoughts of mind.
We need to change our heartland miles,
or the future will wipe away our children's smiles.
The air's so thick and gray above,
our land's in need of our undying love.
We've reaped the gold from our green lands,
out of greed and deceit to put money in hands.
Our future's outlook is looking dim; to start right now, our time is slim.
Our wildlife is running thin.
Our wilderness is in remorse.
We've destroyed the way of nature's course.
God looks down from up above, unhappy with our dying love.
Together all, as one nation together and fight,
To flee from wrong to do what's right.
We have the opportunity at hand
to save our once pure, righteous land.
Our waters are in deep despair.
From coast to coast they need repair.
My heart has broken right in two,
as I see the filth in our great deep blue.

Catrina A. DeMicelli

Our Dad

As we sit and watch you peacefully sleep, the memories they do come from
deep as time we spent together as Father and Children,
Of times we will never be able to replace.

Of all the times of anger for things we so stupidly had done,
And then of pride, in all the things that we had accomplished,
Of times we use to make you so mad,
and then the others that made you so glad,

The strength was always there with you, guiding us and steering us,
On what you hoped was the right road to walk, never telling us what to do,
But giving us our own mind to use, whether it was right or wrong always
there and always strong,

Your strength was enduring and came from deep within,
the tenderness and caring that was part of you,
You taught giving and caring ways and were always there to show us the way
to be good and gentle kids and to respect what God had given,

To respect our mother and love her dear you taught us right throughout
our years, hands all gnarled and crippled,
still soft and gentle within us they came.

Now we sit and ask the Lord to take you on his golden road where you
will once again be our guardian and protector to guide us to thee!

Naomie Lucius

My Love for You

Looking into your eyes, I could melt away
I never imagined I could ever feel this way
Touching my heart, skipping a beat
Knew one day my soul mate I would meet

Feeling so good, feeling so right
Taking me on an emotional high
Coming into my life felt like a dream come true
I knew I wanted to spend the rest of my life with you

With all the struggles we had to overcome,
We banded together, we became one
I give you my heart; I share with you my life
From the day you and I became husband and wife

I vow to always keep my love close and near
The thought of losing you I shall never fear
Because throughout the lies and all the doubt,
You've never given up hope, showing me what your love was truly about

I promise to love you and always be there
Never forgetting the special memories that we share
Promises to be made, years to go by
I belong to only you, for my love shall never die

Janelle Lee Mack

Run and Hide

I listen as the wind blows.
Its song is a sad one.
I don't want to listen.
The sound I try to outrun.

Over my head, danger leers.
I try and try to hide my fears
But sometimes someone treads inside
And I have to run and I have to hide.

T. J. Currey

Euphony

Dedicated to the sweet sounds of song
E-asy swinging of a clarinet
U-ndaunted cough of the tuba
P-iercing piccolo
H-ypnotic harmony
O-rotund oboe
N-octurne of the violin:
Y-easy . . . rising beauty of music

Shari Gellman Dince

Merciless Hunt

The owl cries in the night.
All of the world is still.
He finally takes flight
For the hunt and the kill.

The field mouse hides
For fear of his soul.
His fears subside.
The owl has control.

As if knowing all too well
Where the mouse stays,
He swoops down like a bat out of hell
And carries away his prey.

Desiree Rose King

Lasting

birth screaming out
growing up from without
people make you be
who you are
by exposing you to that
they wish they were
by and by you who
you are
as an adult
you see very far
by the setting sun
you say I lived this
life my own way

William Boyd Nix

Mi Amor

I sit here and think, without a wink.
Did I do the right thing,
Or did I blow the wing?
Can I take it all back?
Can we give it another whack?
You made me feel special.
You made me think you cared.
You made me feel wanted.
You've taken away my despair.
I wish you'll come back
To be together once more,
Come back to me, my lover, my baby,
Mi amor.

Suzanne Ford

Three in One

Connie, Special Connie, she was loved by all.
Need something done or just for fun, all she needed was a call.
Deep down, an open spot she kept for that special one she met.
He loved her through good times and bad, so many memories—so, so sad.
Way up and above all the other, she was Melissa and Nathan's Mother.
She loved her kids with all her heart, never will they be apart.

Melissa was born in 1982—she was Mommy's precious baby girl.
Little outfits all in pink, she always had that special twirl.
Up and down and all around, this one just could not sit down.
Eyes a sparkling, always smiling; on the phone, she'd be a dialing.
Basketball she loved to play, she was excited come game day.
A Li'l Lady she grew to be—special to Grandma and Sharry and Thee.

Then in 1986, Nathan came a bouncing in.
This one was a boy—ALL BOY, and yes, he had his Father's grin.
And as he grew, upon his face Angel Kisses fell in place.
Oh, how he loved to tease; the look, the laugh and "Pretty Please."
The farm is where he loved to be—fishing, gardening—what'd it be?
Wintertime was where it's at, hockey and his "Kitty Cat."
He was Daddy's Little Boy and Grandpa's "Buddy"—Bundle of Joy.
Little Nathan, oh, so sweet, GOD'S SPECIAL TREAT.

    Annette Shane

The Rocket Boys

"Well, just don't blow yourselves up, boys.
Those rockets aren't toys."
Is what Elsie Hickam says
on just about any old day.

That spelled trouble for Homer, O'Dell, and Roy Lee.
One of their rockets took a wild turn, and from Coalwood they had to flee.
They had to go to Snakeroot
to do a rocket shoot.

The rocket took off with a vroom;
two seconds later it ended with a boom.
They couldn't figure out what they would need,
so they went and asked Quentin for help and he said yes indeed.

Now they are on track,
instead of being slack.
They went to the science fair
because they had their rockets go up into the air.

At the fair, they won,
then at home they shot off the last one.
Homer now works at NASA as an engineer,
but he holds those old days very dear.

    Dawn Kindley

Thoughts of Her

As I lie awake, waiting to fall into a dream of her,
my mind fills with thoughts of her and of the joy that they bring me.
I think of the way my body quivers with excitement
at my first glance of her every presence.
I think of how her smile can brighten my worst of moods
and bring me happiness from within.
I think of the beauty that flows from her
and into me when her arms are around me.
I think of the times when she is by my side and we are as one,
holding hands and the feeling of bliss that runs through me.
I think of the gentleness that flows from her hands when they caress my skin.
I think of how her gestures makes me feel of worth and of her desire.
I think of how her voice soothes me even when she is afar.
I think of the moments that I spend lying by her side
in the quietness of the night, feeling her heart beat next to mine,
hoping that some day our hearts beat as one.
But as I begin to fall asleep, a feeling of sadness comes from within
when she is a far and I have missed her smiles for the day
that have brought her joy and happiness
and that she might have forgotten me.
But as the sadness sets in, I fall asleep and fall into a dream of her
and the joy once again is within me.

    Travis Burrows

A Gift for You

A gift for you, you will find
undercover and behind,
waiting to be filled with memories
of travels far and wide.
As you begin your journey
to places yet unknown,
the key is yours to unlock
the trunk of treasures it will hold.

    Marcia Sandahl

Melting Me

Building up over and over
Its ultimate power deceived me
It conquers it all from poison to flower

Grounding it up slower and slower
My overconfidence convicted me
It forced itself bolder and bolder

Running from it colder and colder
My heart of stone consumed me
Blind and sinking lower and lower

Until the day, when over my shoulder
My lonely cloak of emptiness lifted
Then and now your love melts me
With you in my life, I am truly gifted

    Joe E. Kruse

I Am

I am the night
plain
monochrome
plagued by day
aargh!
the sun
it blinds
my darkened eyes
rainbows
do so outdo me
sunset is my only
salvation
that is when I am
beautiful
but no one
is awake
to see
so I have
only me

    Brandy Churchill

Birth

Days—as clouds
Whisking by
'Mid the torrent of my life
The sun—my friend
Its rays—my foe
To sear me 'mid my strife

The grass beneath
The boughs about
The purging of the rain
To struggle on
Seeking martyrdom
Born from out of the pain

What angels plea
Or gods becry
O'er me—'mid this plight
From darkness came
Thrust out—accursed
Into this feigning light

    Ward Strickland

The Light

Days go by like the rain . . . washing away the dirt from the streets.
I look around and do not see.
I look around, does anyone even see me?
Movement . . . the hustle and bustle of passersby everywhere.
No one seems aware.
If only they would open their eyes . . . perhaps, they might see me.
The days go by without the hint of life.
We move in opposite directions . . .
Away from that which seems to be . . . our destiny.
The rain darkens the sky and our souls, and yet we still do not see.
If only we would open our eyes,
What would there be?
Are we such fools we cannot see . . . the light ahead of our destiny?
Love, life, and all that's good;
These things are all around, if only we could . . . see.
Days come and go,
Perhaps, there will be a day not far away.
A day that just <u>one</u> stands up to search the sky.
Just one to say . . . I see.

    Susan Lee Vaughn

Blades of Green

Fresh new leaves are filling the trees
making shade for a cool place in the grass
Away from the tip of the tongue of a burning Sun
Motionless in splendor, I lie while a breeze gently swirls
around my soul, against my skin,
one daydream ends and another begins
Sweet smells of honeysuckle and lilac deeply permeate me
while the birds of day sing soothing songs
How without can one get along?

Across my bed in blades of green, at one with earth, wind, and fire
I shine like a star at nature's desire across my bed in blades of green

A sky so blue it makes me cry
Puffy clouds so soak up the tears that fall
A butterfly flits from flower to flower, making minutes evolve into hours
The hum of the bee, the branches that creak,
some of the first sounds that Man may recall
For millions of moons have come and gone,
and still bees and branches of trees live on

Across my bed in blades of green, eyes are closed, senses clear,
I dream a wish to lie with she, my senses full when she is here
Across my bed in blades of green

    Jimmy Kennedy

I Wonder Why

I saw a lady struggling with her wheelchair one day in downtown.
I thought she was so lucky. I wonder why?

I wonder why people ask what happened to my wrist.
You see, I slit my wrist one Sunday afternoon. I felt nobody loved me.

I wonder why I have a 7-inch mark on my stomach.
It only takes a second to realize that I had to remove a swizzle stick
I had taken a long time ago.
The doctor said, "Remove it, or else the thing you desire, death, will follow you."

I wonder why I see scars on my back.
Is it because I threw paint thinner on myself? I wanted to immolate myself.

After all this, is it any wonder that I had to go to
Queen's Psychiatric Unit, called Puu,
and Kaneohe State Hospital's Guarded Pali in the 1970s.
About ten years ago, I had to go to Kekela, Queen's Psychiatric Unit,
now because of burnout.

But the only real person who really knows about suffering is my mother.
She told me once, "I gave you a clean body, now you've ruined it."
We both felt devastated and so unhappy.

I wonder how I will live for another 49 years.

I wonder how a child of Buddha can even say, "Namu Amida Butsu,"
now with so much conviction that maybe things will improve.

    Edna F. Wada

Don't Go

Don't go from these shattered dreams
Don't leave and pull away the seams
I will miss you more than you know
But alas, there is no way I can show
My affection towards your life
And please, don't go

Your smile makes me delighted
And your spirit has been sighted
By my eyes but mostly my heart
Reached out and grabbed me so
Oh, but please, love, don't go

The last time we spoke was love
Nothing came near, down, or above
That time we had was sweet
And someday I hope to meet
The true love of your life
And once again this proves that
Love will never prevail but lose
All it has to offer but again I say no,
Don't go, don't go, don't go

    Travis McCollum Leonard

just a little note of thanks

For those who know life doesn't end after breaking up

thank you
for hurting me
thank you
for not caring
thank you
for breaking my heart
thank you
for turning me away
thank you
for lying
thank you
for making me cry
thank you
for letting me go
thank you
for opening my eyes
thank you
for letting me know
thank you
now i can move on

    Desiree Amber Lauzon

Pain

Pain is there, it shouldn't be
Something we don't deserve
Tests our character and nerve
Brings back the memories

Pain is there, it shouldn't be
Tears flowing down the cheek
Knowing of the accident, so bleak
Brings back the memories

Pain is there, it shouldn't be
Drugs and alcohol in him
I became a victim
Bringing back the memory

Pain is there, it shouldn't be
Like a storm moving near
God is with me, I need not fear
Brings back the memory

Pain is there, it shouldn't be
My body, mind, it has torn
But through his strength I am a victor
Bringing back the memory

    Teresa Clark

Legacy

They never thought of the little child, who should have been so dear.
They screamed out all their hatreds, and there he was to hear.
Barely more than an infant, with this pressure he'd have to deal.
With his immature judgement, he will see how "big" people feel.
Watch him grow and reason, "It is better not to care."
For the turmoil that's inside him, he's become afraid to share.
Now he's grown in to adulthood, and his hurt is coming out.
Not with understanding; no, instead, he'll scream and shout!
And his wife returns the screaming, for there's pain in her heart too.
From their parents they have learned this; it is all they know to do.
They never thought of the little child, who should have been so dear.
They screamed out all their hatreds, and there she was to hear.

Margret Lance Lassich

Inspiration

I looked for inspiration; inspiration found I none.
And then at last, unbidden, inspiration, it did come.
Was it buried or suppressed? Was it hidden or denied?
Then it shone forth bright as day; don't let it be denied.

Inspiration comes from where? To us a mystery.
Yet when it comes it opens eyes; it sets our spirits free.
Perhaps it was a babe's first cry roused dormant thoughts long buried.
Or when a bird takes to the sky . . . ideas formed are varied.

Was it someone I met today? A scented flower's bloom?
A special word or deed from one who freed our thoughts from doom?
Inspiration, let it flow; don't bank it up inside.
Let the well spring open wide, and ride upon the tide.

Elaine Uonelli

The Lonely Cat

It lounges in the easy chair
Alone it sits, friendless
Staring steadily into oblivion
Static now;
Alive yet curiously nonliving
A bewitching feline shape
I walk, unhesitant, the sound of my footsteps follows me to the animal
And its steady gaze shifts
Guarded green eyes . . . wander lazily across the room,
To rest at me
In the mutual gaze we share now
An exchange is carried out
The utter simplicity
Of complete understanding
We both know what it's like—
To be lonely.

Talia Shahbaz

The Way I See the World

I see the world around me as I sit in the corner with fright.
There's a woman being beaten by her husband, and no one seems to care.
How can I make it stop?
I look at my world in disbelief as I watch the news.
A 7-year-old went to school with a gun and killed a classmate.
When will this stop?
I look at my world with caution as I see my family and friends.
Will they be the next victims of this cold world?
I look at my world in confusion as I look out the window.
A gay man is being harassed for who he is.
Why can't they just accept him?
I look at my world in grief as I listen to the radio.
My friend was killed by a drunk driver.
Why did it have to be her?
I look at my world in determination at the number of volunteers.
We are going to make a difference.
I look at my world in hope as I walk down the hall.
A new kid is welcomed into a group of friends;
Please, can we keep it this way?

Pamela Brown

Not the Same

Although my heart longs to sing,
From within, it feels the sting
Of a love that would not bring
The joy and fulfillment I longed for.

Selfishness is our worst foe,
It overtakes and suppresses
The purest of all emotions
Without taking much notion.
Like a storm in forward motion,
Unrelentlessly to plunder,
And soon the love gone asunder,
Vanishes leaving a void.

Oh, what a needless ploy . . .
My heart is not a mere toy!

If we could just understand
That true caring can withstand
Dark clouds, lightning, and the thunder
With love, forgiveness, and sincerity,
We would experience the wonder
That was meant for all eternity.

Estrella Terry

The Greatest Gift

Chosen whispers never heard
Longing for the light.
Memories from yesterday
Closed in the darkest night.

Fear and coldness great despair
Wanting me to know.
Lingering in silent sleep
Wherever I shall go?

The hold of gloom, so close within
For many, many years.
But every bit of strength I have
Can't hold back all the tears.

The time is now to bid farewell
To thoughts that seem in vain.
Triumphantly I stay the course
My life I will reclaim.

So look inside and realize
You're very much of worth.
To know one's self in every way
Is the greatest gift on Earth.

Cheryl Wiley

Tears of Bitterness

My heart has gone out
To children in need,
Society's outcasts
People take heed!

Why are the children
Beaten and abused?
Were they ever asked if
This life they wanted to use?

Why so much cruelty
Especially to those
Too young for the attack,
Too young to fight back.

I cannot understand
Why people have desires
To take frustrations out
On an innocent little child.

Whenever it rains,
Just remember this:
The Lord is crying tears,
Tears of bitterness!

Betty Louise Durham

Step Close to Me

Step close to me, put your head on my shoulder.
Tonight is the night I just might get a little bolder.
Let's slow dance to the music like we've never done before,
and everything around us we'll make sure to ignore.
It's cold outside, but tonight you won't freeze,
I'll be all over you like a blanket, giving you all of me.
Step close to me, I'm phening for your love,
It's like the angels sent you from the heavens above.
I was so alone until I found you,
I can feel it in my heart that this love is true.
This moment is just for you and me, this relationship will last eternity,
so baby, step close to me.

Ambria Fike

The Game

Five fifth grade boys hit the floor a ballin'.
Their feet are bigger than the rest of their bodies,
but not one is fallin'.
They run the floor from end to end.
They know which basket is theirs to defend.
They dribble and pass and shoot the ball.
A foul or not is the referees' call.
They play three quarters, the game is close.
It looks like it will come down to "who wants it the most."
With only seconds left, the game is even.
A guard from the other team has the ball and
towards the basket is weavin'.
There's a pause, a last look then both feet are set.
The ball flies through the air, and then the swish of "nothin' but net."
The other team screams and brushes back their curls.
Our guys were beat by a team of fifth grade girls.

Joanne Prescott

Sorrowful Tear

It's almost like I'm tearing my hair out and no one notices I'm going bald
screaming at the top of my lungs and no one notices a bit
It's like I'm dying little by little and no one really cares
I repeat myself over and over and no one gets my drift
I repeat myself over and over and no one gets my drift
I'm wandering around this big work with no one to take my hand
No one seems to understand me
No one
They say they love me but how can that be
after everything I've said and done
Everything's unreal to me
A new world starting
Night around the bend
Will I lose what I know?
Will anything be the same?
Give me a hug and tell me you love me before I am completely gone

Kayte Junek

In Sympathy

Know that I feel your hurt and your sorrow. But from experience, I
can promise you that your pain will lessen over time.
And in its stead will be those memories of him that will make you
laugh, and yes, will make you cry. Your father is still there!

And, after all the times you complained about not wanting to look
like your father and you look into the mirror and see
characteristics of him in you or you see them in your kids.
Your father is still there!

And when your father comes to you in your dreams, know that you will
be able to tell him all those things that you think he didn't know
(although he knew them all the time)
Your father is still there!

And when you think you can hurt no more or that your sorrow will
never cease, know that your Father in Heaven is still there and
will give you no more than you can handle for He will be there to comfort you!

Consuelo G. Lopez

Goodbye

To M. L. B.
Well, years went by, and we grew older,
More mature in our ways.
And even though she might be gone,
The memory still stays.
Is this all my fault?
Could I have drastically changed?
Or maybe this is for the best,
My life being rearranged.
So maybe life won't be like
I remembered it yesterday.
And maybe she won't be there
On my wedding day.
But I wish the best for her
And her life as it goes by.
And all the other friendships
That she's willing to give a try.
I guess it will never be
The way it was again.
But it was fun while it lasted,
And this is now the end.

Nicole Beauchaine

Where Love No Longer Lies

We fought with our hearts;
holding them up high,
offering all that they had
for the good of all.

But we could not shield them
from the spite and vengeance
being thrown.

The people on the sidelines,
the ones to decide the outcome,
just stood behind the wall. . . .
blind . . .
deceived . . .
never knowing what was being thrown.

We cried out for help
but no one could hear us;
hope seemed so far away.

Our hearts stand screaming. . . .
I love you!

Tears roll from our eyes
as our hearts bleed.

Amy Louise Hagenbuch

Extending

When you proclaimed
Your love to me,
Was it just for me
Or an extension to my family?

When you saw me
You made a quick judgement
You moved from me
To the next person you thought was sent.

What's up with the looks?
What happened to that smile,
The one you flashed,
The one I saw for a mile?

I got there first
My sister second.
Who would you pick
If you only had a second?

I guess I'll never know
How you feel.
So from now on,
How about keepin' it real?

Alicia Reneé McKee

Untitled

This is a poem to my father, who I'll no longer call dad,
Whose insensitive ways has given me no respect.
Whose tired excuses have made me feel low.
Watching your medium build walk about with no words to mutter.
Never assuring me of your tender loving and care,
I can never tell if hatred gets in the way.
Miserly ways have deprived me of good birthdays.
I don't blame you for the decisions you make . . . I know you're a fake!
Uncaring and distant are two more of your characteristics.
I seek no answers or explanations. . . .
I know you are just one of God's bad creations.
So I write for truth, for meaning, heart and soul.
Cry no more tears . . . because I know my light will forever shine gold!

Tyronza Williams

Her

I take a stroll through emerald blades of grass
And take time to smell her flowers
Golden roses with peridot stems
Sometimes, I'm there for hours
Amethyst daisies speckle the diamond sky
Opal clouds join the topaz sun
Which glitters in her bluebird eyes
Ginger oak and cinnamon pines are dabbled here and there
But with the mighty sugar redwood
They just cannot compare
The cunning Alexandrine eagle sails high up in the atmosphere
And it gazes down on pearly mountaintops that grow throughout the year
And they grow only for you, my dear

Tom G. Haren

Hearts of Hate

A tribute to the victims of September 11, 2001
Hearts filled with hate, such a violent, desperate display.
An unbridled passion gone hopelessly astray.
What initiates this evil that would bring forth such pain?
All these lives now, forever gone.
What a terrible waste, the actions from those hearts filled with hate!
These evil souls are a timeless ill
For all those who fight for goodwill.
This, a battle which will forever be instilled.
Maybe one great day, they will meet their malicious fate.
They will crumble.
As we continue to pray for the power of love to end forever
This ill will and dismay!

Christie L. Morgans

My Outlook on Life

Let me take off the mask
Let me find the key that has bound me
For I sit alone in darkness
Bound by chains of hopelessness
Condemned to remain in silence until I have become the silence
Even though I know nothing, I am still tortured
by the knowledge that I do not hold
Unwind my soul, so I may know
Let me live in peace as I am
Let myself show at the masquerade, for the mask I put on is deceiving
Rather than a reflected image of myself
Let me unravel the string I've wound tightly around my soul
Let me live with the truth of my past
May I understand what I can't seem to grasp
For the truth slides through my hands and down to the ground
Because understanding is not something I know
I can't bear this loneliness and emptiness I feel inside
For I am lonely and lost with nowhere to turn
This is what I see and know
It has swallowed me up and shown me the painful reality
Of my newly reformed outlook on life

Jessica Meeter

Love of Carnations

To my mother
As spring blooms with love
So also my woman beams forth
With subtlety and sensuousness
She is fresh as carnations
Rare to be found yet loved
Carnations flood me with memories
Of my love blossoming in her teens
Her cheeks like apple orchids
Are passionately painted
She is a woman of substance
She soothes me when she talks
She is strong on her will
Her determination for success
It could move mountains
She is fragrant as roses
They sway to touch tender strings
She is my inspiration to life
Beauty is inspiration
For a poet of aesthetic waves
She is my carnation bloom

Shivani Chethana Banappa

Long Lost Friend

In childhood days
We never knew
The fun we had
Would soon be through

Come summertime
Without a plan
You moved away
Didn't understand

Our lives moved on
No questions asked
And then a voice
From out of the past

It's really you
My long lost friend
Some calls to make
Some notes to send

We'll meet again
I'll hold you soon
More fun to share
And memories too

Mary J. Lazoration

An Ode to Mom

Do you know how special you are?
Don't say you cannot see.
Doesn't matter if you're near or far,
You're always there for me.

You've turned my skies sunny and blue
Every day for all these years.
Don't ever say that it isn't true,
You've been there to dry my tears.

Forever my inspiration you'll be,
My everything, my all.
Always you're in back of me
In the case that I should fall.

So on cloudy days, don't feel down.
Keep a smile on your face
Instead of making a frown.
You made my world a better place.

Do you know how special you are?
Don't say you cannot see.
Doesn't matter if you're near or far,
You're always there for me.

Danielle Nicole Nelson

Boundaries . . .

Be there for them; sometimes they just need you to listen.
Open your heart; let them see the REAL you.
Unconditional love; don't ever let them doubt your love and commitment.
Never go back on your word; if you say you will do it, DO IT.
Discipline; teach their hearts right from wrong.
Always follow discipline with love.
Remember that they are not yours, but Angels on loan from God.
In good times and bad, Love them with all your heart.
Eventually, you will have to let them make their own decisions, right or wrong.
Sometimes, even when you want to be their friend, you have to be their parent first.

Jon W. Birky

Her

She is in my head, in my heart. I think of her by day and dark.
Who is she, what is she—but most important, where is she?
Is she fat? Maybe. Is she ugly? Possibly. But . . . as long as SHE IS.
An image invades my mind: she is looking at me. She has a smile.
Her smile makes my smile look like a frown and her joy alike.

Her manners are soft, kind, tender, and sweet. I watch them and
delight upon them.
In the depths of my mind, after opening a door with her eyes as
gates, I find myself in a world ideal.
In it she moves, she talks and even kisses . . . in the dark. I shake my
head in desperation, hoping to wake and wishing to remain, both at
the same time.

Alex Liu

A Song for the Homeless

If I were a rusted barrel in a jungle of cement,
I would grow limbs and embrace the thunderstorms.
I would make my branches into silver canteens
And unite them as crystal clear canals.
The sallow faces and lonely spirits would drink me in,
Swimming delightfully within my belly of brilliant sunsets.
It would be a night full of mosquitoes kissing ears—
A midnight in July, muggy with moss in my veins.
Like the mother's tender hand on the babe's head,
I would sway back and forth, flamenco-ing to the bass of thunder
And the percussion of God's tears hammering the topsoil.
The homeless would have satin silk's quilt
Wrapped placidly about their torso.
They would dance with the quilt as I clicked my castanets wildly Together.
I would give them my own air. I would give them my own feathers.
I would melt my iris like a lavender wax crayon
And pour it into their concave hearts of gold.
O downtrodden! O distraught! O dejected heirs of adversity!
I am satin silk's quilt and I am a rusted barrel in a jungle of cement.

Ryan Russell Johnson

My First, My Last, My Only Love

When I look into your eyes, I see a world of love,
filled with rivers with white feathered doves,
leading to oceans of lust and mountains of trust,
with the outside painted with collages of just us.
When I look into your mind, I see a man and a wife,
creating a life without struggle or strife.
Building a society, not based with anxiety,
but a variety of cultures of breeders, parents and teachers,
and oh, yes, seekers of the knowledge of the holy one.
When I look into soul, I see the mother of the Earth,
giving an aspect of what she's worth by giving life through birth,
and yet still connected to this woman of the Lord
by an invisible umbilical cord that can be cut by any sharp sword,
so on one accord we remain, 'cause disconnected, we are slain.
When I walk into your heart, I feel a warm embrace.
That is not a gesture of disgrace,
but feels as soft as a material we call lace,
but just in case you didn't know, her strength derives from up above.
She's everything I need 'cause she's My First, My Last, My Only Love.

Charles Edward Council, Jr.

The Flowers that Dance in the Wind

Softly dancing,
Dancing, dancing in the wind.
No worry, no fears—
I'm softly dancing in the wind.

Tossed to and fro,
To and fro, to and fro in the wind.
Fears and worries fill my soul;
I'm being tossed to and fro.

Stormy skies!
The skies, the skies,
The wind! Anger, fear, sadness—
I am roughly flying in the wind.

Softly landing,
Landing, landing on the ground.
This is my home the wind chose for me.
No worries, no fear.
I have my foundation.
He is God.

April J. Moore

The Blue Spring Moon

Once upon a dream
I dreamed a moon
It was a moon that was blue
As blue as could be

It rose during the spring
Like a goddess smiling
It told me to start

The next day is when it started
It was my labor of love
All through the spring and summer
I watched as it grew

It started again in the fall
Once again I had a dream
It was the moon like a goddess
It told me it was over

I picked it all the next day
Half for me half for the moon
I burned the moons and prayed all night
When I woke the flames
Were gone but my feast had just begun

James Lee, Jr.

Stained Glass

My eyes peer thoughtfully outward
Twisting up and yet downward
The light shining brightly inward
A cry sending shudders along my skin

The glass glitters like a rainbow
While the men prepare to row
And row they shall for my love
Which shall come like a dove

Across the waters dead as can be
While a thought wanders through me
And no smiles cross my face
Since my love is lost

A sheep wandering through the valley
A warrior preparing to kill
Nothing more but instead a gallery
Of pictures once made from will

Pictures that adorn the glass
Glass that shows a lass
One that is coming through the hills
And one who is nothing more than my will

Andy K.H. Yeoh

The City

The city life is exciting to me.
With its buildings everywhere and on every block, there sits a tree.
The young people all racing to get somewhere.
The elderly people are strolling down the street without a care.
The cars are rushing to get from place to place.
The boss might be there, so be on time just in case.
In the daytime the sun comes up letting you know it's time to move.
At night the lights come on letting you know it's time to groove.
Lights, cameras, action! Do you believe all you can see.
All this is exciting, about the city to me.

Felicia Maria Noble-Willaims

To You, My Love!

There was something I wanted to say,
The one thing that I always wanted to convey:
That I had loved you from the bottom of my heart,
Which is as deep as the ocean and as bright as the star.

I love the way you smile; I love the way you feel.
I love every moment that you shared and spent with me.
The first time I saw you, I failed to realize
that you were the one for me.
You had everything that I ever dreamt of, the love, the warmth, the feel.

But alas! I think it's too late now.
I ask myself, my heart . . . why so was the setback?
I couldn't say that which was on the tip of my tongue:
That I had loved the one who was in front of me!

Ramachandra Yellapragada

My Tiny Ballerina—Not an Illusion

Darkness of night slowly disappears as rays from bright morning Sun
shine through the window, an illusionary spotlight for my tiny ballerina.
Sparkling tiara adorns her long auburn hair flecked with gold;
her delicate body, sculptured, wearing a pink tutu,
matching ballet toe shoes with satin ribbon
spiraling around her shapely legs, a captivating beauty
poised in position as a bird ready for flight. . . .

Music begins to play. . . . my tiny ballerina starts twirling
around and around on her tiny platform stage;
music ends, as did her dance. . . .
with amazed enthusiasm, I heard my voice cry out, bravo! Encore!
My fingers automatically reacted to the command. . . .
I quickly wound my new music box for another display
of exceptional beauty in action.

My tiny ballerina, an intriguing porcelain statuette artistically created
with a highly technical instrumental mechanism,
giving ultimate viewing pleasure for all who see her. . . .

Evelyn Giles

The Eternal Wind

The wind, forever blowing across the rolling landscape
Bringing sweet fragrance of blooming flowers, giving feelings of peace
Bending the broad leaves of dark corn stalks in a farmer's field
Rustling the leaves of a willow tree growing by a stream

Bearing up songbirds gliding through the evening sky
Causing ghostly moans as it sweeps
Through the soft needles of a pine tree
Transporting precious seeds to being life anew on barren soils
Making rolling waves along a seashore

Touching a hot, tired face with fingers of soothing coolness
Creating flowing waves of motion in the lush, tall prairie grass . . .
Carrying across the valley the faraway sound of a train whistle
Forming every-changing shapes in the soft white clouds, high above . . .

Embracing crimson colored leaves drifting to earth in the crisp fall air
Making falling snowflakes dance, as if alive!
May the sweeping winds forever blow
Giving mankind a touch of lasting peace for the weary soul!

Michael McNeal

Happy Mother's Day for a Teacher

On this beautiful morning,
there is just one thing to say.
I only wanted to wish for you
a very Happy Mother's Day.
Your teachings are a blessing;
your scolds do not bother.
You have been more than a teacher;
you have been a second mother.
This is the very truth;
a sounding truth in Heaven.
If I have to say it again, I will,
but seventy times seven.
You have bestowed your warmth
with firmness and consistence.
You have proved yourself a teacher
for my life and my existence.
I will say no more now,
in this glorious month of May.
Just remember, it is my wish:
Have a Happy Mother's Day!

Angel Enrique Mercado

Child of the Past

Life's bridges are broken,
and I am unskilled.
Will it take me forever,
to learn how to build?

Emotions are thrashing,
like the ocean in rage.
I'm trapped in a current,
holding me in its cage.

I'm lost in a forest,
saturated with fear.
My scream is an echo,
that no one can hear.

I flee from a volcano,
whose fury is mine.
The eruption takes over,
before there's a sign .

The cave of abandonment,
a place I could hide.
The child forgotten,
I found her inside.

Lori J. Van Wagoner

The Way Life Is

Life is an eternal spring,
an indiscriminate lapse of time,
and of the unweary happening,
we hope our time will be divine.

For life is short and tragic; for most
people can't really live,
and God, our most hospitable host,
will help our souls themselves to give.

It's said better to have loved and lost
than never to have loved at all,
but tragically, as some must boast,
the losing of love is not without fall.

So I say it's not true
about what people say to love,
and to be feeling mortally blue,
consoled by only the stars above.

Life, you're lost to me now,
a bright but dead thing in time,
and i never knew quite how,
but i wish life were mine.

David Michael Vaughan

On Our Way

As we leave this place to start over again
We look back at the empty halls and lockers, and many new and old friends.
We realize that soon, too soon in fact, that this all came to an end.
But now we go on our way to bigger things like jobs and college and wedding rings.
In our heart we fear this giant change but we take it with courage and pride,
And with a whole new set of rules to abide.
Our friends and teachers we will never forget,
In our hearts we store them safely away
As we go off on our way.

Allison Potter

Our World Destroying Our Truth

Another tiny boy drifts away to dream.
He daydreams of dragons and mystical sorts of things.
Soaring past the cotton clouds he lands the mountaintops,
Holds his hands high in victory as the world below simply stops.
Seven hundred pairs of eyes gaze up toward his face.
Eyes fixed on the boy living in the four corners of the sun.
But the sixth of seven hundred turns his face away.
Our boy disappointedly drops his arms, for his journey's just begun.
Knowledge of the world strikes him from the mount,
And the river of his dreams dries up at the fount.
Though the promises are always kept, he loses sight of the truth.
Sadly he forgets what to bind and what to loose.
Pain, betrayal; he sees them avail, but it is revelation of the blind,
When everything he seems to find is seldom what he had in mind.
Oh, please spare him more time. . . .

Michael Wayne Waters

Who We Are?

Who am I:
I am the person who watches you in jealousy.
I am the person who awakens expecting to get
beaten once more.
I am the person whose only reason to go to school
is to be laughed at.
I am the person who has a disorder of being too
nervous around people.
I am the person that goes to the doctor every month
from a butt rash caused by too many wedgies.

Who are you:
You are the person who later makes me want to accept suicide.
You are the person who awakens to feel the joy of humiliating me once again.
You are the person who does not know the meaning of love.
You are the person whose only reason to go to school is to
impersonate my silly acts.

Melissa Esther Montes

You (Stephanie)

You knew what it took to be a great person in a not so great world
You took your time to understand the soul behind the face
You saw that there was more to a person than just the shield
They put up to protect themselves
You humble us.

Your love, compassion and optimism will transcend the boundaries
Of flesh and time and will forever be the light that brightens our paths
Your strength, wisdom and endurance will continue
To inspire us to levels we thought unachievable
You guide us.

The glow of your smile is burned into the dimly lit areas of our minds
Adding color, texture and depth to the most pale of memories
The presence of your spirit will always be felt and our love
Unlike our bodies is everlasting
We continue to mourn your physical death but we
All recognize that in this state you touch us more than ever before
You keep us.

Benjamin Gilbert, Jr.

You

If rainbows had an earthly form,
If beauty fell like dew
And gathered in one treasury,
Its name would be called . . . you.

If song that fills the heart so sweet
That flows like liquid joy
Would touch the fires of my love,
Its fervent heat employ,
Each note, in dazzling crystal form,
Once heard, would shine anew,
And one by one, when all were done,
Their beauty would be . . . you.

If love that lifts me through the night
On rapturous wings of peace
Could to my longing hand be known,
Its velvet heart release,
'Twould wrap me in its sensuous folds
And thrill me through and through—
Oh, such exquisite luxury,
It only could be . . . you.

Shirley Yvonne McCoy

September 11, 2001

As we shed the tears
for those we have lost
we look to the sky
where our God reigns,
and he smiles at me,
and he says, it will be okay.
The injured are safe,
the dead are with me,
and I smile upon you.
September 11th will
live with me forever;
the sound of the planes,
the look of the fire
and the voice of Congress
singing "God Bless America"
is stuck in my brain.
There are mothers without children,
children without parents,
wives without husbands
and husbands without wives.
But I say, God Bless America,
our home sweet home.

Erica Luviano

Branches of Life

My branches sway in the gentle breeze
My blooms kissed by the sun
My bark a roughened texture to touch
My roots how deep they do run

My life began with a simplistic seed
Nurtured and grown with love
Some years I did not long to thrive
Some I flew like the dove

The winds and storms of Mother Nature
Tested my will and endurance
But then again with each new spring
I was mended with assurance

And now I stand and find myself
With ages yet to come
That I am strong and willfully made
From years of life's wisdom

My branches sway in the gentle breeze
My blooms kissed by the sun
My bark a roughened texture to touch
My roots how deep they do run

Shannon M. Baker

Paper Dolls

All of you are one.
You are like little paper dolls.
Copies of one another.
Afraid to be different.
Too concerned you won't fit in.
Why do you care so much?
Is it acceptance you crave?
None of you care that you're being used
Or maybe you do care and are afraid you'll be tossed aside if you admit it.
I don't know. . . . it just seems like you're wasting your lives.
If only you cared about yourself . . . not your outsides . . . but what's
inside . . . your soul.

    Anna Barsuglia

To Self

A beautiful woman of God.
Treasure yourself and love who you are.
A strong soul, a soft heart, wise mind, and a giving spirit.
You are ever changing while reaching for that mark.
Very desirable, sexy to some, a challenge to many, but only special to one.
To understand me is to know my creator and His will for me.
A woman from man can only be a gift from thee.
To know who I am and where I came;
without me, my marriage wouldn't be the same.
A beautiful woman of God,
I am indeed.
My soul mate's treasure he has received!

    Tuesday Gaylord

When a Man Loves a Woman

when a Man—BORN as a boy, RAISED as a prince to LIVE as a King
Loves—a POWERFUL force of CONNECTION and DEDICATION often dreamed yet seldom seen
a Woman—the BUTTERFLIES of eternal lives who broke the cocoon from which demeaned
TRANSFORMED into a Queen
it's such a BEAUTIFUL thing when a Man loves a Woman
'cause that Man will feel WITH that Woman
HER pain becomes THEIR pain
as I no longer exist and ME was infiltrated by WE while YOU are
surrounded by ME
surrounded by YOU
REBIRTHED as Us
CONNECTED by Trust
BONDED by Faith
CRAVED by Forever
DREADED by Never
WELCOMED by the fact that ALWAYS can NEVER die with YOU and I together
it's funny how LIFE is a little better
when a Man loves a Woman

    Keith Washington

My Journey

Why should I apologize for who I am when I choose it so?
Because I choose spirituality over religion to be closer to my God?
Because my quest of knowledge doesn't rely on a college education
With professors who choose to teach me what they feel I need to know,
Yet have the same degree which I am seeking?
But my quest of knowledge extends to curiosity
With questions of how and why and trips to the library
And strolls through the ghetto reading the faces of my people.
A picture is worth a thousand words; yet the blind see so much more.
Why should I apologize for the road you decided to take?
Because my faith is stronger than your bible intake?
But I'm suppose to feel there is something wrong with me.
When my soul is older than my grandmother's, I bless her soul.
And my heart is warmer than the core.
Should I smile
and pretend to be happy with lies?
When it's knowledge I seek, with frustration from most, read my eyes.
I know everything; I know nothing; my quest, my journey never ends.

    Najla Slowe

Sleepless Nights and the Break in Time

Tracing the shadows in my mind
Tracing the things I left behind

Looking for a safe place to stay
Looking for some other way

For the sake of time
For the sake of love

Send the rhyme
To the lord above

Treasure the jewelry
Treasure the grime

Sold to the world
In the light of lime

Stretch the summer rain
Stretch to avoid the pain

Risk it all and let her go
Break it off but don't let it show

    Adam Cory MacKinnon

Untitled

Alone in the darkness
Nothing to fill the void
The world is full of filth
The sky begins to fall

The world's pawns look on
Bewilderment is the expression
Bystanders are we
But none the innocent

Prevalent is the ignorance
Stupidity leads us forward
Paving the path
With purple haze

And the sky
Still it comes down
Boulders gaining momentum
Spiraling towards the earth

The downward mass overpowers us
The purple haze has taken control
We are fighting with ourselves
Unable to overcome the ignorance

    Darcy Finical

Take Me

God,
I can see your face
right through that open gate.
Maybe if I die,
it would be my fate.

Oh, God, I can see the light.
I am trying and trying
with all my might.

My heart won't stop.
Why won't you let me go?
All I can see is
your lips mouthing "no."

I want a casket
with flowers that are blue
and a pillow that smells
exactly like you.

My limp head
and my fat little chest
will be laid down
and finally put to rest.

    Nikki Marie Galles

Look for Me

In memory of Betty Sue Hill
The other day I heard the voice of Jesus say, come home.
I heard my children cry, Mother don't leave us alone.
I know my children will miss me
But I know that Jesus will set me free.
So on that day that I heard my name,
I went to be with Jesus because I knew that only he can remove my Pain.
To my children: Don't cry for me,
Because in your heart I will always be.
So look for me—I will be with the sun shining so bright.
Look for me—I will be with the moon that brightens your night.
No matter where you are, I will always be there, so look for me.

Michael Gerone Moore

God, My Father

Father, I love you with all my heart and soul.
You are my light in the midst of darkness
You are my sight in the midst of unclearness
I will hold on to you and give you praise
For it is only your hand that has held me always.
When I cry, you wipe all my tears away.
When I fall you are there to steady me gracefully.
When I call you hear my every word and respond with a father's care.
You know just what to say to make my day.
So I am glad to have you as a father, and in your presence I will stay.
Under your wings will I abide and learn your ways
As I stare into your face.
For I know you are always near.
You're really just a whisper's prayer away.
Besides, I know you really care.

Tisha Daskalakis

To Know Love

Have you ever stopped to ponder love
The feeling of it
The taste of it
The smell of it
The sight of it
The sound of it
Just sat and pondered
To have that person touch you and the smile that looms on your face
The saltiness and sweetness of one's lips after a long passionate kiss
The sweet smell of cologne even after they've left the room
The look in their eyes when you enter a room
The music only you can hear when
They look at you in that special way
If you sat and pondered love
You'd be able to hold on to it forever

Lauren Danielle Wooditch

Calie the Cutest

I love my Calie every day and tell her that she's here to stay.
Yes, I love my kitty all the way who came to me in Hawaii one day.

As I brush the fur I love to touch, I stop to thank my God so much
for the joy I've found in her so sweet. Lord, how did You create such
pretty feet? Or those tiger-stripe legs and tortoise shell coat?
They're beautiful, you see, as anyone would note.
And those white-tip paws forever melt my heart.
Oh, what will I do when someday we must part?

How precious she is beside me all night, and come early morn,
I put up no fight, for "Shuggie Time" is here as she bumps my face.
With a bow of her head the first shuggie takes place!
Shuggies and shuggies go on for a bit 'til enough is enough—
Hey Mom! Time to quit!

Never was a kitty as cute as this
who first greeted me with only a hiss!
A new mom with two babies unloved and alone.
Surely God meant that I take them home.

Nancy Gail Barham

Unrelinquished Love

In a simple rhyme
I couldn't even begin
When so short of time
To tell you of how
I've loved and lusted for her
But now
While the setting of the sun
Sheds golden light
On my thoughts un-spun
I think back to when
My obsession for this goddess
Had affected living then
Her beauty you could not compare
For an equal search anywhere
And would not find
Such a perfect creature
Except within your mind
Within her life
Oh, to have part
I envy the one
Who has captured her heart

Keith Edward Lewis

Understanding Our Love . . .

My mama always said, love is blind,
but this man I have chosen
is one of a kind.

He respects me highly,
he tells me no lies.
He loves me truly,
he's opened my eyes.

He's made me see
through thick and thin.
He's made me know
I can't always win.

I now understand our
love for each other.
It's about putting all
your trust and faith
in one another.

It's not about being
right or wrong.
It's about how much you care
to keep the other one strong.

Jennifer Renee La Rocca

Attributes

The attributes are many,
Some projections we all see
Are those of Sonkhja's gunas—
Sattva, rajas, tamas—three.

The cornucopia of humanity,
A rock cast by the way,
The moon up in the Heavens,
The Sun to rule the day.

A garden filled with lotus,
A mandala round and true,
A paradoxing instrument . . .
This one of great value.

A gender of complexity
Wherein deep waters rage.
Yet silent, bold, unveiling truth
Unfolding page by page.

The nucleus a composite
Of emptiness and form . . .
The making of this being
Is weathered through the storm.

Cynthia Clark Bantau

I Know Now

When a person takes a long walk I'd rather be with you.
I cannot say goodbye nor walk away, for I hide from you.
Hiding from the burn inside my heart, a smile
consoles me when I talk to you.
I hear your name and respond as if it were mine.
Your name is so sweet and soft, I wish it were you.
I watch the sun come out from the clouds with happy golden rays
that remind me of you.
I am so happy that I was led to you with comfort for my pain.
You made me smile when I thought I was nothing.
Vivid images run through my mind which capture memories of you.
I was scared when I had to leave you, scared of never talking to you.
Now I know why the spell of love was released;
it was released because I fell in love with you.

Kayla M. Pula

Someday!

Someday, I'd like us to be more than friends, the way two lovers drift
off and sail into blue skies.

Someday, I'd like to hold your hand beneath the silver moon and
watch the shooting stars, as I caress your body close to mine.

Someday, I'd like to show you all of my favorite places where I go,
when the world doesn't make sense.

Someday, I'd like us to talk of making solid plans, building a
prosperous future, if it's meant to be . . . one day at a time.

Someday, I hope you'll hold my hand and give me that peaceful,
romantic stare, you know the one when two hearts become one.

Someday, I hope we get the chance to say exactly how we feel for
each other, if not today, maybe . . . someday!

Kim Montgomery

Beauty Is in the Eyes of the Beholder

Beauty is in the eyes of the beholder,
but the one you want gives you the cold shoulder.
So are you not beautiful but beastly, that girl's not cute to me.
She is too thin, has too many friends, can't wait 'til the week ends.
Am I beautiful, to myself and others.
Friends can keep your looks undercover.
Telling you that your outfit is cute, knowing it looks like puke.
Does it make you a better person to get picked up or turned down?
A smile is the same as a backwards frown.
You're lucky that the boys don't bother you like they bother me.
That bothers me, 'cause anyone can get a love.
It just depends on the person the eyes are made of.
So when you are ignored or complimented remember the cold facts.
To everybody you ain't all that, but to some one you are.

Tonita Serwaa Osei

Hidden Secrets

There is a place where we keep all of our secrets locked away,
Guarded by golden gates and three-headed dogs that lie in a bed of hay.
There are things here that only I can see,
Because I am the one and I have the key.
I see all of the things hidden deep within;
All of the hurt, the anger, the tears, and sin.
I see all of the world hidden in fear,
And when I look back, I shed one more tear.
I wonder how much longer this can go on;
Will the fight be over, will someone have won?
I stand here and wonder what can I do
To save a world in despair and very much askew?
Now I lie and wonder more,
How the effects will be felt shore to shore.
The hearts of many will grieve with pain
For the losses that the world may never tame.
All of the secrets in the gate they must stay,
Forever and ever to be locked away.

Audrey Valdez

Rejoice

the leaves rustle singing to the breeze
the clouds float by with the harmony
they sing "Rejoice"
but I cannot for I am but the mere wind
that softly moves among them

Ainsley Elizabeth McCarthy

Baseball

B eginning in the start of spring
A time when church bells ring
S ummer begins and it's time to boast
E xciting kids from coast to coast
B aseball season is here
A nd it's time to let out a cheer
L aughter and joy fills the air
L etting kids have fun without a care

Ben S. Abzug

Anger

Fire devours my sore being,
Leaving not but a nimbus shadow
Of nauseating egocentricity
Fanning life to its scorching glow.

Relentless pursuit of useless hatred;
Pain reminiscent of old sores
As the Wheel of Life rolls, lost forever
Through fathom depths—no more—no more.

Cheryl Agueda de los Angeles de Joya

The Thunderstorm

The thunderstorm
Rips through the night
It does not stay
It rips and bites
While everyone goes
In and hides
The thunderstorm
Is in a fight

Michael Nicholas Keks

My Wish

I wish being on my way forever
to finally arrive there, never
And striving for perfection
always to need correction

My goals always at hand
will be found in no land
Like horizons that fly
ever remaining nearby

Michael Prantounas

Dreaming of a Time

Dreaming of a time
Sipping white wine
Watching the glowing fire
With a new man I admire
Cuddling by the fireplace
Snowing, just a trace
Looking at the stars
Wrapped warmly in your arms
Fingers tenderly caress my face
Kisses you gently take
Love, do we make?
Then I awake. . . .
Just dreaming again, this time

Juanita Pfeiler

Forbidden

Her eyes can pierce a man's soul and conquer his every fear.
A speech so soothing and tranquil echoing within his ear.
Her lips shine with hopes of a seductive kiss from her lover.
And as her beauty captivates my eyes, my heart flutters
'cause I know she is forbidden.
She probably tastes like strawberries, I truly wonder.
I want her to shower me and cause me to shake underneath her thunder.
The fragrance she wears sends me into a paradox of bliss.
I long to see her face and discover a taste of her sacred lips
but I know she is forbidden.
She is intricate and time has molded her in every dimension.
Her walk is enchanting as she strides with so much intention.
I ache with the thought of knowing she is so distant.
But I hope she'll one day recognize my persistence,
though I know she's forbidden.

Colby Curry

We All Drown

You struggle,
You try to breathe, but the water rushes over you, and you choke.
Then you gasp and sputter, and try to swim.
But the tide pulls you under.
It sucks you down into the mud,
until you just lay there,
being absorbed into the earth,
and the need to struggle passes, and you think toward the future. . . .
Will anyone miss you? Will they care?
When will I feel warmth again?
All I feel is cold, and now I feel nothing
And I'm cold and the world is new.
But I'm too soon and no one wants me.
My mother wanted me dead. So I die,
and enter the realm of my Lord and live forever "in Peace."

Amy Featherer

Letting Go

You can't let go because that means you have
to accept that they are gone.
Your heart aches; it's hard to breathe as reality hits you.
You have their memories as well as the ones you had with them.
You have their face and their old embrace. You have their influence.
You have pictures of them.
They will be with you step by step.
They will teach you to remember the good times from the past
and look toward the new ones in the future.
When it is your time to pass through the gates
to a place so pure and delicate,
they will walk with you.
And all your questions will be answered and you will understand.
To those who don't believe, this is your awakening.
You can let go.

Dinah Elizabeth Thompson

Eye of the Storm

When adversity strikes time and time again,
One becomes accustomed to the pangs of its relentless blows
Assaults upon one's morale arrives at a state of impertinent normalcy
All notice of its vile presence slowly fades,
Misery becoming a permanent resident in a day's droning existence
Now, as such adversities are eventually overcome,
And the plagued blanket of misery is lifted,
One grows uneasy
Sitting in a transient sea of false serenity
Surely, the calm before the storm
Awaiting in trepidation for the next wave of bludgeoning conflict
Anxiously hoping for the next blow to be delivered
Certain that such placidity would soon be unmasked
Faltering sanity, counting each excruciating second
Prisoner within the Eye of the Storm

Diana T. Ho

You

All I am is because of you,
my ways and my time are same as yours,
my lips repeat your words,
and my mind your thoughts.
My heart beats for you, just for you
because I am you,
I am your reflection, your other you.

Maria Teresa Rodriguez Almazan

Sun

She woke up,
she looked up.
The day was glorious.
She came up.
Enormous and glimmering,
she is a shining star.
She makes your day glow.

Katia Nectaria Penemenos

Fierce Gale

Sometimes I feel like
Like I'm alone in this life
No one there to take my frail hand

In these times, tears
Flee the refuge of my eyes
Are You there? Do You understand?

These thoughts, they flood my mind
Your face I cannot find
Are You waiting just beyond this veil?

The lie, it tears in two
And You come crashing through
In Your fierce and raging gale of love

Now in the tempest
I find my rest
In Your arms, it's incredible

And when my soul is grieved
You grant my reprieve
Inner peace incomprehensible

Here is that warm comfort
Here is peace . . . enveloping me

Triton Lloyd Stellflug

Birds

In memory of Jake Redlinger
I sit on a park bench
All alone and sad
With a pain in my heart
From thoughts of my Dad

The wind starts to blow
As I look toward the sky
And shout to the heavens
"Why? Tell me why!"

In a flutter of wings
I'm surrounded by birds
To sing me a song
That will never need words

My heart starts to soar
As they sing their sweet song
And I feel a great love
That's been gone for so long

I feel his protection
From way up above
And I know I will live
In the light of his love

Joan Marie Redlinger

Color of Red

Red is the color of the blood Jesus shed, a color that was seen when
The thorns went on his head. It's a color that was seen when he died
For you and me; when he promised us his love for all eternity.
It's the color of the anger that was felt by all as they stood there
To watch their mighty Jesus fall.
Jesus gave this color to the blood he shed, and this bright color
Is the color of red.

Jonathan Hughes

What Was

I have wanted to be held in your arms,
just one more time, for so long.
What happened to us?
I thought that our love was so strong.
I know we are over with, the relationship done and through.
But I think about it a lot of times, and I just don't know what to do.
Sometimes it gets to me and I just want to scream and shout.
Then others, I want to call and maybe work things out.
I'm sorry that I still have these feelings,
But I really don't know just what to do,
But I just want you to know that I still and will always love you!

Holly Reigle

A Memory Forever

emotions run high when I think back
heart pumps at the speed of light
replaying the memory is like repeating a track
knowing every word, every line; the beat doesn't skip, hits just right
every tear that was rolled is never miscounted
since this kind of joy is never forgotten
because it doesn't come around often
with my eyes closed, I can push away all the negativity
which brings strain and makes me feel surrounded
the hardest of the hearts can be softened is my opinion
being placed in my arms for the first time made me realize
you're my reason for living, looking at me with transparent eyes
sat me on top of the world, lost in a world of excitement
when the doctor said, congratulations, you're a father
to a beautiful, brand new, baby girl; a gift from God
a great enlightenment, my fifteen minutes of fame
a privilege to have been there
proud to have given you my last name, my memory forever
my memory to take when no longer in this world, but elsewhere

Raul Guillen

Before Time

In the beginning, there was chaos;
there was light, an aurora of extreme blindness.
I was the spark of nothing bathed in lucidity.
I was darkness. I was truth.
When I became, the universe became. . . .
anything that can be named became.
I am nothing, the untrue . . . Oblivion. You call me god.

The day that I sinned, time began.
The image is motionless and animated in me.
When I caressed the princess of light, she made a gesture of devotion.
I never had a desire so strong.
We laid down beside the river of forget and made love for an eternity.
When it was over, she wept.
Her tears brought colors to chaos.

I am nothing. I am the spark of darkness in light.
When my seed ripened in her, the end of the beginning began,
destruction of unity and purity began.
Time began.
You call me god.

James H. Trinh

Company Comin'

They come from the mines today,
Three men in a jeep.
Across the holler, Annie screamed,
And we all began to weep.

I seen 'em drive down here,
Must be ten times afore.
Footsteps crunch in black gravel
On their way to the door.

They come from the mines today,
Three men in a jeep,
And stood on my porch, silent,
Until we began to weep.

Rosa B. Lester

Difference

I am black
So people say I am dirt

But my mind is
Free
Alive
Working

While their minds are
Creeping
Crawling
Searching

Over the emptiness
Of prejudice

Ruth E. Todd

Missing a Loved One

One day you're with them,
Laughing and having fun.
The next thing you know,
They're in an accident,
And now they're gone.

That's what happened to me,
On this horrid day.
I'm with him one minute,
And the next he's gone.

My family and I are the ones,
Left behind to feel the sorrow and pain.
That's what happened to me,
This sad and sorrow day.

Jennifer Jill Gobeli

Fossils

We cast our spells.
We kiss, we tell.
And build our walls on other walls
That lie in ruins far below.
An ancient snow that buried autumn,
And tender shoots of an early spring.
Layered legends, histories
Of each of us,
Concentric rings.
Like redwood trees
And Paleolithic clay:
The fossils of our former days
Are buried deep beneath their time,
And won't see sunlight
'Til they're mined.
And brought to conscious memory
To dissipate
A rain of rust
And scattered o'er
The living crust.

Steven Martin Zink

You . . .

You're the one I turn to when everything seems so bleak.
You're the one that listens to me every time I speak.
You're the one I hold on to, the one who fuels my fire.
You're the one I need to touch, you ignite my desire.

You're the one I dream about each and every night.
You're the one I need to hug and hold so very tight.
You're the one that found the true me that I thought I hid so well.
You're the one that pulled me out of my lonely shell.

You're the one I trust completely, and that you know is true.
You're the one who completes my life . . . by just being you.

Sharon L. Niesen

I Am . . .

I am not the one who sits in front with a hand raised high.
I am not the one next to that person who is beautiful and smart.
I am not the jock that sits behind her.
I am not the one who can never be quiet, yelling out wrong answers.
I am not the one who sits quietly in the corner, quiet as a mouse.
I am not the one who sits next to the jock lazily sleeping class away.
I am the newcomer, the "new kid."
I am eager to answer questions and to please the teacher.
I am strong yet lazy, and never know when to shut my mouth.
I am also the quiet one, not knowing everyone, making me the "new kid."
I am the newcomer, the "new kid."

Clarence Johnson

Daddy Please

Daddy please don't hurt me, can't you see my tears?
Daddy please don't hurt my mommy, don't you see her tears?
Daddy please don't hurt my sister, don't you see her tears?
Can't you see our tears of trust and friendship going down our faces?
Don't you see the love we had together and our days of enjoyment
streaming down our faces?
This is hard seeing you hurting our family and our hearts that are so
sweet and pure.
So daddy please don't hurt our family, please don't make me cry
because it hurts my heart and it just kills me to see you in this state of
mind.
So please stop hurting us so we can start being a family again.
Stop the madness and be our friend. Just because we can't live
together, we can love again.
So stop the tears in our eyes so we can be the best family we can be.
Will you please stop the tears in our eyes, so we can feel loved and
safe again.

Kalen Anderson

Heroes of Our Times and Lives

What is a hero and what does he do?
Someone who'll sacrifice something for you.
Someone inspiring, someone who cares,
He may give up his life, do what nobody dares.

For someone a hero may be Superman,
Or simply a person who offered a hand.
Some of us want to be like them someday,
Others find comfort in what they do or say.
We all have our heroes which we'll love all our lives,
We'll praise their brave deeds that brought tears to our eyes.

My personal heroes are my mother and dad,
The most caring and dedicated parents one has ever had.
They left their home in Russia, their native motherland.
They left their jobs and parents, their colleagues and their friends.
Through obstacles and hardships, my parents had to strive
To give me and my brother a free and better life.

Anna Bokarius

Serenity in Silhouettes

*To my friends who attend my
annual shore pool party at summer's end*

Autumn is coming to the shore,
But summer will return once more.
Soon you will hear the flapping wings.
Listen as a chirping bird sings.

They are the sounds of sad goodbyes,
As great flocks in formation rise.
In perfect V's, they'll fly so high.
Wings flap to echo their goodbye.

Autumn is coming to the shore,
But summer will return once more.

Arline June Pearce

Him

He came to me in the dark of night,
Gingerly sweet and eager.
He longed so to be close to me,
For my love, however meager.
With smiling eyes I welcomed him,
Receptive, warm, and tender.
I reached to take his hand in mine
And sighed in sweet surrender.
I stroked his cheek.
I kissed him there,
Admired his form, so fine,
As I watched him drift to dreamland,
This little son of mine.

Angela Sims Hayden

The Warm Gardens

Amid bushes, grass, trees green
Amid flowers,
Shadows are short,
Sun in ruler . . .
It is noon.

Breeze is praying,
Silent in the Churchyard,
Birds observe in quiet,
The Church bell tolls. . . .
In the warm garden.

The Church is the Garden. . . .
The Garden, the Church.

Jo-Ann Cicchetti

A Mystical Place

The sea is a mystical place
Where enchantment and adventure lie;
You may see God's shining face
In the water, if you try.
Some people visit for pleasure,
Some people weep and cry;
But I go there to treasure
Strong feelings that do not lie.
Secrets float at the bottom,
Mysteries creep through the sky.
Sweethearts come here often
And ask their lovers: why?
Many strange ships have sailed
And many old ships have roamed,
And while great boats have failed,
Others have found new homes.
Since mysteries of the ocean
Will always remain untold,
There will always live the notion
That the sea is filled with gold.

Lindsey Fosse

All Men

Heart and mind rarely coincide;
in the absence of truth all suffer,
but what is truth, look for the roots,
find that of which we ponder;
anything can be rationalized.
The truest form lies in one's eyes,
for the devil is at play.
Whether or not admitted,
EVIL carries the masses through the day.
Have you ever sat upon the mountain tops,
looking down upon the world?
What you observed might surprise you
when you take away the meaningless words.
Action dictates intention,
while intention stems from the soul.
A man can be pious or spiteful, but this cannot be told.
The heart of man can be misleading while the mind can be deceiving;
it takes time to heal wounds and it sometimes takes believing.
It takes understanding to heal pain and need, so you must understand this—
most men live and feed off greed, but ALL men, all men bleed.

    Michael E. Chin

Molly the Cow, the Gift of Life

To the brother I always wanted, had, and may have lost
Not spiritually, not emotionally, not mentally, but physically.
Since your disappearance, I wanted to give up
because the deepest hole that could ever exist was found, my heart!
Your words of simplicity when you gave me "that" gift were:
"I can't afford anything expensive to give you, wish I could give you much more."
My sweet brother, wherever you are, it's not the expensive things that count,
But yes, whatever is given without pressure but with pleasure,
sincerity, satisfaction, love, and a great smile like the one you had
and that will never be forgotten. Yes it was Molly the Cow.
She sleeps with me, goes everywhere I go, she's basically glued to me.
I can smell you through her, that simplest Molly has given me
so much courage to fight life.
There is no money in this world that could have bought my courage.
So, as you see, you have given me through Molly a priceless gift:
The gift of life! She will always be with me.
Every time I look at her she tells me not to give up.
If I do then I will lose you forever and everybody else I love.
So, thank you for giving me the best and thoughtful gift ever!
Molly the Cow, the Gift of Life.

    Doris Garcia

My Mother's Hands

They held my father's, wore his ring, fed and comforted two children,
And still were beautiful. As a child, I admired their grace.
Holding a cigarette or glass of Chablis,
They were elegant and fragile, like sparrows.
I used to compare them to mine, small fingers, tomboy hands.
Hers grew worn over time, buried both her brothers.
She began to lose her grip. Their memory made her try to escape.
Alcohol, mental illness, then her parents died, and she just let go.
Now homelessness. Her beautiful hands now scraped and clawed,
Fighting for food and shelter on the streets of Baltimore.
She lived in our backyard 'til we turned the water off.
Years passed as I tried to forget, pretend I hadn't loved them,
Tried to forget their birdlike grace, 'til one day they became my own.
One day, I looked at my hands, my life, and saw my mother in me.
My drinking, almost losing my brother—I hadn't planned any of it,
Neither had she. Like living with a part of her, my pain lessened,
Compassion grew in me. Her hands are different now,
But still hold mine in love and caring.
I love having my mother's hands.
Like suede over steel, they have softness and strength.

    Bronwen West

Perfect Unity

With the passage of time
we only draw closer together.
More than friends,
more than lovers.

We're paired for life,
the two of us,
bound in more ways than one.

Our bodies,
our minds,
our souls.

Forever together,
one.

    Bennett Paul Williamson, Jr.

Sleep and Death . . . Or Is It the Same

Sleep is just a little taste of death
If we fear death
why don't we fear sleep

When we sleep
we are in a deathlike state
for hours upon hours

Also in that deathlike state
when dream
maybe in death

We just dream forever

    Jack David McKee

Lion's Breath

In thy fury
In thy might
Awaken on a sleepless night.

To conquer beauty
And tame the maiden
Boost his altar, golden-laden.

No foe to dare
His Kingly mane
To wallow his
Inflicted pain.

In lion's breath
Thou will succumb
Be it no more the lonely one.

    Mark Maynor

Incomparable

My heart sings a song
sweeter than a bee's honey
My hand tingles with a feeling
that isn't bought with money
My world is motionless
everything is right
My mind is calm
my eyes fill with light
No words can describe
my feelings for her
As everything else
becomes a blur
She is the one
I truly desire
The only one to fill me
with passion and fire
To have her in my life
would bring me bliss
To feel her lips against mine
giving me a gentle kiss

    Junius Joseph Taville

Love's Power

May you kiss me with the kisses of your mouth
For your touches of endearment are finer than wine
Your fragrance is as good as the finest oils
Let them be poured out upon me
For this, many have loved you
Let me run off with you; do let me be with you
This is a love finer than pure gold
For your love I have passionately desired
Upon my beauty you will lay
Your right hand under my head; while the left embraces me
O, how I long to hear your voice
I lie on my bed at night, here I sought for the one my soul has loved
With sweetness your lips entice
As your words depart like flowing milk and honey
About you I tell others
O, how sweet to my palate is your love
How sweet love is to be compared with the bitterness of death
Here the seal of your love is placed upon my heart
For the force of many waters could not wash it away
Here it will forever stay; here I will forever lay

Tiffany Bacon

The Arrival of Spring

Soft, delicate leaves fluttering, innocent birds chirping
and tweeting, flower petals blossoming forth in full bloom,
announcing the arrival of spring.
A healthy field of dense grass, becoming greener, encouraging growth,
seeds implant their roots in the wholesome soil,
shooting forth their stamens into the air of spring.
Fish leaping out of small ponds, frogs hopping from lily pad
to lily pad, turtles dragging themselves to the shore,
coming out of the water to welcome the spring.
The sun wakes up earlier now, taking more time to heat the earth,
blessing the people with its gentle rays,
warming the land for the coming of spring.
The ice is now melted, the water is now evaporated,
clouds are forming in the heavens,
to shower us with the rain of spring.
If only someone knew, how quickly the winter flew,
where has all the snow gone, and the wintry spirit too?
It is now time to move along, stop glancing back in disappointment,
look ahead in awe and amazement,
and marvel at the world in which we live.

Stephen Hopkins

Holding On

Back in the day when I was growing up
Things were bad but we always stuck it out
It was nine brothers and sisters living all together
Sticking together, conquering all types of weather
For Mom, things got tough, 'cause she was doing it all alone
Trying to raise her kids in a single parent home
We would pray together, play together, laugh together and cry together
Mom continued to assure us that one day things would get better
In spite of our condition our house was our home
Every day mom would remind us to keep "Holding on"
In the break of a new year, mom's up late
Figuring how to keep her bills up to date
Christmas did not miss us, we all got toys
Dolls for the girls and trucks for the boys
Back then we did not understand what mom was going through
To keep clothes on our backs and each of us a pair or shoes
Throughout the weekdays she worked as a maid
Working herself sick, trying to keep the bills paid
At times I'd watch her pray from night to morn
Begging the Lord to help her kids to keep holding on

Alexander Brown

Dawn Chorus

Toaster pops
Coffee spills
Dog barks
Phone shrills
Kids are whining up the stairs
Newspaper warns
Beware! Beware!
Birds sing crazy in the trees
Trouble travels on the breeze

Susan Superson

An Exaltation to My Prince

Joyously, my soul loves a man
who speaks with truth in his heart
not of a demand,
who bravely stands among the crowd
with all his strength and grace around.
This man I exalt for such heroic deeds,
to me is noble and worthy indeed.
For him I can give a million praise.
My prince, with love, meet my embrace!

Ma. Mylionette Maghoyop Dioquino

Wait for Me

I did not know you were going to die;
I had no time to say goodbye.
God took your hand;
We had to part.
He closed your eyes and broke my heart.
You can't come back;
I know that's true,
But one day, Dad,
I'll come to you. . . .

Ronald David Fry

Girl of Color

Here I start,
A little girl of color,
Wishing this, dreaming that,
Playing games, being names.
Learning things, forgetting things,
Loving beings, hurting some.
Feeling pride, all in stride,
O, this little girl of color,
Now, all grown up, a little tougher.

Juanita R. Morgan

To My Papa, Happy Father's Day:
A Poem for You

You are special and nice
and a man that likes rice.
You shine like the sun
and know how to have fun.
You don't were a tie,
but you always want to try.
You glow in my heart,
like a lightening bug part.
You don't were boots, nor suits,
but you are very smart
and have a good heart.
You play in the snow
and I say " You go!"
You are my lion protecting me brave,
I am thankful for that.
And I just want to say,
"HAPPY FATHER'S DAY."
Love, Izzy

Isabella Fidanza

Livin' Life

Livin' life to its fullest is the only way to live.
Don't hold back, give life all you have to give.
Change the things you can, don't worry about the things you can't.
Don't worry about those who stress you, let them rave and rant.
Easy does it, one step and stride at a time.
Livin' life to its fullest is definitely not a crime.
It's kinda hard livin' life to its fullest in this world we have.
One thing you gotta know is not to be mad.
You gotta keep your head up and stand tall and proud.
And remember to keep your head out of the clouds.
Remember to not get lost in the crowd.
Don't let it grow cold in this world of hate.
Keep happiness in your heart and happiness will be your fate.
Even when some people get under your skin.
You'll smile and think that you're not like them.
Be thankful of your life even if it's kinda hard.
Keep your dreams on your mind, and someday you'll go far.
Far beyond this world of violence and crime.
To a place of inner peace and a higher state of mind.
Live life to its fullest 'cause I just proved it's the only way to live.

  Peter Sackett

Smoke

The darkness filled my lungs when I awoke,
And the feelings locked inside are covered with a cloak.
When I invoke your spirit I only seem to choke,
It's so hard to see in a world lit with smoke.
The smoke I inhale will go to my brain,
To where my spiritual and mental pains are the same.
I want to ask Jesus to heal His lame,
But I can't even find myself in this smoke to call out His name.
But who am I to blame?
For I am too within myself, I am not the same!
And I don't question God's power or position,
But when I seek Him I usually find myself in opposition.
The choice is up to me of who I want to serve,
But how can you accept something you don't even deserve?
Or better yet, how can I picture something I can't even grasp?
I only get a brief glimpse of His love and I can only gasp.
But a glimpse does not last, and soon I am overwhelmed by my past. . . .
And I am left stripped of position and without a way,
But maybe a love so great isn't meant to be obtained?
For something tangible is so easily thrown away. . . .

  Jon Mooneyham

Happiness

As I sit here and contemplate
I wonder why the sky is so never ending
I wonder why the grass is so green
I am now befuddled
Still in a state of confusion
I confirm myself lost
I can feel the gust of the wind blowing my mind away
I now look beyond the sky at the sun
I see the most beautiful face smiling upon me
The UV rays now blinding me
I shut my eyes for a few seconds
I look again the smile of my face was gone
I had to double check myself
I shut my eyes again then I shall look one last time
Now that I looked again no more face or smile appeared
I look in front of me with despair in my eyes
I am soul shocked for that face I saw is no longer a face
I am now staring at the most beautiful girl of my dreams
I shall now know my soul mate is awaiting me in the eyes of eternity
Finally my heart has been fulfilled and my happiness has been restored

  Mark Anderson

Darling, My Butterfly

Roses are red
Love is blind
You opened my mind
To love I could not find
When I look in your eyes
I find love of the same kind
Which is why I say
Darling my butterfly, will you
Could you always be mine?

  Thomas Brauer

Time

What is time?
It is wished to be delayed,
It is wished to be sped up.
It is the race of life.
It can be as long as an eternity,
Or less than a blink of the eye.
It can be wasted, or cherished,
Happy or sad.
That is time.

  Lauren G. Ponta

I Wonder

I wonder
what makes the wind howl
and the stars glitter bright.
Is it Mother Nature
and Father Light?
What makes him smile at me
and me smile back?
Is it Cupid?
I can't seem to keep track!

  Marika Pers Faytell

Snowflake

Shining on a
Nice December night floating
Onto the streets of the town
White flakes
Falling silently while bringing
Love
And peace, holding and
Keeping
Everyone together this chilly night

  Jenny Glick

Thoughts

If I were to write, where would I begin
My imaginative thoughts have no end
They run like a thousand waterfalls
And a trillion phone calls
Conclusions lead to delusions
Of memories past
Yet I've found freedom at last

Walking the path
Divided in half
By my own good intention
Not to mention
The music behind it all

Running down an endless hall
Searching for my spiral galaxy
My infinitude
The intimacy
Of my youth
When my elements were still aloof

  Jeanette Meade

The Roach Brigade

Once upon a time, there was a mouse who lived in my house
And he left a piece of cheese beside the sink above the floor.
It attracted many roaches and they came in motor coaches
And Blackie, who's my cat, was scared to death.

Then she hid behind the table
While a roach, the one named Mabel,
Gave orders to line up in twenty rows.

The roaches started talkin' when their rows had started walkin'
And they missed the turn up by the kitchen sink.

If they had just been listening to the mouse who's always whistling,
They'd have found his stash of cheese without a fight.

But they kept right on a walkin' and they kept right on a talkin'
'Til they marched right out our great big front room door.

It was quite a sight to see and just between you and me,
I'm quite glad we only have mouse;

'Cause if we had to please all those roaches with more cheese,
I'm afraid we'd have to pack our bags and leave.
    Linda D. Altavilla

My Mom Is Gone

In memory of Minnie Pelzer Shell
Those arms that held me close to her bosom
And cradled my helpless tiny frame
Those hands that changed my soiled pants
And prepared meals for me time and again
Those eyes that pierced the depths of my soul
And scooped out truths I tried in vain to conceal;
Those lips that guarded her soft voice,
and instructed, corrected, and consoled with zeal;
Those feet that once chased after me
and allowed her to walk here and there;
Those ears so quick to listen and to hear
unspoken thoughts that showed her care;
Those body parts move no more for me.
For I peered down into an empty shell—
a cold facsimile of what used to be a warm and loving, life-giving well.
Those days with Mom—forever etched in my memory—
and cherished by a grateful heart were merely sprinkles of God's love for me—
the same God who now assures me
that with Him my Mom is gone to spend eternity.
    Gloria Shell Mitchell

Our Wedding Vows

No eyes have seen, nor ears heard, nor the heart of man
Conceived what God has prepared for those who love Him.
1 Corinthians 2:9.

When our Father was making all our souls, there were those
He decided to break in half and place into separate bodies.
There are those few who, with God's help, guidance and
Blessing, search until they find their other half—as we have
Done.
Judy, I sense your presence before you enter my sight; when
You are in pain, I feel it; when there is joy in your heart, I'm in
Heaven.
If you ever doubt my love, look into my eyes.
If you ever doubt my strength, let me hold you in my arms.
If you ever doubt my heart, look in the palm of your hand, for
It's there that you hold it.
If you ever doubt my wisdom, look in the mirror.
If you ever doubt my words, look at my actions.
If you ever doubt this marriage, look to our Father in Heaven,
For it was there that this was set in motion; but it is here,
Today, that it is complete, and we are made whole again.
    Judy Patterson

Mom

Three little letters
Two of which are the same
Represent the dearest person
A truly cherished name

Everybody everywhere
Have someone whom they treasure
But nobody, anywhere
Can ever, ever measure
Up to mom and what she's done
For his loved ones everywhere
    Josephine M. Thomas

Falling in Love

The gold of your hair
The pink of your lips
The love in your eyes
The magic of your hands
The message of your mind
The language of your body
The velvet of your skin
The marble of your breast

All this makes me fall
In love with you
    Giuseppe A. De Giuli

The Stories of My Tongue

Remember me forever please
my time is almost done
and in these passing moments now
the stories of my tongue
The story of the wilderness
wild, safe, and free
is nearing its extinction now
if you simply let it be
Story of the people now
is filled with hurt and pain
genocide and homicide
tears fall like acid rain
The story of the children
cast away through time
neglected and abused through life
the parents, yours and mine
It doesn't have to be this way
my years on Earth are done
but you can change the future
with the stories of my tongue
    Whitney Gilbert

A Family Photo

Who's all in the photo?
Does time stop in this photo?
Thirteen of us smothered together,
Lined up forever.
Although I sit up perched and proper,
I wasn't so happy.
Instead of a forced smile
I should of reached for awhile.
One, two have passed on;
I try to look beyond,
Pressed against my breast
As I lay here to rest.
What dear ones I'm tied in time with;
This family photo
Will go on without us.
Someday there will be no one alive
To capture the eyes
Of a family photo
I'm tied up with.
    Barbara J. Sanzotta

Harden

rubbing back and forth
splitting the once united skin
letting the blood run down my fingers
rubbing still back and forth
cheese grating my epidermis
stinging pain
subtle pain
no pain
numbness
it builds up
callousing
now I have a calloused hear

Beth Cutler

That Computer Poem

I saw you in the disco
Last night in San Francisco
The way you used your joystick
It really makes my mouse click
Come sit down on my laptop
Lets do a little hiphop
Let's go into a chatroom
And do a little boom boom
I saw you in the disco
Last night in the San Francisco
One way you used your joystick
Has really made me feel sick
Doctor checked my hard drive
A virus in my archive
My disc was not protected
And now I am infected

Mankaran Singh

Robbed of Innocence

To anyone who's been sexually abused or molested by a family member

He crept into my room each time
like a thief into the night.
I lay feigning peaceful sleep
my body trembling with fright.
He stood beside my bed
just staring at me asleep.
I prayed to God each time
I wouldn't make a peep.
He came and sat down on my bed;
his hands my body did explore.
Never did he speak to me;
my pleas he would ignore.
A little girl's innocence
is what he took away.
A woman with mixed emotions
is all there is left today.
Too scared to fight him off,
too ashamed to tell another.
The one who robbed me of my youth,
no stranger, but my brother.

Kathy Lou Cordova

What Friends Should Do

Friends should love you, no matter what
Friends should comfort you when you've been dropped
Friends should defend you when they're wrong
Friends should be the ones to buy you that thong
Friends should help you with that work
Friends should buy you a knife to threaten that jerk
Friends should help your band get a start
Friends should crack a smile when your teacher farts
Friends should be there when you're down
Friends should help you when you feel like you're about to drown
Friends should see that you're depressed
Friends should motivate you when you don't feel like getting dressed
If you were a friend, you'd notice a change
If you were a friend, you'd help me up
If you were a friend, I'd feel more loved
If you were a friend, I'd be free as a dove
If you were a friend, I wouldn't be writing this
If you were a friend, these wouldn't be my last words
So I'll go now and have some fun
Goodbye, my so-called-friend

Sally Jane Houlden

Just Want a One-Night Stand

All I want is just a one night stand,
I don't want no permanent man.
No commitments, no hangin' on,
No one to say if you don't I'm gone.
I want it simple and want a smile,
I need to touch and hold you awhile.
Don't have to worry if I stay the night,
Just don't make me cry, don't make me fight.
I don't want no permanent man,
All I want is just a one night stand.
No name, no tears, no worry, no fears,
Cuddle and kiss, just one night—do this.
A tender kiss and caress of the hand,
Fingers through hair, try and understand.
No commitments at all, not even a name,
No worries, no fears, no feeling of shame.

I don't want no permanent man,
All I want is just a one night stand.

Terry L. Morris

The Game

When I was little, I played the game;
now I'm older and the game is still the same.
It has always been my first love,
the game with the bat and the glove.
I love the game, it is so intense,
especially hitting the ball over the fence.
I played third base with much love,
I played third base; I had a golden glove.
At the plate, I used an air attack.
For all my damn critics—guess what?
I'm back.
Don't think I'm cocky; I know I'm not the best,
but next year I'll put my game to the test.
This is a game truly about the team;
to play this game again, that is my dream.
This is a game that everyone should play;
any given team can win on any given day.
There's only one thing in life that
cannot be changed,
and that is the love I have for the game.

Todd Andrew Garris

Do You Feel?

Do you feel it's right
To disregard my emotions?
To leave me with my memory of this fight?
Do you feel you're just
In your actions against me
And my lonely heart?
Do you feel you can proceed
Without love in your life?
Without someone to care for you?
Do you feel any remorse
For any sins you've done, old and new?
Do you feel and sorrow
For anyone you've done this to?
Do you feel any pleasure
When I do this to you?
When I tell you it's all over
And I pull the gun to your head?
Do you feel any worry
When you're lying on the floor dead?

Amy Michelle Suddleson

Forbidden Fruit

Electricity! Eye to eye.
Hey! Don't I know you? I can't speak.
The room is spinning out of control.
I've never been so defenseless.
I can't even make sense of this.
You speak, but I don't hear a word.
What would happen if we kissed?
Would your tongue slip past my lips?
Would you run? Or, would I melt into you?
Mouth to mouth—lust to lust,
Spontaneously, we combust.
Forbidden fruit—ring on my finger.
You are such a moral woman.
To throw it all away, no questions asked.
Will I pretend I am innocent?
What would happen if we kissed?
Would your tongue slip past my lips?
Would you run? Or, would I melt into you?
Mouth to mouth—lust to lust,
Spontaneously, we combust.

Cari Ann Johnson

Battered Woman, Unbreakable Woman

By nightfall he shattered
Your wedding dreams with heavy punches.
Your mouth's blood a crimson flower,
Staining the conjugal bed.

For six years you hid
From the truth,
Until too many black eyes
Ended your blindness forever.

Shaking, you signed the complaint,
But the shelter escort
Held your other hand,
Keeping your heartbeat steady.

The callous judge assigned "counseling,"
And called you a loser,
But you stood strong and said for all
To hear, "No, I'm a survivor!"

Henry Lovett Howard

Unbridled Passions

In the middle of the night
I wake up with a jolt
Can this be really me
I cannot imagine
Strange and unknown passions
Of another world pierce my insides
I grapple the sheets and arch my body
Uttering cries of pain and pleasure
Can I go to such extremes?
I am horrified and intrigued
I am trapped in the burning pleasures
'Til the light of the dawn comes to my rescue and I adorn the garb
Of respectability

Hemjit Bharathan

Broha

I reach to the sky calling out your name
In the dark the moon gazes down sharing a familiar glow
Setting the scene for four souls, when we
Parted time did not reflect the changes that
Occur so suddenly, but did we change?
If so, for better or worse
The turn is full circle and once again we
Embrace as four united souls, the time away is
Not truly time away, we partake of memories
And times of the past
Looking only to the future for outtakes of
Our history
God created greatness in the four of us
Is it true?
The things we can do broha
The things we can f*cking do
You and I together

A piece of me is gone, that piece is you

John Hubert Cross

Green through the Black

I fade away—don't look back
Disappear—into the black
Leave you here—to die alone
The more I think—the more I feel
The closer I get—the more I need to run away
Kill me again like the other day
I'd do it to you in thirteen different ways
when you die, I'd like you to know
the pain will ease, but very slow
I want to—hear you speak
You won't say it
I don't blame you—for the bullet
I was born dead
You're so jealous
I saw you stab me
In my back
It was clear, like green through the black

Jeffrey McLaurin

Sullen Anthem

You seem to have found a peace you can
safely call your own; when will I find mine?
Troubled in my eyes—chaotic and
moronic are the things we do. Nothing seems
to change, not even in time, or in age.
I've had enough of these stupid games we
play. I'm sick of the tired words we say.
Blood is spilled, innocents drilled, because
justice is truly blind. Youth are killed
because they don't have the strength to
find a way to free their minds. We'll never
have peace because we're all too blind to
see the damage we have done.
Children cry because they can't afford to
eat and are too afraid to sleep. Your
mother sells her body just to afford what
little you can buy. I won't even try to
understand. Neglected and affected—the pain
has to stop.

Johnny Palacios

Victim

Have you ever been raped
If so did you escape
Were you forever damaged
Did you turn him in for what he did
Or did you go on and try to forget
You can't forget when he totally changed your image
After he took what he wanted he could not look you in the face
Then he hoped he never sees you again in any case
You thought he was your friend
You didn't think that's how your relationship would end
He knew you trusted him
You almost had love for him
He took advantage of your trust
Selfishly only thinking of lust
The reason why you trust so easily
Is because you get lonely continuously
Searching for someone to give you attention
You got attention through something your mind did not mention

Tia Smith

Bullies Don't Control Shootings

I woke up early to go to school any day like the rest.
There was this kid who I was always a pest.
I was supposed to go take a math test.
Instead he pulled out a gun and I took two to the chest.

He got his revenge on me.
In a distant voice I heard him say "Whoopee!"
Now that I'm dying, it's hard for me to see.
Because of my meanness, my life's done unfortunately.

With my life coming to a close.
I hear multiple "Oh, no's."
Another kid shot me and my life just froze.
I guess I had multiple foes.

Now that I'm dead I live to regret.
My words became a serious threat.
I'll never do it again you can bet.
But Saint Peter I just met.

Joe Wezner

don't care

you say you pick and choose but you don't care
you get between the legs running through the hairs
you don't want love you don't want to care
is it fun to crack your gun and shoot those flares?
spread the burning love in between her legs
keep it unsafe because you don't care
keep them sick—but you're unaware
of the fire you hold deep down there.
the ring of flames—are your dues
because you don't know you keep it cool
but do you know all those females catch up to you?
the cycle is near coming to an end
your life is on the line burning to a thread
you start to know—you start getting scared
now you start to wonder—which love affair?
smoky haze starts to cloud your eyes
your mind flashes back—back in time
as your life turns to ashes and dust
to dust
all for the satisfaction of carnal lust.

Janielle Frazier

The Lost Girl

They found her body in the water
Floating in the weeds
She had been cut badly
Choked with a piano cord the cut was deep
She had been in the water for at least three weeks
The blood had washed away
Her tissue had begun to decay
A lump began to form in my throat
As they loaded a young girl into the boat
To bring her in out of the water
To get an identification from her mother

Randi-Lynn Nicole Semler

A Conch, a Crab, a Leech

I saw a glimpse of the ocean,
and forgot about the shackle 'round my neck.
I threw this wretched iron ball from off the cliff,
and it pulled me off the deck.
A lung full of water?
A throat devoid of air?
But not the first, nor the latter!
My skin, it did not tear!
A new array of senses have invaded my being.
I finally savor the taste of me.
There is so much more than simply seeing.
I know what it is to be.
Don't dare to throw the lifeline;
You won't receive a response.
Let me rest in this joy of maritime;
Your repulsiveness never taunts.

Jonathan Ernest Parrott

Jane Doe, Dead Doe

Mangled decomposing corpse lay in the dirt
Mud caked hair, torn blouse, ripped skirt.
Who she was nobody can say
Why was she murdered in such a brutal way
Once a woman with a future so bright
Why was a cord 'round her neck so tight?
Knife wounds down deep to the bone
How much she suffered nobody had known.
Child abuse made her turn to the street
To survive she'd sell herself to men she'd meet
Now she just lays there, a nameless face
Stripped of beauty, life, and grace.
Was the degradation of this demoralized, desensitized society of hate
The reason this woman met her murderous fate?

Margaret Colleen Johnson

The Tale of Sleeping Beauty

A celestial beauty stepped up inside his spectrum
Behold the intervention where Goliath simply wrecked him
With David she would kick it, but this beauty would be sleeping
Slowly driftin' away . . . only to watch his heart weaken
The following evening, Beauty hooked up with Goliath
Dry between the eyelids, but inside David's cryin' from the torment
Now it's more than just an average crush, it's something he can't touch
His heart will slowly turn into rust
Collecting dust while Beauty sleeps, not giving David's heart a chance
Sleeping Beauty found Goliath and mistook it for romance

Brendan Carlin

All You Want to Do

Distinct rhythms . . . dramatic upbeats . . . fiery lyrics . . . this
unbelievable music vibrating inside my bones—passionate dancing—
sweaty but sweet bodies rubbing up against each other—holding each
other . . . looking deep into each others eyes . . . breathing heavily,
carefully trying to seduce one another . . . the dancing speaks their
real words, feelings . . . as you move closer and closer, smelling his
delicious cologne . . . feeling his every muscle contract . . . the music
unnoticed getting faster and faster but the movement, the
dancing, getting slower and slower . . . sexy whispers travelling back
and forth yet you don't want to talk or even get to know him . . . just
dance . . . that's all you want to do . . .

Michelle Soroka

A Lonely Jew Forever Known

Take a look into my eyes
The blood and death of a thousand generations
Are reflected upon them
The sorrow of a thousand more lay behind them
In my eyes
The burnt bodies of a hundred babies are held in each fiery abyss
The blood of their murdered mothers runs cold throughout them
The lonely hearts of a thousand orphans scream out for comfort
The corpses of their fathers lay stiff on the cold gas chamber floors
Take a look into my eyes
The faces of a thousand children stare back
Their cheeks sunken
Their hearts stopped
Their ribs shown
My eyes
An ocean of tears from torn brothers flows there
The sound of a billion bullets piercing bleeding heads are heard there
Into my eyes
The touch of dead fingertips
The sounds of dead voices
The feeling of dead love remains there

Jonathan Barker

My Kat

When I woke up on my first birthday,
My parents shouted, "Stupfind@34#@!"
And as I wiggled and squirmed and sat up straight,
I noticed something furry and soft hiding in the blankets.
"6$^GNC@#HGFD$," said Mom, "GdsgKUXN%&*#2," said Dad.
Bursting with enthusiasm—oh, but what is this?
It's got four short legs and furry feet, and a wet, pink nose.
It's got long; pointy things sticking out at the sides and
It's black and white and its ears are on top of its head!
And it's furry all around. Sheesh, what is this thing?
Let me see, it's got a long curling tail and it moves
Around a lot. What could this be? What could this be?
Just then Mom and Dad both leaned towards me
As they excitedly whispered. I smiled and giggled
And went back to this creature. Aha! Then it struck me:
This is a elephant! No, wait, that doesn't sound right—hmmm . . .
Yes, I've got it now, it's a kat!

Mina L. Acevedo

Night Swim

I swim to your sun
Through my sea of dreams
Tasting wishing stars
As night draws breath.

I am driven by immutable fate
To the spawning shore
Of your fire's corona
Planting my seed,

Waiting, waiting . . .
For the dawn of your love's spring.

Marsi Camille Salmi

tribute to america

america
though the towers are no more
our life has changed for sure
we will still prove america is the best
will only be a lot stronger from this test

we will take our time to do our healing
and try to get over this horrific feeling
but when we do, you'll hear us say
all the terrorists, they must now pay

united we stand is what we say
you had yours, now it's our day
after all is said and done
america is still number one

your cowardly act only dampened our spirit
now we're coming for you, better feel it
soon there will be no more talking
bin laden, you're the dead man walking

Jack A. Fulper

War

What is war but a shameless whore,
Her iniquities imposed
With eternal lust and desire that must
Be tended to by those . . .
Who anguish, bleed, and die.

This bawd is to blame for the grief and pain
That we bestow one on another!
Her selfish wit to plot and to pit
Brother against brother . . .
Has put the world awry

Gary L. Good

Life

On a cold rainy night, sitting lonely in a
room. thinking, wondering about life.
How life has been, how life should be,
how life can be so f***ing cold at times.

Thoughts of the world that we the people
have every day, every night, every minute,
every second.
These are thoughts
that we, the people, think about,
the questions that we, the people,
ask ourselves to help us to decide,
shall we move on with our lives,
or shall we stay and die
with the lives we have lived?

We, as the people,
can only answer that as individuals.

Billie Jo Bunting

No Tit for Tat

How can I develop affinity
for a soul without sympathy
of the smallest quantity,

I mesh with no tit for tat
but when there's only brutal attack
tell me, who will relate to that

Not fighting back is a common sense
while a reliable fence
is a good defense

Muhammad Deji Adiat

Mysterious Smile

Mysterious smile
Kiss tattooed on my hand
Fingers touching my piano
Rejoicing sound
So close to me

Stars turn pale
Nights stop breathing
Empty flat echoes
Old piano cries
So far away

Béatrice Kvist

Christmas Past

Tiptoe on the Lino
So cold on your feet
But today you don't seem to mind
Because who shall you meet?
The coals are crackling in the fire
Causing shadows on the wall
Whispering laughter and smiles
The soft snow that goes for miles
Has Santa left a stocking?
Bulging at our feet
All five of us, our little hands
Find the tangerines and nuts
All the while She's watching
Her heart bursting with love for us
She made all this possible, She did
All the warmth and love from Her
Makes Her quite unique
Our Mum is who She is
Nobody could ever compete

Tracy Livingston Savage

The Sky So Gold

The wind blows.
The sky so gold,
Never lies,
And the trees so tall never judge.
The grass so green,
Whispers to you its comforts.
The world around is full of beauty.
The flowers on a spring day,
Sing you their glory,
And the evergreens whistle their love,
In the winter.
But fading fast is the gold in the sky,
And coming soon is the dark of night.
Yet,
I know,
Tomorrow is another day to listen,
To the sky so gold,
And the trees so tall,
That never lie.

Brittany Brinser

Worth Living

Life is worth living again
I've found a lover that's also a friend
I've found a home to live on my own
Yes
Life is worth living again
Yesterdays are long and forgotten
Tomorrows I'm longing to see
I wake with the Sun
My todays have begun
My dreams are returning to me

Kathleen Kiefer

Volunteers

With people working day to day
And no one caring for another
How we can go our separate ways
Not looking at each other.
There are those among us
Who know no other feeling
Than to volunteer
And be there to help healing.
In times of shedding a tear
They're always there to help.

Brett Anthony Patterson

Why Children Chase Birds

The pigeon that waddles dumbly away
is the tantalizing easy problem
that's confoundedly difficult to solve
and so must be pursued
because a big kid would get it.
The blue jay dropping down from a
low branch to snag a morsel
is the bright color that you can spell,
and only by holding it can you
point and recite to prove your talent.
The sparrow that flits from ground
to bush to eave to tree
and sings its presence to the world
knows the same fascination and fear
of the world as your own mind and heart.
The wings of living flight
scatter in the face of newfound power
and remain that goal of reaching,
that which will not be caught,
but returns to present the challenge.

James Alfred Martin, III

Who Is She?

Is she the golden angel
Who soared into your life
To set your world to spinning
And then became your wife?
Is she the perfect mother
You want to raise your child?
Is she always even-tempered?
Does she always wear a smile?
Does she keep your household tidy
And prepare your meals on time?
Does she cut down on expenses
And does she always draw the line
On the ones who would exploit you
To cause you money woes?
Does she smile at you at breakfast
And wrinkle up her nose
As she tells you that she loves you
And wouldn't have another life?
If so, I've got to tell you
That she is the perfect wife!

E. Widger

The Touch

The touch of an angel
I wish to see
From the greatest of all
Who lives on the sea.

The touch of an angel
I wish to feel,
Like the love of a letter
With a sweet kiss to seal.

The touch of an angel
So like a nice wife,
Unfortunate the cruel world
Had to soon take her life.

Kenzie Nichols

Don't Throw Him Away

I know what he did was wrong
that is all there is to say.
Even though you say you are ready
you shouldn't completely throw him away.
Keep him in your heart
for all the good times you had.
But remember this one thing
for every good their is always a bad.
You found this out the hard way
there is not always an answer to why.
But you try to say inside
underneath all that bad
there really might be a good guy.

Marla Marie Kemp

Summer's Island

Hidden little windows,
shining white walls,
summer's own
geometry

Faint herbal smells,
below
a salty
steel blue sea

Sensual lavender,
a winding sandy path,
riding donkeys,
picnic
in the shades

I kiss you softly,
lost in dreams
on sun-dried grass

Chris Wanten

Secret

Shhh, I have a secret
And it's one I cannot sell
It was told to me in confidence
And I swore I would not tell

I cannot explain its details
So I'll try to change it some
Give it another name
And try to make it sound more fun

But surely you must have known
What everyone's suspected
It's something very obvious
I'm sure it was detected

Let me give you a little clue
So I cannot be to blame
Try and constantly guess
About this certain person's name

Helen Margaret Fezer

A Sunny Day

Birds singing
Flowers blooming
Butterflies flying
People saying
Oh! It's a
Sunny day

Making up games
Calling out names
Having fun in the sun
Children playing
And saying
Oh! It's a
Sunny day

David Jamal Watkins

When Your Freedom Dies

Why do the trees and flowers sigh?
Why do they fade and die?
Who do the mountains hide the sun?
Who do the years pass by?

Why can't we keep the morning sun
fresh with eternal dew?

Life is but an empty shadow show
Kings and fools must go.
Life is but a passing by
All of us shall go.

Life is but a dream that dies
When your freedom dies.

Antonio Campasas Roldan, Jr.

Hiding from Life

I sit idle on a bench of stone
Searching for thoughts much my own
Wondering when my life will unfold
Wondering why I feel so alone

I sit here on this cold, hard bench
Not knowing who or what I'll become
Gazing into the herd of smiles
Caring only for the pure warmth of some

I sit too long on this lifeless bench
Staring out at the world from a perch
Life does not look good from the outside
Life is good in active search

So I get up from this stagnant bench
And stretch my sleeping legs. . . . wow
Life certainly has a different view
When not hiding on a cold, hard perch

Fred Neff

Every Time

Every Time I close my eyes
A lonely teardrop falls
Then suddenly I realize
Strong are not my walls

And Every Time I go to sleep
His vision clouds my mind
These memories I cannot keep
Why won't they stay behind

So Every Time I wake up
I will pray for you to go
Your visions and your memories
No longer eating at my soul

Now Every Time I want to smile
I will remember all I've asked
And maybe in a little while
Every Time will be surpassed

Arlene Michelle Warren

Rest in Your Arms

Every angel in the sky cries.
Tears stroll down their cheeks
because you say goodbye.
Every star in the sky shall
remind me of the day when darkness
filled the night.
Vulgar laughter clings to your soul
like wet clothing, in the tiny
body of your innocence.
The sun still shines. It kills
slowly; darkness is full of light.
'Til that day that you are present,
forever I will rest in your arms.

Sergio Antonio Diaz

I Believe, I'm Sorry

Horror stories from books and friends,
Telling my fate when I reach my end.
Is it wisdom or untrue?
The choice to believe is up to you.
Tales of a city made of gold,
Angels with wings that unfold,
Some of the stories I've been told.

This sounds crazy, I admit,
Fire and brimstone in a pit.
A demon with horns
And a tongue that is split.
I'm sorry,
I don't believe any of it.

Daniel Arthur Wolcott

The Head Nod!

Wsup! Head Nod, eyebrow raise.
Every day in the halls
This is how guys communicate.
Wsup! Head Nod, eyebrow raise.

Girls don't understand it.
In fact, neither do we,
But nevertheless, it's always:
Wsup! Head Nod, eyebrow raise.

No hugging, screaming, giggling.
Guys are much more simple.
We get the job done quicker.
Wsup! Head Nod, eyebrow raise.

It's a greeting unparalleled,
Means more than a hug.
Getting acknowledged means all.
Wsup! Head Nod, eyebrow raise.

Benjamin A. Taft

Love of a Lifetime . . . With You

I can't remember a time
when I did not love you
That is how I know
that our love is true
we've stood through
our ups and downs
and I realize that I am lucky
for the love that we found
I've never wanted anyone
like this before
the way I want this love
to last forever more
I can't believe it
but it's true
I found the love of a lifetime
with you

Jennifer Mary Barba

One Seed

All men created from one seed.
From one seed grew trees.
From tree grew branches.
From branch grew stems.
From stem grew leaves.
From leaves create colors.
From color create human races.
From human race create differences.
From difference create life.
From life create death.
From death create spirit.
From spirit create
"The womb of the Heaven and the Earth."

Lucinda Jones

Making Up after a Fight

They said when it rains it pours.
You told me love doesn't hurt
But who's perfect.
They said when it rains it pours.
My heart hurts like a slamming door.
Without a fuss or fight
Everything is bright.
With a fuss or fight
Nothing is right.
Let's spend more time together
No matter the weather.
I love you with all my heart
Let's not break that apart.

Jesse J. Belin

I

I
Here I
Sit, riddled with
Pits of self-loathing,
Pierced with arrows of hatred,
Destroyed by the blades of depression.
The world is a dark place where
I, I will live never happy,
Never loving, never feeling alive.
Blood drips, sparkling rubies
Stain the earth
So beautiful
I . . .

Joseph Bozdech

A Time to Dance

I feel it when you look at me,
I can see it in your eyes,
the words you find so hard to say,
your silence can't disguise.
The nervousness between us,
the way we get along,
all the things we have in common,
how could we be so wrong?

Wrong because the book of rules
says that we cannot be,
can't be, to laugh or talk together
for what others might see?
Our hearts joined for a reason—
they deserve to have their chance
to live, to love, to laugh, to grow
. . . our hearts deserve to dance.

I cannot speak all the words
of what there is to say,
I just hope we have the moment,
to dance our dance . . . someday.

Jamie Cooper

Miracle

You asked me for a miracle;
It can mean most anything,
A baby's cry, a flower's bloom,
The hope in every spring.

I gladly give you all I am,
My heart, my soul, and more,
A life to share, a tender kiss,
A love completely pure.

You asked me for a miracle,
It's in everything we do;
I see it every single day,
My love, the miracle is you.

Jeffrey Gould

Love's Prick

Speak not of love to me.
For as a thorn pricks the finger,
So has love pricked my heart!

Cupid's arrow flies steadfast
With aim to please,
Yet spites those with eyes for truth.

Souls who seek love, with gentle lips
promise, then waiver
When love presents itself.

Eyes steady with passion, flee
When true love weaves its spell.
I'll not escape, nor repel love's magic.

Monique Alyce Young

To Love a Son

This love is often scary,
Terrifying at best.
It often overwhelms me
As I hold him near my breast.

I have felt love before,
But this is like no other.
It is the love I felt
The moment I became a mother.

Yes, this love is so powerful
And it brings me endless joy,
As I gaze into the face
Of my beautiful baby boy.

Catherine Ann Hoadley-Doyle

America, Stand Tall

The heart beats still in the chest
Of a dying man
Shards of glass through his hand
As breath leaves lips he cries out
America stand tall.

The tears fall soft on the cheek
Of a dying child
Chunks of concrete will land
Round, over and under . . . oh,
America stand tall.

The hands reach for the husband
Of a dying wife
She lays her ring in dust
As her soul whispers and prays—
America stand tall.

The ribs—our buildings of trade—
Of a dying hulk
Falls into the fiery pit
As its gleaming frame shatters
America stand tall.

Bonnie F. Becker

Untitled

After the harvest
The first snowfall

Dagmar Suzuki

Israel

I watched her
Flaring to the sky
Battling pain and fate
Striving to conquer
The opponent
That never
Loses

I watched her
Gleaming negative image
Counterpoint white against black
Pain against pleasure
Life against death
And everything outside
All color, light, sound
Vanished as the focus
Glaring on the stage of
Sun-drenched letters
Luminous against the cosmos

Jerry Harry Jacobs

I Am Myself

Minutes seem like hours,
And weeds seem like flowers.
Time seems endless
When you're friendless.
I find it hard to rhyme
When I don't have the time.
Where has it gone?
Sitting up 'til dawn,
Watching the moon
And holding a balloon.
Seeing the sun,
And thinking I've won.
What have I won? I've won none.
Delirious and furious,
Emotional and critical.
I like to be unique, I'm not weak.
Proven to the world I can make it.
Unlike those who fake it.
Intelligent, creative, and interesting
As opposed to stupid, boring, and dull.

Tiffany Joella Hedges

Countenance

Has anyone told you
how stormy your eyes
even when smiling your half-smiles
or grinning your lopsided grins?
Or has anyone ever dared drown
in those dark pools
even if only to catch a thread of light
into your being?

Already the noonday
has worked its magic into your eyes
tame-tender, wild-stormy;
but always the inscrutable silence
of impenetrable thoughts

And I wonder:
if I probe deeper,
fall into you
will I surface in time
to catch my breath
and still the beatings of my heart

Christine Villafuerte Flores

Pete

There once was a boy named Pete
He had very stinky feet
It took him an hour
To take a shower
But now his feet are neat

Meredith Legare Brown

Katie

Which Wright is newest and fine?
Katie is! Katie is!

Who's the latest in our family line?
Katie is! Katie is!

Who used Vaseline on her hair?
Katie did! Katie did!

Who has eyes so bright and fair?
Katie does! Katie does!

Who'll be Miss America in her time?
Katie will! Katie! Katie will!

Who'll be the student so sublime?
Katie . . .
Of course she will!
Who wraps us 'round her little finger?
Well . . .
Katie does! Katie does!

James L. Smith

Love Cascades

Sweet cascades of icy cold
in shimmering colored waves,
splash in drops of golden hue
on rocks and hidden caves.

Deep within its sheltering walls
the creature huddles, shivering,
staring at the brilliant light
entranced, bewitched, and quivering.

Slowly one hand reaches out
to touch the rainbow veil.
Quickly then, the hand withdraws,
shaking, cold, and pale.

The light of rainbows in his palm
guides him out into the day.
He fears no more the sunshine.
Love sometimes is that way.

Jared Brandley

Guardian Angel

*To my niece, Anna, and my friend, Brittany,
who lost her father*
Every step you have taken
I have taken with you
Every heart you had broken
I had broken with you
Every kiss you have kissed
I have kissed with you
When you were in trouble
I was in trouble too
Now you are gone
And I am too,
But now I'll go back
To sing your song for you
Your song of "Amazing Grace"
Saying please remember me
Excuse me now and you will see
Just remember that I am your
Guardian Angel and forever will be

Jessica Marie Green

One Love

Sitting here all alone, nothing new,
Just me, thinking about you, my one true
Love; the day we will meet again to be
Together as one, to love, to honor,
To cherish forever as one heart.

Shelby Nichol Ball

Pegasus

Oh, for a horse with wings
A winged stallion
To carry me over these heavy hills
To a peaceful valley of cool ripples
And sweet, warm grass under my toes

Oh, for that stallion
That strong stallion
Take me from this hard oppression
To that airy heaven in the valley
Where the wind urges my bare heels to
Take flight with you among the
Shimmering tree tops

Oh, young winged stallion
Do not leave me here
But take me
Take me

Grace Ellen Selogy

every time

every time you cry
i will cry with you
every time you laugh
i will laugh too
every time i see you smile
my eyes begin to glow
every time i see you hurt
the pain i feel will show
every time you give up hope
i'll have faith in you
every time you need to talk
i will be there too
every time means anytime
whether night or day
my love for you
continues to grow
in each and every way

Kimberlee Lach

Angel Tears

The evil beating in the men's hearts as
they planned.
God watched and grieved.

The passengers laughing and so
joyful boarding on a morning bright.
As God watched and grieved.

The panic rising up off the silver
wings glistening.
While God watched and grieved.

The first searing thrust into pillars
of glass and steel.
God only watched and grieved.

As heroes rushed in to give their souls
to crushing stone.
Still God watched and grieved.

The search in the midst of dust and ash
for what each one fears.
And finally God opened the heavens
for the angels' tears.

Sherry Diane Cannon

To Show My Love

Here's a card to show my love,
I thank the man from up above. . . .

He blessed me with you, as you can see,
My love for you will always be.

Yvonne R. M. Candelaria

I Feel It

Addiction, addiction,
I feel it.
My caffeine, my sugar,
I feel it.
My beer, my nicotine,
I feel it.
Occasionally I quit,
I still feel it.
Forgetting why I quit,
Because I feel it.
Quitting's an illusion,
When you feel it.
My habits, my cravings,
I feel it.
My soul, my cancer,
I feel it,
My death, my decay,
I felt it.

Travis Neal Wells

He Is Me

He is my dreams,
or rather,
where they come from.
He is my night,
or rather,
the star that lets me see.
He is my storybook here,
or rather,
the storyteller.
He is my skin,
or rather,
the youth it holds on to.
He is my drive,
or rather,
what keeps me from crashing.
He is my laughter,
or rather,
the sounds that make it mine.
He is me, and I love him.

Tatiana Blania

Darkness

As I lie here all alone
I shiver
from the freezing cold
that's in my mind
I don't even know how much time
I have 'til I break
My whole life is a fake
and I'm all alone
in my own box
It's like a deadly zone
growing old
watching my skin wither
My hair grows long
as I wait all alone
becoming an old, ugly crone
with brittle, bent bones
I wait, all alone
shivering in the darkness
that I call home . . .

Britton Michael Taubenfeld

Halloween

Thunder, thunder up above.
What is it, mother? Shhhhh, my love.
It's just the thump of creature feet—
A creature in a windy sheet.
His claws are dragging on the floor;
He's crashing, smashing at the door.

Brandon L. St.George

Nightmares

These nightmares
are the only thing that scare me
because of the things I see
I view myself
with failing health
I'm dying
but not crying
I'm unable to care
where my life will end
I lived with no friends
and that's how I'll die
Why?
As I lie on my death bed
with my head on a pillow
and know when I cease
I'll have no peace in my soul
because it has too big a hole

James Amaral

I'll Sit

I'll sit and wait;
My eyes are blinking.
Wondering what you are thinking,
I'll sit and think about your face,
And dream about when we embrace.
I'll sit and think about your eyes
And wonder what kind of surprise
Is standing there outside my door.
For you are the one,
The one I adore.
I'll sit in a field and stare at a star.
I wonder how far apart we are.
For all I do is think about you,
I wonder when I'll see you.
But for now my love
I'll stay strong.
And hope this time
Is not too long.

Melesa Rose Carson

Do You Love Me?

Do you love me?
Do you not?
Can't you see
This lonely feeling I've got?
Sometimes you do
Sometimes you don't
You can say I love you
But you won't
Why is that?
You can hide your feelings
But I can't hide mine
Can't you say I love you
Just this one time?
So do you love me
The same way I love you?
'Cause for your love
Anything I'll do
So do you love me?

Anh Truong

Dreams?!

D-disjointed memories
R-recompensing of our moments
E-engrossing day and night slumber
A-absent visions
M-marinating soul and mind passions
S-simply wonderful?!

Printress Lavon Holland

Think about It

Have you ever thought of sleeping
Of forever, shutting your eyes,
Of hibernating in ignorance?
Have you ever thought of quitting
Of putting down your books
Of dulling your cognition?
Have you ever thought of dying
Of releasing all your burdens
Of escaping from your body?
Wouldn't it be relaxing if I
Could extricate
From the boundaries, the burdens?
I wanted to go,
Yet something holds me.
Flashbacks of simple things
Memories of stupid events
That kept me happy
Even for only a second.

Alfie Lam

Under

Understand . . .
Him:
Undernourished.
Underprivileged.
Underachiever.
Underdog . . .
Decision:
Underworld.
Undercover . . .
Outcome:
Under influence of drugs.
Under interrogation.
Undertakes escape.
Under car
Undertaker
Under us,
Forever . . .
Understand . . .

Kunal Singh Pal

Whole

Don't look into my eyes
I don't want you to see
All the misery and anguish
That lives inside of me

Don't look into my eyes
I don't want you to know
There is a hole in my heart
That continues to grow

Don't look into my eyes
I don't want you to feel
The extent of my grief
That I beg not to be real

Don't look into my eyes
It is the window to my soul
A piece of me has been taken
That only when reunited
I again will be whole

Jeanenne D. Nelson

Sweet Sunshine

Sweet sunshine
I embraced her and made her mine
Tried to take my time
To show her how
And I lost my sweet sunshine
Forever and now

Allen Deegan

Love So Pure

Love . . .
So pure as it awakens
So innocent as it forms
So incited
As it extends instinctively
With its crystal-like fingers
For the placid and vigilant love
Within another's heart
Snuggling it lovingly
Ardently
'Til they become
but one.
Love . . .
Don't ever depart
For my heart would wither
And my soul
Would for ever dwell
In the house of solitude

Helio Ruiz

Darkness

In darkness there is no shade,
No comfort or fade.
To feel lost, alone, and ashamed
In that unknown place
Where guidance is gone
And all faith betrayed.
Never to be seen but always heard
The outcome of a lie
In a misspoken word.
So easy to shatter and break the glass
That holds a dream, which never lasts.
The bellows and cries
Of unconquered fears
Seep into corners
Of dreaded nightmares.
The screams of pain are always bare
They follow in search
Of what was never there.

Kazia Marie Reeves

Popular

It's something that I never was
It's something that I'll never be
But always wanted
To be popular
Be with the "in" crowd
But I'm just an outcast
Waiting to be brought in from the cold
Time's almost out
Nothing yet
The sand is running thin
Damn!
Why do I have to be left out?
As the fine sand runs thinner,
Still no change
I guess there never will be
Because I wasn't part of the "in" crowd
Or
Popular

Andrea Erin LeBarge

Memories

More and more years go by
But many will not remember
What is heard
Around the world
Which will mean a lot to us
In years to come

Ashley Marie Castellano

United, Ready Always!

I'm a proud STARLET of URA.
We're United, Ready Always!
I put my service before self,
Am trustworthy as a pal.
I make myself accessible,
As well as being reliable.
I learn, I excel, and I teach.
Nothing is beyond my reach.

STARLETS are united, you see,
For we serve in Unity.
Relate with others Neighborly
And do our work with Integrity.
We learn and use Technology
And strive for Excellency.
Customers love us finally,
'Cause we serve Delightfully.
I'm a proud STARLET of URA.
It's this that makes my day.

David Tan

Body Rocking

I wish you'd just tell me
To screw off
Go jump in a lake
Or kiss your butt
I would
Well, the last one
At least
Dancing this dance
Would be easier
How close can I hold you
How slow can I dance
How long can I smell you
How many promises can I make
How long can this last
Before the music stops
Feet slide still
I'm left inhaling
Body rocking

Ike Lee

Just Open Your Eyes and See

Just open your eyes and see
Those things uncool with me
They rule your life in spite
But of course they are not right
Doing drugs is uncool to me
Those very people just can't see
What is happening to their body
They just make it a hobby
Picking on people younger than you
Is not very cool
You think you are so big and bad
But it makes them sad
When you don't try your best
You are not encouraging the rest
So don't give in
You will make it through thick and thin
Every night while lying in bed
Think of your life ahead

Tammy Reilly

Remarkable

something remarkable
something called you
happened to me once
and i'll never forget it
and i'll never forget you
and how remarkable you are

Julianne Naughton

The Futility of Flares

The living live;
They can die.
The dying die;
Will they die?
The dead lived;
They can want to live once more.
Do they?

Death and life, good and bad.

The churning of the motor engine
Rises through the air;
Voices of discordance
Are heard everywhere.
I hear one call my name;
I turn; no one is there.
Stars burn bright in the deep, dark sky;
Bright;

Bright as flares.

Nian Long Ng

Dreams

I dream of my life. . . .
How it could be
How it should be
Rainbows with vivid colors
Happily, smiling faces . . .
Going places
Not locked up inside
In a world of hate
A mile wide
Brilliant conversation
With no hesitation
No regret, no dying sorrow
Just laughter, tranquility
Fills my much needed tomorrow
Then suddenly it stops
My dreaming ends for now
I am back in a life of darkness
Trying to escape . . . somehow.

Annette S. Ziegler

The Way I Am

I used to be so proud
Now I can barely hear your words
But actions speak so loud
That every syllable could be heard
Inside a faded reality
Awakening from a silent dream
Is it truth or fantasy
Ripping apart at the seams
Take your time, inhale
A little more awake now
With our eyes wide shut so tight
Yet someway, somehow
I can see better when blind
I used to be so afraid
Truth is bleeding through
My mind's edges are so frayed
No one there to follow through
You made your mind, exhale

Garrin Matthew Allen

The Flower

The flower is pretty.
Pick a flower and you will be silly.
Hope you like a flower
'Cause you like to shower.
Flowers, flowers everywhere.
Flowers, flowers over there.

Jessica Noreen Spina

Civil War

In the battle of my emotions
The negative prevailed . . .
And I stand wounded on the battlefield
With no apparent home front
Without a USO
Without a future in my sight
And no clear way to go
The cannons have retreated
The artillery's been cleared
And still I stand here wounded
Wallowing in fear
Not worthy of my homeland
My all too humiliated soul
Not worthy of its soldiers
The friends who tried in vain
To save my soul
From
Me

Raquel Santiago

Lost

In the shadows of life,
The darkness, I can't see!
Lost!
Depression of what has
Been done,
Sadness of what has been
Said!
Lost!
Confused and lonely without you,
Desperately wanting to talk to you!
Lost!
No one to talk to,
Caught beneath the doors of Hell!
Lost!
Terrified to believe the fact
That we are not together!
Sadness because I love you!
Lost, because I can't live without you!

Elizabeth Rose Lambert

Not That It Matters Much

Not that it matters much,
but my toe kind of hurts.
I stubbed it on the washer,
doing underwear and shirts.

Not that it matters much,
but at eleven at night,
I get kind of tired,
and want to roll up tight—

into a ball.
The days are long,
and the demands are relentless.
Three children and a mortgage,
the work is endless.

I am not a great poet,
just want some free stuff.
So I am sending this poem,
if I don't get it, that's tough.

Kristine Denyse Lilly

Peace

Peace is forever blue.
It sounds of a harmonious chorus.
It tastes like sweet candy
And smells as a rose.
Peace looks like a smile.
It makes you feel calm.

Samantha Anne Tymon

How Can One . . .

How can one man love one woman
as much as I love you?
How can one man's body yearn and
heart burn for just your touch?
How can one man live or let live
without knowing that you will be there?
How can one man write something
that words can't describe?
How can one man read when he only
wants to learn more about you?
How can one man sleep when
he only dreams of you?
How can one man travel when
he would go no where without you?
For it is you who leads me,
my heart that guides me.
Whatever I do, I do for you.
Remember this always: I love you.

Jason Matthew Hatfield

Your Eyes

Your blue eyes
Bright as a brilliant light
Can't you see
When you look at me
You light up my life
With your caring eyes
Your deep blue eyes
The windows to your soul
Tell me your thoughts
Through a slight glance
Your blue eyes
Saying everything
Yet no words spoken
Your deep blues eyes
Always be with me
Can't you see
When you look at me
You're everything I need

Cassandra Koch

Summer Fun

Summer is fun
A great time to run
In the Sun
You have fun
Freedom from school
Go to the pool
A sunny day
Is a time to play
The temperature is hot
We sweat a lot
Visit friends
Let it never end
We play volleyball
It is not allowed to fall
Look at flowers
Rest for hours
At the park
Stay 'til dark

Maria C. Coca

Yesterday

Yesterday is gone,
No more
Unchangeable.
Today is quickly becoming yesterday,
Tomorrow is quickly becoming today.
The cycle never ends. . . .

Kim Fisk

What We Know?

We know what happened today,
but know not what will happen tomorrow.
We know what we are,
but know not what we will be.
We know what we do,
but know not what we will do.
We know what is our hands,
but know not what is in our minds.
We know what this year brought us,
but know not what next year will bring.
We know the mask,
but know not the face behind the mask.
We know the deed,
but know not the reason behind the deed.
We know the present,
but know not the future.
We know what we have to know,
but know not what we don't have to know.

Jennifer Rosario

Gone

Hush little baby
It's all right
Just follow the Father
Into the light
We grieved the day you left
Daddy cried in bed
I hate the way this happened
Now my baby's dead
Smiles are missed
The world is black
What I wouldn't give
To have my darling back
Eyes of blue
Curly hair too
Need him so
He can't be that far below
Precious child
Was my angel

Lacey Michelle Hatmaker

The Doll

She tries to sleep, she tries to dream
Her eyes won't close and hide the world
She tries to speak, she tries to scream
She has no voice and no one hears
She tries to cry, no tears will fall
She's numb and frayed and dead inside
She's like a doll
Paint and porcelain
Empty within, flawless without
No one sees beyond her skin
Time wears her
It breaks her down
Her cheeks crack from
The strain of her chipped smile
Her colors fade
And no one notices
As she falls from her shelf
And shatters

Danielle Rystedt

Jesus Laughing

A good laugh is
A sign of love
It may be said;
To give us a glimpse of
Or a first lesson in the love
That God bears for every one of us

Betty J. O'Connor

My Best Friend

Here's a story of a girl
She had so much to live for
So many dreams
She had a great life
Or it seemed on the outside
Inside she was trembling, insecure
She had low self-esteem
There was no family love
So many problems
Nobody knew, not even I
And she was my best friend

She saw pills, knives, guns
Seconds before her last breath
I look at the blood-soaked sheets
As tears run down our cheeks
My body numb
I sit beside her, hand in hand
She tells me, "You're my best friend"

Sarah Courtney Spires

The Fear of Us

Restaurants busy with mouths
Houses fluster with dreams
Schools divided in gangs
In the fear of us

Governments choke on politics
Cartoons seep with clarity
Parents love unconditionally
In the fear of us

Nations terrorize individuals
Buildings blockade families
Humans trust life
In the fear of us

In the fear of us
We find a nation undivided
We find humans with hope
We find each other
The United States

Megan Long

Hope Lies on the Racks

Hope lies on the racks
while the hand changes numbers
And its arm twists once
while the hand begins to fade
Innocence once pure
Becomes no sense at all
For a blindfolded world
Digresses our children
To progress its greed alone

Our world is falling
To the depths of the demon
Gradually netherward
As the Earth turns a page
Morals fight with knives
But society with guns
And the people hide still
In the confines of work
Merely shadows on a wall

Robert Edwin Price

Stars and Flowers

As I looked out my castle towers
Saw many lands but little flowers
Been many places near and far
Saw many faces but never one star
Lands and faces are here to stay
Stars and flowers seemed so far away
But since I met you, I see them every day

Davis John

Shattered Dreams

The windmill has stopped turning;
There's no water in the well and
If only they could tell us what a
Sad tale they would tell

Of farm machinery rusting
Of the house no longer a home because
The elements having taken toll
Of the people without a name.

The old truck bearing the stock crate
Has rusted beyond repair and
The drilling rig is immobilized
It's a desolate scene out there.

The sad thoughts which come
To mind as one drives along are of
Shattered dreams and broken hearts
Out west of the town of Penong.

Poet Shirlark

A Friend

Your finger graces mine,
Felt throughout every nerve.
Eyes glaring into his,
This finger turns benign.

These eyes feed into me
To utter sweet words.
Curving past my face,
Meaning nothing more than hot air.

Attempt to coax my gift,
My disposable flower.
Plastic, plagued with dust,
Too ignorant to fly adrift.

Sleeping with this thought
Next to another.
In a guise of friendship,
A mask not easily bought.

Jon Benito

Red Snow

It's a dark day for us, my love,
For you have left me here alone.
The snow is no longer white,
But red with your blood.
My hands are stained with your
Once warm blood,
Now cold and running down
Your lifeless body.
I scream in agony while cold tears
Stream down my rose colored cheeks!
I raise your lifeless but muscular body
To my soft living body,
Hoping to give some warmth.
Yet I know your soul has left you,
Your loving, clean soul.
Please come back to me, my love!
Embrace me with your strong
Arms once again.
My love, come back to me!

Ursula Corrin Speicher

rain

as the rain comes pouring down
from the rooftops of the town
its gentle fingers touch my face
i feel as if there's not a trace
of anyone or anything
it makes me want to laugh and sing
a springtime shower, a summer storm
watching from your home so warm

Elsie Mae Keister

The Reason

My mother once told me
that I am the reason
for living, for loving.
My mother once told me
that I am the reason
she believes in miracles,
in blissful lives.
I believe that
my mother is the reason
I am alive today
and walking by her side.
My mother is the reason
for everything I do,
for my unconditional love
for my devoted life.
My mother is the one and only
reason I am alive today.

Stephanie Marie Ricard

Whispered Secrets

Though kind friend
It is you I vow
Who catches my whisper
Only heaven knows how

For a whisper on the wind
Comes from who knows where
Floating like thistledown
Thence to your ear

I whisper I whisper
To the wind dear friend
But few even hear it
And none comprehend

I, who dream of things mystical
Can with the wind share
My secrets, my dreams
Breathed out on the air . . .

Nyree Marilyn Burt

I Am

I am sweet and helpful
I wonder who my biological parents are
I hear music
I see things around me
I want to be a dancer
I am sweet and helpful
I pretend to ride a whale
I feel bad when I do things wrong
I touch things that are beautiful
I worry about my family
I cry when people close to me are crying
I am sweet and helpful
I understand right and wrong
I say what's on my mind
I dream about owning a whale
I try to be kind
I hope to get good grades
I am sweet and helpful

Megan Roth

Life's Success

Life's journey on the road to happiness
Unphased by growing trend of worldliness

Emphasis placed on goodwill to mankind
Love for family and God the mastermind

Harbor a sense of contentment
Actions required in testament

Work for a desirable tomorrow
Before the world ends in sorrow

Debby Sue Weis

In the Barracks

Laughter and boredom,
passed the time,
too quickly.
Friendship makes me a God,
resilient,
on a concrete path.
Until,
The Sound
of a voice ushers in,
The Smells
and
The Touch,
and no longer do I see,
The Loyalty,
but the lack of
Her,
in their eyes.

Gavin Mark Whittle

I'm Sorry, Allison

I'm sorry Allison, so sorry Allison—
Ewings was its name.
I'm sorry Allison, so sorry Allison—
you didn't win this game.

I'm sorry Allison, so sorry Allison—
I couldn't find a cure.
I'm sorry Allison, so sorry Allison—
the pain you had endured.

I'm sorry Allison, so sorry Allison,
we have to be apart.
I'm sorry Allison, so sorry Allison—
there's a hole in my heart.

I'm sorry Allison, so sorry Allison—
you're now in God's light.
I'm sorry Allison, so sorry Allison—
I cry for you tonight.

Tammy Marie Lyngen

Expression

There goes the dancer
Dancing upon the wind
Behind her the singer
Whose song comes from deep within

Then there's the drummer
Chiming along
And the guitar player
Lazily strumming his song

Don't forget the dreamer
Such as I—who follows along
Feeling the passions
Of the music deep inside

Expression—for the one true love
Which is the way to create
The many different faces of music
Which is the gift from above

J. J. Scaduto

Remember Me

Within my books of memories,
there's happy ones of you.

The joys we've shared together,
the things we like to do.

The way you understand me,
your thoughtful kindness, too.
Within your heart, remember me,
for I still think of you.

Tisha Renee Hicks

I Love To

I love to read
I love to write
I love to dream
while asleep at night

I love to play
I love to run
I love to sit
beneath the bright yellow sun

I love to laugh
I love to sing
mostly I guess
I love everything

I love to draw
I love to talk
and across God's land
I love to walk

Brandi Lynne Hypes

Hold Me Gently

Hold me gently
for the whisperings
to an untamed heart
are not unlike
a warm breeze
to ruffled feathers—
inviting
adventurous . . .
consumed with mystery
and intrigue
possessed of all things
exotic and otherworldly.

Hold me gently
for no promises can come
from a heart
that has yet to take rest
under the Sun

Amelia AnneMarie Moses

Friends

Friends
to be without no point in life.
The absence of what means the most
some minds may not be clear
but then it's lost, cannot express,
the love that was so near.
Realize now most things change
life is just that way.
To have a friend true in the heart
who could ask for more?
Near or far
together, apart,
images of time lost.
Nothing equals
true friendship in life
and for that
there is no cost.

Steven J. Anderson

Shadows of Someone You Once Loved

In your sweet dreams
I will be there
In your nightmares
I will save you
In your waking hours
You will not remember
I will be but a memory
In some half-remembered dream

Jennifer Marie Traver

love online

This is for my lost online love.
i would give you the sky
you are a star
but i'm just some guy
i wish i was where you are
i wished to die
but then you came
but you would not say bye
i am so lame
i hope you are happy
even if it is not with me
i am so sappy
someday people will see
my heart was a rock
you made me care
my heart is unlocked
it is not fair

Jeffery Wayen Thrash, II

Rainbows

God created rainbows
As a promise and a truth.
God gave us tears,
So we could see the rainbows.

Without the tears of healing,
We have no rainbows.
Time to let your healing begin,
So the rainbows can be seen.

Who ever told us to be strong,
We cannot cry.
If you do not cry these precious tears,
How will your rainbow shine?

The rains are tears from Heaven,
Then the rainbow can be seen.
So it is time to let them flow,
Let your Rainbow of Healing begin.

Norva Lloyd Haskins

Fragile Blue

Your eyes gaze into mine
but they don't see me.
Once blue, now faded; I am
haunted by their fragility.

What are you seeing now?
Do you remember
those happier days
when you were younger?

Playing with your brother,
dancing with your wife,
and then producing children
you had to guide through life?

Are you in there?
Do you somehow know
that I am here? Can you hear me
tell you now it's okay to let go?

Wanda D. Robertson

Comfort a Child

God hold us in your hands
Away from the evil of man

Rock us gently to sleep
Out of harms reach

Keep us safe through the night
Shake us gently with morning light

Guide us through our day
Until again we come to pray

Jacqueline Gwyn Lozier

The Wolf

In remembrance of Kamots
A movement in the bushes nearby
A shadow moving silent and sly
A ghost in the darkest night
Climbs to the greatest height
To sing its mournful song

Running in the distance far
Underneath the moon and stars
Is an animal like no other
Who runs and hunts with his brothers
In the dead of night

Growling, snarling, biting, bleeding
The other one is not receding
The fight for leader must go on
Until the other one is gone
To reach another day

Angela F. Corley

Murder

Breaking up is murder
Your heart is broken in two
A little piece of your soul is missing
With everyone you go through
Tears run down your face
You might as well be dead
Your heart feels like it's bleeding
You think blood will consume your soul
Your heart is crushed
You can hardly breathe
Tears won't erase this memory
"Everything will be all right"
Is what is said to you
You don't think it's true
You know you can't improve
Breaking up is murder
Something everyone goes through

Deaven LaShae Coggins

Will I

Will I be my dream and become a
photographer,
or be a scientist and study
thermometers?
Will I be a teacher like my mom
and my dad,
or get a divorce and be very sad?
Will I be poor and need some more money,
or be a food tester and
test new honey?
Will I be the greatest person of all
time,
or give it all up and be a
weird mime?
I don't know what I'll be,
but I know that I am special,
and that is just me.

Sarah Rachelle Cheek

Untitled

As we lie here looking at the sky
I wonder how it can be
That you and me found each other

The clouds float by with ease
Just as I knew you loved me

Now I lie here in this somber
With a gun in my hand
And a rose in the other

Valerie Lavrenz

Remembering You

Late at night when I'm all alone,
I lie awake and think of you.
Times we shared together,
Remembering you.

During the day when the sun's high,
I blindly stumble and fumble through
Life and all its turns
Remembering you.

I wish I could hold you tight,
Make everything be the same, too.
Wondering what you're doing,
Remembering you.

I remember you in all your ways,
In all my life, all day through.
Wishing you were here with me,
Remembering you.

Casey Mae Hite

Truth

Many dreams set beyond the stars
set up very high,
yet the reach is so far
parched up so nigh.

The sound of light within hands
just beyond ones reach,
yet the music flows so bland
sucking each note as a leach.

Memories come and go
to not escape one's life,
yet each thought is a foe
upon heedful strife.

Every spoken word is said
thought to be heard from someone,
yet every language is dead
just blinds no one and everyone.

Katherine Lee

More Than Friends

More than friends,
that's what we should be.
More than a friendship
between you and me.

More than friends,
I hope it comes true.
With a girl like me
and a guy like you.

More than friends,
I know what I feel.
The sweet surrender of a crush,
waiting to form real.

More than friends,
that's what we should be.
Because I love you
and I hope you love me.

Damaris Martinez

Friendship Is Forever

Dedicated to friends lost on September 11, 2001
Friendship is a bond
That never dies, and
While it changes over time,
It remains the fiber that ties
Together who we were. Who we are.
And who we become.

Friendship is forever.

Nick D. Anthony

The M.I.L. Club

The M.I.L. club is not exclusive
Though infamous it may be
The key phrase is "sense of humor"
To keep your sanity!

Throughout the world you see them
They're really everywhere
All dazed and rather shocked
So handle them with care!

An interesting breed these M.I.L.'s
All "wicked" and interfering
They love to attack their prey
For nothing more than being!

All girls become a member
It's part of life for sure
You're one of the M.I.L.'s now honey
A fully fledged Mother-In-Law!

Rachel Vardi

Pieces of Me

I can't feel my body,
I can't feel at all.
I am on the edge,
I am taking the fall.

Pieces of me
Burning in the fire,
like the flame.
So untamed.

Falling to the ground.
My life flashes beyond my eyes.
Thinking about family and friends.
As I look to the sky.

Pieces of me.
Lying on the floor.
Like dirty laundry,
I feel torn.

Daniel Wayne Wilkerson

His Father's Eyes

He is simply wise;
listen closely
to knowledge passed on.

Gained from boyhood,
an honesty
that carries him as a man.

As with his father
before him,
knows strength within.

With subtle shyness,
a sensuality
that is only given.

He, with dark eyes,
knows all
of this man.

Nancy A. LaCosse

Kansas

Kansas is our Cocker Spaniel.
Her friend's name is Daniel.
She is blind as a bat.
Can't even see the cat.
But we love our Cocker Spaniel.

Amber Lynn Anthony

Collapsed

First son, first loss
Taken over by the world
With one but still without meaning
Pain is the soundtrack of his life

Woke up and another life is destroyed
His expressions remain blank
Numb by this that he is facing
Getting used to the catastrophe

The invisible side that is never seen
Chosen to ignore and overlooked
Raised on the pedestal by others
Only to be knocked down and ridiculed

Having trouble to discover
The direction that's been taken
Trying to find meaning out of this one
Because there will be no other—

Adam Ray Rothenberger

When I Look into Her Eyes

When I look into her eyes I see
yearning to know everything.
When I look into her eyes I see
her love, compassion, and hurts.
When I look into her eyes I see
wonder, excitement, trepidation,
and love.
I see her fears, I see her questions,
I see her searching for the unknown.
When I look into her eyes I see
her mom and her dad.
When I look into her eyes I see
their love, their admiration, and
the patience.
When I look into her eyes I see
a child who is loved, honored, and
respected.
When I look into her eyes I see . . .
me.

*Jennifer Renae
Mercedes Schneeberger*

So, I Weep and I Write

Sorrow
Pain
And Loneliness,
These things I feel for you.
I wilt like a flower,
My heart feels black and blue.

I try to sleep, but cannot.
I stay awake instead,
So, I weep and I write
With your voice inside my head.

My spirit is diminishing,
I feel like I can't go on.
Every day seems the same,
Every day seems so long.

My memory is fading fast,
It will soon be night,
I am all alone
So, I weep and I write.

Rebekah Lyn Brooks

thank you

thank you for being here
thank you for the fine beer
thank you for driving in the first gear
thank you for accepting my fear
thank you

Bennie Post

Man Ipulation

At God you play
Manipulating DNA
Not one iota of creation

Light coming out of darkness
A singularity expands, universe
A peculiar Play-doh

Your building blocks A C E G
Arranged so for a reason
Solve a simple riddle

Ignore the complexities
Dive into the incomprehensible
A littie knowledge is dangerous

Gather up your Nobel Prize
The future unveils the answer
Grand opening of Pandora's box

Merrill Morgan Barlow, III

Stand or Fall Love

Gorgeous
eyes that make you melt
Evil
how you were treated
when he knew how you felt
Tears
things that you were so used to
Wishing
why did he treat me like that if he knew
Stranger
mysterious in a way
Induces
a new love to be thought about all day
You see past his outer being
his personality is what you're seeing
This could be right
but you don't know at all
Will I stay on my feet
or completely fall. . . .

Andrea Lynn DeSantis

my love story

i love you.
the sound of your voice melts me.
when i look in your eyes,
i know you are looking into my soul.
you are my best friend,
no one knows me the way you do.
but you aren't here,
i'm alone.
i hate that you left,
you knew how much i needed you.
but i know you didn't decide to leave,
why did that car hit yours?
i think of you every day,
everything reminds me of you;
the ocean, the sunsets, the rain.
i wish you were here to hold me again,
you'd whisper "i love you" in my ear.
and i'd know
everything was going to be okay.

Michelle Mo Vega

has this been said before?

there will be no peace
in the world of humanity
until there are no more americans
no more arabs
only humans

David T. Frary

Emerging

Emerging,
Karma comes full circle. . . .
I can only control my reaction.
Ascending,
Will you come with me?
Rebirth,
I need this
Please need it, too.

David Reuben Kiferbaum

Rain

For my mom, dad, and two sisters
Pat pat pitter pat
It's the sound of rain.
Refreshing and relaxing
Sounds so peaceful.
Sit back, close your eyes
And listen to the sound.
Let it carry your worries away.

Rebecca Deall

proclamation of peace

destruction is what i see
destruction is what i feel
inside it is all falling apart
what i thought i knew
is now not known
is this possible?
lives taken so fast
too fast to comprehend
we are all falling victim
to endless acts of hatred
yet there is one glimpse of hope
instead of falling victim we recover
fight the evils of hatred
and destruction becomes extinct
a word with no meaning
and in its place a word of peace
its name . . . harmony

Lindsay Nichole Erhardt

Hidden Tears

It's not easy to hide tears,
when you only want to hide your fears.
I just want to close my eyes
and hope everything disappears.

I want to enter a reality,
one that's not my own.
Where nothing can reach me.
Just me, all alone.

Sometimes I think I'll go blind,
and my excitement is overwhelming.
Then pity this, pity that,
the world is far too understanding.

I just want to shut my eyes,
and make everything go away,
But the tears are still there,
and there the tears will stay.

Nikki Leonard

Sorrow

You want to borrow some sorrow?
It's like a boulder on my shoulders.
I can't feel my chest.
I can't explain the rest,
And now, I die.

Kyle Eric Gale

Grandma

You always made me smile
You would always go the extra mile
You always made me feel loved
You were like an angel from up above
Why did you have to drink
Why didn't you stop and think
I loved you so
Why did you have to go?

Mindy Lynn Price

Crying Out

My eyes are looking away
But my heart is crying out
The cries are coming your way
You got to help me
Help me out
Before I drown
In this sadness
That is holding me down

Melissa Ann Ruffino

In Memory of the World Trade Center

Crash. Crash. Crash.
Here comes the ash
From our dear old building.
Fell from bottom to ceiling.
Men and women screamed inside
From the tremble of the awful ride.
Smash. Smash. Smash.
It hit the ground.
People eked at the sound
When dear old Trade Center fell
Down. Down. Down.
More ash fogged the air all around.
Run. Run. Run.
Dirt covered the sun.
The planes had won.
Killing 10,000 with one.

Sarah Ann Koehler

Beloved Imagery

I know you so well
with a depth I cannot fathom!
And yet
I know you not at all.
I peer upon your photograph,
gazing into your eyes;
examining the features
of a stranger. . . .

But then
I close my eyes.
There before me is my beloved,
familiar as my breath,
the beating of my heart,
my well-known friend.
He
who shall exist within my soul
forever!

Lois D. Morgan

Angel of Mine

Heavenly Father full of grace
Bless this grandchild's
Precious little face
Bless her little toes and nose
Keep her safe wherever she goes
Bless her hair that always curls
But keep her safe
From this cruel world
We love her, Lord, and keep her well
For we are truly blessed
To be given such a gift
For she is our little girl

Barbara Sue Ramirez

Days Gone By

Oh, how I wish for days gone by
My time sure does seem to fly
Children knew wrong from right
You weren't afraid to walk at night
I sometimes wish for the good old days
I remember all the ways
We used to have fun without TV
Computer games or DVDs
Parents taught kids right from wrong
They knew how to be strong
And children respected their parents too
And did what they were told to do
And families were brought up in love
Faithful to the Lord above
Times have changed now, that is true
But sometimes I wish for déjà vu!

Lisa M. Coulombe

Beyond My Reach

There is a world beyond
my vision and I don't know
why I can't see it.
Is it because my mind is clouded,
or is it because I am in love?
This world, I hear, is a wonderful
place, filled with laughter and
fun, and I know I want to be there
but don't want to leave your side.
I know you are not ready to go
there, so we will not say goodbye.
When the time comes for us to
go together, I'll be ready with open
arms to just to hold while we
take the ride.
In forever happiness.

Justin Michael Bernal

Lost

I cannot see;
I can only hear
And grope about in the darkness.
I seek you out
But cannot find you.
I trip over weeds
And into the water.
I gasp for air
And only draw in water.
I drift to the bank,
But my body is cold;
My heart is still.
I cry out to you again;
I will not leave you.
But you are gone too,
And soon your cold body joins mine.

Heather Marie Posey

How to Impress a Woman

How to impress
A woman
Compliment her, cuddle her
Kiss her, caress her
Love her, stroke her
Tease her, comfort her, protect her
Hug her, hold her
Spend money on her, wine and dine her
Buy things for her, dance with her
Listen to her, care for her
Stand by her, support her
Go to the ends of the earth for her

Brad James Miller

A Warrior

I could feel the spirit as you
Came riding on a dove
Our brief encounter marking
A path through time

I could feel the spirit as you
Tied the necklace on
While listening to the drums
With every heartbeat

I could feel the spirit as you
Danced to the music
As you cried the warrior song
To our creator

As I looked upon your face
Your sweet embrace
I could feel the spirit

Juanita M. Medbury-Walkabout

Anything

I feel as if I can't do anything.
I am trapped
Lost, forgotten,
And afraid.
Help me please.
I am sad,
Alone, wanting something,
Needing someone.
I need this person
To hold, hug
And talk to.
This person will
Comfort me,
Help me, and
Cry for me.
But I feel as if I can't do anything.

Jennifer Elizabeth Jarina

No Place to Turn

I feel I am trapped in a corner.
No way to get out.
I just keep getting tired
The louder I try to shout.
No one seems to hear me
I feel I'm in a prison.
If they could hear my cries
I doubt they would even listen.
I want to have someone near.
No one can handle how I am.
People look the other way.
With their minds they try to condemn.
I once trusted them.
They once had me ruled.
Don't let them get to you.
Don't let yourself be fooled.

Stephanie Marie Burt

Silent Emotions

Just as silent as a leaf,
falling to the ground.
My emotions run through me,
all my feelings bound.
The poor unsettled memories,
the sad sadistic lies.
The demented truth comes suddenly,
the theories drop like flies.
Scary thoughts creep through my mind,
screams ringing through the night.
Falling from the very night,
my dreams took off in flight.

Danielle Marie Zsuzsics

Love Waits

We both know he can't stay long with me,
for his life will not yet allow.
But if his heart has room for me,
I will love him anyhow.
I'll wait until he's broken Free
of the burden of his past.
Someday he'll be truly free;
I know his pain last.
I'll go on singing songs of hope
in the secret of my heart.
We are never going to be alone,
and we'll never be apart.
I have joy, for I somehow know
that the day will come
when my angel and I will fly far away
and our two hearts will be one.

Rachel Dianna Sturgill

A Prayerful Heart

I am young
The day is new
Lord I pray to thee
To help me through
Please give me strength
The tempest is strong
I will not give up
I'll carry on
I'll search the scriptures
Diligently
Lord I love thee
'Cause thou feedeth me
With knowledge
And wisdom
I strive to earn
Your kingdom

Natalie Joy Gibbons

The Turkey Named Goon

There once was a turkey named Goon
Who thought he was born on the moon
He'd float in the air
Without ever a care
From evening until about noon

Then quickly he'd land on the ground
Without even making a sound
His thin legs would wobble
He'd let out a gobble
For the air he would leave with a bound

But then one November he blew it
He came to earth before he knew it
And that fat feathered beast
Was Thanksgiving feast
And that was all there was to it

Ryan Michael Harvey

Untitled

Words of wisdom,
wasted in rhymes.
A weary man's mind,
just passing the time.
A scribbling hand,
the man sits alone.
A page filled with nothing,
its meaning unknown. . . .

Trapped in the verses,
and lost in the lines.
The words that mean nothing,
bring tears to his eyes.

Chad E. Shambaugh

My Unknown Love

Even though I've never seen you
I want you to know
that I will always cherish you
even when the times seem low
God has promised you to me
and He never breaks his word
I know you're out there somewhere
and I know this sounds absurd
that I would tell how I feel
and I've yet to see your face
Had the chance to hear your laugh
or felt your warm embrace
I know you will be Heaven-sent
just like a precious dove
When we meet—you'll have my heart
You are my unknown love

Shawn Phillip Briggs

That Moment

A moment of glee,
A moment of grief,
A moment between,
The one you don't see.
That moment is gone
A moment too soon
That moment gets lost,
Like the sun loses the moon.
What if we all knew
Of that moment we know not?
Could we prevent grief
And sorrows we got?
A moment of glee,
Please set it free
And fill in the gap,
And unlock the key.

Nicole Lord

mr. balloon man

i heard them say you'd float away
but i never believed you would do it
so full of hot air
and i always thought
that you'd be there

bye-bye mr. balloon man
tell me if you ever hit the sand
mr. balloon man

and when i met you flying high
in the cold like that guy
from the bible with the bush
and i saw in you so many things

bye-bye mr. balloon man
tell me if you ever hit the sand
my mr. balloon man

Myriah Lynne Scarpati

Love/Hate

I love the way he talks to me,
I hate the way he sweet talks her.

I love the way he touches me,
I hate the way he holds her.

I love the way he watches me,
I hate the way he stares at her.

I love the way he listens to me,
I hate the way he's all ears for her.

I love the way I love him,
I hate the way he loves her.

Julie Ann Shreve

How Could This Happen?

How could this happen
Before it began
You and I were a team
And I was your biggest fan
How could this happen
Right from the start
Before we even knew it
We were already torn apart
How could this happen
Before we were through
I couldn't even figure out
My feelings toward you
How could this happen
With each falling tear
With wishing and wanting
That you're somehow here

Kelsi Page Cornelius

The Long-Distance Phone Call

Tonight we talked,
And there was too much to say;
So I just balked,
And only asked about your day.
I wanted to know your insights.
I wanted to know what you were learning,
But our conversations flew like kites,
Just like wheels turning.
I wanted to stop and pray,
Especially after what you said;
But instead all I could say,
"I hope our friendship won't go dead."
Please forgive me for the call tonight,
I was just homesick for you,
I just wanted you in my sight,
But I guess I only can listen to you.

Abigail Mosebrook

Rhododendron Flower

Comely flower, bloom!
Wrest your wrapped cocoon,
Spread your petals high,
Greet the butterfly.

Behold, although the sparrow rests
Upon your nestled bud, she warms
You not; to her own nest's
Care yearns her feathered arms,
Untended shelled-brood grows cold.

For it has been provided,
According to your kind,
That you be warmed and grown
Within, nourished by the downy Spring
'Til you are loath to stay,
And must emerge into the light of day.

David J. Bullis

Love

As the wind is blowing through—
The grass is green, the sky is blue;
You love me and I love you.
The sunset rises through and through—
Love is what? A bowl of soup?
A tiny cloud loop to loop?
Can you feel it in the air?
Love is here and love is there.
Love is free, fast, and quick;
Sometimes it doesn't turn out so slick.
What you say is what you feel,
Riding on the lover's wheel.

Kristie Mae Swindell

I Am Me

I am me
And you are you.
They think there's one,
But really, there's two
I'm my own person
I have my own mind.
I have my own past,
which I've left behind.
I'm standing tall
and saying it loud,
"I am me,
and I am proud."
One day,
We'll be set apart.
Until then, we're different
and that's a start.

Chelsea McCarty

Questions Unanswered

Why
the grass it grows green
the sky it glows blue
their unanswered questions
what can you do

Why
days are numbered
payment is due
their unanswered questions
what can you do

Why
lives are ended
and souls haven't a clue
their questions unanswered
what can you do

Joshua Stephen Freeman

Low Esteem, High Esteem

Low esteem, yeeeeeeeeee!
I think I shall never see
A person more stupid than he
Who looks back at me
Yes, every morn I'm torn
Yes, I look so forlorn
For he in the mirror is true
Oh, boo-hoo, boo-hoo, boo-hoo!

High esteem, yeee-haaahhh!
I think I shall never see
A person more handsome than he
Who looks back at me
Yes, every morn I'm sworn
Yes, I love to adorn
For he in the mirror is me
Ho-ho, hee-hee, and hee-hee!

David Stanion

Have You Ever Wondered?

Have you ever wondered,
Why I care?
Have you ever wondered,
Why I share?
Have you ever wondered,
What I thought?

I care,
Because you wonder.
I share,
Because I can.
And I wondered,
What you thought.

Danielle Renee Pelkey

But Never Belonging

I am free,
for like dust
at the mercy of the wind
I soar
traveling the world over
but never belonging . . .

And if one day
a gentle drop of water
traps me
and forces me to descend,
a warm and clear
ray of sun
will help me
to resume my journey
going from place to place
but never belonging . . .

Victor E. Bonilla-Rodriguez

Cold War

A time of war,
a time of despair.
A time of fear,
growing in the air.
There was a great race,
that possessed no runners.
Instead of people,
there were bombs, planes, and gunners.
Two great nations
fought on the world's stage.
The stories of their struggles
go on for page after page after page.
Some thought peace would come;
they were not believed.
Yet through great leaders,
peace was achieved.

Lucas Franchi

Peach

It is soft like the skin of a newborn
With hairs on a woman's cheek
The smell so much like summer
Orange, yellow, peach, and pink
One taste of the temptation
With pithy meat and wild juice
Epidermis ever stronger
Than the dessert of which it clings to
This tantalizing tasty treat
Blessed by the lips' first kiss
A nibble and a lick
Nothing as orgasmic as this
It comes from a woman's basket
So ready to teach:
The best gift to offer
Is your Southern Peach

Heather Amber O'Brien Makela

Pain

I sit here with tears in my eyes;
not seeing the sky.

All is dark and gray;
the pain stays.

People say not to cry,
but it hurts so much inside.

The struggle continues;
the pain never ends.

I feel so alone
that all I do is stay home.

Michele Choate

Snow

Snow, snow, snow
Glow, glow, glow
In all its brightness
In all its whiteness
Winter is calling
Snow is falling
Snowflakes blowing
Warm coals glowing
Walks on virgin snow
Is where I would go
Oh! What a sight
As it lights up the night
Soft slow snow
Melting
Weeping
Please don't go

Will Mitchell

Lee's Endeavor

Torn between country and state
Contemplating the rebel's fate
In between a brothers' quarrel
Against slavery and the soft white pearl
Boundless is our country's pride
While up upon my ghostly ride
I lead my men on a sea of blood
Through the snow and in the mud
I heard a Stonewall crashing down
Almost drowning out the sound
Of a tired hero's lonesome moan
From the numbing bravery he has shown
Praying an end is close ahead
But only Grant is there instead
On bended knee we all now pray
For this Civil War to end today

Robert Lee Poe

The Cat Who Sleeps on the Bed

Every morning she's there,
Always without a care,
The cat who sleeps on the bed.

Curled up neat as can be,
Tucked up tight against me,
The cat who sleeps on the bed.

She purrs me to sleep
And makes sure I'm all right.
Does she make her patrols
For dangers during the night?

I can't say for sure,
But I'll ever endure,
The cat who sleeps on the bed.

Carmela R. Bozulich

To

To see you smile in the night,
to know love at first sight.
To see you cry in the day,
to my saviour on my knees I'd pray.
To hear you whisper in my ear,
to life, I'd no longer fear.
To tell me your love for me is real,
to know how the angels in heaven feel.
To feel your kiss on my brow,
to realize God is with me now.
To have you for my wife,
to have fulfilled a beautiful life.

Serj L. Piro

Courting Friendship

They knew it couldn't last.
The fools rush in too fast!
For better, for worse,
through thick and thin,
each vow will take its toll.
But one year passed, and then two.
Then five and ten and twenty-two.
Now it's twenty-five
and we've just begun to grow.
I guess they didn't know you,
they didn't know me,
nor that the Lord had destined it to be.
At first, infatuation,
then love began to grow.
Then we courted friendship;
in retrospect, how were they to know?

Desmond Allen

Aphrodite Can Kill

She wears a mask of deceit
Shampoos with adrenaline
Rinse, wash, repeat
She shaves her body to clean the scabs
Bathes in alcohol
Clean skin she has
Future savior
We praise her

Armed with a corset and knife
Developed with strife
Seduces her prey
Fixes them with just one swipe
Blessed with brains and hair red
She's two steps ahead
Blinded by lust
Another victory when they're dead

Charly Beckham Tichenor

Bootcamp '98

A specter shines before my eyes
a haunting, ethereal sprite
Forever present, ever near
to guide my dreams at night
Her beauty, love, and joy I feel
she softens all my fear
And sometimes, when I sleep at night
she lets me think you're near

Memories compose and trace
her image ever fair
For when I reach to touch her face
my fingers find but air
We talk each day for hours sometimes
while making not a sound
I sing to her; she smiles at me . . .
It's you that I have found

William Samuel Jackson, II

A Lost Son

In memory of my son,
Michael Andrew Jones (7/21/66–6/6/00)
I wept on your grave today.
The pain of my soul gave way,
A flood of tears
I've kept through the years
Soaked into the ground where you lay.

Someday, I'll see you again.
You'll flash that cute boyish grin;
Your arms around me sweet,
I'll hear your heart beat,
And healing, at last, will begin.

Doris Jamison

A Prayer

God, give us Your desire;
Awake our hearts from sleeping.
Lord, cleanse us with Your fire,
That for the lost we're weeping.
Remind us of our purpose—
The labor's not in vain;
That Satan cannot hurt us
For death in Christ is gain.
Let courage never waiver;
Give strength to win the fight.
We trust in you, dear Savior,
To guide us with Your light.
God, thank you for Your love
And mercies that You send.
Lord, though you rule above,
You're still our truest friend.

Nicole Renee Beaudin

Dragon's Dream

Breathing smoke, breathing fire
burning each one's desire
peeking through the rising flame
destroying everything without no shame
through the night skies
the dragon flies
seeking for its soul
mysteries untold
red fire among my face
ashes spread all over the place
as if only to be a dream
but what does it mean
are the dragons a sign?
questions fill my mind
only the dragons know
when I stay, when I go

Anna Elizabeth Downey

True Love

Have you ever loved somebody
With all your heart, body, and soul,
Not wanting to live without them
Never wanting to let them go?
You'll know it when you find them
True love is wonderful but rare
To desire someone so passionately
Having these feelings you both share
It happens but once in a lifetime
If you are one of the blessed few
Able to find that someone special
Sharing your life and all you do
May everyone find their soul mate
And feel how special it can be
That you never have to lose them
Is my prayer for all humanity . . .

Dave L. Creg

Struggle

Crying out inside this darkness
The eternal night of my soul
Longing for that stolen child
I need for my life to be whole
Ripping off the pleasant masks
That hide my pain from this world
I was robbed of my purity
A flower plucked instead of unfurled
No one can know the void I face
The constant ache that nothing can kill
I have chosen life over deaths kiss
Surviving by mere force of will

Catheryn Alanna Moonsong

Beginning to End

Feeling for love,
streaming of pain,
engaged in these thoughts,
the loses and gains.
Binding and breaking,
the feelings not tamed,
love stays together,
held like a frame.
It begins to grow old,
it withers away,
like frozen with time,
the memories stay.
When the feelings crash,
you may gain a new friend,
but it all happens,
beginning to end.

Ashley Lynn DeMarco

The Way God Made Us

I am not made of rock,
Nor am I made of stone.
I am made of human bone.
I am not ugly,
Nor am I fat.
I am just the way God made me.
I am not weird,
Nor am I strange.
I am just my own type.
I am not better,
Nor am I lower.
I am just the average height.
I know God loves me and you,
And I know you know too.
Let's be equal and remember
We're all the way God made us.

Stephanie Elizabeth Rodill

Flat Feet

I had a dream last night,
a conversation with myself.
Why can't I fit in this world?
The sky made a mistake.
"Explain yourself," I said to me.
Flat feet—suitable for clouds,
itching back, missing limbs,
or wings.
Willingness to give—
ask me, tell me,
hurt me, hate me,
spit at me, and I will still be there
smiling.
Looking up at the sky for answers on
why I can be so hurt.
Because you are an angel!

Regina Gutierrez

Wilderness

To live inside a moment
And grasp onto it so tight
Every second gasps for air
And it will never be right
Killed in passing silence
With only a soft cry
And the whispered words
Of calm, quiet lies
Facing truths I must accept
A thousand dreams of false belief
A few seconds of discontent
Just one hope compelling me

Justin Ellis Robinson

Sparkling . . .

Desire to believe in clinging
Desire to believe in jingles
Desire to believe in snow
Desire to believe in frost
Desire to believe in the moon
Desire to believe in stars
Desire to believe in reindeer
Desire to believe in fir trees
Desire to believe in fire
Desire to believe in Grandma
Desire to believe in fairy tales . . .
My reason tells me to go
My heart tells me to stay . . .
It is cold outside
It is colder inside.
Sparkling . . .

Zoe Onutu

Papaw's Knee

Sitting on your knee,
listening as you tell
stories of the war
and how life had been.
Tales of true heroes
that will never be forgotten
from a time we all think of
as way back when. . . .
when everyone dreamed
of an end to the war.
Way back then
before I was born.
I saw it all clearly
as I sat on your knee
and listened to stories
of way back when.

Talita Williams

Understanding

Does anybody understand
The hurt that comes from words?
The wishes of a child
To end it all?
Does anybody understand
The pain that comes with silence?
The quiet knife
That tears out a child's heart.
Does anybody understand
The anguish of the yelling?
The mental torture
That a child is put through?
Does anybody understand?
Yes, people do.
But they are just people,
People like me and you.

Catherine Sanchez

Love

When I love,
it is for real.
Love is it,
so let's just deal.
Deal with love,
'cause I love you.
I would love
if you loved me too.
So please tell me,
is that what you want?
To love me too,
or love me not?

Susie Ann Gates

Ghosts

The sounds of apparitions
whisk the air from the lungs
of young children,
but ghosts do not walk
among us.
They sit at the table,
passing green apples
between themselves
like conversation,
lightly sprinkling them
with salt
before ingesting the pulp.
And when they are finished,
we breath them again
through our nostrils,
back into our chests.

Jason Andrew Libby

Camelot Dreams

Where are those days of beauty,
Seeing Camelot in my dreams,
With knights in shining armor,
Fighting for honor, so it seems?
Where went those days of childhood,
Of romance and legends read,
Of moonlit-scented nights
Rushing to my head?
Of genteel ladies swooning
Into strong awaiting arms,
Fans and eyelids aflutter,
Showing a woman's charms?
Where went those gentle times,
The ones of which I've read,
Igniting the childish fantasies
On which my dreams were fed?

Connie Marie Naab

New Dawn

The window shutters remain open
Each night as I retire to bed;
Allowing the morning's new dawn
To float over my head.
Gently and quietly it slips in
Without making a sound;
As it brushes my face,
My heart begins to pound.
All at once without prior fanfare,
Are radiant shades making their debut;
Like feathery fingers long and thin,
Of sparkling gold's, silvers and blues.
To take in the majesty of the morn
Awakening to its new birth;
Is such a joy and blessing,
Of immeasurable pleasure and worth.

Sherry L. Plummer

The Kiss I Never Had

You loved me for a little,
You didn't love me long.
You gave me wings of gladness,
You sung my heart a song.
You loved for a hour,
but only with your eyes.
Your lips I could not capture,
by storm or by surprise.
Out of a world of laughter,
suddenly I'm sad.
Day and night it haunts me,
the kiss I never had.

Jamie Leigh Naquin

Spiraling

The wing moves her
Gracefully gliding
Closing her eyes she shut out emotion
Simply shining.
Twirling until she fall
Drunkenly dizzy
Her breath leaves her
Mournfully moaning.
Memories begin to surface
Painfully prickling
She beats against the earth
Hazardously hammering.
Multicolored leaves drift down
Faithfully floating
She let tears surface
Whimsically weeping.

Candice Currey

The Wall

There it is, The Wall
Filled with memories of past,
Pain, built strong and tall,
From loves that didn't last.
You're on one side,
I'm on the other.
Afraid to love, we hide.
We gaze at each other.
My friend, I need you,
The Wall is in your mind;
I will not hurt you.
Love—together, we will bind.
The remaining time in this life
To each other, we give.
Living each day of this life,
Loving each other, we live!

Beverly J. Kuen

A Song of Life

If my heart was a poem
then my life could be a song
a sweet and bitter melody
that would play all the day long
a song of God's forgiveness
and how He's always there
a song of all my doubts and fears
that nobody knows are there
a song of all my love inside
a song of sweet relief
a song of all the things I've done
and a song of my belief
and if this song was sung today
then forever it would take
for I will go to heaven and live
and in that there is no mistake

Matthew Cole Roberts

Imaginative Galaxies

My imagination is like the
Nighttime sky,
Alien places sit unexplored.
You cannot gaze the entire
Galaxy with unaided peepers,
Yet you know it is over yonder.
Shimmering, scattered stars
Are my thoughts,
Ideas of UFOs capture my mind.
Meteorites mingle with my
Mentality at midnight
As I soar the solar system.

Emily Marie Smith

death and life

she was silent never a word spoken
fighting to live
filled with pain
near us yet far away
hope was fading
tears flowed steady
hearts were breaking
goodbyes were said
words of love filled the room
confusion, heartache
never-ending prayers
touching her face, her hands
afraid
waiting for that final breath
then peace
death and life so close

Dorothy A. Kettlety

No Cure

People walking aimlessly.
Nowhere to turn;
Minds are all a blur.
Can't seem to think on their own.
Doing things in a robot form.
Mechanical engines turning gears.
Soon they burn, soon.
No heroes, nothing.
The world we are killing.
Snakes that bite, no cure.
No cure.
Diseases that lurk in dark places.
"That won't happen to me."
Who knew a robot can get a virus?
No cure.
No cure.

M. L. Rocca

vita terrestre

tree of knowledge, you say
life everlasting, you offer
only you have legs, lover, so how
did you
slither into my head
tempting serpent you are, how
did you
climb the stairs to my bed
the gold of heaven dulled
beside your brilliant fires
i sacrificed my god
to gain your respect
and myself to have your devotion
but hell was a little boring for me
and i'm not persephone
i never have to stay

Amber Brooke Carter

My Definition of Retirement (Teachers)

R is for Rest
E is for Excitement
T is for Terrific
I is for me, myself, and I
R is for Recreation
E is for Enjoying my freedom
M is for no more Morning traffic
E is for Everybody's working but me
N is for No more kids
T is for Traveling when I get ready

Felicia S. Martin

My Aunt Kathy

Kathy was so kind,
she knew a lot in her mind.
Kathy, oh, she was so strong,
she fought the cancer for so long.

She knew she'd win and not lose,
and still she fought, while she snoozed.

Time came for the battle to end,
and still the doctors could not mend
what was already through,
she went to Heaven just like God knew.

Jessica Page

Musical Words

Books are my life.
Did I mention they're the words
That I whisper,
The words that I speak,
And deep down inside,
They're the feelings that weep?
Some of them happy
And some of them blue
But boy, how I love to read
Yes, I do!
So ask! I'll read.

Dixon Barth

Forward

Mind set,
better attitude,
crazy or just dazed.
Hearts of stone
now grown.
No regrets,
no resets.
Just move on with time.
Crazy or not
we mustn't stop
to look far behind.

Natasha Marie Cromoga

Forgotten

Forgotten forevermore
Forgotten as before
Forgotten as broken toys
Forgotten as a lonely child
Forgotten as a tear runs dry

Forgotten as a starving pet
Forgotten without a fret
Forgotten as I was never here
Forgotten without a care
Forgotten now I'm dead
In my earthly bed!

Tyrone Pitt

My future

I know of no future
except the one
you have ruined
mom
and
dad
and every other adult
thank you
wise men
for
your wonderful help

Bjorg Edberg

My Pain

My pain it seems
Is caused by everything
Haunted dreams
Of a life gone wrong
I try to cry out
But no one listens
Is anybody there?
Scars of a horrible past
That never fade away
Why can't I just forget
My pain that plagues me every day

Jennifer Leigh Price

[glass]

I have no regrets
Except your Lie

(always with me)

Plaguing
Piercing
Not quite cutting

Like that shard of glass
I found
In the thin sole of my
sandal

Kerry Marsh

My Life

I sit and type
I type and sit
Day by day
Night by night
One day, a job will come
One night, sleep will not elude
Then the sun will shine
And the moon will be full
Until then
I sit and type
And type and sit

Lisa Hornickel

Life and Death

Born here, laugh here,
Cry here, die here.
Life is only but a dialectic
Of reciprocity;
Here, then, and vanish.
Antagonism is a brother,
A sister, and an enemy,
All in perpetual blindness
And abject vanity.

Keep me off "niflheim."
Die here.

Felix Walters Ekezie

My Mind

My mind is a city that never dies.
It is a steal trap, holding all my
mistakes, a trap that catches me
every time.
It is as invasive as the skyscraper,
ever present that blocks the warming
rays of the sun.
It is dirty and in need of prayer, a
messiah to lead me to the valley
saving me from myself and delivering
me to God.

Tanya Shlosman

Sun

Upon the rise
all is golden.
In its life,
it burn and heats.
From its fall,
coldness and darkness
set up the soul.
The sun
is to be much like love,
perfect then strong,
strong then left behind.

Mark Adams

Grandmother's 75th Birthday

What I want to say
No money could ever begin to pay.
This comes from deep inside my heart,
Wherever you may be,
We will never be apart.
For your love will always mend,
And it will never end.
For this much is true,
I will always love you.
So for this happy day so fine,
Let's toast with a glass of wine.

Tisha M. Rosenau

The Old Man

With unsteady footsteps
leaning on a stick
the old man passes by.

A lined face,
two eyes that seem
to accept eternity
knowing he has no tomorrow.

He stares into my soul.
I understand the message.
The fleeing of life.

Sylvana M. Swinburne

Stand

there are so many brokenhearted songs
so true to make us cry
for i, the saddest, remains unwritten
of the day you left me standing alone
deep within i feel the moment, the end
forever and for true, rot the them world
always together—me, yours, you, mine
until our eyes closed for the last time
into the night and then the door closed
and i was by myself
and the future had played a trick on me

Steven Hannigan

Content

I stand here alone,
Although the room is crowded.
I am not seen.
I am not heard.
I am not noticed,
But I am not discontent.
I see people for who they are,
Not for what they do.
Although many mistake it for anger,
It is just confusion
In this world full of conflict.

Alison Bowden Osborn

Just Say Know

Judge others as you wish to be judged.
Use enough half-truths,
Say it enough times,
Then a nation can be brainwashed.
So that its citizens
Are reduced to mindlessness,
You know, not thinking for oneself,
Knowledge comes from experience,
Not blind obedience.
Oh, America,
Will you ever learn?

Rodney J. Shimmon

Why Me?

I live alone
No one else
Just me on my own
Maybe I'll live or
Maybe I'll die
But for now the question is
Why
Why I see the darkness and
Not the light
To tell you the truth I just want to
Live right

Abrina Carlos

Discrimination

Who made these rules?
I don't like them at all.
My skin is too dark
to buy a new vase.
They say I'm too old
to work in this place.
Less pay I get
for being a woman.
I wish I knew where
it all began.
Who made these rules?

Kristina Barrios

Secrets

Secrets are a bond between
One person and another.
It's an urge to tell
Conflicting with a promise not to.
We all have secrets.
Deep, dark, or simply
Scratching the surface.
Some secrets are meant
To be shared with a friend.
Some are meant to be kept inside
The soul.

Rachel Toth

Simple

Love is simple.
Love is sweet.
Love will bow
at your feet.

Some think love
is beauty or sex.
But . . .
if you break its heart—
it hurts
and you've lost it.

Evelyn Wright

Love Denied

*A tribute to my sister, Michaelena,
deceased at two months of age in 1939*
One special day a child was born
home she went but not for long
they say she cried they knew not why
I know she cried from love denied

She struggled hard with all her might
eventually she lost the fight
my sister not as strong as I
finally died from love denied

Dolores Pasarell Rosner

A Moment

A moment's a moment,
A moment's not long,
And after a moment,
That moment's gone.

It passes so quickly,
And yet leaves a song,
Of fun-filled memories,
When the moment has gone.

And while you think about it,
Slips by another one.

Terri Berry Waldron

On Stage

The entertainer holds the stage,
Commands the audience to view
Impressions only, in a cage,
Where music is a Merlin tool,
And magic may prevent a rage
Of truer passion's purer fuel.

Still echoes of the moment touch
A deeper calm, yet leave no trace
Of inner poise. So very much
Is never shown. Each one must reach
A bargain lacking terms as such,
And rhythms of a separate piece.

Mike Doran

A New Day

A new day has dawned.
A new beginning has spawned.
New seeds are planted.
New growths become.
New possibilities emerge.
New experiences happen.
New friends are made.
Relationships become.
Love grows.
Each moment is one of Love.
Make each moment one of Love.
Joy is produced by Love.

Marley Francis Jones

Presley Taylor

A precious brand new life
two years ago today
brought so much love into our hearts
there are no words to say
please know we'll keep you safe and warm
and in our hearts you'll stay
forever our precious little girl
that's two years old today

Timothy James Frawley

Tears

All around, tears of sorrow
flow like a waterfall.
No rainbows to catch,
colors faded to grey.
Lost in a forest of darkness
until thy love returns.
Her heart beats slowly;
it echoes back with no answer.

Kathleen Eva Ashton

Once upon a Time

Once you told me to never run.
Once you told me to always have fun.
Once you told me to never hide.
Once you told me to always have pride.
Once you told me it was okay to cry.
Once you told me to always try.
Once you told me you would never leave.
Once upon a time in you I believed.

Jimmie Lee Henderson

Time

Time is now.
Time was then.
Time has no beginning.
Time has no end.

Time is not a minute.
Time is not a year.
Time is not to be wasted.
Time is very rare.

Judith E. Littell

For My Little Angel

I love you with all my heart.
I respect you for the person you are.
You are with me in everything I do;
I know God has blessed me with you.
I know God will bless us both because
My love for you is so true.
You really are my little angel
And I really love you!

Sam A. Roberts

Life

Life is experience
Experience is tutor of life
Joy and grief are brief
And both make life ripe
Birth and death are routine
But both make life repeat
Sky and all elements are there
To witness life forever
Life becomes beautiful
When experience is painful

Mohan Thulasingam

Moon's Wind

The moon eternal,
Its cycle diurnal,
Moving on ethereal wind,
I know not its spirit,
Or what lies within it,
Arriving at night,
And even day in its plight,
travelling on Moon's Wind.

Matthew Keith Bailey

Deceived

I trusted you.
I thought you felt the same.
You lied to me.
You made me feel really lame.
I thought we had something going on.
I thought we really had it good.
I guess my eyes were closed too tight.
I guess I never understood.

Tiffany Lacy

Timeless

Timeless are the lessons learned.
Timeless are the ways you turn.
To the river's edge and mountains high.
Timeless as I watch and pray.
Timeless are my cares today.
Timeless to the very end.
Timeless,
For my life has just begun.

Cynthia Annette Dugas

Insomnia

Peeking at the clock
the combat starts.
I think to myself,
What if I don't wake up?
Sweeter extras. Maybe that's
what I'm looking for.
How does that work again?
Amplify. Rectify. Get rid of it.

Abilene Smith

Fremily

Words can't possibly describe
The feelings that we have inside.
Whenever we're with all of you,
Our hearts are filled with love so true.

So far from friends,
Much more than family,
You're neither . . . but both,
You are our fremily!

Michael J. Abbruscato

Altruism

To give freely,
no expectation of a return
Who claims this,
in their heart burns?
From the depths of a soul,
a sacrifice
The inspiration for life
not for vice
An altruistic gift for each
They chose to teach

Tara Hilton

The Dawn

I look forward to each and every dawn
I know I shall soon be with you
And we shall be as one
I long to soothe the aching
By holding you in my arms
I suffer 'til our lips can meet
Igniting all the passions
That sustain and keep me warm

Joseph Allan McQueen

Shades of Crimson

The blood in my veins
a shade of crimson.
That beautifully flows
from head to toe.
Scarlet streams
carry emotions,
so every part of me
feels the same.

Danalynn Rambo

Blind and Fractured

I had stardust in my eyes—
I saw you backlit,
the corona of the sun turning you into
a thousand shiny pieces of mirror.
I dulled those pieces,
rubbed the shine away,
and broke you into a million more.

Please accept my apologies.

Emily Chovanec

Time Goes On

Friends may come and go
But friendships never end
We may lose touch
We may not talk
But you are always in my mind
The same can be said for more
Lovers may come and go
But love can last forever

Kellie Vogelsong

A Persian Princess

I fell into a dream last night
Where I could rule the land.
I ruled with care and devotion,
I ruled with a loving hand.
And all my people did come to see
All across the sand
That truth and love will hold them tight
And lead them to the Holy Land.

HRH Princess of Persia

Perfection to Dust: A Love Chronicle

Astonish; amazed with sweet curiosity—
Will it flourish? Will it be?
Can't I possibly live within you?
Or will you reject, yet still love me?

Can my soul possibly glow
With the sight of you?
My love is stronger than any other,
If only that you knew . . .

Ryan Tyler Bryant

Believe in Yourself

Believe in yourself
as much as you can
Believe in yourself
as you walk through the sand
Life can surprise you
if you are not prepared
Life can surprise you
it can really turn you scared
All can be cherished
instead of set on a shelf
All can be cherished
as long as you believe in yourself

Stefanie Ann Hicks

Little Baby

Little baby who I wanted to know,
Why did you leave me and hurt me so?
I counted your fingers,
I counted your toes;
They were all there, why did you go?
I fought for you
From beginning 'til end,
Why couldn't I
Just one time win?
A son I wanted, a son I had;
Why didn't you trust me,
Did you think I was sad?
Little baby who I wanted to know,
Why did you leave me and hurt me so?

Sandra Dawn Taylor

My Country

Come on, everybody,
This is a tragedy in our US history.
We are brothers and sisters,
We got to work together.

Nothing is an end.
There is no use in crying.
We got manpower.
We can come up, remember.

Thousands of friends we lost.
They all remain forever in our heart.
Evil will come to an end.
For that we do anything.

We are Americans,
We are true citizens,
We don't give up our heart,
We have courage in our thought.

Arulselvi Amirrthalingam

Footsteps in the Sand

A solitary stranger,
Journeys through a foreign land.
Over miles and miles of desert,
Leaving footsteps in the sand.

Walking ever onward,
Never quite sure where to go.
Searching for a brother,
That nobody seems to know.

His path is rife with dangers,
In this land of cutthroat thieves,
But with deft and deadly hands,
He'll defend what he believes.

Wherever trouble lingers,
He will surely lend a hand.
At its passing he will vanish,
Leaving footsteps in the sand.

Edward Tipton

Deep in the Wood

Deep in the Wood
a silent man walks slowly,
surrounded by familiar sounds,
each step painfully poignant,
pressing the ground with grace.
A gentle breeze blows,
thick leaves rustle,
is there a voice?
More of a knowing
he is not alone.

Camilla Crist

Hero

Up in the sky
Be glory awaiting
Those many souls are nothing
Knowing
Helpful and tender
Receiving no fee
Just gracious and courageous
For all that be
When time runs out
Forever will they stay
Friends in our hearts
Heroes in our minds

Daniel Bryan Barr

Constant Reminder

Did you forget your ticket—
It's lying on the table—
That it's your mother's birthday?
That you must water the flowers?
That you must give in order to receive?
Did you forget I have a name—
Or to inquire of it—
Or my favorite song?
Did you forget the Golden Rule
That as people we are all the same?
To leave your hate
In place of your ticket?
That God loves us all?
That in summer, snowflakes don't fall?
That everyone bleeds red?
Did you forget where you're going
From whence you came?
To follow only love
And forget only hate?

Haley Star Campbell

The Mighty Gauley

Make way, Gauley season begins today.
The water is pumping;
My heart is jumping.
Gauley season is here—
Have you no fear?
The river is high;
Paddle or die!
Stay afloat, stay in the boat!
Rapids are a rush;
Rocks you will brush.
Bones you may break;
Memories you will make.
Respect the river! Do not quiver!
Never cower,
For she will unleash her true power.
Be strong, be smart.
Have a warrior's heart.
Listen to your guide;
Enjoy the ride!

Steven Patrick Walls

Insight

As we visit your aging father
I look into your handsome face
And see the child you once were
And the man that you are

Kimberly Ann Leaman

Write What I Live

I write what I live.
I don't dare, to invent.
If I was happy I'd say it.
Because, reality is something else.

A hypocrite is such one
that lives of pure falseness;
while nothing is known, to anyone
it is to nobody's concern.

But when it's all discovered
in those shoes
I wasn't liking to be.

Jose Valle

A Glimpse of Eternity

From the first day we met
to our last days together,
I know eternity.
From the oceans that are your eyes
to the gentle breeze of your breath,
I know eternity.
From our first kiss
to our final embrace,
I know eternity.
From the beginning of time
to its undoing,
I shall love you
and that is eternity.

David Michael Brown

Our Love

Our love is mighty
Our love is strong
But it can never be
So what went wrong

You say you love me
As I love you
But then you leave me
Oh, so blue

So my darling
Should we never meet
Without your love
I am incomplete

Aline Rich Rodgers

Storm

Comes suddenly
Comes quietly
First drop of rain
Come inside
Wind picks up
Blustery speed
Storm has hit
Thunder crashes
Lightning hits
Huge storm
It stops
Goes suddenly
Goes quietly

Elizabeth Scholz

Joxer

Joxer The Mighty—
he's always nice and tidy.
Every night he goes to bed,
thinking what his father said:
No more chicks in your bed!
Do it again
and you're dead!

Bryant Conan Tan

untitled

pressure bearing down on me
heavy
want to break
pop like a bubble under the pressure
of your oppressive hands
feigned disinterest
false bravado
clinging
desperate
cast off dispassionately
reaching out frantically for something
to give meaning to my untitled soul

Jacob Kaulike Vasconcellos

Never

Never have I known a trust
as deep and pure or true.
Never have I loved someone
as much as I do you.
Never have I felt this happy
or nearly this sure.
It feels as if we've known each other
a hundred times over.
Never do I feel stupid,
or not good enough for you.
You always seem to know me,
no matter what I do.

Courtney Lynne McCarley

Sometimes

sometimes I think
someday I'll be
something worthwhile to
someone.
sometimes I wonder when that
someday will come and
somebody will care and think I'm
someone.
sometimes I believe
some people don't have
someone to love them not for
someday but always.

Stacy Wilts

My Special Friend

I have a special friend,
we will be friends 'til the end.
She helps me when I'm down,
makes me smile instead of frown.
She has been there from the beginning,
giving me the courage to keep winning.
She will always be my supporting team,
to fulfill my goals and every dream.
She has given me the power and the will,
to improve my each and every skill.
Without her I'd never be calm,
my Special friend is my mom!

Ashley M. Ross

Gifts from God

To see your beauty,
To hear your laughter,
To be touch by your hand,
To breath you deep inside,
To taste your passionate kiss—
Through God's grace, you have shared
These gifts with me.

Steven Dwayne Williams

The Hint of Spring

Amid the bleakest skies of winter
Waits a light that pleads to splinter.
It lurks behind the clouds of gray
And seeps into the darkest day.
Ever present, it yearns to unfold
With all its splendor, warm and gold.
It brings along with it a plan—
New life and light across the land.
So fear not what winter seems to bring—
The snow, the ice, the cold and rain—
For when time comes for life anew,
The hint of spring brings skies of blue.

Yvette Lynne Gordon

Summer Sea

The calming sound of the sea.
The crashing of the waves.
A cooling breeze rushes by
and there alone stands you and I.
Running and splashing in the sea;
That's where you and I will be.

Then the sun begins to set,
and there alone we stand all wet.
As it darkens by the sea
a moonlight walk I will take with thee.
Hand in hand we stroll
until a new day takes its toll.

Tamara Gabrielle Smith

True Power

Everything seems different now
Our lives all rearranged
All the things that used to be
Have somehow all been changed
Money, guns, and drugs
The tools of their game
With a false sense of power
They all strive to obtain
Why can't they understand it
True power lies within
It's too bad they won't see it
'Til their world comes to an end

Steve W. Marshall

The Ballpark

The ballpark is a dirty place
With mud and dirt and rocks
That get inside my leather sandals
And my cotton socks.
And when I try to scuff them out
They increase more and more,
Which makes the bottoms of my feet
Get really, really sore!
Why people bother wearing shoes,
Goodness only knows!
It's so much better to feel the ground
Underneath your toes.

Caroline Gillian Sebastian

Poem on Mother

I have a special mother—
She helps everybody and their brother.
No job is too large—
She is always in charge.
Mom wants to be right
Because she is very bright—
Like a star in the night.

Alexander Leon Moore

Behind the Lines

My guns were gone, my ammo lost;
I could not bear that dreadful cost.
As I headed back to allied land,
I realized my death was soon at hand.
I fought for food, I fought for water;
I tried to avoid the endless slaughter.
Hitler's pawns were all around,
shooting friends to the ground.
I picked up a gun to defend this land;
I wanted to shoot that awful man.
We won the long and dreary fight
on that cold, dark, and loathsome night.

Marcus Lee Stansfield

My Unborn Child

Every night when I try to sleep
I can't help but start to weep
Every time I close my eyes
All I hear is your cries
I've done some things that go unforgiven
To insanity I'm almost driven
To have you here is all I desire
The rage inside me burns like fire
To my unborn child I write
I hope one day we will reunite
For my unborn child I yearn
And for now the fire brightly burns

Matthew David Hukill

Secret Place

Open space
what a place
to be alone
all, all alone
Think.
Concentrate.
Decide.
Deep feelings.
Thoughts exposed.
Brought out into open.
—An intruder!
My moment is over.

Nichelle Okafor

Tim

I love your dark eyes
And the warmth of your skin
When you tell me you love me
I feel alive again
Your spirit is fire
You set me ablaze
And when we make love
I become your slave
Babe, you are gentle
And cruel, all the same
I dream of you often
As I whisper your name

Debby Ann Melton

My Life

My life is mine, no one else's.
Does anyone see my life?
Can they see what I see?
Hear what I hear?
Why do I feel the pain that I feel?
Does anyone else feel this pain?
No, they don't, because it's my life.

Sherry Borke

Dad, a Poem for You

It has been many years
Since I have first met you.
I have given out many cheers
So that attention-wise I could get you.
I do this because I can trust
That you'll lead me in the right path;
I trust you because you are strong
And so far you've raised me right,
Yes you have.
With all my heart,
Happy Father's Day.
I love you, Dad.

Gatlin Cheyenne Johnson

If Tomorrow Doesn't Come

If I died tomorrow
Would you regret today?
If I took my last breath
Would you wish for the past?
If today is all we had
Would you know what to say?
If there was no future for us
Would your love still last?
These things that come between us
Trivial they would be
If tomorrow doesn't come for you
Or for me.

Melissa Feury Rosario

To My Love

There is a place within my heart
Where only you can dwell.
It is a place where no one's touched,
A place you know so well.
Together we shall walk our path
To the future shining bright.
We'll cherish every memory,
As we hold each other tight.
And as the days and years go by,
Time will bless us with much love.
For we have found each other
With the help from God above.

Crystal R. Carier

New Patriots

When you feel the world around you
Is crashing to the ground
Look up amidst the rubble
And listen for the sound
Of our nation standing together
Hand in hand and heart to heart
You'll feel a rush of loyalty
You'll know we've made a start
To awaken as new patriots
A new sense of unity
Our hearts to God, while hands applaud
New Patriots all are we

Roz Bingaman

Voices

voices whispering down the hall
voices heard but not seen at all
voices snickering, voices laughing
voices cackling
fire snapping
while winter napping
voices whispered down the hall

Lindsay Curtiss

Life Is Like an Ocean

Life is like an ocean,
So beautiful at times.
When looking from afar,
It's as though nothing is wrong,
But as you get in deeper,
You find things aren't that great.
What you thought was love
Has now turned to hate.
Always living in fear,
Never knowing how to be free.
Things ever getting better
Just doesn't seem to be.

Joelle Ann Zicarelli

America's Attack

The World Trade Center no longer stands.
It was destroyed by cowards' hands.
Airplanes crashed into their sides,
Many innocent people lost their lives.
The Pentagon was damaged too,
For reasons no one knew.
Through soot and ash our heroes worked,
Overlooking all their pain and hurt.
America has strength and pride.
You cannot destroy what we have inside,
Although many tried at our despair.
We will survive with God and prayer.

Vicki M. Ewing

Soul Searching

Tiptoeing through the fall
Tulips full bloom in the trees
A gentle breeze sings your name
An angel Heaven-sent
To test my resolve
To crack under pressure
To go farther into the uncharted depths
Insanity the only sane option left
In this world of norms and rules
I stand alone, outside, unused
What is the purpose?
What is my pain?

Nathan Olmstead

How I Came to Be

The world around me turned
and I saw a shining light.
The path of my being
torn 'tween wrong and right.
I saw the flames;
I saw the robes;
I saw the choices
fall down in droves.
Forever will I remember then
the hardships that I'll see,
and I will always know
how I came to be.

Jessica Myer

Oh, Little Ones

Oh, little ones,
you think
that your spirit
does not yearn
for the master,
but it does.

It deeply does.

Lisa Milam

He Lifted Them Up

Two airplanes flying in the sky,
He lifted them up.
Two buildings reached just as high,
He lifted them up.
As the airplanes hit their marks,
He lifted them up.
As the buildings burnt and sparked,
He lifted them up.
When the buildings down were tossed,
He lifted them up.
No souls were ever really lost,
For He lifted them up.

Mary Jo Ruebusch

The Clock

Twelve numbers and three hands;
Behind them, desert sands.
The footprints in the sand
Tell a story about the land.
The woodwork without its paint
Makes it look very quaint.
With a mahogany colored coat,
Words are caught in my throat.
There it sits on the mantel
With beauty only sight could tell.
Standing there in shock,
I could only admire the clock.

Kirsten Hall

first love

first love unexpected
tiptoed in surprise
whole life rejected
but this reprise
has unwarranted whoa
for love enters your life
when your eyes are closed
open 'em i say
let it pour in
nothing is the same
the heart will lose or win
risk it and you'll be without

Natalie Laniewicz

Dear Lord

Hold me in Your arms, dear Lord
and help me on my way
I pray to You, sweet Jesus
to guide me through this day
I know I need You constantly
though sometimes I forget
Remind me that You love me
and keep my feet in step
Cradle me, Your little child
through me, Your love shall show
Hold me in Your arms, dear Lord
and never let me go

Carla Thompson

Reflection

Reversed complexion
Elaborate illusion
Flourishing artwork rippling in water
Lovely description
Exquisite perfection
Calling from a different world
Tangible to no one
Inscrutable mystery
Obscured proportionally
Nowhere; only an image

Ann Koscki

Man's Achievement

The night is dark but not for long.
The sun arise, birds sing their song.
The day is here with man at best.
The sun will shine upon his chest.
The herded cattle that run so wild;
the ears of corn to feed his child.
And if should come a little trouble,
his valiant effort sure will double
For this man is the only one,
to support his family and raise his son.

Edward Vasquez

A Storm Unexpected

She is a storm unexpected
Rising from a hot summer evening
A comfort only to evil
Her smile is the devil
With a halo
Making you believe she is heaven
Giving you hell
Her lips drip with beauty
She is wretched inside
Do not touch what you can't resist

Melissa A. Walker

Life Is Ending

Show me everything you have,
And I see nothing but emptiness.
Speak all powerful words,
And I will listen.
Step up to your responsibilities,
And I will see your results.
Shed a tear,
And I will comfort you;
Why do you weep, my soul?
For the souls of many,
Why do you cry?
LIFE

Gail Lennett Tittle

A Psalm

Oh, Lord;
I do not ask for proof of Thee
Yet I find it all around me,
In winter's incandescent glow
On snowy pines bent low,
Or the lacy fringe along the lane—
Artistry from my window pane.
In the flicker of a firefly
The rapture of a starry sky
The slow meandering of a brook—
In every flowering cove I look.
In Sun and wind and sand,
There is the imprint of Thy hand.

Mary T. Hobbs

Paths of Life

You choose your path
I choose my own
And in the end
Whose kingdom has grown
I, on path of Righteous rule
Or you, who chose the Path of Fools
Of military Might and War
Your people dying by the Score
Tell me, King
The use of this
Your name inscribed
On Satan's List
Tell me, King
What can be gained
From a History of Blood and Pain

Brandon Michael Wade

Roll Away the Stone

Angels roll the stone away,
So my friends can clearly see
That I am not inside
Where they're expecting me to be!
And angels wait and tell them
I have risen from the dead
And tell them to remember
All the other things I said.
Tell them I am going
Before them to Galilee,
And if they will only follow,
There shall they see me!

And the disciples went to Galilee, and
When they saw Him, they fell down
And worshiped Him!

Frances Lanter

She

Her eyes, like the ocean so deep;
Always beautiful, calm or stormy,
awake or asleep.
Her hair, like the wind so flowy;
That shine, above the black,
but never too showy.
Her lips, like the rose so pink;
Even the heavens, all applaud,
and the Gods could sink.
Her hands, like the cloth so silky;
Rise only, to the worship,
Thee Almighty.
She, herself knows not what she is;
A creation of the God's, so great,
no eye on earth could miss.

Deepak Talwar

What Is Death?

What is death
is it gone
or is it here
can we stop death
or does it feel good to let go
how does death happen
or do we care
should we be afraid of death
or excited to meet it
do we know when death will come
or does it take us by surprise
should we cry about death
or should we laugh
if death didn't happen
would everyone be happier?

Jennifer Nicole Kosidowski

The Love I Found in You

You aroused emotions
that feel so unsinkable;
to wear anything less than a smile
would be the unthinkable.
You changed my world
when I felt like I was trapped
in a small little cage,
and showed me that
there are going to be better days.
You pranced into my life
and made it all just right;
and now here you are, holding me tight.
Can it be possible, is it true
that I have finally found love
and it came with you?

Tabatha Marie Deese

My Best Friend

There is a person
Whose name just about everyone has heard
He listens when you talk
Gives advice on what to do
He knows your name
As well as your heart
He heals the sick
And gives to the poor
He says that those who are last
Shall be first
He loves me with his whole being
And lives in my heart
He's my best friend and could be yours
His name is Jesus Christ
The son of the one true God

Lesley Barkley

Breathe

Stand in moonlight,
let the silver shade your face,
look at me,
melt me,
ignore my lack of grace.
Listen to my dreams,
dance with me,
give my heart wings,
keep me forever,
you possess the key.
Kiss me softly,
pick a star,
make a wish for me,
know that I love you
for who you are.

Tracie Noel Trog

Obsidian Pupils See Far More. . . .

Obsidian pupils see far more
Appear not to focus
Certainly not on you

Burn right past you
Cold, solid, yet shining and reflective
Pools of tar, you sink
Searing, seething
Overflowing with anger
Flash at you and remain

Either stoic or fierce
No gray areas
Accentuated by churning blood
But I have lost my spark

Ashley Hart Walker

Blossom

As I came out of the fast,
I knew spring was here at last;
I could hear the wind breathing,
Whispering into my ear. . . .
Look! Look! Open up and peer!

It was a blossom so full of beauty,
Rose in color;
Shining forth soft delicate petals
That glowed with all its splendor.

And then I knew, deep inside,
The seeds of love surely grew
With a silent whisper. . . .
She spun a web around my name.
Love began to brew.

Rahi Choudhury

Life's End

Life is pain
That brings life,
Cutting as deep
As the surgeon's knife.
This pain could end
In suicide.
We've nothing to lose,
Nothing to hide.
Free are our dejected souls,
To suffer eternally
Our fevered roles.
Could we survive
Life's minuscule pains?
Just ask those
Who are tangled in chains.

Lisa Condreay

Missing You

Missing you
Here I sit missing you
Day by day I am alone
Wishing you would just come home
Even though you're far away
Here I sit most every day
My love for you is so strong
Even though I know it's wrong
Missing you each day I will
It's just a feeling that I feel
I love so deep within my heart
It's there our love shall never part
Yes my love
My love is true
That's why I am missing you

Diana L. Channel

Survival of the Heart

Thorns supplied abundantly
were piercing restlessly
my heart
drowning drops of life into
rejection
sea
draining me of hope
tearing me apart

Along came then
the friend of time
and helped me mend
my broken heart
pumping now with drops
of love
linking heart to heart

Bahàr Lilian Wallström

Void

As it began it will continue
I look up at the stars and still see you
But now I walk the streets alone
No longer wondering what I've done
The melted block of ice around my heart
Got a brand new frozen start
And now the only thing I feel is cold
It will not last forever
But it is more than never
All I want to do is laugh insane
Not the way I do now in pain
I wish what I felt would leave
Then I could be relieved
Then the only thing I knew would be gone
But in my heart I still feel it there

Nathan St. Pierre

In Little Ryan

In little Ryan's eyes I see
A special part of you and me
The smile is yours
It is so clear, it is almost like
You are near.
A new generation has begun
I know you watch him
Like a son.
We miss you almost as much
As the day you left us
Even more your gentle touch.
It is the forth year
I've said goodbye and even now
I sit and cry and wish you were here
To laugh with me when Ryan smiles.

Sandra McLaughlin

Space

Up to space
We all race
Have to leave this earth behind
We must have lost our minds

Trashing parks
Killing sharks
Cutting trees
Poisoning bees
Polluting water
Son against father
Toxic waste
Wars of hate

Hopefully when we land
We would act less like man

Timothy DeAngelo Wood

Liquefied Solid Sea

A liquefied solid of green and blue
Flows surrounding the world
With perfect timing
Of her waves
Calm then angered
Reluctant to relaxed
Wild and so free
Becomes of this sea
Which cradles objects toward shore
Difficult to endure
With light shining from above
Into her liquefied solid covering
Down deep dark depths
Like space
Such void

Elizabeth Jane Schlosbon

A Mere Glimpse

A glance can be made,
brief but holding
so much meaning.
I take it as an embrace,
though perhaps that
was not the intent.
My own feeling mirrors
that sensation of a
skipped beat.
I hardly breathe,
but cannot contain
my ready smile.
The moment, I decided,
is mine to place
in my heart.

R. D. Zaragoza

Innocence

Today the world woke up
And a shadow fell over a great nation

Eliot once said
The world would end with a whimper
But it was awakened by a bang

Once great buildings
Reduced to piles of ash and bone

A monument to innocence
An epitaph that reads:
Innocence
Gone, but not forgotten
Born September 2, 1945
Died September 11, 2001
Rest In Peace

Billy Dwain Neill

Fermata

anna awakens,
her sweet memories dancing
with dreams of chopin.
silence around her,
anna waits for sleep to fill
her thoughts with music.
god listens, you know.
hallelujahs for prayers:
a fair exchange.
what of it? she asks.
the screams of the morning light
will tear her to shreds.
still safe in her songs,
anna awakens to find
a fermata on her pillow.

Joanna Schwab

Feeling of Love

It's a heart,
and it's a home.
It's everything you've loved,
and everything you've known.

It's a love inside
that burns like fire.
That soothes our soul
and will never tire.

It's the love we share
between us two,
always faithful,
and always true.

Love forever,
me and you.

Amanda Jane Keys

Knowing

Reality is the Unreality
Where do we go?
Reality is the Unreality
Who's to know?

Reality is the Unreality
Life.
Reality is the Unreality
Strife.

Reality is the Unreality
Love sown?
Reality is the Unreality
Love grown.

Reality is the Unreality
This is all I know.

Katherine M. Dunneback

Almost Gone

A mouthful of words
That you dare not speak.
Continuous tears
Fall down your cheeks.
Little by little you breathe
Soft pillowy death that sees.
Colors only seen in black.
Cold chills
Running up and down your back.
Antagonizing hours of pain—
Difficult choices
You have made.
Silence that comes of age.
Locked up.
Trapped in a cage.

Christine Marie Jones

Unlock

through the ocean of darkness
tides pull me closer
star bright
light our path tonight
search the deepest oceans
wander through the hottest deserts
find the key to my heart
unlock the door
climb the highest peak
run through the meadows
please unlock the door
hold my hand as the world turns
love me as I am
unlock the door
please, please, unlock the door

Monica LeeAnn Chavez

Third Bridge from the End

Dark chocolate
Velvet cream
Undulating flowers
Seedy blue film
Riptide skidding out
Foreign interloper
Crushed inside
A sensual tsunami
Saxophone jazz dizziness
Scorched water crashing down
Windy hurricane addiction
Madness
Cured by confederation
Eraser apology
Consuming delicious distractions

Amber G. Webb

The Mighty Dragon

I once had a dream
I saw a fiery beam,
then a mighty dragon of red,
sleeping on his bed.

His heart burnt with rage.
He learned evil from the old mage.
His eyes screaming a pain
of sadness because of his bane.

He sat angry and sad, all alone
on his single mighty throne.
I was surprised to see
that the mighty dragon was me.

Michael Gregory Humpherys

Gifts

Each new day that goes by
brings someone new to our lives
Do we close our eyes and cast them away
Or do we stand before them
our arms and hearts open wide
By closing our eyes
we miss what God has put before us
Yet when our hearts are open
and our souls brought together
then and only then
do we feel the gifts that are given
Those of sharing, caring, faith and love
Only given by our Lord God above

Ladana Lynn Lohn

The Boss

I'm so hungry that I can eat a horse
After pulling a billion hoses.
But wait a minute, I made a pause,
I should pray to the Boss.

Someone asked me, "Who's the Boss?"
I just replied, "He's the Host.
Someone who died and rose,
But absolutely not a scary ghost."

I hope you guessed the name of my Boss,
Because I believe He's our Boss.
He knows you and me;
even the problems of everybody.

Ronwaldo A. Tecson

Crushing the Orchid

Strolling across a field of lilies
he stumbled upon an orchid
stemming from a barren patch
Releasing the lily from his hand,
he kneads the orchid's petals soft
then plucks it from its haven
He glides the bloom 'cross his nose
shrouding himself in her essence
then looked about and realized
he left his lily behind
Turning about he reached for his lily
still laying there beside the patch
Looking at the orchid he said,
"Did you think I could walk through here
and ignore so many lilies?
You are only one, the lilies are many."
He laid her down, gently, by the root
from which he took her
then left her there in barren soil
so she can wilt and wither

Adeline Rivera

Rain

The sky is crying its eyes out
Crying cold tears
We all feel the same way
Follow the heavy rain down
Follow the sheets of cold tears
All the way to where the grass lays
The green of it has drained
It's cloaked in shadowy water
My eyes are becoming the same
Two puddles spilling over
Like the one at my feet
The rain is still beating down
Still is just a blur

Jessica Anne Marie Baker

(The Beauty) Diving Out the Dark

Seven seas across the ocean
burning soul passing through the life
being conscious never lonely
mixing precious never dies
close the open edge of sun
bring the darkness through the shame
memory just never ends
something wrong has fallen down
love you I will never do
strongly touch you I will die
justify the love regret
never lonely once again

Nevena Niagolova

He Led the Way

A cloud by day,
And a fire by night,
This is how He led the way
Through desert land
To the sea of red.
But Pharaoh wanted them to stay.

The parted sea
Let the people 'cross
On dry land where once water lay.
Soon Pharaoh followed
In the midst of the sea
'Til falling waters end his days
And the cloud still led the way.

Doreen K. Schultz

my life

if i take another hit
will i forget what it's like
to be losing my mind
feeling it vanish over time
if i drink another beer
will i forget that i'm here
i'm going crazy being
a stranger to myself
sometimes i don't feel like me
can't remember who i am
i've played pretend so much
i've forgotten who the real me is
if i quit all of that
will an opportunity come
my soul has died
my body gone numb
is there any point to living
if i'm not sure i'm alive
i've forgotten the truth
and believed my own lies

Elisabeth Ami Smith

Trail of Tears

The trail of tears
Was a long and sad journey
For the early Cherokee nation.

The Cherokee owned land for many years
Had to leave behind many belongings
To start a new life on the reservation.

The white man caused their fears
Making them leave their homes
They had for many a generation.

On the trail of tears
Many lives were lost
Causing the end of the Cherokee nation.

Sherry Ann Burditt

For Her Happiness

Last night, I used to wish that
I could live in her kiss.
But tonight, it's her love
That I will try not to miss.

Yesterday, I was selfish,
Because I wanted to be with her.
But today, I know
She will be happier with another.

When she is gone,
I know I'm going to cry.
But for her happiness,
I'll say goodbye.

Richard Ravindra Mohabeer

Three Days

Three days ago you loved me
Three days ago you cared
But now you are gone forever
How could you not be there

Three days ago I was happy
Three days ago I smiled
But now I sit in agony
Crying like a child

You promised me forever
But it was all a lie
And now because of you
Three days ago I died

Iesah Broyles

The Rising and Falling Sun

The sun rises above the skies,
Therein all her beauty lies.
She rose to say, "Hello, my friend,
A new day has yet to begin."
She glistens and beams,
She hides behind a few clouds.
Her beauty flows all day,
Her hurt and pain she hides.
She wakes the world
With her beauty.
She shines on those that she loves,
She has a special time
When her day's work is done.
Just as she rises before us,
She also sets the same.
Her beauty keeps on glowing;
She has to hide all hurt and pain.
Her day's work is never over.
Her children come to play,
Still shine in perfect honor of her name.

Deidre DeNea Williams

The Unseen Hand

An unseen hand entwined with mine
A love, a friend, a soul mate
One heart, one soul, one mind

Future visions shared,
Songs of west coast dreams, baby prayers
and delighted children's screams

A roaring fire, a peaceful night,
holding close, contented faces bathed
in fire light

My love so far and yet so near
Her touch, her laugh, her love
Upon my heart is seared

David H. Wheeler

An Eagle's Tears

I saw the sign of evil
in the highest of the sky
and the tears of an eagle
as a sign of righteous wrath.

It is soaring through the rubbish
with a keen sight of the scene
looking up for signs from heaven
to protect this earthy home.

Since I do not have the wisdom
to help out, in this fight,
I do pray for those in power
fighting for a peaceful kingdom.

Elena R. Jiménez

Fighting Insomnia

The light creeping under the door
always finds my eyes.
No matter how tight,
No matter how hard I try.
No matter how I fight,
I can't get back to sleep.
I can't get passed the first sheep.

The radio could care less
about the sad state I am in.
No matter how much I cry
and block it out, my friend.
No matter how hard I try
to count that first sheep.
I can't get back to sleep.

Brian Wettstein

I Once Knew

I once knew a peaceful world,
I once knew friendship,
I once knew life.
I don't know these things now.
War destroyed the world,
Hate destroyed friendship;
You destroyed me,
I destroyed you.
For what did we do this?
For what did billions die?
For freedom, life, love, and
The right to say I'm better than you.
But who will say I'm better than
You as the defeated lie dead at his
Feet? The person who is worse.
Why have war but to ask the same
Questions.
Why die? Why live?
Why? Why? Why?

Aaron Louis Haueisen

By Any Other Name

It's out there.
Silent and watching
Waiting to ensnare.

It's still there.
Checking the time
Waiting to declare.

It is always there!
Lurking even in sunshine
Evil, using a nom de guerre.

Jacqueline Curley Deeck

A Single Moment

A room can be lit up
With just a smile;
A heart can skip a beat
From a single touch;
But when you look into my eyes,
I just seem to melt.
A second with you
Is what I long for;
Some time alone
To feel secure in your arms.

Gabriella Julianna Vásárhelyi

The Eyes of Truth

The eyes of truth
peer deep into your soul;
piercing, burning, longing to come out.
Consumed by fear of exposing
the lies you've told.
Time deteriorating your very being
your sins blackening your heart.
Dying slowly from this disease.
Time, showing the truth
behind your myriad of secrets.

Jenny Marie Domingues

It's Not the Same

I knew her so well,
that vibrant flowery smell.
I wish she were still mine,
The one I have not treats me fine.
the little things you don't forget,
Make me think I'm not happy yet.
But I'll wait and see,
for a that lovely bee.
Who brought a shimmer,
to a dark lake.

Adam Regan Gendro

Dying

I watch as the petals fall
One by one to the floor
I feel like that flower
I am falling apart, dying
With no will to fight anymore
You watch as this flower dies
Withering to the ground
And yet you do not pick up the petals
And try to put it together again
You watch as this face dies
Smothering in my own pain
And yet you do not even try
To put my life together again
You just watch as we both die

Angela Marie Coulter

A Soul Found

Blue eyes, a devilish smile,
Intelligence and humor,
sexier than any broad chest.
Soft, gentle hands
stroking, teasing, pleasing.
Urgent, demanding kisses
filled with promise and passion.
Soft spring nights spent
sharing love, laughter, and friendship.
Moments remembered and cherished.

Laura E. Atkinson

Grandad 1924–2001

In an instant
a spirit free—
What a joyous affair
all the angels sing—
We join—they hear
with great delight—
Ecstasy expanded
to share without words—
acceptance of the memory
of who he always was.

Dallas Malloy

The Running Dream

The city streets are covered
in an early morning mist.
A dog barks,
a child whines,
an engine chokes to life.
But no one seems to notice—
they're asleep beneath their sheets.
But there is a figure out
on these city streets
and he's running for his life.

Daniel A. Boris

self-worth

behind ugly black shadows
the sun lights life and beauty
spring day is sweet like a rose
so my friend . . .
stop, for it is not the time to cry
recall not the death storm
blow away the void and apparatus
worship not the moon but you
you who are so bright
brighter than the moon itself

Gaosong Ly

Cancun

I wish I was in Cancun
to look at the beautiful moon.
When I think of the stars so bright
I also dream I'm with Mr. Right.
Cancun, Cancun
oh, I want to go soon.
I wish I was in Cancun
I wouldn't want to leave soon.
I'd walk along the beach
while eating a sweet Georgia peach.
I want to see the sunrise
while I gaze in to my loved one's eyes.
You'd see the best of me
'cause Cancun's my destiny.

Davida Grant

Inside Me

Should I or could I
Will I or won't I
Is it right or is it wrong
Should I bend or be strong
Do I scream and cry
Or lie down and die
I will just live
And learn how to give
To a person in need
To never see them bleed

Christi Daniels

Morbidity

The days are gone,
The flowers have passed.
The Sun, the moon, the stars,
Thoughts remain, the dreams . . .
They were dreams.

Trees won't grow,
Grass never turns green anymore.
As Life waits to be born anew,
What is the future to be? . . .
Only shadows of the past.

Matthew T. Love

October

Leaves
turn color
disengage
and carpet the earth
multicolored mums
begin to fade
corn husks
become brittle
pumpkins
crowd the pasture

Summer Parks

New Day, New Way

Ghostly flashes in the night.
People screaming at the sight.
Blackened bodies on the ground.
All is quiet, not a sound.
Stillness broken! Just a moan.
Then another! Now a groan.
People rising from the dirt.
Some are blinded, some are hurt.
Merge together, holding hands.
Come to form a brave new land!

Patricia P. Scheid

I, the Epileptic

An epileptic such as I
am all too often viewed
with prejudice,
an ugly word,
yet one which rings so true.
We are seen as "different"
"lesser than" or viewed
with sympathy.
How absurd and insane it is,
a damned hypocrisy!
An epileptic such as I
must stand against this view.
As but one man, not more
nor less, among the rest of you.

Eric Lathrop Giese

Your Friend

your friend is the one,
who always is next to you,
who says the hardest words,
who always want to see you happy,
who says the truth to your face.
your friend is the one,
who feels the same as you,
who never tells you a lie,
who helps you in everything you need.
your friend is the one,
who makes you happy during bad times,
who keep his promises,
who says I LOVE YOU,
and always is TRUE.

Janet Sanchez

A New Member of the Family

A child conceived out of love,
a gift from the heavens above.

A sparkle in his mother's eye,
a sound of love from his father's sigh.

A proud aunt anxiously waits,
as uncles pray he won't be late.

Cousins can hardly wait to play,
while we wait for the special day.

A beloved grandson to the parents
of the parents-to-be,
Ian Duane Flatt
is who he will be.

Rebecca Dawn Thorpe

Lil' Broken Chair

Look at Mr. Chair,
He is sitting there.

He's falling all apart
It is breaking my heart.

Would you throw him away?
Or would you let him stay?

I really do care,
It's surely not fair,

To see him that way.
Now what would you say?

Would you sing a blue?
Oh, what would you do?

Kathleen E. Montgomery

Soft Whisper

Soft whisper comes to my ear
Lets me know you are near.
Soft whisper floating in the air,
Run my fingers through your hair.
Soft whisper from all around,
Lift my feet from the ground.
Soft whisper in my arms,
I am free from any harm.
Soft whisper when I hear
Fills my soul with good cheer.
Soft whisper, my dear good friend,
May our days together never end.
Soft whisper whose words of love
Lets me know there is a God above.

Ronald G. Touketto

Missing You

I think of you often when I am all alone
wondering if I'll see you soon
or if you'll ever phone.
I can't explain what's happened
to the special times we've shared;
I often ponder on if you really cared.
The way you used to look at me,
oh, how my heart did soar,
and the warmth of your tender touch
made me long for so much more.
There are no words to explain my pain.
If only you really knew
just how much I care. . . .
how much I'm missing you.

Cynthia Kaye Alexander

Crazy

I am . . .
Constantly inconsistent,
Normally strange,
Cheerfully depressed,
Ingeniously smart,
Softly loud,
Harmlessly dangerous,
Seriously joking,
Simply confusing,
In love, out of love,
Spastically calm,
I am . . .
Just me
So call me crazy

Heather Lynn Blalock

Explain to Me

Explain this to me again,
How things got to be this way.
I haven't a clue where to begin,
Nor the slightest thing to say.
Your callow drivel engulfs me;
Can't pull away from your stare.
Why did this come to be?
This mistake has quite a glare.
What was I possibly thinking?
Wasn't much going on in there;
Feel as though my mind is sinking.
Maybe I should get some air.
Still can't understand how or why;
Maybe I'll learn it by and by.

Nicole Dasnoit

My Guiding Light

I dare not write
What I wish to speak
Although at night
I sometimes think
How life would be if you stayed with me
Instead of running off in your fantasy
Sometimes I scream, I grieve, I cry
You didn't think to say goodbye
Now I'm considered to be a great man
Better than Clinton and Abraham
To many, I'm a shining star
But still I'm looking to distances afar
For you, my angel, my guiding light
Oh, what I'd give to kiss you good night

Jason Allen Wellman

Pretty Little Star

Oh, there you are, pretty little star—
Up up and afar.
Gazing down upon the naked clouds
Beneath your lovely light.
Kissing the sky closely a distant sight.
Endless skies surround thee
As the heavens sing a gracious melody.
A melody heard by all,
Of freedom and of loneliness.
Pretty little star—
Up up and afar.
You are lonely
But will see more than I will see
For all eternity.

Lawrence David Smalls

Marriage to You

At first it's so right.
The heart is in flight.
But soon time takes a toll.
I watch him become a mole.
As time went on, dreams did fade;
the hope in the promises we made.
Divorce was not foreseen.
I can't let you be mean.
I must take care of my children first,
and protect them from your curse.
For you are a baby yet inside,
and not the man I thought I would find.
We must move on,
and learn a new song.

Cori D. O'Connor

No One Is Alone

I see you there
All alone and bare.
I feel the pain we share
Thinking that it's not fair.
I look to the ground
Pilling on the frown.
I try to hold it in
When you look back again.
I let it all out
When you let out a shout.
Will this be the end?
Will I no longer be alone?
No one is completely alone.
Everyone has someone.

Yvonne Lynnette Castleberry

Because We Are Americans

Again we have been attacked
By horrendous senseless acts,
But we will bounce back
Because We Are Americans

Numerous times we've been tested,
Numerous times we've passed the test,
Because We Are Americans

So all you terrorists, beware!
We will be here long after your scare
Because We Are Americans.

Our souls are crying,
But our flags are flying,
Because We Are Americans

Linda Lou Mills

Once More

Here we are once more
Looking death in the face
One of us has died
As well as a part of ourselves
How are we to know
When it will all end
Will it end suddenly and swiftly
As his did
Or will it be slow and painful
As so many others
It is unknown
Until our time comes
To look death in the face and say
Here I am

Kathy Rachael Mounce

The Essence of You

It shines as bright as the sun,
drawing to it all who dare to
inquire, to inspire

Your armor is solid, supportive,
yet yields its strength

Magnifying, mystifying, gratifying
the soul and its desires

Allowing for insight, foresight,
to pursue what may seem
unobtainable

God's gift within you,
the essence of you

Lorena D. Huggins

Morning's Gone

To Sarah, with love

Once I dreamt a fantasy,
Of in your arms that I would be.

Then came along morning's dawn,
And from my arms were you gone.

Love's embrace so warm and tight,
Only passed at sun's first light.

Loneliness be now my friend,
With emptiness, 'til the end.

Thus, I hope see will she,
How oft my heart longs to be,

Again . . .

Ian Michael Bollinger

The Pillars Fall

I saw two pillars fall today
this was not an accident
I thought
I saw two birds fly and swallow whole
that is what made the pillars fall
I knew
they wanted the pillars to fall
to make us pay for crimes unknown
to bring our people to a crawl
and to show who had the power
today I saw innocence lost
and the beast has awakened
from its sixty-year sleep
we are angry

Wilson Young

Sorry

Did you ever feel bad
Or did you ever feel sad
Have you ever seen a dove
As pure as love
In all its glory
Sometimes, you can be sorry
At high stakes
We all make mistakes
I have done you wrong
You don't even know for how long
You are leaving tomorrow
And I'm filled with sorrow
I would ask you to stay
But it's better if you go away
I don't want to hurt you
Just know I never meant to
I love you with all my heart
And when you're gone, I'll fall apart
Your life will be better
You can thank me later

Alexandra Culbertson

Fire

Oh, passionate fire
Its flames are in need
Air to help it live
Air to help it breathe
In need of air
Completely dependent on it
Raging fire in need
But air independent from it
Air barely acknowledges fire
Air, with no effort to give
So very thankful for air
The only way fire can live
Air, however, needs its flowers
And the flowers depend on the air
Content with only each other
Content if fire wasn't there
The flames need the air
The air is merely there
Fire couldn't make it alone
But does the air really care?

Josh Clay Davis

Life?

The right hath wronged
The good gone bad
The day is night
And the happy are sad
No one knows why
Only time can tell
Someday it will pass
Or maybe it's hell
Maybe we are all destined
To live life long
Or maybe some are destined
To die very young
Is the choice really ours
Or is it left up to others
Can we choose our destiny
As well as we can choose our mothers
Some believe we can
Others not so sure
Maybe the truth
Is an obstacle left for us to endure

Kyle Matthew Miller

Footsteps

Lying face down,
Crying on the bed,
That sounds like footsteps
Running through my head.
But it's just my own heartbeat
Pounding in my ears.
A monster in my closet,
Confirming my worst fears.
Another note on the door
Saying, "Maybe I'll be back. . . ."
Another ex-boyfriend added
To my ever-growing stack.
Not one logical word
To put into a sentence,
Not one ounce of magic
In those good luck pendants.
So while you wither
In your aura of black,
I'll watch for the end
Of it all as a pack.

Andrea Carrie Boog

For My Martini Man

Shake me
Stir me
Straight up will
Certainly do

In a side car
On the rocks
Laced by something sweet.

Add a splash
Or a spray
Perhaps the mist of a twist
Or hinted juice
Of fermented fruit.

Followed it with the rhythmic
Dance of a swizzle stick.

Shiver with chill
When touched to my lips
This, of course, you knew
My tall drink of choice is you!

Christine Loock

The Mission

There is a place he likes to go
Where adventure lurks about—
A world of color, shape and sound
Just screaming to get out.
He sees not a simple instrument,
But a noisy, deadly foe;
He'll never rest 'til he's done his best
To let his comrades go.
The spoons go first and then the knives,
The kettle with the spout;
He frees them all from cloistered space
And flings them all about.
Another happy mission
Accomplished yet with pride—
The troops a little haggard,
But he's called them to his side.
He fought the long hard battle,
Their leader now is "him;"
This ragtag army he must now deploy
'Cause "General mom" walked in.

Chris Grant

Darkness Is Coming

The sun is setting in the west,
I can feel the uncertainty,
My world is caving in.
Darkness is coming.
I am truly afraid
Of what I don't know,
Of what might be coming for me.
I can feel the coldness
Of the ending day.
Darkness is coming.
Don't say I'm just paranoid,
I already know that for sure.
It just makes me run blindly in,
The dark whispers of the night.
Darkness is coming.
Far away, someone is dying,
Crying to stay awake.
Be afraid to fall asleep,
For one thing is certain,
Darkness is coming.

Rachael Louise Hillegass

Picture of Perfection

To my mother,
Moira Jean Paton (nee McGugan)
I close my eyes and see
A Picture of Perfection
That no one else could be.

That unforgettable smile
Brings the warmth of her soul.
Those sparkling blue eyes
With their fiery glow.

My guardian angel—
She comforts me when I feel alone.
She lifts me up.
She carries me home,

And as her arms embrace me,
I am empowered once more.
She is the Picture of Perfection
And she has blessed me with
her Picture-Perfect Soul.

Linsey Kathryn Stuart Paton

I and Life

I alone in this room
My Friend only computer and modem
Fill all my day until the doom
When loneliness I call a madam

Passes the night with passion
Laying in the bed until she is gone
I sleep over the night
Explore in cyber web for fashion
Look at the skin outside the bone
Choosing armor like the knight

I fight with my sickness
I go with my work
I walk with my dream
I hang up with my hope
I sleep over with my horn
I close my eyes with my computer

Seven years I pretend strong
Seven years I fight my cancer
Seven years I breathe before I go

Handoyo

Little Clown

You are a charming little clown
With eyes of crystal blue
And hair with woven silver strands
A smile of crimson hue
With clothes of naught but tatters
And shoes of different size
A pocket full of sunshine
That you gathered from the sky
And doing all the mystic things
That only clowns can do
You taught me how to smile again
And forget that I was blue
And with your dreams you wove a spell
That changed my lows to highs
And I saw the magic gifts of life
By looking through your eyes
So to the funny little clown
Who of my sorrows knew
My new found dreams and happiness
I gladly owe to you

Libby L. Joseph

Childhood

Striking sticks with medieval minds
Dressing dollies for tea times
Climbing trees to eat so sweet
Running in snow—cold little feet
Colorful walls with paint from our trays
Reading stories to lands far away
Grandma's cookies all over our faces
Puppy kisses leave no traces
Baskets full with things so yummy
Eating too much—"oh, boy" my tummy
Grandpa's workshop—world of wood
Sunday church—we'd better be good
Holes in jeans, tears on faces
Losing teeth to smile with spaces
Scary monsters under the bed
Crossing eyes stay that way it's said
Ice cream cones melting fast
A picture painted of the past
With some tears and tough times
But all experiences tucked in mind

Nicole Markham

Time Stymie

Looking back, at my liver lack
I hold my head up high
I find my mind, by grand design
was freed despite my cries
Compost heaps, and rising yeast
I declare this world a storm
The sharpest knife, ain't livin' life
'til he shucks a bag of corn
Lounging mountain, spouting fountain
cash in stacks, tracked by accountants.
I ask you, who knows what to do
Can you really see?
Walk with me, talk with me
but mostly let me be
in waste we jest,
in haste we're pressed,
to chase this race of time.
I laugh at the mess.
I pass the test.
Yet never free my mind

Mitchel Damon Ober

angels, angels, angels

angels, angels, angels
flying around me
kissing my cheeks
i don't feel it
because i ache for god
i can't feel that either

bless me father
for i have done nothing
teach me how to live
i lost it on the road to death
i saw the flames of hell
fueled on hate and sadness
it stared me in the eyes
and the devil said to me:

"you carry the disease of hope"

i do
it courses through my veins
infecting me
i only wish i could feel it

Claudia Maria Camporeale

Life

Life . . .
What is its meaning
So mysterious
And so fragile
Yet so profound
And hard as a rock
Life . . .
Fun and loving
Deceitful and hateful
Life . . .
Why are we here
What is our purpose
Life . . .
Living and dead
Courage and fear
Life . . .
Carefree and exuberant
Life . . .
Life . . .
Life

Sam Howard Perkins

What People Say

People say
That when you find
Your one true love
You'll know
Everything
Will fall into place
You'll see yourself
Growing old
With your lover
See your future
Your lives together
Children you both created
They look just like you
And your lover too
One day they'll grow up
And ask you
How do you know when you find
Your one true love?
And you tell them
What people say

Allison Kimiko Suzuki

Stop Shining

There is a fine line
Between being civil
And bending over backwards

What's yours isn't mine
I just need a little
Less of these shiny lacquers

Honesty is more
Potent than you'll ever
Condone to whatever asks

Sincerity tore
A whole new you, never
To be mended by your tasks

You don't like the way
I bounded over you
With only a single hop

I don't like the way
You reflect what you do
But your shining can't just stop

Leif Alan Thomas

Some Kind of Wonderful

She lifts my spirits
When I'm feeling down
Or she'll share my joy
When I'm goofing around
She'll open up her heart
In time of my sorrow
And she'll say she'll be here
If I need her tomorrow
She's always seemed to rescue me
From time and time again
And I wonder if she realized this
She should have been a shrink instead
She listens when she should
And doesn't give advice
She's a sweetie of a pal
And she's just so darn nice
If anyone should be rewarded
For their kindhearted soul
It should be my best friend
Undoubtedly, this I know

Lisa Kehoe

intertwined paths

an *Alice in Wonderland* scene
nowhere to turn . . . no longer keen
deserted from straight minds
too many paths as a maze winds
torturous days in the midst of it
seeking aid, courage, and wit
shadow in wonder of you and them
repeated question again and again
"who are you?" do not lie
i cannot answer, "who am i?"
stranger, "which road shall you choose
in a game you neither win or lose?"
imagery of short and smooth paths
when it's illusions an eye truly hath
though there's no other eye or heart
no place to end, continue or start
standing still in the middle here
staring "nowhere" in such complete fear
how will i end? how will i begin?
when will the decisions no longer spin?

Christina Marie Trajano

The Paper Doll Curse

Here I exist in this dead shell.
My face is drawn on,
My clothes colored in by crayons;
Joined to all these other people,
These other faces,
These different faces
That are all me.
A different face for every day.
A new doll for every emotion.
A new me for every mood.
Different colors for every whim.
Yet all of them
Shallow, empty, pale, hollow;
Attached at the arms and feet
To each and every face and costume,
Yet all still identical in their
Two-dimensional imperfections.
This joy,
This shallow existence,
Is my paper doll curse!

Peter Daniel Griffiths

Ginkgo

It is easy
in the season of renewal
to take a greening twig for a sign
that life is not a losing
proposition,
or that maybe we aren't
a pinch of food
hanging uneaten on the lip of God
when
past the hemline,
flesh leaps in dolphin curves,
tracing warm trajectories
beneath synthetic seas;
a swish, a dimple,
spring's message is simple.
Bifurcate and beat the curve,
which is why
the oldest phylum tree
still blossoms
in the shadow of cities.

Daniel Maron

Mamaw Burd

Once young & vibrant
Early to rise
Late to bed
Cooking & cleaning
So many mouths
She has fed
Working the fields
Caring for the house
Raising a family
She was blessed
Now at a ripe old age
No more tears
No more pain
One hundred six
Such a long life
Not many have seen
The changes in time
I remember she would just say
"Live life clean & believe
That's the secret to a long life"

Lisa D.A. Bender

Determined

Beating the odds
fascinated by countless
dreams
of overcoming
obstacles set before you
Some only because you
took your first breath
some because you made a mistake
To be driven by sheer determination
to fight and to climb
Though not easy—
you maintained strength
only the Lord could provide
He acted upon the prayers and rivers
of tears
You kept the faith
knowing and believing
it's only a matter of time
That
this too, shall pass . . .

Tewanna Darcel Bright

God's Touch

I watch the autumn sun go down
I see the changing colors
Green, gold, and brown
I marvel at the beauty
As darkness covers the land
For truly it can't be duplicated
By human hands
I hear the rustle of leaves
Touched by a gentle breeze
I see intricate shadows
As the moon light touches the trees
The heavens sparkle with the light
Of a million stars
They twinkle so near yet are so far
I stand spellbound at the awesome sight
As darkness slowly turned to light
The dawning of a new day
The sun comes up
In all this beauty
I see God's infinite love

Norman R. Noble

Listen to the Children

Listen to the children
for they are not bad
Listen to the children
for they are so sad
Listen to the children
for they are so real
Listen to the children
it's time for us to heal
Listen to the children
their highs and their lows
Listen to the children
for they have no where to go
Listen to the children
the time is now
Listen to the children
they will show you how
Listen to the children
for you were once young
Listen to the children
it's okay to have fun

Mary Wright

Love of a Friend

There are times when
I wish it would rain
Just so the sunlight
Could take away the pain.
Then the rain comes.
It seems to know no wrath
As it washes away
All in its path.
As I sit and watch the drops,
It is so plain to see:
The pattern they are spelling out
Is leading you to me.
So I will be patient
And let the time slide by,
Even when the others
Stop and wonder why.
I watch and smile,
For it is you in the end
In whom I will have found
The love of a friend.

Angel Breannda Sharpe

Midnight Tears

One single warm teardrop
Falls to my pillow
One single warm teardrop
But they'll never know
One single warm teardrop
Glides down my face
One single warm teardrop
To lay curse on this place
One single warm teardrop
In my heart love was born
One single warm teardrop
From my love was I torn
One single warm teardrop
Although deep in my heart
One single warm teardrop
I'd known someday we'd part
One single warm teardrop
My heart weeps after you
One single warm teardrop
For our love was true

Athena Marie Kauffman

Count the Breath Holders

With silent minds,
They're doing nothing but standing.
Watching with troubled eyes,
Waiting for death to come reaping.
Life has become mirrored;
Every day a shadow of the last.
No longer acknowledging life
Or memories past.
See it in their faces,
The forgotten wait for death.
Loved ones feel no compassion,
The troubled hold their breath.
They are fragments,
They are our family & friends.
With hidden or lost wills when born,
They never had the insight to live.
Count the breath holders.
Help to open their minds.
Once gone, they are helpless,
They see no signs and they die.

Dana Cole Brodie

What if

What if, when they see me,
they don't accept me;
they look down on me
and say I'm not good enough
and I can't be a part of it.
What if I'm turned away;
they don't want me;
they can't look beyond
and say I should go home
and forget about it.
What if, in the end,
all my dreams die
and all I have is nothing
and I can't go on
and I stop living.
What if it wasn't worth it
to dream and pretend;
to hope and pray;
to have faith in God;
to believe in myself.

Karla Casco

I Who See

Look and see
I see me
Looking at I
Can't help but why
This feeling
Very cold
Not young nor old
See the ceiling
Like stars I cannot reach
Far beyond is my defeat
Look and see
See me I
Look at me I
Never question why
For sadness will await
Lost in an endless state
Rise above your soul
Not young nor old
Look at I see me
For you shall see

Lee Blanco

A Rose in Life's Garden

I planted a garden a long time ago,
Summer, autumn, winter.
Under the ground, soaking the rain,
Pitter, patter, pitter.
It was in a town, little and sweet,
Applauded in the scene,
When it came up with silent bloom
Among the rippling green.
The bees, they flew to it to greet,
They drank my flower dry.
Petals to ground did quickly fall,
In drink of death did die.
My rose, I feed thee with my tears,
While holding on so tight.
Like a little baby's toy,
You make the darkness light.
A thousand thorns make a thousand cuts
And I am left with nothing.
I give it away, each bloom I've plucked,
In hope of gaining something.

Bethany Baird

Heart of Glass

You'll never know just how I feel
And what I'd do for you
A chance I missed you'll never taste
The joy that I consume
This bitter fruit that fell when ripe
Has far been gone and spoiled
The clock ticks by; its hands spin wild
To regain what was foiled
Too blind to notice what was there
A chance I should have taken
Too late to change what I had missed
A heart of glass now shaken
Look into my heart of glass
My inspiration, lame
I can see the pain inside
In you, in me, the same
Look into my heart of glass
And feel the pain within
Reaching out to be set free
Inside this man of tin

John Berry

My Angel

As the light shines from downward
and sparkles into a green aqua sea,
I just can't imagine
why God created such an angel
that flies beneath a rainbow,
that makes me tremble beneath my knees.
Was she shot from a shooting star?
Did she crawl atop Venus?
Was she dropped from the heavens above?
Did it hurt when she landed
as she shook our hearts with ease?
The warm, sweet breeze
that brushed my shivering cheek
sent a fire through my blood
into a river released through my eyes.
My heart thumped with pleasure.
My body trembled passionately,
I was in heaven,
or at least,
it was brought to me.

Ian Ashley

Hear My Voice

Who are you
that you cannot see past
the color of my skin

Who are you
that you cannot see that
I breathe the same air as you

Who are you
that you cannot see that
I laugh, cry, and feel as you

Close your eyes please and
listen to my voice
listen to my heartbeat
you hear the beat?
you hear the rhythm?

That is because we are
one and the same.

If only you can see
past the color of my skin

Ravinia Denise Ray

Last Year

Responsibilities were minimal
Schoolwork was a breeze
Teachers were lenient
The year passed by with ease.
I chose my own classes
I did what I liked
No personal obligation
No overwhelming inundation.
I ran track for pleasure
No burden of the oppressed athlete
Leave that to the upperclassmen
No real pressure to compete.
Now I have a full schedule
With no time left for me
Time to study, work, and run
Just let me sleep, I plea.
Everything seemed so clear
I knew who I was
And what it was I wanted
But that was all last year.

Karina McCabe

Diary

Projects-place
Where 2-year-olds turn
Double dutch and boys are men.
For their seeing . . . and blue.
Foreseeing anything equal to bullets.
Ring contrary
To a church's chime.
Maybe a drop of a dime
Maybe the tear of a child
For whatever reason it's called blues.
Blues is blues because
It maintains its color
Of cloudy beauty because
Of its unique cultural effect.
It sustains a stench that effects
every jazz bone, agilely settling
to a constant reminder.
To a constant reminder that all
Ancestral prey of all members.
As long as blue.

Brathwaite Donna

Chosen Fate

I go to prom
I go to graduate
I leave my home
I leave my current fate
All alone I stand
As one student
Lost I feel in this land
Until I meet that moment
When all of my dreams
Are met up 'til now
The pot boils and steams
I wake up and wonder how
I'll ever make it so far
One step at a time
I get in my car
And hear the chime
Of the city clock
My bags are packed
I'm driving to dock
Knowing what I have lacked

Anna Reardon

As I Stare

I gaze at your picture
But I know you will not move.
Your face holds a stillness,
Nothing left of your smile.
The look on your sullen face
Makes tears well up inside.
I wanted to touch you,
Hold your hand,
Put your head in my arms.
I want to look away,
But where can I look?
I had no one to go to,
But you housed my emotions.
Now you are still, silent, cold.
I feel rage inside,
But I cannot hate you.
Never will I feel this much pain,
Except when I think of you.
I never imagined you'd do it;
Can't believe you could do it.

Shannon Carline Huhn

The Mailman

I did it, I did it—
What else was there to do?
My hair died green,
My lips painted red—
The mask I wear, the shadow follows me.
He was of no use—
tricking, teasing, toiling with my mind.
He knows no meaning of it.
Struggle, hurt, pain—
the Mailman,
he delivers it all to me.
Straight to my heart, to my head.
But the letters, I still await.
The sweat trickles down my head.
My tears fall down my face—
the rain from the grey sky.
I see green running off of me,
the red running out of me.
What else was there to do?
I did it, I did it.

Angela Silvestri

A Simple Word

Love, four simple letters
that represent all that is good.
Hate, four simple letters
that represent all that is evil.
Two small words,
both powerful and unrelenting.
Used too often, they lose meaning.
Used seldom are strong.
Love is a need, a want, a desire,
something everybody needs to feel.
The sentence, "I Love you"
holds more passion than any other.
Hate is a deep, implanted feeling.
It is learned.
It cannot be relinquished
and only grows stronger with time.
Both Powerful, both harsh.
Both ingrained in the world today.
Both drive us to insanity.
Both drive us to demise.

Stephanie Roberts

Unquenched

With one taste I was trapped—
The sweetness of forbidden fruit.
One small sip was not enough,
But a gallon wouldn't quench my thirst.
Though I know I will never
Taste of that fruit again,
I will always thirst
For its sweet taste again.
You are close, but still far away;
Love or lust I do not know,
But my heart aches for
That sweetness yet again.
Your arms were strong
And warmed my heart;
All I want is to be held so tight—
Hold me like you do.
But not as a lover, as a friend.
So my sweet, I will not taste,
But I cannot stop the thirst that
Will not be quenched.

Victoria Marie Labian

To My Angel

To my angel
I prayed for you this night
I prayed to hold you
And see this starlit sight
I need you here
Living in my life
I need you eternally
To hold you as my wife
I need you dear
With no sweet sorrow
Need you in my arms
When I wake tomorrow
I love you angel
Higher than the skies
I fall deeper in love
With every look in your eyes
So good night my angel
Until again I wake
I need you to know
That it is my heart you did take

Matthew Haynes Molloy

Pipe Dreams

The star
of Alice's dreams,
three inch caterpillar though
he be, spoke on high in
smoky rings: "Oo R U?"
The vowels grow in opium clouds.
Sounds intensify his song,
surrounding and resounding around her.
CRACKLING
stars,
transformation,
wings of colored dust,
the butterfly
floats and
SCREAMS
One side small, the other high!
The mushroom—
another dream.
Behold
pandemonium.

Ariane Vaughn Godfrey

My Little Palace

I have a little palace
That's deep inside of me.
I keep it there safely,
For soon the world will see
The beauty of the palace,
In each and every way.
It will keep them safe and happy
Through each and every day.
The sky is filled with clouds
For a simple, thrilling ride.
The road is easy to follow,
With a garden on each side.
The waters are fresh and clean
For everyone to share,
So come and join the palace,
Surrounded with love and care.
The palace is filled with happiness,
No evil is allowed.
So leave your troubles on the porch,
And ride in on a cloud.

            Rachel Penticuff

Over and Over

I feel the need to say something
About the other day
I need to express myself
How I cannot truly say
The world is full of hate and sin
Not from the outside
But from within
Where do we learn these things
Some would like to know
How did we come to this
And when did hate start to grow
Do we inherit these traits
Should be our parents' concern
Do they not know
Or will they ever learn
That to be free from oppression
Hate and sin
One should love God
Love one another
Again and again

        Shila Faye Brown

Blue Wonders

Eyes with gray skies,
Drops of blue rain,
Dripping so soft,
Like showers of sprinkles at night.
Sparkling blue crystals,
Woven in the white atmosphere,
Capture the season,
While falling so calm.
Quiet the white moon
That leads the blue distinct creatures,
Uprising to freedom,
But falling with blue.
Wide and blue that can cover us all,
Empty yet full,
With all sorts of creations
That get left in a memory.
With all these blue wonders
Painting a great picture,
Where everything has its origin,
Where everything has its blue image.

            Jessie Li

Sorrowful Pride

Tragedy tempted America's pride
The day will never be forgotten
People wept in pain and sorrow
But our unity will never turn rotten
Mr. President has shown his remorse
To our country's horrific loss
Some families will never be the same
As they pray upon the cross
It's comforting to know and see
The selfless support we have received
There are heroes working hard out there
Whose dedication can't be perceived
We must find this heartless enemy
And show to him our strength
For America will grow and prosper
Despite an attack at any length
Our hearts continue to bleed
For the Americans who have died
But the best thing for our country
Is to exemplify our infinite pride

            Jamie Carlone

Too Young

You say I am too young.
Too young for love,
And to know what love is.
I don't think I am.
I know how I feel
When I am around you.
You make me feel special
When you talk to me.
I like the happiness
You put in my life.
Why do you insist I am too young?
You say I can't feel that way,
I can't possibly know what love is.
Well, I will inform you I do.
You make me love you,
Though I don't know why.
It may be the way you laugh
Or the way you smile.
But I do know what love is,
Even if I am too young.

        Kaycee Nicole McMullan

Stop the Hate

What is the problem?
What has gone wrong?
Why did they attack
A nation so strong?
Where does this come from,
This hatred so deep?
Our country stays together;
Our patriotism we will keep.
We will always remember
The citizens we've lost—
Our family, our friends
That were the ultimate cost.
Of this terrorism, this crisis,
This time of pain—
These hugs we are given;
These tears we restrain.
My prayers are with
The country tonight.
My faith in peace
To stop this fight.

            Melissa Alvarez

Brokenness

In brokenness I lay
Before the throne
Of my loving Father
This love I do not deserve
Is overwhelming
In its midst
Humbling myself at the feet
Of the Lord my God
As I weep in sorrow
What love is this
That I receive
This love I take for granted
As His son
Hangs from the cross
His pain for my gain
The unjustness of His death
Brings grace into my world

This loving Father of mine
How sweet Thou art
To save this wretched life of mine

            Amy M. Varley

Epiphany

A feather falling
Gracefully, slowly, pulling
On air
The full extent
Of every molecule, keeping it
Afloat
Taking advantage
Of indefinite amounts
Of definite time
Short
Full of meaning
And joy, until the sudden
End
An abrupt realization
Epiphany
Its journey is over
Sucked the life from glorious flight
Gravity is its downfall
The grave situation of innermost tragedy
Abusing the gift

            Tom J. Amorim

The Pick Up

One and one makes two.
I need a drink—do you?
How droll in a warped sense of way
That is a look of dismay!
Perhaps some wine may do you some good.
Oh, please! No, maybe you misunderstood.
I'm trying to cheer you up—to no avail!
Here, take a sip of some of this ale.

There's that face again.
Do you smell something foreign?
Oh—my drink?
As I reply with a smile and wink
And deciding to skip the preambles—
Are you willing to gamble?
His eyebrow raised
And he looked amazed!
Did I say something wrong?
Don't be fooled—I'm strong!
A curved line appears on his face
Because he knows I have an ace.

            Shirley Aubin

Burnt Rose

Isolating myself from society,
Heavily pulsating ricochets,
Off the wall of dead calmness;
Transparent tears
Coil from the corner of my eyes;
Anger trickles
From the wounds of my knuckles;
Self-mutilation
Conjures up suicidal conceptions;
The pupils in my eyes
Arise as the flow of caffeine
Trails through my bloodstream;
Illusionary preludes
Cause hypnotizing stares,
Relinquishing demonic nightmares;
Deep breaths, cold sweats,
Quivering, unmanageable shivering
Erupts onto my satin sheets;
Therefore I'm labelled
As a burnt rose

Jonathan JLoxly Polk

God's Angel

God lent us his favorite angel
thirty-five years ago today,
He just forgot to tell us
how long He'd let her stay.
She always had a moment
to listen and to share.
I guess we took for granted
she always would be there.
We miss her oh, so dearly,
her beauty and her grace,
the smile she gave so freely
that lit up her lovely face.
Pictures and fond memories
are what she left behind.
Happy days and laughter
are what they call to mind.
She left us way too early,
and although she had to go,
It broke our hearts completely
when God called his angel home.

Catherine Anne Stewart

Me, the Oblivious

This world,
A world of war,
peace,
death,
happiness,
isn't a world anymore.

It's a setup for a great scheme,
A scheme so large that it seems
so very real in the aspect of
everyday life as a sovereign of
the people and their lives.

It is no more a protector of the people
As it once was, or never was.
It is now, or maybe always has been,
a place where everything dies but
not without some type of pride or
Honor of your very beliefs.
Me on the other hand, am one of the few
who don't care.

Elxzander Swenson

Angels

Angels are in Heaven
to greet us when we die,
to teach us all the fun things,
like learning how to fly.
They give out many praises
and always say, that's great.
They give you great big hugs,
no one ever makes mistakes.
Music is always playing;
the Angels love to sing.
They teach you all the songs
that are favorites of the King.
They help you plant the flowers
that make Heaven look oh, so grand.
We should all be thrilled to go there,
this must be the greatest Land.
Oh, I want to go there
and walk on all those clouds.
Just to be one of the Angels
would make me oh, so proud.

Nancye T. Williams

What I Call Fate

I am caught in the middle
Of what I call fate.
On one side there's love,
On the other side there's hate.
I don't know what to do,
I don't know what to say;
I don't even know how
To get through each day.
But I know that if I hold on
That there should be
Bigger and better things
That come along for me.
I'm turned one way
And twisted the other;
When I want to sit and rest,
Everyone says, "don't bother."
Sometimes I'm impatient
And don't like to wait,
But there's no way to hurry
What I call fate.

Traci S. Roberts

First Dream

For Julie
Sunshine falls across the pillow
As you lie sleeping
I watch you in slumber
So peaceful, so quiet
You begin to awaken, slowly
You rub your eyes
Grinning sheepishly, you sit up
I kiss you gently
The sun stabs my eyes
The alarm envelops me
I grope for it
The noise begins to drone
It's 7 a.m.
Another day is just begun
Another dream is over
My feet on the floor
I start the day
I look over my shoulder
Sunshine falls across the pillow

Michael Spencer Levy

9/11

There once were two towers
that were often cleaned with a broom,
but within a few hours,
they became a tomb.

There was a lot of dust in the air,
like smoke from a cabin.
No one dare stare,
Just run and no grabbin'.

The planes struck with force,
like blasts from a cannon.
Like a Trojan horse
came Osama bin Laden.

David Keith Jacobson

Immortal Love

Kisses so sweet
Enjoyable chocolate to eat
Music to hear
Immortal love in the air
Long nights of cuddling
Long nights of snuggling
A bed of roses
Noses touching noses
Dinner with a lit candle
Set near the mantel
Hugs so warm with care
And still . . .
Immortal love in the air
Now and forever we have to share

Kemill Loreto Logarta

Only in Time

My memory lays so well in my mind
Your picture is all I could find
Our love, it faded only in time
Your words still fresh
It's almost as if
I can still feel your breath
Our words stand still
And soon our hearts will heal
Still as we hurt
Our love will change
But only in time
Might we find
That maybe we will love again
But only in time

Lavonna Suzanne Wolf

Don't They Realize?

Don't they realize
That I am not
Like a new shirt,
To be used until
Worn out and discarded?
Don't they realize
That I am not
Like a rock,
Strong and secure?
Don't they realize
That I am
Quiet because they
Used me to make them better
And hurt me with their lies?

Alicia Nicolet

The Last Musical Note

The old man loved his violin
His nimble fingers
Gently held the bow
Playing melodies
Of heartfelt memories
That echoed
Within his heart

One summer afternoon
Sitting under a shady oak
He filled the air with music
Before playing the last note
Of a beloved song
A string broke on his violin

The old man fell
Into a deep sleep
Drifting into hopeful dreams
Searching for the final note
That was never played

Berdenna Thompson

All Alone

Here I am
All alone
In a rocking chair,
Watching the rain fall,
And letting my cat sleep
Thinking of what is to
Become of me in the future
Thinking my thoughts
And writing them down
I'm so depressed
Because my parents left
Now they are in a place
With no worries at all
I wish I was with them
But here I am
All alone
In a rocking chair,
Watching the rain fall
And letting my cat sleep.

Alicia Leann DeMoss

The Foxy Lady

Tasting and touching
Clinging and clutching
Her lips, her eyes
Her hips, her thighs
The moans and the sighs
The little love cries
Was her love real?
It was amazing to feel!
And beyond the bed
So much in her head
She knows where she's going
She'll get there no slowing
Such energy and drive
She's truly alive
Intelligent mind
So sexy and kind
Her love made me tender
I wish I could "send" her
Her first name is Sher
She no longer cares

Howard O. Thrall

Dead

Melt, crumble, fall apart
Let go of my brain
Hold onto my heart

Burn, die, breathe no more
I'm my heart, sitting,
Bleeding, in the pile on the floor

Crash, implode, all else is gone
And my world crumples over
Lying dead on the lawn.

Breathe, surge, heal again?
No.
Dead.

Ben Saufley

Why Me?

Why me?
Why me, eh?
When things go wrong, I am blamed;
When I make mistakes, I am blamed.
Why me? My people, why me?

Why me?
Why me, my people?
When I do good, no one remembers;
When I am sick, no one cares.
But why does it have to be me?

Why me?
Why me, why?

William N. C. Caranda

Generation X

Never been beckoned
Never been called
Considered a worthless disgrace

Never been challenged
Never been dared
Yet thought to be a tragic waste

Never been listened to
Never been heard
Though we all have so much to give

Never been so scared
Never been so sure
Now is our time to live

Page Alison Sohl

Montana Rose

I met a charming lady
On a night the storm winds rode.
Her manner was light and merry,
This pretty Montana rose.

Her hair was like a golden pool
As she lay in comfort's pose.
Her laughter my ear with pleasure ruled.
O, sweet Montana rose!

Her charms won o'er the ramparts
'round my heart imposed.
Sad it was our paths must part,
My enchanting Montana rose.

Richard E. Wood, Jr.

My Silent Self

I cannot tell you what's inside,
and not because of foolish pride.
What I do, think and say,
are truly me from day to day.
Not always right, sometimes more wrong,
I often fear my fellows' scorn,
and yet to open as a book
would allow too many eyes to look
and read my inner feelings fine
and somehow read inside my mind.
I need a certain silent side
to hold the little hurts I hide
and also for small joys of mine
that cause my silent side to shine.

Mary Alice McDonough

Black

Taken from a place so black and warm,
stranded so open and alone.
What brings us to light that is so cold,
a place that has become our home?
To bend and form us to the will,
how can we know what lies ahead?
Strife and happiness so close at hand,
why to this place have we been led?
Away from the suffering we strive to be,
the moments of pleasures others bring.
How to endure this pain and joy,
ecstasy and misery?
In steps along the road we share,
taking from each what sense we may.
Where it takes us, we cannot see,
as we feel along the darkened way.
How can we forgive what brought us here?
To blame or reward we surely may.
Our spark may shine for all to see,
or fade to black and go away.

Samuel Thomas Minervino

Unsettled Confusion

Sitting here, thinking
Not knowing what's going to happen
Not knowing what to say
What she'll say
How it will end
How it will start
Words are not said
Both are speechless
Neither know what to do or say
Finally it is said
She doesn't respond
Time goes by, and nothing is said
She finally responds
She says she can't
He's okay
Sad but okay
They will still be friends
But it will all be different
The moral
Never be friends first and be yourself

Gary L. Dean, Jr

Hard Times

Eager and emotional, all in one,
Disgusted at the other one.
Doesn't let her make guy friends;
Ignores the fact she even has them.
Emotionally he tears her down.

Angered at each other,
For now he will yell at her.
"Don't do this," he says, but she will anyway.
Scared—cold of her life;
How stupid for doing this.
Ashamed of the other one,
For now she will take a stand.
No one can tell her to leave,
Outraged that she would do this,
For now she has left.

Tiffany Marie Jensen

Just Missing You

As the winds blows, so does
your fragrance of perfume come
across my face.

As the moon shines to light the
dark sky, I remember your eyes as
they glitter in the night.

Oh, how the power of your love
has caught me up in a web of
passion always ready to spin.

I love you with a fire that
has pierced my heart; just wishing
you were here in the safety of my arms.

Just missing you!

Angela Michelle Darien

Given an Unbelievable Chance

Yesterday, a child was placed behind a wall
That made her not so very glad.
She was told that she couldn't do certain things at all
Because of her disability, which made her sort of sad.

Today, an incredible teacher tore it down
And gave the lonely girl an unbelievable chance.
This got rid of the girl's saddening frown
Because she remarkably learned how to dance.

Tomorrow, you will see this amazing, happy child
On a stage in the golden bright spotlight
The crowd will cheer and go totally wild
As she smiles that night with all her might.

So always give everybody a chance,
Like I did when I helped this girl learn to dance.

Amanda Kay Dickerson

The Light

I slowly walked through the gate without a second glance.
A symphony of memories filled my thoughts; a single tear shed.
Thoughts of leaving brought sorrow and immense misery.
My broken heart was being viciously torn from my chest.
My shame dissolved all felicity in my weeping soul—
Infinite emptiness, suffering, and complete defeat.
Untouchable love and translucent adoration given to another.
Your concerns, affections and devotion have become extinct.
You have found real love, ignoring my plea for warmth.
Alone in the darkness, I yearn for a gleam of acceptance.
You're a rainbow after a sun shower—bright and strong.
I'm a shadow hiding from the light—afraid and weak.
I diminish because of your radiance and beauty.
I pray the sun will soon embrace me with a brilliant glow.
I will forever gleam with the knowledge of fulfillment.

Jennifer Leahanne Gagne

Night around You

It smells like snow and getting cold.
Come inside and we'll warm up.
Dashing for the door.
Moving, Dancing, Touching, Talking
Just walking downstairs will make your temp go up.
Stepping on the floor. Grab two drinks.
It's time to start as the alcohol takes control.
Doing things you've never done before.
Moving, Dancing, Touching, Talking
Just being near you makes my heart start to thump.
Stepping off the floor. Two o'clock already.
I can drive if when we get there you'll come inside.
Dashing for the door.
It started to snow but, I can't feel the cold.
Next to you, I'm high.

Sarah S. Deneau

Ghost Call

I sit next to the phone,
Waiting for your call.
Each time it rings, I think that it's you.
When I pick it up,
The wish of it being you is gone
For it is someone else.
You called one night and acted very strange.
You knew it was the last time you'd call.
You should have had the nerve to say goodbye.
Instead you make me sit here and wait
When deep down I know you won't ever call.
That is why I have given up
And am no longer waiting.
For I have understood
That you are not worth waiting.

Maria Guadalupe Aguilar

It Is Better To . . .

It is better to forgive just
Once then never to forgive at all.

It is better to humble yourself
Than to allow false pride to
Bring about your fall.

It is better to avoid temptation
Than to give into a sudden impulse
And go out and break the law.

It is better to seek the moral
High ground than to fall into the valley of despair.

So set the proper example; in the eyes of the world,
You will suddenly appear to be ten feet tall.

For you will do well to heed and obey the voice of God's call.

Robert A. Calhoun

Change

For a lot of people it's hard to change.
Always worrying their lives will rearrange.
But after some time, when they clear their minds,
Good things will happen eventually in time.
I know it's hard to forgive and forget,
It's also hard just to admit,
Admit you were wrong to the people you hurt,
And always wondering why you were put on this Earth.
So hold on to whoever you hold dear,
And remember good people are always near.
But always remember when you are in doubt,
There are good people that will help figure it out.
Life's too short to have regrets
So always remember, just try your best.
Good luck!

Paula Rzendzian

Storms of Love

Love is like a summer storm
Coming and going without ever a warn
Sometimes it burns you deep in your skin
Leaving scars of undying sin
But sometimes you can't help but taste
The sweet serenity of the rain in this place
How it feels so soft and tastes so sweet
When it touches you your heart skips a beat
Love can be lustful or love can be grand
But never forget it will always leave a brand
A brand on the soul or a brand on the heart
Making you feel as if love will never part
Though one day the sweet rains will fade away
As the love you once had
On those vigorous summer days

Chelsea L. Kellogg

In Black and White

For all those who died at Columbine
As the shots ring
My heart yearns to sing
for a stop to the violence between the young
to blend away the black and white into gray
to see the religions walk together
on the walkway of non-denomination
to hear the acceptance of difference
which is what God so intended us all to be
and in someway
find the new confidence needed
in the silence that shall never fill
this terrorized world
Adam and Eve created with the simple bite of an apple
If it was only that easy to fix!

Karen Angela Maxwell

The Rain

The rain comes quietly and peacefully,
Then slowly dies away, leaving a trace of its coming.
The rain cleans our air and our ground.
It cleans our souls and our minds.
But what we don't know
Is that the rain is the crying of the heavens;
Crying out for our help,
Crying out for its security and for its health.
The more it rains, the more we are needed
To plant the seedling of a new beginning.
The beginning is the end,
The end of the Earth's pleading.
Seeing the Earth in this much pain
Brings sorrow and devastation to the sane.
I say we must stay and answer to the crying of the rain.

Nicolle Franchot

Angel of Mercy

Born in 1910
She lived a life of more than 10 men.
Pure and sweet
Simple and true
She would do just about anything for you.
By the age of 14 she heard her call.
Through her life she has helped many have a peaceful fall.
Faith like a mustard seed
She helped so many in need.
The Nobel Peace Prize and so many awards has she won
But she gave all the glory to the one and only son.
She lived a life of example so that one soul could see the truth.
Inside her heart was nothing but proof.
But there is more to this woman than what you read here.
Because when the angel of mercy died the world shed a tear.

Robert E. Denbow

Fallin'

Sitting alone listening to melodic beats
hoping to hear my heart speak
At the climax of the moment when I arrived
I am left silent because my heart fails to speak
My mind is longing to speak out to you, out for you
I would give my all every day every hour every minute
For all to know of you like I do
But I can't because my heart is not in it
Though I am not scared my words hide inside wanting not to be shared
And though there are many like me and none like you
I am thankful for all that you do
Let me stop stalling
GOD I want to thank you
because even when my heart stopped speaking . . .
you kept me from fallin'

Conrad Hill

Patterns of Life

Patterns that crisscross,
A webbing of shadow across the window.
The sun never sets on images
They stop before the sky bleeds orange.
Who tells them when to go?

Slowly the light fades.
Patterns melt, dissolving into themselves.
No longer can one line be distinguished.
Lives meld together.
New patterns emerge
As if woven by some ghost spider.
What is real becomes the shadows.

All is part of the very first pattern,
The crisscrossing shadow cast by who we are.

Vicky Elaine Teas

Why Must I Wear This Mask?

Why must I wear this mask?
This mask that is in no way, shape, or form in my likeness.
This mask that hides my inner beauty
And keeps who I am from being seen.
No on tells me or forces me to wear this horrid mask,
But yet I know I must.
O, this miserable mask!
The mask that hides me from the world
That I despise and abhor, but yet that I am afraid to remove.
This mask that is like a prison
That hides me from the sun.
This mask that traps me, binds me,
And strangles my soul.
This horrible mask that we all wear.
This hideous mask that we must break free from.

Karlene Karrfalt

The Day You Left!

When God came and took you,
it broke my heart.
It was a pain that I felt, I never knew would start.
As my brother, you were always there for me,
As you lay dying, I fell to my knees.
I knew you were going to a much better place,
but the heartache I felt slapped me in my face.
You told me you loved me and would watch over me,
But not having you here still hasn't set me free.
I long for our talks, our walks and our times,
But when I look up, I see you with my eyes.
You're an angel now, that I know,
But our memories will forever grow and grow!
I love you David,
Your sister, Krystal

Krystal Irene Gloss

An Ode to the Fallen Beauty

To the Twin Towers of the World Trade Center
Two glowing, bold, imposing structures,
Mighty giants lining Manhattan's south shores,
Sure symbols of hope, youth, glory, and vision,
Romantic, eloquent, ethereal as a poem.

Why did you take that beauty away?
You nasty fellow of hatred and lunacy!
Now, with heavy hearts, we say:
"Goodbye . . . old glory"
You'll forever live in our memory.

As you reached your end, I must confess I wept,
That tragedy so bizarre I thought it's a dream, but it's not,
Amidst the rubbles and your deaths, defiant voices came out:
"A stronger united U.S.A. will live, and will rise up."

Abraham S. Ronquillo

Re: Your Memo

Pain unfurled itself
A ball of fire
A blast from hell
There was no way out
But open space, a howling bellow
And silence—terrible, terrible silence
Damn your walls of concrete and steel
They can be made to bleed. . . .
They can be made to tumble down. . . .
Raining ash and metal and paper
And grisly unspeakable horror.
What vengeful god asked you to leave
That hateful memo burned into our hearts. . . .
My God tells me to forgive
But oh, my God, tell me how

D. A. Hopper

God, Love Colors

On this summer day she'll roll the windows down.
Driving slowly, the breeze flowing through her hair.
Observing the wonders of nature in all its splendors.

She is on her way to the rain forest to observe nature's habitat.
She drives slowly looking across the grasslands,
Observing the beautiful trees. She stares in awe.
Flowers fanning in the breeze, pink, white, red . . . an array
Of colors, She marvel: GOD, LOVE COLORS.

She passed a playground, observing the children playing.
They were white, black, brown, yellow. . . an array of colors.
She marvel: GOD, LOVE COLORS.

She reaches the rain forest. She drives slowly through
Observing the zebra, the tigress, the leopard, the lion . . .
What exquisite colors, She marvel: GOD, LOVE COLORS.

Vivian M. Thomas

Give to You

Unto this world I bear my soul,
Giving a part of myself I couldn't
Or didn't think I was able to give.
Some deepened, crimson taste of berry wine
Flowing from my lips,
Running down my face,
Covering my shrouded thoughts and dreams,
Cloaking my eyes, shielding them from the light,
Ending the pain and suffering inside.
I close my eyes and memorize the strands
Of gold-dipped silk dangling from a candle.
Here I give of myself my memories,
Here I give of myself my perceptions.
Unto you, I bleed my every whisper,
For you are the one who can light my dawn.

Angelique Wilkie

No Hold

While thinking about today
And tomorrow
All that comes is the grief and the sorrow
Life has changed inside and out
From all the events that have come about
But
Life and love have no end
Even when tragedy has you
In hand you still have a reason to stand
As a county we must go on
Fighting and showing that we are strong
Get what is ours and
Protect our land
We don't have to die in
Tragedy's hand.

Ben H. Burt

Untouchable

For Quinton
Tall, handsome, and proud you stand with all of your glory.
Yet your eyes they reveal a different story.
I knew you were like this the moment I met you.
When you first spoke to me I knew it was true.
But the intrigue was too much to resist.
I wanted to feel your body and taste your kiss.
I had a plan to get inside your mind.
To touch your heart and show you that love is kind.
But the story remains the same—you're untouchable.
Still my love for you is undeniable.
You hide your heart well, yet you hold mine
loosely in your hands.
So be gentle, try not to break it as you let
me know where I stand.

Anna Michelle McCumbers

Remembrance

In remembrance of September 11, 2001
Many lives were taken
America was shaken
As they were planning
To destroy our nation

We remember those who died
Those who tried and tried
But they just couldn't escape
Their future and their fate

Those who are trapped in the rubble
Are in a lot of trouble
Many of them won't survive
But their families just keep their strive
To find them dead or alive

Sarah Lynn Hammye

Drinking 'n Driving

Snow falls on the ground, glowing in white.
Watching the leaves fall at the dead of night.
Spring brings the rain to fall on the couple's head.
But when the summer comes, the couple is dead.
They didn't know that their time was running out.
When they left, there was no pain;
You could hear no one shout.
The man in the car forgot the law.
No one stopped him from drinking, yet they all saw.
One too many drinks he had at the bar.
Two hours later, he hit the couple's car.
One nineteen, the other just a year ahead.
They won't see their families, their room, their bed.
You can cry and weep for the tragic loss,
But don't drink and drive at any cost.

Cassandra Renee Stanford

Soul Mates

I used to ask everyone I met
either on the street or on the net,
"Do you believe there's someone for everyone—
like a soul mate? Is there one?"
Their answers came back somewhat rude.
"You're living in a fairy tale world."
I finally gave up asking for fear I was naive.
I felt my hopes and wishes were too hard too retrieve.
You then came into my life and after a few dates,
you asked me and it took me back,
"Do you believe in soul mates?"
I tried to respond, but tears filled my eyes.
My heart felt so full and I came back to life.
You'd answered my question with one of your own.
I knew in a heartbeat, I wasn't alone.

        Maureen Kay DeBlaey

I Am

I am the young and the old.
I am the proud and the strong.
I am the feeble and the lonely.
I am the feared and the fearful.
I am nowhere and I am everywhere.
I am the one who gives you life.
I am the one you meet in death.
I am like nature vast and free.
I am like a young child helpless and waiting.
I am the one you pass on the street and ignore.
I am the one you want to be.
I am closed in and yet free to roam.
I am all people and all cultures.
I am all places and all nations.
I am the world.

        Krystyna Shaffer

Ode to My Bankie

Soft, yellow, cuddly
My bankie is so special
Silky edges that no one can rub but me
Little pictures of bunnies, blossoms, and birds
Made with lots and lots of love
Grandma Betty's hands working so swiftly
To make a bankie for baby Shannon
Trailing around with me everywhere
Outside, inside, on the grass, and in my stroller
In my bed with me at night
While I sleep peacefully
I wrap up my baby dolls and stuffed animals in it

Now I'm older and it lays across my bed
Tattered and torn
But worn with love

        Shannon Elizabeth Smith

From Dusk 'til Dawn

The dusk surrounds us intimately,
Closing on us like depression.
It conceals us in the womb of its radiant moon.
We are confined.
Can we really live like this,
Kept only to our own thoughts,
Heard only by our own ears?
We are isolated, pending the return of the dawn,
In anticipation of a mother's love,
A brother's words of encouragement,
Even a human's touch.
We must push through the night
For the dusk surrounds us intimately,
Closing on us like depression.
It conceals us in the womb of its radiant moon.

        Justin Grace

Just Another Day?

Our faith was stolen
from the heart of a sleeping dove.
The piercing cries from the morning after
will echo for an eternity.
Vengeful pulses race
while a nation is left in chaos.
Enthrall the assailants,
sacrifice them to Mars.
The peaceful heavens casting down shadows,
now a haunting relic.
Martyrs show us boundless fortitude.
Our heroes define valor.
A mighty breath has been cast upon us.
Our candle flickered,
Only to burn twice as bright.

        Corissa L. James

There Is a Place

There is a place where the wind blows softly
and the sky never loses its light
where some are clothed in wings harmoniously in flight
a place where harps are stung by the fingers
of God to soothe the listener's ear
where time is no longer measured in day, weeks, and years
a place where we all once were before the rise of our fall
where one day we all shall return to the golden hall
a place where the only food that's needed
is the love within one's heart
where one's that shared love on Earth shall never be apart
a place that in words is too hard to explain
where the clouds in the sky bring no rain
a place that one day we will all see
a place where once again we all will be

        Robin R. Shaw

What Does It All Mean?

To love is to know both joy and pain.
To lose is to open opportunities to gain.
To cry is to let your feelings show.
To laugh is to make your inner child grow.
To kiss is to show another you care.
To hug is to show another you're a teddy bear.
To dream is to wish for something more.
To grow up is to be loved and cared for.
To hope is to have no control of now.
To comfort is to be there, no matter how.
To understand is to relate to another.
To marry is to prove your love to a significant other.
To remember is to constantly relive the past.
To die is to finally realize life doesn't last.
What does it all mean?

        Cassandra Wegner

Love As Intended

One can search a lifetime
For the true understanding of what it is to love,
But will never fully understand it
Because it transcends human existence,
Which in itself causes one to marvel.

Love is an idealized notion that most of the time
Is an illusion of mind, which we search for
Until the moment it resonates
Deep inside our innate self-conscious.

It is not what we bring to the relationship,
But what we receive as well
That shapes the definition of love.

Once you find your love, hold on to it,
For once it's gone, you may never get it back.

        Neil Anthony Tyrone Frederick

It's Springtime!

In our footsteps there is a spring

As we turn our work into play
And when we work with our fingertips
We linger within our thoughts at this time of day
For all others as we all go along life's way
As we work and rest or if we are at play
Whether it's spring, summer, or fall
We are listening to someone's call
To hire happiness so we will not miss
The glories of spring
That we shall remember as the time goes by
In the month of September
Within the last song that quiets our hearts 'til spring

Paulla Alberta Poe-Smith

Jasmine

Where is the warmth this place once felt?
Where happiness and friendship knelt?
Where you once were to bring us joy
Before fate played its tragic toy?

Tragedy took its bitter toll;
Its emptiness will touch our souls.
To you we dedicate this rhyme
And hope our hearts will heal, in time.

We have lost in life's great game;
This place will never be the same.
Your destiny was our inner beast
And we pray to God you rest in peace.

Katrina Kent

Fragile Glass

As soon as you opened your mouth
it fell to the floor
and
s
h
a
t
t
e
r
e
d
into millions of pieces.
When we tried to glue it back together
we noticed that pieces were still missing.
All of the memories kept coming back and I couldn't forget
trust. . . fragile glass.

Tiffany Neal

When Hearts Collide

What happens when two hearts collide?
Do they join as one?
Do they bounce apart and hide?

When they collide, they meet,
If only for a moment.
The hearts, then one, finally become complete.

If they bounce apart, do they always bruise?
Sore and tender, full of angst and pain.
Yet if they passed by each other, what more there is to lose?

When our hearts collided, I finally knew you.
Your kindness, goodness, and gentleness.
I was aglow with joy, my face beamed with a merry hue.

You enriched me, dear friend; you made me feel worthy of love.
My cold, lonely heart grew warm again
Because our hearts collided, guided from above.

Daniel Eric Autrey

Soldiers of God

Like long lines of weathered posts
Staggering against the elements
Held together by strands of barbed wire
Brave soldiers of God face the battlefront
Determined to stand against the foe
Held together by strands of faith
Nailed to the wooden cross

Bonnie Jo Duckworth

The Breath of God

In a mist on hills and valleys below
the breath of God creates the snow
Its color-flow is not the same
as a picture painted that lies in a frame

Boughs heavy laden yet they have not broke
as sunshine is risen to take up the yoke
Shadows now faded, in part they have past
with many snows melted, the die has been cast

For this is the morrow and so be it well
to live in a place I don't have to dwell
A mist on a hill and lo
the breath of God creates the snow

Lester Dean Bailey

In the Heavens

Today, as I drove,
I saw a rainbow through the clouds of heavy rain.
I always marvel at this sight, no matter how many times I see it.
A rainbow is more than a spectrum of light through water.
It's God's covenant with man,
A promise written in the sky. . . .
A thing of beauty in all that God has created.
God is with us in so many ways;
Today, tomorrow, and always.
Rejoice at the promise written in the sky
And know there is a purpose. . . .
In all God has made.

Susan Weber

For the Love of My Life

To my husband, Ed Olson
I was pure and I was simple.
Pressed my thumb into my cheek, 'cause I wanted a dimple.
My hair was all curly from mom's home-given perms.
My legs were all skinny, not lanky, but firm.
I started running and jumping and flipping in air.
Gymnastics became my passion, my pleasure, my flair.
My studies all faltered because of interest in boys.
I tossed caution aside and threw away my toys.
As I grew older my heart broke in two.
My sweetest of sweets, he said it's over, we're through.
Years passed me by and one after one, those boys became men,
but still wanted just fun.
My girlfriends all settled into a neat little nest
with babies and cradles and a husband to rest.
I cried and I prayed, "Lord, what shall I do?"
I wanted what they had, I needed it too.
Then I grew older than most single girls are,
when I met my true love, oh how bizarre!
He loves me and holds me for all the lost time.
He sprinkles his stardust like sweet smelling pine.
He tells me there's no other that he'd want to share
the rest of his life with, because how we care.
We're together now, from day to day.
Sometimes we work and sometimes we play.
Every moment is better than you can imagine,
because we are soul mates, a match made in Heaven!

Jeannette Ann Olson

A Thought of Hope

One's day is a precious one,
Just to know you've awaken to a new day.
Even though some days may be very unpleasant,
You can only count them as a yesterday.
The good days, the good times are the
Yesterday's to remember,
And the tomorrows to hope for.

Bob Roberts

The Rescue

It must have been a lonely place that brought you to despair
A place so full of darkness that you couldn't see Him there
Yet there He stood beside you with His arms around you tight
Holding you, protecting you, 'til you regained your sight
He must have sensed your agony and certainly your pain
So He joined you on that fateful night in the thunder and the rain
And He fought off the demons so eager to destroy
Because He knew the life in you had much more to enjoy
He must have sensed the danger and watched you lose control
Yet he knew that Heaven wasn't ready for your soul
And though you felt so helpless in the darkness with your strife
There He stood beside you with His hands upon your life

Barbara Jean Henry

Life

Life is hard
There are all sorts of things that knock you down
But if you continue to try
You'll see the blue sky
Filled with all sorts of stuff to see
That will make feel so free
So don't quit now
You're almost there
If you smile, you'll believe
That even life can be fair
So look inside and you'll recover
All the things so great once discovered

Jessica Ann Sanque

Angels

Angels live in Heaven above,
Showering us with their love,

Worshiping and praising God night and day
In every single way.

Angels guide and protect God's people,
Helping through each day.

Each of you have a guardian angel
God has given to you.

And any time you need your angel,
He will see you through.

Erica Dawley

Never Giving Up

Never giving up on what you believe.
People can discourage you and also be mean.
Do what you do best and be good at it.
Because you never know who's going to like it.
Hold your dreams and fly with it.
Hold your head up high and never drop it.
Never give up just because someone say you can't do it.
Look at them smile and keep on pushing it.
Show no fear in what you do.
Stand up and be proud just for you.
Never give up all your hope and dreams.
Because you look back and wonder that could have been me.

Olean Scott Campbell

The Night We Kissed

It's dark out and the stars are shining bright.
We stare at each other in a tight lock.
Suddenly an unknown force brings us together.
When we kiss the world melts away.
Suddenly we're the only two people in the universe.
As we embrace I still feel and sense the magic around us and I know
You are my soul mate.

Sarah Cloyd

Let Us Pray

Dear Lord!
Hold me close to your heart,
Reassure me that it is only a nightmare.
Soon, I will awaken to one of your glorious, sunny days.
If in fact my eyes are wide open, and
I'm standing in the middle of this atrocious reality,
Please, Lord, hold me even closer to you.
Permeate my heart and soul of your love
So that I may find within me the strength
Not to let in the claws of hatred,
Somehow go on living.
Amen.

Yvelle Fleury

The Camps

Dark, Demonic, Depressing. The Train Ride is never Diminishing.
Stygian, Satanic, Saddening. The Illness is only Draining.
Aphotic, Atrocious, Antagonizing. The Shots are Ever-Deafening.
Morose, Malefic, Mortifying. The Gas is always Debilitating.
Heavy, Hellish, Heart-sickening. The Work is entirely Desolating.
Gloomy, Gluttonous, Glowering. The Death is utterly Dispiriting.
Disheartened
Somber
Annihilated
Muted
Humiliated
Gored, We leave this Bleak, Cruel land.

Sarah Ann Miller

My Spirit's Song

Success is what every man desires to obtain,
Yet this gratification is not so easily rewarded to those that wait.
Pursuit will bring achievement,
But does the heart know satisfaction when rewarded?
Easily told is the lie to refrain from acknowledging the truth.
Frustration to a nation multiplied in persuasion;
Chaos? No, merely simplicity.
But what is simple?
Reality or falsity?
Definition hangs on the shelf, neglected by the arrogant.
Explanation lies buried under the confident.
Reasoning . . . hidden forever.

Dorren Rogers

The Line of Love and Hate

Forged between the lines of love and hate
here I stand and now I wait.
Unforgettable was our passion, unsurpassed
was our love. Forged between the line of
love and hate, there I stood and here I to
the gates. To the gates of Hell I have to
wait to find that love that chose our fate.
Damned are we that choose our fate. Forged
through the lines of love and hate. More
towards hate, than to despair. And upon
our judgement we stand and wait to be given
that last chance to let love recreate.

Mark Brandon Bullard

Untitled

There is no up with out a down
There is no smile without a frown
There is no heartache without an undying love
There is no Hell without the Heaven above
There is no hero without a rival
That's why all things complimentary . . .
Are needed for survival

Martin P. Carroll

Truth

Friends get in fights and friends make up,
But what if you never made up?
Well, this once happened to me,
But although we eventually made up,
My life was hell in that time period.
I mean, friends are hard to lose,
But your best friend—that's horrible,
And it all happened to me.
I don't know what you think,
But it's the truth, and friends
Are the worst things to lose,
And it all happened to me.

Jennifer Weathers

Why I Proceed to Live

sometimes it crosses my mind:
why am I here?
why am I born?
why do I proceed to live?
what can I do to make it right—
I'm just a boy,
someone's son, someone's little brother,
someone's nephew, someone's boyfriend,
or maybe
someone's father, someone's older brother,
someone's uncle, someone's husband,
or someone's reason . . . to . . . live.

Phouvong Vongkeomany

Dream Becomes Reality

It seems like a dream and couldn't be real
My eyes were playing tricks but my body did feel.
The sensational feeling when your lips were pressed against mine.
My body became weak and I thought I would die.
From this point of view I've always dreamed of having
You in my life, which is so delighting.
Every second I live brings you closer to me.
The way you make me feel I wish you could see
How good it felt when your lips were against mine.
When I'm with you, I could never be shy.
My feelings for you are so very strong
I love you like a brother, so nothing can go wrong.

William Joseph Andrews

Good Morning, My Love

Good morning, my love
The Sun shines like the light in your eyes
As I awaken alone to the new day
The scent of your skin on the pillows
Memory of your kiss on my lips
Dreams of your love in my heart
Good morning, my love
I face the glorious day with a spring in my step
And a smile on my face
Knowing that at day's end
With a loving heart
I'll be in your arms again

Crystal Lee Robinson

Smiling

I smile when the sun shines.
I smile when I hear the birds singing after a hard rain.
I laugh when my daughter says something funny.
I smile when I think of someone special who has touched my heart.
No matter how down I am,
No matter how angry I might be,
But to the ones I love I am always smiling.

Kellie Nance

Love's Smell

I've forgotten how forbidden your fruit was.
The sweet smell of your sweat drying on
my face as I walk home in the cold air.
My thighs brush together and whisper about you.
The air smells like she's held you,
and I know my lip gloss has tasted you.
But I'm not jealous, I'll breath you in,
and put you on.
I'll take the leftovers.
I'll pull myself away, and you tighten my
strings so my face hurts.
I'll run from you tomorrow.

Melissa Ann Hartle

One

One smile the more, one tear the less
One tender kiss, one soft caress
One minute of joy, one hour of sorrow
One hopeful dream of what may come tomorrow
One word calls you lover
One word calls you friend
One prayer begs forgiveness
One prayer pleads, "Please don't let it end"
One is so small a number
One always seems too few
But one is all I need
One lifetime of loving you

Johnny R. Self

There He Sat

He had sat here before
On four legs of sturdy and strong
He remembered the little hands
That once had played here
Sitting on the legs of sturdy and strong
As he sat he couldn't help but run his hands on the fine finish
Admire the darkest black, shiny white
And despair over the nicks and scratches
There he sat as images of his daughter
Flooded his head
Innumerable there were
His memories

Peter Eshenaur

One and the Same

The world is such a bliss of torment,
It doesn't know which way to go.
There are streams that run and do not stop.
Because we keep on adding to them.
The world revolves but we do not
because we want to stay the same.
The world goes one way and we another,
because we do not want to follow its ways.
There are so many sides of this world
that race is all we seem to think about.
But really we are all one and the same,
to the universe alone.

Teri Marie Taylor

Poverty Beautified

A falling fence around shaky house
Pickets broken; roses open, fascinating

A jumping kid on the junky yard
Steps light; eyes bright, radiating

The impartial sun on the endless heights
Warm grows; light glows, balancing

Anja Bohrer

The Valley

We walk this desolate wasteland
We long for Your peace to fall
We cry out for Your mercy and grace
We cast down every evil and pretentious thought
We long for You, we cry for You
We live for You, we die for You
I see the path before me
But I can't seem to find the way
I feel like I'm wrapped in chains
Please, tell me that there's an escape
I long for You, I cry for You
I live for You, I die for You

Brittany Smedley

Stop Loving Me

Silently behind these hands,
Eyes circled in darkness weep.
Memories surface, one by one,
Scars from the secrets I keep.
Quaking with despair, my body folds
Along the wall beside your door.
Huddling in fear, I am paralyzed;
Inside, I beg you to hurt me no more.
Stop loving me, just leave me alone,
Hear my desperate plea.
Your arms crush me every time we embrace,
Why can't I make you see?

Kristine G. Yarwood

The Rattlesnake

One night late as I was at the puppy pen,
I reached in to give them a treat.
I saw out of the corner of my eye
A rattlesnake coiled and ready to attack and eat!
Slowly I backed away and screamed,
Rattlesnake, rattlesnake!
Bill came out with the shotgun loaded,
And then there was no more snake.
The puppies and I were left untouched,
Much to our relief.
For that night we had a terrible fright,
One we never want to experience again.

Jerilyn Rich

red fox

watchful wanderer at dawn
sylvan shadow slipping silently through the grass seeking
purposeful pause at a clearing's edge
alerted keen eye
crouching
tufted ears listening among golden summer grasses rustling
feathered flyer feeding
blur of sunset fur and grey feathers
a victor of survival
carrying home the prize
two bright-eyed kits emerge from the den
legacy of the red fox

Karen Ruth Heath

Angel

No more pain, just the clouds to walk on.
Everyone loved you, and we still do, even though you're gone.
You're up in Heaven, watching us as we speak.
When I heard the news, the tears began to roll down my cheek.
Have fun in your new home, but still remember me.
You are the most important person in my life,
An Angel I can no longer see.

Heather Fortune

Bathtub Reason

Honeydew and coconut seeping down the drain
Falling, falling, washing away my pain.
Soapy clean, I cry no more
I am free behind the bathroom door.
Lukewarm water passes through my strands of hair
In my bathtub, my soul is completely bare.
Wrinkled fingers turn the rust bitten handle
As a breeze flows through and puts out the candle.
The cotton towel wraps around my hip
As my foot glides out, I am careful not to slip.
Outside this room, my life lies in wait
For my spirit to take control of its fate.

Valerie Sawicki

Never Forgotten

Darkness falls as I feel this pain
Hitting me like a violent rain
I am sad and I cannot deal
I wish this feeling was not real
I try to hide my pain with a smile
But that will only last for a short while
Wishing you were here alive and well
Without your existence my life is hell
I cannot live another day without you near
My days are full of anger and fear
The love I had for you I can never replace
My memories of you I will forever retrace

Wesley John Candage, III

Dreams

If you've lost your way,
to turn or what,

Just stay on track,
and don't look back,

Remember your focus and,
watch the signs,

Leave your fear behind,
let the dark clouds pass,

Wake up and seize your dreams,
or sleep and watch them pass.

Howard Medford Culwell

You Are Always There

Your heart has reached many people,
Your soul has reached many lives.
From now until eternity your love will cross many miles.

You are there to make them laugh,
You are there when they need to cry.
From good to bad your heart is there and truly made of gold.

I fell and you were there to pick me up.
I cried and you were there to make me smile.
I made a mistake and you were there to make it right.

You are always there for everyone.
So be proud of yourself, because you are who you are.

Theresa Lynn Hart

Making a Way

Felicia,
I want you to know that there will always be a way.
I want you to feel that you will always find a way.

But you need to know that there is a way.

Just find it, do it, and most of all, make way—
For there will always be a way.

Laura Scholastica Staniland

Tear

A love for someone so strong goes unexplained
This tear they bring stands alone on a darkened night with rain
The tear comes from deep depths of a soul
From inside a place this tear made whole
The tear a key that unlocked a hidden treasure
It completed a whole and bought great pleasure
At the same time this tear bought wretched pain
From acts of unknown and words not sane
A tear that is needed and yet longed for
A tear that is wanted does it know that it's the core
The core of sanity for this one now depends
On this tear if not the sanity will end

Tomeika Lynn Ganges

An Eternal Smile

A great day such as this has brought a smile upon my face.
The sun is shining, the sky is clear.
The wind blows a cool summer breeze.
The afternoon comes, then it goes.
The sun begins to set, and the night arises.
Still, a great day such as this has kept a smile upon my face.
We've said our vows, then our "I do's."
There is nothing left but a forever lasting lifetime with you.
It may have been a great day.
It may have been a great afternoon.
But knowing that I will be forever with you
Will keep this smile upon my face for all eternity.

Kahaku Oleilehua Reimann

The Great Mother Earth

Times have changed as much as her land
Technology has built, not long it will stand.
She'll take us all before we destroy.
Humans are nothing but her little toys.
We've ripped her apart with no remorse.
We've taken the land and natural resource.
No one will ever feel her pain.
Her weeps and cries drive me insane.
I've watched evil dwell all around,
Yet no one seems to hear her sounds.
Mother Earth, soon to be lost,
It's all our fault, it's at our cost.

Jacqueline Susann Astor

Iris Effigy

The others watch as you pluck their sister from her bed.
Their violet eyes cry tears of sorrow,
For the most beautiful now is dead.
Why must we covet their beauty so, and take away their life?
We claim to love their elegance,
Then cut them with a knife.
In a grave of water pure, you placed her pale visage,
Surrounded by such loveless awe.
Chestnut death claims her once-proud image.
A very morbid crucifixion for one so fine and fair.
You wrote her one fine epitaph
Amongst your lover's hair.

Lezlie Curtis

Once

I once loved you beyond words
And yet always knew what to say. . . .
I once believed in you completely,
Until my heart you ripped away.
I even hoped once to somehow recapture what was left,
But still, my cries go unanswered. . . .
On ears that remain deaf.

Tim Canino

Times to Come

The seas are cold and waves will flow,
which brings the ice and bitter snow.
Icebergs floating and drawing near.
To chill all bones and hide your fear.

With the warmth you give and love you share,
the walls of protection have been broken
and the life within can now be spoken.
With your will and devotion,
anything is possible for all to hear.

If my life without you was as such an iceberg,
then my time has come to open.

Barney Anthony Andrade

My Tears

The flow of a thunderstorm
Is similar to my tears,
Which pour like cats and dogs
With lighting that promotes fears.
So emotional am I,
Like a lost puppy in a hailstorm.
I just want someone to hold me
Day and night and keep me warm.
My tears, I cannot stop them
From falling from my eyes,
Just like a thunderstorm when the heavy rain
Suddenly begins to fly.

Tangela Jelonda Robinson

Learned to Leave

You are like a tumor growing in my soul
Like a favorite treat with too much cholesterol.
Warm sometimes, like a morning shower
But too erratic for me to surrender any power.
I loved you so much, most of it physical
I hate you now, isn't that typical?
How does love pass so fast from joy to sorrow?
How could I just draw the line tomorrow?
You hurt me in your drunken rage
And tore the fabric of our weave.
It's a bad habit you learned at home,
Whereas I just learned to leave.

Christine L. Egor

Nighttime

The bright shining stars on a brisk gray night,
The sound of rolling cars awaiting daylight.
All little kids tucked away in their beds,
Their tiny eyelids closed with love and care shed.
The town was asleep and businesses were closed,
Not even a peep as the calm wind flowed.
Tree branches swayed while the ponds remained sleek,
Mother Nature displayed her extravagant physique.
The dawn was awakening as the sun slowly rise,
Now up and taking in the wondrous sky.
Evening has left us as we remain cool,
Off to the bus and away on to school.

Christopher Mansolf

barrel of laughs

the day i met him was a day of bliss
that was the day that we had our first kiss
i felt so different, all these flies in my stomach
he made me laugh, he's a regular comic
all of a sudden, i let out a little gas
and he said about our date, he'd have to pass
i haven't seen him since

Belinda Sheppard

You

I'm reaching out, but I'm not reaching in.
I need someone else when it comes to the end.
You said you'd never hurt me and that our love would never die.
But after you said that, all I did was cry.
Now I'm forced to live alone in this world.
I can't believe I fell in love when I was still a little girl.
Time has passed and you're no longer there.
My life without you was something I thought I could not bear.
But now I've opened up and looked deep within
And realized that boys your age will never be grown men.
I know I don't need you and my life is no longer blue.
I just can't believe that I let myself fall in love with you.

Amber Bayliss

War?

War is around us where ever we go
and many people wonder
how can others hate so.

They kill and they maim
and shoot bombs in the air,
giving no hope, only misery and despair.

They fight over a piece of land
and call it a holy war.
If it is so holy
and God is love,
what are they fighting for?

Sherry L. Johnson

Last One to Know

I look into eyes, eyes so beautiful.
I hear words so distant from lips so sweet.
I feel a touch indifferent yet once so warm.
Where are you tonight?
Not with me.
Your eyes gaze into the sky.
Your words are so hollow.
You don't hold me close.
Where are you tonight?
Your heart has flown away some time ago.
Wherever you are tonight, it is not with me.
Parting can be bittersweet but you are already gone . . .

R.L. Pratt

Dream a Midnight Dream

To float along the wafting seams,
is to dream a midnight dream.

To fly away on butterfly wings,
to lands where birds and zebras sing.

Purple clouds and children's dreams,
dance along these little wings.

It's here I take in all these things,
in hopes I'll hold forever the songs she sings.

Alas, the sun takes hold of everything,
and so ends my midnight dream.

Corey Miles Sheeley

When I Think of You

When I think of you
I think of the sky
When I think of the sky I think of heaven
When I think of heaven
I think of angels
When I think of angels
I think of you

Katie Jane Sommer

Sensing the Sea

Limbs planted firmly in the sand;
Extended arms, welcoming.

Lie back . . . drift free . . . let go . . .

Vanished sight, conceive the image.
Listen close, conduct the muse.
Breathe deep, consume the wind.
Move slow, caress the surface.
Dance closer, embrace the tale.

Savage, slumber, breaking foam,
Crashing, sweeping, swells of spray,
Slipping back peacefully whence it came.

Roxanne Reese

Nelly

An expounded feeling at first sight.
To explore her passion was my delight;
Her remote spirit somewhat vivid,
Yet her elegant smile slightly timid.
A sigh of relief of thoughtful feelings.
I felt devotion with whom I was dealing.
The beauty of a gentlewoman I must conquer;
Hoping someday I do not daunt her.
A special person is whom I perceive.
Fulfilling her dreams, I must agree.
A distinctive bond is what I see.
'Cause you're always on my mind, Nelly.

Artemio Salazar, Sr.

Without You

Without you, all would be lost,
If you hadn't paid the cost.
Without you would be pain and despair,
life will have lost its worth and no one would care.
Without you would be doom for all,
because of the angels you could have called.
Without you would be agony and grief,
gone would be a world of religion and true belief.
Without you, the suffering would never cease,
but because of you, we have everlasting peace,
Without you, all would be lost,
we are so very grateful for your sacrifice on the cross.

Courtney Parker

The Guilty One

What great joy it doth bring to witness the bird in flight
and stars that shine against the black
as a hoot owl screams into the night

Homage paid to nature's king
a whispered struggle to be heard
and we that live here devour its life
without a single word

Granted be encumbered breast
of all we have undone
and shame bestowed upon us all . . .
for each of us . . . The Guilty One.

Margaret Ellen Mitchell

So I Say . . .

Stop it.
Stop telling me what to wear, say, do!
I am a living, breathing, feeling entity.
Yet you refuse.
You refuse to even acknowledge

Stephen P. Reilly

The Seed of Doubt

Why would you want to plant the seed of doubt?
Once planted in the mind, there is no way out.
The seed of doubt is very strong.
To grow doesn't take very long.
It feeds itself within the mind.
You seek trust, but trust you cannot find.
You seek love, but love is nowhere is sight.
For to plant the seed of doubt,
Love will always take flight.

Lu Anne MoLina

Break of Dawn

Well, I don't believe in heaven or hell
As being far away liquid places,
But last night I kissed an angel
Who whispered and giggled through my embraces.
The sun tapped me awake this morning,
Clutching my empty bed,
Chuckling softly,
Silly boy, had you never let go,
You'd have let heaven go to your head.

Damien Fuzz Thompson

My Heart

My heart is hungry,
hungry for love.
My heart is curious,
curious whether this girl would make my heart full.
I wish she would make my hunger stop;
I wish she would make my heart stop being curious,
But would another girl fill my heart as she would?
No one will fill my heart as she would;
To me, she is one special girl.

Peter Dragan

Days of Hope

Fallen dreams from fallen ideals;
Reign of terror to rain of disaster.
The pain each fully feels—
Most enduring forever.
When comes the time placing pain behind us;
This possible only through human kindness.
Watch for times anew, strength abound;
What is given often comes around.
Keep hope alive.

Jeffery Lee

If Life Had No Color

If life had no color, it would be dark,
dark as the night in spring.
If life had no color, it would be speechless,
speechless as a quiet winter night.
If life had no color, it would be meaningless,
meaningless as a blank sheet of paper.
Empty hearts flow without wonder.
Eyes see without colors.
If life had no color, are we all the same?

Stephanie Chambers

Angels

Angels listen.
Angels hear.
Angels clap when no one cheers.
Angels warn when danger is near.
Angels sing sweet melodies in your ear.
Angels are always looking out for you and me.
Angels never leave they are always here.

Beverly Lynn Stewart

Pardon

Bumping arms, a passer's delight
Excuse me, sorry, you where out of sight
Toiling as I roll and bite the lip
Turn, twist, oops I made you slip
Sorry, may I help
Please sir leave, hold hand and manner your
Existence and if you may, pardon me

Robert Waylon Kerr

The Beating Heart

I taste a beating heart
So stiff and cold
I can hardly feel what emotions I have inside
I try to express them, but I get rejected.
How can that be?

I smell the echo of a beating heart
Are you kind and thoughtful?
Can you hear me when I scream?
I feel that I am lost, lost in my own heart.

Kristin Brittany Giles

Rose

We started work while in our teens,
And many changes we have seen.
Emotions and decisions made,
Shared tears of sadness and tears of pain,
Heartfelt wishes and laughter and love,
Joys of life and dreams to come.
Throughout the years our friendship grew,
Now God has something better planned—
For us to do. Forever Friends . . .

Mary J. Kloppenburg

House of Sorrow

Upon the hill lies a strange house.
A gray cloud hovers over the roof;
rain drops shaped as tears fall gently
from this cloud as if in mourning.
Spring is here, no flowers bloom,
no trees or bushes grow.
Yet every night the upstairs light comes on.
Who lives in this house of sorrow; are they
alone?

Bernadine G. Nobles

Waterfall

Caressing the brow of a smoothed-out stone,
water reaches the point of no return.
Trying to fly and stretching for the air,
water fails and plummets—
exploding like white fireworks on the rocks below
as a river of fragile snow-globs froth to the surface
and baby waves fight like lions,
gaining and losing ground
as they once again rush downstream.

John Colin Merchant

Dewdrops in Spring

The whisper of summer showers to come—
Love is sailing in the air.
A touch of warmth on my shoulders still so fair;
Sweet chirps of the bluebirds talking over the mulberry trees;
The scent of wildflowers gently rides the breeze.
Embrace these feelings so tender and true.
The beauty of a softly budding rose
Entrances the delicate drops of dew.

   Rachael Leslie Ryan

Forbidden Love

you take the broken and try to repair with
words of comfort to lighten despair
i came along, a challenge unlike the rest
you needed me in this quest; i failed you this
as time grew long in this endless plight
we gave up on each other to end the fight
love is still strong and worth the fight but
were taking a break to get it right

   Tonja Lynn Galvan

Mediocre

Dissolve into towering backdrops of
empty dreams
to be smothered in conformist ways.
Make dark passages through a concrete jungle.
Unleash your pain on another. Steal
one
more
life.
Release all rage and systematically
mow down all saints standing before you.
Discover your fantasy and be silenced
eternal.
Hate is a flower that blooms in the winter.

   Christina Caruccio

Lost Princess

Battered up shoes, uncombed wind blown hair
Sweet innocence gone from her eyes
Can he not hear or can he not bear
the silent tears that she cries

The years are passing yet nothing ends
The truth traded in for the lies
It is okay, they now all pretend
Never knowing the tears that she cries

Eventually honesty overtook the lie
She came forward to share her pain
To her silent tears she said goodbye
The love and forgiveness then came

   Bobbie Mechtel

Lovin'

A rose is given by one
Whose aim is to satisfy one's nose.
Flowers will last for several hours
Before they dry up and lose their powers.

Candy is sweet and can be very handy
And will show up around one's fanny.
A gem is given to a special friend,
But all that you can do is look at them.

Now, lovin'? Let me tell you about lovin'.
Lovin' is for you and I and everyone;
It's from the heart with lots of
Caring and kissing and huggin'.

   Vito D'Amico, Jr.

Is It for Me

On Christmas day children wake early in the morn,
Rushing, pushing, screaming, and smiling down to the tree.
Father, holding a gift in hand, children yell, "Is it for me?"
Father smiles and says, "I'm glad you were born!"

   Henry Marcum

Wheat

As I walk through the waving wheat
I feel the soft crunch under my feet
The smell is overwhelming it's so sweet
I'll always love walking through the wheat

   Rob J. Floersch

Watching

The mountains were grey in the hazy distance—
The moon shone bright in the new dawns sun—
The trees were a bright contrast against the brown dirt—
And I—I just sat and watched.

   Heather Andria Stevens

A Question?

I stand looking at the world
Wondering what makes some people hate.
Everyone has ten fingers and ten toes.
Does that not make us all equal, except for the ones that hate?

   Melanie Jensma

Silent Storm

Through life, you are placed through many storms.
It seems as if no one cares for you but you.
You begin to realize that you should take nothing for granted.
The silent storm begins to diminish.
You should not take life for granted.

   Kortland Whalum

Who Cares

The world is round, who cares.
The sky is blue, who cares.
The grass is green, who cares.
But one thing I want you to know is that I will always care for you.
Friends, strangers, and loved ones.

   John Rutledge

The Slide Show

Slide shows picture memories of childhood
How innocent we were
The smile so pure (not forced or fake)
The ideas so premature (not premeditated and questioned)
As we grow into something we're not
Look at a child
I wish I were a child

   Nathan Gass

Time

Time cannot be held, but is a constant
presence behind us laughing,
laughing at the sound of our hurrying,
retreating footsteps.
We can run, but cannot hide, for it is at our tails.
Continuously, unstopping predator stalks prey;
an unending, unrelenting chase.

   Lynne Anne Darga

Spring

Spring is near.
I can feel it in my hair.
I can feel the warm breeze.
It almost brings me to my knees.
When I look at the lush trees,
I pray upon my knees.
I pray this day will never leave,
Because a warm spring day is exactly what I need.

Douglas Vincent Nowak

Fly

Someday, I hope to soar in the sky,
to fly like a summer's breeze,
and to whisper sweet melodies in your ear
like the wind going through
orange, red, and yellow leaves.
I'll sing you a song that reminds you of
the cold winter nights and hope of the day
that I'll surely take flight.

Shaina M. Borders

Speed and Time

Deep thoughts of unforeseen consequences
have slowed my time.
They're robbing me of that which is dear:
hours, days, weeks, years,
spent thinking about the past and the future,
but never the here and now
because it passes so quickly,
from the future, to the past.

Terry Alan Gowens

i will be there

when the sun is down i will be there
when you're scared of a storm i will be there
when you feel lost like no one is there i will be there
when you are hurt i will be there
when you are scared that no one cares i will be there
when you need someone to talk to i will be there
when you need a hug i will be there
when you are down and need some love i will be there
i will be there for you forever that's why i have to say
i love you and congratulations on this great day!

Tammy Marie Henry

Late Admittance

Your
soul
I
knew
across
four square tiles upon which our knees sank
into prayer that first hour—you, to your
Baptist God
Me to my Revelatory God.
Forever bound now we were, through our
conflagrations of heart and mind that
brought us to the barred windows of
"This is for your own good," "This is
for my own good."
Your cure came as soft white coverlet
which your face sank into
too easily and too often.
Autumn curled around the bars like leaves
unseen, escorted me home, suddenly cured,
when I was out of money.

Wendy Stewart

Random Thoughts

Lying naked in the grass
Dew clinging to my curves
Curled up with a blanket of ignorance
I hum softly the story of my life to the moisture droplets.
They listen without judgement
Sliding softly as I speak
But all too soon the sunlight comes
And dries my body up
And in the harsh light I sigh
Alone once more

Stacey Lee Bach

Come, You Are My Beloved

You water me with tenderness to make the flower grow
And with every winter's day you become my footprints in the snow.
The fallen leaves of autumn will kiss and caress our heads
As we grow through the many changes,
Changes wandering inside our heads.
We can meet our friend, the robin, whenever we choose to do so,
And his song can be heard high on the mountain tops,
Even when there is snow.
The brooks become our drummer boys
And play symphonies on the winds,
And the echo in the valley calls and we are one again.
The season may change and we shall grow,
And the Lord will reside over us, this I do know.

Tere A. Williams

Beat of a Heart

Sight is blinded by the wind;
Only sound is the beat of a heart.
Smells blend into a concoction of numbness;
Death has frozen over touch.
Only sound is the beat of a heart.
Blood and sweat mingle into the taste of one
Last breath.
The sun has set in the depths of the mind,
But the moon still wavers in the distance.
Thump, thump, thump—beat of heart.
The once green leaves of the trees now lay
Upon the ground,
Shriveled and covered with snow.
Beneath the frozen surface lay tiny seeds of
Chance.
Thump, thump, thump—beat of a heart.
A life to save a life.
Silence!

Michelle Ellena Flevotomas

Heaven

Heaven is like a flowery bed
We can't really see but it is over our heads.
Heaven is where the angels play
And watched over Jesus day by day
When He was just a babe newly born
On that wonderful Christmas morn.
Heaven is a place of everlasting joy
Easily accessible to girls and boys.
Heaven is a place of eternal living
Attained by us because of giving.
Heaven is the ultimate goal
It does not differ from young to old.
Heaven invites us all to share
So in this life we should all act fair.
Read the Lord's Word—it is a light.
Live each day with love in sight.
God will protect us and Satan won't win
If only we choose not to sin.

Mary V. Dunbar

The Light in the Darkness

There is a light in the darkness
that no one can see.
It's only there to help you out,
or at least it helped me.
If by any chance you should get lost,
all you have to do is believe.
So, don't despair or give up hope,
because that light in the darkness is always there.

Alison Marie Jones

My Friend, a Gem

Good friends are like gold
Priceless and uncommon to find
Their stories always waiting to be told
By those they have touched the heart and mind

I am so happy and very bold
To declare that you are one of this kind
And as passing days unfold
To your thoughts my memory will always bind

You have indeed been a friend
And for this I will ever be grateful
Your love, care and inspiration I will always defend
And to our friendship I will forever be faithful

Olamide Abimbola Adams

The Waking of the Poet

He wakes when dawn disrupts
The restive dreams of paltry somnolence.
He showers in the precipitate mist
Of iridescent shimmers as mock rainbows
Chase the stirrings of his reveries
To the slippery brink
Of the light of the morning sun.
The ghosts of everyday things dissipate
In the cunning ostentation of lucid day,
So he walks where shadows precede him
And the sound of pattering footsteps
Drops backwards in time,
Fading and fainting on the blank asphalt
Of the moment before,
While in the eternal calm
Of ignorant human memorabilia,
Restless dancers gather their airy garments
And without waiting for applause,
Suddenly disappear.

Steven Scheer

The Secret Torment

Sometimes, I wonder about the mysteries of life,
the tales untold.
Sometimes, I gaze at the presence of the stars.
How their brilliance speaks boldly,
yet they burn in silence.
Often I am lost
in this wilderness called life.
Crying in my silence.
Never truly finding the way out.
And I wonder.
Then I wander.
Can this be my lot?
To be alien in this unforgiving world.
To never truly be anything more than . . .
alone and desolate.
Even though my heart cries out for companionship,
I am left here.
And I do not understand
why it has to be this way.

Devera Sutherlin

My Lord

My Lord is the person who will comfort me when I'm down.
My Lord is the only lord I will ever need.
My Lord is a heavenly angel in the skies of heaven.
My Lord is who protects me from harm.
My Lord is who will guide me from wrong doings.
My Lord is who would hear me at all times.
My Lord is who will always have time for me.
My Lord is who does no wrong.
My Lord is who can make me do stuff that I cannot do.
My Lord.

Meredith Anne Grantham

The Key

if i had The Key
i'd open the doors
just for me and no one more
inside the doors i would find inspiration
inspiration for life, anticipation
if i had The Key
i'd open your soul
to look for your dreams and your thoughts and your goals
if i had They Key i'd open my heart
i'd search and search and find where to start

Camila Malena Romero

A Gift for Each of Us from Mom

April 17, 1983
This gift of diamonds we shall share;
For each of us has half a pair.
The value is not in the gem or in the beauty it presents,
But the bond of a mother's love for her daughter
Is what it represents.
A lasting reminder to each of us—across great distances or
Problems our love endures.
It shall mean—I'm here,
I love you, until the day both gems are yours.

Joan Pascouau

The Safe Place

Blue skies speckled with white glide above in the heavens
Cool breezes rustle through the strands of your hair
Soft wind brushes against the cheeks of your face
Eyes closed, you point your face toward the heavens
Your body begins to sway
Feelings of peace and contentment slowly fill your soul
As your breathing slows and body muscles relax
Peacefully, so peacefully, your mind drifts to that place
Another place, a peaceful place, a place where no one can touch you
The safe place, your inner self

Donna Corso

Untitled

A room with no window
A room with no door
A room with an ugly dirty gray floor
A room where to you no exit exists
And the walls are punched with your weak bloody wrists
A room filled with sadness
And a room filled with sorrow
A room where you curse at the thought of tomorrow
Yet a room also happy and a room so free
A room where tomorrow your eyes wish to see
So frustrating and furious
Yet at times so mysterious
It's life

Paulina "Febuary" Karina Sliwa

Our Farewell

What can we say
Because you up and left today?
But then we guessed that's what you'd do
For that big bright light was there for you;
With no resistance you walked on through
And looked on Heaven, oh, what a view.
Your heart's in ours,
Your soul flies free.
And wherever we look,
Whether land, sky, or sea,
We will be strong—
Forever and a day—
Just for knowing you in a special way.

Kay Ryan

Poetry

Poetry is slow,
I'd rather watch my toe grow.
It is full of rhythm and rhyme,
I simply have no time.

I rather do volleyball, basketball, anything
Than read about some fling that happened in 1817.
Poems are everywhere—in books, some plays;
It's impossible to get away!

Poetry is not worth it, it's a waste of time.
Personally if it was on my dime, I'd have it a crime!
Anyway, what is poetry?
There must be something I don't see.

Hannah Lea Pobanz

No More

I will wander through this life aimlessly,
no more,
I will struggle with pain and sorrow, no more
I will watch humanity crumble, no more
I will see love and compassion destroyed, no more
I will watch youth being swallowed up, no more
I will feel this broken, crippled heart, no more
I will feel tears burn my cheeks, no more
I will hear the groaning from my soul, no more
I will feel the winds of hell ripping at my mind, no more
I will fill my nostrils with this foul air,
no more,
no more.

Bonnie Jeanne Edwards

Dust

Don't speak to me of love
and foolish notions,
For I am sand,
Rolling and shifting,
Endlessly changing,
Blown by the wind. . . .

Don't whisper to me of passion
and trifling fancies,
For I am desert,
Empty and barren,
Dry and lonely,
Burnt by the sun. . . .

Don't hint to me of mercy
and worthless ideals,
For I am no mirage
or sweet oasis
or even happy ending;
I am, as far as the eye can see, dust. . . .

Deborah Anne Carr

Questing

From whence the saintly songs so soon forgotten?
From whence the sound of summers in the glen?
From whence the joy of babes just now begotten?
From whence the love of flowers at age ten?

The saintly songs you wonder about are memories.
The memories of the glen are all that are left.
The babes rejoice for they will soon be angels.
The flowers are the voices of the deaf.

Marissa Louise Robie

Take Me

Take me to the place where love can grow free.
Take me to the place where my soul mate holds the key.
Take me to the place where no harm is done.
Take me to the place where my spirit can run.
Take me to the place where my world will never die.
Take me to the place where no one says goodbye.
Take me to the place where inner beauty plays a part.
Take me to the place that I call my heart.

Katrina M. Keller

Seasons Rule the World

Seasons rule the world, like no leader ever could.
No questions, no concerns, simply changing what seemed good.
Dictates color to the leaves, and fashion to the people.
Causes happiness to freeze; covers brilliance with white evil.
Thaws away the pain, sometimes teasing just a bit.
Feeds life with all its rain, waking beauty with its kiss.
Gives us satisfying warmth, in colors gray and blue.
Then just takes it all away, such a cold, cold thing to do.

Robert Louis McGrath

A Mother's Love . . .

A mother's love is the kind of love
that will listen and understand,
the kind that's shown
in the way a mother always lends a hand; it's love that makes warm
memories of caring and sharing together. . . .
A mother's love is a special love
that you know
you can count on forever.

Svetlana Kryzhanovskaya

rainbow goddess

the rainbow goddess soars through the day
looking for a path that will take her away
to that brave and courageous knight
that she must have with all her might.
as hard as she tries and tries
he still cries and fantasizes
about the time they would have had
if only it wasn't for her dad.

Andrea Leanne Forbis

To My Lost Love

Oh, Dear Love!
I cry out your name, but no answer seems to return.
I lay under the stars waiting for my lucky star to fall.
But it seems all that falls are tears from my eyes.
I must say our memories were many that we shared. Oh, Dear Love!
Those summer evenings will never go far from this heart of mine.
I feel those sweet words escape your lips in my mind's eye.
It seems now they numb my heart in fear that you'll never be near.

Michelle Gotch

Twilight Zone

Between two worlds in a twilight zone
far far away but still so close
you can feel the tension
shiver through the room

don't try to understand, it's too complicated
it is a dimension you once will see
but only when . . .
the time is yours
Marcel Gerrits

Time

Time doesn't stop.
It doesn't stop for the man late for work.
It doesn't for the child late for class.
It didn't stop for the teen who's mother's car she crashed.
It didn't stop for Romeo and Juliet.
It didn't stop for the soul mates that never met.
It won't stop at five past two.
So what makes you think it will stop for you?
Shanna Lee Brown

Reality or Legacy

Time goes by so fast it seems
We don't have time to realize our dreams
Our thoughts are on material means
Security for our families and other schemes
But life will fly whatever we do
And only a few things are really true
Our best memories will be tied to people we love
And hopefully to our God above
George Issac Kidwiler, Jr.

Bonnie Bee

God looked in his garden and found an empty space.
Then he looked down on the Earth and saw your tired face.
He put his arms around you and lifted you to rest.
God's garden must be beautiful; He only takes the best.
So he closed your weary eyelids and whispered, come to me.
Now you're up in Heaven, the Lord and Bonnie Bee.
It broke our hearts to lose you, but you didn't go alone
For part of us went with you the day God called you home.
Ricky James Slate

scars

memories of mosquito bites
of damp grass
a voyage of sneakers: two pairs
shuffling across sparkling stepping stones
a palatial evergreen
spacious for two
alone? together alone . . .
your eyes now show muddy jeans and a red rose
Julie Keil Garson

True Love

Is true love real?
Is how I feel about you real?
Is seeing the sun rise and set in your eyes true love?
Is being taken breathless each time I see you true love?
Is seeing you more and more beautiful each day true love?
Is being more and more in love with you each day true love?
If true love does exist, then with you I must of found it
My life is your life forever. . . .
Joseph Michael Kopf

Tomorrow

Don't cry for me,
For I am not the one to be mourned,
Cry for the dusk that will never see the dawn,
Mourn for the night that will never touch tomorrow,

I have known your love,
And felt that joy,
So if my life ends this night,
I'll not miss tomorrow.
Echo ReJoyce Stickland

Reality's Truth

The feelings are eternal
The memories never fade
What's here today is gone tomorrow with only
dreams to carry on
Another day in life's sweet journal the
promises we made
A glimpse of yesterday brings sorrow with
time and hope now gone
Pauline Bernice Nielsen

What I See in Me

In me I see the little one that cried on mom's shoulder
In me I see the wonder of a new world that is yet to be explored
In me I see the rebellion of finding new independence
In me I see the knowing that something special will soon arrive
In me I see the wisdom that comes from within
In me I see the understanding of what knowledge can do
In me I see someone who is important
In me I see someone who is
Crystal Box

When I Die

When I die,
no one will know.
The sound of my breath with fade
with the incessant laughter of happiness.
My insignificance grew
as my importance shrunk.
My life diminished
as I let it.
Kendra Zacher

Share with Me

You show you love me each and every day
You care for me in so many different ways
I tried for the longest to put up a fight
But now I know it was love at first sight
Your kiss is so tender
To tell me "I love you," you always remember
Because all these things you give to me
I give you my heart, love, and my life to share with me
Dusty Stanley

9-11-01

The dust will clear,
And the wounds will heal/
I cry for those who will never hear,
Their kids' happiness and their parents' joy.
I cry for every little girl and boy
Who is gone from us forever,
But we will never, ever
Let the memories fade.
Sarah Colleen Davenport

The Four Seasons

Fall
Leaves are falling.
The wind is calling.
The air is also crisp.
Most of the animals disappear.

Winter
Fresh snow floats to the ground.
Walk around and you'll hear no sound.
It's freezing cold
And the trees look so bold.

Spring
It's now spring.
Baby birds will linger around and sing.
You can plant some corn.
Warning animals are hungry because baby animals have been born.

Summer
In this season it gets so hot
And it gets hot a lot.
So bad you don't care to go outside for more than an hour.
So get with a friend and turn the radio up loud.

Shyla Hoff

An Understanding

Open your eyes and look at me.
Tell me what you see.
We see the same, but what you cannot see
Is what I feel.
And what you cannot feel
Is what you judge me upon.

In my darkest and loneliest hours of depression,
I have often wondered . . . what if
I take one too many pills, or
Accidentally cut my wrist.

But in all my contemplating, my fear of death
Overrides my fear of life.
I may not have lived much, much at all, but
I know what to expect.
It is the fear of death that binds me here to stay
For just one more day.

I don't want pity, nor sympathy, nor friendship;
Just comfort.
I just want to know I'm not the only one
Because it feels as though I am.

Amanda Brooke Newbold

Flight of Destination

I rest upon the wings of the sacred bird.
His flight shall take me high, higher, higher.
He shall take me to faraway lands,
whose wonder I shall see no such beauty as the like.
We soar, as the whisper of wind, through the clouds.
The Sun smiles down upon my back,
warming the whole of my being, outside and within.
The surface of a world I am leaving behind
is now a mere painting,
perhaps created long ago
by a great and divine civilization.
The world with which I am destined
is yet a vision within my soul.
My eyes no longer guide me
toward the sight of beauty and wonderment
for which I have sought to find,
for there is a stronger force from deep within
which enhances my heart with such beauty
my eyes cannot envision.
I reach forth a hand
in which to grasp the clutch of fate. . . .

Tonya Marie Holoubek

Your Love

To my mother
I've been a fool for far too long.
And you have always been so strong.
Through thick and thin,
you've stuck by me, right 'til the end.
And I thank you for loving me so long.
My angel in disguise,
always a twinkle in your eyes.
You never gave up on me.
You're my best friend,
and I'll never abuse your trust again.
I love you and thank you for loving me.
Forgive me for all those tears you cried.
Just know that I'll always try to be the best that I can be,
you'll be so proud of me.
I love you and thank you for loving me.
These words come from the bottom of my heart.
I know you will always be here for me.
You beat the odd's endeavor,
and in my heart you'll stay alive forever.
I love you and thank you for loving me.

Joni Brooks Williams

A Little Longer

What I would give
To feel his arms around me
To hear his voice whisper to me
To feel his lips brush against mine
To hear his heart thump as he holds me close

Once more
That's all I ask
I didn't know it would be the last time
I would have held on a little tighter
A little longer
If I had known

Life is unpredictable
You never know when you will lose the one you love
Maybe for a short period of time
Maybe forever
You never know

I tell you from experience
Hold on a little tighter
A little longer
For you never know if it's going to be the last time

Karen Leslie Cope

My Heart Belongs to You

For Ronnie Lee Russell, Jr.
You are the first one I've ever loved or
shared a love so true.
The only one I'd do anything for, so my
heart belongs to you.
You make me so very happy, you make me feel
things I've never felt before.
You opened your heart to me and I promised
never to shut the door.
I never thought I'd do anything you wanted
me to do. You made me feel special in every
way possible, so my heart belongs to you.
How is it possible for one man to be so kind
and sweet? I know I'll long for your kiss
until our lips meet.
I truly believe you'll be here for me, no
matter what I'm going through, and because
of that, my heart belongs to you.
The thought of making love to you is my
every night's dream. My feelings for you are
worth much more than this world can ever bring.

Latorree Sanchell Powe

Outside

Outside,
the wind on my skin.
The soft grass on my feet.
The sun reaches out and touches my face.
The birds chirp and fly across the deep blue sky,
touched only by the white, puffy clouds.
They fly to the trees, perch.
Build their beautiful nests
on the branches of the beautiful, alive trees
moving with the cool breeze.
I lie down and shut my eyes.
The only smells are of the freshly planted flowers.
Everything is so peaceful.
Why can't our world be like this?

Andrew James Hinderaker

Exams

Why I think exams are torture:
They've got nothing to do with our future.
Exams, I think, spoil our day;
Learning makes it hard to play.
Instead of playing any game,
We learn and learn and learn again.
I think all schools should get the blame
Because they keep on repeating the same.
Centimeters, decimeters, kilometers, grams;
Learn these HORRIBLE things for exams?
I think it is very hard to learn;
You'll know about it when it'll be your turn.
So I think instead of providing exams,
We should start avoiding exams!

Mashaal Mubasher Khan

Teachers

A teacher can be mean
A teacher can scream
A teacher can be funny
Also they can be sunny
Teachers taught me lots of things
One teacher taught me how to sing
Another taught me how to care
Another taught me how to share
They also taught me how to care
As a prize they gave a bear
One thing they all taught me was to think
So my grades wouldn't sink
So today I have to try to say goodbye
But I know I will just cry

Annamarie Catherine Chamberlain

Valley of My Tears

Fifteen years ago today,
The Lord Jesus came and took you away.
Throughout all of these sad years,
This has been the Valley of My Tears.
I'm moving away from here, dear son,
But in my heart you'll always be the one.
The one who makes me smile the most,
The one who makes me cry,
When I think of all the memories,
As time goes slowly by.
I know we'll meet again someday,
In minutes, days or years,
But I must leave this saddened place,
The Valley of My Tears.

Linda Zacher

Ode to Superchris

What manner of man by nature rises
Above all trials and tribulation
Undaunted, and he many despises
His courage charm and iron duration?
Who is this who all hardship surmounts, looks
Good in a cape and through staunch morals and
Valor will no doubt be honored in books
A hero to all, foremost in the land?
Invincible, confounding all foes with
Countenance calm and impeccable style,
Purveyor of justice, bringer of blithe
Possessing great strength and uncanny wile,
Righting wrongs wherever aught is amiss
With powers supreme, he's called Superchris.

Christopher Collins, II

Who Am I?

Who am I?
Where am I from?
Where am I destined?
What are my rights?
How do I actualize my rights?
What is my inheritance?
How do I walk in my inheritance?
What are my benefits?
How do I claim my benefits?

Every day I seek answers to many questions.
I know myself more by the day.
Though I have other questions.
But I am more fulfilled and purposeful
I have to know my true identity.

Akinola Idowu

The Road of Life

What is going on?
What is becoming of me?
I am doing things I would not normally do,
but when I really think about it,
I am just doing what my heart says.
Is this a new road I am now bound to take?
I know there is no turning back, but I still have two choices:
Stay on the road I am on now or take a different path.
What is the right road for me to take?
I don't know anymore. I don't even recognize myself.
But if the right road to take is to follow my heart,
then I am on the right road.
But if not, then I must find the road that best fits me,
and that is the road that my heart tells me to take.

Heather Kapitan

I Believe

I believe in God.
What if God decided to
Be mean for a few seconds?
Where would we be then?
I often think about how God has the
Power to blink, and we could all be gone.
It's really that simple.
It really scares me to know that
If He wanted to, a simple thought could
Pass through the air,
And all the oxygen in the
World would be eliminated.
Wouldn't you believe in God
Knowing this information too?

Christina Marie Cooper

am i all i can be?

if i didn't push myself, i would never know
what i could or couldn't do or how far i could go
i wouldn't know what i could be or what i could become
that i should overcome my fears
and push the limit some
and if i didn't hurt myself in any way
then, tomorrow i'd be stronger
then what i was today
and if i tried my hardest to do the best i could
if it doesn't fit your standards, i wish you understood
step by step to reach my goal, it may take some time
please, understand it's not your mountain, but mine i have to climb
and when the tables turn and you are in the race
i hope when someone ridicules YOU, it slaps you in the face

Brett Dillon

The Feeling of Love

Not the beating brain,
Not the swirling stomach,
Love is the deep pounding of the heart.

When the heart takes control,
Without a warning, you're caught staring.
Lazy eyes,
Clumsy hands,
Buttery fingers;
There's still that deep pounding of a heart.

The whirling wind, unnoticed;
The booming thunder, silenced.
May everything be still for this special moment,
All except for the deep pounding of a heart.

Kayla Ann Erickson

The Yearning

I want so much, I think
sometimes it is too much.
I want to love and help and give to others
something of myself.

How to do these things I want,
to write words dressed and coupled,
to share concepts, ideas,
thoughts and theories, theologies
and philosophies to expectant ears,
anxious eyes, hesitant hearts,
and intellect.

Hoping to soothe the longing
and satisfy my soul's yearning.

T. J. Johnson

My First Love

My first thought as I awake every day
Last before I go to sleep
I care about him in every way
But it doesn't quite get that deep
The love that he gives is so intense
Just as my favorite pecan dish
Acts as if he has perfect sense
Even still, I'll make my wish
Be as kindhearted to me as those surrounding
Love them as much as you do me
Lift the heads of those who are frowning
Lead them to light so they can see
My love for you is stronger than your heart will ever know
The longer we stay together, the more room we'll have to grow

Veneisha Coulter

The Crumbling of My Life

Right before my eyes my life crumbles.
My mother abandons me for a controlling husband.
I do the only thing I know how,
I clutch a man. I love him to death,
but it is so soon. We've only been dating
for six months. I've run out of options
and he's all I've got. I'm scared and hurt.
I don't know what to do. He's picked me up,
wiped my tears, and took my fears.
He's given me love and given me strength.
He reminded me why I'm here, to care for kids.
I have so much love to give.
He made me realize, I still have my whole life.
So here we are three years later, THANKS TO GOD'S GOOD GRACE.

Corina Benavente

The Poor Little Girl (Part 2)

Dedicated to a very sad girl I know
The boy she loves has gone away
and left her there with nothing to say.
Packed his bags and ran away,
said, "I wish there were a better way."

The girl looks out the window again.
Another tear falls down and then.
The old man wipes the tear off her cheek,
but this time the little girl begins to weep.

In silence, in fear, in anger, and lust,
this poor little girl has had it rough.
Every night her cries are heard,
hoping he will come back to her.

Ryan Nguyen

Dream

Sink your teeth into the fruit,
The fruit of never-ending bliss.
You are flying,
Motionlessly soaring through the clouds
Of fluffy gold.
Breathe in the pleasant scent of flesh.
Fill your eyes with the vibrant shades of white.
Listen to the calming voices of the dead children.
Awaken,
Awaken from this restless dream of peace.
Find the fruit on the floor,
The gold sold for no soul,
The flesh of the shadeless children at your feet.
Why wake up?

Ruth Bratcher

The Secret of Life

"I wandered through all the deserts vast;
I survived the winter's chilling cast;

I swam beneath the deepest fountains;
I climbed over the highest mountains;

I was hungry for the boulder's moss;
I was thirsty for the heavens' frost;

I've been torn and stabbed by nature's knife,
To ask you, guru, the secret of life."

The guru straightened his back and lifted his head.
He looked into my soul, and then he said,

"The secret of how to live life long . . .
Keep on breathing, and don't do it wrong."

Ed N. Price

Bottled Up

Bottled up inside are these feelings that I keep,
they're always on my mind; sometimes I can't even sleep.
Bottled up inside is all the sadness that I feel,
one problem after the next; it all seems unreal.
Bottled up inside are the memories of the past;
those times that I was happy, yet those times that didn't last.
Bottled up inside are these visions that I see
of my family being together and the dreams that cannot be.
Bottled up inside are these feelings I can't express,
from loneliness to depression; my life is full of stress.
Bottled up inside there is so much to find,
yet nobody to talk to so it stays on my mind.
Bottled up inside is the salt that forms tears
and the crying out for help that nobody hears.

Amanda Kay Olaby

Corps

A low, pulsing growl swells
into an encompassing roar.
Leaning forward in deliberate anticipation
hearts pounding,
lips trembling,
fingers agitating shaped metal valves
shoulders square, heads high
pride, courage, determination
strength.
Crash!
The sound of harmonic synchronization.
A voice
unbroken from a mass of marching metal.
Precision.

Erin R. Tippets

A Mother's Day Poem

I am sorry my words are still inside of me,
But today my thoughts are here for you to see.

Thank you for each time you hold my hand,
For I wish I could touch you back on command.

Bless you every day when you look into my eyes,
And for those times your aching heart has cried.

Through adversity your face has kept a smile;
Your only survival are memories of when I was a child.

Remember that you are always number one with me,
For the love you have is my precious golden key.

From the man with the silver wheels,
Please don't hurt for me, my spirit is healed.

Jeanette Joy Vance

Passing Year

Being in love with you is a thrill. . . .
I love you today, and I always will
Love you with pride and tend to your needs
And discard the sorrows like unwanted weeds. . . .
In the garden of life with flowers of bliss,
I ache for your touch and your tender kiss
To fill me with joy and kindle my fire. . . .
The love you provide is my only desire.
No matter the weather, no matter the task . . .
My heart strives to answer whatever you ask.
As time falls behind us,
And we treasure what's dear . . .
We'll look back with fondness on
This passing year.

Rollin M. J. Huelsman

Choices

The choices you make
Determines the path you take

As you go through the valley
Remember not to dally

Because you will find
The comfort level may be unkind

When going uphill to the peak
Pray to God as you seek

Consider your fellow man as you rise
Please give him a helping hand as a prize

Think of the happy winner you will be
As others cheer and shout with glee

Carol Reed

Divorce

Even though life has suddenly been a struggle to bear
You always have a friend in a mother with whom you too can share
Just know you done nothing wrong to begin with
It's time to put the hurt felt feelings into a passing myth
Divorce is hard on everyone no matter who you are
But the sun still shines as there's still a twinkle in a star
It's hard to deal with these feelings that soon come to pass
So that you can get on with life at a pace somewhat fast
Please talk to me and remind me how you still feel
'Cause I know those feelings are there and are very real
In a year from now we won't forget what's been
Instead we'll see how life can go on and begin again
Remember I love you and am always here for you then
As well as God above us; He will make it all soon end

Lisa Clanton

Blind Ambition

Unlinked with hope that thee would free
Me from the dark slavery
Of love, where isolation and
Embarrassment reign.
My heart still longs for the
Immortal sensation of love.
Still in the house of the forlorn, where
Love is nothing more than a
Calling for the tormented.
Yet my heart still thwarts these mind games,
And in ardent hopes,
I seek thee for my heart's desire;
With coveted love, which fuels the fire of
Convictions that embody my immortal love.

Andrew Ryan Stafford

Nature's Love

My love for you is like the flower,
Warm, beautiful, and full of power.

When the sun does shine,
I think of you and wish you were only mine.

While the wind hits my face,
I think of us in another place.

With the cold grass under my feet,
It's like I can feel your heart's steady beat.

The clouds up in the sky
Make me think of you and I.

As day turns into night,
I try not to think of you, leaving me in fright.

Kira Beatrice Naquin

Never Apart

Distance in body but not in mind to the
heart in love is so unkind.
Our bond is stretched but never to break,
the connection too strong—make no
mistake.
Like the sun and horizon from night into
day, whenever apart always finding the
way.
It is time spent away, so hard to endure,
that shows us our love is so real and so
pure.
Oddly enough we are never apart, our
souls intertwined—always together at
heart.

Stephen A. Koos

They Already Know

They're not picking up the phone,
because they already know,
about the little massacres.
They found your writing on the wall,
I was hoping I wouldn't have to give them an explanation.
They breathe me in,
they thought they knew me oh, so well.
I thought I wouldn't have to tell them the truth.
I took my lover off the wall,
and ripped him into pieces.
I thought I would never feel the things I feel now.
Nothing is ever going to be the same,
no one is picking up the phone.
They already know that the massacre is me.

Jennifer Evans

My Life

It's probably 'cause I'm blind 2 the fact
That I've been stabbed in the back
By my own friends and now I don't know how 2 act
But now my dream of happiness is dying
So now it's like what's the point of even tryin'?!
I was once told that the world's a cold place
and you can't let it get'cha
But what am I supposed 2 do
when my girl leaves me 4 some 1 'cause he's rich'a?
So now my only friend is my misery
'Cause I let my loneliness get 2 me
But what doesn't kill ya only makes you stronger right?
That's 2 bad 'cause I'd rather be dead
than live with fake people any longer.

Jeffrey Paul Moyer

The Swings

Down like a slow departure
From a milky white mass of sky
The wind immodestly lifting up my skirt.
Thursday black string underwear
Can you see him?

Ideas of a slow-world wind chime
Enter my bloodstream as I
Climb on the swings
The mercurial substance weighing me down.

But my feet keep running

And running
Until I reach the edge of the cliff
And I am finally flying.

Celia B. Parada

Grandpa

I pray for the day to see you again
To put this sorrow to an end.
God took you with no warning. . . .
Left my heart with so much mourning.
Grandpa, I miss you so much. . . .
What I would do for one more touch.
The days go by and you're not here,
But in my heart you will always be near.
I remember the last words you said to me,
And as long as I live they will always be.
You were always one of the best men in my life;
No one can change that no matter the price.
Our day will come when we meet again;
I will be expecting an embrace that never ends.

Tebeth Erin Brooks

Each and Every Day

I covet not what is in my heart,
but of my mind's desire,
but dare not say, for thoughts of loneliness.
Of the hardships we have,
I know in you burns a passion for me,
but nor you even whisper it, for your fear of end,
fear of change of time and place
and everything thereof.
But let not your silence end this passion,
for it drives the soul on it,
pushes your sanity with an angel's touch
to keep you living it, to let you find comfort in mine eyes,
to feel ease in my touch, to know this is what I live for
each and every day.

Derick Rhinehart

Because I Love You

To my older brother, Lachlan: I hate to love you.
I'm scared that he will leave me.
I'm scared that he will go.
I'm scared something will happen and I will be left alone.
I'm scared that our closeness has been lost in time.
I'm scared that you're getting too caught up in crime.
I'm scared that you will forget me and never ring or call.
I'm scared that you don't love me anymore at all.
I'm scared because I miss you so much that it hurts.
I'm scared because you make me cry.
I'm so scared that, like Mum, you will die.
I'm scared that you will find a life somewhere other.
I'm scared because I love you,
My one and only brother.

Courtney Lee St. Clair

Alone

Being alone is really so sad,
going through memories, the things that you had.
To sit and to think one day at a time,
no person to hold, no mountain to climb.
Your body is still, no motion no grace,
you put your head down or stare into space.
Your mind starts to think of things you should do,
but you don't do anything as if stuck down with glue.
The more your ALONE the harder it gets,
to escape your prison like dolphins in nets.
You become a recluse and cannot break free,
will anybody save you, Please, "who has the key?"
What has life in store, do you have the strength to get out,
because your mouth is wide open and no one hears your shout.

Brian Robinson

The Pig Am I

I sat down to a meeting between the pig and I.
I said the pig was baleful. It turned out to be a lie.

He said he saw me eating a missing minced meat pie.
I said they should be grateful for all the pies I buy.

He said, "Clean up your house, it stinks just like a sty."
I said, "Just one more plateful . . . or wait 'til pigs can fly."

I added, "You're a louse," and this was his reply:
"Don't think that I am hateful. To do my job I try."

But then the end was looming beneath the starry sky.
In truth I wasn't spiteful; I opened up my eye.

I ceased my pie consuming, and washed it down with rye.
It came clear before I ate full: The real pig was I.

Roger Neal Christenson

My Dream

My dream is everlasting until I wake up.
Then I live a nightmare that just won't give up.

At times my life seems hopeless, I feel I can't go on.
But death itself scares me, just the thought of being gone.

My friends try to help me, they say all I have to do is tell.
They don't seem to realize I live life as a total hell.

My heart has been broken time and time again.
But I can't help myself, and I trust him again.

Well, here I am; it's just me and this gun.
I'm saying goodbye, even though my life has just begun.

My dream is everlasting, I'll never wake up.
I won't have to live a nightmare that just won't give up.

Thrisha Ann Wilder

Dreams

If you are wondering why I am here,
There is a simple answer. For I am a dream,
A dream of whose? you may ask. There is a simple answer.
For this person you may not know. But I know her very well.
Are you still wondering why I am here and who this person is?
If so, please realize that I am someone
That she was never able to be. For I am her dream.
Are you wondering why I am her dream? I am her dream!
For I am her daughter living out her dream.
Why? you may ask. There is a simple answer.
She left this evil world to help guide me;
Now my job is to fulfill her dream and to live out my own dreams.
Soon we will see who will live my dreams.
Will it be me, or someone who is special to me?

Natasha D. Smith

Ever Changing World

The frozen wind that once burdened our breath gradually melts away.
Our world boasts signs of a warmth to our souls coming in near day.
When the glorious day entwines with our world,
we sense joy begins to stir and swirl.
Our heart of ice is conquered
for the great coming of the new beginning.
The world of Spring, warm and carefree,
changes our heart for a new you and me.
What is this perplexing sensation, this dawn of creation?
It's Spring! Our time of change when our heart, once of ice,
transforms to gold.
We greet the great new, and bid farewell to the old.
Our forever-living wishes finally unfurled,
we are once again reminded of our ever-changing world.

Daniel Peter Mancini

Dan

A mother's love is like an underground stream
Everlasting, calm, but strong.

Though daily it's shown, but not too extreme,
Until the day when something goes wrong.

A shot rang out that shattered the night.
"There's been an accident." I think it was murder.

A mother prays to God, "This just isn't right."
But for family and friends, the stream was a girder.

All alone now, the stream's just a trickle,
Allowing the tears which last so long,

To fill the Earth and filter down.
Everlasting, calm, and strong.

Carol Frances Nelson

An Austere Place Called Earth

It's too damn arduous to live in this world these days
where violence displays!
Terrorists, serial killers, and rapists roam.
To most, the only safe place is home.
Young girls having babies, only to abort.
Ambitious people yearning more, only to extort.
Illegal drugs spread, altering people into robots.
Blood spills universally as a lunatic fires shots.
With no way out,
this world a perilous place without a doubt.
So to God we give praise
while trapped in a maze.
Like a prisoner in a cell,
Planet earth's a living hell.

Raul Ochoa Alcaraz

Mother's Lullabies

As we were driving, I caught her eyes,
While she was singing our lullabies.
The singing was sweet, and the love so great,
As I sat in my seat, the spirit left no hate.
Then all was quiet, and she started to cry,
While she was singing our lullabies.
On the drive home, she sang them to us,
Each one so special, and filled with love.
Then I began to wonder at that time why,
Why did she sing to us our lullabies.
In that moment, the tears coming down,
I felt my mother's love, I felt it all around.
I want to see my mother, and her shining eyes.
And hear her sing to us, our lullabies.

Dustin Cade Barnum

Soul Searching

You told me I was trying too hard
To find the one true love to fill this void in my heart

You said all good things come to those who wait
And my search would come to an end by a meeting of fate

I searched for the missing part of my soul
In every man I came to meet and know

Each attempt to find my chosen partner
Made my heart grow weary and harder

You were the one I relied on each time
To help me pick me up the pieces of my broken life

Taking risks and falling down made me realize you were right
All along, my one true love was right before my eyes

Janet L. Pifer

The Next Time

Next time
. . . I will understand
. . . I will speak less and listen more
. . . I will smile a little more
. . . I will not judge
. . . I will think before I speak
. . . I will be less critical
. . . I will ask you how you feel
. . . I will give you your space
. . . I will nag less and encourage more
. . . I will take your advice
. . . I will ask your opinion
. . . I will laugh with you
. . . I will love you more . . .

Michele Ann Burpee

Afraid to Cry

Never bite off more than you can chew
Don't let your heart get the best of you
Always believe in love at first sight
Always stand up for what you know is right
Smile when you answer the phone
They'll hear it in your voice
Always be proud of this country's freedom
The freedom of choice
Walk a mile in their shoes
Before you criticize
When you talk to someone you care about
Look them in the eye
And never ever, ever
Be afraid to cry

Mikala Andrea Cryder

Why Can't He See Me?

Hey you, see that guy over there?
One day he is gonna care.
He likes to play hard to get.
He likes blondes, I bet.
Why does it hurt so much
When he walks away and acts so tough?
Why can't he just turn around and look at me?
Am I see-through, is that why he can't see?
I can never defend myself on my behalf,
So all he does is sit there and laugh.
Why can't I control the way I feel?
He doesn't even notice that I'm real.
I guess that teaches me the greatest lesson of all:
You can lead a heart to love, but you can't make it fall.

Connie Jay Cordell

One More Day

We thought we had it made, but look at us now.
On the Black Tuesday, our lives turned upside down.
"Mommy, I'm tired, when's daddy coming come?"
"Mommy, I'm hungry, when are we gonna eat?"
What's one more day? Why am I so scared?
Of one more day, living in this nightmare.
I'll never forget that day, when we had
To give it all away. The memories of my dad.
From a warm farmhouse, out into the streets.
From food on the table, to hardly anything to eat.
"Honey, I don't know when your daddy's coming home."
"Baby, I'm sorry, but there's nothing to eat."
"And baby, I wish I knew how I'm gonna get us through
just one more day."

Lori Herman

Chipped Nail Polish, Monday Mornings

Chipped nail polish, Monday morning
And you're still in my head.

You still haven't returned the calls
Of my hollow, longing voice lingering on your machine.

Your haunting smile on your chiseled face
Still diddles here in my mind.

Your look of excitement in those velvety chocolate eyes
No longer surfaces in real life.

My dreams of you are tattered and torn
Like my chipped nail polish,

Monday mornings,
And your absent phone calls.

Char-lynn Antonette Griego

The Incontestable

Death, the immortal pursuer of life,
Perpetually stalking through time and space,
Tirelessly wielding the dreaded scythe.
Eternally looming in every place,
Until the moment when the time has come,
For Death to strike and overtake its prey,
The deadly scythe falls and the deed is done,
And the prey never sees the light of day.
The victim lies within Mother Earth,
Eventually decaying into dust,
Which as the foundation of life gives birth,
to the impending victim of Death's lust.
The predator of life gives back to it,
Only to extinguish the light it lit.

Steven Ng

Man of Contradiction

His hair is as dark as night,
but in his eyes I can see a bright light.
His spirit is as free as the wind,
yet his heart is as heavy as a ten-pound weight.
His soul is like an open book,
yet he is tight-lipped and won't say a word.
What's in his mind is a total mystery,
yet you can read his face like a book.
He's full of love, yet there is hatred;
he's full of wit, yet he's extremely serious;
he's hard-working, yet he's as playful as a child;
he's self-confident, yet there is fear;
he's a man of contradiction.
He's the man I love.

Julie A. Strong

Death's Burden

Black Death stalks me throughout the endless night.
He comes in many guises in my dreams.
Death follows me as I search for the light.
No single soul heeds my terrified screams.
I meet Death as he creeps in darkened streets,
While he searches for unenlightened souls,
For men who live their lives in self-deceit.
Death gives mankind no mercy or parole.
He's filled with vengeance, for he cannot live.
Death cares not for the fate of pointless lives.
His heart is cold and he cannot forgive,
Yet I watch him with my impartial eyes.
Death lies bared in an unguarded moment.
I've seen his face and it's filled with torment.

Rebecca Lane

Repentant Heart

Oh, how the repentant heart
When the pleasure and moment are ripped apart
The ecstasy is gone and pushed away
Yet the reminder of her continues to stay
He warned, pleaded and asked of me
But I chose to be blind with every plea
"My child why do you ruin your body and my temple
Is not my law very simple?"

I dwelt in the den of sin
No stronger than other men
Yet I am to be a different man
One that follows a righteous stand
My body aches for the night
To seek evil with all my might

James Wine Nellis, II

Mornings, Days, 'n Nights

In the morning when I wake up, I think
Think about how lucky I really am
Lucky to have you, my best friend and love
My heart and soul long for you at my side
During the long days, I gaze into space
Thinking of your luscious lips and soft kiss
Dreaming of holding you and touching you
Feeling your smooth skin and caressing it
Knowing that you care for me above all
And that true love controls your heart and mine
At night, I fall asleep with you in mind
I stare at the moon and drift to dreamland
I dream of you and I getting married
And us living together forever

Derek M. T. Hoff

Journey

Feeling so sad, always melancholy,
Getting so hurt the heart starts to feel fear,
Again forsaken by Love's own folly,
Thyself alone with solitary tear.
Oneself's own strength inside is the fortress,
That binds and envelops morose and shame.
With tenderness of Love and vast kindness,
Journey begins to the wavering flame.
From the darkness beyond shadow and night,
Hope lies eternal for the task ahead,
To find the soul completing one's own light,
Merging even deeper than lovers wed.
Travel from loneliness through pain and fear,
The blue sky will become forever clear.

Young Chang

Star

In my dreams I fly above the sky,
watching the world slowly passing by.

With my sorrows left behind so far,
I am free to be among the stars.
Their beauty burns so bright,
like guiding lights in the dark night,
leading to hope and love,
sent to troubled souls from the heavens above.

When the world is cold,
and your heart hasn't the strength to be bold,
remember the end has yet to be told.

Happiness is never far;
just look up and find your star.

Vanessa K. Hodgson

Have You Ever Found the One?

Have you ever been scared
You wouldn't find the one
The one God meant you to be with
The one God put you on the Earth to love?
Have you met someone you love
And got excited
Thinking that person is the one?
Then you split up
Now you're heartbroken
Then one day you bump into a woman or a man
And it's love at first sight
Then you spend the rest of your lives together
So
Have you ever found the one?

Danielle B. F. Walker

Today Is Tomorrow

There are many obstacles in my life that I have overcome
Yet, at the same time, I feel my life has just begun
Like a ball of yarn that has been unthreaded
You would think there is nothing left
But look again and the ball has re-thread
A chance to reclaim one's self
Not to say that our past will be erased
After all, that is how the present, we create
If you look inside a heart unclosed
The whole wide world, you could expose
So be careful what you do
The choices you make could be deja vu
And be careful what you say
Consequences once served before, you just might reclaim

Marjorie Robinson

Bad Timing

To the moon that connects me with you love,
Thank you for never abandoning me.
Your body warmed me—my soul's winter glove.
Still, it restricts me from turning my key,
Unlatching a girl from her small town.
I want to stand on the rock where we danced
Just to remember how our bodies bound,
Not with each other; with the moon, in a trance.
The distance of love, weary of our trust;
Our bittersweet endings marked by daybreak.
Our hearts know passion will finally rust;
The moon falls away and now we're awake.
Our lives after all fall into strange places,
Like a deck of cards and its two red aces.

Laura Parker

Baggage

I see all this baggage on a man
Only I can see the baggage that he carries
He has a shopping cart and some pans
But I can see what he truly hides and carries
He carries the backpack of pain
The sack of greed
And the book of hate
All this nastiness he contains
He considers death to be his mate
I can see his silent complaints
All this baggage might seem like a lot
But look in you and you might find some of his bags too
And you should give this poem a thought
That you are this man and you have his bags too

William James Brownlie

Isolated

The lake was still, calm.
Animals drank from it, fed from it, yet it was calm.
My heart felt like exploding, but no—still, calm.
There was nothing around, not anywhere near-isolation.
I was deep inside my soul, locked within.
The only living things near it were
animals
trees
plants.
Things with no human language, no one to hear a cry in the night.
Faint ripples appeared on the lake, growing larger. Then they stop.
Still.
Calm.
Isolation.

Kara Marie Bensley

Loneliness

Oh, what a mess I am!
Out for attention . . . could that be it?
I feel so alone, yet my friends are always there.
I slide out the door and no one seems to care.
I lie, I dream.
I cry, I scream.
Wanting and waiting for everything to come out right.

My life is a mess, a great big mess.
Dreaming doesn't help
And neither does lying,
But I can't stop this never-ending pattern of confusion.
I lie, I dream.
I cry, I scream.
Wishing and hoping that everything will be okay.

Laura Pilcher

My Life, My Heart, My Soul

My Life holds meaning with you near my side
I cannot seem to feel enough of you
Although I sometimes let my selfish pride
Act as a shield, blocking my feelings true.
My Heart yearns for return of the same love
Bright crimson it burns, bright until the end
With Fate watching and guiding from above
To no one else will my heart ever bend.
My Soul cries out for comfort and for peace
Which only you seem able to bring me
Please do not leave me, not myself release
For from myself to you, I often flee.
The thought of losing you I will not fear
You must know that I love you true and dear. . . .

Daphne Shutt

In Ways

In ways, you are the one.
In ways, you make me laugh to the fullest.
In ways, you are the best friend in the whole world.
In ways, you are always here.

In ways, you are not always here.
In ways, you are so mean.
In ways, you ignore me.
In ways, you're cruel.

But, in ways, you make me smile.
In ways, you make me forget my worries.
In ways, you make me fantasize a thousand dreams.
In ways, you make me complete.

In ways, you are the one and only one for me.

Jay Lim

You Can't Understand

If you only knew
I was there
I saw it happen
You couldn't think of the pain I saw that night.
You could never imagine it
You weren't there
You didn't see it
You didn't see the pain in her eyes
When she was there
You didn't hear the screams
You didn't listen to her cries
You weren't there
You couldn't feel the pain
You couldn't see it either

Stacy L. Wagner

Lost

I watch him daily.
He falls.
He forgets.
I don't understand.
This is the hardest time in life.
God, I don't want to give up life to prolong his.
How can he just wither away?
I watch him fall deeper and deeper
Into nothingness of his past.
This disease takes him away.
My love makes him stay.
His mind goes, his body stays,
His life slowly drifting into

Katie Buckley

A Mother's Day in Heaven

In loving memory of my mom
You were the one that meant so much,
it seems to me you were the crutch
that held me up when I was down.
And every time I hear the sound
of someone's voice that sounds like yours,
I turn to look and you're behind closed doors.
What I can't touch or I can't see
that person I know is missing me.
But someday I know we'll meet again
And we will sit in heaven's den.
I just can't imagine how happy you must be,
Leaving behind your every thought,
and much good deeds.

Amanda Roberts

My Dear Friend, Wess

A harsh grave and a nearly end
A brief but beautiful life, my friend
I miss you—why did you have to go?
But you are happy somehow, I know
When they told me best friend had died
I felt so cold, I never cried
Where the car wrecked, there's still a stain
As in agony you had lain
The people don't notice, they drive on
I want to tell them, stop, cry with me—he's gone
I am going to cry again
For one last time
Goodbye, my friend
I will miss you forever

Shentel Trahan

The Enemy Within

Our dead are still with us, their spirits linger on.
Unseen yet felt, as hearts do melt and tears fill the dawn.
We pray for forgiveness with weak, uplifted hands,
As we plan to strike down men who hide in foreign, faraway lands.
Terrorists came with cancer's stealth,
They plundered our land and stole our wealth.
The wealth of innocent, precious lives;
Our children, elderly, husbands, wives . . .
I struggle daily with my soul, angry and upset.
I wonder how to kill them all, repenting with regrets.
Like poor men begging at God's door, I ask to enter in;
Then pray to God to make us wise, as we struggle with these sins.
I can't imagine playing fair, while wondering more and more
About the evil of men's intent that sends us off to war.

Carolyn Tann-Starr

Heaven's Omen

Rainfall falls from my eyes like teardrops.
Flowers wilt and die from my pain.
My heart pounds on my ribs and rips in two.
I jump off a fluffy cloud into the moist, warm air.
I land into a heaven with hells throughout the lights and rainbows.
I'm crying; a flower collects all my tears dripping off my face.
I faint to the ground, thinking of someone special.
I love that person so.
It breaks my heart to even think of him.
I cry and weep like a flower.
I think of him like a butterfly, landing on my petal of tears.
They are blow away by the cold, dark, and gruesome wind.
It blows on my eyes of tears.
The light shines down on my Heaven's omen.

Michelle Laster

Conscious

To the tear spotted eyes and the sign detector of the lies.
Currents trace around dream routes.
Fighting the strongest wind force thrown at you every day.
Around to every indented angle.
Walking in a tolerance condition.
Balancing on the clutches of uncertainty, threatening of solitary.
Dead thoughts float from insincerity.
Swimming with fallacies and lies.
Fighting the storm.
With inner part of temper.
Adorning the outside with waves.
Covering with a blanket of stars and security.
Puddles outcry soft words of rebellion.
Everything is the way it has to be.

Katherine Varrati

Live On!

Praise be, I'm 88 and I feel just fine!
So why not tempt fate, and shoot for 99?
With help from the Almighty, why not go for 90?
90's good, but it's lots more fun to hit the number 91.
On and on it's mighty few who ever reach 92.
So why not a darer be, and trudge along to 93.
And as I have said before, what's wrong with 94?
And since I'm still alive, I'll head on into 95.
And barring any unlucky tricks, I'll coast on into 96.
Though I think I'd like Heaven, I think I'll try for 97.
On and on, tempting fate, why not go for 98?
And since I'm feeling fine, why not go for 99?
One hundred, good grief, I'll reach it with a sigh of relief.
Beyond that I cannot rightly tell, it all depends if I'm feeling well!

Anice R. Badie

My Story

Why do you treat me like you do?
You scream, you yell, you make me blue.
You say you love me, never untrue.
I always believe you, I need to get a clue.
You flirt with my friends, do you love them too?
Might as well, you're lying to me, I need to get a new.
Into a million pieces you've broken my heart.
Why can't I move on, why can't I part?
You have a way with words
To make me believe you, then get hurt.
I think I've learned my lesson this time.
So I'm through with you, I'm gonna get what's mine.
And that's the story, sad but true.
That's how I left him to start anew.

Shelly Davies

Cold Rain

Running down the dark path,
a feeling of grief,
with knots in my stomach.
I collapse and fall to my knees.
I am panting, trying to catch my breath.
In the silent night begins the drizzle of the soft cold rain.
I close my eyes as I succumb to my emotions. I begin to cry.
The warm tears mixing with the cold rain,
as they stream down my face.
I never felt so alone.
Fond memories of the past have all been shattered.
Why did it happen?
What have I done?
I saw her with another.

William Lorenzo Doleatto

In All Eyes

As I stand at the bus stop,
I hear nothing but I see all.
I smell the cigarettes and that darn cigar.
What kind of world was I dragged into?
With my heart raging for boys
But not able to make up my mind.
Still, I sit at the bus stop and wait.
I wait for visions of love.
As I stand at the bus stop
I look at them,
They look at me.
I get offered a cigarette,
And yet, still look away
Am I also looking away from love?

Bobbie Sue Tuxford

The Insanity of Relationships

The maddening thoughts of the tortured mind
Happiness we've lost and cannot find
Hopeless, helpless, and consider our life of no worldly use
We peek over the fence for an excuse
Searching for greener grass
Instead of researching the vested past
Is life really easier with someone new
Is the intense excitement clouding your view
The grass is no greener
The water no cleaner
The time has come to reflect
On the pain you so easily subject
Focus on your ability to process the facts
Work on getting your happiness back

Dale Arthur Gluck

From the First Time . . .

From the first time I saw you
I thought your were fine

From the first time I heard you talk
I thought you were cool

From the first time you made me laugh
I thought you were funny

From the first time you told me you liked me
I thought you were sweet

From the first time you hugged me
I thought you were great

From the first time you told me you loved me
I knew everything I thought was true

Jessica Anita Patrick

Reflection

Being
To Exist can be exhausting
To try and fail
To try and succeed
This is what drives us
In the end, what do deeds amount to?
When accomplishments show no sign of spirit, are they just?
To Exist can be exhausting
Fatigue thinking leaves ideas lost
Troublesome habits only spiral downward
Idols are not always what they seem,
Are they?
When you sleep, when you dream, that is anyone's only peace.
Existing is exhausting.

Stephen Kimbrough

The Spiritless Eight and Six

Where from womb to worms is vindication?
Gathering this orb's intangible dust?
Healthy accumulation festers! Lust!
Power? Struggle for quarterless traction,
Emerge singular! Lacking compassion?
Beliefs swirled in educational gusts.
Bookish indulgers maw, I say, you must!
Why? To earn forever. How? Direction;

Believing the snail trails a silver streak.
Thus, secreted through pen, brush, tool and sword,
Achievement is the residue of Man.
Being, with eternity in its beak.
The bird inherits the loft of the Lord.
Striving, free-willed mortals do what they can.

Jack Flynn

It Used to Be

It used to be that I could walk fast with no slack.
Now it's one step forward and five steps back.
It used to be that I could dance to a fast beat.
Now it's rheumatism and poor aching feet.
It used to be that my face was taunt and clear.
Now, it's laugh lines and wrinkles everywhere.
It used to be that I had 20/20 vision.
Now it's glasses to see television.
It used to be that my hair was long and brown.
Now it's short and white on my crown.
It used to be that I could eat anything, anytime.
Now it's medicine every day, on time.
It used to be that I took care of my daughter, you see.
Now my daughter takes care of me!

Rosa DaGraca

Time

The cold system of efficiency—it haunts me every day
A lifetime portrayed by diagram—the basis for my dismay
Laws of numerical functions are engraved inside my head
These imaginary deadlines are destined to make me dead
Maintained in endless suffering by the walls I cannot climb
Tears of manifested fears flow with the dreadful sounding chime
The merciless hands of Grandfather Clock—perfectly aligned
There can be no evasion of the tick-tock, tick-tock bind
The never-ending propinquity of the edifice of time
Guarantees my unhappiness, even as you read this rhyme

Jeffrey Walter Ekhardt

Joy

Joy is what I feel when you enter the room.
Joy is what I feel when I see you.
Joy is what I feel when I see you smiling.
Joy is what I feel when I'm in your arms.
Joy is what I feel when I hear your voice.
Joy is what I feel when we are just relaxing.
Joy is talking to you about nothing.
Joy is spending time with you.
Joy is what I feel when I'm with you.
Joy is what I feel now.

Juanita Nance Gatewood

Freedom

The musty smell of the earth after several days of rain
Gives me a high and takes away my emotional pain
I'm thankful for my life, my ability to breathe
My home, in this life, I'll never leave
I feel a part of the earth and hope when I'm gone
I become the air, the wind and can kick up a storm
I want to feel free to move, to go anywhere I please
I want to fly, to travel and see what's over all the seas
I'll do it one day that's my final aim
To become an element and never feel pain

Leonella H. Akong

You're Seven Today

Dedicated to my granddaughter, Jessica Lynn Rago
Happy birthday, sweet little girl,
You're more precious than the rarest pearl.

I can't believe that you're already seven,
It seems just like yesterday, you were sent from heaven.

The prettiest brown eyes and hair,
With a smile that can warm the coolest air.

No matter how far we're apart,
There's always a place for you in my heart.

C. R. Brown

Heart

The key to freedom and peace of mind
Is a smile and a kind word to share with mankind
The rich and the poor should walk hand in hand
Religious differences should be respected throughout each land
Our world can be such a perilous place
Hatred and distrust have shown their monstrous faces
I have decided to change the world
Every man, woman, boy, and girl
I will listen, share, and work for the future generations
So we can live in peace and harmony in all situations

Kimberly Nicole Nettles

Rain

The sky is gloomy and trees are talking
cover your head because it is going to rain
The birds are stirring and cats are running
cover your head because it is going to rain
The air is blowing and the water controlling
cover your head because it is going to rain
My knees are shaking and my back aching
cover your head because it is going to rain
The clouds are full and waiting to drain
cover your head because it is going to rain

Danielle Stafford

All Alone

Somebody help me I'm all alone.
I have nobody to call my own.
It seems I'm the last in everyone's line.
Nobody here wants to be mine.
Please just give me someone to hold.
I just need somebody to help me grow old.
Anger and rage don't help one bit.
Yet I'm too old to just throw a fit.
Somebody help me I'm all alone.
I now know I'll never have someone to call my own.

Wayne Carl Westcott

Weakness

Struggle is the defining word of life,
Yet how true it is when the waves of life
pound down and the weaknesses so buried
within intensify with this continuing tide.
The definitions of humanity
seem to underline this principle,
but can you conquer and transcend the deeply
woven strands of imperfection?
What need we do to conquer the sealed
fate of an imperfect soul.

Russell Brant Stout

Someday

Someday you'll love me,
Someday you'll care,
Someday you'll treasure the moments we've shared.
My heart will have left you,
My soul will have died,
And then you'll realize the tears that I've cried.
Someday you'll love me,
Someday you'll care,
Someday you'll want me
and I won't be there.

Bethanie Ann Waner

Life Goes On . . .

I thought that I knew you like the back of my hand. . . .
Everything seemed as though it would work out as planned.
I told you so many things and gave you so much more. . . .
What did I get in return: I got to watch you walk out the door.
You broke my heart and took my breath away. . . .
You always said that no matter what, you would always stay.
Now here I am, all by myself. . . .
Lookin' up at your picture that is still sittin' on my shelf.
Will life go on? Will I be able to make it through?
Of course it will, 'cause baby, I no longer need you!

Kristina Marie Giglio

Angel

This angel, independent, stands alone.
A victor's wreath is poised, a brow to crown—
Could this but be the prince for whom she seeks?
Her feet, stilled, will walk the earth below;
Yet wings will give her conquest of the skies.
A restless spirit, moving yet serene
No home she knows within this temporal realm.
That which she seeks is purely spiritual—
A mortal I look on, still wondering
If I could share that final destiny.

John Walton Smith

Hate

I hate how you would look at me.
I hate that you would stare.
I hate the way you smile.
I hate the clothes that you would wear.
I hate how you'd listen to me whenever I would talk.
I hate how you'd look whenever I would walk.
I hate that I wanted to cry when I would look in your eyes.
I hate how you had me looking when you walked by.
I hate all these things and so much more. . . .
But what I hate the most is that I still care for . . .

Crissy Napoliello

Untitled

I don't know why the world is round.
Why ducks are yellow, why snow is white.
I don't know why I cry at night.
Why I put on this face to make others think it's right.
I don't know why my feet are small, why some buildings are tall.
I don't know why I smile at all.
But what I do know is this: I'm a human, and so are you.
I know you didn't mean to do that too.
I know that once upon a time I was just fine.
I drew the line.

Sadie Miranda Hillis

Lone Rose

The field full of swaying long grass
Memories of yesterday and far gone pasts
Love gained, love lost
Though remaining locked in my heart

A grave stands alone
Bare and cold
Nobody cares, nobody knows
The bluest of skies turning black though my eyes
One lone rose remained standing
Now it has died.

Colleen Dionne Cooper

The Crowd

As I look upon this faceless crowd
I see smiles with just one frown
Why does this sadness become distinctive
When it takes control of those who are weakened
Soon this sadness has everyone down
When it began as a joyful crowd
Now the one whose face was gloom
Is brightened with glory throughout the room
Then the sadness is swept away
And no longer are the clouds gray

Heather Lynn Wade

Summer Boys

Summer is da best
you meet new guys and leave da rest
guys from school are, oh, soo old
but da hotties we met were as shiny as gold
BuShY EyEbRoWs-n-a TiGhT 6 PaCk
leave da rest b.c. they aren't comin' back
you know you're wanted when you see their glare
strong muscular arms you can hardly bare
and now this leaves us at da end of da summa
we'll be comin' back next year so it won't be a bumma!

Lisa Paige Cohen

First Love

You're the light in the dark staircase of my soul
It's only in your eyes I see what is truly divine
It is you that puts hope in my soul

Just your presence, please no words
Just let me look into your eyes
The light all the way to your soul
Just let me be to you what you are to me—everything
Or at least pretend—the actor in my finest tragedy
Pretend to yourself that I am someone in your life
Just let me be here with you and pretend you'll never leave

Melodie Anne Gillmor

Nature's Loving Fury

I was born of the Earth's nourishing blanket,
of the Wind's ever-changing secrets,
of the Sea's refreshing kiss,
of the Sun's warm embrace,
and of the Moon's watchful guidance.

When I die, the Earth will surround my body,
the Winds will take in my mind,
the Seas will swallow my love,
the Sun will burn my hate,
and the Moon will guide my Spirit to Freedom.

Sarah Michelle Horken

Heartbroken

Rain, rain, go away
you took away my sunny day
brought me sadness and despair
made my flower disappear.
I loved this flower more than life
gave her the best soil and plenty light.
Did everything to keep her near
hoping your clouds would not come here.
But I started neglecting my flower and she went away
That's why the rain is here today.

Adam Dustin Foust

Dead Inside

I cry because my heart is breaking.
I laugh to hide the pain.
I shout to ease the stress
caused by him when he walked away.
I smile to try and show him I'll be fine on my own,
when in reality, I've lost the only love I've ever known.

So when you see me happy,
just know I'm trying to hide
from everyone around me
that I am dead inside.

Katherine Ballard

Dream

I dream of you night and day
I picture us happy as we lay
We laugh so hard we cry
But now it is all gone because I had to lie
I broke my vow and my commitment
You broke my heart and I can barely live with it
And as the Sun rises and another day comes
I awake to your sweet hum
But it is only my mind playing games
And again I am left alone in pain

James Robert Smith

Blue Doggie

I saw Blue Doggie run by today,
Down the street and up the driveway.
He sat outside our orange home,
And begged for a new bone.
I asked Mommy if we had one to spare,
But when she looked out the window Blue Doggie wasn't there.
I said, "He's right there, Mommy, can't you see?"
I did not know that to her, Blue Doggie could not be.
So, I took a pink bone and went out the door,
And sure enough, Blue Doggie came back once more.

Maura Cullinan

Forever

A look tore my heart in two
In a breath of a moment I knew
I could never love another
Or I might as well smother
And die, and lie, and never breathe again.

And maybe if we were separated forever
I could still never love another
And maybe if we could be together
Nothing could ever sever
My love, for my dear, again.

Sarah Elizabeth Covert-Flory

My Daughter

She has my eyes, she has my face.
She has my wit, she has my grace.

She has my fingers, she has my nose.
She even has my little toes.

When I look at her, all I see
Is a spitting image of who I used to be.

I love her some much, you couldn't possibly know.

I would be so sad if she was ever to go.

Samantha Lee Smith

Sweet Child

I remember you, with love, my son,
and will 'til the end of time.
I remember you with laughter and tears,
and know that once you were mine.

You were here with me for awhile my son,
now you've gone to the heavens above,
the angels look after you now, sweet child,
as you abide in the realm of Gods love.

With love always, Mom.

Sandra Kay Dupell

One Day . . .

One day I'll be on top of this game
One day I'll never be the same
One day I'll be in control of my life
One day I'll be happy with a nice wife
One day I'll have a smile on my face
One day I'll have finished in first place
One day I'll grab hold of my prize
One day I'll look into the skies
And see that I'm as happy as a dove
Because I'm totally completely in love

Jimi Werbe

Just Us

Just you and me
alone . . . outside . . . under the stars
feelings of warmth and love for each other
the presence of God
being never alone with each other
having faith in one another
trust, true happiness
not what is ahead or behind us
what's inside us
that's the difference

Tami Zimmerman

Why

I live in a world of hate.
I see it every day.
Just can't get away.

It's all around!
And sucking me in!
What can I do, I try not to sin.

I see happy things, they don't make me grin.
I see sad things, that burns a fire within.
My world is so great, a world full of hate?

Nicholas Charles Chesna

Why God?

Why God?
Do you do these things to me?
Why do you make me sad?
Why do you make me mad?
How can you let these things happen?
Why did so many die?
Why do I live a lie?
Why do so many hate?
Why are so many so ignorant?
If this is only Earth, I cannot imagine Hell.

Andy William Saxton

9/11

It was the eleventh of September and all through the land
the media was buzzing with crisis at hand.
Two planes had cavorted with buildings, it seemed,
by propelling themselves into the stiff iron beams.
Not once, but twice the twin towers did shake.
Those planes in the sky with chaos in wake.
Many are hurt,
too many lives lost,
for this thing called world peace
but I can't take the loss.

Aaron Lingenfelter

Wonderful Day

In this world where there is war,
Some days I think I can stand no more.
Lying in my bed at night,
asking god to hold me tight.
I turned on the TV today
and thought, this is going to be a wonderful day.
People helping people everywhere
Thank you god, I guess people do care.
Lets hope it stays this way because this is one wonderful day.
September 15, 2001

Julie Ann Poulin

9/11

So many deaths
so much suffering for thousands of people
as the destruction hits New York City
the debris from the building is overwhelming
it will take a miracle to help all of the people
but there is still hope
but there is also despair
everybody asking "what to do next" no one knows
the abominable crash made by the cowardly terrorists
will leave the nation in an uproar!

Nicole West

Never a Darker Day

Looking around I see a place.
It's full of death and disgrace.
I see no kids playing,
For they are all laying
With huge tears in their eyes.
Their fathers and mothers didn't come home.
Their parents last moments will always be shown.
Something must be done,
Yet there is nowhere to run,
For we are helpless, too.

Bethany Brown

Daddy's Little Girl

Your beautiful girl whom you believed in so much.
Your hope for the future, your pride for today.
Your faith in the world was renewed through her.
Your eyes spoke the words your mouth couldn't say.
That girl whom you'd rush home to see each day.
The one with the smile that would take your breath away.
She embodied everything good and kind in this world.
Your heart shattered into pieces the day you were told.
She's no longer a ray of goodness for the world to see.
Don't worry, little Sarah, you will live on in me.

Prudence Amana Alexander

Time

If time would stand still only to keep this
moment from ending, I would wish it,
for your love showers me
every moment your eyes fall upon mine.
Our souls has become one;
they are so intertwined, it will never be torn.
True love is what this is
from me to you and you to me.
Be mine, for I'm yours forever and always.

So shall time stop for us?

Earllee Lafradez

Burn

Burning sin fills my life
Echoes of laughter surround me
Burning pain tortures my soul
Just thinking of you brings pain
How could you torture me like this?
Forcing so much pain into my life,
How do I put up with you?
You're a pain in my side I just can't erase.
Just leave me be
And go away.

Leah Marie Cunningham

Castle War

Demons surrounded the iron-gated castle.
Castle that would fall in a slaughter of evil.
Evil that would stretch its vile roots down into earth.
Earth that would be ravished and stripped of life.
Life that would wail in mourning for a soul.
Soul that would pass through the trial of birth.
Birth that would rally the tormented humans.
Humans that would take up arms for battle.
Battle that would lay siege to the twisted castle.
Castle that would be cleansed of its demons.

Brendan Murphy Meany

Voices

Estranged thoughts flow
through my mind.
As I sit and stare at the wall.
I hear so many voices past and present,
voices that are distant with unknown origin.
Sounding so familiar yet, so strange.
They keep me from going so far into
my fantasy world that I may never return
and at the same time protect me from
the dangers of reality.

Jessica Cathryn Driscoll

Trust

Keeping with the moment, I peer
Across the darkened starlit sky.
Realizing that though we are far apart,
I cannot shake this sense that we are together.

Staring deep into a single star, I lose myself and
Touch your soul with my heart.
Opening my deepest most inner being, I
Recognize that though we are apart,
Eternity awaits our weary souls, and I am comforted.
You are loved.

B. Tyler Miller

After the Night

After the night the wind is calm.
The sky is clear.
I do no fear.
After the night
The fight of the sunlight is done.
The world is asleep, and the day is done.
For I don't fear.
The wind is not there.
For the night is done.

We go to sleep and awake and have fun.

Julia Desantis

Control

It takes everything I have
To control my thoughts, feelings, around
everyone.
Yet, when I'm alone
I let go, and cry and scream, or try to
scream.
Tears rolling down my face
As I curl up on the carpet
Trying to hold myself together.
It hurts, to control,
When you don't want to.
Hit the wall,
No! Don't, it'll make things worse.
So you clinch your fists
And fall to your knees,
And you breathe . . .
Then the door opens, people come in.
Quickly, you dry your eyes,
Pull yourself together,
And smile.

Charles Robert Aquilino

Challenge

I am myself; there are none the same.
Some have classified me "the sweet one,"
Easy to take advantage of and even easier to ignore.

Those who encounter my blatant honesty
Often choose to run or in spite cause me pain.
I never intend to offend and often fail to succeed
In accepting my wants and retrieving my needs.

I can't accept your gift; I am not worthy.
If you could only understand the reason you don't see me
Is the result of this wallflower's allowance to be painted upon.

I've waited to be challenged, only to watch it pass by.
And I sit in resentment as you all unknowingly walk away.
Even though, in bitter shame, I turned my back on you yesterday.

I have admitted to seeing this problem full view.
Yet I am not certain I can use these newfound legs.
So, in fear I will sit idle and in hope I will venture.
Given time, we will see if I can brave the challenge.
I have yet to endure.

Amanda R. Erickson

Octoroon Odyssey!

The old white towns people were craning like
ogres, they were, as they ogled the ochre
colored octet! The octet was soulfully
harmonizing to the sounds of a marimba and
bongos, as they belted out the lyrics of "Burn
Old Dixie Down!" They had came from out of the
Bayou, just outside New Orleans, celebrating
their liberation and freedom from the old
Brier Patch! Dressed in colorful Mardi Gras
fashion, they danced joyfully on the banks
of the mighty Mississippi! Never before and
never again would the evil Klan-like
town's people witness the flamboyant octet,
this group, all 8 of them, with high yellow
skin, silky curls of golden streaked hair, and
eyes like sparkling diamonds of coal! Cajun/
Creole Indians, true Octoroons, they were!
An odyssey of epic proportion! Here, in plain
view for the entire little evil town to see!
YES! AN OCTOROON ODYSSEY!

Pamela Jo Roper

Happiness Sometimes Hard 2 Find

I close my eyes but never my mind.
I try not 2 cry, knowing happiness
is sometimes hard 2 find.
But I strive on an ocean and ride the tides
Leading 2 the sea of tranquility.
Distilled is my body, 4 I see something
starring at me.
Contemplating on its silly games,
so still I remain,
starring at the new looks and getting new feelings.
In all actuality not real!
So I reach out my hand 2 touch it, know it.
Feels 2 good I wanna love it.
The music plays, but still it won't dance.
Shh! I heard it say; I'm your love in the
still of the night, but I'm not what you see
come morning light. I'm just an mirage in your heart.
You're looking in all the wrong places and faces.
Just open your eyes—happiness you'll find.
4 happiness has been there all the time.

Fredrick Shepherd

Disabled

The sun rose with a blazing golden glory,
but I did not see its rising
as I lay with my eyes open.
I have always loved the sunrise,
and the emotional pain took hold of
my chest with a grip that hurt.
I tried to stand and then to walk,
but my legs felt like rubber
and did not respond.
I have always loved to walk—
to walk through the bush and smell
the scent of the eucalyptus,
to hear the call of the bellbirds.
I touched the hot metal, but I
did not feel the heat until it was pain.
I have always loved to feel—
to feel the silky velvet of a cat's ear
or the warm outside of my coffee mug.
I am not the same person. MS has seen to that.
I am now classed as "disabled."

Lorna Beverley Gray

Dream Theater

The Earth has swallowed the Sun
And now the time has come to enter my dream theater
I draw the covers close as sleep settles in
It's time . . . let the show begin
I have a front row seat to my subconscious play
Onto the stage the cast makes their way
In the orchestra pit the conductor raises his wand
It's time the show goes on.
The curtain is raised, music echoes through the hall
To my emotions it seems to call
Anger and rage take center stage while others wait in the wings
Fear battles strength in a duel to the death
And hope takes its final breath
As the plot plays out within my silent sleep
I feel bound to my theater seat
Act after act and line after line
My most inner fears are clearly defined
Soon it is ending and as the sun finds the day
I am awakened from this sleepy play, but I know this play is life
And that it will only end when the sequel of death begins

James Arron Henson

You and Me

There are people in this world like me
Who never know what to do or be
Who never seem to be good or bad
And make both themselves and others sad
But you, you're different to all the rest
You are the one, the very best
The one I learn from and love the most
I'd tell the world and I would boast
That you alone make life worthwhile
The walk of life worth every mile
The love you give cannot be told
I know it's mine and I should hold
It in my heart 'til the day I die
And never, ever wonder why
I was the one you chose in your heart
The one you miss when were apart
All I can say is I love you, too
And I always want to be with you
As long as we love, we will always be
Together forever, just you and me

John Benjamin Saxton

To the Dad I Never Had

My name is Sierra Nichole, Dad,
I took on my family's last name.
I am now 14 years old, Dad,
but my life will never be the same.
You're always on my mind, Dad,
I will always think of you.
I will always wonder, Dad,
if we one day meet, what would you do?
If some how we were reunited, Dad,
would we be a loving pair?
Would we have a normal relationship, Dad,
or would our lives just tear?
Why did you leave Mom, Dad?
I know you were both young.
But your mistakes will always be here, Dad,
and they can never be undone.
But even though I miss you, Dad,
I still think you could've done more.
You left me without a sign, Dad,
and left my heart so sore.

Sierra Nichole Kleban

Mistakes

Mistakes are thought of as something bad.
Some are scared to make mistakes.
The ones who walk high try to hide their mistakes.
I have one question—why? You learn through your mistakes.
People are afraid they will be judged by their mistakes.
A mistake can open your eyes to something new.
A mistake one day will open your eyes wider the next.
You can ponder on your mistake and try to not make it again
Or you can see what good has come out from it.
Mistakes don't happen by accident.
If we were meant to be perfect, then we wouldn't have mistakes.
They are there for a reason.
Don't try to hide your mistakes.
Some are ashamed,
And some look back on those days and laugh.
Don't try to hide your mistakes.
Shine brightly and don't cover you face.
If you make a mistake, you just learned a new lesson.
Mistakes were meant to be there day and night.
Don't try to hide your mistakes.

Danielle Taylor

I Can Tell You

About the love I have known through the ages
It is the one constant within me forever
Deeply interwoven like the grapevine
into my heart and soul completely
this love is connecting as one us all

I can tell you in song
about our universal connection in love
musical notes flowing freely and in harmony
melodies as deep as the oceans
rhythms as high as the heavens

I can tell you in nature
Sunrise, sunset, and rainbows
Sky, clouds, planets, stars in our galaxy
Existing harmoniously and completely as one

The love is there
The love is within me
The one constant that is held nearest
While dearest to our hearts and souls
Forever as one completely

Anne Marie Schoefer Smith

So Confused

I am still in junior high;
my life is still quite new.
But already I wonder:
what am I to do?
I'm still a young kid,
at least my mom thinks so;
but when I finish school,
where am I to go?
Will I work at a fast food restaurant?
Or shall I set off to college?
Will I become a lazy bum?
Or shall I be eager to expand my knowledge?
I have a few more years to ponder this,
But they are depleting fast.
I often find myself searching
For a way to make them last.
What am I to do?
Where am I to go?
At this moment, I am thoughtless,
But hopefully someday I will know.

Tyler Alexander Willis

Competition

I love this awesome thing,
Fast moving and thinking it will bring
Sweat pouring off your brow,
Working even harder now,
Ripping past the farthest limit,
Though it is hard I must admit.
Finally fulfilling a lifelong dream,
Sacrificing it all just for the team.
Recalling what your instructor said,
Filling your opponent's heart with dread.
Whether athletic or academic sport,
You've always got a friend's support.
We never gave up, we never gave in,
Our effort paid off for this incredible win.
They never broke through our immovable guard,
Oh, what a feeling to have competed so hard!
I just can't wait until I next compete,
Can't wait to overcome an impossible feat.
Showing the world how great you can be,
That's the reason I compete!

Johnica Jo Fetsch

Life

Struggle, survive—it's all about life
Living to die, dying to live, don't take
Just give—true love and inner peace
Touched by an angel in your sleep
You laugh and weep, your heart, your soul
Is so much more, feel pain, feel joy
Embrace your life, don't destroy
Be true, be yourself
Health and happiness is the measure of wealth
No regrets, just lessons learnt
Knowledge is freedom—be strong, assert
Take a chance, overcome your fears
Smile and shed a tear
Love yourself for who you are
Love your neighbors near and far
Beauty of nature is all around
Look up, look down
Rejoice in a rainbow, wish upon a star
Watch day turn into night
Be thankful for your life . . .

Gail Maytom

After You Left

My eyes always longing to see the sight of you
My heart desperately searching to find you
My soul feeling incomplete at the loss of you
Never felt so lonely
You were supposed to always be my one and only
Why did you have to go? I wish you had never left
Every day I wanted to tell you how I felt
But now you're gone and I'm stranded
You're gone and I feel abandoned
Why couldn't it be a different way?
Being together forever and a day
The thought of you put me to sleep at night
And I would get up thinking of you at the break of light
Now the thought of you gives me sleepless nights
And I wake up wishing we had never had those fights
Brought hope into my life and broke my heart when you had to leave
I think of you not being there and I can hardly breathe
I lost my best friend and it seems like the world was taken from me
I found the key to your heart but I couldn't unlock the door
I'll leave a special place for you in my heart forevermore

Armen Yedalyan

Me

I am just a teenage girl
Trying to live in this crazy world
It is not always easy for me
As I go on each day, I begin to see
I see people that call me names
I see them going on for days
But when those days soon are done
They see how they made me strong
I fall, because I have realized
Realized that strength is not my prize
I've just become weak all over again
And crawl into my own little den
I might not come out for a while
But when I do, you will see my smile
My smile will be as bright as ever
Because I know that I am clever
Clever because now, I know
That this world is always on the go
So, now, I know that I have become strong
Because my learning days have just begun

Erika Elizabeth Riley

as you walk through the valley

as a newborn child
the world is new
everything is interesting
as you walk through the valley
as a young child
things become more and more familiar
the world is now starting to make sense
as you walk through the valley
as a teenager
you think you know everything
but your life has really just begun
as you walk through the valley
as an adult
there are good times and some bad times
but you stuck in there and made you way through
as you walk through the valley
as one who is dead and gone
you are missed very much
just the person people want to see again
as you walk through the valley

Eric Warren Prioleau

Night Is a Lonely Time

Night is a lonely time when everyone
around you is asleep.
I wake up with the fragments of a dream
in my head.
I stare into the dark at the face
I see in my dreams.
My body feels hollow and there's an emptiness
where my heart used to be.
My mind shudders as I wonder,
how long will I miss him?
How many nights will he come to me
only in my dreams?
How many nights will I wake and cry
for someone who's not here?
How long will it be before I stop hating
the fall of night?
If I could, at this moment, have
but one wish granted,
I would wish for an endless sleep
with no dreams to haunt me!

Sharon Mosser

Dream of Love

We feel secure, understood, appreciated;
We enjoy being together.
We communicate an unconditional love. . . .
We stare into each other's eyes;
Our souls connect as the Sun sets.
Smell the moisture in the air . . .
Hear the sounds of the surf . . .
Feel the cool breeze . . .
Warm sand tickles our bare feet.
Roses surround the wooden porch.
This is not a house, but our home;
It has seen a few tears,
But it has also felt great joy. . . .
We express our passions,
Enjoy fun and laughter;
On the walls art collections hang;
Music fills the air;
Family and friends feel welcome here.
Cherished memories of moments shared . . .
This is my dream of love. . . .

Alice Swann

My Place

This is my place; it is where I belong.
You can find me here when things go wrong.
I sit and stare at the sunset sky,
Wishing that someday I will fly.
Thinking of things that need to be done,
Things that need to be said before I am gone.
Let my loved ones know what they mean to me
Before God leads me away and sets me free.
Set the right goals; find the right way,
Rest myself at the close of day.
These are some things I think of there
As I sit there and I stare.
As the Sun goes down, my thoughts go clear,
And suddenly, I feel you near.
I get a chill up my spine;
Everything is right, everything is fine.
You see, My Place may never be found.
It isn't in the sky or on the ground.
Look into my eyes and you will see
My Place is here, inside of me.

Lindsey Swanson

Spiraling into Forever

Spiraling down this road to forever
No one to help me
And the only other travelers here spiral as well as I
I do not know anymore and
I have to live every day like it's my last
Because I can't figure out what's coming next
I'm so unprepared for what I've already seen
For what I've already done
And spiraling on this road to forever is a dangerous one
Ferocious thorns and things hitting me
Hitting me like a bad blow to the stomach and it turns inside me
Spinning like I spiral down the road called forever
Is what it seems will take me nowhere
That's not how I saw it
But considering I am still learning
What I should already know by now
Doesn't surprise me much
'Cause the road called forever doesn't stop spinning,
Doesn't stop spiraling
As my road called forever keeps on spinning

Breanna Woicekowski

The Preeminent Player

He's a myth, but also real,
he'll block a shot or make a steal,
but that's not why he is the best,
it is because he passed the test.
The test of every boy and girl,
that live in this fanatic world.
He is now bigger than himself,
than the trophies on his shelf.
He now exists in every mind,
in every heart of all mankind.
He is now an epic story,
of pain, endurance, and most of all glory.
He does more than just play ball,
he fulfills our dreams, he makes the call;
the call to do what we cannot,
to make the pass and make the shot.
So even after he is gone,
his legendary story will go on.
He gave our dreams their beginnings and starts,
the day that he touched our hearts.

James Russell Poteet

Caterpillar Sting

The caterpillar sting that Stings,
an already hurt wound will not heal.
I don't think it will ever heal.
This caterpillar sting keeps coming
back up into my mind. Why?
Why does it have to come back?
This caterpillar sting hurts my Pride.
I cry because it hurts.
I cry because of the memory of the Sting.
The caterpillar sting will never leave my mind.
Every time I see a Black-eyed Susan,
I will think of the Sting.
We had picked Black-eyed Susans
before the Sting.
Every time I think of a fight,
I will think of the Sting.
We fought before the Sting too.
Why does it hurt?
Why does it come back every year on January third?
Why?

Sarah Marie Roth

Wings of a Mother

God gave our mothers wings
wings to scoop us up when we are down
God gave our mothers wings
wings of protection from all harm around
God gave our mothers wings
wings to hold us close to her heart
God gave our mothers wings
wings to push us each day to a new start
God gave our mothers wings
wings of hope and love in our times of despair
God gave our mothers wings
wings of hugs to show us how much she really cares
God gave our mothers wings
wings to wipe our weary eyes
God gave our mothers wings
wings of passion to let us know that everything will be all right
God gave our mothers wings
wings of strength and courage to carry us when she is gone
God gave our mothers wings
wings to hold onto until our days are done

Yolanda Joyce Hearns

Screwed, Yet Again . . .

I'm not blind. Nor can I see,
the countless times we disagree.
I think it's perfect. You "know" it's not.
Those angry words . . . that I forgot.
I thought it true. You thought it fake.
Your freedom came, my heart did break.
Contented, you dejected me. . . .
Our time to come, you cannot see.
I now can see. . . . I am not blind.
The love we had, you cannot find.
You found it once. I found it twice.
You cannot see, it does suffice.
Our love was strong, but we were weak.
Our hearts were young. . . . our love, antique.
The past is past, and that we were.
The love we had, we shall inter.
But if our love, it does exhume.
It will not cease. It shall resume!
Don't call me blind, for I can see,
the love that burns . . . in you and me.

Tiffany Alexandra Nunez

Departure

Stranded in the desert of despair
Wandering deep into its lair
I trusted you so, but was deceived
Betrayal is all I've ever received
I absorbed your words of love and passion
Now I'm hanging to dry in pathetic fashion
You promised me forever, left the next day
Promised you wouldn't let go, pushed me away
I never seem to learn, but remain so naive
Against better judgment, I always believe
But this is it, I will not take anymore
I've hardened my heart, frozen my core
I'll never put my faith into anyone again
For this monster called love, I have no yen
You've taught me the nature of this reality
I am now but a machine without morality
I want to hurt you just as you've hurt me
These tears are caused by you, don't you see?
Still loving you is the worst part of all
Yet it's too late—you didn't break my fall

Andrea Lee Aicher

I Knew a Man

I knew a man so big and strong,
Who tweaked my ear when I did wrong,
And stood betide when I did pray,
Confessing my sins at end of day.
I knew a man as a stripling lad,
Who taught me good and cautioned me bad.
Unhappy and depressed, where future led?
Trust in the Lord, was all he said.
I knew a man, so happy was he,
When I stood up, a man to be.
Watched with a smile my trembling hand,
As I slipped on the golden band.
I knew a man who lay weak and dying,
Still comforting me when I a-crying.
Why, father mine! Lord? His work undone,
But 'tis time for you now to be one.
I once knew a man, a father was he,
A better man or father one could not see,
And maybe, just maybe, he'll help me be,
A fraction, just a fraction, of what was he.

Kaustuv Das

Moments

For the moment, take a deep breath.
For the moment, know I am thinking of you.
Just for the moment, picture a place of happiness.
For the moment, let go of your troubles and
Empty your mind of all thoughts of stress.

For the moment, there is nothing but love.
For the moment, there is nothing but peace.
Just for the moment, picture the world as
You want it to be.
For the moment, serenity is now.

For the moment, your thoughts are your future.
For the moment, you feel alive.
Just for the moment, true love is yours.
For the moment, you control your destiny.

For the moment, I am somewhere in my moment.
For the moment, nothing else matters.
Just for the moment, thoughts of us continue.
For the moment, we are together, undisturbed.
We are together in the moment, but I am yours forever.

Scott D. Privette

Brian

We never knew a day so bright
Could turn into our greatest fright
For it was one year ago in May
We lost our friend, for whom we'd pray
We hear he had been driving home
Coming from where, still no one knows
When suddenly he lost control
And then began to lose his soul
Didn't see that semi until it was too late
A simple drive home had controlled his fate
Brian has kids, ages three and one
Who won't remember things they had done
But when we gaze at those tiny faces
We see Brian, and remember past times and places
Our memories will pull us through
Because that is what they are made to do
He was closest to us; my husband's best friend
God saw that they made up, right before the end
We mourn Brian now, and we always will
We lost a best friend, who now rests upon a hill

      Cindy McMullen

Bubble World

You are the reason everything's alive
I have created this world and all of time
I blew bubbles to create, and planted us here
To grow and make love within our atmosphere
Whenever anything falls from the sky
It's falling for you (the way I do . . .)
Whenever tides heave their crying sobs
They're crying for you
Whenever life is born again
Whenever I can kiss your hand . . .
All that is made and done is done for you
All so I could look upon your face
Your existence shines in all of this God's grace
Yet I worship you—
My love for whom I've made our Earth spin 'round
My love for whom I've painted sight and sound
My love with whom new life I long to create,
Breaking all past molds of time and space—
I blew bubbles to make universes and planted us here
In live lingering magic of destiny clear . . .

      Elizabeth Rose McKeown

Don't Forget

Sometimes we forget to breathe.
We forget that trivial problems
will pass with time.
We are often in need of someone to remind us
that life does go on
with the never-ending cycle of our universe.
 So take a "delicate few" to think about that.
That one thought should put it all in perspective.
And I hope you remember that in this short life
math problems don't matter
and clothes don't count.
And in the end,
We won't remember if we won, or if we lost
because that isn't what's important.
But our memories will be of the seemingly insignificant times,
like phone calls until 4 am
and listening to each other cry.
And we'll remember the times when
we truly lived, laughed, and loved.
Thank you for giving me so much to remember.

      Fallon Marie Such

Feeling Alone

As I sit in my bedroom staring at the wall
I feel as if I'm alone in the world, no one cares at all
I thought I had friends and that they cared
I don't know what to do!
This pain is too hard to bear
I feel angry, I feel sad
I feel betrayed by the friends I had
So, as I sit in my room staring at the wall
I wonder and wonder
Does anyone care at all?
Because if they did, maybe they'd act more like a grown-up
And not so much like a kid
Though I may be sad and my heart is torn apart
This prayer that I have is that
People will have a change of heart
So, when you feel alone and without a friend in the world
One friend is never gone
He is a true friend you can rely on
All you have to do is
Close your eyes and fall on your knees

      Tonya Marie Wilson

What Time Is It?

To the Hudson, Massachusetts, firefighters
There are times throughout our lives, when
we are faced with terrible sorrow. There are
times we would say that this could never
happen to me. There are times we want to do
what is right for me and you. There are
times when we just can't express what you
truly mean to us. There are times when
disaster strikes, and it costs someone's
life. There are times when we say good night,
with the hope we'll see another night.
Whatever the time may be about, it is
comforting to know you are there,
although we pray not to see you, knocking at
our door. If you do so have to arrive, we
pray also, to survive.
We offer you these words, as a symbol of our
faith. That the Hudson firefighters
continue with their desire to extinguish
yet another fire!

      Steve Madden

Invisible and Silent

Invisible tears stream down my face.
Silent screams are heard within.
What you see isn't what I feel.
I feel a mess.

My heart is being squeezed.
My ears aren't really hearing.
My mind is denying.
I understand what you're saying
it's not hard to comprehend.
But what you just said hits right where it hurts
because I myself have said those words.
Those words were only uttered in an
attempt to save the other from suffering.
Now I know better. . . .
It doesn't work.

The pain builds and builds
until I can bear no more.
But I don't know how to express my pain.
So for now I'll keep my tears and screams invisible and silent.

      Krystle Angie Torrau

Our Journey

Our journey is like the growth of a tree.
As a seedling, we stretch upward,
With straight intent, toward Heaven.

However, a crossroads may appear,
And we follow the path
Of an off-shooting branch,
Going sideways, out on a limb perhaps.

In an attempt to secure growth and survival
We return to the trunk;
Ever-reaching, ever-stretching upward,
Strong, yet yielding in a windstorm.

Trees, branches, roots, limbs—
It's all part of the circle;
If we just remember that even tree trunks
Aren't perfectly straight.

The gift is to recognize and allow for
Gentleness with ourselves,
As God is with trees.

Elizabeth Tait

The Dance

Looking back at that night
I remember every moment of joy
How could I forget
When he walked in that night
Looking like a young man
He was no longer a boy
When I found him looking my way
I could not believe he wanted to talk to me
He started to walk towards me and
I wanted to go the other way
He asked me to dance and I said, "who, me?"
The night was almost over
We had danced all night
Holding him made me feel
Everything would be all right
Now it's all over
All that's left is a memory
Now all I feel is pain
My memories have now
Turned into a dream

Vanessa Arthur

Three Weird Sisters

Of crooked essence and frightful smell,
These hideous creatures crawl from hell.
And through their throats, their words do spew
To tell the tales that no one knew.
Fair is foul, and foul is fair;
But why is it that they do dare
To warn Macbeth of times to come
And not tell where they know it from?
Are they merely hallucinations
Which fill Macbeth with anticipation;
Or three old hags grown senile and feeble
Roaming around and scaring people?
Those explanations are Banquo's beliefs
Which, perhaps, he gives for his own relief.
But the truth that Macbeth will soon validate
Is the three weird sisters are tellers of fate.
All these horrors to you I mention
And all beware their cruel intentions.
Their sole purpose: to interfere
And ruin the lives of those they come near.

Nathan Allison

Fragility

Our nascent souls
Are delicate as the wings of dragonflies
Soft and lustrous, light as a whisper
Glowing with God
Molded delicate and transparent
Reborn in illumination
No longer stained by blood and soil
The blood and soil we once wore proudly
Trophies of a life of pyrrhic victories
And tearful catharsis
A life in which we struggled even to breathe
Where our souls became callused and hard
When we choked on polluted air
And swam in brown estuaries
Before we knew internal illumination
We once hid in shadows
Ashamed of the truth in human frailty
Wallowing in the deception
Of our brute strength
Unaware of the power of fragility

Alexa Woodward

Our Chance

You made my life so livable,
I'd praise you to the sky.
Then you did something unforgivable,
You made me cry.
I can't keep myself from crying,
It hurts so very bad.
I feel like I am dying,
I just can't stop thinking of what we had.
Now that we are no longer together,
I feel pain every day.
I had thought we would be forever,
But then you went your own way.
I remember the first time you kissed me,
How I melted like ice.
Then when you said we couldn't be,
How I could see the pain in your lovely eyes.
We took the chance,
We had our fun.
We had our dance,
But now, it's done.

Deidra Elizabeth Shelton

At Close Hand

Aged,
much older than their years.
Beautiful and delicate.
Comforting and nurturing.
I look at my mother's hands and hold back my tears.
Emotional?
Yes . . . I am.
These are the hands that held me,
picked me up when I fell,
healed my wounds.
Real
and imagined.
They've pushed me to shoot for the moon
and held on to me so I wouldn't go too far.
But someday these hands won't be here
to pat me on my back
or wipe away my tears.
And I fear this.
The hands that molded me and hold me together
won't be there to catch me when I fall.

Gail Dawn Haenze

Heaven or Hell

Can you tell Heaven from Hell?
Crippled in the gutter, tears running down your cheek,
Diving in and feeling a bit higher than before,
Finding what has already been found,
Trying to feel when your body is numb.
Breathe in the air and close your eyes.
The crimson sun is perishing from your world.
Are you afraid?
Does the darkness frighten you,
Or could it be what is found in this tunnel of black?
Floating through the unreal sanction of chaos.
Seeing what should be hidden.
"Just a pin prick," you say, "I feel no pain."
Treachery amongst a dominant force,
Dwelling deep in every shadow is depression and remorse.
Compelling moons, they will soon perish, just as the sun.
Let all of your beauty shine!
Try reaching up, rather than jumping down.
Acknowledge the fact that you may drown.
Your lips move, but no sound is heard.

     Mary Lou M. Snow

I'm Mad at Us

Run with feet, faster
quickly, run faster

arms gaping, fingers crawling through air
like flies, screaming palms and rippling elbows, gray

I jump with feet from the clutches

right into cradling arms, supported by
strong limbs, they run now, faster and faster

hand stops us,

motions for me to come down, I follow the

rules,
hand flicks me away, a pile of arms and legs
false,

lying, stealing, killing, raping, adultery,

secrets, rumors—

stop, you have more than arms and legs

     John Weylin Gibbons

Music (A Gift)

The violin wounds
like twilight.
The guitar soothes
like water.
The first bird singing at dawn.
And dangerous water—
now calm river,
now swift rapids.
The drums, like a rapid dance
down a narrow, cobbled street.
And the voice of twilight tells you
its truth in every tongue
and calls you somewhere distant,
'til you want to become a cloud,
orange in a golden sky,
propelled by the flutter of wings.
A dance by a stream at sunset
down the cool stones of the path,
faster and faster,
'til a bird song flows through your veins.

     Victoria Kosaya

The Queen of Rings

A vengeful Hell doth pulse within thee
Death and despair rage all around me.
I must at thy hand feel death's anguish,
Or I shall nevermore myself be.
Every creature feels love's rapture,
Am I not of flesh and blood?
To live ever without a woman
Were all my days in Hell to brood?
Ah, come swiftly! Ah, come swiftly!
Is not it that I have caught thee now?
Bring me hither iron fetters.
Who dares much, much oft shall gain!
Only friendship's harmony softens every sorrow
Without this sympathy, ne'er could face the morrow.
Ay, that can a woman racked with woe,
Oppressed me with grief, the livelong day.
Come, my lovely chime of bells!
Ring ye little bells again.
Come, my lovely chime of rings!
Let all ears now hear thy knells.

     Bojan Peovski

Emotions

What are these emotions I feel inside?
Some I show, but others I hide.
Sometimes I ask myself, Why me?
Is this how I was intended to be?
How do I put up with the things I do?
Is it because God wants me to?
When others go through this how do they feel?
Are these emotions even real?
Sometimes I think I have a friend
But I am alone 'til the end.
Sad and alone that's how I will be;
People say it's weird, but that's me.
There are other emotions that I've had
But they cannot overpower why I'm sad.
Dying I think would end it all;
If I died I'd do it standing tall.
Filled with hope and joy I'd cry
With a glimmer in my eye.
I now know why these emotions I hide,
It's because I was meant to be alone 'til the day I die.

     Erika Early

That Special Word

As I sit here on my porch writing a letter to you
I pause at such curiosity for I don't know what to do
My sentence isn't finished my handwriting's okay
My letter isn't long but I worked on it all day
I think I'll start over since it isn't that good
Or maybe I'm not in that writing type of mood
I crumple the paper and rethink it again
And scribble some words this letter I can't end
I write it once more, is there something else I should do?
For the words I have chosen where just beyond two
The first word was "I" then "love" as the next
But the next few I'm not sure of this is far more complex
A word far more important just to be called the way it is
It's worth money and riches far more than just this
How exotic like wild animals it is
How much better IT feels than when you receive your first kiss
But it's not just SOMETHING and it's not just IT
This word that's worth riches it's YOU that I pick
Just writing "I love you" just isn't enough
Because I love you way more, way more than just love

     Jillian Michiko Nakamura

Truth Returned

Vision of love in a sunlit night,
blinded by emotion on a darkened afternoon.
Feelings confused by surroundings—
time construed by hastened events.
I see you but misunderstand
as I hear nothing but black.
I see your shadow down the hall,
but you left only a song.
I see your voice when I speak
and hear your eyes when I look to the sky.
They scream for something you lost
and seem to think I immediately found.
The air thickens as the moon rises;
I see one star, too far away to notice.
The sound gets louder as I walk away,
now replaced in my mind as before.
Everything about me is a lie;
the truth I possessed was returned
to a place I dare not understand,
for I may perceive it too clearly.

    Kristin Ilene Edwards

Hurt Heart

This is dedicated to those whose hearts have been hurt at least once. . . .

My heart is bleeding,
waiting for a new love,
that light on the darkness
after a strong wind turned off.
Even though some guys had tried to help me
they had failed in their hopes. . . .
My hurt heart is bleeding,
and there's nobody capable to stop him.
There's a heart hurt! My heart is hurt!
Why is life so cruel!
After all the happiness that you brought me!
My hurt heart lost its shine
and confronted its destiny cruel.
Hurt heart . . .
someday you'll find
that love that you're looking for,
and the hurt heart
won't be hurt back.

    Zoila Villarreal

Black

Black, all black
As you spiral downwards toward your fiery grave
Your snowy white turned to black
Your eight-part harmony turned to nails on a blackboard
Bloodied, broken, burdened you fall
Fallen to the hell reserved for me
Taking my stain, my stench, my sin
The end? Not quite, not yet
You lay
The last ace on the table with the chips
The chips white, red, yellow, brown
Black
Black the look on the card shark's face
You stacked the deck and won fair and square
Your black, my black, disappears
The soot, the ash, the dirt is gone from you
Radiant white, perhaps more glorious than before
You step forth from your blackened tomb
And leave that awful burden there
Hidden in the blackness forever

    Fred P. Swartz

Loved Too Much

When is it possible to love too much,
To think never of yourself
But the one you love above all;
To feel elated . . . the love surging . . .
The heart pounding . . . the soul warmed . . .
And the smile ever-present,
And yet with one word . . .
Or one deed, be devastated,
Shattered into a thousand shards.
Then the heartache takes you over,
The pain seemingly unmerciful,
Knowing maybe for the first time
The love you received was not given
But only a reflection of yourself,
Your gift . . . your heart . . . your love . . .
Without one ounce of sharing from the one you love so deeply
That realization is the moment. . . .
That is the clue. . . .
That is the lightning strike that breaks your heart
And tells you, you have loved too much.

    Rose Marie Neri

The Month of March

I'm glad I was born in this month,
the month of winter's last gasp,
the birth of the promise
of warm days and nights,
mint juleps and barbecues.
To lie under a full moon on a warm night
with little beads of moisture forming on my flesh
that glistens with the moonlight.
Of warm summer mornings when
my feet barely touch the earth as I hurry off to work.
The wonderful fragrances of spring,
nature's melodic and tender sounds
that float on the breeze and caress my senses.
They trigger memories of happy times
and wonderful friends and all the gifts
God has given me.
Thank you, Lord, for this body,
a most awesome machine
that allows me to experience the pleasure
of these springtime gifts!

    Larry Monette Caley

Angel

come, O angel of love
pierce my skin with poisoned arrow
make my dreams come true
let her see and love me

come, O, angel of love
pierce her skin with your poisoned arrow
make her love me
O, angel of love
why do you torment me so
what is your sick pleasure of my torture
O, angel of love
why have you forsaken me
why should I not have one to call my own
now I see you are no angel but a demon
you make us dress a certain way, act a certain way
for what
for the emotion of another
why, O, why do we seek the affection of another
is it merely for the pleasure of you, O, demon
or is it to help us feel good about ourselves

    Philip Andrew Williamson

My Home in Me

In this place this place my home,
This place alone my thoughts do roam,
not the place where grass is green,
but where my dreams within are seen,
This is a place that few will see,
The place within you, them, and me,
The world within us is who we are,
whether it is small, or extending far,
let the world within you shine bright,
To all around, all day all night,
In order to see look with your heart and mind,
and you will be surprised at what you find,
If you really want to see don't look with your eyes,
What really exists your five senses denies,
Look at life for what is really there,
Most overlook it or just don't care,
How beautiful it is when it is true,
How ugly it is from the wrong view,
When you find yourself from deep within,
You will focus on where you're going and not where you've been.

Joel Singleton

My Distant Dreams

She glides through the doorway
The dimly lit room turns bright
Walking up to the stage
She's going to play her music tonight
Putting down my cold glass
I stop looking at an empty chair
I turn around to see her throw back her hair
She dances to the rhythm of her violin bow
A crowd gathers around the star of the show
She slides to my table and sends me a wink
Blows a kiss my way as I raise my drink
She appears in my distant dreams
Every day we're apart
That sweet lady's music captivated my heart
The band packs, it's late and time to close
I ask where the lady went but nobody knows
Stepping from the stage she turned around
To throw back her hair
And then she slipped through that doorway
Into the cold night air

Joseph Paul Calitri

Benji

His voice is singing,
Of my love, my troubles, my life.
His bondage pants have me in a net.
Like catching fish at sea,
Reeling me into him.
Every crank of the pole or
Every pull of the net
Pulls me closer and deeper into his heart.
His pink and black hair has me in a crazy daze.
My twin is nonconformist. Proud.
His piercings and his tattoos
Are another way of taking me into him.
I get trapped in the stories of his tattoos.
Unrealistic. And his piercings hook onto me,
Keeping me close to him, for all time.
But when he finds a girl, and it's not me,
He stomps on my heart with his grinder boots,
And the once good bondage pants
Choke me with the love that he is spreading,
That's not to me!

Alyssa Capillo

Someday Soon

I'm writing this so someday he will realize I care
He'll know exactly how I feel and that I'm always there

I think of him just like a God or master I obey
I'd give him money, treasures, gifts (whatever) any day

To feel our lips connect again could power me to fly
And if we do not hug again I swear to God I'll die!

I need this boy so bad that I can hardly breathe the air
To find and make his heart love me, I'd search just anywhere

I love this boy with all my heart, whatever should I do?
Am I too ugly for this boy to ever love me too?

His friends say he has met his mate, his true, undying love
I cried so much after they told me that she was the one

Why must they kiss in front of me, they know it makes me mad?
Is seeing me in pain the thing that he needs to be glad?

I have so many questions, yet I'm running out of time
I'm learning now but hoping that someday he'll soon be
Mine . . . someday soon

Sara Schroeder

The Night Sky

The sky is dark.
I wonder, when will I make my mark?
I look to the south sky.
I look to the north sky.
The owl is hooting.
What will I be doing?
I look to the west sky.
I look to the east sky.
I wonder, who am I?
I look at the stars.
I wonder, where is the planet Mars?
I look at the moon.
I think about noon.
I think and I think.
How many more hours are there before noon?
I look up and I look down.
I wonder, where will I be at noon?
Am I planning too soon, for noon?
I think what a beautiful moon.
I look, and look, and I wonder.

Angela Buck

Pride's Fall

As a little girl I chased all day,
But my brothers would not let me play.
You're too small, you're a girl,
I often felt alone in this world.
One day to prove I was brave,
I climbed a fence on a dare made.
I reached the top three times my size,
Then the stench and huge pigs caught my eye.
Next thing I knew dad pulled me out,
They were laughing and rolling about.
Even mom and dad joined in the roar,
It wasn't funny what were they laughing for?
Then I realized as mom hosed me down,
I was buried in the mire of pig town.
Two shiny holes revealed my eyes,
And my teeth were shining as I cried.
Everyone sneered yuck! stay away from me,
That impression brought em to their knees.
But eventually there came the day,
A new baby sister and the boys let me play.

Shirley Rose Kidd

Who Am I?

Who am I, conceived by a black father and a
Native American mother.
Born to a nation, born from many nations.
So I ask myself, "Who am I?"

Do I see myself as others see me,
A traditional Native with a nontraditional look?
Who am I?

My father said, "No matter what the mixture,
you are considered black in the minds of others."
In his mind, am I black? Who am I?

My mother said, "No matter what the mixture,
you are Native American."
In her mind, am I an Indian? Who am I?

Some people profile and/or stereotype me,
but I have my own sense of being.
I make my own way in this world
using my intelligence and ingenuity.
Who am I? I'm just me.

 Dale J. Ricks

A Letter

You treated me like a princess;
the next day it was all a mess.
Was I invisible; could you not see?
There was no happy ending for you and me.
Do I exist? Do you care?
You wanted to be friends—if you dare.
My feelings have been ripped,
But why the end of our friendship?
"Avoid" must be your new word.
I never asked you to give me your world.
Now there are misunderstandings and confusion,
but there is no more compassion.
"What did I do?" keeps going through my head,
but when I turn around, you have already fled.
There has been no words said.
I'm done, your game for me was too far led.
You played me for a fool;
ignorance must have been your tool.
It's your loss, I can do much better.
Now I close this letter.

 Kayla Marie Polliard

Closing Moment

As I sit and stare I wonder if life's truly fair
Here lies a great woman that I know
should she stay or should she go
that is the direction she needs to choose
What's best for her is best for us
so why must there be so much family fuss
We should be with one another for family support
not putting up walls to defend a fort
a woman of good uniqueness and heart
so much to say and no idea where to start
different kinds of love to express the way
not knowing if today is the day
Give us a sign to know the end is near
for the unanswered is where most build fear
A sister, a mother, a daughter and a wife
Please end what she feels is a difficult life
She need not be uncomfortable or scared just aware
that all her family wants her to know they care
To all, she has become a great friend
and this will remain even in the end

 Raymond E. Spinelli

Memories of the World

I see an angel.
He comes before me
And I stare into his eyes.
I see a sweet soul
Filled with memories of the world.
The past, all is forgotten,
But all is remembered.
Myths are legends,
Legends are reality.
Destiny is soon to be discovered.
Religion rules and is a way of life.
The world is young and has much to learn.
Peace is proclaimed
And broken promises line the road ahead.
I see a faith-forgotten future
Where hate outlives hope,
Where technology turns against truth
And lies are loved.
I see all this in an instant
And a single tear is shed.

 Natascha Maree Somo

The Love I Lost

From the time you looked at me
I knew we were meant to be
We lived so far apart
It really broke my heart
When I found out you had to leave
I knew we had to be a long distance love
Days grew into months and months turned into years
You never returned to this place so dear
I dreamed of the day you would come
But alas you never came
I found a different game
But I still knew that I loved you
I believed you would come, someday, someone
Would meet me on that road of life
And help me through my times of strife
I hoped that someone would be you
But somehow I knew
That you were gone
And I had to go on
'Cause life is too precious to lose

 Cassia Backwater

My Pure Bliss

I watch him from afar
hoping he'll notice me.
He grabs my hand
and asks me my name;
at this time,
I'm on cloud nine.

Things are going well
until I turn my head and there she is.
They engage in conversation
and soon I am all alone.
I do all I can to impress him
but I can't catch his eye.

He glances over with a gorgeous smile
and tells me to wait there.
It's getting late, I'm about to give up.
Then he appears and says, thanks for waiting.
I say, you're all I've ever dreamed of;
I would wait for an eternity.
He slips his number in my pocket, smiled, and walked away.

 Victoria Marie Lemus

Poem

I'm going to try and get this poem thing done right
This line by line rhyming I'm attempting tonight
This poem is about love, about pain, like many others
It's filled with the clichés you read one poem to another
Its title is "Poem," represented in a word or two
Perhaps "Hate," "Happiness," or "I Love You"
One way or another it's a poem nonetheless
A simple writing of words one uses to confess
Confess or express, it's all the same
Feelings are let out freely, wild and untamed
Just make sure one writes well and remember to rhyme
But wait not all poems rhyme, well not all the time
Silly these poets, they just cannot decide
Whether it's childish to rhyme about what they're feeling inside
The simple poem, a form of art and expression
But all this expression leaves me with some questions
Must every poem express a feeling or emotion?
Must every poem have a purpose and a notion?
Because certainly this poem does have a purpose my friend
Heck, I just wanted to rhyme, from the beginning to the end

Eric Le

The Painter

I sigh at the image before me
And pick up the powder,
Smearing natural tones
On shadowed skin,
Smoothing textured eyes.
I sigh at the image before me
And pick up the blush,
Illuminating a false, inner light
Upon my cheeks,
Brightening pale skin.
I sigh at the image before me
And pick up the liner,
Materializing striking features
Above saddened eyes,
Bringing sunken pupils forward.
I sigh at the image before me
And smile . . .
But cannot believe that smile,
Because covered is the masterpiece that was
Me.

Angela Marie Smith

A Seascape of Wonder

A swirl of brilliance
A blue fantasy
Silver and gold streaks darting
Here, there, and everywhere, whirling with energy
Splashes of dazzling colors
Sparkling light skipping on the surface
Surreal visions dance before the eyes
A flash of teeth, a flick of tail
A wild array of power and strength
The birth
The life
The death
A gold hush covers all
Blue stains pink
Sparkles blush ruby red
Golden ribbons wind across the crimson waters
Baby breezes curl the waves
The cycle continues
Life and death intertwined
The ocean sings its song

Christine Mary Paiva

Coming Down

And my eyes closed
as my hands reached for the clouds to cover me.

And it rained down on my body
like the tears from an unseen god.
It rained.

And it thundered in my ears
like my father's voice
scolding me,
leading me,
calling me,
judging me.

And my body fell
as I found my way.
My body fell
and the world was spinning

and I was falling and it was raining
and it all began to make sense
as I came down and laid queerly on the bathroom floor.

Tyra J. Louis

Good Night

He sways into the dimly lit hallway
Grabbing another glass of brandy
Gulps . . . It down
He slouches against the wall
Wrinkles flow through his clothes like
Small waves . . . drifting in an ocean
Fine lines caress his face
Painting a picture of a young man
Aging . . . faster than most
His piercing blue eyes scream out his pain
Like the wailing of a fire truck
Racing . . . to find flames of a burning building
"Hi, honey."
Sluggish words
Slurred words . . . painful words
He staggers to the staircase
Slams into the wall
Falls . . . unconsciously to the floor
He sleeps like a pile of old crumpled clothes
"Good night, sweet daddy"

Krystal Allen

To the Void inside My Soul

Someone once told you regret nothing
Since then, you've regretted everything
But by not taking risks, you lose your dreams
Dreams that get you through the present
Even as it slips into the past
Where emotional confusion becomes tangled
With broken friendships, painful memories
It bothers you to never know
Where you're headed in this life
Like walking down a dark alley
Underneath a starless sky
You search your soul for answers
Fearing what you might find
Are you the person you thought you were?
You ask, what do I want from myself?
And wait for a response
Then the stars appear, one by one,
To light your way, and then you see
Before being true to others,
I want to be true to myself

Brittany Paige Thompson

Realism Strikes Back

Picture yourself in a race to the finish
With nothing but a hurdle in the way.
As hard as you train, as hard as you try
The hurdle's too high, and you just cannot fly!
Take a look at the crowd and see if they notice.
The will is still there; the ability is missed.
They always say a big heart can go a long way,
But now I know a broken back cannot be remade.
Life will go on without a stop for me.
I'm just afraid I may not ever catch up, you see.
There is but one thing to force me out of bed.
That is the woman I love and hope to someday wed.
I must just face the truth of the mire.
I'll never become Elliott, Chelios, Sosa, or McGuire.
There will always be Jager, sports, and sex.
It's just my muscles I cannot flex.
So if you're reading this and you are sad,
Just know that it does make me mad.
However as long as Stephanie holds my hand,
It will never matter how my life will land!

     Timothy Brehm

The Sniper's Vow

Oh, Lord strengthen my body
Help me strike my enemies down
Let me shield my fellow soldiers
And let me rid our enemies
With each bullet I fire
Let it take with it my wrath
The blood and memories of my dear dead friends
The anger of our entire nation
And let it plunge itself
Deep into the heart of my enemy
Killing him with the instant it strikes
Many friends have I lost to this war
Let me lose no more
Help me serve and protect my nation's people
I shall stay here concealed among nature
Preventing enemy advancement
For as long as I survive without being seen
Or running out of ammunition
Let my sacrifice be of some use
To aid my friends to victory

     Yohan Desmond Spencer

To Find the Worth of Poem

In truth my lyrics are quite dull;
Of stanza's I know not.
Some things I say are quite full
Of meaningless phrases and the lot.
I try to write grand things like Shakespeare,
And I bore myself to death.
I do not write for overseers,
For it's the cowboy poet I know best.
A poem is a thought,
One once said to me.
Not meant for worthless change or to be bought,
Not meant for foreign eyes to see.
In my heart, a few rhymes sound more fun
Than descriptions of the seas.
To find worth in poem,
Lies in the hearts of you and me.
So I write for the healing of my heart;
Prizes do not matter.
Because the writings I put forth
Count for something better.

     Paul Cannon

The Coming Spring

S l o w l y
the green comes,
hesitant at first,
as though winter were a hungry wolf
and spring a new lamb.
But soon,
when the fear of cruel clawing ice and snow has passed,
she comes
shyly peeking out into the pale blue sky,
creeping out from her earthen cover,
spreading tiny leafy buds and spears of grass;
draping skeletal trees with green gossamer
with every step she takes.
Summer will come
arrogant and brassy with blazing heat;
displaying every hue of green possible.
But for now, spring reigns
gentle and serene;
content to knit her lacy cobwebs
and wait.

     Jana Lynn Nyman

Perdita

don't tell me you've got problems.
everybody does but some just think
they're the only ones. so suffer
to the moon for it's being the lunatic
laughing at the sane
who think they're mad enough
as the man-on-the-moon.
no, but believe me, i was the man-on-the-moon
once
and yes, caiman saw me up there,
so stop moaning.
you know what thom says:
being miserable is easy;
being happy is tougher
and cooler.

go and look for your mind
'cause you're never going to find it.
you're sane
'cause you never look at the water.
no, you never look at the water.

     Oya Nuzumlali

More Than Just

A friend of mine once told me a wife was only this,
One who does your housework and is paid with just a kiss.
Can you believe to my surprise, I found this was not true,
A wife is much more than this, so I'm telling you.
A partner and a lover, the one who holds our hand,
When everything in life goes wrong, she helps you make a stand.
To wake up in the morning and smell the coffee brew,
You realize she cares for you through just the things she'll do.
A friendly face across the table, such a lovely view,
Who listens to your daily gripes and cheers you when you're blue.
That bears your children, washes clothes, and irons skillfully,
She keeps the whole house in order, efficient as can be.
When the children all are gone, the house a quiet place,
And there's only the two of you, just look into her face.
See the one who's always been close by your side,
To make your life what it was and helped to ease the ride.
Many dreams she gave away to help you follow yours,
The feelings she did not show as she cried behind closed doors.
So, if you think a wife is just a maid that kisses pay,
You better take a deeper look at what you have today.

     Albert H. Moir

Sadness

What are these lies that cloud my mind?
This madness mixed with desire,
This sadness mixed with confusion . . .
What is this pain that ruins me?
The pain that weakens me.
The pain that brings me to my knees . . .
What is this madness?
The madness that destroys lives,
The madness that destroys minds . . .
What is this disease that infects me?
This disease that eats me alive,
This disease that muddles my thoughts . . .
What is this sadness?
The reaper of souls,
The master of madness,
The creeping death,
The boiling anger,
The conductor of the symphony of destruction,
This, which is the beginning of my end,
or the end of my beginning . . .

Josh Levine

A Night without Stars

You left me here, alone with the night.
The stars, they fade.
The darkness sets in.
I look for an escape,
But the door shut in my face.
I run through the night,
Searching, striving
For an answer that has ceased to exist.
I stand detached at the end of one world,
Looking down, pondering the memories.
The wind in my hair
And the pain in my heart.
My hope is exhausted,
I surrender, I give in.
I don't have the strength
To find the light from within.
My stars are gone,
And in their place
Are drops of water,
Tears fall with grace.

Heather Duran

Shattered

He lies on the bed with such silence—
Silence that makes the heart stop.
My eyes strain in the somber surroundings:
Visions of a still silhouette, a small child.
I stretch and settle my hand over his chest,
Searching for a selfish satisfaction.
Silliness steals away my fear.
His chest soars and sinks with a steady pace.
Slumber steals our last soundless bond.
Dirk is gone.
Sanity is at a standstill.
Split-second knowledge shatters my world;
Stabs my soul.
Slowly his body enters the space of earth;
Soon under a shroud of soil.
Something I await—anything from the shallow.
Sorrow engulfs me.
Suffer for eternity times seven.
Sleep my angel.
Sleep.

Erik M. Dalton

"Splash" the Duck

Going down the road
We saw a duck that strode
With wings stretched
And claws that scratched
Belonged to the cat
The cat was fat
But the duck had no chance
The cat had only to prance
All of a sudden
The duck started struttin'
The cat was surprised
But the wings hadn't arisen
The duck started grinin'
The cat's mind was spinin'
The duck pointed behind
And there were nine
The cat was shocked,
More ducks were stocked
It was gone in a flash
And no longer bothered the duck named "Splash."

Heather Marie Divin

Never the Way I Planned

Somewhere we went wrong,
Took the wrong road, misjudged precious time,
Time that can never be regained.
Judgments have been made,
Restrictions set forth,
It's all over now.

I thought we were careful, but that doesn't matter.
We lost something today,
Their trust, our freedom.
I hope our love is strong enough to keep breathing,
But it seems as if Fate has dealt another crushing blow.
Will I lose him?

We're no longer kids, there's no one else to blame,
Only with the falling sands of the hourglass
Will the ramifications be made known.
Oh, how they are feared!

It wasn't supposed to be this way,
But things never went the way I planned,
And I guess they never will.

Lindsay Anne Lesser

Enduring the Pride

Pride is the heat coming off my face
The victory of running and winning a race
The glory of defending and stealing the ball
The revenge when I'm dribbling past them all.
Pride is lending a helping hand
The choice to lead by taking a stand
The decisions I make to better the future
The example I give to those who are younger.
Pride is the "A" I strive to reach
The step toward my dream to teach
The desire I have to succeed well in school
The entrance into the college rule.
Pride is meeting the mountain top
The unending devotion I pledge not to stop
The tears in my eyes—frustration and despair
The smile on my face when I'm finally there.
Pride is my drive to be the best
The work that I use when put to the test
The times I've had to go through steep bends
The greatest of feelings that never ends.

Kristin Noel Kline

Cast Off

Cast into my dungeon, Shackled and chained,
Shadowed in blackness, immersed in pain.
Desolation, my creation, a curse to this world
In ravaging anguish, my existence is swirled.
Caged by my psyche, my conscience devoid
Castrated confidence, my life is destroyed.
Bow to my master, a gesture obscene
No light in the tunnel, only death serene.
Take up the rapier, glistening and strong,
Embattled, embroiled, the passage is long.
Dash for the exit, an end to this fray
Tussle and toil, for a victory this day.
Cast off my armor, relinquish my sword,
The robes of the mortal are mine no more.
Riding winds of hope, that eternity brings
Soar to my future, on angelic wings.
Upon this province, winged future in flight,
Celestial divinity, heavenly right.
Shadowed no more, spirit aloft,
Dreams surreal, prison cast off.

Clement Allen Barnes, III

Glare in the Dark

Did you see that?
The twisted shapes with their twisted motion
Swirling in and out of the bleak
and utter darkness
The shuffling of deformed flesh
Their demented mumbling and laughter
Oh, that horrid laughter!
Piercing into my brain
Ripping from me my sanity
I am not crazy!
I have seen them! I know them!
They are coming for me!
You do not believe me! Look!
Look! Do you not see them?
They are coming closer! Closer!
There! In the shadows behind you!
Then the muffled cackling
of horrific laughter
Trickles across the room
like so much warm crimson.

Michael P. Williams

Open Your Heart

Open your heart, love again
It's been seven years of rain.
Time to let go of the suffering and pain,
'Cause there's really know one to blame.

Open your heart, let love in,
You know, of course, it's a sin
To keep such great love to yourself;
Are you afraid to love someone else?

Open your heart, love again
Look around, it's everywhere.
Love can be found in many places,
Just look into the people's faces.

Open your heart, let love in,
For you know the time is right.
Just look, you'll see the light,
Then you can love again.

Open your heart,
Love will come in.

Carol Jane Lonergan

A Peek into My Soul

I never let people see my work
at least, not people I know
yet, I would read it to a total stranger
my work is a window into my soul
and I'm scared
I'm scared if you get that peek into my soul. . . .
if you see the true me . . .
if you knew who I really was . . .
you wouldn't want to know me anymore
my poetry is the blood of my soul
my drawings are its limbs
my music is its heartbeat
I must write to keep my soul alive
if I gave you my heartbeat my soul would die
but, perhaps, when I meet that one who knows my soul
I will show them
but I am sure
that they will have already seen
anything I would have for them to see
in me

Diana Purcell

Meet Me . . .

Meet me in my dreams tonight,
I think my request is very slight.
You cannot be here to comfort me,
But in our dreams, together we'll be.
As you trace my cheeks and kiss my eyes,
The emptiness within me sinks and dies.
We go wherever we wish in our dream,
The ocean, the desert, or visit the queen.
All I wish is that the dream would last,
Night becomes day and it happens too fast.
With dreams we can be together more,
Climbing up mountains or walking the shore.
Holding hands, we can go anyplace.
In our dreams, we always have a space.
I am busy now and so are you,
With various tasks we must do.
I will need you tonight when day is done,
When the sky is dark and there is no Sun.
I will ask you this favor when the time is right;
Will you meet me in my dreams tonight?

Gabrielle Koczab

Life

The rain is lightly pouring
Right outside my window.
It seems a hidden reminder
Of the way every life must go.
It has been said
That rain must fall into everyone's life.
It seems my rain hasn't yet ended.
The rain started the day I was brought here
And continues yet to fall.
Where is the end,
If there is any end at all?
Do we not all deserve a chance to dry our feathers and fly?
It seems to me
That in my life I will not get a try.
I may never see the mountaintops,
Never fly above the clouds in the sky.
Because of the unrelenting rain,
Forever pelting me down.
My life will soon have gain,
And that shall be the end of the rain.

Danielle K. Soldner

The Ways We Are

If one person says he likes those ways
The other will grieve about it for many days
If one asked for the color white
The other would ask for gray or blue
If you have one way of doing things
The other will do the opposite of that
If one could sit around forever
The other would run until the end of days
If one likes the calm and serene
The other likes the fast and chaotic
If one likes the way society works
The other will stand in an anarchy of disorder
If one reads Shakespeare and Nelson and Hemingway
The other reads King and mysteries and horror
If one loves the beach and the waves and the sand
The other loves indoors and the couch and TV
If one chases dreams and fulfills their destiny
Then the other will just stay and rot and wither
If one stays here and the other goes far
That just defines the ways we are

Michael Olinzock

If I Did What You Want Most

If I did what you want most
If I changed without a boast
If the colors in the rainbow
Signified my love for you
All the colors would be pictures
Of my memories in you
For I've grieved of past mistakes we've made
And dreamed of starting new
Of the words spoken so often
That have truly hurt
The inward parts of you
I am beginning new this day of change
You've prayed and hoped for true
For weight loss
For new thought processes
For words to lift and give
Life so abundantly has changed the way I live
I am a new beginning
Because of the one who's beginning
Has given me new life

Emily Carvallo

The New Kid

I was walking down the hall
And I saw some kid new.
His skin was black,
But for all I cared it could have been blue.
Some people were laughing,
Some people were staring,
Some people pushed him,
With out even caring.
It made me mad
To see them stare.
So I went up and
Touched his hair.
I said, "come on new kid,
You don't need this."
And as we walked away
He gave me a kiss.
So to all of you
Who don't like blacks,
Whites are no different
As a matter of fact.

Krista Lynn Dingman

Without You

I sit and think, what would I do
If you ever left, if our love was through
I'd feel so sad, I'd be so blue
I don't think I could make it, without you
My life would be empty, my heart would break
I think I'd pray my life he'd take
It would be hard to make it through
In this life without you
I'd sit and cry all night long
While listening to sad, old songs
I'd cry myself to sleep at night
Hoping tomorrow, it would be all right
Tomorrow would come, it would be the same
I'd feel no happiness, I'd feel only pain
So I sat and thought what would I do
If you ever said our love was through
Then it hit me, that you are here
I should be loving you, while you are near
Not thinking of you leaving or being gone
Just making sure that you stay in a happy home

Patricia Harris

Confounded Soul

Sweet silent tones of grace pour forth from
your lips as words unspoken, unutterable for
fear of loss to another unworthy of their
mellifluous sound. With words do I see through
your every mask and fallacy into the soul
untouched by unfamiliar eyes. You see into the
depths of your darkened soul to rekindle that
light once aflame, but the ever-growing fear
of rejection and immutable consequence
persists. Overcome the reluctant mannerism to
allow another into your world. A world not
discovered by means of search, but rather
through willingness revealed to those most
worthy of such a gift. Show me the world that
has yet to be claimed. Speak of nothing, but
tell me everything. I can still see through
the closed doors behind which you hide. Allow,
instead, this ground not yet tread upon, to
become the path upon which I travel, in search
of the soul I once lost.

Catherine Anne Green

3:46 a.m.

Restless nights . . . lost and lonely.
Move around tossing, turning.
Images of plenty run wild
I cannot sleep, screams this child
Of school, of work, of his one true love.
Change positions, toss the sheets.
Thinking of her, his heart does beat,
Going mad, going crazy, does some chores . . . but is lazy.
Gets a drink, spits in the sink,
Then sits down and begins to think.
This is MY night, what a mess.
All I want is some rest!
I keep on dreaming; my eyes remain open. . . .
Thoughts of love and the ocean.
Can I run to her? Can I swim?
The stars, once bright, start to dim.
Here comes that Sun,
Oh, where is my hun?
Another lonely moment . . .
The night has won.

Leonceo Vasquez Angsioco

Rant

Cover my eyes so I cannot see the lies.
Inside I scream for something to seem
to make some sense in my thoughts of craziness.
I can't figure out
what these feelings are about:
gloom, hate, indifference,
passiveness, no control.
What am I doing?
Where am I going?
What will I find
inside the maze of my mind?
frustration is building within,
but of what I don't know.
I want to show them, but don't know how or where to start.
What is my part in this place they call life?
Nothing seems to suffice:
the filth I feel around me,
the filth I see controlling.
Sweep away these cobwebs in the back of my mind
so that I can find the answers or a sign
of why I'm so confined.

Shirley Yang

She Sings

This is about Britney Spears.
She sings for everyone, smiling.
Then leaves for her room,
Not home, never home.
Home is no more that a word to her.
Though some cheer, others don't,
They make fun, and say things that hurt.
She learned not to cry in front of them,
Or else the cameras flash, and stories spread.
But still she sings, never slowing,
Never showing, how they hurt her by what they say.
Still, she sings.
They talk about the bad things she does,
But they never say the good.
Sometimes they don't see the things missing
In her life, but she does.
Tomorrow she will wake up,
And no matter what they say,
She'll sing,
Still smiling.

Jenny Secretan

The Pleasures of Love

We have definitely had our share of innocent fights
Which made me feel restless throughout the night.
The fights ended and I was back in your loving embrace
Filling my eyes with the wonders of your beautiful face
I find exquisite pleasure in simple glimpses of you
I could gaze at you all night if you would allow me to.
We have shared many hours of darkness exploring explicit delight
Only to find ourselves interrupted by the horrific time of night!
I feel completely alone and empty inside when you are gone
Left to remember the times just shared, anticipating the new dawn
When I awake disappointed to find that you are not there beside me
I think quietly to myself. . . . where might my beloved lover be.
I found you as soon as possible and just held on to you tight.
Amazed how I could feel so vulnerable and yet easy to fright.
I love you with all my heart and soul, you are the only one
If you were not there by my side my life would surely be done.
Although we may have disagreements that last a few days
I know deep down inside my heart this is only a trial phase.
I am thankful and appreciative of the moments we shared together
I truly hope we will remain in each other's heart forever and ever!

Shauna Marie Bandy

One More . . .

one more day . . .
. . . the birds sing
. . . the children play
. . . the dogs bark.

one more night . . .
. . . the stars come out
. . . the streetlights come on
. . . the crickets chirp.

one more day . . .
. . . i cry
. . . i look from the inside out
. . . i die inside.

one more night . . .
. . . i sing of loneliness
. . . i sleep
. . . i dream.

one more time i look out from my world and watch
yours pass by in happiness. one more day, i dream, then i die.

Maranda Zilk

I Know

God give me strength. The strength to do what
I know what I feel is right. But it's hard. My mind is
out of control. My feelings have run
wild. My heart aches. It throbs. It gives me a headache.
Because It knows. It feels the truth. My feelings have
lost my train of thought. Focus! I know what I have to
do. I know definitely. God give me strength. The strength to
stop feeling. But it's hard. It's so hard! Give me strength
to gain control of my mind. My mind is the key to free my heart.
I'm confused. God give me strength. The strength to just walk away.
To walk away from the pain that is burning me on the
inside. Burning me so bad that I'll be scarred for life.
Scarred enough to make hard. So hard and unmoving. Cold
and heartless. But I know what I have to do. I know
definitely. But God it is so hard! Please give me strength. I'm
begging you. I cry out please take away this pain! Make
me numb. Make me cold to the heat. It's my only way out.
Can't you hear it? My heart? Hasn't is suffered enough?
Can you hear it? Free it. Free me! Damn it, my heart
will die! God give me strength, it's my salvation. I know.

Marion Louise Hudson

Judge for Yourself

The teacher I never wanted
Is the teacher I'll always remember.
Caring, loving, devoted human being,
Standing as tall as a giant.
Rumors sprang up all around about her
That I never should have listened to.
Stories that were untrue and exaggerated,
Making her sound like an awful teacher.
The principal's office here I come—
You must take me out of this class
Or I am moving to another school.
"Give her a chance," was the principal's response.
As a terrified ten-year-old, I walked into class
Giving her a chance and forgetting the rumors.
Getting to know my favorite teacher
Is the best thing I have ever done.
Don't listen to rumors, judge for yourself.
Do not miss out on knowing
Some important people
Who may become your favorite teacher.

Crystal Canole

At All Costs

You say you are so tired,
And your muscles are weak and sore.
You say you just can't go on.
Well, I know the feeling.
But we are working towards a goal
And if it means success,
No price is too high, no practice too long
And no pain too horrible.
Perhaps you would rather take it easy,
But you would fail.
I would rather endure the pain and suffering,
For then I will succeed.
You say enough is enough,
But that's not so with me.
I believe in victory at all costs
And fighting to achieve a goal.
So don't speak to me of pain or exhaustion.
I know them well
For they are akin to victory,
And therefore friends to me.

Laura Elizabeth Mooneyhan

A King's Letter

Great paintings by King of England,
You treasure with your lives
Great songs by King of Pop,
You value in your hearts
Great satires by King of Comedy,
You savor with your ears

How come seas you pollute into deterioration?
How come animals you butcher into extinction?
How come forests you sentence to destruction?
How come children you murder through abortion?

You do not treasure them as great paintings
You do not savor them as great satires
You do not value them as great songs
You do not love them as I LOVE YOU

For these things were given to you by ME. . . .

The Sole Creator of your kings of this world
Love,
The King of Kings

Carlos Sumagui Angeles

September 11, 2001

I cannot look my children in the eyes without crying.
Because people are so full of hate.
So full of hate,
they become blind to everything.
Because people are so vulnerable.
How did it feel
to sit in the departure lounge
of an anonymous airport,
looking at the faces of the other passengers?
Families.
Knowing that soon they would all be dead.
Watched by millions around the world,
their death, a piece of film
on TV news;
from every angle,
repeated over and over.
Your head was so full of hate.
It became all you could see.
Children are celebrating in the streets.
What will happen now?

Rebecca Helen Galloway

Why Did My Love Have to Say Goodbye?

Why did the man
that I showed and gave my love to
say goodbye to me?
There are so many ways you can say goodbye to someone,
but this goodbye means that he was never coming back,
Every night, after I say my prayers,
I ask myself,
Why did he say hello,
But he really meant goodbye,
As I lie in my empty bed,
I ask myself,
What will I do without love,
Memories of the man that I love beside me?
As I look to the other side of my bed,
I don't see the man I love.
I just close my eyes and cry myself to sleep.
When I wake up the next morning,
The cycle starts over again.
Memories of the one that I love
That told me hello, but meant goodbye.

Danielle Jones

Hold On to the E

It was the perfect match from the start
Whatever she wanted, I gave from the heart
Going above and beyond was no problem for me
My life was filled with purpose and meaning
I would always get lost in her
Anxious to greet her in the mornings
Filled with thoughts of her in my dreams
No problem that she sometimes exhausted me
She was my world, second to none
So how can I live now that our time is done?
I don't want this life without her
There is nothing left inside
There could never be another
Those that were second
Try to piece together this shattered soul
There's no reason to go on; I want to live in what was
What a tremendous loss of a great L.O.V.
But was it complete? There is no E.
It was . . . just . . . a J.O.B.
I can use that to keep the sanity

J. D. Johnson

Dear Mom

Even though we don't always go some days
And sometimes we don't agree in the same ways,
I've always looked up to you for your guiding hand,
And in return, you've helped keep me out of the quicksand.
You have stayed tall, beautiful and strong
Even when it seemed as though everything went wrong.
You are always right there by my side, day and night,
Whenever I am sick, not leaving unless everything's right.
You are there for me with your loving care,
Taught me my manners, and not to stare.
You are always there to protect me
But making sure the real world I can see.
Still doing your absolute best
In keeping me from any harmful pest.
You are there finding some safe route,
When I could swear, there's no way out.
You are careful to warn me of a one's way,
And when with them to my instincts stay.
You are my very "bestest" friend
With a friendship that will never end.

Kaila Gretchen

Pain

Love. What an ever changing word.
When you say it to your parents, it's compassionate.
There is brotherly love, warm and caring.
We love our God with fear.
But when you love another person,
There is pain. It is unique, this pain.
Some will pretend not to know this feeling.
They will ignore it;
Try to make it disappear.
But anytime they love someone, it is there watching,
And when the object of their affection leaves,
It pounces with a fury.
Life stops, and everything they touch
Is the love that has left their heart frigid.
Nothing is safe
When that love leaves;
It takes something with them
And will never be replaced.
The pain that remains will lessen over time.
Maybe.

Jonathan Olmos

Go Inside

When times are tough and you feel there's no hope,
Go inside.
Find your inner strength,
The strength for the tougher times.
Pick up the broken pieces of you life
And put them back together.
Smile when problems are thrown your way
Because you have the strength to win.
Look up. Look proud.
For you were struck down and got up again.
You were losing and fought to survive.
When the chips were down,
You picked them up and went on.
You fought to survive
And you won another victory
For your towering collection.
Claim your reward,
For you have won it.
You will be able to say,
"This problem is solved; now give me another."

Duston Anthony Roark

Disaster in America

September eleventh,
I awoke with hope and laughter,
Never hearing about this disaster,
It was eight thirty when the news hit me,
I turned on the news channel,
To see pain and sorrow.
First the Twin Towers,
And then the Pentagon,
All those lives,
Were all so gone.
Then the last one,
Location I do not recall.
My heart goes out,
To all those people,
Their families and friends,
Never knew that was their end.
Be strong America,
For we WILL fight back,
And take back our rights,
To live freely.

Alaina Nicole Niece-Vaughan

Love Unreturned

I remember that night, when we kissed for the very first time
You made me shiver
Now, I shiver alone,
in the cold wind of the night,
as tears roll down my face
for the love I have given you
is neither welcomed nor returned
I thought my love mattered to you,
I thought you felt the same
I thought you wanted to be with me,
but by your actions and not your words
I am again proven wrong
I might have been lying to myself
about the way you felt
Or were you lying to me
to avoid the painful truth?
The truth might hurt, but lies hurt more
So I guess I hurt myself
In fantasies you've loved me for it seems like forever
In reality, did your love ever begin?

Angela Sturgill

I'm Not Yours

You might think I'm weak
Falling for the things you say to me
All I ever wanted you gave to me
But now it's time for you to realize
I'm not yours, you can't use me
My heart knows better, I'm stronger than you
So just leave and go because I'm not yours
Stop trying to make my mind
Think you're mine
'Cause my heart will lead me
In the right direction
Away from you
Now I know better
I don't need you anymore
You make me do things
You say you'll always love me
But please baby just let me go
I'm not yours, you can't use me
My heart knows better, I'm stronger than you
So just leave and go because I'm not yours

Cassandra Laeng

Fear

Swept away with good words
Up in the clouds in a daze
Getting caught up in the cords
Running around in a maze
Contemplating thoughts about you
Wondering if this could really be
And if you're true
True enough to be with me
Your actions have spoken loud and clear
I was too blind to notice
Now in my heart there is a tear
Happened because I didn't focus
In his hands was my heart
Without any thought of my feelings
He took it and tore it apart
I ask myself "when will I start healing?"
It may take days or months
Probably even a year
No matter what it will be done
As soon as I get over my fear

Alba Diva Cabrera

The Flow

Water slowly creeps,
From under the door,
Making a puddle.
The water rushes, the puddle grows,
Into a creek,
A huge, gushing river,
Inside my mind,
Spilling out, all at once,
Open the gates, free the flow,
Let everything out,
But keep it coming,
In a never ending flood,
Engulfing me,
Dragged down, by forceful currents,
Pushed in a direction,
I don't want to go, no fighting it,
Shoved into a crevice,
Trapped, I can't breathe!
Drowning . . .
Without a sound, a small trickle flows. . . .

Sara Jane Henceroth

Today Our Nation Saw Evil

antifreeze me.
blood becomes blue juice in plastic
like small coolers keep my ham and American.
bloody body fallen frozen.
memory leave.
evil hatches and licks its fangs of pain.
fortress's turncoat to collide life with life.
did you hear what they said?
O God O God O God O God
world pause.
steel castles fuse intercourse in the sky
legs of the great giant fall, arm of the
shield amputated, dissolved to powder; no,
that white sprinkle is not baby but
death stagger wrench heart.
fly flag.
judgment day looms ferocious, foaming.
the dogs are hunting, hungry while
hands clasp, love prays, people stand.
hope faith time tomorrow.

Lauren Nicole Wood

New York Aftermath

Chaos spews out of the ruptured fuel tanks.
Flames fanned by anger and hate.
Devastation inflicted on people unknown;
World spins and turns upside down.
Spreading destruction, death close behind.
Reason and logic ignored.
How can you help? What is there to do?
Tears give the only release.
Behind are families; their lives torn apart.
A country is under attack.
Who has the answer? Where will it come from?
Can we feel safe once again?
September 11, I wish I'd forget.
The memory will live with us all.
The lessons we've learned at so great a cost;
We'll build on and then move ahead.
The terror we've seen. The scars on our soul.
We'll never be naive again.
The bill for this action can never be paid.
And yet we must send the bill out.

Thomas A. Lamb

September 11, 2001

What took 4 years to create,
Took only seconds to destroy.
The pain, so hard to alleviate,
All from a madman's ploy.
The number of souls lost
Will take months to know for sure.
While the families ponder the cost
Of starting all out war.
Debris and smoke filled the city,
As innocent people ran for their life.
People watching on TV thought what a pity
And pondered who would have such strife.
The planes that hit had instantly vaporized,
Along with the precious cargo they carried.
While those on the ground realized
To many of victims were they married.
Symbols of Capitalism crumbled,
As a nation watched in horror.
And when speaking, we did stumble
To try and describe our terror.

Robert Christian Reustle

the sky

i remember looking at the sky,
and thinking, will i go there when i die?
all the things i have done and said,
all dissolving overhead.
there are things that i regret,
the most things that i won't forget.
i lie back, looking at the clouds,
beyond them, vast darknesses, like shrouds.
it was all peaceful and serene,
as if it was all a dream.
i see a plane up above,
filled with people, filled with love.
i feel the grass between my fingers,
when in my mind, a single thought lingers,
when people die, what do they feel?
do they see what they have done, even steal,
or just their last and middle years?
death, the thing most people fear
because the time will come someday,
no matter what you do, it'll happen anyway.

Christopher Davis Ginther

Happiness

Happiness isn't something you get with money
Or the way you feel when you walk out and it is sunny.
Happiness is only one thing—
God the Almighty King.
He hung on the cross for you and me.
Can you imagine how it would be
As the thorns were slowly pushed through His skin
All He could think about was dying for our sins.
While He cried out in pain.
The crowd thought He was insane.
The sky went dark, the Earth began to tremble.
Our God is truly a symbol!
Each day I want to strive to be like Him.
To walk in His footsteps and never sin.
Thank you, Lord, for all you have done;
You have shown your people you are the true Son.
Lord, I know you keep me in your sight,
And help me to spread your light.
You are the true Almighty King,
And to you I will forever sing.

Tosha Dawn McCloud

Evil vs. Salvation—My Testimony

Head spinning confusion
Hurtling toward an atmosphere
So deep into darkness that midnight does not compare.
Anger and hate combine as one in this place of evil,
Piercing my heart and soul.
Weeping and gnashing of teeth are heard in the distance.
A loud voice calling my name,
Temptation beckoning me to come forward.
I go and I fall, falling into a
Deep abyss of pain and sadness.
The loud voice turns to laughter; I scream out for help.
Then, as I think that this is my eternity,
A strong hand catches me and lifts me up.
I now stand firm in the Light of Love, Peace, and Hope.
I now have an armor of truth.
I have strength to overcome
Whatever is placed in my path.
Evil tries to come like a lion to pounce and devour.
My armor is there protectively,
And my life has changed forever, like a butterfly in a cocoon.

Jessica Erin Latham

Wondering Out Loud

As I look into the dark night sky,
I wonder how, I wonder why.
As I look into the deep night sky,
I wonder why she never tries.
I wonder if she cries at times.
I wonder if I've lost my mind.
As I look at the black night sky,
I wander out, I wonder why.
I dream of two warm hearts in kind.
I wonder what walls must be climbed,
Searching for answers in my tortured mind.
I wonder if her love's divine.
As I float into the deep black sky,
I close my eyes, my mind takes flight;
the dreams begin and all is right.
I wonder why. I wonder why
Each heart must melt at each sunrise.
I wonder why love isn't blind.
As I look into the starlit sky,
I yield to love and recover life!

Mitchell B. Baruchowitz

Insane

I sit upon the windowsill,
Waiting for the day to come,
When all the world turns upside down,
And I will rule the world around.
They don't want to listen,
But they're going to hear it soon,
The noise I make behind the walls,
My cries for help, my screeching calls,
They all will soon be heard.
You think I'm mad and that is what you see,
For all I seek is your misery,
You cannot overpower me,
For soon I will be coming for thee.
You are now a fright,
Scared to see,
The light ahead,
From what I be,
You think of what or who I am,
Look out, Mack;
I'm the Gingerbread Man!

Jason Abofsky

Uncertainty

Questions.
Everywhere.
Now and again kind enough to subdue to whispers,
Other eras not.
Whirling, twisting, a few earth-shattering,
Others barely audible.
Dost thou have a hold on thy life?
Dost thou shudder at the thought of knowing thy soul?
Questions.
They be the tiny tugs at thy ear when gazing upon the stars,
The murderous cries when a babe dies.
Heaven summons its citizens with questions.
Hell begs like a dog with question's unspeakable pain.
They cry to be answered—no, they shriek!
For all life is bending to their will,
And answering—I know not.
I know not!
For it is death, not life, that answers them.
Questions.
Everywhere.

Jessie Weis

Judy

She goes into her bedroom and she looks in the mirror,
She sees someone she doesn't know,
And her eyes start to tear.
She wonders why she feels so bad,
When others feel so good.
But she doesn't want their help or pity
And she wishes that she could just move on,
Just carry on without all this ache and pain.
And she doesn't realize that we would gladly share the strain.
She doesn't have to try to handle everything,
Because if she does she'll never hear the pretty birds sing.
Now I don't know if she will take off the mask she wears,
But if she looks around,
She'll see someone who cares.
And maybe if she wants to,
She can look ahead and live her life,
Really make it last.
She's a fighter and I know she is strong.
And when she leaves she won't be gone,
Because her name will carry on.

Amanda Jane Walworth

One Word to Say

To see you is breathtaking,
Your smile and soft touch
Always warms my heart,
Your kind words and inspirations
Always lifts me off my feet,
Your understanding, caring and compassion
Truly an incredible feat
Thank you for all that you have done
Giving your shoulder, when I needed to cry
Kind words when I needed to sigh
Your strong support and
conviction to lift my spirits
Thank you again for all your merits
How can I be so lucky in love I prayed to God,
to send someone from up above,
I truly believe that I have found my soul mate
Maybe, God does give to those who wait
My best friend in the whole world
There is only one word to say
"I love you" (Well maybe three words)

Jeromy D. McMahon

Waiting

When will time unveil
the true love of mine
I prayed a prayer long and hard
for this to come to be
I have searched in endless time
to dwell in a house as one
to be apart from this is what
I want not to be done
I am still searching for her hand
I have searched far and wide from sand to sand
and still I have found not one hand
I struggle to keep my mind from straying
from analyzing each as they appear
for this I am sorry my dear
I am still in waiting for her hand
I will not push it and I will wait
for her to appear on the sand
Father your servant is waiting
for you to place her by my side
for that is true love for you and I

Aaron Duke

Inspiration

When I look into your eyes
It's the way you make me feel
It's not that I can't live without you
It's just that I don't want to even know life without you
I don't need eyes to see the love you give to me
I've been blessed
I found what most people search for
Their entire lives . . . but few ever find
That one person in the world
I was born to love the rest of my life
I found that special person
That will never let me down
That understands it all
All that I am
All that I'll ever be
It's because of you
Your faith in me
I'll always be on your side
Watching over you in all do
I love you

Joseph Luciano

Grandpa

To Maurice J. Coyle, 1918–1995

I was a year ago tomorrow
then we all felt such sorrow,
for with all of your hard work,
and always giving it your best,
God took you from us
so you could have eternal rest.

Grandpa,
I want you to know that because
of all your loving, caring and generosity
you have touched the lives
of all your family and friends,
this is something that will never end.

And always remember
that as you look down at us
with your Irish eyes smiling away,
that as we think of you our
Irish eyes smile the same way.

We all miss you and love you so much.

Dawn Burgus

The Giant's Toe

I woke up early on a sunny day.
Life was good, we were ready to play,
Then a great terror fell from the sky.
All we could do was sit and cry.
Five thousand gone in just one blow,
We looked around—where did they go?
Fanatics fell upon our head,
Innocent people were left dead.
Our people rose to the occasion.
People pitched in from around the nation.
Firemen and rescue workers from everywhere
Merged together to show our nation's care.
They have hit us in our heart.
We bled and we were torn apart,
But through it all, we will stand
A mighty, strong, united land.
Fanatics, you would be best to know,
You have stomped a giant's little toe.
We are a true united land.
On your heads, we will stand.

Laura Terry

Dancing On

A truly remarkable person, Morrie Schwartz,
touching so many lives
with his profound wisdom and insight.
A well-respected college professor, Morrie Schwartz,
perceiving students as raw jewels
to be cut and polished to a proud shine.
A person who enjoys life's pleasures, Morrie Schwartz, dancing
his way of capturing the simplicity beyond the complexities of life.
A victim of the Lou Gehrig's disease, Morrie Schwartz,
enduring the brutal affliction;
leaving his soul burning in a mass of wax.
A man with a positive spirit, Morrie Schwartz,
refusing to wither and disappear;
making death his final project.
A teacher, Morrie Schwartz,
teaching lessons in his final days;
denying anything as being "too late."
To love and be loved . . . Morrie Schwartz,
understanding the greatest gift
dancing on in our hearts.

Meagan Johnson

Bed of Angels

Hundreds of lives were lost today
Tonight they sleep on the bed of angels
War was not declared, nor was a battle fought
They were innocent!
A cowardly act, to say the least
An enemy without name or face
Struck at the heart of this nation
The act was not random
It was an intentional and outright attack
The site of devastation
Appears to be exactly what it is—a war zone
The impact of this tragedy
Will be felt for days, weeks, months
And even years to come
Smoke and ash billowed forth
First blocking the light of day
Then raining down on the recent casualties
In a war yet to be declared
The collapse of the Twin Towers struck a heavy blow
But as a nation, we will go on!

Adam James Telford

Dreaming of You

Countless nights I've lain awake,
Carefully thinking my life through.
With every vision I imagine,
I can only recall memories of you.
The sun shines in your sparkling eyes.
You shade it to see.
I wonder what you're gazing at
And then I realize it's me.
You're like a ray of sunlight,
Beaming in the darkness of the night.
When I am with you,
Everything suddenly seems so right.
I reach out my hand to you
In hopes that we will touch.
I long to feel the electricity
I need to feel so much.
Each day we spend together,
I love you more than I did only yesterday,
And I will continue to love you
More and more each day.

Korin Marie Butler

God Cried

Today God was sad.
I know this because
He cried all day.
He flooded the streets,
He flooded basements.
Today was a sad day
because God cried,
He cried out in pain.
He was in pain because
God couldn't understand
why someone would kill so many.
God couldn't understand
how someone could be so cruel,
how someone could kill thousands.
So God cried all day,
wondering why someone could be so cruel,
to you, to me, to everyone.
He let his tears flood streets and alleys,
while hundreds of volunteers
helped dig through the rubble in New York.

Amber Nichole Futchko

My Dream Last Night

The stars gaze down. The moon is out.
And where are you? In my thoughts about.
I lie asleep, dreams flooding with you;
A smile o familiar, a feeling so new.
With me is the spring. A beautiful life.
No envy, no hatred. A time void of strife.
And what better a sight than me there in your arms?
A feeling so lovely—my world without harm.
The breeze kisses our faces, so soothing, so slow;
The wind sings our song and your smile gives a glow.
But your smile is not it, for the sun also laughs.
And our heaven is happy—She too took her day off.
From your lips rise the words, those so soothing to me,
Those which come from a book most cherished to thee.
And as I sit there, I pray never for the moment to end
And hope that God receives the favor I have sent.
My happiness halted as I woke up in resentment—
"It was only a dream," I thought, as I cried in disappointment.
And foolishly I realized my prayers had been sung
My dream was not over, my dream had just begun.

Maya Lottati

Moment

Disengaged today
Non-engagement
Meant not to be, beaten to the end
Enveloped in tissue
Owed more than possible
More pain than new beginnings
Beginnings coming to ends
Compassion no longer
Longevity questionable
Questions unknown to ask
Known but not spoken
Spoken to the last word
Lasting impressions, pressure in the heart
Hard like a hammer
Mercy not seen, senile to become
Complexity in full embrace
Bracing after each hour, our bond no further
A warden of my own pride
Milestones of memories
Stone-aged memories in time

Rachel Marie Sosnowy

Remembrances

In depths and darkness of a sleepless night
Or in the mists of secretive daydreaming
Remembrances creep slyly in my sight
With misadventures and misfortunes teeming
Remembrances of my tempestuous past
Remembrances of sins still unforgiven
Remembrances of targets hit at last
Of treasures lost, accounts broken
Even remembrances of all my loves and hates
Remembrances of praises and offenses
Remembrances of friends and lost playmates
With whom I rarely managed mending fences
Remembrances of many traveled roads
Of stumbling over roadblocks and boulders
Of bulky and incalculable loads
And heavy burdens pressing on my shoulders
Remembrances of every stepping stone
Imprinting marks on all romantic souls . . .
Yet I don't live by memories alone
And move ahead to new and tempting goals

Yakov M. Zilberberg

Reshith

Reshith, supreme point
Nexus of the dialectic, point of the coincidence of opposites
Point of darkness, point of light
From you the ten Sphiroth, the Merkebah, the wind of the moon
Oh, Reshith, fire flows through your divine centers
And infinity stands in your sun and your moon
From you Kether and Malkuth, Netzoch and Hod
The Supernals the Middle Pillar Binah and Chokmah

Reshith, point of the moon
Point of the Sun, splendor of Yahweh
In the shadow of the Sun and the moon

Oh, Reshith, you guide the Merkebah and the hosts of Israel
The heavenly kingdoms, the Sephiroth, the Sun, and the moon
Your shadow crosses night and brings fire to the moon

From you the archetypal worlds endless fire endless night
The fire of Shin flows through your Sephira
From your shadow and night the templates of creation
In a cosmic explosion of matter and antimatter
As God's shadow crosses creation and creates the World Soul

Dr. Antoinette Voget

As Quiet As It's Kept

Poets are born with better dispositions
Than politicians and thieves,
For poets enrich their social circles via
Suave art-of-word choices that celebrate life.
The scope of a poet's love is higher than most,
For a poet's love starts with an unending obsession
With life's dreams, velocity, and perceived
Universal Truths.
A poet fights better than soldiers, for, through
The power of his pen, a poet can colonize
New hopes and inspirations for generations.
God, the father, blessed the world with
Artists, musicians, writers, and poets,
For he certainly knew that Man's survival
(Chances to survive) could only be enhanced
By how they spark our imagination of true wisdom.
Otherwise, the true quality of our society
Without them would be very, very
Different and much less enlightened,
As quiet as it's kept.

James Anthony Johnson

Ode to a Great Dad

When I was born,
I had a dad that up and went away. . . .
No one could ever want that kind of dad
Not even one; no way!
But I was blessed from that day on,
And this I say to you:
That my Kentuckian uncle, who raised me,
Was the only dad I knew.
He was there to see to my needs;
He always seemed to care.
He gave me a lifetime of love,
And saw to my welfare.
He did this in spite of his own needs
Never thinking of his own self,
'Cause his family was what he cared for.
We were what he considered his "wealth."
Now, don't you think that God has a place
For dads, like the dad I just spoke of?
May God keep my dad in His great care,
In that great eternal love.

Andrea Brown

Two Towers

Two towers fell today,
But our country did not.
The pentagon burned today,
But not as bright as our spirit.
Loved ones died today,
But their memories will forever live.
The skies are dark today,
But a light is burning smoke cannot quench.
Good friends died today,
But we found others we didn't know we had.
Policemen died today,
A hundred more took their place.
Firefighters were lost today,
More are there, holding out their hands.
Prayers were said today,
Asking for strength to carry on.
Our country was attacked today,
But we are not broken.
Our hearts were torn today,
But our flag and our faith stand strong.

Dale A. Sullivan

Just a Little Bit

I wanted to be loved by you, but i can't
anymore, i have to go now, i'm sorry for the
pain i've given you, it will be better this
way, maybe someday we can actually be
together, i know we didn't talk much,
i think we're runnin' out, you never
understood how much i loved you, i guess
this is the only way to get through to you,
i'd rather leave (die) than have you hurt,
my love for you was so strong, and it
still is but i have to move on, you don't get
it do you? how much i'd go through just
for you so i have to leave just for a
little but i'll be back someday, will you
still love me or will your love fade away,
my heart will always be in your hands
waiting for your command, that's enough
assurance to believe i'm true so just hold on
i'll be back for you, maybe this is what's
best for us, maybe our love won't be such a fuss anymore

Tricia Rose Stewart

Perfection

You look at me, and think I'm beautiful
Like the winter sun shining down upon
freshly made snow angels
You look at me, and think I'm smart
Like the sly fox who can sense when danger
is approaching
You look at me, and see the sun
A bright, warm, summer sun, reaching its
rays out to everyone and drawing them
towards it
You see me as a gift
But, if you could read my thoughts
You'd see that I'm ugly and hideous,
not pretty
I'm stupid and mental, not wise
And I'm lonely, sad, and hurting
I'm dying inside
You look at me, and think I'm perfect
But, that's the difference between you and me
I don't

Jennifer Lynn Sullivan

I Wish

I wish it were you I could hold oh, so tight
To whisper I love you as we kiss good night
I wish every night to the stars up above
That I could show you my undying love
I wish to be with you and that's where I'll stay
Sharing each moment of night and of day
I wish I could feel you take your hands in mine
Your touch soft and tender your love so divine
I wish to stare deeply and die in your eyes
Distance my obstacle you are my prize
I wish life were simple and that would just be
Living forever just you and just me
I wish you were here right by my side
Long walks on the beach we'd take stride for stride
I wish I could tell you it's you on my mind
My search has been long you're my ultimate find
I wish to tell someone that person is you
You are so special my feelings are true
I wish once this happens to just let you know
That once I have you I'll never let go

D'Juane Fletcher

Forever Remember

He staggers down the moonlit trail,
his whole life a fairy tale.
He takes a nip of old Jim Beam,
approaches the cabin few have seen—
across the threshold and through the door,
all alone, unlike before.
His life was perfect, a young man's dream.
They'd been together since seventeen.
The memories raged throughout his mind,
looking for a peace he'd never find.
He gave his all, he gave his life
to the lying witch he called his wife.
His hopes had withered, his dreams have died,
the door swung open as he cried.
He placed the stock upon the floor,
and stared into the rifle's bore.
She plead with him to change his mind.
The solution was clear, not hard to find.
You never cared, it's plain to see,
but one thing's certain, you won't forget me!"

Troy David Bertagnoli

Winds of Love

Remembering September 11, 2001
Winds of love blew upon America
when free people embraced and
held their neighbor's hand.
That day those thoughtless acts of evil
flew on terror's wings on our homeland.
Our hearts were broken as our loved
ones swept away.
But evil cannot break the loving spirit
of the good, old USA.

Freedom is the song the world is singing,
words of love and peace are in the air.
Winds of love are blowing peace and freedom
upon all the lands and people everywhere.

Love is the song the world is singing,
the words are ringing in my ear.
Soon, all the world will see—
we are brothers and sisters,
holding freedom dear.

Shirley Van Osdale

Another Day

As the world watched in horror, our lives, as
Americans, were shook. Cities stopped
around the globe; and a few planes were all it
took. Tears began to flow as we gazed into
the screen. Barely able to imagine how it
felt to be on the scene. Planes shot through
those towers, and sadly, that wasn't all.
The Pentagon was challenged; then the towers
began to fall. During this confusion, another
plane crashed down. The destruction that
rang abroad brought a halt to every town.
Bush took stand, he said punishment would be
enforced. And, now, as cleanup begins, we
let time and preparation take its course.
Prayers are steadily rising as tears steadily
stream. Know that we will prevail, no
matter how bad it may seem. With our faith in
God and a great man to lead the way,
America will stand its ground and see
another day!

Steve Michael Smith

Something Special

Love is something that means a lot.
It's said to the ones we love so dear;
Sometimes it's the words our loved ones want to hear.
In times of sickness and grief, love can be the strongest thing.
Some people say it without a care when deep down they don't care—
They feel something that's not there.
Wanting to be loved is the most sacred thing.
Love is a very special thing!

Richard Francis Zuber

Lost

Oh, dear! Oh, dear!
Where could I be?
I think I'm lost inside of me!
I've walked and walked through tunnels far.
My legs hurt, I need a car.
Oh, my!
I'll make this short (It's sick, you see . . .).
I've just come out the other side of me!

Laura Swoboda

my day

i wake up in the morning not yet stressed
i roll out of bed and go get dressed
i rush to catch the bus
when i miss it i start to cuss
my nose is stuffed so i can't smell
teacher just called on me but i can't tell
after i get out i go skate
there go some people spreading hate
i go in to listen to some punk
i think it's better than rap and funk
i get my homework done
now it's time to skate and have fun
more people ride by and yell at me
they're mad because they can't do what they see
after i'm done having fun for the day
i get a shower then hit the hay
i lie in bed and think about the day
then i realize that i'm doing okay

Kristopher Allen Smith

Our Voices Will Be Heard

Anger, violence, hatred, inhabit all our streets.
Too many youth with our Maker too soon they meet.
We are always quick to judge, also to place the blame.
Suppressing the truth, so not to feel our shame.
There are children with guns, roaming through our schools.
Prejudiced lawmakers establishing all the rules.
More rigid laws are made, still God is not allowed.
Gun laws against the innocent, will this protect the crowd?
We have no time for children, or to teach them of His life.
Instead we turn the other cheek, ignoring all their strife.
So anger burns inside, they find their way with violence.
We pay no heed to them, we find solace in our silence.
I have no expression, as tears stream down my face.
What has gone wrong in the hearts of the human race?
This world that we live, it is filled with evil ways.
Hatred, racism, murder are a part of every day.
Where friendships and compassion used to stand with pride.
Now they stand alone, hoping the tribulations will all hide.
We need to turn from transgression, start teaching of His word.
I know our youth will listen, our voices will be heard!

Kitsy L. Golemon

The Bleeding of the Silence

It's the way the wind blows
On those warm sunny days
And how the moon glows
In the dark woods and its mysterious ways.
Or the way you can sit
And let some things go unspoken,
Knowing that every day
My heart will get broken.
It's the way I sit and wait,
Hoping, praying, and pleading
That you can hear my heart
And all of its silent bleeding.
But I know that it is the way
More hearts get broken
Because someone stopped caring,
And more and more words are left unspoken
Because you couldn't see; you couldn't hear.
Now here I am left
With only the sound of silence and no one to dry my tear.

Kirsten Lauren Wiggins

In the Deep Dark

it's in the deep dark
that i want to make love to you
i want everything to be black,
dark, mysterious

i sit here
listening to the music
that makes me think of you
and lying in bed with you
and it makes me feel . . .

my jaw drops—
the music takes control
of my body, of my soul,
and into you i fall
like an angel from heaven,
and i find my innerself
somewhere out in the middle of space,
and i tend to forget what i am doing here
and how long i have stayed

Melissa Ann Arnold

The Power of Emotions

Hate is the thing that makes you wrong
Just listen to all hate related songs
Makes you full of anger inside
If no one had this then the world would be fine
Get rid of this and life is sublime

Anger is something that is not sane
Seems to be everywhere here, there again
If I was the one to decide what to do
Then I'd make a law against lust and this too

Lust I just wish would be a thing of the past
It's always somewhere and you know it'll never last
I wish, oh, I wish it'll never happen to me
Because I know how wrong it is you see

Love the emotion that sets you right
Fills you with warm feelings throughout all the night
Even when you're having fun
Thinking about a cherished one
Love is just happiness forevermore

Adam P. Saunders

We Are All Equal

We are all equal no matter what color we are.
People always talk about one another.
They think it's cool to see someone hurt.
It's not cool to see someone cry or kill him or herself
Because of what other people say about him or her.
God made us to be friends and to love one another.
He did not make us to hate one another or to kill one another.
He made us different colors for a reason.
He wants us to not hate each other but love each other.
It really doesn't matter what color you are.
God made us the color we are for his own reason.
So don't talk about one another.
If everyone thinks about it, we are all the same color.
We all look different.
We should always remember that we are all equal
So we don't see any more people die
Because of what other people say about their skin color.
We should never make fun of someone.
We all need to remember we are all equal in this world.

Laura Ann Deall

why do i love you

This is a song for my Love Bong. You'll always be my baby! Ilysm!
i don't know why—why do i love you?
somebody told me it doesn't have to be this way
but what can i do, no one i found but you.
nothing compares about how i feel for you!

'cause every time i see you,
you brighten up my day!
'cause every time i'm with you,
i laugh all the way!
so many questions—
i don't know what to say!
oh why do people ask me,
why do i love you?

and now i know why—why i'm actin' this way
for now i'm so sure, i'm gonna love you all the way—
and what about you, do you feel the same way too?
that is the question which can only be answered by you!

Cynthia Amian Fortuna

Quotes

"Choke on your forked tongue as you lie to
me again; I could never swallow your false
ideals of a lifeless, happy ending"

"The way the rain comes falling down hard,
that's how I feel inside, sometimes"

"This is my favorite sad story, forget
me not or I'll forget myself. I've got a
few things that I'm afraid of sometimes.
I just can't face myself, I guess
I'll just tuck myself away tonight.
You know it's been one of
those days . . . every pretty flower,
every lovely flower, every deadly flower,
hides its life inside of shame. Well, a stem
is not a rose, but that's just how my garden grows."

"The voice of Death can only be heard by
the ones who fear it."

Jennifer Lynn Fecht

My Loved Friend, Adam

I loved you friend but now you're gone,
but please don't fear your soul lives on.
We miss you much down here on earth,
but up in heaven you'll have rebirth.
So let me ask you a question,
although it pains me to say:
Were you ready? Were you scared?
Or did you need another day?
No one can answer me but you
and you're not talking at this time.
No one could understand but you,
but you are now lost for all time.
Is heaven better? Better than this?
A place where you can hug and kiss
and make up for all time lost?
Forgive and forget with no hate or regret.
We miss you much and forever more;
until the day we meet again,
in my heart is where I'll keep you, friend.

Susan Fedorka

I Am

I am adventurous and questionable
I wonder how we became humans
I hear the rain and thunder
I see the wild horses in the morning light
I want to own horses of my own

I am adventurous and questionable
I pretend to fly like a butterfly in the sky
I feel excited when I'm with my family
I touch the clouds
I worry about my family when I'm gone
I cry when I am sad

I am adventurous and questionable
I understand school
I say love conquers all
I dream to have more friendships
I try different foods
I hope to go around the world
I am adventurous and questionable

Erin Leona Tobison

God's War—Not Ours

We may live on this plain of humanity.
We do not battle the humanity of this plain.
Weapons we fight with are not of this reality.
We're here to help remove the pain.
We must throw aside our imaginations,
and throw aside everything.
We must take into captivity
every single thought we think
and give it as an offering
to the obedience of Christ.
For His Spirit is on the rise.
My defense is of God,
for the LORD is my defense.
And the Holy One is my King;
and my God is the rock of my refuge.
That is why I sing;
be still, and know that I am God:
I will be exalted among the heathen,
I will be exalted in the Earth.

Daniel Lloyd Dummer

Age Was the Answer

I can feel you there And I can feel you care.
For we were meant to be; why can you not see?

There's this wondrous feeling deep within our souls;
It connects our being, no matter what unfolds.

Age is your issue, but give us a chance
To reconnect our souls and continue this dance!

You were in my heart from the very start.
We were so connected, so why were we to part?

A need for younger? Why? I do not know?
We always felt connected and you told me so.

Now I feel your spirit as it fights to see
Age as the answer. Why does it have to be?

Let the old dream die for what is meant to be
Our ages do not count, why can you not see?

I feel you with me, but I need to know
That age is not the answer. Will you tell me so?

Mari Rozett

The Real Me

So who am I anyway—Marilyn Monroe or Doris Day?
Am I wicked or am I pure? Either way, I'm not that sure.
Because most people I know today think that I'm a certain way,
I'm really not that way at all,
I've just built up this giant wall.
I can't get out, you can't get in, so I keep it all locked within.
If I keep it in, I can't get hurt.
There's no key to insert.
The only way to break this wall is through a crack, so very small.
So tiny, I cannot get out, not even by some secret route.
The only one who's found the key is Jesus, who's inside of me,
For with him, I share all things, because of this salvation brings
Hope to my life, both big and small,
It might be enough to break this wall.
So every so often, if you make it quick,
You could break off just one tiny brick.
For that one brick would make a hole
So you could gaze into my soul, into my heart, into my mind,
And gaze in awe at what's behind.

Amanda Rucker

The Me You See

The me you see is who I be; were you looking for another me?
Glad to be in the skin I am in. Why do you ask me where I've been?
Haven't you heard that I am black as night?
Come close, it's all right
The me you see is who I be
Hips full as the moon
Beauty just now bout to bloom
Ain't no price attached to me
'Cause the me you see is who I be
Taste the honey gushing out of me
This is who I be, who I be
I am my mother's mother and her mother too
I can even be a mother to you
A thousand babies have passed through my womb set
Love often was a vacant room but
In the clouds of today, I claim victory
Over all the years, for I am today's black woman, kinked and curled
And free
The me you see is who I be

Carolyn Dyson

The Man Downstairs

There is this man who lives downstairs.
I rarely see him, but I know he's there.
He works all day and comes home at night.
He washes his hands, then eats a bite.
This man grows tired, so he heads off to bed.
But not before his "good nights" are said.
He makes his rounds throughout the house.
Up the stairs and to the right,
He stops to tell one child good night.
Across the hall to the next room he goes.
The light comes on, and his baby glows.
His words are soft, and to her he says,
"Good night my princess. I'll see you in the morning."
Then he turns to leave without any warning.
I then sit up and quickly say, "Hello there. How was your day?"
He tells me his stories; then it's off to bed.
He fluffs up his pillow, then lays down his head.
My daddy sleeps just down the stairs.
I rarely see him, but I know he's there.

      Loretta Kay Smith

Realization

I remember a time when each day was long,
when the world was a playground and life was a song.
And we fluttered through years with barely
a care, ignoring the future and what waited
there. But as I grow up,
darkness sets in.
My bright world has turned to
concrete and tin.
I now see violence I looked past
before. You died and my heart hit the
floor. There are days when I just
want to break down and cry.
There are days I want to throw
in the towel and give up.
But I hold my head high and
push my way through.
Because no matter what I do,
I'll never get the chance to
say goodbye to you.

      Kristin Milom

My Soul

I have a soul, a ticket to my life, a
passport to death; what is it?
Physical forensics have the biggest play,
So let's all check my DNA.
A bunch of markers is who I was when here,
So check 'em out, read my markers, never fear;
My markers stay and you can tell it's me,
But my soul, it's gone? Eternally?
Was I a fingerprint and is that all?
That makes me feel so very small,
And if we loved, am I an echo in your mind?
That seems much better and in real time.
But will I perish when you go too?
Or will I stay, immortal, in the cosmic glue?
Will my soul be dormant like a stone, a
Spiritual marker in God's domain?
I think when I find out the answers here,
You'll know I'm gone, so never fear—
Within the cosmic glue I'm here.

      Alfred W. Babb

In My Dreams

There's hope in the darkness
Only when I'm near you
But you don't do what I want you to do
You don't hold my hand, you hold my heart
You don't kiss me, you kiss my life with light
I die inside when you leave my side
But I still haven't heard you say
What I want you to say
It gets darkest before the light
You can't take my heart without takin' chances
When you are near me
There's something in your eyes. . . . fear
You don't touch me
You won't take my hand
To know you don't love me like I love you
I just don't know what to do
The pain feels so real and it's deep in my heart
So please my love
Love me like in my dreams

      Wendy Rebecca Gabbert

Psycho

Days of silence
echo through my head.
Loud and restless,
disturbing my thoughts of innocence.
Trouble and corruption
linger in my mind.
The screams of agony,
the only noise of silence breaking through.
The silence is deafening
as it echoes through the empty space.
I barricade my ears,
yet I still hear the agony.
The screams rip through me
and I go crazy.
You wave the flag of surrender,
but I only see red.
I continue on my way;
I go too far
and now you're gone.

      Kerri Hyde

Enchanted Forest

In the dark starry night,
I walk through this beautiful place,
big tall trees cover the ground
tiny fairies sit on the leaves of colorful trees
It is a clear night, warm, a little misty
I hear the songs of different birds
nesting in the trees
twisted around the branches and trunks
are beautiful silver jewelry
a lovely place to be and think about everything
no one knows of this place, but me,
I come at night so no one will see
I sit by a tree and just breathe
let the time pass and feel free
I go there every night
to think about the things that came
and the things to come
then I open my eyes and it all disappears
just a dream, an enchanted forest of a dream

      Ali Nichole Evans

The Phoenix

Thoughts have flown so needlessly for a passion unfulfilled.
So dazed and confused by reality that dreams oblivate.
Futile feelings lay strewn in fractal disarray
For hope and faith cannot piece the past.
So shattered, yet reborn, we foray again,
Outright into the superunknown.
Arcane hatred, senile with suppression,
Rips naked your mortal soul.
To live, to lust is a feverish thought,
So carnal, yet sublime.
The peril of mundanity warps out,
And a vortex of emotional scourge begins.
A twilight smile flirts with your New Year's resolves.
Normalcy is no more than a betrayal
Of the educated reasoning of our daily sins.
After forever has come and gone,
Reason will still prevail.
It is then, I shall rise once more
From my immortal ashes.

Soumik Sanyal

Dreaming

From the barren mountaintop,
standing quietly alone;
totally absorbed in the creation
of a changing sunset.
My thoughts transcend the darkness.
My heart begins to quicken,
and I dream, I dream, I dream!
To fly! To fly!
Oh, Dear Father, let me soar;
lift me on the wings of dreams,
to soar above the eagle's flight.
Let me taste the cool breath of life;
let me soar to heights never known.
Let me dream and climb higher, yet higher.
To feel Your strength, to know Your love,
to be in Your presence, to climb even higher.
To reach for the quest of Life,
to soar, 'til I am fulfilled of Thee.
Then to return, to return to Life and to be!

Theodore D. Stanton

Apology

Children, we apologize
for putting you in this world as it is,
in such misery and hunger
with so little justice,
so little integrity,
and so much free hatred and wars;
for the past ones, those happening just now . . .
and we still leave you Yugoslavia,
the Middle East, the Far East
the neo-slavery, the neo-Nazis,
and so much more and more.
Children, we apologize
by tearing apart the ozone layer
for the filthy, muddy, dirty and stinky waters,
and for the cancers you get from it. . . . and AIDS, too!
Children, we apologize
for the sad scenario where poverty reaches so far.
We apologize for all the trash, the crack, the grass,
instead of being happy. . . . being you!

Mary Clar Amar

Freedom Denied

Walking down this dirt path of age
With drops of rain across my face,
I see in dreams the plight of my fate.
My ancestors came this way in force
To build the road I now trod on.

I hear the river down below
Trying to tell its story in vain.
It saw the horrors we now can share,
But just in whispers for fear of whom
We all know, but must pretend to spare
Ourselves the shame of knowing the truth.

The school house atop the hill
Is where we go to learn not our past,
But the past that did us in.
The bondage of ages past
Has put us where we are.
Just where we should be, so they thought,
Never to think for ourselves.

Che J. Sunday

America, the One

Here we stand
Each American hand in hand
Eyes to our flag, terrorists brag
The new war begins, innocent dead
Terrible sadness fills each American's head
Heroes gone
Their wives and children long
Just like the saddest song
Together we embrace, every heart every race
We shall join hands together
And fight this enemy that hides behind religion
America's GOD does not kill
The unexpected, the children
America's GOD does not hate
The innocent, the free
Under GOD and country,
We shall stand strong
United we shall be
Bonded together and always FREE

Lisa Ann Wright-Clegg

I Love You

I love you now,
I loved you yesterday,
I will love you tomorrow,
I will love you forever.
When you're around me I feel safe,
And when you're not,
There's always that empty space.
The gleam in your eye gives me a feeling,
A feeling that I've never felt before.
One day we will be together, and when that day comes,
I will be free,
Free from all the sadness,
Free from all the tears,
Free from all the stress,
Free from all the fears.
The day we are together
Is when two become one;
When that day comes,
You will always know that I love you.

Nicole Lynn Frazier

Last Dance

On this weary drizzling night
Faultless souls danced in silken moonlight
Stuck in a blissful state
For one cause to live and delight
Bounding upward and soaring down
Mortal beings pranced around
As ancient and aged ones of eras before
Gazed with rapt-filled reverence at love and ardor
Between the null was you and I
Moving together in frozen time
But ever slowly seasons past
Together we were, as one we danced
Forever I shall dance with you
When our music slowed then faded
Inside my head I carried on and played it
I danced with your picture on that wall
I danced with memories as I waited to go
And now I dance with you as time takes the
Last of this weary soul

Doug Wade Cunnington

Advice

I was once told from the wise but old,
to be warmhearted and not cold.
Do not show arrogance, nor show pride;
the Lord replied, "You'll receive a bumpy ride."
Take search to the book of proverbs,
and then take heed to those words.
You'll then take flight with the eagles and birds.
Remember the teachings,
and take heed to the readings.
Like a cup of wine, He'll pour out your blessings.
Bind them around your fingers;
wear them around your neck;
show your Father's wisdom that much respect.
He's told you once;
he's told you twice;
honor His name for a prosperous life.
This is my advice to you.
Now you do what you need to do,
and I pray I see you in a life that's new.

Marcus Mills

Clue

Even after all the things I've been through
I still do things the same.
I always jump too quick, move too fast,
And am always the one to end up
With all the pain. And even though every time
I promise myself, "No, never again,"
I seem to find myself back where I began.
"You need to be treated like a lady,"
Is what they all say, and the new one
Is always perfect for at least a day.
But something always changes, and I'm always
Left in the rain trying to hold onto
Something that's no good, just letting them
Find another part of me the last one
Forgot to drain.
And every time it's over I think
I've learned something new, a trick
I'd never seen before, when the truth is
I still don't have a clue.

Jodi Danielle Vance

My Grandmother

Many years in a sin-filled world took their
toll. Aging, pain, disease, and ultimately
death are the fruits thereof.
But weep not, for this one was a believer.
She lived her faith publicly and fed it to
her flock of ten.
She was strong, courageous, and loving as is
her Saviour.
She didn't "try" to be like this, it was
easy. She was this way.
And now she is gone. Not dead, but more
alive than ever.
Now she lies in our Father's bosom just an
arm's length from her beautiful Saviour,
and a whisper from her God.
Holiness becomes her, now that it is
actually possible.
Holiness that was not achieved, but imparted
to her by a benevolent Creator.

Andrew Dowey Dickson

At a Loss

Awaiting the hour of eternal life
Great despair fills those around him
The evil cancerous entity that entered his body,
Now taking him from us.
He can't speak, for it causes great pain,
But lying on his death bed
Still has the strength to grasp my hand.
These are his final hours.
Yet faces them with a look of courage and great love in his eyes.
Not prepared for his departure I can't control my emotions.
Ready to burst, trembling, I abandon him.
At a moment which we needed each other the most.
I didn't want him to see me cry.
I needed him to see me strong, but let him down.
Not returning to his room, I play his song silvery and sweet.
Maybe he heard it, my goodbye
For when I return he is gone—an empty shell left behind.
I'm still angry with myself, for not staying with him,
but his eyes sent a spear through my heart.

Denisse Angulo

Hope Is Near

Believe,
I Can . . .
Believe,
I Must . . .
To Conquer Obstacles,
Will Never Be Much Trouble,
Always Present . . .
Always Alive . . .
The Function of My Ability is Always to Rise
Is My Skin Different?
From Yours?
Or Has Fear . . . Power Turned You Sour,
Never Look Down . . .
Always Revolve . . .
Continue to Learn . . .
Continue to Love . . .
Continue to Solve . . .
Continue to Strive . . .
Continue . . .

Clarence Beaver, Jr.

One Love Life

She said that she would stay; she said just for a day.
This was the way, this was a happy day.
She said that she could smile, and we smiled for a little while.
I put it all on file, and I carried it many a mile.
We could dream of many things,
birds that sing of Pegasus wings.
Problems occur that stop and frustrate,
make us speechless and keep us up late.
Moments that move us through the day
change us all in little ways.
After a while, it all disappears,
and the moments that moved us have turned into years.
She said that she could leave;
she said that I would grieve;
this was not untruth (cause),
then she brought me another guy as proof.
I did not want to believe
until I was staring at her leave.
One love life, one love life.

David Brian Eddleston

A. J. McLean: Our Angel

Oh, sweet angel
you've inspired me.
You've taught me.
You've presented yourself as a role model.
And now you're filled with pain and heartache
Which makes millions of hearts ache as well.
To see you suffer, we weep.
To see you in agony, we hurt.
If you think we're giving up on you,
then you're crazy.
If you think we don't believe in you,
then you couldn't be more wrong.
We look up to you for your strength.
We feel an overwhelming bond which
no one can destroy.
Always remember the support that you have—
Your family, friends, and fans.
We know you can better yourself.
We know who you are, and who you can become.

Tracey Ann Evans

We Are from Mars

We are from Mars, we don't like the heat.
We come in most colors, we are good to eat.
We come in different sizes.
We come in different shapes.
Different people have to come to know us.
I tell you now, we are not made of grapes.
Sometimes, we are solid;
Sometimes, we are crunchy.
Sometimes, we are just plain nuts.
People like us in many ways.
We travel near and far,
Sometimes, people store us in a jar.
We come with a letter, it is not unique.
We are not hard to hold.
We are always fun to seek.
We have been around a long time,
And have changed in many ways.
Now, it's time to tell me what you think I can be.
Answer: M&M candies

Kaitlyn Janee Zimmitti

Waste

Life.
The difference between breathing or not.
Deciding if effort and time are fruitless.
If a temporary feeling will last.
Whether a relationship means everything
Or anything.

Why does one choose to live with fight
While another fights to live without choice.
Or not to live.
We who are left behind to pick up the pieces,
Wonder why life is so bereft of value;
That setbacks and losses mean ending it.

Breath in our bodies is so fragile;
Too easily broken
While those still struggling with pain
And the rainbow at the end of the tunnel,
Wonder why they made their choice
A waste.

Stephen Schaefer

An Unsung Song

There's a song in my heart for you unsung.
Your life had only begun. . . .

There's a pain in my heart so deep; there is
a void like no other. I have to go on for your brothers.

You see, nothing seems important now that you're gone. . . .

You touched so many lives; you never knew . . .
you were loved through and through. . . .

I will wait in hope beyond a thousand years
to see and hug you again. . . .

Don't think I will sit back and say what's
done is done. . . . The evil one's pain has just begun. . . .

Until I see you again, my love song to you
will remain unsung. . . .

Lana Escobar

An Answer

Couches and coffee, and their tip cups
Things with no wires, and electronic alphabet soup

I'm tired of e-everything.
I miss hearing a voice.
Sometimes, I don't want to have a choice.

I want my favorite player
To stay on my favorite team.

I like mail made of paper
Because I don't need a password to open it.

I like it sometimes
When a store has only a few things.

I miss the ice cream man.
I miss hot dog stands.

This is my time. And I don't want it.
Why?
Fax me.

Jason Meyers

A Child's Cry

I saw my daddy hurt my mommy,
I cried for help no one heard me.
I saw my mommy with blood all over her face,
I cried for help no one heard me.
I saw my mommy cry herself to sleep,
I cried for help no one heard me.
A strange man kidnapped me from my family,
I cried for help no one heard me.
This strange man is now hurting me,
I cried for help no one heard me.
My daddy found me,
but nothing was ever said,
I cried for help no one heard me.
When my mommy and daddy got a divorce,
I cried for help no one heard me.
A year later my friend got killed by a train,
I cried for help no one heard me.
Now I'm grown with kids,
When they cry I know I'll listen.

Patricia Leaver

The Perfect Moment

Snuggled up beside you
Sleeping like lovers
Feelin' your breathin'
Smellin' the wonderful scent that is you
Wantin' to stay in this moment forever
Knowin' it must end
Afraid it will never come again
For we are not the lovers of my dreams
Merely friends who live too far apart
How deep my love is
How sad I am to leave you
How lost I am without you
How I long for what can never be
Thank you for that moment
When I could hold you and smell you
That you were mine alone
When we snuggled and slept like lovers
My dream became reality
And never again

Jonathan Craig Hutchins

Free

Life has lead me down some rocky paths.
Troubled times tore my heart in two.
The future seemed so unsteady and unsure. . . .
So afraid to love, then He gave me you.

Free my heart, take me where I've never been.
Free my soul, teach me to love again.
Free my dreams, believe where they can take me.
Free my fears, calm them like a gentle sea.

The pain can seem so unsubsiding.
When the ones you trust the most have broken your heart.
But there you were to wipe the tears away
And show me that it's worth a brand new start.

Free my heart, take me where I've never been.
Free my soul, teach me to love again.
Free my dreams, believe where they can take me.
Free my fears, calm them like a gentle sea.

With you, I am free.

Ann Marie Margaret Tomulis

Regret

My thoughts turn to rain
Dance with me and see you ending a beginning
Raw materials waste convincing shadows
Darkness echoing rain drops
Forehead washes down, slowly pain and grief
Imagine only now what have I done
Given in dreary looks to color my bed
Hopefully gaining perspective on the day
Tomorrow comes, no day
Pain, anguish, anger, fear
What is
Will it die
Never, no, go away, relentless pain
Cry, vision lambs of wool
Cool water, gentle breeze, missing art
Wandering fool, look not to the wind
Be free, dream, caress, love
Endure loss
No matter what given time

Cara Camilli

Weep

If he were here right now, he'd say, "Oh, baby doll, don't be sad"
With his arms wrapped around me, giving me strength and love
My head would rest on his shoulder while he held me close
I would weep for the mistakes I have made
For those I'm going to make
I would weep for the past, the present, and the future
For the lies and deception
For the relationships gone bad
I would weep for the love and the hate
For the good times and the bad times
I would weep for all
And as sleep set in while tears still fell, I would drift off
Lying in the arms that held me during the weeping
The arms that will continue to hold me
If not physically, but in my heart
Until beyond, when time no longer exists
When the physical no longer exists
When the mistakes and the relationships
When the good and bad love and hate cease to exist

Melanie Falor

Endeavor of the Soul

A sterling soul searching for peace, that's
what keeps my heart at ease. I've seen the
soul strive to fight the luring evils of the
night, which search to keep his spirit under
the ponderous weight to chemical slumber.
But now the soul has new eyes! He sees
deception, hate and lies, and how the blinded
soul shall die. "I surmise a better life,
exempt of slavery, throes and strife.
Freedom has removed death's knife!"
Now you see why I can last through moments
when my strength has passed. I have seen
this newborn gaze; a goal, a glimpse of
greener days, is in his sight to see the hour
when he can let his spirit flower. Blissful,
clean and not a slave to poisons leading
to the grave. Now he's seen where he can be,
a vision of himself free. Beside him stands
his soul and me.

Ashley Laine Stack

My Pay Back

The ground has fallen above me; greeting me.
I spare every last breath; scaring me.
What comes next? The crossroads of life?
And it all came to welcome me,
because of one little knife?
Tearing, scaring, replacing my soul;
How do I repay thee?
Don't replay me, I'll pay my toll.
Suffering and learning, while looking back
at my past; I came to wonder, how did I ever last?
I know I've done wrong, but I've also done right.
You should know, you walked beside me.
I never quit.
Something is startling me, is it true?
I need to be something, or someone new.
You replay my emotions,
Spinning me around,
While in a deep sleep you changed me,
While I was being put in the ground.

Leyla Mardel Korpela

Vinyl, Yellow Raincoats

I walk along the sidewalk we call life,
and some days it's happy, smiling, and blissful.
Yellow sunshine trickles down everywhere,
but that's just some days, because
just before I forget all the hate in this world,
I see a little crack,
and just beyond that a pool of lonely water.
I just keep tripping, falling into these puddles
dripping with great depression.
Most of the time, I can stumble out and
keep walking along my path, my sidewalk, my life.
Other times, I have no energy to pull myself out,
so I slip away and drown in 2 feet of water.
Usually right before I lose what I am
and drain my veins of who I am,
someone reaches in and grabs my arm, pulling me out,
pushing me back on my path;
the way I want to go, the way I'm supposed to go.
One day though, I'm going to sink.

Kristina Tamny

Since We Met

Ever since I've been on the net,
There have been so many people I have met.
Some short and fat; thin and tall.
But you are the one I like most of all.
When I first met you I thought, "How neat!"
But then I wondered, "Is he a cheat?"
As time went on and I talked to you more,
I discovered I was liking you more and more.
Time went on, more questions grew;
I had to ask all about you.
I asked if you were married; you said "no"—
I was thrilled!
But when you asked me, I knew I was killed.
I told you the truth and said, "I am married"
Where we stand now is really great!
I have a true friend, a forever "Web-mate."
I have you in my heart forever, dear.
And it's only because we are not near.
You're kind and honest and forever true.

Cindy J. Magle

To My Best Friend

He loved me deeply with all his heart;
He once told me that he loved me and dreamed
Of he and I in love. I told him, as I looked into his eyes,
"I do not love you."
We became partners in studies, plays, and dreams;
Together we won all, the world was ours.
And he told me one day in the warm fall sun
That he loved me. And I looked into his eyes and said,
"I do not love you."
He called for me on a cold, distraught day
When winter winds blew ice and fear and bitterness.
He asked for my hand to hold; he was scared.
Before he left me, he whispered that he loved me.
I looked into the dying sparkle of his blue eyes
And kissed his lips. "I love you," I said,
As I began to cry.
He smiled, closed his eyes, and died.
"I love you," I repeated mournfully as I saw
He still clutched my hand.

Ali Carter

Letting Go

On the inside is hurt and pain,
Even further is sin and blame.
On the outside is an image of happiness and joy.
Is it real? No one will know.
I feel like time is closing me in.
I don't know what to do.
I don't know how to win.
I hear the game of life is really something hard.
I guess it's time to put up my guard.
But something keeps me here; I'm not sure what.
Maybe an emotional tie that won't give up.
As days go past and weeks go by,
I can feel these bonds break.
No more chains to hold me down,
No more people to make me frown.
Free at last, the feelings are gone,
A happy body once again.
A free soul, no blame or sin.
A true image, outside and in.

Jennifer Leigh Neuhaus

Quiet Prayers

Lord, I know that you can hear me
So I guess I won't shout.
To you my prayers I now send;
My dreams I must let out.
The little boy, the growing man—
They need some help, a guiding hand.

No matter what I say or do—
Your message received loud and clear.
Any fear that captures my mind—
Reassured you are near.
Life has problems, trying to serve;
Follow the straight, not round the curve.

The angels sent down to this world,
Disguised though they might be.
Their eyes watching o'er us all
And ours beginning to see.
The entire world hears words you send.
Our prayers to you. Listen. Amen.

Douglas James Pavkovich

Control

Control is fake; control is
fleeting. There is no control.
Anarchy rules; pain is forever; love is
nowhere; hope is lost; death stalks all, and
control is lost. The living are dead; the
dead are living; the circle spins; the wheel
goes round, and when it stops, we all fall
down. The role of control is lost; society
crumples; all is dust. The world rots; the
word is lost; all that we have worked for
is gone. All that we have found is lost; all
that was lost is found again, found
again are ways of old, found again is the old
world, where hope is found, where love
is everywhere, where pain is gone. The wheel
of power is hard, and those with power fall
to those without, and those without destroy
those with. Control—fear—control, in all its forms.

Ben T. Retmier

Shadows of the Past

Chaotic thoughts abetting unbearable distress
The calm you seek you cannot possess
Afflictive memories that will forever remain
Countless nights spent engorged in disdain

The demons of your past generating relentless affliction
Teeming with turmoil and malice, a vehement disposition
Aggravating recollections that you cannot contain
Comfort, calm and contentment you fail to attain

I am your angel, I am your strength
Look into my eyes, for you heaven awaits
Take my hands, with me you will ascend
Your pain and sorrow I will amend
Your troubles will soon come to an end

A dark world within your heart and mind
That some day you will leave behind
The peace you desire I will help you find
The haunting shadows of the past will disappear
And new dreams shall arise

Nohemy Alvarado

The Struggle

Back and forth I struggle
From one way of living to another.
Many life-styles I've adapted to
And many I've unadapted to.
Rules and authorities change
As often as I see a new moon.
It's tiring to learn and unlearn.
It's confusing to know what's right and wrong;
Which path to take and which to ignore.
To follow my heart and feelings is considered wrong,
And to go by rules is right.
But they don't make sense.
Why should one obey rules and be obedient?
Why not live life and make the right choices by act?
Instincts should be ruled through a person,
Not controlled by "authority figures."
Going through stress day after day
Doesn't help one grow strong and stable,
But weak and feeble.

Heather Divin

The Angel and the Caterpillar

Alone on his branch did sit he. Waiting for
someday, something to be. What shall come of
me? He thought in his tree. Am I to grow,
love, be free? From the clouds he did
descend. His teachings would now soon begin.
For this would be his last good deed. This
Angel's work would find new lead. Up in the
tree tops did sit they. Swaying with the
breeze, to and fray. I've heard your
prayers and have come for you, for we are a
pair of lovers true. You've touched my
heart and my soul. We'll never part;
together grow old. Look at this, I had no
clue. I now have bliss, I now am new. With
that said, I must retreat. Your heart's
not dead; my deed's complete. Please Angel,
his voice did cry, I need you here, don't
say bye. Now I must go; with love,
I leave. Awaits my beau, awaits my reprieve.

Joshua Augustus Thompson

Iron-Rose

It in itself is a prophecy.
It stands alone at the brink of the horizon,
As the moon lights its back.
It is determined,
It is intense.
In its own way, it truly is an enigma.
It is the answer to all questions
And the question that is left unanswered.
It draws forth the immovable object
And walks from the irresistible force.
It is your enemy.
It is your friend.
It is your ally.
It is content, yet sustained.
It is itself
And no one other.
It is its own ruler, yet everyone's servant.
It in itself is great.
What is it to you?

Matthew L. Stewart

Believe

Walk the road that knows your step
Sing the song you can't forget
Feel the mountain from the distance
Love your worth, live this existence

Tell the stars your secrets
Whisper love to the streams
Sing lullabies to the moon
Make reality listen to your dreams

You can cry forever if you need to
But you'd miss out on the laughter
If you let the tears dry
You will believe again in happily ever after

Maybe you will never sing like the angels
Or dance like a ballerina
It's okay, it does not matter
As long as you can look in the mirror
And love what you see
And become what you believe

Laura Danielle Piana

Sun to the Midnight Sky

You came into my life
Like the Sun to the midnight sky
Like seeing a sunset
Through the eyes of the blind
You showed me how much fun life could be
How much you could really mean to me
Just when I thought my life was going down
You came to me from out of the crowd
Now I live my life to see you each to day
To feel your arms around me
Knowing this won't go away
I think of you by day
Dream of you by night
And when I'm scared
The thought of you erases my fright
You're what I looked for
Through all of my sorrows
And I know you'll be with me
Through all of my tomorrows

Erin Rosa Moore

Desire in the Night

On this night, most every year
The storm is there for you to hear
The winds kick up and spread the leaves
For that special someone, he still grieves
Blowing, whirling through the night
Thundering, streaking purple sky's a sight
The winds die down; rains continue
His thoughts of her the main venue
The hour grows late and still he sees
The peace amongst chaos, just past the trees
Rumbling, whisping, producing rain
Administering a calming medicine, not in vain
A hope for a better tomorrow is in his grasp
Just, must let go of his past.
Although his love for her shall remain
Doesn't mean he can't love again . . .
It's growing later still; he must retire
Certainly will regain his desire . . .
Rekindling the fire . . .

Ryan Gregory Waldorf

Brave New Me

I said I needed a home of my own
A chance to be free, stand tall and alone
Thought I was more than half of you and I
I believed I was my own best disguise
Now no one is left to call me wrong
I am at home and summer is gone

Every day is a cold bitter fall
With my voice echoing off each bare wall
I have what I desired and can't turn back
Fearing you'd moved on with nothing to lack
I'm not as tall as I pretended
My perfect life is now upended

Those words I now eat are an uncooked meal
And unlike me, you have begun to heal
Freedom from you is now bondage for me
In my brave new world it is hard to breathe
Now I wish you had asked me to stay
But memories of us push me away

Richard Brownell

Blessings

This is for you, Mrs. Copeland!
Sometimes things that seem the worst
are blessings undercover,
like when one special to you leaves,
you can't help but still love her.
Sometimes things are not what they seem.
Sometimes life has a surprise to bring.
Whether it's awesome or awful at the time,
you can't ever put your life on rewind.
You have to put your faith in Him,
trust everything's going to be okay in the end.
You know that I know that you knew.
There's nothing about the past you can do,
so always keep focused ahead,
not back on a dead pet that you hadn't fed.
Don't worry about the past things,
just think about what tomorrow brings.
Even if you've lost one you held dear,
remember, to your heart, they shall always be near.

Brittney Nichole Dorris

A Message for the World

Take a walk with me and I'll show you
places you've never seen.
Sit and talk with me and you'll discover
things only felt in dreams.
Hold my hand and you will understand
all the mysteries of the universe.
Look into my eyes and you will find
that which will become my curse.
See yourself through my window
and feel the pain you've caused.
Regret times passed that we could have shared
if only you took a moment to pause.
Hate yourself for being you and all the things you've said and done.
Hurt inside because now I'm gone.
I've got my freedom. I've finally won.
Laugh with me and wake to the magic stirring in your soul.
Discover who you are and try alone to become whole.
Cry with me and pull forgiveness from my heart.
Love with me and let me leave so I can try another start.

Shannon Howell

My Heavenly Father

Ever since the beginning, you were there
You gave me nothing but love and care
Through hard times when I was going to fall
You kept me up and through it all
You allowed my life to go on
I thank you—that is why I created this poem
In the world, there are a lot of decisions to make
But I know you have my back with every step I take
Without you, who would I be?
Just another lost soul
Playing a sad, sad role with no goals
But with the love of Christ
I have a feeling my future is going to be all right
There's no stressing from me
'Cause my heavenly father is watching over me
Night and day, day and night
He's got my back through all my struggles and fights
Every morning when I open my eyes
I'm blessed you allowed me to live another day and rise

Keli White

Happiness

To smell the fragrance of spring flowers on the breeze
or feel the warmth of a summer shower.
To see the night sky with its simple brilliance
or see the ballerina in her flighty dance.
These things are happiness.

To dry the face of a tearful child
or feel the depth of a lifelong love.
These things are happiness.

To see but a glimpse of tomorrow and to awake
to the morning light.
To snuggle in the warmth of a feather comforter
when the cold bites at your nose.

These things are happiness.

The simple things that bind us like a ball of
twine unravel as we feel the pulse of time
and embrace the gift of life.

This is happiness.

Sharon Lynn Haymes

Lost

Hands reach for your soul while eyes steal
your heart. Falling quickly into darkness,
void of light, your mind slips from your
grasp, and raindrops like stars from above.
Hearts are torn in two by distance, love
holds together what bodies destroy. Betrayal
befalls the world and truth floods forth.
Gasping, drowning water fills all space.
Praying for the end, wishing for the pain of
knots and needles to subside pulled beneath
the surface, held fast by tears of torment.
Memories return, each with more force then
the last. Rain falls. Music is played. Masks
are worn. Each knows the dance step by step
move by move. Games are played, walls are
built. Safety is nestled away in a cool dark
corner peeking through holes watching souls
play in the warm light. The pain of love is
gone. But what is left?

Christine A. Chonka

If I Saw You

If I saw you lifeless, would I lose my hope?
Helplessly and fragile;
So tenderly frightened;
Looking far beyond;
Crying out for help;
Not making a sound.

"May I say I love you"—
I know you cannot hear.
The doctor says I must choose
But I know it is up to you.
So as I cry this tear of life
And say a little prayer,
I must let them take off
The machines that hold you there.

I must walk out for if I stay,
I may never leave.
My heart will always remain
Next to your loving face.

Latasha Kay Gilliam

On Seeing Yehuda Pen's Painting, *Letter from America*

She looks like my grandmother: babushka wrapped,
Face stern with care not enmity,
Dark eyes hooded;
Protecting the last vestige of private dreams.

But it cannot be my grandmother.
The letter is from America,
The land of promises to which Grandma fled
So she would not have to wear her mother's face.

In her vagabond pack of rebellion,
Had Grandma mistakenly tucked her mother's face?
Had she taken from the old world age-old forbiddance
That thwarted dream-blossoming even in new soil?

Or was Grandma, like her mother, protecting a vision,
Distant but worthy of her patience,
That allowed her to glimpse herself
As the conduit to future carefree faces?

Sonya Oppenheimer

Eden's Door

The doors of Eden close at my countenance
And a single drop of despair falls to my cheek
Life seems not to find me
Yet I overturn rocks searching for its glow
Impeccably brilliant the gates enrapture my soul
Angels of hope embrace my heart with freedom
Opening my heart to love but also to hate
Closing my eyes I see the cruelty of painful searching
I pray the truth will reach me
But still; life seems a breath away
Broken
I turn from Eden's judgeful door
And weep at my lost innocence
Mindful now of all evil
The terror of nothing creeps through my veins
Am I to be punished for all eternity?
Will beauty ever fill my soul with pleasure?
Perhaps knowing pain
Is better than being ungrateful to pleasure.

Kathryn Westervelt

Why?

Flowers, gifts, notes and sex
Waiting for what will happen next
Movies, dinners, walks and fun
Something exciting has just begun
Plans, goals, dreams and conversations
Discussing ideas about future situations
Promises, rehearsals, rings and marriage
It's time to shop for a baby carriage
Hours, days, months and years
Things are more different than they appeared
Disagreements, arguments, fights and tears
Beginning to wonder what happened here
His, hers, yours, theirs and mine
Wondering what will happen in time
Love, anger, happiness and sadness
What can I do to stop this madness
Cheating, stealing, secrets and lies
It all ends in divorce with one question in mind
Why?

Roger Dale Pope, Jr.

mourning music

sometimes felt like sugar-sweet morphine
slipped into my bloodstream
blood streamed
streaming flags
i could be you so,
please no please no please no misguided retaliation
we all want blood and revenge
hell i'm thirsty too
but i could be you
i could be the ghostly
dust-covered man buried in the rubble
i could be
the innocent foreign-born man now in deep, deep trouble
so let's sing a song
honor the memory of naive and free america
because we're all grown ups now
we're all grown up now
and dearest youthful america
i miss you already

Kent Brockman

We Are Still Free

We go to bed each night
And we never give it a thought, not even once
That we are not safe, because we have that assurance
That we are the most powerful nation in the whole world
And we are reminded each time we see Old Glory unfurl
But there are those that life and liberty, they mean nothing
As for freedom, they have no bell that they can ring
So like a thief in the night, they came to rob us of our freedom
In such horrid ways, that it left us all totally numb
So many innocent lives were taken by this thief
And just left America to deal with all the grief
We will deal with the pain and the grief, and we will go on
But we will do it together, making sure no one stands alone
To do otherwise would be playing right into the enemy's hand
And we are Americans, so together we will stand
And when we lay our heads on our pillows each night
We will still believe that America stands for all that is right
But we can rest easy knowing that punishment will be swift and just
Because we are still in America, and in God, we still trust

Susan L. Dunsford

She Cries

She looks down on her fallen children and
can't help but be sad. Not only that, she's
angry, confused, she's just plain mad. First
reaction, retaliate, hurt back, make someone
else feel this pain. This lady, she cries
freedom, and her nerves have been strained.
She needs an explanation, she needs to know
why. Wait, did you hear it, an entire
nation just sigh? She's helped so many
others, who could attempt to hurt her so?
Terrorism hasn't destroyed her, but she's
suffered a severe blow.
She'll get composed, do what's right, those
responsible will be made to pay. 9-1-1
which stood for help, now represents a
very dark, bleak day. It will forever
symbolize the desperation and helplessness
placed in her eyes, It will remind us that a
nation and a lady named Liberty cries.

Gerry A. Spooner

Gift of Sight

I can smell the roses from the bottom of my grave,
I'm six feet under with nothing to give,
In the life that is draining, the spirit remaining,
I'm in the web of the wealthy and the soul of the poor,
And I can't take it anymore.
Yesterday I was alive and didn't know they existed,
The weeds were tall and the flowers were twisted.
Roses can't grow in a heart unattended,
Feelings won't show unless the spirit be mended.
The dirt's been packed and the caskets been kissed,
Now that I am free, I see what I missed.
Compassion is hidden behind fear and doubt,
Only with your help can I hope to get out.
I can smell the roses from the bottom of my grave,
The world above I could not brave,
In the web of the wealthy and the soul of the poor.
With a deep thought of someone,
And a good thought from you,
Dig deep in the dirt and help me break through.

Anthony Todd Massey

untitled

she clasps my hand in a mournful farewell
her brown eyes glisten
protecting her spirit from the world as a mother
dove shielding her eggs
her soul losing strength with every tear
i ask why her heart aches, but her tongue has
placed that secret under lock and key
so with quivering lips she murmurs her wellness
turning her eyes to focus on the horizon behind me

i see her though she does not see me

i gaze upon her tragic beauty and all else flees
from sight
her countenance the sun putting night to flight
and though many moons threaten to eclipse her
she refuses to grow dim
and it is then
that i realize

that i love her

Mario Ramos

Distance

Time is not on our side
It only stands against us
Something beyond our control separates us
We fight but can't fight the distance

Time is all we have
Why does it go so fast
We're trying to make the best of our lives
We only want to go the distance

Time erases pain
If you knew what I held inside
Could you see
I've fought the distance

Time is too much
I only want to be by your side
Back in your arms
Hear your voice
If there's love
We can fight any distance

Nathaniel David Taylor

Time

Ounces and ounces go by
Time will never be something you can buy
Gallons and gallons go past
Time always goes too fast
Ounces and ounces go by
Time was never anything that kind
When the moment is there it passes away
Time spoils the moment for me
Time was never on my side
The tidal is there but it never hits me
I push it but it never comes towards me
So why try because the moment will never come again
Ounces and ounces go by
Time was never anything that kind
Gallons and gallons go past
Time never desires to last
Ounces and ounces go by
Time leaves me there to lie
Torn and bruised from you

     AnJulie K. Rogers

City Fish

An immense, cluttered city;
A confusing maze.
Sun filters down
Splashing luminous light on the tops,
Making the shadows seem that much darker.
Streaks of florescent orange, electric blue,
And neon green flash before my eyes
As I weave my way through the coral towers.
The other fish look all the same at a glance,
But when you pause and take the time, you see
They are all so different and unique—
Each with their own path and purpose.
I'm vaguely aware of the sharks and danger
Lurking in the same enormous ocean.
Hooks with worms and nets await
For one of us to succumb to the temptation.
There are so many of us, I'll never be chosen
To be plucked from my spectacular, salty home,
To be left in a glass cage in someone's basement.

     Megan Moser

Microscopic

Dust particles dance in the beam of light
peeking through my curtains.
They invade my eyes,
dissolving on the moist surface.
Not good enough to blind,
shadow world's bitter agony.
Constant pressure.
A button on fat woman's jeans, two sizes
too small.
Poor button.
Why won't it just pop?
Be free.
Darkness tarps over beating lives,
engulfed by sour lemon drops on my tongue.
Pale gray shatters dreams
in mirrors gazed upon.
Thank God I can see
those dust particles
dance.

     Jessica Therese Jager

Your Last Goodbye

Your world comes apart at the seams.
A huge weight is on your shoulder,
Like a mountain crumpled down on top of you.
You feel all alone, yet you are surrounded by many.
All dressed in suits and ties, they all cry with their Last Goodbye.
Like magic, your loved one is here one minute,
And gone the next.
You hug another, hoping for a miracle,
But you know your loved one is gone for good.
All that's left now are your memories.
Oh, how you'll cherish them; they call to you all the time.
You are so vulnerable that instantly you begin to cry.
You begin to ask yourself, am I ready to say goodbye,
And then you decide that you're not.
But is anyone ever really ready?
You'll have to live with this for the rest of your life.
But just remember the days when they were here,
And not the day you said,
Your Last Goodbye.

     Daniel Basile

The War That Cannot Be Won

As the walls of America come tumbling down,
The people of Palestine seem to be proud.

Could they be proud of the lives being taken?
The foundation of humanity has surely been shaken.

Do they not see the consequences of their actions?
Sorrow and mourning are America's only reactions.

Is there a reason for the fear being seeded?
These battles and bombs are surely not needed.

These wars we fight only hurt one another,
Fighting amongst ourselves, destroying each other.

These petty squabbles don't need to be won,
They are already lost before they've begun.

Fighting human against human to settle the scores,
Do we not see these are civil wars?

Unless we can all come together and unite,
Freedom and safety are surely out of sight.

     Dustin Lee Engelhardt

Society's Machine

A silent night, a counter strike,
two dead soldiers and one casualty of war.
Families forgotten, children crying,
My life destroyed by corporate lying.
Why am I always dealt an unappreciated hand?
Is the dealer mad because I called Him a fake?
I only used His name in vain
A million times for Christ's sake!
Make that a million and one.
But who cares?
I don't, let you try and keep me down.
I won't go away, I've been through too much.
I seen too many things that would scare an adult.
I will not go, I will not fade, for I am a soldier of my own cult.
I bleed my way, I cry my way.
As usual circumstances, trends, beliefs, in the end
make me die your way.
Society; once again,
Clutched another victim from mother's hands.

     David John Drab

Summertime

Summertime
Beaches and people
Sea gulls screech
Sand castles and ice cream
Little girls and boys
Grown-ups with their toys
Skies of blue eyes only for you
Rock and roll, hands in love to hold
A kiss on the board walk, full moon nights
Hot sticky August days
Sunsets in the country
Skies of gold and blues
Then October, things turn colder
As we stop for corn along a roadside stand
And remember our summer
Hot warm and fast
Three beautiful months it lasts

Summertime
A few words of rhyme
    Alan Norman White

what's what

what do you view life as?
some say it's all about choosing a right path.
i ask, "what's right?"
is right as a baby—what you were taught?
i hear some people are brainwashed.
i ask, "what's a brainwashed person?"
a person who has different beliefs
than another person.
if that
other person is viewed as brainwashed by
the person he/she believes is brainwashed;
what is love?
i hear love is blind.
i also here life is love and love is life.
does that mean that life is blind?
could life see?
you may wonder, "what's life to me"—
i could only express my interpretation of it through sighs,
but i can envision it with or without eyes
    Henry Mainer

Heaven Inside

As I close my eyes and listen to the seas,
What do I hear?
What do I feel?
I hear the crashing waves beating on the shores
To a melody written by the gods.
I feel a peace inside and I ask myself,
Is this heaven inside?

Walking on the sands with the sun above,
What do I feel?
Can this be love?
I feel a sea breeze run across my face
And caress my soul with a warm embrace.
I feel a peace inside and I tell myself,
This must be heaven inside!

I feel the love of life from every living thing.
I can feel that harmony, which life could really bring.
This is what the gods had meant for our lives to be,
A little bit of heaven, heaven inside.
    Allan P. Briggs

Dream of Solitude

Here is a place where I can be alone,
a place which no one else has dreamed about.
Around me, I can hear the whistling wind
hum a lonely tune that spills through the
dangling leaves of the towering trees
which cast their shifting shadows
on the earth below.
Every now and then, the rush of the wind whips
a few scattered leaves from their branch
to flutter like the butterflies
that stain my view.
Upon my pedestal of solitude,
nothing of the outside world
seems to reach my thoughts.
My only companion, the golden Sun,
which beats its shining rays of light upon me,
is allowed to share my silent reverie
of the past, present, and future.
This is my time, my world.
    Michelle Amorin

garden symphonies

a blue symphony of clouds
soaring above my dreams
like those moments of delicious sunshine
and deep, forest shadows
in my white, diamond garden bed
surrounded by two thousand wild daffodils
lovely, blood-red roses
and luscious, purple violets
budding by a sea of languid waters
reflecting the beautiful, starry sky
through the trees flooded with moonlight
after a thunderous summer rain storm

hear the whispered language
of mother earth and her goddesses
worshiping the flowers
climbing my garden trellis
and blessing them with crystal drops
of morning dew and the last
of the swirling, nighttime, silver mists
    Molly Dietrich

Brother, Son . . .

I love you as a brother,
I love you as a son.
I'm proud of you. . . .
and all you do.
But lately,
I have seen myself in you.
The hurt and knowing are in your eyes,
the depression is in your posture.
How did you come to be this way?
Did you get it from me?
I love you too much to see you go through
what I went through. . . .
I can't stand the image of a blade at your wrist. . . .
pills in your hand . . .
drunk . . . passed out on the floor . . .
You needn't feel the way you feel. . . .
I'm right here beside you. . . .
Brother, son . . .
Let me help you.
    Carrie Janelle Bufford

The African Burden

What is the matter
are you okay
you look hungry
can I get you anything
I admire you
from where I stand, you carry the whole world on your shoulders
does it hurt
I think so
is that why you are sad
please answer me
I want to help but I don't know where to start
please don't die
can someone help her please!
I guess nobody cares
But I do
Because I am your child
I will go and get help
I will return
And the burden will hurt no more
              Christopher O. Dule

Darkness

It fills my soul and surrounds me
Darkness, powerful and menacing
closing in, engulfing me, taking control.
Why did it come, no one knows
when will it go and leave me alone;
when will the pain cease.
In the distance, there is a ring,
a ring of pure white light;
it is slowly moving towards me.
I am supposed to be a light to the world,
but the world is so full of darkness and hatred,
it would over power me and dim my light.
There are other lights that shine like me;
they move towards me to join me,
help me lighten the world.
The ring that was moving towards me,
they are other lights coming to help,
joining hands so they lose not one of them, but we still need help;
maybe you are the light that will make the difference—help us!
              Heather Leach

Disasters

Disasters are frightful, unexpected things
They last much longer than a fling
One disaster was Saddam Hussien
Another involved four big planes
They crashed into the World Trade Centers
Killing many, many family members
They were hijacked by about three men
After a while they flew right in
This was an act of terrorism
When these people are caught they'll do more then go to prison
God bless the USA
And all the people in every which way
We will always stay together
For we are the people of the United States
And we will never, ever loose faith
So raise your flags up high to the sky
And pray that we will catch this guy
Osama bin Laden is his name
And killing people is his game
              Jessica R. Chittenden

Natural Beauty

You don't need makeup or cover-up
You don't need tight jeans or dress-up
Just be yourself and you will see
All your natural beauty

I have always been told that beauty is skin deep
I have always believed this to be true
I have never had to wear makeup and such
Because I am as beautiful as you

So what are you trying to hide
And what do you have to fear
Are you scared that someone will see
All your natural beauty
              Ellen M. Wright

Because I Know What Love Is

So many people seem to be confused about real love.
Not knowing where to find it when push has turned to shove.
But if they knew my mother, there'd be no doubt I'm sure.
Because I know what love is, I learned it straight from her.

Her children rise and bless her, she showed them love each one,
As she complimented and praised them for silly things they'd done.
She cared for them in sickness, through trials and in woe.
Because I know what love is a debt to her I owe.

My life is ever changing, it's changing as I write.
I'm finding as I'm losing, dichotomy in sight.
But some things remain constant, as life goes to and fro.
Because I know what love is I'll make it through mom-o.
              Calvin Carter

A Tribute to Mothers

What is a mother?
She's like no other;
kind, caring, always giving—
her time, forgiveness, patience,
a listening ear, a helping hand,
an extra nickel or more;

often good advice; always encouragement.
She sets the example for her family; and
she sacrifices her needs, temporarily—whatever they may be.

Indeed, there is no other—
exactly like a Mother!
Have a wonderful, relaxing Mother's Day!
              Marsha L. Moore

I'm Just a Boy

I'm just a boy—
things always happen to me.
Live one day in my world and you will see.
The scratches jump on and the bruises appear.
One would think someday they would all disappear,
but they're forever there, day to day and year after year.
I fall, I slip, I tumble to the ground,
I get back up without even a sound.
You see, I'm used to the scrapes, the cuts and the blood,
the dirt, the grime and even the mud.
The world is my playground and I am its toy.
Even though I'm twenty-two,
I'm still just a boy.
              Kevin Lewis

Pain

In the world, children cry
They beg to stop the fighting
Children do not understand the words "racial tension"
They do not understand the word "hate"
Children only know the words love and pain
How quickly they forget their simple language
When adults teach them other words
And other meanings
Suddenly color and background are more important
More important than "who wants to play"
Love fades away
But there is always
Pain

Katherine Kennedy

Clock

Time ticks by without worry.
The time I face might end early.
To see that clock wind down to nothing.
The bitter life.
The bitter hatred.
The heartbeats, knowing that they aren't mine.
Is this clock alive, or is it counting my time?
Tick, tock, tick, tock, the clock is painful.
This tool of destruction.
This wretched thing.
Is this judgement?
Here is my fate.
The time has come; it is not too late.

Thomas Wade Beair

Never Knew

Never lived, never laughed,
Never went into the past.
Never cried, never shared,
Never knew the feeling scared.
Never loved, never lost,
Never thought about the costs.
Now I am looking down upon her,
Her face so pale with death
And never did she wonder what would happen to the rest.
We're all gathered here now,
Taken over by our grief,
That her life had been taken,
By her own disbelief.

Danielle and Tessa Korf

The Striped Hunters: A Tribute to Marine Snipers

Like a crouching tiger death awaits;
from the tall grass arrives a certain fate.
A ruby lens locks onto prey,
waiting to strike from a mile away.
Never detected by the human eye;
in mud and rain, still they lie.
Hear them growl as they reach out with force,
striking their target without remorse.
Again the striped hunters fade away in the mist,
adding another casualty to their list.
Day after day they'll kill once more,
using their rifles to win the war.

Bart Black

Tears for You, Carmen

To my 2-year-old niece, who passed away in March, 2001, from meningitis
Tears of Joy, Tears of Pain
These tears of ours still remain
They are for you, Baby Carmen, we miss you so much
It's you, "MY SWEET," everyone longs to touch
We love you, "Sweet," and it's tears we cry
Because, precious Sweet, you were too young to die
We hope one day soon, God will wake you up
To see you again, drink from your little cup
But this we know it oh, so true
There will never be another you

Love everyone who loves and misses you, Carmen

Denise Jordan

End the Wars

Why must we take all this pain and suffering,
End the wars, end the wars,
Nothing but blood shed this is,
End the wars, end the wars,
Mothers cry out in sorrow,
End the wars, end the wars,
Brothers, sisters, mothers,
Fathers, grandmas, grandpas lie
Breathless with no air to fill
Their dead bodies,
End the wars, end the wars,
Why must our world go through so much grief,
End the wars, end the wars I say!

Kayvan Jordan Fassnacht

She Is the One

She is the one with the beautiful eyes,
The joyous laughs, the saddest cries.
She is the one that talks on the phone;
I kiss her softly when we walk home.

She is the one, always there;
When I tell her my problems I know she cares.
She is the one always in my head,
When I think of her nothing's said.

She is the one I've always wanted;
If she left me I would be daunted.
She is the one I've always dreamed of;
She is my first love, my only true love.

Matt John Holler

In God We Trust

I am sick and tired of the crime in the streets.
It is enough to make my spirit weak.
I walk around all day and night,
Trying to keep myself out of sight,
But, everywhere I look and turn,
There is always someone to fight.
As I fight my battles night and day, I have no place to go.
Suddenly this man entered into my life;
He had so much to show.
I followed this stranger everywhere.
He was the Son of God!
He was sent to me without a fuss
From His Father . . . In God We Trust.

Carmen Brown

To My Broken Toe

Oh, my toe, oh broken toe
You give me so much pain
You hurt me on a cruise ship
You're like a dirty stain

You came to me at a Hampton Inn
In a wet bathroom
That fateful night I slipped and
Fell
I'm sorry I broke you

Oh, broken toe I hate to say
I wish that you would go
AWAY!

Anna Jean Schroeder

Another Day

In the mist of the early
morning dew, as the day begins
all fresh and new, my thoughts turn to you.
My heart swells and tears well in my eyes as I look
upon the beauty that has become our life;
We have come so far.
We have learned so much.
Sometimes I can't believe our luck,
Or was it fate.
The twists and turns that brought us together,
The way our lives have changed forever,
carry me through until the glorious colors of the evening
sun close in and around us with the hope of another day.

Deborah Seitler

Amnesia

Hello my name is . . .
I don't know who I am anymore.
I thought I knew,
but my perceptions change every little
second.
The seconds and my identity pass like the
wind.
Who am I?
Who are you?
Does anybody know who they truly are?
I think I do.
Yes, as a matter of fact I do;
how about you?

Brian Lynn Breiten

Life (in the eyes of a 16-year-old)

To many life is fresh and new
sweeter than any fruit

I sometimes wonder why we are here
Why would God put us on Earth
knowing that we would, in fact, kill ourselves

Life is like a fruit
growing up ripe and uneaten
or shriveling up and dying without a purpose

Life is funny in my eyes, but then
I can hardly see what's in front of me
Life will stop some day
and we will end never knowing

Deborah D. Rehm

Lamentation

I wanted to show you the world,
Its beauty and nature, every landscape and acre,
But you did not want to see.

I wanted to play you a song,
A well-crafted art, derived from the heart,
But you did not want to listen.

I wanted to tell you my life,
Of the joy that was you, how my heart filled with blue,
But you did not understand.

And now my world is in shambles,
The music now silent, on this lone desert island,
Since you departed me.

Miguel Francisco Lee

Sobriety

A new vision we now have seen,
A new answer that married our sobriety into our dreams;
Hope based on being there, that's you and me,
A dream hooked into everyday realities.

Sobriety a new vision every day,
A dream we can remember into tomorrow and even yesterday;
We now remember the names of friends,
And friends now like us for who we are.

A new song now sings within our hearts,
And our hearts now linked into sober thinking;
The answers simple, and answers clear,
The answer is actually just being here.

Donald Alfred Cooper

storm clouds

spring frost that melted in summer's heat.
no more snow on hot summer streets.
no more storm clouds in light blue skies.
no more tears in bright blue eyes.
things are always pleasant when you're around.
things are even better when the sun goes down.
we look above at who we are.
your smile is brighter than any shiny star.
the down fall to this story
is when i woke up this morning,
when i looked outside and what i saw.
you were gone like the summer's sun
that faded into the fall.

Dann Lee Hufford

Blessed

As I walk outside
I notice the wind brush through my hair
As I close my eyes and wish for my dreams to come true
And that's when I see you
Day by day I look at you and ponder how it could be
All my dreams came true
When I fell in love with you
I must have been an angel
to be as blessed as I am
I have you holding my hand
Blessed as blessed can be
To have you with me
Until eternity

Jennifer Perez

Christmas Mourning

'Tis the season for holiday cheer
'Tis the time for a child's fear
On the night when Santa should come
A child lies quiet, facing a gun

Jingle Bells should ring, snow should fall
Another child cries as he's thrown down the hall
A boy in tears lies tied in chains
As Santa flies by, snapping his reigns

Christmas mourning for all who cry
The tears and the fears hidden in Christmas lights
Merry Christmas to all and to all a good night
Another abused child dies in the night

            Melody Lyn Wilson

Avalanche

The falling tumbling whiteness spiraled down
Upon the ground the accumulation piles
Upon the ground the suffocating town
Descends the ivory mountain that engulfs
The unsuspecting people trapped within
The buildings like the subs within the sea
This cannot be the bottom line for me
The pudding river raging on the town
The never ending sound of churning snow
The massive mountain reached outer space
Estates below the snow the ground
The scraping, burrowing extremities
The people undertake a great escape

            Michael Gay

Drugs or Life

Dedicated to David Rowe
Drugs may come and

drugs may go.

Drugs will kill the ones who do and don't
know. Some may sniff and some may swallow.

But even though they still make you
hollow, like a tree. They make you sick like
a dog. They make you ribbit like a frog.

Even if you do not get these things you
sniff and swallow, it's better off because
they make you hollow. . . .

            Tasha Lashai Rowe

Untitled

Without you, Jason,
Where Unicorns run free
And Pegasus' fly above me,
Where Elves and Gnomes play all around,
This fantasy world is where I'm bound.
A land where Dragons roar
And Phoenix still soar,
A place where Fairies go,
The end of the rainbow,
A wrinkle in time
That I could call mine,
And have my dreams come true.
It would mean nothing without being loved by you.

            Jamie Eugenea Eacret

The Puppy

He opened his eyes to a whole new world,
Lying in the grass with his furry tail curled.
He tried to get up and walk around,
But all he did was fall to the ground.

Again and again he tried to walk;
The people were laughing and couldn't talk,
But the puppy kept trying, as hard as he could.
And then, all of a sudden, there he stood.

No one noticed, but there he was,
At the top of the hill, a great ball of fuzz.
"How'd he get up there?" someone cried out.
That's what growing up is all about.

            Brian Kebel

There's Love Every Day

The persona of love . . . Mom
To rise in the morning,
and look on a new day
is God's way of saying there's love every day.
To hear a child sing,
see an eagle take wing,
is God's way of saying there's love every day.
To know children, then grandkids,
as you work and you play
is God's way of saying there's love every day.
God's calling you home at the end of the day,
when you're so tired and weary, you traveled so far,
it's God's way of saying love's here and will stay.

            Rose Lereane Graner

I Remember Once

I remember once
drowning in a fountain of tears—
The pain so unbearable;
the emptiness so dark I lay breathlessly in a room full of silence.
The chills that danced on my skin;
the dampness that enveloped my presence—
suddenly I am alone in the world.
Every thought,
every feeling,
every tear seems highly concentrated.
I could hear my heartbeat
and the night grew on.
That's all I remember. . . .

            Lori Ann Cammllarie

When Love Runs Strong

When love runs strong
Clouds seem less threatening
Fear to hurt will produce the clouds
Residing at the horizon
The threat of loss is never far away
Rivers of hope and guilt run deep
Something however succeeds in growing strong
Ever so fragile
Almost not of this world
And when morning dawns
There is but one comfort
To know there's somebody standing beside me
So alone is not a concept anymore

            Dominique Maria Berton

The Portraits

Mother Nature sure had fun tonight
She lined up her cans of sprays
And painted portraits in the sky
With reds and golds and grays

There were blues mixed in,
and purples too, with little dabs
of white that drifted through the
tree lined scene—Oh! It was such a sight

The portraits that she painted
grabbed my heart and held on tight
I looked in awe at her creations
She sure had fun tonight

Sandra Gail Churchill

I'm Going Home to Jesus

If you should go before I do,
Please say hello to those I knew.
Tell them I'll be coming soon;
I hear the trumpets—a merry tune.

Soon I'll see my savior's face
And thank him for this heavenly place.
Don't be sad and do not cry—
Remember God's own words: "nobody dies."

I'll walk the places I loved best
And on a cloud my head I'll rest.
I'll never more be racked with pain;
With Jesus now, my burdens I have lain.

Shirley Theresa Lukaschunis

The Power of Time

O, wretched time! How
Thou pilfers away sweet youth,
Leaving the face which once was
Satin and silk, etched and scarred
Like old leather. 'Tis brutish time
Who devours the supple strength of our tender age,
Making us frail and ever brittle.
Time, the thieving knave, e'en
Reaches his cold hand into the vaulted
Chambers of the mind to pluck out
Cherished memories of our past days.
But, in my heart, time doth powerless be,
For it is there I keep locked up my love for thee.

David Withers Mcaliley

Raggedy Ann

Ah! My poor old Raggedy Ann!
Oh! My poor old friend!
You're tattered and torn, for you I mourn,
My poor old Raggedy Ann.

You've been torn and mended as many times
As I have fingers and toes.
You were my friend through my childhood days,
You shared all my joys and woes.

Even now as I look upon your face,
Your smile, crooked and wan,
I know, no matter how old I get . . .
I'll still love you, Raggedy Ann.

Carol L. Williams

How to Reject Rejection

When I think of the word rejection
It's like getting one vote in an election
Or you're last when it comes to selection
Or first when it comes to ejection

Other meanings for this hurtful word
All terms you have probably heard
To be cast off or thrown back
Refused acceptance or given the sack

But me I've learned how not to be rejected
It's by making sure you're not accepted
So don't get down when you're not wanted
Just get even by appearing undaunted

Michael Leo White

Dream for a Day

It's a dream for you and me
The sweet smell of the morning dew
The joys of the land
Flowing through your hand

The Sun rising up in the sky
Radiating the light of the day
In beauty pictured so true
Allowing thoughts to wander from you to me

A dream for a day
So light and bright, happy in sight
It brings the dream of you
To become ever so true . . .

Paul S. Lambertson

A Love Poem (?)

They say there's someone for everyone,
Me, I don't think it's true,
'Cause if there's someone for everyone,
Why hasn't she found me, too?

Day after day I spend searching,
Trying to find someone who's true.
But when that Sun comes a-setting,
I always come crawling to you.

Now when that black death comes calling,
And the Sun sets on me one last time,
Will I have found that special someone
To have and to hold and make mine?

Robert Lee McGee

I Met a Bug

I was down on the floor with no aim to do more,
When I noticed a dot. He certainly was not
as big as a bumblebee
but rather like a flea.
He ran fast as heck and avoided any speck
which might eat him up or put him in a cup.
To that end he ran fast and so at the last,
I watched him go down a hole that was round.

So sadly my meeting with a bug was so
fleeting that I really don't know
what makes a bug go.

Betty Absher

Grandpa's Tree

Grand purple lilac tree
Rapidly blooming in spring. Every
Afternoon I go to sit inside its branches;
Navigating each and every beautiful flower
Bushel.
Deep in the center of the wonderful tree;
Peering out to see the yard. My grandpa
Alongside my
Sister watching the many cars go by.

Today and tomorrow for the
Rest of my life, I will sit inside its
Enchanted, wonderfully scented branches.
Entering my own little world of daydream.

Rebecca Dawn Marchiando

Cloud Magic

Traveling through the sky
to a magical place so high
Where dreams come true
and happiness is brewed
Red, orange, yellow, green,
wonderful colors are such a gleam
Sweet smelling carnivals have a smell
of cotton candy and Sweet'N Low
Traveling to magical castles,
seeing wonderful unicorns soar through the sky
Fluffy, puffy clouds flow around the sky, way up high
Rainbows sparkling through and through,
'round and 'round a unicorn's horn

Avery Elizabeth Moore

When You Walk in the Pathway of Duty

When you walk in the pathway of duty,
praying to God as you go,
look up and thank the Savior,
He will carry you through.

The trials down here may be heavy
but the one you trust is on the throne,
look up to Jesus and thank Him,
He will carry you through.

When you come to the end of life's journey
and your troubles and trials are over,
look up to Jesus and thank Him
because you are on your way home.

Susie Jones

The Purity of Innocence

Love is a baby, a blade of grass, the moon, stars, sky, clouds,
a flower, a tree, a stream, a breeze, and all the things
which retain their purity.
These things are redolent and are the epitome and
essence of pure love, for they have no malice,
seek no vengeance or retribution,
do not undermine through treachery and greed.
They do not, with intent or purpose, cause hurt or pain.
They do not express anger, jealousy, envy, spitefulness,
or any other negativity.
They are all beautiful, unblemished, and pure.
They are truly what is good and beautiful.
This is love.

Raul Ortega, Jr.

Redeem

Who remembers the words to "Redemption Song,"
now that every Elvis tune has gone
to the top of the charts, to the top of the hill,
to fill minds and thrill kids and make the first kill?

When oil's been found, why harvest the rice?
Trade oil for labor and take their advice;
take off those rags, dress up in their cloak
and after a long day, relax with a Coke.

Looked into the future, tradition was lost,
and we used their currency to pay up the cost.
To clean up the mess, they sent in their best,
but they forgot the Sun sets in the west.

Brian Alessi

The Lantern

Misty, dark and gloomy night
Tumbling feet searching for light

People in the world, in profound obscurity
Trying to find the way in uncertainty

Steps of shivering uneasy despair
Staggering in darkness unaware

Seeking for a rewarding future,
But finding none in the bitterness of a human creature

Look ahead, look closely, find the lantern
Words of wisdom, accurate knowledge that shines brightly
and changes the wicked worldly pattern

Ricardo Romo

Do It for You!

Sometimes you need to get away,
And others you know it is best to stay,
But whatever it is you decide to do . . .
Don't do it for them, do it for YOU!

Pressure will probably eat at your brain,
Pressure to have sex, or do drugs, like cocaine.
They'll convince you to cave, and you'll know it is wrong,
But do it for YOU, you've got to be strong!

Do it for you, you've got to believe
That you've got the power that you can achieve!
And choose the right path, you cannot turn back.
We've seen too many people take the wrong track.

Ashley Mae Ziegler

An Island (Love Is . . .)

Love is an island the which we are on
It lingers. . . . inhabitants are gone
Surrounded by water a piece of dry land
It weathers storms with the touch of a hand.

Love understands, love forgives
Love helps us. . . . to live
Shelters us, like an island at sea
Leaves us amazed sets us free.

If you a shipwreck in life have had
And you think all has gone bad
Look for the island, the help from above
And please . . . try love.

Ryan Unruh

The Old Man and the Lad

He was old cold tattered and gray
As he trudged along on his way
To where he was headed I did not know
But it was a cold cold winter's day

Down the street loud and clear
The sounds of voices children near
As the old man raised his eyes to see
A lad so young so strong so tall

With outstretched arms and gentle smile
He said I will help you along as far as I go
Unsteady of gait and trembling hand
They walked along arm in arm

And the lad so young so strong so tall
Led the old man along to the old man's place
Walking beside him at the old man's pace

And on that night before to going sleep
As the old man bowed his head to pray
He asked the God above to please keep watch
Over the lad so young so strong so tall
      Corine Tucker King

Country Boy

A country boy sent out of country
seeing the world through bloodshot eyes
experiencing a war which extinguished many like him for this land
He would own only a part of fighting for a white picket fence,
A true love, a story to tell the grandkids.
It was mid-March before he realized
The six months he had been in country had passed in two days.
He waited in his foxhole for one more moving
Target to grace the scope of his gun.
Mud-stained hands and face, shoes not removed from weeks before,
The steam from the hot ground rising around him.
It made the moonlight unwelcome, much like the Enemy he fought.
Though more years have passed than the 20 I have lived
Memories and thoughts are still fresh in his mind.
Restless nights, ones in cold sweats,
waking to remember how he could have saved his friend,
A friend who died gracefully, proudly, motherless in his arms.
Tears fell down the cheeks of his mud-stained face.
He held on with strong hands, laying the shoes,
Not removed for weeks before, steam from the hot ground
Rising around them.
      Marti Kelly

In Forever Glide

In glide quickly, soaring with no fears, as I see you up there.
 No rush in time, as forever, has you. Up high.
As my inner wings surround my heart, I float to you.
As I feel my spirit shine out in endless rays.
My eyes watch the clouds take the very make of peace and pure
love and sincerity. No conscience, for all is clear—
there's no steering gears, shifting you back to tears.
It's only pure, pure and dear, that's you, Kelly. As I steer near.
I'm left amazed, in ease, now dazed. So soft as you there lay, embraced.
As I feel to face a loss but a trace. As I know your grace, beatitude.
As words have no expression for what my eyes behold above.
Screened in its very own. Light that soars endlessly, you hold all true.
I watch thee in my heart, to never depart.
I cling to art that you beautified within my heart.
I love true, forever you, beau.
This is for you, as I feel you shining through.
Music take me, to beatitude, beatitude, to my beau.
Your my tune, to my soul, Chiming Harmony, as I hear.
Comfort glides, sadness slides, rainbows arrive,
"Beatitude" be bop beau.
Voices of embrace puts a smile upon this face.
Lift me take me out of this place, into grace.
Bebop beau, bebop melodies of tunes, rhythm as I sooth.
A music world, a poem, a connection alive in it
"Antiphony" take me, lift me, swirl me.
      Toni Bruff

Cold

Transparent as glass, you know I want you.
My breath you see. I'm cold, you see my soul.
Hold me safe as a birds nesting in a birch tree.
Cold. You see my need. Need like clay to be molded,
like a child needs to be scolded and loved. I'm cold
needing you, my constant glow, my constant fire.
I feel you tangible like the smell of a peeled orange,
like an arousing aura warms to the core.
Time can't do without you. My mind can't do without you.
Cold like the icebergs in the Arctic, longing your reassuring arms.
Cold as a breeze ten below.
Stinging cold, only to be chilled even more by your absence.
my existence stands still for you.
Blue flame, bring life to this berg.
Light two to make one. One existence, soul to soul.
I'm transparent, only you know.
Take hold of one who is forever.
Rather fever than to linger in cold.
      Tamiko French

Talks with Dad

I spoke to my father for a spell the other night.
It's been five years since he passed, five years out of sight.
These chats are one-sided; I'm the only one to talk.
 I might be in my car, maybe out for a walk.
I tell him that I miss him, I sure could use a hand.
The response is consistent, his silence a command.
Just think of the memories, a solution can be found.
The past has all the answers, all the ones that are sound.
Do it for God, family, community, all that is right.
When you work with that purpose, you can sleep through the night.
      David J. Smith

Tomorrow

Counting down the days until I can set myself free.
Next in line to see my spirit fly and learn to clear
my mind. Clear my mind from all this mischief
and these rebellious things. Counting down the days
of renewal. To renew myself and my values.
Counting down the days it takes to make myself
stronger in mind, body and soul.
Counting down the days it takes to change myself for the better.
Counting down how long it takes to grasp
the reality of a teenager's life. Starting from scratch
I will change. Change for myself to live a long
productive life. Counting down no more.
I start today and live a
life of beautiful tomorrows.
      Mary Rogers

James Randolph Knaub, My Father, My Hero

In a B-17 in World War II—
the 91st Bomb Group is with whom he flew.
He flew thirty missions with seven in the lead plane
and prayed for peace for our country again.
An honorable man who never patted himself on the back,
he fought an Me163B Rocket Fighter attack.
He treated a wounded comrade, then turned to his waist gun
and fought bravely as the Mustangs
finished what he and his crew begun.
There were many brave missions,
and more stories to tell about the love of his
country, and devotion to family as well.
He believed in our nation, our flag and her glory;
I am only beginning to tell of a hero and his story.
The honors, awards and the medals he wore are a fitting
tribute to the man I adore.
His Distinguished Flying Cross was among many received,
yet he had a quiet dignity about all he achieved.

Now he is resting with folded wings,
but I won't be silent about my pride in him.
Just look through the clouds in the faraway sky,
for to protect us again, my hero flies.

Jean Hughes

It Takes Three

How does one make a marriage last, so many people ask?
It's my belief that not just two, but three complete this task.

For God must be the cornerstone on which your home is made.
Otherwise it won't be long before your love will fade.

Men, as husbands it's your role to go where the Lord leads.
To love your wife and children, and to supply their needs.

Women, your role is to be submissive to your spouse;
Love, respect, and honor him, and keep a peaceful house.

As parents, don't take lightly the job that's given you;
To train up Godly children who'll love and obey you.

Basically, I want to say, this road ahead of you,
Must be travelled at all times, by three instead of two.

Jenny Lynn Bean

I Was Born When I Met You

Take a look, burn your vision, and make a decision.
Speak to me oh, rising sun, teach me your beauty,
your most inner thoughts.
I have died, raise my mortal conscience, raise it to your level.
Oh, rising sun, kiss me and allow me to breathe,
stare into my hollow eyes and touch me;
kiss me so I can burst into flames.
Let me melt in this seeded garden.
Just for a moment let me open my eyes for I can feel your warmth.
Oh, highest love, the outlines of your image carve out my words
with tears that seeped out through my eyes,
I whisper my feelings with fears. Dear Father, why am I
trapped in this forsaken body, why is my masked soul breathless?
Tell me what is this I see? Her essence elevates to a higher degree.
My sorrowful eyes cannot bear, as I sprinkle out my cries.
Oh, beautiful one, late have I loved you,
I recognize the signs of these ancient flames,
once washed with blood and stained with mortal tears.
I know that my true love is near.
In this angelic place, I find streams of flowers
to which your presence consumes my every desire.
There I stand; your image brightens the sun's flames.
You stand before me as I capture your majestic smile.
My love, when I was unborn in darkness filled with sorrows,
the desire to find the truth surged from your beautiful light,
my unborn soul has emerged.

Niko Mitsiopoulos

I Had a Dream

One night, I saw a black man
walking through a field of dirty, white cotton.
As he approached the edge, the Kudzu reached up
and grabbed his legs.
He struggled to free himself
but the vines clung to his body, unmercifully.
Finally, he was able to rip the wretched restraints from his body.
Now freedom, the open road, lay only a few feet in front of him.
I woke to find it was merely a dream.

One day I saw a black man chained to the back of a pick up truck.
His body was dragged along miles of Southern country road,
until a passing drain pipe severed his head from his body.
In horror, I fought to wake up, but soon realized it was a reality
and not merely a dream.

One evening, I settled in to ease my troubled mind.
A flame flickering outside the window created awkward shadows
for my eyes to unravel.
As I reached the window, I could see the fire feeding on a back man.
The flames seemed intent to consume his body.
I struggle to unlock the window, but would not budge.
I could merely watch.

Richard Edward Riddle

An Answer

Behind my dark brown eyes and girlish smile
There is something much deeper. . . .
Fear, heartache, sorrow . . .
Each day, it grows a little stronger. . . .
Living life the way you're expected . . .
Knowing the terror that will come upon you if you do not . . .
Looking someone in the eye saying, "Everything is fine!"
Even though you want to tell them what is going on in your mind . . .
What can I do to make this pain go away?
That is the question I have asked myself since I was a little girl. . . .
Maybe one day I will receive my answer. . . .

Shannon Marie Frommelt

Angels in the Architecture

Angels in the architecture
Reaching for my face
I tell 'em there's no need
I already packed my suitcase
Angels in the architecture
They're shutting this place down
Tired of working through the night
In this God-forsaken town
And my body is silent
It welcomes the night
And my spirit is broken
Receptive to the light
Angels in the architecture
Still alone and still in need
If I could just see them
I'd grab my bags and leave
And my body is silent
It's slowing right down
And my spirit is broken
It's too damn late to send in the clowns

Timothy Piper

Warriors Born in Captivity

Have a past, but no future.
In their eyes can be seen generations of fireside councils
Discussing the day's events, the marriages witnessed, the rugs braided,
the elders buried. But no future.
They live on the reservation, producing more
blue-eyed warriors teaching them the ways of the Cherokee,
but not the ways of the blue-eyed visitor who came generations ago
and gave them their blue eyes but not their freedom.
What a legacy! To see in their genes a proud history of Scots, but no future.
The future is buried on the reservation in the ways of the Cherokee.
It stopped! Frozen in time, revealing itself in the haunting gaze of the blue-eyed Cherokee.
No eagerness, no anticipation, no excitement.
He carves an ancient history in ancient stone of the prowess of the hunter,
but he can't take if off the reservation.
So his blue eyes tell another story of his Scot ancestors who visited,
pleasured, and left no future,
only a past of smallpox, pollution, and dying fish and herbs;
of creek-beds dry, and smoke-filled casinos, and hopelessness.

Annabelle Herrada

My Peaches

She was six months grown.
April sixteenth she was supposed to be born.
Nothing better could've happened to my family.
We couldn't wait for her to arrive.
Christmas night we got the call, to find out she wasn't alive.
My sister had to give birth to her.
But instead of pronouncing her time of birth, it was time of death.
I got to hold her.
She was so beautiful even though she wasn't fully grown.
On her tiny little head she wore a peach colored hat.
That's why she'll always be my Peaches.
I wonder about her eyes, because they weren't open yet.
My sister told me no doubt, they would be Whitney eyes.

Whitney Leigh Rhodes

You

When it is dark, You are the light in my life.
When I weep, You are the strength for me.
When I stay the same, You bring a difference.
When I get a prideful heart, You become humbleness.
When it begins to rain outside, You bring me sunshine inside.
When I forget all that I am, You remember and remind me.
When I loosen life's belt and start to float away, You keep my feet on the ground.
When I fall down, You pick me up.
When I have no words left to say, You speak up.
When I just cannot see, You open up my eyes.
When I begin to sink, You throw out the lifeline for all to grab hold to.
When the storm never ceases, You calm the waves and wind.
When I do not seem to hear, You become my ears to listen.
When I just cannot stand alone, You stand for me.
When I get tripped up, You open up Your arms to catch me.
When I just do not want to say the words, You show me the nail prints in Your hand.
When I forget my purpose, You remind me that I raise my head to the sky to see the Heavens.
When I just do not get it, You pray that I would know and fathom Your love.
When I just seem to forget, You show me Your cross and say, "I love you!"

Faith O.

Poet
Profiles

ABSHER, BETTY

[a.] North Wilkesboro, NC [title] "I Met a Bug" [pers.] I am a retired teacher who was greatly influenced by Dr. Seuss and others who write children's books in rhyme. As a child, my daughter loved all such books, just as my kindergarten classes did. I hope to write a children's book in rhyme someday. As a child, my mother wrote poetry and would write a poem to me on my birthday or other special days. I firmly believe my talent was inherited. I have written poems for retirements, birthdays, dedications of buildings, and for no reason at all. I simply enjoy writing poetry.

ACEVEDO, MINA

[a.] Morton Grove, IL [title] "My Kat" [pers.] I'm honored and pleased beyond words to have my poem published. I wrote this poem shortly after my cat disappeared. I think this is a great way to remember him. Adding a little honor always makes grief a little bit more bearable. I'd like to thank one of my best friends, Aron To, for always making me laugh with jokes about the way my cat was named. It isn't one of the most intense and complex poems, but nothing could be closer to my heart.

ADAMS, DANIEL

[a.] Madison, CT [title] "Inside" [pers.] Poetry is my own way of trying to let things out and expressing my feelings. It's almost like my own personal therapy. This poem is about a previous girlfriend who cheated on me and broke my heart. Everything happens for a reason. If she didn't cheat on me, I wouldn't have written this, and I wouldn't be going out with the girl I love now. Poetry has opened more doors for me than I ever thought possible; it has helped me express who I am, not what people see.

ADAMS, OLAMIDE

[a.] Shomolu, Lagos [title] "My Friend, a Gem" [pers.] For me, poetry is an in-born hobby that compliments my love for music. I must acknowledge the inspiration and encouragement that came from my parents, Tunde and Adefileji; my brothers, Jide, Bode, Wande, Lekan; and of course, Tolu Okeowo, my pal. "My Friend, a Gem" was written for Olufunmilayo Demuren, a girl I highly respect and love dearly, and her charming twin sister, Olufunmilola. I thank the Almighty Above for endowing me with a gift of artistic creativity. This poem is dedicated to all my "Good Friends" all around the world.

ADIAT, MUHAMMAD

[a.] Walthanston, London [title] "Not Tit for Tat" [pers.] About one-and-a-half decades ago, my family was going through some real trying times. It was self-inflicted, caused by members of the family. Mother, realizing the stress, the trials, and tribulation on her children was overwhelming, called me and said: "The path of life is a plain strife, yet journey the wilderness with fearless heart. Perchance devils reign, withstand the pain, and live without reason (hatred) for a goodly reward." Ever since, I've been able to see each human being (whether evil or angel-like) as human beings being natural.

AKONG, LEONELLA

[a.] D'Abadie, Trinidad and Tobago [title] "Freedom" [pers.] I live in the countryside and enjoy my time away from work at home, my private retreat from the rest of the world. For me, the best times of the day are just before dusk and as dawn breaks, when there is a period of stillness. I love nature and I love to write, and I hope that my words evoke the same feelings of freedom I had while I was writing them.

ALCARAZ, RAUL

[a.] Richmond, CA [title] "An Austere Place Called Earth" [pers.] This poem was subconsciously inspired by the Oklahoma City bombing. However, it can also be applied to the tragedies of September 11, 2001. I

would like to take this moment and honor every victim of violent acts. I realize my poem is dark and heavy, but it reflects a part of today's society that cannot be overlooked. Let's do everything we can to put an end to this and find a positive solution. There's still hope lingering. Thank you!

ALEXANDER, VIRGINIA

[a.] Edgewater, Co [title] "A Smile" [pers.] Growing up in a family of writers, and raising a family of writers, has taught me how truly blessed I am. I hope I can pass on to my grandsons, Cameron Lee and Desmond Lee, the strength of spirit that they may realize the importance of their words. I would like to teach them that in the master equation, words are parallel to the actions that follow them, bringing forth the sum of our character. We can be beautiful in word, thinking ourselves rich; however, if we are not equal in deed, we are left exposed, empty, and poor in spirit.

ALLEN, DESMOND

[a.] Roseto, PA [title] "Courting Friendship" [pers.] I wrote this as a gift to my wife, Merrill, for our twenty-fifth wedding anniversary

AMAR, MARY

[a.] Hadera, Israel [title] "Apology" [pers.] I was born in Brazil, and I am a trained surgical pathologist who has been living in Middle East for 24 years. In my profession and surroundings, especially recently, I've seen so much trouble, so much suffering, and so many tragedies. Poetry was the only good way to express these feelings in public. I'm sorry for all of these sorrows.

AMBRUSON, DENISE

[a.] Spencer, MA [title] "The Wish" [pers.] "The Wish" was written for a special person in my life, as a "creation-celebration." What better gift than the gift of song! I loved the lyrics and wanted to share them in their poetic form. I thank God for His divine inspiration in my life, and for those I have met along the way. To Him be the glory!

ANDREJCO, CARLA

[a.] Trenton, NJ [title] "Life Less Ordinary" [pers.] Poetry is the language in which the world interprets itself to me, the manner in which my subconscious and my true self are revealed. One evening, I gazed upon the face of someone I loved very dearly. When I asked him what he was thinking, his response was, "I think you'd be bored with my life." All I could say in response was, "I don't think so." The gift of poetry allowed me to convey my true feelings. "Life Less Ordinary" was the proclamation of my love for him, regardless of how unappealing sharing a life with him appeared.

ANDREWS, DEAN THOMAS

[a.] Acme, PA [title] "Lightning" [pers.] "Lightning" is a poem I wrote for many reasons, one being the not so complex being and the intensity of a storm. It actually is a paradigm for the way we live our lives. Some making make quick, bright, awe-taking flashes, and some do exactly the same with slow, meticulous steps. Steps that, in and of themselves, do not flash, but in the whole might make a better biography. I was born and raised in Pittsburgh, PA, where I studied as an English student at the University of Pittsburgh. I am now in the process of attaining a business management degree at the University of Phoenix. All of my poems are dedicated to those significant in my life, while leaving them purposely unnamed, indeed names them.

ANDREWS, WILLIAM

[a.] Punta Gorda, FL [title] "Dream Becomes Reality" [pers.] The poems I write come from my heart. The feelings I have, I put into a poem.

This poem, "Dream Becomes Reality," is about someone I care for and always wanted. One night that dream of a kiss came true.

ANTHONY, AMBER

[a.] Mount Holly Springs, PA [title] "Kansas" [pers.] This poem is special to me because it is about my dog; her name is Kansas, and she is a Cocker Spaniel. I made that poem after she died, to remember her. She was blind, and she didn't have a friend named Daniel. I hope if you have a pet, you love it as much as I did.

ARDENEAUX, C.

[a.] Mandeville, LA [title] "My Wife" [pers.] This poem is dedicated to my wife, Deane, who is an inspiration in my life. I am the senior of six children: Loretta, David, Jeanette, Patricia, and Gary. Each one has contributed to my challenge to write. The love expressed in some of my writings was taught to me by my loving mother, Esther. The strength is a display received from my Aunt Lillian. I am a graduate of Tulane University College, New Orleans, LA. My writings are from a free expression of thoughts.

ARTHUR, GARFIELD

[a.] West Falmouth, MA [title] "West Falmouth Harbor" [pers.] Having boated, sailed, kayaked, fished, and swam in West Falmouth Harbor, my attachment to it is great. A very special friend who lives on its shore inspired this poem. My background embraces engineering and work as a Director of Photography. Poetry is a recent endeavor, one encouraged by peers. Being able to express one's feelings in this fashion brings pleasure and gratification, and I am continuing to experience both.

AVELLA, MICHAEL

[a.] Dunmont, NJ [title] "The Surf" [pers.] I am 17 years old and live in a small town in New Jersey. My English teacher wanted the class to write a poem for extra credit, and I needed all the help I could get. I was heavily into drugs, and this poem explains how I felt and still feel when I got the help I needed with that problem. If I was still using, I would have never written this poem. This poem is very special to me.

BARAJAS, PETRA K.

[a.] Tollhouse, Ca [title] "Amazin' Tales" [pers.] Ms. Barajas lives with her husband, five cats, and two dogs in scenic Tollhouse, California. At present, she writes only in her spare time, but hopes one day for her hobby to become her vocation. This poem describes only in part her love and joy in her feeling companions.

BARNES, CLEMENT, III

[a.] Elkridge, MD [title] "Cast Off" [pers.] I am 24 years old and I have been writing as long as I can remember. I am an aspiring novelist, but I write poetry and song lyrics in my spare time. I find writing to be therapeutic and I don't know what I'd do without it. I only hope that others can find my poetry inspirational or as meaningful as I do.

BARNUM, DUSTIN

[a.] Mesquite, NV [title] "Mother's Lullabies" [pers.] I wrote this poem to remember my mother. We were driving home when she sang to my brothers, Alex Joyce Britton and Challis, and I our lullabies. She would do this often and there was never a time she got through the five lullabies without crying. My mother passed away in 1998. This poem describes one of my vivid memories of her. I love you, mom. Love, Dustin

BEAN, JENNY

[a.] Sidney, ME [title] "It Takes Three" [pers.] I believe that writing is a gift give to me by God. It is my desire to use this gift to glorify Him and to share Him with others. My family seeks to live a life that is an example of obedience to Christ. My husband and I live in Sidney, Maine, and we have been blessed with three wonderful children. If you enjoyed my poem, please read the book that inspired it—The Bible. John 5:24 says, "Whoever hears my word believes Him who sent me has eternal life."

BELL, ANGELA
[a.] Hercules, Ca [title] "Forgetfulness" [pers.] This poem represents all the encouragement, faith, and devotion that have been given to me over the years. It tells the story of new beginnings, old endings, and special memories. I thank God for the talent, my parents for their support, and family and friends for their enthusiasm for my written words. I give a special thanks to Angela Lopez, for providing life stories for me to turn into heartfelt lines of poetry. To my husband, I give the biggest thanks. I love you, Barry, and thank you for always encouraging my devotion to poetry.

BELLUCCI, JOSEPH
[a.] Staten Island, NY [title] "Mamma Cat" [pers.] I am an avid animal lover who owns five animals. I also feed and provide shelter for several stray cats. Mama Cat was one of these strays. She was a sick cat who came to us pregnant. Her three kittens lived for six months to one year. She survived four years after her kittens. She was a cat so timid that the birds would actually eat next to her. Her life inspired me to write this poem. The five animals I own were strays. My favorite just died, Rex a long haired Akita who will be the subject of my next poem.

BENNER, JOSH
[a.] Fitchburg, MA [title] "The Fallen Soldier" [pers.] Growing up on a military base, I was always fascinated by the brave men and women that I saw around me. I often wondered why anyone would dedicate their life to serving their country, but through the years I realized why. I realized that there is an understanding of what we have been given by the earlier brave men and women. War is as American as apple pie, and is also the original creator of heroes in our country. Anyone who says we lack heroes these days needs to take a long hard look at those who are willing to die for us, those who are just waiting for their chance to give back what they feel they owe. They are the real superheroes. Unfortunately war can leave some people unsatisfied, this is the case for the character in my poem.

BERGER, CARRON
[a.] Cockeysville, MD [title] "A Mother's Love" [pers.] I would like to thank my two-year-old daughter, Lindsay Elizabeth, for inspiring my love and thoughts to write the poem "A Mother's Love." Having my poem actually published is such a great honor, and it is something that my daughter and I will both cherish forever. It has also given me the courage and the hope of someday writing a children's book. I hope everyone who reads it will enjoy it and remember what a wonderful gift our children really are.

BERRY, JOHN
[a.] Houston, TX [title] "Hearts of Glass" [pers.] I once had a friend; she was smart, funny, attractive, but most of all a true friend. I always had feelings for her, but was afraid to show them until it was too late. She is now with a wonderful man and I am with a wonderful woman, but what she never knew is that I loved her.

BHARATHAN, HEMJIT
[a.] Cochin, India [title] "Unbridled Passions" [pers.] True poetry comes from within the soul. This poem was written in an instant when I was swept by deep and powerful emotions. It was a strange and magical moment when my inner-self took charge.

BITSIS, SHARI
[a.] Seekonk, MA [title] "Reflections" [pers.] This poem is about my childhood fears. It is about growth and how the experience gained from passing years has strengthened me as a human being, and allowed me to conquer many fears and see through to my soul.

BLACK, BART
[a.] Prescott, AZ [title] "The Striped Hunters: A Tribute to Marine Snipers" [pers.] For ten years of my life, I was blessed to live in Guatemala, a Central American country. During this time, I spent many days running through jungles and ravines, learning to rappel, and living a mock life of a soldier. It has long been my dream to earn such a prestigious title as a United States Marine. This, however, can only be a dream. I have come to respect the US Special Forces, including their snipers. This poem is a way for me to live a dream, but also to show my respect for the soldiers who suffered through the worst of conditions in an effort to rise above their limitations, and to defend their country with all they possessed.

BLANCO, LEE
[a.] Bay Area, CA [title] "I Who See" [pers.] Art is life and life is art. It's the best way and only way that I can express every aspect of myself. Photography expresses what I see. Music allows me to use my physicality. Poetry signifies what I think and feel mentally. This poem has a lot of personal meaning to me. It describes a moment in my life where I took time out and looked at myself, for the first time ever. I eventually walked away and told myself that a life that's not lived is a life that's not earned.

BLANIA, TATIANA
[a.] Windsor, VT [title] "He Is Me" [pers.] This poem is for Ernie. My soon-to-be-husband. It came to be because we were going on our first vacation, our anniversary was a couple of weeks before. To save money for our trip, we promised not buy presents. I just had to do something. So I wrote a poem and mounted in on slate. On our day he said he loved it, and then gave me a beautiful bouquet of flowers he had purchased. I gave him a playful tap on the shoulder for spending money, then I hugged him for a very long time.

BOHRER, ANJA
[a.] Carmel, CA [title] "Poverty Beautified" [pers.] That decayed city villa in Oakland, CA, incited my curiosity with the beauty of its neglected wild garden. Rumors echoed that the building was uninhabitable, but there was life. Stretching my neck over the blossoming rose bushes, I caught many glances of Latin women occupied with their outdoor tasks. A peacefully happy atmosphere prevailed in that community, hidden behind the combined picket and rose busy fence. I was forced to revaluate my concept of happiness.

BONILLA, VICTOR
[a.] Chicago, IL [title] "But Never Belonging" [pers.] Every work of art has a special link with its creator. Through art, the artist can hold a moment in time and forever treasure an event of his or her life. Everything we create carries a little piece of ourselves and that is what makes it special. Being able to communicate through our creations is a gift that one cannot overlook; we must be forever grateful.

BORDER, DANIAL
[a.] Belfair, WA [title] "What If?" [pers.] I am a 13 year old who lives in the small town of Belfair, Washington. Poetry is a fun way to express an idea, thought, or feeling. I'm a student at Hawkins Middle School. I like extreme sports, Blink 182, and anything fun. Thanks to poetry.com; this is really cool!

BOUTCHER, FREDERICK
[a.] Bayside, NY [title] "I Wish I Wasn't So Stupid!" [pers.] I spent 25 years living a dark, lifeless existence, fighting with the demons of three-and-a-half years in Vietnam. In June of 1995, I came to Saudi Arabia hoping to escape my demons. It was August 15, 1995, when Priny came into my life. I feel like I died and was reborn. Priny, my beautiful Filipina, put reason back into my life and sparkle in my eyes. We are living in Saudi where I teach Electrical Physics and share home between Bayside, New York and Pangasinan, Philippines.

BOZULICH, CARMELA
[a.] Rowland Heights, CA [title] "The Cat Who Sleeps on the Bed" [pers.] This poem came to me in the dark hours before dawn. I awoke from a fitful sleep and one of our cats was stretched out against my side, purring loudly. She tends to spend most of her day on our bed, and we now have a special little mattress for her. I dedicate this to her, Star, my own furry hot-water bottle.

BRAUER, THOMAS
[a.] Palm Springs, FL [title] "Darling, My Butterfly" [pers.] This poem was written for a girlfriend of mine. It shows how much I care for her. I got the name "Darling, My Butterfly" from the pet name I gave her, "Butterfly." I believe that poetry is a gift, as well as a source of entertainment. I write poetry for fun, entertainment, to express my feelings and say things that are hard for me to say. I do wish to dedicate this poem to two girls that are very important to me in my life as of now: Kathleen Brodbeck and Brandi Hagan. Thank you both so very, very, much.

BREHM, TIMOTHY
[a.] Hanover Park, IL [title] "Realism Strikes Back" [pers.] This poem was written during the hardest, greatest, and worst time of my life. At the age of 23, I was diagnosed with spinal stenosis (narrowing of the spinal canal) and degenerative disk disease. The doctors told me I have the back of a 70-year-old man and the worst they've ever seen in someone so young. I was in so much pain that I couldn't get out of bed half the time. I was able to get through it only because I met my future wife, Stephanie. This poem expresses my feelings at this particular time of my life.

BROOKS, REBEKAH
[a.] Durham, NC [title] "So, I Weep and I Write" [pers.] "So, I Weep and I Write" is a very poignant poem. It explains how I felt going through a breakup with someone special in my life. I find writing when I'm sad or lonely is the best time for me to show sentiment and self-expression. Poetry is more than art; it is an outlet for emotion and feelings. I hope that my poetry will not only move you, but also inspire you.

BROWN, ALEXANDER
[a.] Ridgeland, SC [title] "Holding On" [pers.] This poem is special to me, as it exemplifies my mother's love, care, and dedication for her children. Even though she is now deceased, she lives forever in our hearts and minds. To my faithful supporters, I would like to thank them by name: sisters, Joann, Samella, Felita, Rebecca, Corenthia and Mary Lou; brothers, Wendell, Nathaniel, Frankie, David and Joseph; my daughter, Alexria Sukia Robinson. Special thanks to Ms. M. Williams and Mr. M. Riley. Thanks for being there. Last but not least, thanks to all my friends and family in my hometown of Georgetown, South Carolina.

BROWN, BRANDY
[a.] Pascolena, CA [title] "One True Love" [pers.] Usually I have a hard time saying the things that are on my mind, like when it comes to telling a guy how I feel. Poetry has always been an easy way for me to get my words out. This poem was written to tell this guy who I have been talking to for a while how I felt about him. He means something to me and I would be hurt if I was to lose him. This was the best way to get the words from my mind to his heart so he would understand where I was coming from.

BRUFF, TONI
[a.] Kalispell, MT [title] "In Forever Glide" [pers.] Love's Profile . . . The deep affection is devoted, honest, and endless. Fountains of waterfalls are breathtaking, beautiful, caught in, like wings of doves. As the sky unfolds, like a scroll of ribbon released, love is written, received, circling a zillion times over in words never upon ink: the highest repeat a heart can speak. Love is complete, timeless, priceless, sealed upon the heart. It is inspired and lead by the author of life. Love, light, power, peace, beauty, and joy—Countless in all, within one.

BULLIS, DAVID
[a.] Sandy, OR [title] "Rhododendron Flower" [pers.] As Frost said of poetry, so I also delight in nature, and find it exceeding instructive, a well from which sweet lyric may be drawn.

BURNS, JASON
[a.] Denver, CO [title] "The Perfect Tan" [pers.] This is one of only a few poems that I have ever shared with anyone. The poem is not about getting a tan at all, but rather the wonderful feeling of being part of everything around you. I was sunbathing one July day in beautiful Cheesman Park, when these words were channeled to me. I wrote as fast as I could and finished in about two minutes . . . it was a wonderful feeling. I want to give thanks and dedicate this poem to Shirley Klinehamer and Mark Robichau. You will be in my heart forever.

BURT, STEPHANIE
[a.] Saginaw, MI [title] "No Place to Turn" [pers.] My poem is written in the hopes that young people like myself will learn that popularity is a trap. If you're in the "in crowd," they own you; if not, they disregard you. I was owned and then left by myself, and this poem expresses my sorrow and pain.

BUTLER, DIAJA
[a.] Los Angeles, CA [title] "The Wings of Love" [pers.] Much too often, the power and intensity of love is taken for granted. It has been confined to spouses and children, limited to so-called "loved ones," and restricted to only those with whom we associate closely. The true meaning of love has become but a marginalized concept and lost on us. We have forgotten to share our passion, our adoration, our gift of love with those around us. This poem was written to remind the people of the world that love is the core of inner and communal peace. I would like to dedicate this poem to my mother, Rosilyn, who helped me fly; my dear family and friends; and my husband, Tooki, from whom the splendor of love has brought me incredible happiness.

CALEY, LARRY
[a.] Egg Harbor Township, NJ [title] "The Month of March" [pers.] "The Month of March" occurred to me on a warm morning in March, a few days after my birthday. I am fortunate that my birthday coincides with the rebirth of nature in springtime, as expressed in this poem. I would like to dedicate this poem to all the artists who have struggled in the face of the rising tide of technology and the few resources to teach our children the beauty of artistic expression.

CANNON, JANICE
[a.] Dallas, NC [title] "Legacy" [pers.] When I reflect on God's awesome creations, I am reminded of my responsibilities as a soul that is currently experiencing physical life. I believe that our souls were created in the beginning, when God yearned for companionship. Since then, and throughout eternity, I believe that we experience reality in infinite dimensions as our souls grow in spirituality through trials and tribulations. We separated ourselves from God through sin, but Christ came to earth and provided us with a plan of salvation. If we follow that plan, we can eventually find our way back to God. My poem expresses this ideal.

CAPILLO, ALYSSA
[a.] Evanston, IL [title] "Benji" [pers.] I love music, and my poem "Benji" is about a member of my favorite band, Good Charlotte. I would like to dedicate this poem to all my friends (especially Becca, because she got me writing, and Lynda, Edytka, and Deneen), for always being there; to my family; and of course, to Benji. This poem is for you!

CARTER, ALI
[a.] Martinez, GA [title] "To My Best Friend" [pers.] This poem is very important to me because it shows the strong bond between my best friend, Jeremy, and I. For a long time, I was not close to him because I was consumed with too many superficial activities. It took a near-tragedy for me to realize what an important part of my life he is. I wrote this poem during that hard time in our lives. This poem is for me to show Jeremy how important he is in my life, and that I will love him for the rest of our lives.

CARTER, PAMELA
[a.] Minneapolis, MN [title] "My Father" [pers.] I wrote this verse one evening while finishing up my last requirements for college graduation. It is in honor of God and my father, Clarence Carter. My father's spirit and strength have been an inspiration to me. The memories he left help guide me and give me courage and strength. Through unconditional love and faith, I've learned that life is not a destination but a journey. My family and I have truly been blessed!

CAULDWELL, ATHENA
[a.] Omaha, NE [title] "The Greatest Gift" [pers.] "The Greatest Gift" is a poem I composed as I began to understand the value that each human has! Writing this poem enabled me to accept who I am. Poetry provides an opportunity to express my honest feelings from the heart and soul. Most importantly, I hope that my poetry will inspire others, despite their problems, to know their self-worth. Hopefully this poem will increase their understanding that there is something special about them. They need only look inward to find peace, happiness, and the knowledge that they do have value and worth in this world.

CAZA, HEATHER
[a.] Syracuse, NY [title] "Only One" [pers.] "Only One" is in memory of a special little boy. It is entitled "Only One" because when I visited a cemetery near a campground that I visit yearly, the headstone seemed to jump out at me. I love children—they say and do the darnest things—and I couldn't imagine the pain of these parents when they lost their little angel. Therefore, every year I leave them a little poem on their son's headstone. "Only One" is the most recent; it was left in the fall of 2000. I can't imagine the pain that they have felt, but I do offer my deepest condolences.

CHANNEL, DIANA
[a.] Eustis, FL [title] "Missing You" [pers.] I wrote this poem from love. To me, the most important thing to possess in life is a loving heart. It is important to remember always, if only in a memory of days gone by, someone who has touched your heart, as well as your very soul, so much that you will never forget them.

CHOATE, MICHELE
[a.] Dallas, TX [title] "Pain" [pers.] I was born in West Germany in 1964. My father was in the service, which made us come to the States in 1967. I was only three. I was a scared child. My mom and dad always argued. We came to Texas in 1969, where I was abandoned by my mother, left at my grandmother's door. I was again scared and confused. In 1969, I was placed in a children's home for six very long years before finally being adopted by my current parents. As you can tell, I have been through a lot of heartache and pain, thus the title of my poem, "Pain."

CLANTON, LISA
[a.] Fox, OK [title] "Divorce" [pers.] Writing has been a part of my life for as long as I can remember, from poems, short stories, cookbooks, to my favorite children's book. My girls, Misty, Amanda, and DeOnna, have all been raised to express themselves in writing. The three of them have always encouraged me to write, and I continue to do so every day. I really hope to become a well-known author someday soon, with children's books and my mystery novels. I would also enjoy using my poetry in greeting cards. I feel that through the power of words, great things can happen.

CLEMENS, CHANDRA
[a.] Hanson, MA [title] "Traveling to Australia" [pers.] This poem was written about my experience traveling as a student Ambassador to Australia. Throughout the poem, I mention some of the locations that I visited and experienced in Australia. Australia is a beautiful place and it was a trip of a lifetime.

CLICK, CINDI
[a.] Quinton, AL [title] "Goodbye" [pers.] This poem is very special to me. I loved my school very much. The state closed our high school down from the 9-12 grade. We all had to leave and go somewhere else, and it was really hard for us all. We were a very unique and special school; we were family. We thought we had a great things. We were the Martin Warriors. The board of education, Congress, and State—no one would listen to us. So, Martin High School is no more and it is a great loss to everyone, including myself. My heart will forever belong to T.W. Martin!

COLLINS, CHRISTOPHER
[a.] Victorville, CA [title] "Ode to Superchris" [pers.] This past year in English class, Mr. Petruschin, the teacher, encouraged us to get intimate with our poetry. So I decided to poeticize myself. I feel that this sonnet depicts my confidence and good humor, as all poems depict some facet of their author's lives. Poetry is a great medium of self expression. Through poetry, we share ourselves; for this poem is Superchris, and Superchris am I

CONWAY, TRESSIE
[a.] Dade City, FL [title] "Woes of a Third-Shift Technician" [pers.] I have been a third-shift technician for several years. And though I love my job and my shift, it often gets very lonely being on a schedule which is opposite from the rest of the world. We are a rare breed and a forgotten minority who deserve a little more recognition and respect for the part we play in today's society. My poem, "Woes of a Third Shift Technician," is just my small way of helping the rest of the world to remember and understand us a little better.

CORDELL, CONNIE
[a.] Keysville, VA [title] "Why Can't He See Me?" [pers.] I have been writing since I was very little. I write poetry to let people know they are never alone. I wrote this poem after a boy I liked so much walked away. I just want to give readers an insight to my love of poetry. I also want them to know that in any given situation, someone will always feel their pain.

CORSO, DONNA
[a.] Lafayette, TN [title] "The Safe Place" [pers.] Writing is a way to express and share the thoughts and feelings I discovered when I love a child. Somewhere in time, in the midst of daily life, I forgot the magic of poetry. I forgot how writing and sharing feelings can bring a smile of someone's face. lift a sad spirit, share love and compassion, and feelings. I'm grateful for the gift of words, for poetry has purpose and meaning, and lives on forever. I dedicate all my writings to those who fill my heart with joy and peace, the Lord, and my family

COSTNER, WILLIAM
[a.] Hickory, NC [title] "Mending Heart" [pers.] This poem was written to show my emotions about a wreck that killed four of my friends. Cole, Keona, Robin, and Ashley were killed in a car wreck in February of 2001. Their loss was tragic, but the tree that they ran into survived the crash and are growing the lost bark back.

CRAIG, JOHN
[a.] Kamloops, Canada [title] "Babies" [pers.] Try to be careful on how you treat babies because they can see it. Thank you for publishing my poem. I've never written a poem and I took a lot of time thinking about what I should write! Thanks again.

CULBERTSON, ALEXANDRA
[a.] Gulfport, MS [title] "Sorry" [pers.] I am a Junior at Harrison Central High in Gulfport, MS. I just want to say that I am very proud that another one of my poems is being published. I want to thank my friends and family for supporting me. I would also like to thank God for giving me this opportunity. I love you all.

D'AMICO, VITO, JR.
[a.] Manchester, NH [title] "Lovin'" [pers.] "Lovin'" is a testament of words that I was able to put on paper wile expressing my feelings of passion and love. This poem consists of my sentiments that were inspired by a woman who entered my life in October of 2000. She has helped make my 2001 better than I could have ever anticipated. She has become and will always be "my very special best friend, always." "Lovin'" is my dedication to this special woman for whom I will always have a special place in my heart.

DALTON, ERIK M.
[a.] Lewiston, ID [title] "Shattered" [pers.] This poem is in memory of my brother, Dirk, who was murdered when he was only four years old. The loss of a loved one can be overwhelming, but the pain does fade away and the love you feel continues to grow stronger. I hope sharing the love and pain I felt will help someone who has experienced the same.

DAS, KAUSTUV
[a.] Pune, India [title] "I Knew a Man" [pers.] This poem is very special to me. The poem highlights the conflict in my mind. I am still not sure whether I have achieved what I wanted to be. The person who had so much influence on me from my early childhood, saw me progress through thick and thin of my life, is no longer here to guide me. My chosen path, now away from him, I ask, "Lord, the work undone, have I come up to his expectations? Shall I achieve a fraction of what was he?" [Dr. Kaustuv Das is a General Surgeon, an artist, a painter and a sculptor. His sensitive mind and artistic vision now weaves his thought into beautiful poems.]

DASKALAKIS, TISHA
[a.] South Ozone Park, NY [title] "God, My Father" [pers.] Poetry is my life. Writing is a gift with which God has graced me. This poem expresses the fatherhood of God. It describes His care for me. Writing enables me to escape the troubles of life and find peace through poetic verse. My godmother, Bishop Daisy B. Garvin, has always been my encouragement and supporter when it comes to writing and my artistic vision. I hold an Associates of Arts in Liberal Arts. I am an Evangelist and plan to pursue a degree in Music at Hunter College in January. My long-term goals are to become a producer in music, and become a writer and a dancer. I love to sing, dance, and write poetry. My life source and greatest influence is God Almighty, who has exclusively been the father I never had, naturally speaking.

DAVIS, JOSH
[a.] Goldsby, OK [title] "Fire" [pers.] The poem "Fire" is very special to me because it is about my daily struggles and fears. I dedicate this poem to Christy, my air; and her children, Adam and Rebecca; they are the flowers. I love you so much, Christy, and I thank you for everything. My prayer is that one day this poem will have no meaning to me. I pray that one day you have need of me and love me like I love you.

DAVIS, SHERRY
[a.] Goldsboro, NC [title] "Do We Dare to Dream?" [pers.] I have found that the best teacher is life. It teaches you to withstand joys and sorrows. I am 40 and have been writing since I was 20. If you feel something in your heart, put it on paper.

DEANS, KRYSTAL
[a.] Kill Devil Hills, NC [title] "Daddy" [pers.] I find my inspiration all around me. At this particular time in my life, my dad happens to be my inspiration. He tries his hardest to make sure that my family and I are well off. Needless to say, my dad is a wonderful husband, son, friend, and father. I dedicate this poem, and any others down the road, to him.

DEEGAN, ALLEN
[a.] Long Beach, CA [title] "Sweet Sunshine" [pers.] I wrote this poem for an ex-girlfriend after we broke up, while I was stuck in my depression. It was only the second poem I ever wrote, but it seemed to get the best reaction from friends. It was inspired when my ex-girlfriend asked me a question, and this poem was my answer. I want this poem to tell people that if you're in a relationship, take it slow, but know when to pick things up—emotionally, not physically.

DeMICELLI, CATRINA
[a.] Lomita, CA [title] "Cry of the Wild" [pers.] I like writing poetry; it reaches to the realm of our souls, and makes you look at life in a new light. My heart expresses itself in words inspired from my soul. It is a gift from my heart to your soul. I wrote this poem for my children, Matthea and Nathan, in hope that our nation can pull together and keep in mind what is really important—our precious land, that we need to live on in our future, in peace. If my writing can touch others in good ways, I can help to do what's right in my life.

DEWITT, ALYSSA
[a.] Grand Rapids, MI [title] "My Mom" [pers.] Hi, my name is Alyssa DeWitt, and I'm 11 years old. The reason I wrote this poem is because of my natural, unconditional love for my mother. She's a single parent, and I love her will all my heart.

DIAZ, SERGIO
[a.] San Juan, TX [title] "Rest in Your Arms" [pers.] This poem is dedicated to every soul that has touched my life—especially to my mother, the pillar in my life; and to my Dad, my guide. My hands create, my imagination gives life, but the light that guides my hand is Anayanci.

DILLON, BRETT
[a.] Hampstead, MD [title] "am i all i can be?" [pers.] I wrote this poem for all those out there who are told day in and day out that they are never good enough. All my life, I've been told what I'm doing this wrong, and that I never put my best into it. Well, to all those out there—I still don't care what you think about my life! And to all those who supported me: Thank you! For all those out there who feel this way: Live your life for you and God. Anyone else's opinion does not matter! I hope my poem inspires someone! One last thing: If nothing else, let go and let God!

DIOQUINO, MA. MYLIONETTE
[a.] Cagayan de Oro City, Philippines [title] "An Exaltation to My Prince" [pers.] My poem is an example of a terse style and a classic sense of writing. I share this among women who believe in the full character of a man and in the practice of chivalry. I'm fondly called "Miles." I am an educator of Lourdes College taking master's studies in teaching English as a second language. I was born in Cagayan de Oro City, Philippines to Antonio and Juanita Dioquino. I share my passion for singing and writing with my five married sisters: Ma. Luisa, Ma. Victoria, Ma. Teresa, Ma. Antonette, and Marimar, who have greatly contributed to my craft and person. Being the youngest has been an advantage. I've become a dreamer. I consider my pen and my paper as pals; they stand witness to all my crucial and exhilarating moments. I firmly believe in two things: decisions involve strength of character, solidarity of faith, firmness of will, and man's willingness to risk; and that God is the Divine Artist who remains unsurpassed.

DOLEATTO, WILLIAM
[a.] Ottawa, ON [title] "Cold Rain" [pers.] I've always enjoyed creative writing, especially poetry. I find, with poetry, you can tell a story or share a feeling without having to write a novel. This is the first time I have submitted or shared any of my work with an audience. The poem that I have written was a wound that has since healed, but the memory is still etched in my mind. I find that negativity can sometimes breed creativity. I hope my poem can bring out emotions from the reader. I want the reader to be able to relate to the words and feelings that the poem portrays.

DORAN, MIKE
[a.] Redlands, CA [title] "On Stage" [pers.] I have written songs and poetry since high school and have met known many accomplished writers and performers. In its larger view, this poem is for them all. More specifically, this piece is for Maureen, a marvelous singer/songwriter who is, today, a mother and special-education teacher. She once concealed the fact of having placed quite well in a songwriter's festival, fearing she might hurt my feelings, as I had entered the contest but failed to place at all. Her extraordinary kindness and artistry will always remain in my heart. God bless you, Mo. Thanks for the memories.

DUBIN, KIMBERLY
[a.] Selden, NY [title] "Life" [pers.] This poem about life is special to me because it tells about different decisions that you can make as you get older. I couldn't have done this poem without the help of my family and my teacher, Ms. Carella Dean, who inspired me to enter this contest and create a poem that would be special to people all around the world. My hobbies are singing, acting, bowling, and soccer. During my free time, I love to get together with my friends and family. I thank the International Library of Poetry for giving me this chance of a lifetime.

DYSON, CAROLYN
[a.] Vallejo, CA [title] "The Me You See" [pers.] I live in the San Francisco Bay Area. I came to the Bay Area from Florida thirty five years ago. I remember seeing the fog and thinking the city was on fire, only I didn't smell smoke. I have come into womanhood here, and my poetry and other writings allow me to share my journey and growth. I am my mother and her mother, Cesa Leo Goldsmith. I am a part of the story of every black woman. Travel with me and you will see that the me you see is who I be.

EARLY, ERIKA
[a.] Modesto, CA [title] "Emotions" [pers.] I dedicate this poem to my best friend Heather H. I wrote this poem about the basic questions that people ask. The reason why I dedicate this poem to Heather is because she has helped me through some hard times. When I fall, she is always there tc help me up. I just hope that I do for her what she does for me. This poem is for all of the people out there who feel the same way. I guess some people have to be in a certain state of mind to write certain poems. In this case, I was in a mood.

Most poetry comes from the heart. I'd like to thank my mom, Toyia; my step-dad, Cris; my sister, Tiffany; my step-sister, Samantha; and most of all, my best friend, Heather Herrera.

EDWARDS, BONNIE
[a.] Greensboro, NC [title] "No More" [pers.] Although we walk through our daily routines with painted smiles and cheerful greetings to our fellow man, there are many, many who are enduring a nightmare of unending anguish and pain. This is the secret cry of a broken soul who has lost hope for that precious ray of sunshine, that better tomorrow, that one spark of love for which the heart so desperately longs.

ELDRED, TASHA
[a.] Peoria, AZ [title] "Backstreet Boys" [pers.] This poem means so much to me because I am such a huge Backstreet Boys fan. I never in my life would have thought that this poem would be published. My life revolves around the Backstreet Boys. A.J. McLean from the Backstreet Boys inspired me to write poetry because he is a poetry writer himself. That would be so awesome if the Backstreet Boys actually read my poem. I also want to thank my family for being there for me all my life. BSB, if you are out there, I really want to meet you!

EMERT, MIKE
[a.] Toccoa Halls, GA [title] "Seed" [pers.] I am a college student who likes to write poetry when it comes to my mind. I am not a professional or an amateur writer, but I love to do it when I get the chance. I was inspired to write this poem by my girlfriend, Natalie. God bless!

ETTER, KAITLYN
[a.] San Dimas, CA [title] "Waiting" [pers.] Poetry is my outlet; it is something I like to do to escape from the world and my problems. I wrote this poem at a very hard time in my life. One day, I just sat down with my journal and all of these powerful emotions started to form on my paper. I am going to be a sophomore in high school. I live in San Dimas, California. My friends from theatre, (which is one of my hobbies) and school mean so much to me; I would like to thank them for their support. I would also like to thank my family for everything.

EVANGELISTA, YVETTE
[a.] Fort Washington, MD [title] "My Baby, Belle" [pers.] This poem is very special to me because it speaks of when I became a first-time mom. The feeling of being a mother is wonderful and is beyond words. I am happy to have expressed it in this manner. I am sharing this poem with my dear husband, Sonny, who stood by me all the way. I am proud of this simple accomplishment, and I am sure that my daughter, Belle, will come to appreciate it.

EVANS, TRACEY
[a.] Taneytown, MD [title] "A.J. McLean: Our Angel" [pers.] When I decided to submit a poem this year, I knew it had to be focusing on something special. I chose A.J. McLean's fight and struggle against alcoholism, depression, and anxiety. What this man is struggling to overcome takes courage. It takes even more not to hide it from the world. He has an incredible amount of support, including myself. Words can't express how proud I am of him for being a man and admitting he needs help. I'll always be here as a fan and supporter. I love him. This is my tribute to A.J. McLean

FEDORKA, SUSAN
[a.] Port Jervis, NY [title] "My Loved Friend Adam" [pers.] This poem is very special to me because it came to me at a very difficult time. I would like to dedicate this poem to Adam's family and friends. Adam could spend only one

second with you and change your life for the better. He was the most charismatic person I had ever met. He will be missed, but never forgotten.

FERNANDO, IRANGANIE
[a.] Saugus, MA [title] "I Still Wonder" [pers.] I am a Sri Lankan, a poet and a writer in the Sinhala language. This is my first English poem. In the poem, I give a slight insight into the kind of life my son had when he was growing up, and how it affected his life. As a child, I learned to find comfort in turning my sad painful experiences into poems and short stories. Today, as an adult, I still find comfort doing so. I have also written my first English novel, a memoir that's not considered for publication.

FETSCH, JOHNICA
[a.] Munday, TX [title] "Competition" [pers.] Competing is the most exhilarating aspect of my life! Regardless of the outcome, that feeling—that breath-taking, heart-racing feeling of giving it your absolute all—is worth more to me than any blue ribbon or gold medal! My grandmother, Martha Jo Lawler, taught me to love poetry. Poetry allows me to express myself and show life's beauty to others. Poetry isn't just writing words; it's searching one's heart and soul to make the reader experience your feelings. I would like to thank my family, teachers, and friends, who have all had a great impact on my life and my poetry.

FINCHUM, TED
[a.] St. George, UT [title] "Birth" [pers.] As I watched a young lady give birth, it occurred to me that the beginning of life was not easy, but seemed to be worth it. It touched my heart and mind. I put on paper what I felt. At times the words just flow, and I am compelled to put them on paper. Life is short. I write what I see and feel. To live, love, and laugh are life's greatest joys.

FLORES, CHRISTINE
[a.] Baguio City, Philippines [title] "Countenance" [pers.] I have the ultimate passion for the texture of words. That is why I chase them around, mull over them, toy with them, and then try to shape them into something which I call my own version of things. I write as an ode to this earthly life, the only thing I know that is certain. I believe that there is nothing like this throbbing present to live, love, and write.

FOGGIA, JEANNIE
[a.] Park Ridge, IL [title] "It Cannot Last" [pers.] In the past two years, I've realized the value of time—days, hours, minutes, even seconds. Time with loved ones is often taken for granted. Now I face the harsh realization that I cannot go back and change things I have done that I now regret; I can't reverse the things I've said. I cannot retrieve time lost with people I care about, or the time I have wasted. I can only take advantage of every moment I have. I know now how little time we are allotted. We must take advantage of what we've got before it's too late.

FORD, SUZANNE
[a.] Stamford, CT [title] "Mi Amor" [pers.] "Mi Amor" is the third poem I've written and have published. I thank God for the talent He has given me. I thank my mom for always being there for me and encouraging me to do my best. I feel blessed to have her as a mother. I dedicate this poem to my half-sister, Sandra, with this message: "I love you—never give up hope." I also dedicate this poem to my boyfriend, Cosmin, with this message: "I love you; I hope our love will last forever."

FORTUNA, CYNTHIA
[a.] Manila, Philippines [title] "Why Do I Love You" [pers.] "In our hearts there's a voice, a voice from our soul!" I listen to that voice and it makes me write things! This poem started with a question: Why am I loving? It's hard to explain love, but it's easy to show

it! When I start to write, everything comes rushing inside me! I should keep on writing! I am a 26-year-old dentist who loves singing, dancing, acting, and writing songs, and poems! My family, relatives, friends, and my love are my inspirations! They keep me living and loving! And I send my thanks to God, who made all things for us!

FORTUNE, HEATHER
[a.] Temperance, MI [title] "Angel" [pers.] An angel is a guardian spirit. Even though my grandma passed away, she is still with me wherever I go. She will always be my guardian. "Angel" was not written at the greatest time of my life, but it is still close to my heart, just like my guardian angel, Carolyn Fortune.

FOSSE, LINDSEY
[a.] Diablo, CA [title] "A Mystical Place" [pers.] I am freshman at the University of Arizona. I have loved poetry since I was a child. I would like to dedicate this poem to my parents and my sister. Without their love and support, I would not be here today.

FRIEST, JOHN
[a.] West Orange, NJ [title] "Rocks with Writing" [pers.] Poetry heals our wounds and makes us think. This poem was inspired by a trip to a cemetery when I was in College. My science class went there to chart life expectancies. I wrote this poem after reading a tombstone of a baby. I realize that I have been blessed in many ways: by having had a grandmother who worshiped me; with Diane; by having a saint for a mother and a gentle intelligent father; by being able to write; and having grandparents, aunts, uncles, brothers, teachers, cousins, and friends; and by being able to share this poem with you. Thank you for reading my poem!

FULLER, VIVIAN
[a.] Belfast, ME [title] "Come Walk with Me" [pers.] Poetry, or the ability to write, is truly a gift from God. I thank God for this gift He's given to me. This poem is my way of sharing the hope that is within me, and my way of giving back to God a part of what He's given to me. He is the way, the truth, and the life.

GALLARDO, VICTORIA
[a.] Red Bank, NJ [title] "Don't Knock the Hustle!" [pers.] When I write my poems, I tend to use my own personal experiences. Whenever something bad happens to me, I just get my pen and paper and start to write. A lot of my poems are mind boggling and they are often filled with more than one meaning.

GALVAN, TONJA
[a.] Des Moines, IA [title] "Forbidden Love" [pers.] This poem is about the love of my life, who taught me you can't always fix everyone; but you can fix yourself. When love's strong and true, you can take a break to see things clearly. It's never too late to fix what's broken and save the beauty you onced shared. This is very special to me and perhaps it'll be for you, too

GANTT, JESSE
[a.] New Cumberland, PA [title] "If the World Was Blind" [pers.] I am an aspiring Olympic Ski Racer. I am currently ranked second nationally on the USSA Circuit for my age division. Poetry helps me to put my hopes and feelings into words. I hope they will inspire a kinder and more compassionate world for us all to share. I wrote this poem to express how important it is to judge people by that which is in their heart and soul, rather than by the way they look on the outside.

GARCIA, DORIS
[a.] Vancouver, Canada [title] "Molly the Cow, the Gift of Life" [pers.] This poem was dedicated to my brother, a part of my heart and soul. I was suffocating with great pain, as if I was losing myself and wanted to find that light to give me peace. Instead, I ended up turning everything

around by holding on to faith, hope, and Molly (a Beanie Baby that he had given me). I hope through this poem that I can make people realize that a gift should be seen through the eyes and heart of the giver and not how much it cost. The cheapest gift for someone could be a treasure for another. If it wasn't for Molly, I wouldn't be here today. I am very happy to be able to share this poem with you all and hope you can share it with your loved ones!

GARDNER, VIRGINIA

[a.] Sarasota, FL [title] "Oracle of the Cosmos" [pers.] I live in Sarasota, Florida, with my husband, Ray. The love of poetry was instilled in me by my father, Dr. Fred Hinett, and mother, Trudy Hinett. Robert Louis Stevenson was my first role model, followed by R. A. Milne! I wrote this poem out of a need to express my belief that unless the planet returns to a higher moral code than exists today, we shall bring upon ourselves our own destruction. "Oracle of the Cosmos" was written months before the September 11, 2001 attack on America. Was the oracle trying to tell us something?

GIESE, ERIC

[a.] Irvine, CA [title] "I, the Epileptic" [pers.] This poem is very special to me. You see, when I was five years old, I came down with epilepsy. That was 43 years ago. This poem, in a nutshell, says that while epileptics do have a disorder, we are also people just like the rest of you. This poem comes from my heart.

GODLIN, DANIEL

[a.] Sharon, MA [title] "Soaring" [pers.] I am a sixth grade student in the South Area Solomn Schecter Day School in Stoughton, MA. What inspired me to write this poem was when I was thinking about my Poppy. I wished to see him one more time in Heaven, so I went "Soaring" and saw him. I love poetry, and so did he, and that is what made me write this poem. I hope that others who have special people in their lives who have passed can relate to my love for Poppy. Perhaps those people will share my poem with their loved ones.

GOMBA, OSILA GRACE

[a.] Canber, Australia [title] "Depression" [pers.] My friends call me Syl (Sil). I'm sixteen years old and I have one of those loving families that annoy you and claim to do what's best for you—a big brother, sweet and vicious at the same time; two villains for younger brothers, always scheming devilish episodes; and an innocent, backstabbing sister (spoiled beyond repairs). Anyway, I go to college, Canbessa College in the ACT, Australia, the continent with strange seasons—like winter in July! I'm inspired by reality, things that are right in my face, and some experiences. I enjoy movies, parties, and those priceless things like the wind in my face when driving (actually speeding) down a highway in the night, watching an orange sunset in purple clouds, and falling in love. Everyone thinks Shakespeare is a genius that figured out how to bring out the art in people. At the night time, I'm one of those people. My favorites are *Romeo and Juliet* and *Twelfth Night*.

GOMEZ, HEATHER

[a.] Hyde Park, VT [title] "Sweet Escape" [pers.] I never felt I had a talent in writing until the seventh grade, when my first piece was published in a school book. I kept on writing and found that I was enjoying it more and more. I wrote this poem when my family and I were going through a difficult time and writing down my emotions seemed to help. Before I knew it, I formed this poem. I'm just glad I could share these emotions with you, and hopefully someone can relate to my poem. I would also like to dedicate all my poetry to my sister, Ronilee Gomez.

GOODMAN, ROBIN

[a.] Franklin, TN [title] "I Am Who I Am, Who I Am I Will Be" [pers.] I am 11 years old and I love to sing, dance, and have fun. My sister Jeri writes her thoughts in a journal; I write mine in songs and poems. I wrote this poem because my Dad and friends get mad at me for standing up for what I think is right. But one thing I know is that I have to be me. When we play pretend, my friends pretend to be someone famous. I play myself because I will be famous one day.

GOWENS, TERRY

[a.] Lakewood, WA [title] "Speed and Time" [pers.] I have been influenced in my writing by my depression, and many industrialist writers. In trying to look for a talent, I've never considered poetry. One day, I submitted a poem I'd done after staring at a clock, and now I've found my talent. I'm probably one of the few men in my family to write something publicly and have it published.

GRAHAM, MISTY

[a.] Bay Springs, MS [title] "Since You Left" [pers.] Poetry is one of many pastimes I enjoy. I have so many things to inspire my poems, such as my children, Joseph (6) and Brandon (2); and my niece, Shelby (2). This particular one has its own special meaning, though. It was meant to tell the man in my life, Brandon Bossen, my fiance, how much loneliness I felt while we were apart, to let him know that I love him very much. Each of my poems have their own special meaning for all the special people or moments in my life. I have to thank God for all that He has blessed me with. Without Him, I would be nothing.

GRANER, ROSE

[a.] Bethlemhem, PA [title] "There's Love Every Day" [pers.] A poem is an expression of love, and your innermost thoughts. I'm surrounded by my family, so I have no shortage of love.

GRANT, CHRIS

[a.] Boring, OR [title] "The Mission" [pers.] My vocation and training is in the medical field, where I've learned that good health is one of God's greatest gifts. The other is grandchildren. Michael, my youngest grandchild, is the inspiration for this poem. Every day with Michael is an adventure. I simply record those moments in verse. I didn't write this poem to be published, but to remind me that his life is a constant joy and celebration for me. Michael's mama thought I should share my joy.

GRESHAM, HEATHER

[a.] Cincinnati, OH [title] "Where I'm From" [pers.] I am 17 years old. I am from a broken home and was raised by my grandma for most of my life. This poem has a special meaning to me because it shows people who I am, what I've been through, as well as where I'm going. I hope people and other children can relate to my poem. I hope it becomes an inspiration to others from broken homes, just like it has become an inspiration to me. I also hope that people see the meaning in it, even if they aren't from broken homes!

GRIESE, MARY JO

[a.] Austin, MN [title] "Life" [pers.] I am a mother of four, grandmother of six. "Life" is my poem about my life. Yesterday I was 16, today I'm a grandmother. Life is precious. I sew my husband's shirts, drapes, crochet, and do many crafts. I never tried my hand at poetry until just recently. My youngest sister, whom I called my first born, was a good poet. She passed away two years ago, so maybe I am carrying on for her.

HAGGERTY, PAUL A.

[a.] St. Ives, Cambridge, UK [title] "Sunday, Early Spring" [pers.] Constructed in much the same way as an artist would produce a water color like Emily Dickinson's poetry. Her poetry and diary was for me, "love at first sense." High on my must-do

agenda is a pilgrimage to Amhurst, Massachusetts, to visit "The Homestead." That she could equate the throat constricting loss that death incurs with the quiet tidying around the house in "A Sudden Sweep" placed all the power of her gentle hand warmly on my stiff, chilled back.

HAMMERS, ERIC

[a.] Sun Valley, NV [title] "Breaking Free" [pers.] In 1991, the woman who was to be my wife died in a car accident. The mental aftermath brought forth a number of emotions. The poem "Breaking Free" was one face of those emotions. In memory of Angie L. Vrana.

HANDOYO

[a.] Bintaro, Indonesia [title] "I and Life" [pers.] I wrote this poem because I had feelings for someone like this. This poem has a great meaning to me, and it is my honor to share it with you.

HARBOTTLE, DIANE

[a.] Nattinghamshire, United Kingdom [title] "Thinking of You" [pers.] This is my way of expressing how I feel about people that I care about. I value people and respect their opinions. There is always a place in my heart for my family and friends. I think of them every day.

HAREN, TOM

[a.] Lowellville, OH [title] "Her" [pers.] As you probably have guessed, my name is Tom Haren, and I'm the author of "Her." I'm fifteen years old, and I live with my family in Lowellville, Ohio. "Her," is a poem about a very special person, my girlfriend, Katie. I've never really been at a loss for inspiration, but nothing has inspired me as much as her. Being a huge John Lennon fan, I'm very familiar with the belief that all you need is love. But until meeting Katie, I could never really identify with it. Now it's a way of life. Thanks for reading and happy trails.

HARVEY, RYAN

[a.] Folsom, CA [title] "The Turkey Named Goon" [pers.] I was inspired to write this poem because I always saw turkeys at my old school and one said "goon goon." My hobbies are writing, coloring, drawing, and reading. I live with my mom in Folsom. During the summer, I go to my dad in Crescent City. At the end of summer, I go back to my mom. My dad has a girlfriend, Carrie, and she has two kids, Kiel and Cole. My mom has a boyfriend, Shawn. He has a kid named Andrew.

HATFIELD, JASON

[a.] Hemlock, MI [title] "How Can One . . ." [pers.] The reason I began writing poetry was because it really helped me release some of my innermost feelings. Poets like Shakespeare and Hemmingway have touched so many individual lives. I would love to have this opportunity. I hope to someday write a poetic piece that summarizes all of life's love and loss. As far as "How Can One . . ." goes, things change, people change, but the love remains forever.

HATMAKER, LACEY

[a.] Bartow, FL [title] "Gone" [pers.] All I want in life is to make people see the importance of God and His great sacrifice for us. I did this poem from His mother, Mary's, point of view. My life is His to shape and mold. Give yours too, and you'll be happy always.

HAYDEN, ANGELA

[a.] Dallas, NC [title] "Him" [pers.] Life is poetic; flowing richness pervades every element, every simple thing. To convey to others just a smidgen of the intoxicating emotion that courses through me is the ultimate satisfaction. The mundane, as well as the spiritual, inspires me to pen. I am fond of saying that every road goes somewhere. My hope is to share my discoveries along those roads. I reside in North Carolina with my son, Chad.

HEAD, MARYBETH
[a.] Applegate, OR [title] "My Love for Nature" [pers.] I will be a freshman at Hidden Valley High School. I have to say that I don't consider myself an artist or an author, but because of poetry.com, I truly feel like one. My understanding and love for poetry has been greatly heightened. I am happy to share my poetry with others.

HEARNS, YOLANDA
[a.] Rockford, IL [title] "Wings of a Mother" [pers.] My mother, who has always been an inspiration in my life, inspired me to write this poem. She has always told me to never give up and encouraged me to always believe in myself. She believed in my dreams and has always been my best friend. She pushed me to move further, but she held me with a love that is so genuine. One thing my mother gave me is the wings of courage and strength to make it through each day in life. Every time I want to give up or feel that I can't. My mother says just spread your wings and God will do the rest. Thanks, mom, for being you. I love you for sticking by my side through all of my good times and bad times.

HENRY, BARBARA
[a.] Tulsa, OK [title] "The Rescue" [pers.] I have been writing poetry since I was 16 years old. I believe it to be a gift from God, and I believe I should continue if only for my own personal expression. This poem was inspired by a friend who attempted suicide. When I heard his story, this poem was born. I only met this man once, yet his story touched me in such a way that I sat down immediately and penned "The Rescue." My initial interest began when my father died suddenly while I was in high school. I wrote about his death and the void in my life, and it proved to be a sort of therapy for me. Since that time I would write when I felt sad, scared, or alone, and I would feel better. I learned that writing in rhyme came easy for me. I still write whenever I'm inspired or feel that something in me needs to be expressed. This is my first publication and I am thrilled you found it suitable for print.

HILTON, TARA
[a.] Wichita, KS [title] "Altruism" [pers.] Some of the most influential people in my life have been teachers. This poem is an expression of my feelings about the sacrifice teachers make in order to inspire even just one life.

HODGES, LINDSAY
[a.] Belfast, Ireland [title] "Four Seasons" [pers.] Poetry has always played a central role in my life, marking every important phase, from growing up to developing a love for literature to finally establishing my own creative voice. No for of expression is more personal, emotional or honest. The sharing of my poems with family and friends has been an immensely moving experience and has enhanced my relationships beyond measure. My writing reflects an awareness of the people and places around me, and I hope that my poems convey a special meaning and understanding for those who read them.

HOFFMAN, BETTY
[a.] Merced, CA [title] "Retirement" [pers.] My husband, Stan, and I are retired and live in the San Joaquin Valley in California. We are enjoying the freedom of retirement, but are amazed at how busy we are. When a friend, Linda Aue, retired from the US Postal Service and expressed a concern about being bored and having nothing to do, I wrote this poem for her. My sister, Mary Rausch, has been writing poetry for years. I am just getting started. I was delighted with the invitation to publish my poem.

HOLLAND, PRINTRESS
[a.] Yakima, WA [title] "Dreams?!" [pers.] Dreams are unseen moments of our lives where we, people of unlimited passions, reveal our inner selves in silent thoughts of heart, soul, and mind. This poem was inspired by my silent thinking as I observe the things around my life. To all that read these words along with others: May your inner dreams be awakened from the silent words in your visual presence!

HOWARD, HENRY
[a.] Los Angeles, CA [title] "Battered Woman, Unbreakable Woman" [pers.] This poem is dedicated to Irene, Rebecca, "Broken," and so many other women, survivors all, who have touched my heart, inspired me with their courage, and deepened my commitment to building a world free from violence against women and children. With enough support and compassion, we can be free of our culture's terrible trap of always blaming the victims for their own misfortune. Anyone can ultimately move from being a victim to standing forever tall as a survivor. May this poem contribute to that process. I am proud to be another man against domestic violence!

HUDGENS, JASON
[a.] West Valley, UT [title] "Incomplete" [pers.] I believe that everyone should have an outlet through which they can express emotions that otherwise would stay confined within, eventually boiling over to other less dignified ways of expression, such as physical anger. My poetry is my outlet. It helps me deal with my emotions in a way that is very meaningful and fulfilling to me. I would like to thank my family and friends, and especially Amber Tempest Yang, who has always made it easier for me to be me.

HUELSMAN, ROLLIN
[a.] Mentor, OH [title] "Passing Year" [pers.] Thank you, Michelle, for the inspiration, support, and motivation responsible for my efforts. I love you dearly and eagerly await our wedding date. God bless you, my love.

HUFFORD, DANN
[a.] Danville, IL [title] "Storm Clouds" [pers.] This poem is about a girl who I dated over the summer. One day, she was gone and so was summer. I see life as a big storm. Sometimes it can be stormy; other times, a clear day.

HUI, AIMEE
[a.] Livingston, NJ [title] "Not Like Peter Pan" [pers.] Fairy tales have always been sources of my inspiration, hopes, and dreams. "Not Like Peter Pan" takes the poetic language of fairy tale imagery and infuses it into the experience of growing up. This poem has acted as a mirror for me, reflecting a time of innocence, a time of uncertainty, a time of fear, and a time of departing from childhood. I hope that this poem may serve as a reminder of the childhood optimism and confidence familiar to so many of us.

ISAAK, RYAN
[a.] Dinuba, CA [title] "Let Me Go So I Can Come Back" [pers.] My writing has been inspired by love; she has also inspired my life. I wish I could explain the love I have for her, but words would never do it justice. Thanks, S.V.

JACKSON, VERA
[a.] Saint Louis, MO [title] "Missing You" [pers.] As the pages of our lives continually turn, we are faced with unseen uncertainties that weigh on our emotional being. Our physical expression cannot detail the deep puncture wounds that our hearts consume. Poetry is a way of expressing our innermost being. Sometimes happy, sometimes sad, emotionally written words are all that we have.

JACOBS, JERRY
[a.] Brooklyn, NY [title] "Isabel" [pers.] Calvin Coolidge and I were both inaugurated on March 4, 1925. He as President, and I as a Prince of hopes and dreams. My boyhood ramblings were in the territory of Crotona Park in the Bronx, where I became a bard and a bird watcher, and wandered among magnificent trees, bright yellow birds, and assorted humanity. My poetic instincts were awakened by reading the great poets. My first attempts were appropriate to my age and time. I have always had strong emotional reactions to motion pictures, and it was "The Pawnbroker" that stirred such disturbing feelings that I needed an outlet to express them. I hurried home and wrote my first long, serious poem from beginning to end, without a stop. It came out fully formed and I have never been able to change in a line of it.

JAMISON, DORIS
[a.] Yorktown, VA [title] "A Lost Son" [pers.] This poem was written to my son, Michael Andrew Jones, on the first anniversary of his death. It is an expression of this mother's grief and hope. On June 6, 2000, he lost his life in an automobile accident. He was a beautiful human, whose shining eyes and loving heart were donated to increase the lives of others. I recommend "The Compassionate Friends" to other grieving parents. Michael, words can never express all of our love for you, my son.

JOHN, DAVIS
[a.] Hasbrouck Heights, NJ [title] "Stars and Flowers" [pers.] This is dedicated to Celia Gambale, the woman who showed me my "Stars and Flowers." She is very special to me and I wanted to somehow share that with the world.

JOHNSON, KIM
[a.] District Heights, MD [title] "Why?" [pers.] There were times in my life when I went to church, but evil was always present. I was hurt and abused by different ones in church. Then when my mother died, I really thought God hurt me, too. I got to the point that I didn't want to pray. I then decided to leave God and the church. Because of God's grace and mercy, He kept me. God spoke to me and said, "Kim, it's only a test. Let my will be done; stand still and know that I am God." I know now the secret to living Holy.

JOHNSON, MARGARET
[a.] Surrey, Canada [title] "Jane Doe, Dead Doe" [pers.] So much of today's music glamorizes or glorifies violence, especially that against women. Unfortunately much of this music is available to young people. I didn't want my poem to glamorize or glorify violence (against women), but rather to show just how horrific it truly is. Our society is desensitized by the violence in music, TV, and movies, and this can contribute to the violence we see around us. Thank you to my teachers, Julie, Annette, and AM, for the inspiration to write the poem. I am 22, and live in Canada. My hobbies are drawing, piano, and tarantulas.

JONES, MARLEY FRANCIS
[a.] New Paltz, NY [title] "A New Day" [pers.] Jesus teaches us about love: "Love is patient; love is kind, love is not jealous, it does not put on airs, it is not snobbish; love is never rude, it is not self-seeking, neither does it brood over injuries; love does not rejoice in what is wrong, but rejoices with the truth. There is no limit to love's forbearance. Trust its hope, its power to endure; love never fails" (1 Cor. 13:4-8). With Jesus' help, I try to live this way. Would that every person on this planet live this way, our world would be a much better place. With Jesus in our lives, we can live a life of love. Jesus is an example of perfect love. He died so we can live.

JONES, TRENA
[a.] Jacksonville, FL [title] "She Was Only Seventeen" [pers.] During my senior year of high school, two of my classmates passed away. Writing was my outlet for my great grief. This poem is one of four I wrote in memory of my two friends. Now the world will know I miss my friend, but she will

forever be remembered. Death is a mystery, especially when they die young. Hopefully this poem will help others. It definitely helped heal my broken heart and wounded spirit.

JONES, ZULA RICHARDS
[a.] Austin, TX [title] "Denture Disasters" [pers.] I am 90 years old and have written over 800 poems, ranging from the sublime to the ridiculous, from religious to political, from childhood delights to eschatology, and from philosophical to whimsical. I have had only a few of these poems published. The soul of a poet is bared to the eyes of all who wish to read. A few may judge him to be wise, some may his wisdom heed. Revealed in what he originates is a poet's innermost thoughts. If to some of these you can relate, that's all I have sought.

JORDAN, DENISE
[a.] Campbell, CA [title] "Tears for You, Carmen" [pers.] This poem was written about my two-year-old, who died of meningitis on March 25, 2001. My family has been trying to deal with her death because she didn't have to die. She did because of the negligence of a doctor and his misdiagnosis. This is a way to deal with her death. She was called "Sweet" by my mom and family. My entire family misses her so much. She will never be gone because she will always be in our hearts. My family was tragically hit with meningitis. My four-year-old niece and my mother both got the meningitis, along with Carmen.

KAAYA, DIANA
[a.] Dar es Salaam, Tanzania [title] "Forever Friends" [pers.] I've never thought of my poetry as a talent or gift; I always just believed it was my way of expressing myself. Poetry frees me and lets me say or be anything. The poem "Forever Friends" is about my best friend, Karen, she has almost the same effect on me as poetry does. She helps me be free. With her, I don't need to pretend. The poem was just my way of showing her how much she means to me. Apart from writing poetry, my other hobbies are listening to music, watching TV. I am just your average 15 year old.

KAROUNI, GHALEB
[a.] Vacaville, CA [title] "Knocking on the Chords of the Spirit" [pers.] This experience represents my personal vision into life. It's a call upon the good souls to take life deeply, understand it, and live it based on that understanding. There is no advantage for being evil and no need to await award for being good. Good is endlessly awarding. As a physician, I came to understand that life is so simple. Therefore, my call is: Be good, be good for the sake of good, and do what to you wish the others would.

KEHOE, LISA
[a.] Brant, MI [title] "Some Kind of Wonderful" [pers.] Writing poetry has always been a way for me to express my feelings. It's a way of helping me relieve stress and feel at ease. This poem, in particular, was written for my friend Kelly, who has always been there for me during the rough times in my life. I am so thankful to have a friend like Kelly! She is definitely "some kind of wonderful!"

KEMP, MARLA
[a.] Columbus, OH [title] "Don't Throw Him Away" [pers.] I've been interested in poetry since fifth grade. I started writing in eighth grade. This poem has significant value because of the story behind it. My friend was dating a boy with whom she was very much in love. One day I found a letter he had written to another girl. It was obvious that he was cheating on my friend. One night I stayed at her house. He called, wanting her back, but she wasn't sure. That's what this poem is all about. Even though a special someone may cheat, that doesn't mean they are not worth another chance.

KENNEDY, JIMMY
[a.] Voorhees, NJ [title] "Blades of Green" [pers.] I have been writing poetry for many years, but this is the first time I have sent out some of my work to be critiqued. I also compose original musical compositions, play drums, bass, and sing. It has always been a dream to be published in some fashion, and perhaps this publication of my work will be a door to other opportunities. I am also in the process of attaining a degree in Audio-Engineering, and plan to continue writing lyrical, as well as musical, ideas for the purpose of recording and publishing in the not-too-distant future. Writing poems is a passion that doesn't go away. It is deep on the inside, and I think it is there to stay. At least, I hope so!

KHAN, MISHAAL
[a.] Toronto, Canada [title] "Exams" [pers.] Poetry is a gift of God that only some people have. When I was a small child, I was very interested in poetry. My parents bought me books of my nursery rhymes and I read them with utmost delight. When I started going to school and I was in my fourth grade, my teacher encouraged me to write poems and stories. I became a writer. I wrote poems and stories which were appreciated by my teachers and all my family members. My great-grandfather was a poet, so my grandmother always encouraged me to write poems. I feel very delighted today and I want to thank all my family members and my teachers for all the encouragement they always gave me. This is one of the poems that I have written. I was inspired by a catchy slogan: "No Exams, No Anxiety" That was when I wrote this poem called "Exams."

KIDWILER, GEORGE
[a.] Harpers Ferry, WV [title] "Reality or Legacy" [pers.] While typing a short version of my life after high school for a 40th class reunion, I could not help but to reflect on how fast the 40 years had flown by. The words to the poem seemed appropriate for the reunion, and the poem was printed in a handout which told classmates about our accomplishments. Writing the poem was very special to me, and the reflection on the forty years since graduation was also a special time. Sometimes we join our education and mental capacity with our spiritual side. It is during these "rare" times that true art and enlightenment is achieved. God bless.

KIMARA, WACIUMA
[a.] Bronx, NY [title] "Lawrence of Arabia" [pers.] It took words a-plenty to communicate my "Lawrence of Arabia" to the world. Several thoughts and images, sporting verse and rhyme, were initially all mashed into a pot, 15 lines deep. What stewed in this pot is good enough to be published by the ILP, for which I am truly grateful. I decided to write about Lawrence after spending the summer of 2001 as a hired assistant to City College of New York professor Harold A. Veeser. We worked on a research project that shuttled me back and forth into both the past and present of Edward Said, a professor at Columbia University. My poem attempts to marry the arbitrary (mechanics of poetry) with the natural (my feelings, emotions, and imagination).

KIN, TIA
[a.] Singapore, Singapore [title] "Life Comparison" [pers.] Using all the functional sense within me, I observed and analyzed others around me. It was in 1997 that this poem was written out in my journal with feelings of sadness. Sadness is to have seen and felt a person fall into comparing one's life with others and end up self-destructing. We may or may not live well, be highly educated, have great occupations, or interesting hobbies; but what or who are we to compare things in this world. I heard "Why not?" (Well, compete, don't compare.)

KING, TIM
[a.] Muncie, IN [title] "Masks" [pers.] All poetry should be regarded as intimate communication that attempts to express its creator's personal thoughts, feelings, or political ideologies to other individuals. This poem is my endeavor to encourage people to be genuinely sincere with themselves and others, to share who they really are, and to not modify their behavior (or wear masks) for particular social situations because of what other people might think. Only after this is accomplished (the removal of masks) can we, as humans, embark upon the eternal task of improving our true character, and thus find satisfaction in the magnificent gift of life.

KOCH, CASSANDRA
[a.] Morocco, IN [title] "Your Eyes" [pers.] This poem is about someone I crossed paths with in my journey of life. He will always have a place in my heart. "Your Eyes" is about what went through my mind as our eyes met. It is what I was thinking, but could never say. Poetry has a great impact on my life. It is a way for me to express my true feelings and thoughts. Poetry is a way to set my mind free. My family is very loving and has always been supportive of all my endeavors. I live in Morocco, Indiana. I am a senior at North Newton Jr./Sr. High School. I will be attending the Illinois Institute of Art College in the fall of 2002. I work at Burger King in Kentland, Indiana. Some of my hobbies are sports, art, and poetry. My philosophical point of view: "Poetry is all around us, but very few stop and take the time to truly understand it. For the ones that do understand, they have a new look at life."

KOOS, STEPHEN
[a.] Shaker Heights, OH [title] "Never Apart" [pers.] This was written for the love of my life, Kasia, who is an ocean away. We share a bond that knows no limits, and this poem is just an expression of our special dedication. It often helps me when lonely feelings arise.

KOPF, JOSEPH
[a.] Richardson, TX [title] "True Love" [pers.] I wrote this poem as a reflection of how I view love. This poem is my hope that all the people of world find love in their lives. This poem inspires me to seek love in my daily life. I owe my mother, Nancy, and father, Joseph Mathias, for all their love and support. To my special friend: Thank you. I am fortunate to live in Richardson, TX, in the USA. I hope all who read this poem seek love and peace in their lives. I also wish to thank my grandfather, Roger, for being there when I needed him.

KORF, TESSA & DANIELLE
[a.] Pine City, MN [title] "Never Knew" [pers.] This poem was written about a girl who had to live with many family struggles. She found the lost love of her parents in drugs. Not knowing or caring about her family's true love for her, she committed suicide. Danielle and I live in Pine City, Minnesota, and would like to thank our parents for always showing their love for us. We won't ever end up in the kind of situation in the poem. Thank you to all the people that have been there for us both.

KORPELA, LEYLA
[a.] Sitka, AK [title] "My Payback" [pers.] Can anyone actually define poetry? I know I can't. I do know that it speaks without speaking, and it feels without feeling. Most of all, it needs no explanation. It satisfies mystery. The truth behind a poem is for the writer to know, and the reader to ponder. I dedicate my poem to my father. I love you.

KOTHARI, SANJAY
[a.] Tamilnadu, India [title] "Life and Peace" [pers.] My poetry is a pure inspiration from my father. He is a great Hindi poet. My poem "Life and Peace" talks

about my family. All of my poetry is dedicated to my father. Basically, he is my God. As a man of virtues, principles, and discipline, he has been my role model and my inspiration all my life. I dedicate this poem to my father, Mr. P.C. Kothari; all my family members, especially my mother; and my beloved friends, especially Amit. May God give happiness to all.

KURLE, BONNIE JEAN
[a.] Spokane, WA [title] "Remembering" [pers.] One springtime evening, a friend of mine called to tell me that her husband had shot himself. He had been suffering from severe depression. I stood helplessly by her side as I watched her—and still watch her—adapt to life in the shadow of her husband's gruesome suicide. This is her story.

LABASTIDA, GABBY
[a.] Puebla, Mexico [title] "My Inner Child" [pers.] I have always enjoyed poetry and writing it. It's a way in which I can express myself freely. This poem shows what life is, how we all grow and changes occur. My life has been blessed by God, my creator, who has given me this ability to write poems. God is my inspiration for the poems I write. My family and friends have supported me every time I need support. I enjoyed writing this poem because in a short way, it tells about growing up and facing the world, not alone, but with God and my family by my side.

LAFOND, JOAN
[a.] Kelowna, Canada [title] "Women Child" [pers.] Another poem I wrote inspired me to write "One of Two." I'm 55 years old and only have a sixth-grade education. This poem came from my heart. Not a day goes by without a thought of the child I had to give up.

LAM, ALFIE
[a.] Vancouver, Canada [title] "Think about It" [pers.] This poem is greatly inspired by the lyrics of a Chinese song. The simple, yet powerful words used in the song, and the enlightening ideas behind it, moved me and eventually helped me find my own interpretation of life, as seen in "Think about It."

LAWRENCE, FELICIA
[a.] Lansing, MI [title] "Real Life" [pers.] I am the daughter of Jack and Delilah Lawrence. Poetry and writing have been passions of mine for as long as I can remember. This poem reflects some of the love and lessons my parents taught me as I grew. I have remembered them throughout my journeys. Life teaches lessons to us all. Listen to your heart, follow your mind, and the rest will come.

LAXAMANA, ARLENE
[a.] Glenpool, OK [title] "Self Relic" [pers.] This poem is a description of what it is like to be raised in a Western culture as an Asian child. Transplanted to Tulsa, Oklahoma at 11 months old from Manila, Philippines, finding balance between two cultures has not been easy. I feel more pressure from one side than the other. However, there are many people in my life that bring me comfort and play on my team. All of you know who you are, and I love you—especially you, L.J.L. You have brought me so much happiness, and I love you.

LEAVER, PATRICIA
[a.] Gautier, MS [title] "A Child's Cry" [pers.] I hope that my poem will inspire parents to pay close attention to what their children tell them. I would like to thank my husband, Jeff Leaver, and our two beautiful children, Ariel and Makayla Leaver. I would also like to thank my mother-in-law and father-in-law, Chun and John Leaver. I would also like to thank my family: my father, Marvin Miller; my mother, Linda Miller; my grandmother, Lucllie Ledlow; my sister, Vickie Danley; and brothers, Billy and Mike Miller; my uncle, who recently passed away, Larry Miller; and the rest of my family and friends.

LEITH, RYAN
[a.] Port Lincoln, Australia [title] "Sleep" [pers.] This poem is one of my favorites from the many I have written. I wrote it in an English lesson earlier this year. My name is Ryan and I am 14. I live in Port Lincoln in South Australia. My poem "Sleep" is about the wonders of sleep and how the young mind perceives it. I am very proud of it.

LEMUS, VICTORIA
[a.] Spokane, WA [title] "My Pure Bliss" [pers.] When I write poetry, it comes from my heart and soul. If I can't sleep at night, I pick up a pen and the words just seem to flow. My poems are events in my life that have or very well could happen. They are reflections of my innermost feelings, and a tiny slice of my soul. A person's soul is powerful and when put into poetry, the meanings are endless.

LEVINE, JOSH
[a.] Woodmere, NY [title] "Sadness" [pers.] This poem is one of my many poems that reflect on how I look at my life. My writing style is similar to my favorite poet, Edgar Allen Poe. I don't write to share my poetry with people, but to get out my feelings. I'll continue writing despite any criticism I receive. "Sadness" and my other poetry is only a reflection of me and nothing more.

LEWIS, KEVIN
[a.] Mauldin, SC [title] "I'm Just a Boy" [pers.] Writing frees my mind from all the hardships I have encountered throughout my life. It grants me the honor of total self-expression. It makes me free in a world where true freedom has been reduced to select individuals choosing and setting limits for the vast majority. I am forever indebted to my writing for allowing me this priceless privilege.

LIU, ALEX
[a.] Nyack, NY [title] "Her" [pers.] This is actually not a poem but a description a very special girl. Behind the description, there is a face; and behind the face there is an essence so hard to describe—beyond words or recognition. I was born in Quito, Ecuador, and for as long as I remember, I've had that image in my head. A bunch of people who I consider closest to me would understand why I wish to thank them for everything they've done: Amber Beck, Laura, Anne, Meni, Ricardo, Felipe, Isaac, David, Sonya, Belen, Daniela, Kathy, Greg, Amy, Dad, Mom, Grandparents, and ultimately, God.

LOEWEN, KRYSTAL
[a.] Port Coquitlam, Canada [title] "Forgotten Sounds" [pers.] I've been writing poems and stories for about two years. My poems are the way I express my perception of the confused world around me. "Forgotten Sounds" is about the struggle many people wage when trying to come to grips with showing the person they really are. I receive a lot of support from my family, friends, and teachers. Although I have received some harsh criticism, I remember that to be a writer is my dream, so I pick up my pen and write some more. Follow your heart and never give up!

LOOCK, CHRISTINE
[a.] Laguna Niguel, CA [title] "For My Martini Man" [pers.] Once in a great while, you meet someone who makes you want to pull out all the stops. In the words of Katherine Hepburn, "Love has nothing to do with what you are expecting to get, only with what you are prepared to give—which is everything. If you are very lucky, you will be loved back. Anything less is not love. It is a wonderful cocktail party, but it ain't love." I honestly believe this to be true. Perhaps therein lies the gift—not so much that the other person feels the same way, but that we were able to feel that way in the first place.

LOPEZ, CONSUELO G.
[a.] Glendive, MT [title] "In Sympathy" [pers.] Words and feelings flowed when my friend lost his father, and I could still sense the loss of mine. He asked me many times if it would ever stop hurting. When my husband lost his father, these were the same thoughts and feelings I had about how a son sees his father. Over 16 years ago I lost my father, but he comes to me in dreams and I tell him all the things I always wanted him to know. It comforts my heart. When people cannot hear the words in the poem, they can focus on His presence and comfort their soul.

LORD, NICOLE
[a.] Los Angeles, CA [title] "That Moment" [pers.] At the time this poem was written, my fiance was in the Intensive Care Unit at Cedar Sinai Medical Center. He had been shot several times in his abdominal cavity on Easter Sunday. As I sat in the hospital lobby day after day for three months, I often pondered the moment before this tragedy occurred. Our family was ecstatic as we anticipated our traditional Eastern dinner, but in one split second, our lives became distressed. I wish I knew of the moment I knew not! Remarkably, his condition improved and Damian is currently at home awaiting his full recovery.

LOUIS, TYRA
[a.] Chandler, AZ [title] "Coming Down" [pers.] Tyra Louis is currently a resident of Phoenix, Arizona. She graduated from the University of Nebraska-Lincoln. She is currently working on her first book of poetry.

LUKASCHUNIS, SHIRLEY
[a.] Clarksville, AR [title] "I'm Going Home to Jesus" [pers.] My poems have been the way I let my feelings come out. I have never been good in conversations, but in poems I can express myself, my feelings—and it is a legacy for my son, Charles Hazen, and grandsons, Mike and Matt. This is the greatest tribute I could ever receive, thank you. This is a gift given to me from God and it is my way of thanking him for many years of miracles in life. Thank you for making it possible to share my feelings with the world at this time—it couldn't have come at a better time. I have had many heart attacks recently and have only a very limited time left here, as my problem is uncorrectable. I now have this book to share with all.

MADDEN, STEVE
[a.] Hudson, MA [title] "What Time Is It?" [pers.] I dedicate this poem to the Hudson, MA firefighters in December 1999, shortly after their support of a warehouse fire in Worcester, MA. That tragedy resulted in the loss of a half-dozen firefighters. I believe poetry is a way to express one's inner feelings and touch those who also appreciate and respect poetry.

MAGGARD, ASHLEY
[a.] Oldfield, MO [title] "Jesus Christ" [pers.] My name is Ashley Maggard and I'm 15 years old. I have always enjoyed writing, but in December of 2000, I started writing poems. They came to me so much easier than stories. My aunt, Donna, encouraged me by telling me about how she used to send her poems into a certain contest. This told me I wasn't so different and maybe I could win a prize. All of my family and friends have encouraged me to continue writing.

MAGLE, CINDY
[a.] Mary Esther, FL [title] "Since We Met" [pers.] As an amateur in poetry, having my own poem published has made me feel better about myself, and has inspired me to follow through and create more poems in the future.

MANCINI, DANIEL
[a.] Colorado Springs, CO [title] "Ever-Changing World" [pers.] I am 12 years old. I have loved art and creative writing for as long as I can remember. I thank

God for giving me the gift of creatively expressing my thoughts and ideas through poetry. This form of expression gives me a joy and contentment that I hope to cherish and enjoy all the days of my life. I want to thank God for creatively expressing His own thoughts and ideas through this poetry in motion we all know as our very own world. For without His expression of unconditional love, life and poetry, along with the joy they bring, could not exist.

MARSH, KERRY
[a.] New Haven, CT [title] "(glass)" [pers.] I honestly never considered myself to be much of a poet, maybe because I don't write poetry very often. However, when I write from deep, sometimes subconscious feeling, I feel the right words flowing, and something truly and surprisingly beautiful appears. I am proud of this piece, simply because it was a surprise. This poem is made of some feelings hovering just below total consciousness, that manifested themselves as something tangible and meaningful. "Glass" is about a situation I never let myself completely feel, but once I acknowledge the feelings, I felt peace. Thanks to my family, especially mom and Dr. Susan Cole. You helped me realize my potential.

MAYTOM, GAIL
[a.] Airlie Beach, Australia [title] "Life" [pers.] Poetry is a wonderful way to express oneself, and my poem "Life" is a reflection of how I try to live my life. Making the most of every day and seeing the beauty in everyone and everything is certain to enhance your life, and will bring you closer to living the life of your dreams. I hope that this message touches the hearts of everyone who reads my poem.

McALILEY, DAVID WITHERS
[a.] Broadway, NC [title] "The Power of Time" [pers.] To me, poetry is the language of the heart. This particular poem is about the power of love and how that power can overcome anything, even time. The goal of any artist is to connect with the audience, to touch them in some way. I hope this poem touches your hearts as it has mine.

McCARTHY, AINSLEY
[a.] New Hartford, CT [title] "Rejoice" [pers.] I don't write poems very often because I need inspiration. Most of my inspiration comes from nature surrounding me. This poem came to me one day while I was walking through the woods. All my poems are made with full feeling. Poems just come into my head, but normally aren't written down.

McCOLLUM, NICK
[a.] Wheaton, IL [title] "What Is It All Worth?" [pers.] I write poetry according to feelings I have at times. Often at night, I lay in bed and reflect on my day, and the effect it has had on my life. This poem was written when I was in seventh grade, struggling with pressures and friendships. I am currently a freshman at Marmion Academy, and I use my poetry to express myself and my feelings to others.

McMULLEN, CINDY
[a.] Des Moines, IA [title] "Brian" [pers.] My poem was written during a time of mourning. It is a true story of friendship and life, and how quickly it can all be taken away. I was extremely amazed and excited when I was notified my poem would be published, and I hoped that after reading my work others would take the time to mend fences with friends or relatives. Life is precious and short, and no one ever knows when it will be the last time you see or speak to someone for whom you care deeply.

MEADE, JEANETTE
[a.] Laurel, MD [title] "Thoughts" [pers.] My inspiration comes from my Heavenly Father. My motivation to express is found in the struggle of the flesh's will versus God's will. My aspiration requires age and wisdom to be manifested youthfully.

MERCADO, ANGEL
[a.] Mayaguez, Puerto Rico [title] "Happy Mother's Day for a Teacher" [pers.] True teachers are teachers for life. They help us achieve our goals, overcome barriers, and give to us, with their hearts and their minds, the tools to move toward a brighter future. For this and much more, teachers should be acknowledged and thanked with a feeling that emerges from the very essence of sincere gratitude. My poem, "Happy Mother's Day for a Teacher," is my gift for all teachers who are mothers and all mothers who are teachers. Wherever you are, teacher . . . mother . . . thanks!

MEYERS, JASON
[a.] Lindenhurst, NY [title] "An Answer" [pers.] I saw a boy of perhaps 11 or 12 years old as I sat in my car, stopped at a traffic light. He was riding a motorized scooter, steering with one hand as he spoke into the cellular phone he held in his other. 15 years ago, I was a boy his age, and I thought back to that time. That fleeting moment in my car made me long for the time when a pack of baseball cards or a slide on a playground would keep me happy all day. I miss the innocence, the charm, that life seems to have forgotten these days. I wrote "An Answer" that night, and then I probably checked my e-mail.

MHONIE, ATIENO
[a.] Kasane, Botswana [title] "Wounds Unbound" [pers.] I'm no poet, but a Christian nurse. I never wrote a poem before! My motivation is our youth living and dying daily without purpose or hope. I founded ACOBOS, an organization providing holistic care for HIV/AIDS clients in Kenya in 1992. This poem commemorates Edwin, a special son, drowned in drugs, deeply hurt, and angered by his stigmatizing family. To obtain drugs, Edwin was unscrupulous! Drugs didn't heal his hurt, drugs killed him, leaving many infected and wounded! ACOBOS points HIV/AIDS clients to God, creator and sustainer of life. Anti-retrovirals may kill too unless God's love replaces our stigma.

MILLER, KYLE
[a.] Waverly, IA [title] "Life?" [pers.] Many people these days go through depression. It's not uncommon. Sometimes, you don't even know who is going through it. Many, like myself, learned quickly to mask it. So instead of talking to others, we are left with our lonely questions. Questions like in "Life?" How does one deal with questions like this alone? Instead of answering these questions, I chose to write about how it felt, to help others get a grasp on what they're feeling. So, to you out there who don't know how to deal with this inner pain, this is for you.

MILLS, MARCUS
[a.] Cincinnati, OH [title] "Advice" [pers.] First of all, I would like to thank my Savior, Jesus Christ, for this opportunity. Next, I would like to say thank you to my best friend and companion, Kenyatta Hawkins, for her support. My poem is really straight: I am a firm believer in God Almighty. Through Him, all things are possible. And when you start to follow His word, you will soar with the eagles and birds.

MITCHELL, WILL
[a.] Falkir, Scotland [title] "Snow" [pers.] Often we don't realize we have a gift until someone takes time out to notice and to tell us. I have created poetry, mostly for fun, all my life; unfortunately, I have never written my works down on paper—until now, that is. Now I plan to share my thoughts in poetic verse with as many people as will listen or read. I also hope to encourage the talents of my daughter, Rebecca; my sister, Senga; and sister-in-law, Sue; all of whom have been a huge inspiration to me through their own poetry.

MONDT, MARY
[a.] Belleville, IL [title] "Thoughts" [pers.] I have always spent a lot of my life alone, not that I've always wanted it this way. Writing poems has been a way to express my innermost feelings, and was a gift from God to me. It is a way to calm myself and to let others know my feeling in a discrete way.

MONTES, MELISSA
[a.] Laredo, TX [title] "Who We Are?" [pers.] I was never really the poetic type, but as I grew, I learned more. Gathering information from experiences convinced me to put my thoughts and memories in poetic form. This poem is the life that a person goes through and never forgets. This poem shows you how we take advantage of many wonderful things in life, including having the wonderful experience to share this poem with others.

MOONSONG, CATHERYN
[a.] Piqua, OH [title] "Struggle" [pers.] I was molested when I was five. My poetry allowed me to delve into my soul and find the woman I was meant to be. I'd like to thank my mother, Brenda Jean Thomas, for giving me my gift with words; and my men, Aaron Buck and Joseph Losh, for supporting and loving me through all my changes. I would never have been printed without you. To all those who have been molested, raped, etc: We have already survived; now is the time to thrive.

MOORE, APRIL
[a.] Silinsgrove, PA [title] "The Flowers That Dance in the Wind" [pers.] To me, poetry is a wonderful gift from God. All of my poems, including "The Flowers that Dance in the Wind," acknowledge Him. After all He has allowed me to express myself in this unique way. My poem relates to the situations and circumstances and how we can trust God as our foundation.

MOORE, MARSHA
[a.] Washington, DC [title] "A Tribute to Mothers" [pers.] Throughout my life, since graduating from high school (1963) in Washington, DC, I have done extensive writing. These writings include: research papers, short stories, poetry, educational reports, curricula (all levels), and newsletters. I have found that this is my second best tool for communicating with people. I can express my innermost feelings, thoughts, and opinions, while surrounded by music and pictorial memories. My maternal grandmother, mother, and aunt inspired this poem.

MOORE, SUE
[a.] Winnipeg, Canada [title] "Grandmother's Smiles" [pers.] This poem is very special to me; it represents a very special person, my husband's grandmother, who lived with us until her death. Her name was Dorothy Moore (1902-1990).

MORK, TAWNYA
[a.] St. Croix Falls, WI [title] "The Glass Forest" [pers.] Growing up in North Dakota and going to college in Minnesota, I've had plenty of experience with winter. I wrote this poem on the sunny day after an ice storm. The idea came so quickly, and the words spilled out faster than I could write them. My ability is a gift from God. I hope to use it to write children's books, as my high school Creative Writing teacher encouraged me to do. My parents, my three younger siblings, and my loving husband of two years, Aaron—my biggest fan, have also encouraged me to write.

MOSANKO, MARGARET
[a.] Phoenix, AZ [title] "I Love Writing Poetry Each Day!" [pers.] I was a "Depression years" child and couldn't afford the bus fare to go out of state to accept a scholarship (at a college) that had been given to me, because my father was already gone and my dear mother had no funds to help in this matter. I inherited the poetry habit from my dear mother (who wrote it

beautifully), and I've always enjoyed writing poetry, too. I've been a legal secretary in most of my working years, and I've always enjoyed being able to help people adjust to their problems in life and to help secure their future. I'm friendly, honest, and an "unclaimed treasure" because I never married, but I do feel I could have been an outstanding wife and mother, just as my dear mother was! I'm 84 and still writing poetry. I'm still thrilled about it, too! I still drive a car and have a good sense of humor. I enjoy all sports; in my day, I played softball, field hockey, tennis, and basketball. During World War II, I worked (in Detroit, MI) with the Naval division on the torpedo program. I was secretary to one of the Navy officers from WWI, who was called to work on this program. I really enjoyed it

MOSES, AMELIA
[a.] Nespelem, WA [title] "Hold Me Gently" [pers.] To write is to breathe. It is a release, the outlet for all my emotions and the one vacation that I have the luxury to indulge myself in. Ever since I can remember, I have been fascinated by the written word, whether it was the Bible, a newspaper, or a good book. I credit my successes and the motivation of my successes to my loving family, whom I hold in constant awe and appreciation. Thank you for encouraging me to use the gift that God has given me. I can deny you nothing, and will offer you anything.

MOYER, JEFFREY
[a.] Rochester, NY [title] "My Life" [pers.] I'm a sophomore at Hattwick College and a member of the Hattwick football team. Poetry helps me express myself about my everyday life and the world around me. "My Life" was written about all the fake people that have come into my world.

NANCE, KELLIE
[a.] Bryson City, NC [title] "Smiling" [pers.] This poem is for my daughter; she has a way of making me smile. I also write and let my feelings show through my writing. Throughout my years in High School and my next two years in college, my writing is a major part of my job and education. Not only do I write, but I also paint and express my feelings through my work there also. I hope the ones who read my poem sit back and smile.

NAULLS, BRUNO
[a.] Lywood, CA [title] "Thoughts" [pers.] To think, at a younger age I detested writing. My father would make my brother and I write about every place we went and event we attended. This dislike for writing soon faded and writing became a hobby. Now I write primarily about love and its issues. I guess when I love, my heart leads and my words follow. I hope you enjoy. God is my strength, and love is my weakness; my playground lies between the two. The never-ending battle is to unify them on the same field so I may rest. Until then, I write on. God bless.

NELSON, CAROL
[a.] Bradenton, FL [title] "Dan" [pers.] This poem is dedicated to my son, Daniel, who was shot and killed by his friend. The accident was avoidable, but happened nonetheless. My son was 20 years old and looking forward to his 21st birthday. He was a published writer, covering many sports events and had a script accepted by a major TV station. I love you, Dan. I always will.

NELSON, JEANENNE
[a.] Irving, TX [title] "Whole" [pers.] This poem was written in loving memory of my son, Tyler J. Nelson (October 8, 1996 to December 5, 1996), who was lost to Sudden Infant Death Syndrome.

NERI, R.
[a.] Buffalo, NY [title] "Loved Too Much" [pers.] Ever since I was a child, I had a fascination with poetry. The lyrical way words mesh to carry a certain meaning, it touches my musical sense and it intrigues me. It was not until recently, when I gave a poem as a gift, that I realized that my work was of interest to others as well. As I became confident and at the insistence and encouragement of family and dear friends, I submitted "Loved to Much." Sharing myself and my emotions was never my goal. Although it brings me great joy to have my words not only seen, but more importantly felt.

NG, NIAN LONG
[a.] Singapore, Singapore [title] "The Futility of Flares" [pers.] Art is a concise, yet vivid expression of life, and I write to uphold that. I try illustrating in my works the lack of feeling modern man has toward his environment—expanding on the theme prevalent in the works of T.S. Eliot that the modern life is one of utter decadence. Human lives, like flares, burn brightly on this temporal canvas, yet their attempts of infinite incandescence are futile as they fail to realize that no matter how much they try for material accolades, the fact remains that one day, the flares in their lives will extinguish, leaving nothing unique of them.

NICHOLS, KENZIE NICHOLS
[a.] Bastron, TX [title] "The Touch" [pers.] I find that poetry is an expression of yourself. Without poetry, it would be hard to find a way to express yourself. I started writing in second grade, when my mom helped me release my talent. This was the best thing that could of happened to me. I write non-stop now!

NIESEN, SHARON
[a.] Pinellas Park, FL [title] "You" [pers.] After 33 years of thinking I would never meet my prince charming, he finally showed up! And now I know what being happy is all about. He showed me the way. And for that, I will always be thankful. This poem is for him.

NILSSON, LILIANE
[a.] Norrkoping, Sweden [title] "You Go So Far Away from Me" [pers.] Poetry is a part of the life for me. English is a foreign language, as I am Swedish, so it was a big challenge to use English for my piece of poetry! I am pleased to say that I am happy in life to have a lovely family. They give me time to write poems whenever I want to! I will say thank you to my dear family and friends for reading all my poetry I send them all times!

NORD, BARBARA K.
[a.] Castro Valley, CA [title] "Winds of Growth" [pers.] God gave me a special way of expressing my feelings, through verse. However, it wasn't until I accepted Christ as my Savior, and through the encouragement of Sylvia Akl, our pastor's wife, at our Bible study classes, that I was capable of putting my poetry together in the right place.

NUNAMAKER, LAVON
[a.] New Paris, PA [title] "A Tribute to Our Veterans" [pers.] I was asked to write a poem for our church bulletin for Memorial Day. My reaction: If God would give me the words, I'd try. Thus, "A Tribute to Our Veterans," was born. I have always been fascinated with the military. I have never felt they were given enough credit or recognition for all they have done for their country. This poem is just my way of saying thanks to those men who fought for me. Thanks for choosing my poem for publication. This certainly is an honor.

ODOM, JIMMIE
[a.] Haynesville, LA [title] "Prison RN" [pers.] At 39, I graduated from LPN School; at 49, from college for my R.N.; at 59, I graduated from a Correctional Guard Clon. I now work for a state prison. Humor is my way of dealing with stress. Words and reading are the joys of life. My four daughters say I have taught them there is nothing they cannot do if they want it bad enough. Life is one big classroom; I learn more every day. I have been married for 41 years.

OSMUN, LAUREL
[a.] Branford, CT [title] "Ode to Samurai" [pers.] I am one of the luckiest people in the world. I have wonderful friends, family, and have known many special creatures that have left their pawprints lovingly in my heart. I am married to a wonderful man, Mark, who treats me like a goddess. This poem was inspired by a cat who literally moved in with us. He was only able to stay a short while before going to kitty heaven. What an astonishing cat he was, sleek and graceful, fierce and loving. I will miss him dearly. I am a craftsperson and jeweler for a select few. My hobbies include photography, tye dying, batik, gardening, and my newly-acquired skill for writing. My family loves the outdoors, and being from New England, we love these cool autumn nights. Live and let live, leave no footprints. Love those around you. Find inner peace, dwell in yourself.

PAGE, JESSICA
[a.] Yakima, MA [title] "My Aunt Kathy" [pers.] The poem "My Aunt Kathy" was written in one hour, and is dedicated to the memory of my beloved Aunt Kathy. My aunt was diagnosed with cancer July 4, 2000. She was strong, brave, and fought the cancer like a never-ending battle. We enjoyed the time we were able to spend together; these were precious moments. When the hourglass ran out, we hung strong—just like she did. Kathy was only 43 years old when she passed away on June 4, 2001. I hope people can understand this poem and feel the devastation my family and I went through when we lost our friend.

PAL, KUNAL
[a.] Calcutta, India [title] "Under" [pers.] I feel that poetry has universal appeal, and has the power to give enjoyment to all, regardless of differences in culture and age. I have enjoyed writing this poem, which I wish to share with all—young and old alike.

PARROTT, JONATHAN
[a.] Cleveland, TN [title] "A Conch, a Crab, a Leech" [pers.] I enjoy writing poetry because it serves as the most tangible and direct way of connecting with people. My favorite phrases have always been: "Yeah, I feel the same" and "I know what you mean." They seems so real to me. A complete and updated library of my work is available for viewing on the Internet. God bless.

PATON, LINSEY
[a.] Glasgow, Scotland [title] "Picture of Perfection" [pers.] I am a 19-year-old student from Scotland. Having completed an HND in "Leisure Management," I am about to embark on a "sport in the community" degree course at Strathclyde University. "Picture of Perfection" is dedicated to my mother, Moira Jean Paton (nee McGugan), who passed away in August of 1996. "Thank you for the days, they will never be forgotten.

PEARSON, ALICIA
[a.] La Mirada, CA [title] "The Long Goodbye" [pers.] I wrote this poem in honor of my grandfather, Jack Swain. He has always been my hero and for the last ten years, he has suffered from Alzheimer's. He has faced this challenge that God has placed in his life with great courage and strength. His greatness has inspired me, and this is my way of sharing him with you. Thank you to my family and the love of my life, David Ehlers, for encouraging me and always believing in me. I hope my poem can touch other people's lives and help share the love I have for my grandpa.

PENEMENOS, KATIA
[a.] Sydney, Australia [title] "Sun" [pers.] I enjoy poetry because it expresses my inner feelings. My

poem "Sun" talks about a woman as bright as the sun, a woman I would like to grow up to be. This poem reminds me of a woman becoming a mother (giving birth to a child), like the beautiful sun giving light to nature.

PEOVSKI, BOJAN
[a.] Ann Arbor, MI [title] "The Queen of Rings" [pers.] This poem has taught me to relish the intellectual challenge of examining emotions against a broad context of thought. For my part, it provokes innumerable passionate moments of high emotive stimulation, excitement, and delight, all uniting in a collaborative effort to raise the level of modern art. Recurrently, I attempt to relate word to word inside the poem. I employ the essence of family love and support to increase the value of what I can return to the world in verse.

PHILLIPS, MITCHELL
[a.] Las Vegas, NV [title] "She" [pers.] I have lived in Las Vegas, Nevada, almost my entire 43 years. I am a corrections officer and have been for 16 years. I write poetry when my heart feels the need. When life itself turns my life upside-down, I like to express it in words. "She" was inspired by the death of my mother-in-law, who we dearly miss

PINDER, ALETHA
[a.] Spanish Wells, Bahamas [title] "There's a Rainbow" [pers.] "There's a Rainbow" was my very first poem. When I was 16, I made my first big mistake in life. Then my life just got worse to point that I didn't want to live anymore. When I was 27, I met Jesus. He showed me the true meaning of love and gave me such peace and joy, which worldly things never could do. Poems help me to express what I feel and help others to see the light without having to face the darkness. Jesus is the light of the world and without Him there wouldn't be a rainbow.

PORTER, LEONA
[a.] Hutchinson, KS [title] "Hearts Broken in Trusting Hands" [pers.] This poem was written simply for everyone who felt they didn't matter in a world that doesn't care.

POTEET, JAMES
[a.] Riggold, GA [title] "The Preeminent Player" [pers.] When I was younger, I saw my first basketball game with my dad. It was the N.B.A. finals and the Lakers were playing. Magic Johnson did things with a basketball that were beautiful and poetic. He is the reason I play basketball, and this is a tribute to him.

POTTER, ALLISON
[a.] Croydon, PA [title] "On Our Way" [pers.] I am 12 years old and have been writing poetry for a year now. Other than writing, my hobbies are roller skating, reading, and going to school. I love poetry because it is a way for me to express my thoughts and my feelings through words.

POTTER, RICKEY
[a.] Brunswick, GA [title] "The Black Sand Beach" [pers.] I dedicate this poem to my two beautiful children, Erika and Shelby Potter, whom I had waited so long to get (46 years, to be honest). Living on the coastal Georgia beaches for so long, my oldest daughters Erika (4) found a perfect red rose that had washed up on the shore. After a period of time, we walked to a paved road and she began to pick the petals, leaving a trail behind us. She said, "Look, daddy, this is a black sand beach." My daughters are my dream, my life, my everything, and I love them dearly.

POWERS, KYLE
[a.] Olathe, KS [title] "Heartache" [pers.] To err is human, forgive divine. Everyone makes mistakes. It's how you deal with those mistakes that

dictates the kind of person you are. The person in this poem knew he made a mistake and was then pleading for forgiveness.

PRICE, ED
[a.] Bellevue, WA [title] "The Secret of Life" [pers.] I think the true "Secret of Life" is your personal belief system. What do you believe? Did we evolve out of nothing? Is there a God? If so, is there a true religion? Did God send His Son to die on the cross for our sins? That's what I believe, but how about you? Our life is the journey to discovering that secret, and when we die, the guru answers us—the answer is our result when we cease to exist, or when we to go to heaven or to hell. And you thought this was a silly poem!

PRICE, JENNIFER
[a.] Sapulpa, OK [title] "My Pain" [pers.] Everything that has happened in my life affects my writing. I was born in Topeka, Kansas. After four short years of my life, my parents divorced. I lived with my father until the time I was twelve years old. I then moved in with my mother and her husband at the time. In 1998, my mother was divorced for a second time and she and I moved in with my aunt in Oklahoma. With the two divorces, all of the moving, and everything that has happened in between, I've been inspired to write about the emotions that I have felt through it all.

PRIVETTE, SCOTT
[a.] Stuart, FL [title] "Moments" [pers.] The inspiration for this poem came from my true love, Kim. When we can't be together, we can be in our thoughts of each other. My parents are a great inspiration to me in other aspects of my life which continue to appear in my work and various hobbies. Thank you, Kim, Margaret, Forbie, and my extended family for continued support and inspiration. I love you all the most!

RAMIREZ, ERNEY
[a.] Canterbury, CT [title] "For My Love" [pers.] This poem is about the woman I love. These words that you read in this poem are true expressions of my heart. She means the world to me, and this is a way to show the world how much I love her. This poem is perfect for any man to show his true expressions of love.

RAMNARINE, STUART
[a.] San Fernando, Trinidad and Tobego [title] "Do We Really?" [pers.] Poetry is my way of reflecting reality through the eyes of a dreamer. In this world of haste and thoughtlessness, poetry offers a means of retreat. This poem, "Do We, Really?" was written to commemorate the opening of the Operation Smile Home for Children in Poonah, Trinidad. Many children will have a better life because someone, inspired by God, turned his head, and then his heart, in their direction.

RAMSAY, MELISSA
[a.] Red Deer, Canada [title] "Indelible" [pers.] I wrote this poem in memory of one of my friends, Tara Rose Smith, who was killed August 28, 1999, as the result of a drunk driver. She was only days away from beginning her twelfth-grade year, and that struck me the hardest. I realized then that life is more precious than we perceive it to be. I wrote "Indelible" hoping it would help me deal with the death of my friend. I've written other poems about issues that I've had a hard time dealing with in life, and writing has helped me through these times. Poetry has given me a new outlook on life, and I thank my friend, Tara, for that. I know she'll always inspire me and will always be looking over me.

RAVOTTI, NICHOLAS
[a.] Danielsville, GA [title] "An Outing with Daddy" [pers.] This poem is dedicated to all the brave individuals, children and adults alike, who have encountered the horrors of child abuse first hand, from either being abused, or having found out that their children

have been abused by their spouse. Domestic violence is an issue which I believe is strong and smothering throughout the world. Growing up, I knew several people who were victims of domestic violence. Looking back, I regret very much that I did not have the bravery and strength to help them. I hope that in the future, parents will learn from others' mistakes.

REHM, DEBORAH
[a.] Yulee, FL [title] "Life (In the Eyes of a 16 Year Old)" [pers.] This poem was written by my 16-year-old son, who was killed in a car accident in May of 1998. He wrote this poem in his journal just two months before his accident. He was a young Christian and was on his way to church when he died. He had many thoughts about why God put us on earth. We all know now why he was put on this earth—he was such an inspiration to all of us who knew him. I have other poems he wrote that I would like to share. He really gives us a lot to think about. I never knew he was writing this journal until after he died, and I found it in his school backpack. He was my heart and soul, and I miss him dearly. My son's name was Gregory Lee Dyal.

REIGLE, HOLLY
[a.] Moncks Corner, SC [title] "What Was" [pers.] I really love this poem. I hope it touches others as it has touched my heart. I would like to thank my friends and family for encouraging me. Thank you, Mom, Dad, Josh, and Jody. I want to thank my boyfriend, Daniel, for loving me and helping me to forget the past. But most of all, I want to thank someone very special to me, my best friend, Kathleen Stewart. Thank you so much, Kathleen, for reading my poems and always encouraging me to enter them into a contest. Without your encouragement, this poem would have never been published.

RHODES, CHRISTIAN
[a.] Seaford, NY [title] "Closure" [pers.] Pure poetry is a way of expressing one's emotions. It comes from the passion one possesses deep inside his or her soul. Therefore, it is beautiful and cannot be judged. This emotional release changes daily for me. One day, I may try and bottle it until it oozes from my soul. Other days, it cannot be contained and erupts with volcanic tremors.

RHODES, MEGAN
[a.] Flat Rock, NC [title] "When I Was Young" [pers.] This poem is for my mother, who inspired me, and supported all my dreams.

RHODES, WHITNEY
[a.] Lansing, MI [title] "My Peaches" [pers.] I wrote this poem in memory of my niece, Sarah Noel, who passed away. My family was already going through a hard time and it was extremely hard dealing with her death. Writing this poem helped release some of the hurt and pain I was feeling. This poem is my way to remember someone I loved and lost.

RICARD, STEPHANIE
[a.] Albuquerque, NM [title] "The Reason" [pers.] I wrote this poem for my mother for Christmas. I felt that the things, the presents I was going to give her, were not enough to show her how much I love her, and how much I appreciate everything she has done for me. Because I am deaf, a lot of people believed it would be hard for a parent who has never been around a deaf person to raise one. I am one of the many proofs that she has done a wonderful job in raising me so far. I wanted to show her through my poetry how thankful I am to have her as a mother.

RILEY, ERIKA
[a.] West Allis, WI [title] "Me" [pers.] There is no special story behind this poem. I was experimenting with different topics for my poems and decided to write a poem about myself. I am a "typical" fifteen-

year-old sophomore in high school, trying my best to be myself and do well. I hope you all enjoy the poem!

ROBERTSON, WANDA
[a.] Chicago, IL [title] "Fragile Blue" [pers.] My dad died on 8/28/2001. This poem was the direct result of my last visit with him. It is my memorial to him. Poetry helped me deal with his loss.

ROBINSON, BRIAN
[a.] Mississauga, Canada [title] "Alone" [pers.] I dedicate this poem to my son, Stefan Robinson. We were both going through a very difficult time, but he handled it better than I could have imagined. He gave me the strength to see inside myself and express my feelings in verse. Thank you, my sweetheart.

ROBINSON, WARRENE
[a.] Inglewood, CA [title] "The Chains of the Past" [pers.] Renee is what most people call me. I was inspired to write "The Chains of the Past" in honor of anyone who has gone through the metamorphosis of that awesome cocoon of life's adversities. I'm 49 years old and writing has become my passion to release the innermost thoughts of my soul. My goal is to reach just one person, to let them know they are not alone, and that they can come out on the other side— as free as the butterfly. I count it a privilege that my poem was selected to speak to many.

RODRIGUEZ ALMAZAN, MARIA
[a.] Chihuahua, Mexico [title] "You" [pers.] Maria Teresa Rodriguez was born in Chihuahua, Mexico. Since she was a little girl she felt an extraordinary inclination for literature, especially for poetry, perhaps as a refuge for her loneliness or for a way to create new environments in which everything would be perfect. Her poem "You" is dedicated to her best friend, Jesus.

ROGERS, DORREN
[a.] Jacksonville, FL [title] "My Spirit's Song" [pers.] Many individuals find themselves unsatisfied with their well-being. Continuously, we are looking for something more. We take the necessary steps that we think are appropriate, but sometimes there really isn't more. So we find ourselves confused because we are stuck feeling fragmented. I once felt this way, as I believe everybody does. Eventually those mentions succumb to our inner peace.

ROGERS, MARY
[a.] Fayetteville, NC [title] "Tomorrow" [pers.] I am sixteen year old. This poem represents a time when I was struggling to stay out of trouble. It also is a story of negative thinking and making my life more positive.

ROLDAN, ANTONIO C., JR.
[a.] Laguna, Philippines [title] "When Your Freedom Dies" [pers.] Eternal vigilance is the price of liberty. Life is meaningless without freedom. These lessons I learned the hard way, under martial rule. My own sister and brother got thrown behind bars without any warrant. Nobody knows exactly how many citizens got "salvaged" or "hidden from the sun" forever, without a trace. I survived mainly by the faith that God is good, and even kings and fools must go. Today, I have turned myself into a moral reformer, transparency advocate, change management and organization development practitioner. Through lectures, poems, and songs, I wish to keep these lessons alive.

ROSA, EMILY
[a.] Escondido, CA [title] "Time Is" [pers.] I wrote this poem because I've always been pushed by time, as if I am running from time or the problem. My life has been difficult at times, but I smile through all the pain and sorrow. I look at each day as being a good day. Thank you, God! I also thank my family for being there for me, especially my brothers, Eddie and

Eric. I also thank all my good friends and special loved ones. I will keep on writing poems and one day make my own book of poetry like Emily Dickinson. Thank you all!

ROSENAU, TISHA
[a.] Phoenix, AZ [title] "Grandmother's 75th Birthday" [pers.] Poetry doesn't come easy to me, but when the moment strikes, I run with it. Creativity arises at the strangest times. This poem talks about the most courageous, strong, and intelligent woman in my family—my grandmother. She keeps us all in line. She has always been there to see me through all the aspects of my life. Through good times and bad, she's there to find the goodness in every situation. No matter what I talk to her about, she is all ears and an open mind. What an inspiration she has been for me. Happy Birthday, Ruby Severson.

ROSNER, DOLORES
[a.] New York, NY [title] "Love Denied" [pers.] As a neglected child, I often spoke of a sister much to the annoyance of the adults. At eight years, I was finally forbidden to mention her again. They tried to convince me that she was an imaginary friend and or a doll I once had. I harbored her memory all my life. At age 60, I set out to find her. I'll never forget the day I held her death certificate in my hand. I had been 2 1/2 years older than she. Just recently, I found the cemetery where she lies. She has no stone and was buried with thousands of others in an area known as Potter's Field. She never had a proper funeral, the mere mention of her existence was denied. We both suffered from lack of love. I wrote the poem to honor her (she has never had a visitor), and also to bring awareness to all neglected, abused, and abandoned children. I am 65 and it still hurts.

ROTH, SARAH
[a.] New Orleans, LA [title] "Caterpillar Sting" [pers.] This poem is about the loss of a dear friend. When I lost my friend, I turned to poetry to help me move on. I feel that poetry is a very good way to express yourself. Poetry also helps you understand what other people feel, as well as how other people think about different things. Poetry is a universal thing. People all over the world read and write poetry. Poetry is a very private thing. Poetry speaks to us in different ways. When people read it, they feel many different ways. Poetry is a very special gift that is meant to be shared.

ROWE, TASHA
[a.] Raven, VA [title] "Drugs or Life" [pers.] I am 13 years old. I give thanks to God for my talent, and to my uncle for the inspiration. My uncle had a substance abuse problem. When he was hospitalized, I was inspired to write this poem.

RUEHLMANN, MIRANDA
[a.] Burke, VA [title] "Lovesick Fool" [pers.] I'm very happy with how this poem turned out. It was written from the heart and described exactly how I felt at that moment. I never would have been able to write this poem if it wasn't for the person I wrote it for. You know who you are!

RUFFINO, MELISSA
[a.] Chicago, IL [title] "Crying Out" [pers.] The poem I wrote was actually for one of my stories I had started to write. I would just like to thank my family for the inspiration they have gave me through the years, and also for their love and understanding.

RUIZ, ROSALIE
[a.] Corona, CA [title] "Half a Soul" [pers.] One year, I made a needlepoint birthday card for my sister, Maria. Realizing I could not send a blank card, I sat down to write a simple birthday message and before I knew it, I wrote this poem. Perhaps I should say it wrote itself, because it took only 15 minutes for the

feelings in my heart to come through my pen. Throughout my life, I have always enjoyed putting my thoughts and feelings on paper. I am so grateful to God for giving me such a pleasurable gift.

SACKETT, PETER
[a.] Washington, DC [title] "Livin' Life" [pers.] I'm from Washington, D.C. and I am currently a senior at Bishop McNamara High School in Forestville, MD. I always put a piece of myself into my work. So this poem is not only words on a page, but emotion and belief transcribed onto paper. I want to dedicate this poem to my late-grandfather, Major James H. Sackett, retired USAF. Also, this poem is dedicated to my grandmother and mother, as well as my family and friends. They have all molded my perception of life, which made this poem possible. I love every single one of you. God bless and live long.

SANCHEZ, GAY
[a.] Manchesney Park, IL [title] "Janel, God's Gracious Gift" [pers.] This poem was written for my youngest sister, Janel, who lost her life at a very young age. She was a very special person, even with all her difficulties. She was our gift of life and is greatly missed. This poem was meant to keep her light going on in all of us, and hopefully those who have had an experience with a special child, forever.

SANYAL, SOUMIK
[a.] Arrumbakkam Chennai, India [title] "The Phoenix" [pers.] "The Phoenix" is a tribute to that indomitable human spirit, which forever strives. The mere promise of another dawn rejuvenates the desire to live and not merely exist. "The Phoenix" attempts at acknowledging the embattled yet unfazed "spirit" that pulsates through time and space, despite the monotony, pain, and grime it confronts. I dedicate this poem to my grandmother, who has taught me never to say die!

SCARPATI, MYRIAH
[a.] Phoenix, AZ [title] "Mr. Balloon Man" [pers.] I have been writing poetry since I was eight years old. This poem is about coming to terms with things that are gone and won't ever be the same again. Everyone has a balloon man at least once in life.

SCHNEEBERGER, JENNIFER
[a.] Janesville, WI [title] "When I Look into Her Eyes" [pers.] I would like to dedicate this first publication to my mom, dad, and brother, Dan. You all believed in me and in my special talent. Thank you. I would also like to say that nobody can be as proud of me as me. Thank you, mom and dad, for all the confidence and encouragement. I love you.

SCOTT, ANDREA
[a.] Bockhannon, WV [title] "Mother Owl" [pers.] I've recently taken a different journey on my poetry. My past poems focused on my life experience and ideas. Now one might say I'm trying to see the world through another's eyes. "Mother Owl" displays this. I saw the world through my grandma's eyes to try to understand why she is the way she is. I thank God soulfully for my gift of words, and I see his purpose. The purpose is to keep my sanity in a troubled world and to express myself better to my loved ones.

SELF, JOHNNY
[a.] Hoover, AL [title] "One" [pers.] J. L. Self resides in Alabama. He jumps from airplanes, rides a motorcycle, and says he only writes when something or someone affects him deeply. Every accomplishment and success have been affected by his mother, Carolyn; his father, Johnny; and his sister, Angie. The subject of this work, though she remains unnamed, undoubtedly inspired him, as well.

SELOGY, GRACE
[a.] Bothell, WA [title] "Pegasus" [pers.] As a 16-year-old girl, I don't often have the freedom to express myself as well as I should. Poetry is one way that I can place my thoughts together so they make sense, at least to me. Going through rough things in my life has given me the chance to touch other people and made them see the world the way I see it. When I wrote "Pegasus," life was hard and I wanted to get away from the world, so I wrote everything down and it became a beautiful poem. I love writing and hope to continue it.

SEMBA, ALEXANDER
[a.] Moses Lake, WA [title] "A Wasted Life" [pers.] This poem has given me the opportunity to share with you my perspective on life. It gives a different message to people about how life sometimes is taken for granted. I have been given the chance to send a message to the people, and hopefully something can be learned from this poem.

SEMLER, RANDI-LYNN
[a.] Smithburg, MD [title] "The Lost Girl" [pers.] Although I am only 16, I know what I want in life. I want to be able to write and know others can read my words. "The Lost Girl" is the first poem I ever put out for others to read. Some people think this poem may be found disturbing. To me, this poem just tells about a tragedy that does happen in life. Sadly, this does happen. My prayers go out to the family's who have had this or something like this happen.

SHAHBAZ, TALIA
[a.] Lahore, Pakistan [title] "The Lonely Cat" [pers.] Poetry is what I use to say the unspeakable, make it sound sad, or funny, or both. I find that the intensity of certain things can only be expressed in poetry, and if there is any truth-seeker out there, poetry is one field he will definitely have to rake. This is where people say outright what they hide in daily life. The fascinating thing about this poem is the way a person and an animal can connect, but a person and a person have difficulty connecting at all.

SHARPE, ANGEL
[a.] Niagara Falls, NY [title] "Love of a Friend" [pers.] This poem, to me, means more than the words I can write. I wrote it when I first met my fiance. At the age of 20, we met and have since planned our wedding to take place next year (2002). When I wrote this poem, I meant it for him, but never gave it to him. After a year-and-a-half, I finally did once I entered it, and he loved it. My name is Angel Breannda Sharpe. I am currently 22 years old, engaged, and attending school for court stenography. Congrats to all others published in here.

SHELTON, DEIDRA
[a.] Houston, TX [title] "Our Chance" [pers.] All my feelings are expressed through my poetry—my hurts, desires, secrets, and anything else. I feel my poetry lets me get away from my hectic life in Houston. I live with my dad, Mikey (40), my mom Cricket, and my brothers Tommy (18) and Timmy (17). The only sisters I have are not blood-related, but I adopted them as my sisters. They are Tiffany and Heather. Heather is my age, 14. My poetry lets me get away from all that. It lets me get my anguish out. The cause of this certain poem was heartbreak. I cared a lot about a boyfriend that I had, but I got hurt. This poem came out of it. My sisters helped me out, too. But, like I said, my feelings go from my heart to my poems.

SHEPPARD, JOHN
[a.] Glen Allen, VA [title] "My Sunshine" [pers.] I am a police officer, and like many police officers, I have a hard time expressing my feelings. This was my first attempt at poetry. Recently I fell in love with a wonderful woman who inspired me to write this poem. I hope this will not be the end of my creative writings.

SHIRLARK, POET
[a.] Bendigo, Australia [title] "Shattered Dreams" [pers.] My name is Shirley Clark, but I have chosen to use the nom de plume of Poet Shirlark. I am 66 years old, married, with family and grandchildren. My other interests include golf, fishing, sightseeing, gardening, and the computer. I have always had an interest in poetry, preferring verse with rhymes in some way, but have only taken to writing in the last couple of years. My subjects are varied, mainly just "as I see life." I would personally like to achieve my belief that "everything we do should be a picture and everything we say should be music to the ears." Penong is a small town on the eastern side of the Eyre Highway which crosses the Nullarbor Plain, skirting the Great Australian Bight. It was on our return from our winter holiday, heading for Penong across the Nullarbor, that both my husband and I were deeply affected by what was obviously, at one time, someone's "dream," quite shattered by the stronger power of the elements. My husband made the comment, "It's a desolate scene out there!"

SMITH, ANNE MARIE
[a.] Fort Washington, PA [title] "I Can't Tell You" [pers.] I write poetry in joy and delight of life. I go deeply within my heart and soul. The words flow freely. My inspirations are love—agape—nature, the cosmos, and beautiful music of many cultures. Since music bypasses logic and goes straight to the heart and soul, I feel particularly inspired by the songs "Nostalgia," "One Man's Dream," and "In My Time," by multicultural composer Yanni. It's poetry and music converging on the love of life through its beauty and appreciation of life's great joys—all people, nature, the cosmos.

SMITH, JOHN
[a.] Cohoes, NY [title] "Angel" [pers.] "Angel" was composed in Mexico City and was inspired by a famous statue I saw there. The poem was sent on a postcard to my wife, Nika, who then lived in Moscow. I travel extensively and find, if the Muse visits me, that poetry is the most expressive medium to relate feelings which lie deep beneath the woods themselves. The postcard, especially of an evocative subject and through restricted space, can impose the necessary discipline for concise verse.

SMITH, KRYSTAL
[a.] Elk, WA [title] "Set Free" [pers.] My name is Krystal Smith. I'm seventeen years old. I was raised in a log cabin in the woods of Elk, WA, by my grandparents, Jesse and Angela Smith. They began home-schooling me at three. Because of the Lord's help and their willingness to teach me, I don't remember a time when I couldn't read and write. God gave me the gift of poetry. When I'm praying to Him, He turns my prayer into a poem, as He did with "Set Free." I hope it touches those who read it.

SMITH, LORETTA
[a.] Ridgeview, WV [title] "The Man Downstairs" [pers.] The poem I have created is very special to me because it is about my father. He is a big influence in my life and in my writing. The poem expresses how my father works very hard to provide me with everything I need and want, but yet is absent from my daily life. I feel that kids and parents everywhere can relate with my father and myself. Hopefully the fathers realize, just as mine did, that they are loved and missed.

SMITH-GAYLORD, TUESDAY
[a.] APO, AE [title] "To Self" [pers.] This poem is just a sample of many inspiring psalms the Lord has blessed me with. I believe in Jesus Christ as a my saviour and without him, this could not be possible. I thank everyone who encouraged me and prayed for the manifestation of God's promises. My poems are a testimony of my life, created to uplift and help others. I am happily married to an army soldier, John Gaylord. We're currently residing in Baumbolder, Germany. I am very grateful for the opportunity to share my gift with you. Thank you and God bless.

SNYDER, KEITH
[a.] Sandia Park, NM [title] "Cheri" [pers.] Rarely, if ever, does one encounter an individual who's effect is so profound as to change one's life forever. Katrina Cheri Petney did that for me. She opened my eyes to life, filled my soul with joy and passion, and taught me to realize who I really am—an artist. I always knew that I wanted to write, was unsure of what form, and hadn't known until I met Cheri. The poem "Cheri" was my first and I haven't stopped writing since. She holds my heart, is always in my thoughts, and I will love her forever.

SOBER, CARLY
[a.] Magnolia, TX [title] "Sitting There" [pers.] This poem is special to me because it shows my feelings about the sun and how it shows. I think it is a good poem if you can imagine what I see. My name is Carly, and I love writing poems and have for quite some time. I want to be a designer when I get older. Poetry is something I do in my spare time. I hope to give it my best all the time.

SPINELLI, RAYMOND
[a.] Newport, NH [title] "Closing Moment" [pers.] This poem is dedicated to my mother, my best friend, who passed away at the age of 47 from emphysema. She was a truly great person. I love you, mom, and I hope that you are happy and without any pain. Just know you are always in my heart and my thoughts.

ST. GEORGE, BRANDON
[a.] Sturgeon Lake, MN [title] "Halloween" [pers.] I wrote this poem when I was four years old. I am now 13 and live in Minnesota. I enjoy writing short stories and playing football. I live with my mom and dad, Ernie and Rita. I have five brothers and three sisters. Reading and writing allow me an opportunity to use the computer and have time alone. I like reading novels, especially science fiction.

ST. PIERRE, NATHAN
[a.] Prosper, TX [title] "Void" [pers.] I sat down to revise this poem, to make it seem a bit more appealing, to make it flow more naturally, but every word still strikes an exposed nerve, even if the memory of that day has faded. Every unbalanced phrase and asymmetric line is a clear echo of the words spoken by my mind. It is not a heavy dirge written by my heart to drag you down; it is a wailing ballad, composed by my soul to reach out to all who hear it.

STANION, DAVID
[a.] Clarks Summit, PA [title] "Low Esteem, High Esteem" [pers.] I wrote this poem to reflect the humor and philosophy in my life. I reckoned self-esteem to a roller coaster. In my life, it never reached the pinnacle of the first hill! Undaunted, I got out, started pushing, got rolled over, reached up, grabbed, swung up, and found myself in the front seat, facing forward, going backward! Back hill routine: Swinging up, I would find myself facing forward, going forward, last seat, going where? Staying in the human race on the coaster of self-esteem, one must build self-confidence to overcome that first hill to get into the game of life.

STELLFLUG, TRITON
[a.] Zimmerman, MN [title] "Fierce Gale" [pers.] This poem is actually parts pieced together of what I originally wrote as a song. I have taught myself to play guitar and enjoy using music as a creative output, as well as an input. Creativity will continue to be a big part of my life, as I am a graphic design major in college.

STONE, D.
[a.] Houston, TX [title] "Taking Chances" [pers.] This poem is about taking a chance on new love and its uncertainty, but also the excitement and anticipation of a beginning. Originally this was to be a song, but it seems more moving as a poem. I am but a simple wordsmith and the creation makes a life of its own.

STRONG, JULIE
[a.] Billerica, MA [title] "Man of Contradiction" [pers.] I find poetry is a great way of expressing one's thoughts and feelings. I write about people, causes, etc. that inspire me. The man whom this poem is about greatly inspires me. You're one in a million, J.D. I love you. Thanks for the inspiration. I would also like to dedicate this poem to my family and friends. Thank you for your love and support. You (including J.D.) not only inspire me, you make me proud. I hope the readers of my poem have the kind of love and inspiration in their lives that I have in mine.

STROUGHTER, LATINA
[a.] Huntville, TX [title] "Life Is" [pers.] God blessed me to write "Life Is." I thank God for blessing me with His wisdom and insight. I thank my family for their encouragement, love, and support, as I continue to write. "Life Is" is based on, and written from, my experience. Through poetry, God blessed me to communicate that experience. I hope that my poems inspire, touch, and motivate other people to live life!

STURGILL, RACHEL
[a.] Little River, SC [title] "Love Waits" [pers.] This poem is for Johnny Farrell, who has been my love since April '99. Despite consistent obstacles in our relationship, we have loved each other through everything. The friendship and love between us has stood in the face of lies, other relationships, anger, and pain. Love waits, for with true love comes patience and forgiveness. True love knows no end. God will work all things out for good in our lives if we trust in Him, and I thank Him for putting Johnny in my life. I will always love you.

SUCH, FALLON
[a.] Elyria, OH [title] "Don't Forget" [pers.] My poem was written for my friend, Julie, as a graduation present. The love for poetry is something that brought us closer throughout our senior year of high school, and something that has helped me sort out my feelings and emotions for a few years now. I am from Elyria, Ohio and am a freshman at Ohio University.

SUNDAY, CHE
[a.] San Francisco, CA [title] "Freedom Denied" [pers.] I was born in Bafut, Cameroon and educated in Cameroon, Nigeria, and the United States. I am a graduate of the University of Idaho, in Moscow, and Golden Gate in San Francisco. I have a doctorate in public administration. The poem "Freedom Denied" is a reflection on colonialism from an African's perspective. As a kid, one grows up trying so hard to follow in their parent's footsteps, but not quite. Only the natural phenomena around knows how things were before Europeans came. That's what the river represents. Schools taught us about European history, not African. It is where the emphasis is on Europeanizing Africans. No African languages are used as medium of instructions, and the ideology that salvation for Africa lies in Europe in reinforced.

SUTHERLAND, KASENA
[a.] Fries, VA [title] "A Visit with My Thoughts" [pers.] I love wintertime. The snow is so beautiful. I sit in the dining room and watch the birds and squirrels at the feeders. At Christmastime, everything is more beautiful. All my decorations with red bows blow in the wind. I live in the country outside the small town of Fries, VA. I was born in Fries and still

live here. I am married and have four sons and three grandchildren. I love to read and write poetry. Once I think of a title, then I write the poem.

SUZUKI, ALLISON
[a.] Mililani, HI [title] "What People Say" [pers.] This poem was originally written when I was 15 years old, back in 1992. At that time, I questioned the meaning of true love. After talking to many people and getting many different answers on the subject of true love, I came to a conclusion with this poem. Once I came up with the title, the poem seemed to have written itself. I still believe in this poem, and I always will. I hope this poem rings true, not just for myself, but for you as well.

SWANN, ALICE
[a.] Dowagiac, MI [title] "Dream of Love" [pers.] "Dream of Love" was written as my personal vision of true love. By putting my thoughts in words, they empowers my faith that one day I will have that special person to love, who loves me in return. I wish to inspire anyone who reads the poem to never give up searching for love. We all need to love and be loved. We were born to learn to love.

SWINBURNE, SYLVANA
[a.] Middle Village, NY [title] "The Old Man" [pers.] The eyes of the old man reflects the brevity of life. He tries to give a message to every soul to live life to the fullest. Time goes by extremely fast. "The Old Man" symbolizes ourselves. We seem to forget that life is too short, until we reflect on the stone of the old man. We are the old man; we are the every look when we fail to see and to accept life as a gift from the Creator.

TALWAR, DEEPAK
[a.] Limmasol, Cyprus [title] "She" [pers.] This work is dedicated to a woman whom I shall not love for the rest of my life, but for the rest of mine. Of all the beauty of skin and soul I have ever seen, she was simply the best. She is one woman, but I fell in love with her twice. First, with her, and second when she was already mine. Of all the words of pen and paper, these are the saddest it could have been. Never let these words become a part of your thought process. Be a go-getter in life. Someone like "She" is waiting out there for you.

TAN, DAVID
[a.] Singapore, Singapore [title] "United, Ready Always!" [pers.] This poem came into being when I was involved in my company's special project in building and promoting a common vision and shared values among our staff. I would like to dedicate this poem to my company, the Urban Development Authority of Singapore, and all the staff of UDA. I hope one day this poem would become the heartbeat of every employee of UDA.

TAVILLE, JUNIUS
[a.] Houston, TX [title] "Incomparable" [pers.] I am glad that God gave me the ability to express my emotions through poetry. Poetry gives me the chance to feel freedom while I write and to leave my stress and problems behind for an hour or more. The poem I have written describes how a man feels when he meet his soul mate, and how his world can change. He begins to feel emotions he has never felt before and feelings that he never knew were inside of him. I wrote about this subject because I have felt these same feelings and emotions toward a woman.

TAYLOR, BRADSHAW
[a.] Grand Cayman, Cayman Islands [title] "Today and Tomorrow" [pers.] The title derives from a statement/promise I sometimes make: "When tomorrow becomes today!" It is rooted in my hope, knowledge, and belief that promises will be fulfilled, especially the promises of God! The poem developed from a simple four-liner to my former wife at the start of the

New Year. It embodies my beliefs which have developed from, and been vindicated by, my life experiences. I remind Edward and Donovan, my sons, "My glass is half full, not half empty!"

TERRY, ESTRELLA
[a.] Cookeville, TN [title] "Not the Same" [pers.] Conditional love is not the same as unconditional love. Conditional love says, "I will love you as long as . . ." setting boundaries and limitations that one must endure in order to find acceptance with family, friends, or partners. Unconditional love is at the other spectrum saying to us, " Although I may not understand everything about you or agree with everything you say or do, I accept the person in you and will love you the way you are." This poem is dedicated to every man, woman, young person or child out there who longs to feel loved unconditionally.

THOMAS-CARTER, MICHELE
[a.] St. Louis, MO [title] "The Ups, the Downs" [pers.] I write about my experiences with depression. I use writing as a way to cope with depression. I write poems, articles, essays and short stories about mental illness. Writing is my way of unplugging. It helps me to relieve stress. Hopefully my writing can be used as a weapon to battle depression.

THOMPSON, SHARON
[a.] Burtonsville, MD [title] "After All We've Been Through" [pers.] I dedicate this poem to all women, especially those close to my heart. I wanted to create a poem that captures what's really in the hearts of a lot of women who have experienced long-term relationships that have failed. They need to know that it's OK and life goes on. At the beginning, the poem depicts sadness and disappointment, but suddenly ends with a burst of joy, happiness, and new life! I'd like to acknowledge my parents, Rev. and Mrs. Charlie Thompson of Virginia. I love you!

THROCKMORTON, LINDA
[a.] Keosauqua, IA [title] "Day Star" [pers.] The poem "Day Star" is about my thoughts and love for Jesus. My inspiration to write the poem came from meeting a very special man named Billy. He stirred up such creativity within me that I wrote of the love that he brought into my heart when we met. It set me on a pathway of finding my true self. For that, I am thankful and I dedicate this poem to him. Without him, it would never have been written.

TIPPETS, ERIN
[a.] Raymond, ME [title] "Corps" [pers.] I am a 17-year-old high-school student from Vancouver, Washington. As a devoted fan of drum corps and as a future music teacher, I dedicate "Corps" to all of the young people who participate in drum and bugle corps every summer. Whether it be in front of ten people or 10,000 people, these youth perform to the utmost of their abilities and literally put blood, sweat, and tears into the pursuit of perfection.

TOMULIS, ANN MARIE
[a.] York, PA [title] "Free" [pers.] This poem is dedicated to my fiance and best friend, Nicholas Miller. We are planning to be wed in 2002. Thanks also to Mom and Dad, Aunt Rainy, and Ralene and Jimmy, for their love and constant support. I am truly blessed.

TONER, TERRANCE
[a.] Staten Island, NY [title] "Tomorrow" [pers.] I wrote this poem almost twenty years ago, while in high school. It was one of the first I've kept in a collection which I've only recently begun to add to after a five-year hiatus. It's message seems so much more significant in light of the recent tragedies suffered in New York and Washington.

TRUTER, TAMARYN
[a.] Mullingar, Ireland [title] "Forever" [pers.] My whole life I wished for a "soul mate," a "twin flame", and it finally happened. I'm only 16, but true love has found me. This poem is about a time when I was willing to give that up because I was confused and wasn't sure who I was. But this person showed me what true love really is; he never gave up on me, and he taught me to live for now. He helped me find myself by just accepting me for who I am! May true love find you, and may you listen to the signs!

TWALA, FUMU
[a.] Dallas, TX [title] "Mother Earth" [pers.] Poetry is the perfect way to express my thoughts and feelings. My poem, "Mother Earth," is mostly about what everyone goes through when nothing seems to work for them in their lives; these are the questions that they ask themselves. This poem doesn't give solutions or answers to anyone. It's only what I or anybody else feels when they are hurt. I am the only child of a single mom and restaurant manager. At seventeen, I am waiting to join college. I've started tasting the proverbial "life out there." Applying for a scholarship has been an uphill task, let alone securing one. Regardless of my grades (4.0), all these and many more predicaments prompted me to ask: "Do I deserve all these? What's my destiny?"

VARDI, DANIEL
[a.] Ganey-Tikva, Israel [title] "Destined Together" [pers.] My mother writes poems too. At first, I was very proud of her but didn't think about writing stuff of my own. Eventually, the poetry writing started to effect me. That was when I was 14 years old. And now, a year later, I've started to notice my love of poetry, and "Destined Together," among others, was born. I owe everything to my mom for being my inspiration and for encouraging me to express myself in writing. I thank her for giving me her "gift" of poetry.

VARDI, RACHEL
[a.] Ganey-Tikva, Israel [title] "The M.I.L. Club" [pers.] I have always loved to put pen to paper, whether it be philosophical sentiments, short stories, or satirical views of my experiences in life. "The M.I.L. Club" was written as a lighter side of being a mother-in-law, as I one day found myself. Any "girl" who becomes a "member" will vow every word of this poem to be true to the point. May I take this opportunity to mention how proud and honored I am to have this poem of mine published along side a poem written by my son, Daniel Vardi.

VASCONCELLOS, JACOB
[a.] Kailua Kona, HI [title] "untitled" [pers.] I feel that the greatest influences in my life are Jim Morrison and Andy Kaufman. From Jim Morrison, I learned about expressing myself, and my poetry is like my ode to Jim. From Andy Kaufman, I've learned that none of this is so bad that we can't all just have a good time. After combining their two life philosophies, you get mine. Let's all just live free and have a good time. This is life, we're here; it doesn't matter why, just accept it and enjoy the ride.

VAUGHN, SUSAN
[a.] San Diego, CA [title] "The Light" [pers.] The words flowed like water as I sat at my computer and began to type. These words, I feel, are a message to us all to stop living our lives in repetitious circles, to start living with a purpose of loving one another and to begin seeking our spiritual paths. With love and faith on our sides, our lives can only be richer. As for me, I'm trying to do just that after many uneventful and empty years. I've started reading more and writing. It had been many years since I last wrote a poem, so I was very surprised when the words came rolling out. The past ten years I have been earning my keep as an artist. I've come to realize I can offer heirlooms of the future, and now, perhaps, I have something to say by writing.

VILLARREAL, ZOILA
[a.] El Do, Panama [title] "Hurt Heart" [pers.] I was born on February 14, 1973. I live in Panama with my parents and brothers. I have a Degree of Communication Studies at Universidad Santa Maria La Antigua, and while I was studying there, I became a member of the theater group "El Desvan." My hobbies are to watch TV, to read, and to write. Poetry is the easiest way to show my feelings, either when I'm sad, happy, depressed, or glad. This poem was written in April of 1992, and it commemorates a special moment—my first love and the first time my heart was broken.

VONGKEOMANY, PHOUVONG
[a.] East Harford, CT [title] "Why I Proceed to Live" [pers.] To me this poem is very special. Every day I wake up thinking of this question. Is it possible that the man up above gave everyone of us our own destiny? In my mind, he gave me life to be there for someone else, to help or to make someone happy. Life is like a web unfinished. It's my destiny that will finish my side of the web.

WADA, EDNA
[a.] Honolulu, HI [title] "I Wonder Why" [pers.] My father, a Buddhist minister in Hawaii, died in 195, when I was about three. My mother, who is from Japan, raised my four sisters and brothers—I am the youngest. This is not an easy task for any widow, but it was harder because my mom doesn't speak English and has all her relatives in Japan. She is now 91 and has had a stroke. I am her primary care giver. I attended University of Hawaii, where I attempted to become a teacher, but instead had a nervous breakdown while practice teaching. After nine-and-a-half years, I received a B.A. in psychology.

WADE, BRANDON
[a.] South Grafton, MA [title] "Paths of Life" [pers.] This poem, and all of my poetry, is dedicated to the human race. It is my hope that all people will choose the path of peace, rather than the path of fools. To those who strive for peace, keep strength against those who would destroy it.

WALKER, KESHIA
[a.] Pasadena, CA [title] "Turning Point" [pers.] Since I have become a recently-divorced woman, my life has made a 180 degree turn. This poem was ignited from how my soul was feeling. It is the rebirth of the human spirit. It is my hope that women are given strength and power if they have gone through the same experience.

WALSKEY, VERONICA
[a.] South Connellsville, PA [title] "The Angel I Never Saw" [pers.] "The Angel I Never Saw" is a dedication to a very special lady, my mother—Geraldine Speelman. This poem came forth one evening as I sat by the candlelight, reminiscing about days past. In a vision, I saw this wonderful lady in her simple attire working fervently to take care of her family—realizing that she's always been there . . . yesterday and today. These words are a small way for me to say, "Mom, I love you. Thanks for being you." I will always treasure this special angel that God sent to me. May she be immortalized with these words.

WANER, BETHANIE
[a.] Mesa, AZ [title] "Someday" [pers.] Poetry is a way to express my inner feelings. It's very relaxing and comes very naturally. This poem is about abandonment and trying to let the other person know that it hurts. I'm not going to stick around and wait for them to understand, someday they will know—it's called karma. Peace, love, harmony, and special thanks to my fiancee, Anthony Streit, for his support in my writing. Also thanks to my mother for being there through good and bad, and to my father, who is a writer himself. He is a great inspiration to me. Thanks!

WANGERIN, DENNIS
[a.] Meguon, WI [title] "Thy Mountains II" [pers.] Poet stature . . . artist capture . . . siren nature . . . together rapture: Livest thy dream. . . .

WARREN, A.
[a.] Norfolk, MA [title] "Walking in the Autumn Woods" [pers.] A.J. wrote this poem while he was in the fifth grade. He is now 12 years old and a seventh-grade student. A.J. enjoys writing poetry at school and at home.

WASHINGTON, KEITH
[a.] Little Rock, AR [title] "When a Man Loves a Woman" [pers.] I believe God's true gift to a man is a strong, loving woman, and I was blessed enough to receive one. Love is powerful. It can make you see, feel, hear, taste, and smell things a little sweeter than before. It bonds you so tight that you feel what they feel—the laughter and the pain. Love is more than a four-letter word; it's a whole new life. Mine started when I met my wife, who is my real inspiration for "When a Man Loves a Woman."

WEATHERS, JENNIFER
[a.] Medford, OR [title] "Truth" [pers.] I love writing and sports. I am 5'7", blonde hair, and blue eyes. I look up to my family for moral support. Sometimes I can tell my little cousins look up to me for everything.

WEBBER, CHERYL
[a.] Stratford, CT [title] "Ha! Or" [pers.] I was feeling very sorry for myself when I wrote "Ha! Or," I felt that once again I had made the wrong choice in matters of love . . . which was just a misconception on my part, as I am still happily in love and engaged to the same wonderful man. My poetry is usually a little more upbeat and I hope when they are read, they are liked as well.

WEREMY, CHRISTINE
[a.] Omaha, NE [title] "To Wonder" [pers.] Sometimes people just have to write down even the simplest things. Poetry, songs, and lyrics are always to vent the frustrations of life. "To Wonder" was a way for me to express inquiries about what other people do after you can't see them.

WEST, BRONWEN
[a.] Orlando, FL [title] "My Mother's Hands" [pers.] I am a 25-year-old English major and hope to be a professor and singer on the side. This poem was written as an assignment for a creative writing class I took in the Spring of 2001. I am grateful to have it published. Over the past five years much has changed in my relationship with my mother. Today I love her for who she is. For the first twenty years, I was angry at her for her mental illness. I lacked compassion and had no contact with her for years. Today my mother and I have a beautiful relationship.

WETTSTEIN, BRIAN
[a.] Sycamore, IL [title] "Fighting Insomnia" [pers.] Writing poetry heals wounds, solves problems, inhabits souls, lifts spirits, and builds the confidence of people all over the world. How do I know? Because it's done all that for me! But recent song lyrics in the Old 97's song "Book of Poems" brought me back to reality: "I got a book of poems that's gonna set you free . . . I got a real bad feeling that a book of poems ain't enough." I realized actions are stronger than words, but don't stop writing or you will probably take the wrong actions.

WHITE, CARRIE
[a.] Chunky, MS [title] "Happy Anniversary, My Darlin' Tim" [pers.] This poem is about the one true love in my life, my husband. I lost my darling Tim in a car wreck on July 12, 2000. In a split second, my life changed. I had never been able to write poetry before

I lost my husband, and then it just came to me. I put all my pain and sorrow down on paper. It helped me get through a very difficult time in my life. I dedicate this poem to my angel in Heaven, Tim; my three beautiful children: Kayla, T.J., and Shelby; and the love and strength of my mother, Phoebe Quillen.

WIGGINS, TIYA

[a.] Antelope, CA [title] "In This Place" [pers.] Poetry is my song—and so I sing it unto you. This poem is very important to me, it represents a point in my life where my soul was free, free exploring all the beauties of this wonderful world. I am currently a sophomore at Fisk University, the place which has made me a poet. (Fisk Forever!) Fisk definitely opened my eyes to many things going on around me today. From this I write purely what is in my heart and my soul. This is why I am a poet.

WIKRAMANAYAKE, MARISA

[a.] Colombo, Sri Lanka [title] "Dreams" [pers.] "Dreams" captures a feeling of hopelessness and a lack of courage, condensing it to record the emotions felt throughout one long-forgotten moment of time.

WILCOX, CLINTON

[a.] Madera, CA [title] "True Love" [pers.] Too many times today, society sends out the wrong messages about love. They're all over the television and movies. My poem, "True Love," was written to show how love should be. It's not how you look that matters, it's what's inside that counts.

WILLIAMS, TERE

[a.] Mount Pocono, PA [title] "Come You Are, My Beloved" [pers.] Unconditional love, alone, is the one moving force to generate peace upon our planet. Earth is the creator's greatest gift to all mankind. Men must change before nations can change. This writing is dedicated to my mom, Tere, who gave life to me; and my son, Rich, who has been the wind beneath my wings. Although these words have been written by me, I humbly acknowledge the infinite one for the inspiration that continues to flow through me.

WILLIAMS, TYRONZA

[a.] Fort Meyers, FL [title] "Untitled" [pers.] Poetry is a way to free my mind and to get things off my chest. This poem was a way for me to express my true feelings to my father. He will never know the extent of his damage or the amount of pain he has caused unless he reads this poem. This is a way for me to get back at him. It has helped me to keep my head up high, as well as achieve goals I never set for myself. Hopefully, others will read my poem and realize that even the worst things have good qualities.

WILLIAMSON, BENNETT, JR.

[a.] Mount Pleasant, FL [title] "Perfect Unity" [pers.] Poetry is a way to express the feelings and emotions that are so profound that I simply cannot keep them inside. I write poems down so that my friends and family can share in my joys and sorrows. I was born in South Georgia and currently reside in Florida with my lovely wife, Angela.

WINGFIELD, LARAMIE

[a.] Gretna, NE [title] "My Untold Story" [pers.] I have always loved the water. To me, it has a personality all its own. Sometimes it is comical, sometimes it is dramatic, and sometimes, like in "My Untold Story," it is tragic. I dedicate "My Untold Story" to a teacher that shares my love of poetry and drama, Carole Homan.

WOOD, TIMOTHY

[a.] Mobile, AL [title] "Space" [pers.] This poem was written for an eighth-grade English assignment at Semmes Middle School, in Alabama, in 1999. The destruction of our environment and world inspired the poem. It is very satisfying to have my work published,

especially in light of the 9/11/01 disaster. I would like to dedicate this poem to the victims and their families.

WOODRUFF, JESSICA

[a.] Titus, AL [title] "If I Lost You" [pers.] I think poetry is a way to express your feelings. My poem means that if anything ever happened to my best friends, Laura and Jayne, there would be something missing in my life and heart. I wrote "If I Lost You" to tell them how I feel. I hope you will share "If I Lost You" with your friends and family. I also hope you are lucky enough to have friends like I do.

WOODS, ZANIESHA

[a.] San Mateo, CA [title] "A Passage to Heal" [pers.] My grandmother's illness inspired me to write this poem. My grandmother was sick about three months ago. Gangrene had set in her large toe, later spreading to all the others. It was later announced that she would have to have an amputation of all her toes on her right foot. The whole family and I were unprepared for this turmoil, so I just went to my computer and vented with words. Before I knew it I, at thirteen I had written a beautiful poem about life. It was truly "A Passage to Heal!"

WRIGHT, MARY

[a.] Norwalk, IA [title] "Listen to the Children" [pers.] I am currently a psychology major at Upper Iowa University. I moved back to the heartland three years ago. My family has suffered the loss of my little sister, and two brothers have been diagnosed with cancer. Through the pain of family and national tragedy, I was inspired to write poetry, hoping to restore love. I have a whole series of poems. I plan to utilize some for a book.

WYATT, JESS

[a.] Levittown, PA [title] "Panther" [pers.] I became inspired to write this poem after read Amelia Atwater-Rhodes' book *In the Forests of the Night*, which involved a tiger. She described the settings so detailed that I was moved to write the poem. I'd like to thank my family for encouraging me to keep trying; my parents, Marie and Greg Wyatt; and my brothers, Chris and Steven, as well as the rest of my family. I'd also like to thank my friends and classmates for inspiring me to start writing poetry. And I'd like to thank the Lord for blessing me with this wonderful gift.

WYNN, TODD

[a.] Amelia, OH [title] "Thank You, Mother" [pers.] Poetry is more than just vain words—they are words spoken through the soul, an eruption from the spirit yearning to be loved. This poem is about the greatest love of my life, my mother.

ZACHER, LINDA

[a.] Colusa, CA [title] "Valley of My Tears" [pers.] I wrote this poem in memory of my son, Alan Lee Talamantes, because I needed to express my deep sorrow. It made me feel closer to him in my heart. He fell off a cliff into the ocean in 1986, at age nineteen. My other son, Ralph, and daughter, Lori, were both devastated with grief. We all miss him dearly and he is always in our hearts. I felt very bad that I had to move away from where he is buried, but I know his spirit is with us through our Lord, Jesus Christ.

ZIEGLER, ANNETTE

[a.] Anna, OH [title] "Dreams" [pers.] I feel that poetry is not just a creative ability, but can be used as a very helpful mental tool as well. By encapsulating our innermost feelings, we are releasing stress and anxiety. It can help us sort through our most troubled times. Poetry allows us to escape into a world of magical events or tranquil settings of water falls and streams. Wherever your mind wants to journey, poetry and writing can take you.

Maybe you too can begin to write. Take time out for yourself and learn to capture your dreams. When you are writing, the sky is the limit!

ZIMMITTI, KAITLYN

[a.] Branchburg, NJ [title] "We Are from Mars" [pers.] The feeling I got when I first read Shel Silverstein's poetry was wonderful. It inspired me to write poetry wherever I went. I want to be a well-known poet who everybody loves, just like he was. Mrs. Toni Burke, my teacher, also inspired me. She gave me the opportunity for my poetry to shine. Lastly, my mom inspired me. She's always right there guiding me. Without these people, I don't think that my love for poetry would have been as great as it is today. I would like to dedicate this poem to Shel Silverstein, Mrs. Burke, and Mom.

Index
of
Poets

Index